THE WATTS BOOK OF
Music

AUTHOR
Keith Spence

CONSULTANT
Hugo Cole

Watts Books
London • New York • Sydney

Contents

Illustrators
André Amstutz
Ian Beck
Brian Craker
Hugh Dixon
David Godfrey
Bryon Harvey
Robin Jacques
Michael McGuinness
Tony Moore
Ray Pelly
Andrew Popkiewicz
Trevor Ridley
Rodney Shackell
Mark Thomas

Editor
Wendy Boase

Art director
Michael McGuinness

Art editor
Judith Escreet

Designer
Elaine Partington

Picture researchers
Karen Gunnell
Helen Spence
Paul Snelgrove

© Aladdin Books 1993

Published in Great Britain
in 1993 by
Watts Books
96 Leonard Street
London WC2A 4RH

Based on *Living Music*,
published by
Hamish Hamilton Ltd,
London, 1979.

ISBN: 0 7496 1271 1

Foreword

by Sir Robert Mayer

Having watched British musical history in the making for nearly 100 years, during which self-denigration and apathy have given way to self-confidence and eager enthusiasm, I gladly accept this invitation to write a Foreword to *The Watts Book of Music*.

My involvement in music began in 1924. With my wife, a pioneer singer, I put my experience as a businessman and my profound love of music as amateur pianist and ardent concert-goer, to work to launch a series of symphony concerts designed exclusively for an audience of children. Most people were sceptical; but the initial impact on a sector of the population that in the early 1920s had probably never seen or heard a symphony orchestra was so overwhelming that we were encouraged to persist. Fortunately we were strongly supported by influential political figures like Arthur Balfour; our 'New Deal' efforts were applauded by the press; and we gained the confidence of teachers, who in the course of 15 years of concerts leading up to the Second World War brought us something like 1½ million children. Working on our own, unencumbered by committees or red tape, we threw ourselves into our self-imposed task with enthusiasm, and by the time Chapter One of our activities came to an end with the outbreak of war in 1939, we found to our astonishment and satisfaction that we had erected what was described as 'a national structure' – *monumentum aere perennius*, a monument more lasting than bronze.

The second chapter opened in 1954, when we founded 'Youth and Music'. The idea was to extend the structure based on pre-teenage children so as to embrace adolescents in school or college or starting out in business, and build a bridge between school life and after-school life in relation to music. We felt we could go no further with the concerts for children, which had become a self-perpetuating institution with a life of its own. The inclusion of young people in a somewhat more mature and ambitious age group opened up the prospect of developing an interest in other forms of listening, especially opera, as well as encouraging music-making through competitions and participation in youth orchestras, at both national and international levels.

In the context of music in England, these two aspects may be seen as a tributary flowing into the stream that by 1945 – the key year when for the first time in British history the State took a hand in supporting music and the arts – was already showing signs of becoming the noble, mighty river it is today.

Nowadays it is possible to engage in musical planning and to discover and bring forth talent which hitherto had been dormant. *The Watts Book of Music* makes its appearance at a singularly auspicious moment in our musical history, and places the emphasis on what is the paramount aspect of all music – its vitality. This very word implies life, and life-enhancement. Viva! Long may it live!

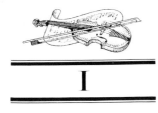

I

THE NATURE OF MUSIC

What is music?

WE ALL know what music is – at least until we try to put into words what we mean. Then we realise that there is no general agreement, and that what is music to one person may be little more than a jumble of noise to someone else. Throughout history anything new has been greeted with the cry: 'It isn't music!' It was said about Bach in the 18th century and about Stravinsky in the 20th. It is said by lovers of classical music about pop, and vice versa. So perhaps we are dealing with various 'musics' rather than one single art of music.

The dictionary makes some attempt at a positive definition, calling music 'that one of the fine arts which is concerned with the combination of sounds with a view to beauty of form and the expression of thought or feeling.' Although this seems adequate, it is not really satisfactory, as it rules out one single sound as music. Chinese musicians can listen to the resonances of a single bell note as it dies away into silence, and for them that is music.

Most people, however, in the East as well as the West, expect something more from their music than contemplation of a single note, no matter how beautiful or evocative it may be. Every piece of music, from a song that lasts little more than a minute to an hour-long symphony, is a living organism – it is born out of silence, it grows with time and finally dies again, either on some triumphant chord or else by a gradual fading away. Again like living organisms, not only are no two pieces of music alike, but all performances of the same piece differ in subtle ways, depending on the skill and personality of the performer. This is as true of the gentlest piece for solo guitar as it is of a huge symphony involving 100 or more players.

In the face of such complexity, it becomes almost impossible to think back to that distant moment when the art of music first came into being. In any case, even the experts do not agree with one another as to what the origins of music actually were. Some claim that it began with singing, while others maintain that it began with rhythmic drumming, perhaps to accompany a dance that would make the crops grow or lead to a successful hunt. What is certain is that it was a primitive activity of intense significance, involving all the family or tribe.

Today we tend to regard music as entertainment, a means of relaxation after a busy day. But this attitude is a recent development as far as the history of music is concerned. The Ancient Greeks believed that certain scales or modes weakened men's resolve, while others made them ready for battle – a belief upheld by such dictators of modern times as Hitler and Stalin, who branded music as being good or bad for the moral health of the people.

Apart from such extreme political attitudes, music that is new and disturbing has always been resisted. Composers tend to build on the complexities of their predecessors, until the music becomes so difficult that a return to simplicity is demanded. This happened about 400 years ago, when opera was established in an attempt to return to the 'simplicity' of Ancient Greek drama. It happened again about 1750, when J.S.Bach's sons turned away from the mighty structures of his music, dismissing him as 'the old periwig'. It has happened again in recent years. After the very advanced and

Music, like this imaginary figure, is made up of many elements, from natural sounds such as birdsong to the instruments of orchestras and bands. It also involves dozens of interlocking activities: the composer's mental powers, the design of instruments and concert halls, a player's skills and personality – even the printing of programmes.

cerebral music of the 1950s and 1960s, many of today's composers have returned to more traditional styles of music.

Whether simple or complex, people create and listen to music because they love it. When Schubert wanted to sum up his feelings for the 'wondrous art' he practiced so miraculously, he set them down in one of the simplest of all his songs, 'To Music', which is an outpouring of affection and thanksgiving. And Beethoven, at the beginning of his 'Solemn Mass', wrote: 'From the heart it came, to the heart may it go.' That is the true meaning of music.

Music around us

In the 18th century high-flown Italian opera was considered absurd by ordinary people. In this William Hogarth cartoon (above) the people in the street enjoy listening to a popular tune from the down-to-earth 'Beggar's Opera', written by Dr Pepusch and the poet John Gay, while the violinist of the Italian opera looks from the window in outrage and dismay.

Buskers in Covent Garden open market, London (above) play traditional Chinese instruments. Such street musicians are often students, who perform for cinema queues or on the underground, and may be of professional standard.

TODAY, APART from the music which we listen to by choice, we are bombarded by musical sounds from every direction, and at most hours of the day and night. There are radios, cassettes and CDs in the home or in the car, piped music at airports and in flight, in hospitals, supermarkets, bars and restaurants. Music of one sort or another is inescapable. This trend has been criticised by those who claim that constant exposure to music tends to make people less discriminating, although the opposite is probably true. The human brain can normally cut out what it does not want to attend to; and this is true of music as well, unless it is so obtrusively loud or repetitive that it compels attention. In fact, the opportunity of hearing anything and everything probably leads to greater selectivity rather than less. The listener finds what he likes by trial and error, and is then able to follow up his newly discovered interest.

All this kind of music has been 'canned' or pre-packed in some way, either by the record companies, by the firms that provide piped background music or by the radio stations. So it is reminiscent of the sort of bland, untroubled music that kings and lords in bygone centuries used to command their musicians to play during mealtimes – like a musical decoration corresponding to the tapestries and pictures that hung on their walls. By the nature of the society of the time, such court music was heard by only a small proportion of the population. The rest had to be content with ceremonial processions and municipal occasions, in which local musicians were put on public view, with the austere music played in church, with the dance music of travelling musicians, and with what they were able to provide in their own homes.

When public concerts developed in the 18th century, they were comparatively expensive to attend, and the number of people who could fit into the fairly modest-sized halls of the time was limited. The only way most people could get to know symphonies and other large-scale works was by playing them at home in four-handed piano arrangements. During the 19th century the building of vast concert halls meant that live music reached more people than ever before.

Standards went up accordingly, and audiences could compare one performance of a work with another – although in the absence of any method of recording, apart from what the critics wrote, they had only memory to carry them over from one concert to the next. Today the problem is not lack of choice: it is that choice has become so bewilderingly difficult. In a capital city such as London or Paris there may be four or five concerts to choose from every evening of the week, and often afternoon concerts as well. Those who prefer an evening's music at home have only to switch to the classical channel that many radio stations put out, or alternatively, put on a CD or cassette.

Much of the music played today is not intended for concentrated listening, but is there to obliterate outside noise; this is the kind of music that is piped into factories, hospital corridors and airport lounges. The Canadian composer Murray Schafer has coined the word 'soundscape' to define 'the vast musical composition which is unfolding round us ceaselessly'. In a medieval city the loudest noise in the soundscape was the clang of the church bell. In a modern city the background is provided by the constant roar of traffic.

A composer's inner ear is bound to be highly sensitive to the external soundscape. If he finds it ugly and repellent, then the music he composes may well reflect his dislike of what he hears all round him. Occasionally a well-known composer may be able to influence the soundscape to his own advantage. Thus, when Benjamin Britten lived at Aldeburgh on the Suffolk coast, he managed to persuade the authorities to alter the flight paths of aircraft that would have disturbed concerts at the Aldeburgh Festival.

The influence of soundscape is perhaps one reason why the music of many composers is so much less easy on the ear than commercial music. One mirrors the soundscape, the other erases it. In the 1920s Edgar Varèse tackled the problem head-on by bringing the sounds of the city, such as bells and sirens, into his music, while in the 1950s *musique concrète* composers used tapes of urban and other noises. But composers have not generally gone to such extremes. They have absorbed the soundscape slowly, and audiences have preferred it that way.

BACKGROUND MUSIC

In all ages there have been two kinds of music: serious works that are meant to be listened to with full attention, and lighter music to provide a background for eating, conversation and other activities. In the 16th-century mural (right) showing a wedding feast given by the nobleman Sir Henry Unton, a group of musicians playing the flute, viols and lute accompany a procession of masquers performing a symbolic drama. The artist has ignored perspective and made the musicians very small.

In Victorian times music was used as a background on every possible occasion. A 'Utopian' Christmas scene (left) shows a distribution of puddings and other food, as a quintet of violin, piano, harp, guitar and singer provides the music. In the 20th century the universal appeal of pop music has led to the emergence of radio disc jockeys (below). They have an enormous influence on which records become popular enough to form the musical background in discothèques, cafés and pubs.

The raw materials

12

EVERY ART has its own basic materials, as well as the techniques of shaping them into a completed work, which have been built up over the centuries. The sculptor has to know how to handle different kinds of stone, metal and wood before he can give solid form to the shape that exists inside his head. The painter, who interprets the three dimensions of the outside world on the two dimensions of a piece of canvas, has to understand the basic principles of perspective, as well as the ways in which all the colours at his disposal complement or counteract each other. The composer's task is even more difficult. He is dealing not with a piece of granite or a tube of paint, but with a fixed amount of time, to be filled with sound that can hold the audience's total attention.

Apart from purely electronic compositions, in which the composer remains in control without the need for a human performer, once the musical work is written down it is literally out of the composer's hands. In the case of an orchestral work, his initial creation will be interpreted by as many as 100 people, playing many kinds of instruments, and controlled by a conductor who may have very different ideas about the work from what was originally in the composer's mind. In the case of a solo piece,

there is the character and technique of the player to be taken into account. Then there is always the acoustic quality of the concert hall to be considered. This will often decide whether a piece emerges clear or muddy in tone, and whether each chord will be cut off dead or merge confusedly into the next.

Before a composer can put a note down on paper, he must learn the tone qualities, range of notes and technical problems of each instrument, and the conventions of traditional harmony, which are based on the laws of acoustics. Of course, in modern music, as in modern sculpture and painting, the traditional rules no longer necessarily apply. But the composer, like the visual artist, has to know them before he can break them with confidence.

Western music, which was ruled by harmony for centuries, originated in the church, with simultaneous singing of two or more lines of plainsong, or religious chant. Singers and listeners grew accustomed to thinking of music 'vertically' as well as 'horizontally' – as chords separated from one another, rather than as interweaving lines of melody. Thus the theory of harmony evolved, which ruled that some groups of notes were harmonious and satisfying, while others were discordant and harsh.

In the Middle Ages, musical notation was quite different from that of modern times. On this 15th-century manuscript of a madrigal (left), the stave has six ruled lines instead of the five of today's stave, and the notes are square or lozenge-shaped, depending on their length. Medieval music, which was originally based on Ancient Greek music, was in a variety of modes or scales. The five-line stave and our familiar major and minor scales were adopted in the 16th and 17th centuries. The medieval modes survive in traditional folksong, and have been revived by 20th-century composers.

Pythagoras (left) not only discovered the famous mathematical theorem, he was also a musician who worked out the various scales or modes of Ancient Greek music. This drawing is based on a medieval woodcarving, which shows the philosopher wearing 15th-century costume.

QUAVER

CROTCHET

RISING QUAVERS

FALLING QUAVERS

RISE FOLLOWED BY A FALL

FALL FOLLOWED BY A RISE

THREE RISING QUAVERS

THREE FALLING QUAVERS

Medieval plainsong was written in a distinctive way (left). Our modern rounded notes derive from the special notation of this period.

But one generation's discord is the next generation's perfectly acceptable harmony. To a medieval monk our so-called 'common chord' – the notes C, E and G on the piano – was a discord to be avoided, although it was the basic building-block of all classical music. The same is true of the discords used in modern music. Sooner or later all chords lose the power to shock, as people grow accustomed to hearing them in a wide variety of pieces.

The 20th century has seen enormous acceleration in the rate at which the raw materials of music have changed. There has been a growing rejection of traditional notions of harmony, ushered in by the music of Wagner and Debussy and leading to the 12-note system of Schoenberg.

Later composers such as Webern and Messiaen added their own revolutionary ideas of instrumental timbre and rhythm, while the tape recorder and the computer have enabled Stockhausen, Xenakis and others to lead music down paths of ever-increasing complexity.

Yet the reality of musical inspiration remains as mysterious as it was when Wagner 'dreamed' the chord of E flat and turned it into the magical opening of 'Rhinegold', or when Stravinsky had a vision of a solemn pagan rite, which surfaced a few years later in the shattering music of 'The Rite of Spring'. Beethoven described the way he composed in unforgettable words: 'I carry my thoughts about with me for a long time, before writing them down . . . I change many things, discard others and try again and again until I am satisfied; then, in my head, I begin to elaborate the work in its breadth, its narrowness, its height and its depth, and as I am aware of what I want to do, the underlying idea never deserts me. It rises, it grows up, I hear and see the image in front of me from every angle, as if it had been cast, and only the labour of writing it down remains.' But without years of experience in handling music's raw materials, the inspired visions of Beethoven, Wagner and Stravinsky would have remained locked inside their heads.

A conductor's working blueprint is the orchestral score. This page (above) is from the overture to Wagner's opera 'The Mastersingers'.

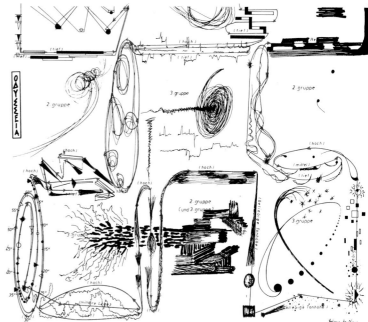

Many modern scores bear little resemblance to those of earlier periods. Some composers use graphic notation (above) instead of notes, as can be seen in this section of the score of 'Odyssey'. Written by Bulgarian-born Anestis Logothetis, it is a ballet score for three groups of players.

Makers of music

PEOPLE IN
MUSIC

composer

orchestral
player

chamber
musician

soloist

accompanist

conductor

solo singer

choral singer

opera singer

librettist

teacher

music therapist

publisher

copyist

concert agent

orchestral
manager

opera producer

concert-hall
manager

instrument-
maker

librarian

critic

musicologist

recording
engineer

radio producer

listener

At London's 'Prom' Concerts the men who heave the piano about the platform and adjust the music stands are always given a good-natured cheer. This is probably the only public applause they ever receive, but it is fully justified, as they are essential to the smooth running of a concert, and the star conductor and pianist, not to mention the first violins and the second trombone, would be lost without them. They emphasise the fact that music is an activity where a vast number of human beings interact, all with special skills of one sort or another. Composer, conductor, orchestral player, publisher, agent and concert-hall manager all make up a structure in delicate balance, in which none of the parts can function fully without all the others working equally well.

Before the end product of symphony, overture or concerto can be enjoyed by the audience, an enormous amount of organisation has to take place. Concerts are planned not months but years ahead. While the final adjustments for tonight's concert are being made in the concert hall, the hall's management already has a complete schedule for the following year, and has worked out what orchestras and what soloists

A London 'Prom' concert could not take place without the work of an army of people with non-musical skills, from removal men to programme-makers.

will be playing on any particular night; while there is at least a rough schedule for the next year but one. This applies even more to opera houses, where the organisation is far more complicated, involving principal singers for every opera, an orchestra and chorus, plus a small army of stage hands and other experts.

All this ant-like activity provides the framework in which the music is played, and in which all musicians are involved. Even the composer, working away at his score in as much peace as he can find, cannot escape. He has to get his music published and performed, and needs any number of contacts before he or anyone else can hear a note of his music in the concert hall. This is nothing new: composers like Mozart and Berlioz spent an enormous amount of time and energy rushing about booking halls for themselves and getting together the musicians to perform their works. In more recent times composers like Stockhausen and Maxwell Davies have founded their own instrumental groups to play their new and controversial music.

Among the most inspiring musical developments of recent years has been the tremendous growth of youth orchestras, where talented young people meet to play music of every kind. A typical example is the London Schools Orchestra (below), which is here conducted by Simon Rattle, one of today's leading British conductors.

Television has brought the basics of music to millions of viewers. The baritone Thomas Hemsley (below) is here giving a master class in singing on BBC television.

St Cecilia, the patron saint of music (left), was martyred in Rome or Sicily about 200AD. It is not certain when she became music's patron, but it was probably not until about 1500, when artists began to paint her playing the organ and singing to it. According to legend, St Cecilia sang so sweetly that an angel came down from heaven to listen. About 1570 the town of Evreux in Normandy began to celebrate her feast day, November 22nd, with special music. In London a musical society was founded in 1683, to sing an ode in her honour every November 22nd. In 1692 Henry Purcell wrote a magnificent ode called 'Hail, bright Cecilia', and Handel wrote an equally fine birthday ode in 1739.

The musicians who actually appear on the concert platform, or have their works played regularly in public, are only a small proportion of the vast number of people who have been trained to a professional standard. In music, as in every other artistic profession, it is tough at the top, and it is becoming tougher all the time as more and more highly skilled players appear. All the same, there are more chances now for catching the public eye, with prestige events like the Tchaikovsky piano competition in Moscow or the BBC's 'Young Musician of the Year' contest in London, which bring unknown young players to the attention of millions, and guarantee them solo recitals and concerts with the world's leading orchestras.

On the other hand, composers probably have a harder time getting their music known than ever before. Today there is little general interest in new music, and even concerts of new works by established composers like Henze and Carter are thinly attended. A young composer stands little chance of hearing a large-scale work performed, unless he is lucky enough to get a commission from one of the big orchestras or from a broadcasting company. Having heard the work once, he may well never hear it again. In the world of modern music, 'first performance' often means 'last performance' as well.

In both the performing and the composing worlds many people end up in the teaching profession, handing on their skills and knowledge to a new generation, most of whom will also teach. This may sound a second-best prospect, but it does not have to be so (see overleaf).

16

In music the old tradition of master and apprentice lives on from the Middle Ages. This relationship forms the basis of Wagner's opera 'The Mastersingers', which is concerned with the competition to become a member of the musicians' guild of Nuremberg. A thin thread of continuity links the greatest composers, either directly or through study of each other's works. Bach taught his sons, and one of them taught Mozart. Haydn and Mozart both learnt from each other. Beethoven taught Czerny, who taught Liszt, who in turn taught generations of young composers and pianists. At the beginning of this century Schoenberg taught Berg and Webern, and the study of Webern's music by Boulez, Stockhausen and other modern composers led to many of the developments of today's music.

At present, the teaching of playing and composing tend to be regarded as separate functions, although that was not always the case. In the 18th century and earlier the two were closely interlinked. Bach taught both playing *and* composition, since any all-round musician was expected to be able to produce music on demand for a patron – at least, if he hoped to get a good job as musical director at a princely court. By Mozart's time the two functions were separate. In modern times this split is almost universal.

Another aspect of music that has appeared – or rather reappeared – in the last 20 years or so, is the use of music in healing, especially in mental healing. The Ancient Greeks were well aware of this connection, and they made the same god, Apollo, the ruler of both music and medicine. The Bible describes how King Saul's fits of depression were cured when David played the harp for him, and an entirely different sickness – physical, rather than mental – caused by the bite of the tarantula spider was supposed to be cured by the tarantella dance of southern Italy. When music lost its mystical or magical associations and came to be regarded almost entirely as entertainment, its healing powers went largely disregarded. But now it has come into its own again, as a group activity in mental homes, and especially as a way of opening up communication with autistic children, who cannot be reached by means of words. Through playing an instrument as simple as a toy drum a child can begin to 'talk' to the outside world and receive a reply. As a music therapist has said, music can bring about a change from mere existence to life.

DANCING THE TARANTELLA

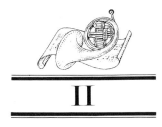

II

INSTRUMENTS IN ACTION

The orchestra at home

18

To LISTEN to a first-class symphony orchestra, faultlessly playing a musical masterpiece, is one of the most exhilarating experiences modern civilisation has to offer. Yet although it seems to have a timeless permanence, the symphony orchestra was a latecomer to the musical scene. In its present form it only dates back to the classical period of Haydn, Mozart and Beethoven. Earlier composers used whatever instruments were available at the local aristocratic court or in the town band. Monteverdi, in the early 1600s, was able to produce a rich instrumental sound to accompany his operas because his patron, the Duke of Mantua, had a band of 40 skilled players. But at Leipzig, a century later, Bach had to make do with about a dozen strings, half that number of woodwind, three trumpets and a drummer.

In those early days there were no halls built exclusively for concerts. Apart from princely palaces, orchestral works were played in churches, theatres and opera houses. As late as the last quarter of the 18th century Mozart gave his concerts either in the theatre in Vienna or in various private palaces. The growth of public concert halls was a 19th-century development, parallel to the growth of an educated middle class with a strong desire to hear good classical music played well, and the money to pay for it. The famous Leipzig Gewandhaus ('Cloth Hall'), from which one of the world's finest modern orchestras has taken its name, was first used for public concerts in 1781.

THE STORY OF THE CONCERT

Before special concert halls were built, orchestral works were played in the grand palaces of wealthy patrons (above), as Haydn's symphonies were at Esterháza in the 1700s. A small group of musicians played in an informal atmosphere, as people ate, drank and talked to each other.

Very few concert halls existed solely for orchestral performances until the end of the 18th century. Europe's oldest surviving concert hall, the Holywell Music Room at Oxford in England (below), was opened in 1748, and concerts have been given there ever since. As concert-going was expensive, people had a greater sense of occasion, bringing a new formality to the concert with their elaborate dress and manners.

London's Royal Albert Hall (below) is famous for its summer season of 'Prom' concerts. The orchestra shown here is the London Symphony. Like all top-line orchestras, the LSO plays in a variety of concert halls, from the Barbican and the Royal Festival (far left) in London to the Palacio de la Musica in Barcelona (near left).

Small groups of players, able to perform almost anywhere, are very popular. The Academy of St Martin-in-the-Fields (below) specialises in 18th-century music.

The vast concert halls which were built in the 19th century (above) meant that thousands of people could listen to music. To fill such huge spaces with sound, orchestras also grew in size.

Recently, the traditions of the 18th century and earlier have returned to music, with much smaller instrumental ensembles playing in informal surroundings (below).

In 1813 London's newly-formed Philharmonic Society gave its first concert in a hall near Oxford Circus, and in 1822 launched itself into musical immortality by commissioning Beethoven's 'Choral' Symphony. The connection between orchestra and concert hall was especially strong in 19th-century America, where wealthy cities such as Boston and Cleveland vied with each other to establish excellent orchestras and build magnificent halls for them to play in.

During the 19th century vast buildings like London's Albert Hall enabled more people to listen to music than at any other time in history, and orchestras grew in size so as to be able to fill such spaces with sound. While 25 or so players had satisfied Mozart, the symphonic works of Mahler and Strauss, composed in the years round 1900, demanded orchestras of 100 or more. Such inflated proportions brought a natural reaction back to smaller groups of players. After the First World War, the 'neo-classical' composers, led by Stravinsky, valued clarity above everything else, and wrote for orchestras of classical dimensions.

As for concert halls of recent decades, buildings like London's Royal Festival Hall incorporate all the latest techniques of controlled acoustics. The hall constructed for Stockhausen at the 1970 World's Fair in Osaka, Japan, pointed the way to unlimited future possibilities. It broke entirely with tradition by being shaped like a sphere, with a platform suspended in the middle for the audience, and sound coming from all sides through an enormous number of loudspeakers – total stereo in the concert hall.

The conductor's role

A T THE beginning of every orchestral piece, after the leader of the orchestra (principal player of the first violins) has taken his place, there is an expectant hush in the concert hall. Then the conductor strides on to the platform, glances round the orchestra, stands with his baton poised for a moment, and the music is under way. At the end of a successful performance the conductor takes the lion's share of the glory, although he always shakes hands with the leader, and waves the orchestra to its feet to acknowledge the applause. He is the star of the concert platform. He may share his stardom briefly with a soloist in a concerto, but for the rest of the concert he is the undisputed ruler.

The conductor's emergence as king of the concert hall has been a slow process. In the 17th and 18th centuries time-keeping was normally carried out from the keyboard of harpsichord or organ, although the rhythm was sometimes given by waving a roll of paper, or thumping a stick against the desk or on the floor. The French composer Lully actually died from this procedure. In 1687, while conducting his own '*Te Deum*', he accidentally brought the stick down on his foot. Gangrene set in and he died a few weeks afterwards – the first conducting fatality.

About this time the accompanist (called the 'continuo-player') was often the composer as well, and since few rehearsals were held, he was probably the only musician who knew how the whole piece should sound. He played from a 'figured bass' – that is, the lowest line of the music, with figures indicating the harmony supported by the bass. Although the continuo-player was normally kept busy, if the performance seemed in danger of breaking down through losing the beat of the music, he could continue to play the bass line with his left hand while beating time with his right. Eighteenth-century music is still often played this way.

Principal conductor of the Berlin Philharmonic from 1954 until his death in 1989, Herbert von Karajan (above) had a meticulous approach to the classics.

It is not known for certain who was the first conductor to leave the keyboard and stand in front of the orchestra waving a baton, but the credit is usually given to Louis Spohr (left). Born in Germany in 1784, he was one of the most brilliant musicians of his day. He is said to have used the baton in 1820, to conduct one of his own symphonies at a concert in England. Spohr died in 1859, aged 75.

Richard Strauss (above) is remembered today for his operas and symphonic poems, but early in his career, at the end of the 19th century, he was one of Europe's leading orchestral conductors.

Born in 1882, Leopold Stokowski (above), who was English-born despite his name, made his reputation with the splendid Philadelphia Orchestra. He was a leading conductor for almost 70 years.

The Hungarian-born Sir Georg Solti (above) had a dazzling conducting career in Britain at the Covent Garden opera. He is now the principal conductor of the Chicago Symphony Orchestra.

The Italian Carlo Maria Giulini (above) began his career in Italy soon after the war. He has won international fame conducting the operas of Verdi, as well as the symphonic repertoire.

As a conductor-composer, Pierre Boulez (above) has cast new light on the music of Debussy and Webern, and has also conducted Wagner at Bayreuth. The Italian Riccardo Muti (below) has come to the fore in the 1970s.

Both Haydn and Mozart directed their symphonies from the keyboard. During the following period, when the keyboard director was beginning to disappear but the baton conductor had not yet become fully established, the leader of the orchestra sometimes gave the beat by waving time with his violin bow.

A slightly later composer, Hector Berlioz, was not only the founder of modern orchestration, but also developed a complete conducting technique. The rules he laid down seem elementary and obvious today, but presumably they were not always followed when he formulated them in the 1850s. 'A conductor,' he said, 'should *see* and *understand*; he should be *agile* and *vigorous*; he should know the composition he conducts and the nature of the instruments; he should be able to read a score.' Berlioz had suffered from incompetent conductors, at least if a story in his memoirs can be believed. At the first performance of his enormous 'Requiem' in 1837, the conductor, François-Antoine Habeneck, had just reached a particularly tricky passage, when he laid down his baton and calmly took a pinch of snuff. But Berlioz was equal to the occasion. Leaping forward, he pushed Habeneck aside and triumphantly conducted the work through to the end.

The line of professional conductors stretches back to Hans von Bülow in the middle of the last century. Many conductors have reached a great age, kept fit by the amount of exercise they have to take. Arturo Toscanini, who was born in 1867, conducted the first performance of Puccini's 'La Bohème' in 1896 and lived on until 1957, unrivalled for the brilliance of his technique and his hypnotic power over the most self-willed orchestras. He was strong-minded in other ways: in 1931 he was assaulted by Mussolini's thugs for refusing to conduct the Italian Fascist March.

Their successors are the modern stars such as Herbert von Karajan, Georg Solti and Colin Davis, while the newly-established conducting competitions are constantly producing the conductors of the future. They may not be as eccentric or flamboyant as the conductors of yesterday, but their streamlined efficiency is better suited to the jet-propelled international life of today's orchestras.

The strings

THE STRINGS are the foundation of the orchestra. With their enormous pitch span, from the lowest notes of the double bass to the highest harmonics of the violin, they cover almost the whole range of audibility. Their tones merge together, so that the violins overlap with the violas and the violas with the cellos, giving a consistent background sonority against which woodwind, brass and percussion can perform their more individualistic roles. The string section far outnumbers all the other players in the average orchestra: out of 100 or so members, two-thirds will be string-players.

The strings have great advantages over other instruments. Whereas wind-players grow tired and need to conserve their energies, so that composers have to give them breathing-spaces between extended passages, the strings are often treated as though they were tireless. In symphonies from Haydn to Shostakovich they have always borne the brunt of the musical argument. Individually, they are the most voice-like of instruments, following the inflexions of speech and song. They can express passion or rejoicing, they can sigh and they can chatter. The violinist and cellist can suggest aggression or gentleness, showmanship or modesty, by the way they apply their bows to the strings.

On a stringed instrument an individual note can be extended almost indefinitely, and swelled or reduced in volume as it proceeds. The strings have other capabilities that make them unique.

VIOLIN
The supreme example of the instrument-maker's craft is the violin. It reached perfection about 1700 in the workshops of the great Italian violin-making families, notably Amati, Guarneri and Stradivari. No one since has been able to improve on the work of these masters, although studies have been made of the wood, glue and varnishes they used. In the early days of the violin, all four strings were made of animal gut, but the drive for greater brilliance and power has led to metal being used for the two lower strings.
Although the violin seems to be supported by the left hand, it is in fact held by being gripped between the chin and the collar-bone (above). The left hand is used for stopping the strings. The average orchestra has 30 or more violins, divided into firsts and seconds.

VIOLA
Slightly larger than the violin, the viola sounds a fifth lower. It has a more veiled and thoughtful character than the brilliant and extrovert violin – a quality appreciated by Mozart, who played the viola himself, and who contrasted the two instruments in his beautiful 'Sinfonia Concertante'. The viola, long treated as the poor relation of the violin, really came into its own in this century, largely through the skilful playing of Lionel Tertis. With its greater weight and longer strings, the viola calls for a larger and stronger hand than the violin, and is more tiring to play. The symphony orchestra has 12 or more viola-players.

For forty years the Amadeus String Quartet (above) was a world-famous ensemble specialising in chamber music. Its members gave regular concert performances in London and abroad.

CELLO
The cello's sonorous and vibrant tones make it the most lyrical of all instruments. It is held with the neck pointing over the player's left shoulder, and is supported on the floor by an adjustable metal peg below the tailpiece (above). The sound is an octave below that of the viola. The role of the cello in underpinning the orchestra is almost as important as that of the first violin in providing the main melodic line. Cellos are very effective when used *pizzicato* (by plucking the strings with the fingers), as in the allegretto movement of Brahms's Second Symphony or the lively scherzo of Tchaikovsky's Fourth. The cello section of an orchestra usually has at least 10 players.

DOUBLE BASS

VIOLIN

DOUBLE BASS BOW

VIOLIN BOW

TUNING PEGS

FINGERBOARD

STRINGS

BRIDGE

The stringed instruments (right) have acquired a special vocabulary to express their many talents. *Pizzicato* describes the twanging sound produced by plucking the strings. *Sul ponticello* is a nasal sound made by drawing the bow across the strings near the bridge, and *sul tasto* is its opposite: a transparent tone made by using the bow near or above the fingerboard. *Col legno* means to strike the strings with the wood of the bow to produce a dry, brittle sound; *con sordino* is to play with a mute on the bridge to make the tone silky and smooth. When the bow is bounced lightly off the strings (*spiccato*), the result is a slight separation between the notes. *Punto d'arco*, which uses only the tip of the bow, is an effect of extreme lightness and delicacy.

By vibrating movements transmitted through the fingers of the left hand (*vibrato*), the string-player can enrich and enliven the tone. Yehudi Menuhin has described the different kinds of *vibrato* as 'narrow and fast, producing a gleaming, penetrating sound', or with so much *vibrato* that it is 'like a brilliant light'.

It is this enormous variety that makes the strings so fascinating, in spite of their outward uniformity. Composers have always revelled in the sounds of a string orchestra playing by itself. Bach's Third 'Brandenburg' Concerto, Elgar's 'Introduction and Allegro' and Bartók's 'Divertimento' for Strings are just a few of dozens of deeply satisfying works that have been written for the strings alone.

DOUBLE BASS
Because of the immense size of the double bass (about 2 metres overall), its player has either to stand, or sit on a high stool (above). In shape this giant instrument of the orchestra differs from the other stringed instruments, as it has sloping shoulders that taper towards the neck, like the old viol family, instead of a single rounded curve. It is also the only instrument in the orchestra to tune its strings a fourth apart,

rather than a fifth. The double bass often plays in unison with the cello, at an octave below. A strikingly effective example occurs in the opening bars of Schubert's 'Unfinished' Symphony. In post-classical works the instrument often has a part entirely separate from the cello. About eight double bass-players are usually included in the symphony orchestra of today.

In the classic jazz trio of piano, drums and bass, the double bass-player (above) usually plucks the instrument.

The smallest stringed instrument, the violin, has the longest bow, while the giant double bass has the shortest.

Strings in the past

FAMOUS STRING PLAYERS
1650-1850
VIOLIN
Corelli
Vivaldi
Tartini
Kreutzer
Paganini
Vieuxtemps
CELLO
Boccherini
J.L.Duport
DOUBLE BASS
Dragonetti
SINCE 1850
VIOLIN
Joachim
Sarasate
Ysaye
Kreisler
Elman
Heifetz
D.Oistrakh
Menuhin
Stern
Zukerman
Kyung Wha Chung
VIOLA
Tertis
Primrose
CELLO
Casals
Fournier
Tortelier
Rostropovich
DOUBLE BASS
Koussevitsky

THE IDEA of producing sound from a stringed instrument by passing a bow across the strings, instead of plucking them, came to Europe from the Middle East. The Arabs had a bowed instrument called a *rabab* which reached Europe in about the 10th or 11th century. The voice-like sustained notes of bowed strings, in contrast to the instantly-dying sounds of the lute or harp, soon became enormously popular. Minstrels played the pear-shaped rebec and the waisted *vielle* or fiddle, and kings kept bands of fiddlers to accompany their dances and provide a musical background to their journeys.

During the Renaissance, the instrumental families began to separate into the forms we know today. As far as the bowed strings were concerned, there were two main groups: the violins and the viols. Although their names are so similar, they were completely different. The violins, like the rebecs, were held with the soundbox under the chin, and the fingerboard away from the player. The viols, on the other hand, no matter how small, were held pointing downwards, with the fingerboard at the top, as with the cello. The viol developed from the guitar (the old Spanish *vihuela*) during the 15th century; like the guitar it normally had six strings, and frets (pieces of gut tied round the fingerboard) to give the position of each note. The violins, on the other hand, had only four strings and no frets.

Italy was the home of early violin-playing, and also of early violin-making. The great violin-makers were established at Cremona in northern Italy by the mid-16th century, and for the best part of 200 years the families of Amati, Guarneri and Stradivari carved, glued, fitted and

The most outstanding of violin-makers, Antonio Stradivari (left), made about 1200 violins in his lifetime (1644-1737). Each one bore a special label (below). Nowadays Stradivari violins fetch vast sums of money.

Antonius Stradivarius Cremonenfis
Faciebat Anno 1732
de Annis 9

varnished their miracles of musical craftsmanship. Their skills mainly went into the production of unrivalled violins, but they also made superb cellos, violas and guitars.

About 1600, the violins and viols were in a state of uneasy truce. The gentle-toned viols, playing in 'consorts' of different-sized instruments, suited aristocratic amateurs. The violins, more rhythmic and brilliant, were ideal for accompanying dance music and tended to be played by experts. But as music became increasingly professional, the violin was bound to triumph. In France, Louis XIII established his *24 Violons du Roi* in the 1620s; 40-odd years later, Charles II followed suit in England. The viol still had admirers, such as Purcell, but by the 18th century this ancient family was obsolete. It was left to our own century to rediscover the viol's grave and eloquent voice.

Meanwhile, the violin went from strength to strength. Composer-violinists like Corelli wrote quantities of violin sonatas and trios at the start of the 18th century, and technique surged ahead, keeping pace with the improvements made by the Cremona instrument-makers. About 1780 the modern bow was perfected by the Frenchman François Tourte, enabling the virtuosos of the time – culminating in Paganini about 1830 – to evolve the dazzling array of bowing techniques now available to every violinist.

Strangest of all the strings was the *tromba marina*, which had a tapering triangular body and a single string, later increased to two. It disappeared about the beginning of the 18th century. The name, meaning 'marine trumpet', is a mystery, although it may refer to the instrument's trumpet-like harmonics.

The rebec (above), often used to accompany dances, was one of the earliest of bowed instruments, and ancestor of the violin.

The viol (above) was superseded by the violin in the 17th century. Its gentle tone could not compete with the brilliance of the violin.

MAKING A VIOLIN

Every good violin has a distinct personality. Made from carefully chosen wood of several different kinds, it is dependent at every stage on the skilful eye and hand of a master-craftsman. During the course of centuries it evolved into the matchless products of Stradivarius and the other great Italian makers, who laid down the guidelines which later craftsmen have followed. The tradition continues, and in the same way as a 'Strad' made in 1700 is still played today, a 20th-century violin will be delighting audiences in the year 2200.

Violin-making involves different kinds of wood – maple for the back, side pieces (or 'ribs'), and neck; pine for the front (or 'belly'), lying under the strings; and ebony for the tailpiece and fingerboard. The craftsman (above) is bending one of the ribs round an electrically-heated bending iron. There are six ribs altogether. When they have all been bent to shape, they are clamped to an inside mould (below) and glued to the corner and end blocks.

After the glue has set, the ribs are removed from the mould, and strengthened at top and bottom with narrow strips of wood called 'linings'.
The back and belly of a violin (below) are each formed from two pieces of wood, which are cut from the same wedge-shaped block and glued edge to edge so that the grain of the wood is a symmetrical match. First, the under side is planed.

Then the shape of the piece is marked out, using a plywood template as a pattern, and sawn to shape. Next the outer surface is 'arched' into a smooth curve (above), using gouges, planes and scrapers.

The inner surface is then hollowed out to a slightly concave shape – a process known as 'thicknessing'. At some stage in the shaping process, depending on the craftsman, a narrow groove is cut right round the back and belly, about 3mm from the edge, and 'purfling' is inserted (above) by tapping lightly with a hammer.

The purfling is a triple inlaid wooden strip, coloured black-white-black. It is decorative, but it also adds strength to the back and belly.

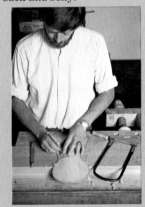

The two graceful 'f' holes in the belly, being marked out with a template (above), allow the sound to escape and also enable the belly to vibrate freely. The bridge's position will be half-way along the 'f' holes. After the holes have been cut, the bass bar is glued inside the belly and running parallel to it. Its purpose is to spread the vibarations and to resist the downward thrust of the strings. The next stage is to glue the back to the ribs, and finally the belly (below), using a number of clamps.

A water-soluble animal glue is used, so that the violin can be taken apart for repair. When the three parts of the body have been assembled, the neck and carved scroll are attached. The ebony fingerboard (above) is fastened to the neck, and final touches are given with the file (below).

The violin is now ready for varnishing with from eight to 12 coats of oil varnish, allowing up to two weeks for each coat to dry. When the varnishing is complete, the sound-post is inserted through one of the 'f' holes, and the pegs, tailpiece, bridge and strings are fitted. The completed violin (below) is given a final polish.

The woodwind

UNLIKE THE strings, which form a unified family, the woodwind instruments are so varied that they are hardly a family at all. In pitch they vary from the high skirling of the piccolo to the low growling of the double bassoon. They can be lyrical, soothing or menacing, and the skill of an orchestral composer is largely his skill with the woodwind.

In their range, the flute and oboe correspond roughly to the violins, and the clarinet and bassoon to the viola and cello. In their construction, flute and clarinet have a cylindrical, parallel-sided bore, while oboe and bassoon are conical, which makes them harder to shape and hence more expensive. There are wide differences in the methods of sound production which lead to very different qualities of tone. The flute and piccolo are bright and agile, the clarinets have a more throaty sound, while the double-reed instruments are pungent in tone. The term 'woodwind' is deceptive today, as the flute is nearly always made of metal, and the clarinet is often made of ebonite.

The standard classical orchestra had its woodwind instruments in pairs. As the 19th century progressed, each member of the family acquired a third instrument: the piccolo as the higher version of the flute, and the cor anglais, bass clarinet and double bassoon as the lower versions of the other instruments.

FLUTE

The modern flute (below), for all its sophistication, is still the shepherd's pipe of Arcadian legends. Debussy knew this when he depicted the calm of a hot afternoon by the long flute solo of his 'Prélude à l'Après-midi d'un Faune'.
The flute has also been accepted in the world of modern jazz, where it is played by such masters as the American soloist, Herbie Mann (right).

KEYS | MOUTHPIECE

The flute is played by blowing across the mouthpiece (below). The lowest notes are warm, and the highest are brilliant.

PICCOLO
The piccolo (below) is the half-size version of the flute. It is played in the same way, but sounds an octave higher. Although the piccolo is one of the smallest instruments in the orchestra, its piercing quality can be easily heard above the full body of players. This versatile instrument can sound humorous, as in Rossini's 'Semiramide' overture, or wildly grotesque, as in Berlioz's 'Fantastic' Symphony.

KEYS

MOUTHPIECE

OBOE
The oboe was probably invented at the French court about 1655. (The French word *hautbois* means 'high wood'.) Its tone is fairly consistent throughout its range, and it is often used as a solo instrument. The oboe can rival the flute in agility, as Ravel showed in the rippling passages of his prelude to 'Le Tombeau de Couperin'. The oboe has a double-reed mouthpiece, which means that there is no contact between the player's mouth and the body of the instrument (below). The double reed is all-important, and many oboists prefer to make their own.

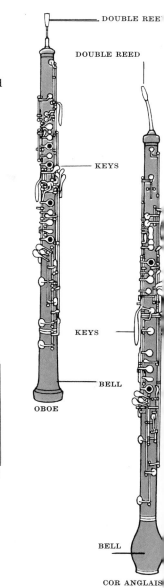

DOUBLE REED

DOUBLE REED

KEYS

KEYS

BELL

OBOE

BELL

COR ANGLAIS

COR ANGLAIS
The tenor version of the oboe is known in English as the 'cor anglais' – literally 'English horn'. Its plaintive quality is brought out in the slow movement of Dvořák's 'New World' Symphony.

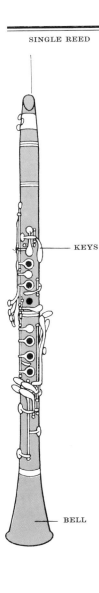

SINGLE REED

CLARINET

Unlike the flute, with its origins in the remote past, the clarinet (left) had a definite inventor: J.C.Denner of Nuremberg. In about 1700 Denner invented a single-reed woodwind instrument. At first it was played with the reed uppermost, but now the reed rests on the lower lip. The clarinet has three distinct registers. The lowest (the *chalumeau*), is dramatic and sometimes sinister.The middle *clarino* notes, from which the clarinet takes its name, are warm and expansive. The highest notes are shrill. Mozart and Brahms, both masters at writing for the clarinet, loved its expressive qualities. The Clarinet Quintet by Mozart, is a popular piece among modern clarinettists like Gervase de Peyer (below), who plays it here in a BBC television programme.

KEYS

BELL

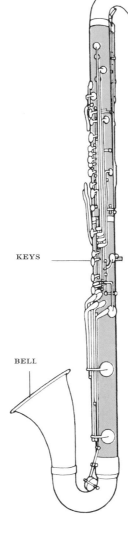

SINGLE REED

KEYS

BELL

BASS CLARINET

The deep and sonorous bass clarinet (above) has roughly the range of a cello. Wagner made great use of the instrument in the four 'Ring' operas, as did Tchaikovsky in his lively 'Nutcracker' ballet music.

Modern orchestras have 12 or more woodwind players, instead of the original eight of Mozart's and Beethoven's symphony orchestras.

Today's players, like Heinz Holliger on the oboe, Severino Gazzelloni on the flute, and Alan Hacker on the clarinet, are constantly pushing back the frontiers of technique, even managing to play 'chords' that give the impression of two notes being sounded at once. Berio has composed '*Sequenza*' pieces for solo flute and other instruments, while Stockhausen's '*Zeitmasse*' is for that rare combination: a woodwind quintet consisting of flute, oboe, cor anglais, clarinet and bassoon, all of which have to cope with rapidly changing speeds and rhythmic patterns.

BASSOON

The bassoon acts as the bass line to the woodwind 'quartet'. Like the oboe, it has a double reed, connected to the body of the instrument by a curved metal mouthpiece called a 'crook' (left). Unlike other woodwind instruments, the sounding tube is so long (about 2.5 metres) that it is doubled back on itself, making the instrument look rather clumsy. The tone quality is mellow, but it can also sound playful. Beethoven used it in both ways.

The double bassoon, a massive instrument twice the length of a bassoon, sounds an octave lower. It often plays the same notes as the double bass.

SAXOPHONE

Invented about 1846 by the Belgian instrument-maker Adolphe Sax, the saxophone is classed as a woodwind instrument, despite being made of brass. It has a single reed (like the clarinet) and a conical bore (like the oboe), and is made in a variety of sizes. Today, the saxophone is mainly a jazz instrument. A well-known soloist such as Sonny Rollins (right) is in great demand among the fans of modern jazz.

A typical woodwind group such as the Venturi Ensemble (left) plays a variety of music from Bach to the latest modern works.

Yesterday's woodwind

ONE OF the world's oldest surviving instruments is a bone flute made by a Stone Age craftsman around 3000BC. Pierced with five fingerholes, it looks like a primitive recorder, and would no doubt sound very similar. In prehistoric times flutes, because they were played with the breath of life, were regarded as symbolic of life itself. This personal, intimate quality is evident in all the woodwind to the present day. The Stone Age piper and the modern orchestral flautist are brothers in music.

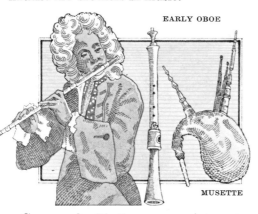

EARLY OBOE

MUSETTE

Jacques Hotteterre (left), who died about 1760, was flute-player to Kings Louis XIV and XV. He was a member of a family of makers and players of woodwind instruments, of whom the most famous, Jean, invented the oboe about 1655. Jean was also a bagpipe player – not today's loud Scottish bagpipe, but the gentler *musette*.

Compared with the more recent past, we are badly off as regards the number of woodwind instruments at our disposal. Our flutes, oboes, clarinets and bassoons do not begin to match the Renaissance shawms, racketts, recorders, curtals and crumhorns for variety of timbre. This dwindling of resources was due to changes in the social role of music; as orchestras became standardised in the 18th century, dozens of different instruments became extinct.

Alone among the modern woodwind, the transverse flute existed before the 16th century, as an addition to the enormous family of recorders. In Bach's time the flute and recorder were still virtually interchangeable – his Fourth 'Brandenburg' Concerto and Suite in B minor sound equally effective with either flute or recorder, although the latter does not balance so well with powerful modern strings. But later composers, such as Mozart, demanded brilliance and panache, neither of which the soft-toned recorder was able to provide.

The oboe, however, can be given a definite origin. It was developed in France between about 1655 and 1660 by Jean Hotteterre, who was both a craftsman and a practising musician.

Hotteterre seems to have been a bagpiper, a member of the group of royal musicians known as the *Grande Ecurie du Roi* (literally 'Great Stable of the King'). When the composer Lully was put in charge of the royal music by Louis XIV in 1655, he banned the loud shawms from court. So Hotteterre, who no doubt played the shawm as well as the bagpipe, produced a milder version of the shawm for Lully's sophisticated music. The bassoon evolved in much the same way, from the harsher-sounding early curtal.

SHAWMS

Apart from the shawms, other families of double-reed instruments, among them the crumhorns and racketts, disappeared during the 17th century, along with the colourful Renaissance pageantry of which they had formed a part.

The fast-shrinking woodwind family was greatly strengthened about 1700 when J.C. Denner of Nuremberg invented the clarinet, the only single-reed orchestral instrument. For a long time the clarinet remained an outsider, and only came into its own with the great virtuoso Anton Stadler, for whom Mozart wrote both his Clarinet Concerto and his Clarinet Quintet. A century later Brahms followed Mozart's example, writing his magnificent Clarinet Quintet for Richard Mühlfeld, together with a clarinet trio and two sonatas. The 19th century saw great refinements in the technology of all the woodwind, especially in the development of reliable systems of keys, to allow for faster and more efficient fingering. The main innovators here were the flautist Theobald Boehm, who developed the flute's key system, and Adolphe Sax, who is chiefly remembered as the inventor of the saxophone, but who also perfected the modern bass clarinet.

In 1846 Adolphe Sax (be-
low, left) invented the
saxophone. A year later
Theobald Boehm (below,
right) produced the first
Boehm flute, which has
remained almost un-
changed to the present.

The ancient shawm can
still be heard today in
Brittany, where the duet
of *bombarde* (shawm) and
biniou (bagpipe) is one of
the most characteris-
tic forms of Breton folk
music (left). It is also
played in Catalonia, in
Spain, where the instru-
ment is used to accom-
pany dances called *sar-
danas*, which are perfor-
med in the open air.

A CONSORT OF RACKETTS

Among the most curious
of Renaissance instru-
ments were the racketts
and the crumhorns. The
rackett, a solid cylinder
of wood with nine parall-
el holes, made a sound
like someone blowing
through a comb. The
crumhorn or 'crooked
horn', a curved double-
reed instrument, had a
full, singing tone.

CRUMHORNS

RECORDERS
Despite the difference in
size, all recorders have
eight holes. Large recorders sometimes have a
metal mouthpiece.
Enormously popular in
the 16th and 17th

centuries, the recorder
played in sets, as well as
being a solo instrument.
By the 20th century,
only a few recorders
existed outide museums.
Arnold Dolmetsch, a
Frenchman who settled
in England, owned two.
When these were lost on

a train in 1919, he was
heartbroken. But he set
to work at once, and in
1920 produced the first
modern recorder. Carl
Dolmetsch (Arnold's
son) and his family
(below) carried on the
tradition of making and
playing fine recorders.

BASS

TENOR

TREBLE

DESCANT

The brass

THE BRASS is the glory of the orchestra. The instruments are magnificent to look at – the shining bells of the trombones, poised to hurl their sound directly at the audience; the convoluted grace of the horns, their mellow gleam corresponding to their gentler notes; the glittering trumpets, compact and efficient, and still carrying faint echoes of their military origin; the squat tuba, slightly comic for all its splendour. As for the sound, it speaks for itself. A somnolent audience can be roused to alertness by a call from the brass, like the fanfare that opens Janáček's exhilarating 'Sinfonietta'. When used to create a solid wall of sound, as in Bruckner's symphonies, the combined weight of the brass makes an overwhelming impact.

The brass instruments are metal tubes, with a cup-shaped mouthpiece at one end and a flared bell at the other. When the player blows into the mouthpiece, the air column in the tube vibrates at a certain frequency; the tighter he compresses his lips, the higher the note. The notes are those of the 'harmonic series': first the fundamental or lowest note, then the octave above that, then the fifth above that, and so on in steadily decreasing intervals. The problem with all brass instruments is that, in order to change key, the length of the tube has to be extended or shortened. Apart from the trombone, all brass instruments change key by means of valves, which alter the tube length by bringing different short lengths of tubing into play.

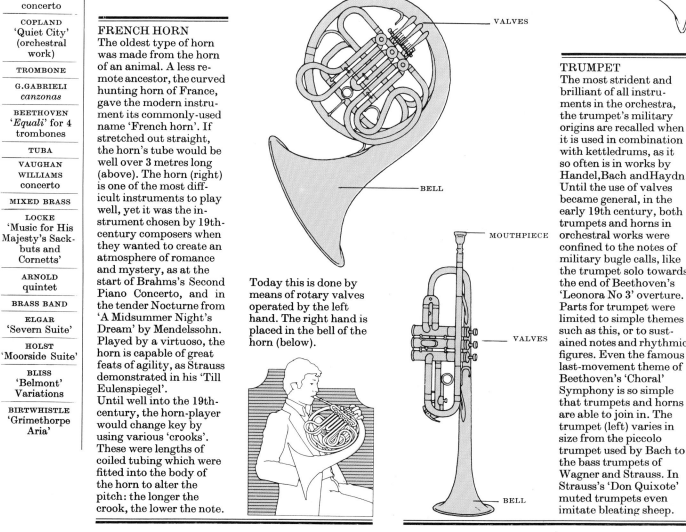

MOUTHPIECE

VALVES

FRENCH HORN

The oldest type of horn was made from the horn of an animal. A less remote ancestor, the curved hunting horn of France, gave the modern instrument its commonly-used name 'French horn'. If stretched out straight, the horn's tube would be well over 3 metres long (above). The horn (right) is one of the most difficult instruments to play well, yet it was the instrument chosen by 19th-century composers when they wanted to create an atmosphere of romance and mystery, as at the start of Brahms's Second Piano Concerto, and in the tender Nocturne from 'A Midsummer Night's Dream' by Mendelssohn. Played by a virtuoso, the horn is capable of great feats of agility, as Strauss demonstrated in his 'Till Eulenspiegel'.
Until well into the 19th-century, the horn-player would change key by using various 'crooks'. These were lengths of coiled tubing which were fitted into the body of the horn to alter the pitch: the longer the crook, the lower the note.

BELL

Today this is done by means of rotary valves operated by the left hand. The right hand is placed in the bell of the horn (below).

TRUMPET

The most strident and brilliant of all instruments in the orchestra, the trumpet's military origins are recalled when it is used in combination with kettledrums, as it so often is in works by Handel, Bach and Haydn. Until the use of valves became general, in the early 19th century, both trumpets and horns in orchestral works were confined to the notes of military bugle calls, like the trumpet solo towards the end of Beethoven's 'Leonora No 3' overture. Parts for trumpet were limited to simple themes such as this, or to sustained notes and rhythmic figures. Even the famous last-movement theme of Beethoven's 'Choral' Symphony is so simple that trumpets and horns are able to join in. The trumpet (left) varies in size from the piccolo trumpet used by Bach to the bass trumpets of Wagner and Strauss. In Strauss's 'Don Quixote' muted trumpets even imitate bleating sheep.

MOUTHPIECE

VALVES

BELL

SOUNDING BRASS

Brass bands are a product of the Industrial Revolution, and are very strong in the towns of northern England. The Brighouse and Rastrick band (above), founded in Yorkshire in 1858, is a completely amateur group. In 1977 the band broke into the pop world with 'The Floral Dance', an arrangement of a traditional Cornish air by their musical director. The recording sold almost a million copies, and won the Brighouse and Rastrick players international fame.

Many brass bands have such skilful players that composers like Vaughan Williams and Holst have written specially for them. Standard bands have 24 brass-players and two drummers. The instruments range from cornets and flugelhorns in the high register to euphoniums and trombones in the bass. The cornet developed from the circular French post-horn, used in coaching days. The flugelhorn, which has a rather plaintive sound, derives from the military bugle.

Classical symphony composers, such as Mozart and Beethoven, were generally content with a brass section of two horns and two trumpets. Berlioz, in his 'Fantastic' Symphony, extended the brass to include 13 instruments. Wagner took the process further: his 'Twilight of the Gods' demands 21 brass players. The brass section reached its greatest size in works of the late romantic period, such as Schoenberg's giant song cycle *Gurrelieder* which calls for 29 brass instruments. Later composers have been more modest. Bartók in his 'Concerto for Orchestra' and Stravinsky in his 'Symphony in Three Movements' used the now-standard brass section of 11 players: four horns, three trumpets, three trombones and a tuba.

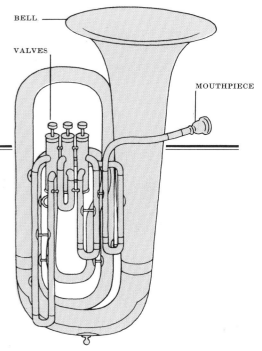

BELL

VALVES

MOUTHPIECE

TROMBONE
Apart from details like the shape of the mouthpiece and widening of the bore, the trombone (left) has hardly changed from the medieval sackbut. It has the simplicity of genius: instead of having a complicated system of valves, the tube of the trombone is shortened or lengthened by means of a slide drawn in or out by the player's right hand; the left hand holds the mouthpiece to the lips. Wagner was especially fond of the instrument's combination of sonorous dignity and power, and he gave it the noble main theme of the overture to his opera 'Tannhaüser'. But the trombone is not always played in such a sober way. When played *glissando* (sliding) it gives a whooping cry, as at the end of Bartók's 'Concerto for Orchestra'. The commonest trombone is the tenor, with a tube length of 3 metres. The bass trombone is found in most orchestral works from the mid-19th century onward.

MOUTHPIECE

BELL

SLIDE

TUBA
Rich and resonant, the tuba (right) provides a powerful foundation for the brass instruments. It developed fairly late in the 19th century, taking over from the ophicleide, for which Berlioz and his contemporaries wrote. In military bands the tuba gives the 'oom-pah' bass. But it can also be a descriptive instrument, as Ravel knew when he orchestrated 'Pictures from an Exhibition' by Mussorgsky, and gave

the tuba the lumbering tune that depicts a heavy Russian ox-cart. The tuba, dwarfing its player (above), is rather

clumsy in appearance. The tuba is made in many sizes, ranging from the euphonium, with a tube length of about 3 metres, to the contrabass tuba (6 metres). The usual orchestral tuba (above) falls between these two (4 metres). The so-called 'Wagner tuba' (right) was a special instrument devised by the composer to add a new colour to the brass in the 'Ring' cycle of operas. It is not a tuba at all and is, in fact, more like a horn.

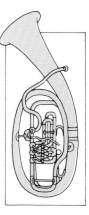

Beginnings of brass

ACCORDING TO the story, a young Bohemian nobleman called Count von Sporck, while on a grand tour of Europe in about 1680, heard the combined horns of the French royal hunt in full cry. So impressed was he with the sound that he had two of his servants taught to play the 'French horn' and when he returned home established it as an orchestral instrument.

The horn's curved shape and conical cross-section go right back to the Roman *cornu*, and even further back to the rams' horns which the Jewish priests blew to bring the walls of Jericho tumbling to the ground. In the Middle Ages one particular horn was awarded to knights as a mark of glory. This was the oliphant, made as its name indicates from an elephant's tusk, often richly carved and inlaid. The most famous oliphant of all time was the one blown by Charlemagne's nephew Roland, on the battlefield of Roncesvalles in the Pyrenees, in 778. As he lay wounded, Roland blew so violently for help that he burst a blood vessel and died.

Two Renaissance relatives of the horn were the cornett (not to be confused with the trumpet-like cornet) and the serpent. Although made of wood, these are usually classed as brass instruments. The cornett, a curved instrument with a cup-shaped mouthpiece, had disappeared by 1750. But the serpent lingered on in military bands and in the church until well into the 19th century, and has recently been brought back to life by Peter Maxwell Davies, who gave it a part in his opera 'Taverner'.

All these instruments have a conical bore. Trumpets and their relatives are cylindrical, which gives them much greater carrying power. A Roman poet, Ennius, described how the trumpet 'blares out *taratantara* with a terrifying sound', as it was to do on the battleground for a further 2000 years or more. Trumpets were used for peaceful ceremonial occasions as well, especially in the renaissance. Trumpeters then were organised into guilds, and guarded their skills jealously. Although their instruments had no valves, they could master such difficult music as the solos in Bach's second 'Brandenburg' concerto and Mass in B minor.

The trombone, with its brilliantly simple slide mechanism, seems to have been invented in the 15th century or earlier. At least, the earliest reference to *sacqueboute* (sackbut) dates from the 1460s, and it must presumably have appeared some time before that. Derived from the minstrel's trumpet, it soon found a place in church music, to which its grandly sonorous tones were well suited. Trombone music reached its height in Venice in the years around 1600, in the magnificent *canzonas* written for St Mark's by Giovanni Gabrieli.

A short-lived member of the brass family was the ophicleide – a brass form of the bugle, which replaced the serpent in orchestral music about 1820, before being itself superseded by the tuba. In Mendelssohn's 'Midsummer Night's Dream' overture, the theme representing Bottom was originally written for the ophicleide.

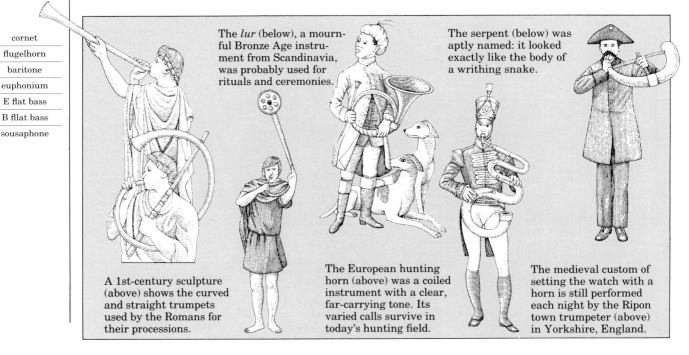

The *lur* (below), a mournful Bronze Age instrument from Scandinavia, was probably used for rituals and ceremonies.

The serpent (below) was aptly named: it looked exactly like the body of a writhing snake.

A 1st-century sculpture (above) shows the curved and straight trumpets used by the Romans for their processions.

The European hunting horn (above) was a coiled instrument with a clear, far-carrying tone. Its varied calls survive in today's hunting field.

The medieval custom of setting the watch with a horn is still performed each night by the Ripon town trumpeter (above) in Yorkshire, England.

MAKING A FRENCH HORN

Making a brass instrument is a fascinating combination of engineering craftsmanship and acoustics. A horn consists of several distinct sections. Its unique tone quality is given by the bell – that is, the 90cm of tubing where the sound emerges from the instrument. This is one high point of the craftsman's skill, as the bell has to be carefully shaped and bent into a graceful curve. Then there is the valve assembly, which lengthens or shortens the distance between mouthpiece and bell, and finally the mouthpiece, which meets the player's lips.

The craftsman begins to shape the horn (above), bending a flat strip of metal round a solid centrepiece to form a tube, and clipping the edges together by small projecting pieces of metal, or lugs. Most horns are made of 'yellow brass', made up of 70 per cent copper and 30 per cent zinc.

The next process (above) is to fill the join with spelter: a metallic compound of granulated brass, borax and water, mixed together into a mustard-like paste. When a blow-torch is directed along the seam (below) the spelter melts, making it airtight.

The craftsman must be extremely careful at this stage, as if the torch is held too long on the joint, the brass of the horn will also melt.

The tube is then forced down over a steel core or mandrel (above), the shape of the horn's bell. When the tube and a separate flare (below) are sufficiently formed they are

brazed together, by using the blow-torch (below). Unevenness in the joint is carefully hammered out.

The bell is then 'spun' on a lathe (below): the flare is turned to adjust the metal's thickness, and the edge is curled back to form a rim.

Next, the bell is filled with molten pitch, which solidifies (below). The craftsman holds the metal rod while he bends the tube round a wooden block, shaped to the required curve of the horn. The solid pitch prevents the horn cracking or buckling.

The outside surface is filed and smoothed with emery while the pitch is inside the tube; this is then melted out, and the inside cleaned with solvent. The bell is complete.

The working parts of the horn are made as a sub-assembly. This consists of the valves, which rotate so as to send the air down different lengths of tube controlled by levers, and bows or slides, which can be adjusted to alter the tuning. The craftsman (above) is attaching these slides to the row of valves. On his bench are slides and other parts. The valve system is connected to the mouthpiece by a further curved length of tube (below), which is carefully bent into the correct shape.

Finally, the whole gleaming instrument is assembled and given a polish (below). On this particular horn the flare unscrews from the instrument, making it more compact.

The percussion

PERCUSSION INSTRUMENTS
timpani (kettledrums)
side drum (snare drum)
tenor drum
bass drum
cymbals
antique cymbals
triangle
tambourine
jingling johnny
tamtam (gong)
Chinese wood block
sleigh bells
cowbell
rattle
anvil
whip
wind machine
thundersheet
maracas
bongos
guiros
claves

FROM THE thunderous boom of the bass drum to the jingling of sleigh bells, from the ear-splitting shriek of the tamtam with its full power unleashed to the clear note of the triangle, the percussion produces an infinity of sound effects that contradicts its disparaging nickname of the orchestra's 'kitchen department'.

Like the trumpets in the brass section, the drums are basically military instruments. The kettledrums (timpani), carried in pairs one on either side of the drummer, were cavalry instruments, used with trumpets to give signals in battle. The smaller snare drums (side drums), with their rattling stridency of tone, were carried by the infantry musicians and were accompanied by the high-pitched skirling of the fife.

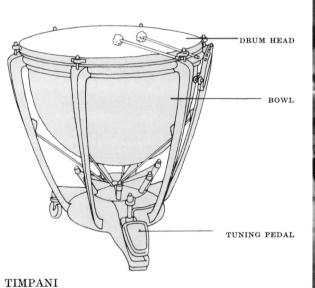

DRUM HEAD

BOWL

TUNING PEDAL

TIMPANI
The timpani or kettledrums carried by Turkish soldiers on camel or horseback (right) were brought to Europe by returning Crusaders. The modern kettledrum (above) consists of a copper bowl with a sheet of calfskin stretched across the top. Sometimes plastic is used. The note sounded depends on the size of the bowl and the tension of the skin. Pedals allow the timpanist to change the pitch by a simple foot movement. Characteristic of the kettledrum is the drum roll, as in the dramatic thunderstorm section of Beethoven's 'Pastoral' Symphony.

The drums for which the classical composers wrote were pitched a fourth or a fifth apart, and their pitch could only be altered by screws labor-iously turned by hand. Modern drums, such as those used by the Royal Philharmonic Orchestra (above), are fitted with pedals to alter pitch.

TAMTAM
The orchestral tamtam is a large gong, as much as 1 metre across. Its appearance and resonance is best known as the Rank film company's trade-mark: a brawny figure who strikes a tamtam before each film. Played softly, a tamtam suggests solemnity and mystery; played loudly, it can drown every other instrument in the orchestra. Berlioz was one of the first composers to use the tamtam.

In Bach and Handel's time, drums were often assembled from any military bands that happened to be available. For open-air music large numbers of drummers might be needed. The 18th-century record probably goes to Handel's 'Music for the Royal Fireworks': no fewer than 16 kettledrums and eight snare drums played in the first performance in 1749.

Beethoven was the first of the classical composers to allow the drums to join intelligently in the orchestral conversation. In the mysterious passage that leads from the menacing scherzo to the blazing finale of the Fifth Symphony, and even more in the Ninth, where the timpani open the scherzo with a hammer-stroke octave leap, the drums are treated as something more than mere producers of percussive noise. Berlioz, a great orchestral innovator and lover of massive effects, increased the twin timpani of the classical orchestra to four in the 'Fantastic' Symphony, and to 16 for the shattering climaxes of his 'Requiem'. The normal number in a symphony orchestra is now three.

Later composers diversified the percussion. Wagner requires 18 anvils to depict the toiling dwarfs in 'Rhinegold', Schoenberg specifies a length of heavy chain in his *Gurrelieder*, while Messiaen's *Et Exspecto Resurrectionem Mortuorum* includes tamtams, gongs and bells. Many modern works include instruments from South American popular music, such as bongos (paired drums) and maracas (gourd rattles).

SIDE DRUM
The side or snare drum (right) has a skin over both ends, with strings (or 'snares') of animal gut stretched across the lower end, to provide a snappy, rattling effect. This drum descended from the small medieval tabor, taken over and enlarged by infantry regiments. The side drum is used rhythmically, or for the threatening close roll. In Ravel's 'Bolero' it plays the same two-bar phrase 169 times.

A CHILDREN'S PERCUSSION GROUP

BASS DRUM
The largest drum of the orchestra, the bass drum, looks and sounds magnificent. It made its debut in western music in the 18th century, when it was used for a 'Turkish' effect, along with the cymbals and triangle. Mozart used it in this way in his overture to 'The Abduction from the Seraglio'. Its heavy thud can also suggest an atmosphere of doom, as in Verdi's 'Requiem'.

CYMBALS
The Ancient Greeks and Romans used cymbals to accompany their religious rituals. Although modern cymbals are larger and sound harsher, they still have a primitive feel about them. Cymbals are not clashed directly together, but are struck at a slightly glancing angle. A single cymbal may also be suspended and played with a drumstick, a wire brush or a metal rod.

TAMBOURINE
Basically a small one-sided drum, with jingles hung round its rim, the tambourine is as ancient as the cymbals. When it is struck, the instrument can outline a rhythm; if shaken, it makes a constant shimmer of sound.

TRIANGLE
The triangle made its first important solo appearance in the 1850s, in Liszt's First Piano Concerto. It can be struck on the outside, to give pure single notes, or the beater can be vibrated rapidly inside it.

DRUMSTICKS
Wire brushes, most often found in jazz bands, also provide special effects in the orchestra; side-drums are played with slim sticks of hickory or lance wood; sticks with large heads of wood and felt are for kettledrums.

The rich and the rare

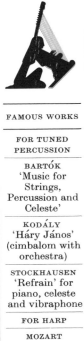

For an instrument to be accepted by composers and orchestral players is rather like joining an exclusive club. Existing members all know one another's capabilities and drawbacks, and any potential new member has to be a good mixer as well as a character in his own right. So it is not surprising that the number that gain acceptance is comparatively small. Some novel instruments have survived for a little while before being superseded; a good example is the ophicleide, a brass instrument welcomed by Berlioz and other composers before vanishing in favour of the tuba. Others, like the electronic *ondes martenot* which produces a swooping, flutelike tone, have never really become popular, although this particular instrument is prominent in at least one modern masterpiece, Messiaen's '*Turangalila*' Symphony.

Many of the instruments that have served their probation period in the last century come under the general heading of 'tuned percussion'. The three main instruments in this category are the glockenspiel, xylophone and vibraphone. These, as well as the marimba and celeste, consist of small tuned bars which are struck with small hammers, and are thus related to the tubular bells, the orchestra's answer to the peal in a church tower. The cimbalom is different in that it has strings instead of bars.

The harp, one of the most ancient of all instruments, had to wait a long time before winning a permanent place in the orchestra. Since early harps were diatonic (unable to play sharps and flats), they could not take part in music that needed changes of key – a problem solved by the invention of the pedal harp in the early 19th century. Here Berlioz was the pioneer, using two harps in the whirling dance movement of the 'Fantastic' Symphony.

Modern composers, from Bartók on, have explored the possibilities of all these instruments. In his 'Music for Strings, Percussion and Celeste', which includes an important part for harp, Bartók makes brilliant use of contrasting sonorities, as does Stockhausen in his 'Refrain', which exploits the tone qualities of piano, celeste and vibraphone. All over the world composers are writing for such instruments, and their players are often the star performers at concerts of contemporary music.

BENJAMIN FRANKLIN'S HARMONICA

Apart from discovering the principle of lightning, Benjamin Franklin (above) also invented a musical instrument that remained popular for 50 years. About 1762 he built a glass harmonica which produced a sound like that made by running a wet finger round the rim of a wine glass. The instrument consisted of a set of tuned glasses mounted on a rotating spindle. The glasses were kept wet by being turned in a trough partly filled with water. The German harmonica (below) shows glass basins arranged in the same way. When the basins are touched with the fingertips they give a gentle chiming sound. Mozart wrote a delicate 'Adagio and Rondo' for glass harmonica.

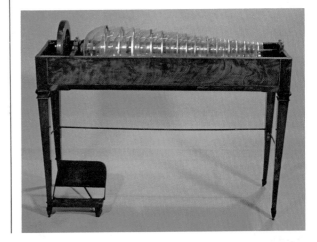

A pioneer percussionist, James Blades (above), is shown here playing the xylophone in about 1930.

XYLOPHONE
The orchestral xylophone consists of wooden bars arranged like the keys of a piano, which are suspended over metal tube resonators to amplify the sound. It is played with two small hammers.

MARIMBA
A larger and deeper version of the xylophone with a more mellow tone, the marimba is sometimes called the xylorimba. Alban Berg used it in his 'Three Pieces for Orchestra' and Milhaud wrote a concerto for marimba and vibraphone.

VIBRAPHONE
This instrument works on the same basic principles as the xylophone, although its sound is altered by electrically-operated discs. Britten used the vibraphone in his 'Spring' Symphony.

GLOCKENSPIEL
The German name of this instrument means 'bell-play', and it sounds like gently-chiming bells. It is fundamentally similar to the xylophone. Mozart used it in his opera 'The Magic Flute' to announce Papageno, the comic bird-catcher.

CELESTE
A metal-barred instrument, the celeste is operated by a keyboard instead of hammers and is played by a pianist rather than a percussionist. It became accepted into the orchestra after it was used by Tchaikovsky in the 'Dance of the Sugarplum Fairy' from his 'Nutcracker' ballet.

CIMBALOM
The Hungarian variety of the medieval dulcimer, the cimbalom is struck with curved beaters to give a resonant and barbaric sound. Stravinsky used it in his '*Renard*' and Kodály gave it an important part in the 'Háry János' suite.

TUBULAR BELLS
A complete set of tubular bells consists of a chime of 18 tubes of different lengths, each giving out a different note. Tubular bells can be incredibly solemn, as in Wagner's 'Parsifal', or jubilant, as in the final bars of Tchaikovsky's '1812' overture. Their reputation spread from the orchestra into the pop world when Mike Oldfield called one of his instrumental pieces 'Tubular Bells'.

Spanish-born harpist Marisa Robles (left) has her own harp trio and is also well known as a solo player.

HARP
The instrument of angelic choirs, played by the young David to soothe the mad rages of King Saul, the harp is the only plucked instrument to have a regular place in the orchestra, and it casts a special radiance over the music in which it takes part.

Early harps were small portable instruments, not the large harps of today. In its modern form, the harp is one of the most beautiful of all instruments to look at, with its hollow sound-chest, gracefully curved neck, and fore-pillar, which is often elaborately carved and lavishly gilded.

The harp is held against the right shoulder and played with the thumb and three largest fingers of each hand. Typical harp sounds are the *arpeggio* (a chord with its notes played one after the other) and the *glissando*, in which the hand sweeps across the strings. Debussy and Ravel used these harp effects with special understanding. Wagner also loved the harp: no fewer than six harps play together as the Gods cross the Rainbow Bridge to Valhalla, in the joyful closing moments of 'Rhinegold'.

The Irish harp (above) is a small instrument with a gracefully curved fore-pillar. Unlike the large orchestral harp, which is played with the finger-tips, it is played with the nails. In days gone by, Irish harpists were sometimes punished by having their fingernails cut. The Welsh harp, with its straight fore-pillar and a longer neck, differs from the Irish. It is the instrument of the eisteddfods (the Welsh festivals of poetry and folk music).

Guitar and lute

APART FROM the piano, the guitar is the only solo instrument that can be guaranteed to pack the largest concert hall. Even 20 years ago this would have seemed extraordinary, since the guitar's repertory is limited, and its carrying power is small. A number of circumstances have contributed to the guitar revolution. Firstly, in its electric form as used in pop music, the guitar is now the most familiar of all melodic instruments. Then there are thousands of amateur guitarists able to pick out a tune and play a few chords, who like to see a master putting the instrument through its paces. Finally, there has been the example of one superb musician, Andrés Segovia. For over half a century he recovered old works from neglect and inspired composers to write new ones, and handed on the torch of classical guitar-playing to the postwar generation of Julian Bream, John Williams and Narciso Yepes.

Although it is now fully internationalised, the guitar has never really lost the traces of its Spanish origins. Until 1600 or so it had a rival in the aristocratic *vihuela*, for which Luis Milán, one of the greatest 16th-century Spanish composers, wrote quantities of magnificent music. The most prolific of all guitar composers, Fernando Sor, who virtually founded the modern repertory, worked in England in the early 19th century and did much to increase the guitar's reputation. Other composers were attracted to the instrument. Schubert tried out his songs on it, and Berlioz, as a young man, roamed Italy with his guitar slung on his back.

Unlike the guitar, which has always remained popular in one form or another, its cousin, the lute, fell into complete neglect for over 200 years. The complexities of its special tablature (notation) did as much as anything else to drive it from the scene, in spite of its great visual beauty and the sweetness of its tone. Although Arnold Dolmetsch began the lute revival about 1900, it is only in the last 20 years or so that a full-scale renaissance has been under way. The lute will always be a minority instrument, but the pioneering work of Julian Bream and his contemporaries means that, after centuries of silence, the stately dances of Dowland and Milán are being heard once more in their full beauty.

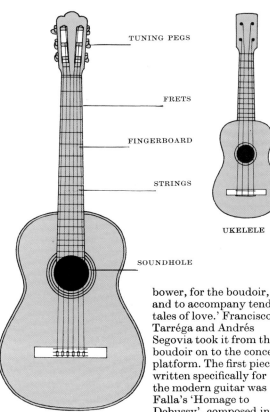

TUNING PEGS

FRETS

FINGERBOARD

STRINGS

UKELELE

SOUNDHOLE

GUITAR

In recent decades the guitar (above) has become a leading concert instrument. The name derives from the Ancient Greek *kithara*, the lyre played by Apollo. The instrument has six strings, the top three of nylon and the lower three of nylon wound with wire. The player finds the notes by means of frets (small strips of metal fixed to the fingerboard at semitone intervals). A ukelele (above, right) is a miniature guitar. The guitar developed in Renaissance times, parallel with the lute. It was played at the courts of Louis XIV and Charles II, and had its various ups and downs of popularity well into the 19th century. Despite the outstanding works composed and played by Fernando Sor and Mauro Giuliani in the early 1800s, the guitar remained an amateur instrument 'for the bower, for the boudoir, and to accompany tender tales of love.' Francisco Tarréga and Andrés Segovia took it from the boudoir on to the concert platform. The first piece written specifically for the modern guitar was Falla's 'Homage to Debussy', composed in 1920. Since then there has been renewed interest among composers. Malcolm Arnold's Guitar Concerto has a slow movement in memory of the jazz guitarist Django Reinhardt, and Britten's 'Nocturnal', written for Julian Bream, is based on a song by Dowland. The guitar is played by plucking the strings with the fingernails (below), although a plectrum is often used by folk and pop musicians.

ELECTRIC GUITAR

The universal instrument of pop music, the electric guitar (below) has six strings and a fretted fingerboard, like the ordinary guitar. A small screw-head placed under each string picks up the sound, which is fed to an amplifier and then played through loudspeakers. A bass guitar has only four strings, and is pop's equivalent of the jazz bass.

Playing his own compositions all over Europe in the years round 1800, Fernando Sor (left) created enormous enthusiasm for the guitar.

MANDOLIN

A miniature lute, the mandolin was popular at the turn of the century (above). It is familiar as the accompaniment to the serenade in Mozart's opera, 'Don Giovanni'. Schoenberg also used it in his 'Variations for Orchestra' of 1928.

BANJO

The banjo enjoyed great popularity in the 19th century. Now, like the ukelele, it is not often heard except where folk music is still a living tradition, as in the deep south of America (left). The body of the banjo is made of parchment stretched tightly over a wooden hoop.

SEGOVIA'S ONE-MAN VICTORY

The guitar owes its present popularity almost entirely to the work of one superb musician, the Spanish master Andrés Segovia (above). Born in 1893, he was largely self-taught. He gave his first recital at the age of 14 and came to international prominence after the First World War. To begin with, he mostly played works by Sor and other early composers, or arrangements of keyboard works. As his fame grew, however, music was written specially for him. By the 1920s he was so well known that the French composer Roussel wrote a guitar piece called simply 'Segovia'.
Naturally, Spanish composers like Turina and Torroba were the first to write extensively for him, but the Mexican, Manuel Ponce, wrote sonatas, preludes and a concerto for Segovia, and the Brazilian, Heitor Villa-Lobos, composed 12 guitar studies for him. The most popular of all modern works for guitar, Rodrigo's 'Concierto de Aranjuez', was in fact written for someone else. But Rodrigo paid Segovia a magnificent tribute with his 'Fantasia para un Gentilhombre' ('Fantasia for a Nobleman'), based on themes by the 17th-century guitarist Gaspar Sanz, which Rodrigo wrote as a link between the two 'noblemen of the guitar'. After the Second World War, Segovia taught the Australian-born John Williams and many other leading guitar players.

LUTE

Our word 'lute' derives from al'ud, the Arabic name for the instrument, which probably reached Europe after the Moorish conquest of Spain.
The lute differs from the guitar in having a pear-shaped back, constructed from wafer-thin segments glued edge to edge. It also has a pegbox bent back at a sharp angle, and a beautifully carved 'rose' below the strings, unlike the guitar, which has a simple round hole. The lute reached perfection about 1500 and vast quantities of music were written for it, culminating in the works of the Elizabethan composer, John Dowland. He wrote songs with lute accompaniment and many solo works. By the 17th century, the lute had become steadily more complicated and unwieldy. In the 18th century it was used by Bach in his 'St John Passion'. Bach also wrote four lute suites, which were the swan song of lute music.
But the lute has been revived today by musicians like Julian Bream (right). Modern notation and new instruments have encouraged a whole new school of lutenists to rediscover the art.

PEGBOX

STRINGS

ROSE

RIBS

The piano

One of the piano giants of this century was the Chilean, Claudio Arrau. Born in 1903, he was a child prodigy. He was famous for his playing of Beethoven sonatas, all of which he recorded, and was also a great interpreter of romantic music, especially that of Schumann and Liszt.

As the piano became more popular, pianists developed their own styles. The greatest pianist after Liszt, the Russian-born Anton Rubinstein (above) was a pupil of the master. Like Liszt, Rubinstein was a composer as well as a performer. In his enthusiasm he often hit wrong notes, yet this did not affect his popularity with audiences.

In recordings made by pianists like Ignacy Jan Paderewski (below) in the early 20th century, the right hand can often be heard playing very slightly after the left. Today this is thought of as old-fashioned, but it was part of the technique of romantic pianists like Chopin and Liszt, who played with much greater rhythmic freedom than the pianists of today.

Apart from the effects a player can produce by touch on the keyboard, the piano has two pedals, which enormously increase the range of expression. The sustaining pedal, operated by the right foot, is the soul of the piano. One of the greatest of all composer-pianists, Ferruccio Busoni (above) called the pedal an 'inimitable device, a photograph of the sky, a ray of moonlight.' By using this pedal a good player can link one note or chord smoothly to the next, disguising the fact that each note on the piano dies almost completely as soon as it is struck. The other pedal is the *una corda*, meaning 'one string'. Worked by the left foot, this pedal shifts the whole keyboard mechanism a little to the left, so that the hammers only strike one string of each note instead of the full three. On upright pianos, the hammer mechanism is moved closer to the strings. Almost as soon as the piano became popular it began to be mechanised. The street piano, popularly and wrongly called the 'barrel organ', appeared soon after 1800. When the operator turned a handle, pins attached to a barrel activated the hammers. A great improvement came when pins were abandoned and the piano

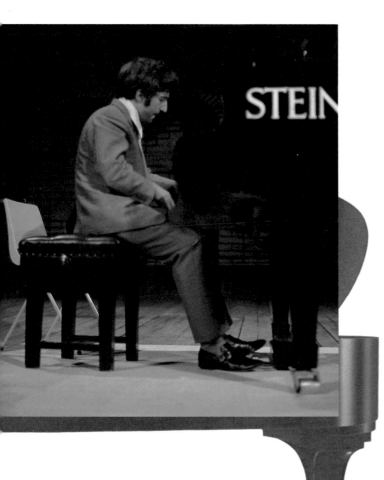

Russian-born Vladimir Ashkenazy
is considered one of the finest
pianists of the post-1950
generation.

41

F ROM THE gleaming black concert grand, dominating the platform and tuned before each recital like a high-performance racing car, to the honky-tonk pub upright covered in beer stains and cigarette burns, the piano is the most versatile of instruments in all kinds of music. It can play so softly as to be almost inaudible, or thunder with all the power of a complete orchestra. It can sing melodiously in a Chopin nocturne or crash percussively in a sonata by Prokofiev. For two centuries composers have hammered out their first thoughts at the key-board, and the attitude of thousands of children towards the art of music have been conditioned, for better or worse, by their struggles with the world of black and white notes.

The piano's full name – 'pianoforte', soft and loud – reveals the first reason for its success. Unlike the harpsichord, which could only be soft *or* loud, and gave the player no control over the duration of a note, the piano put infinite gradations of tone at the fingertips. It was not long before it began to produce virtuoso players. Mozart, Beethoven, Chopin, Liszt, Bartók, Rachmaninov – these are just a few of the composer-pianists, outnumbered a hundred to one by the virtuosos who have played other men's music.

Despite the pessimists who prophesied the decline of the piano with the trend towards smaller homes and greater mobility, this shows no signs of happening. The overall standard of playing has never been higher. Performers still in their teens can cope with the fierce technical demands of works like the Liszt Piano Sonata, which only a generation ago were reserved for the giants of the concert platform.

Composers likewise show no sign of losing interest in the piano. Messiaen, in his vast 'Catalogue des Oiseaux' and 'Vingt Regards sur l'Enfant Jésus', has enormously increased the piano's scope, as has Stockhausen in his series of piano pieces. For a few years composers like John Cage experimented with producing new sounds by adapting the strings and hammers in a variety of ways. A further recent development has been the piano's adoption as an orchestral instrument. Stravinsky led the way in 'Petrushka', and he has been followed by a host of composers from Copland to Britten.

mechanism was activated by air blowing through a perforated paper roll. These 'pianolas', or 'player pianos', reached a high degree of sophistication, although they declined with the popularity of the gramophone. In their most advanced forms, a player's actual performance could be cut into a piano roll and then perfectly reproduced on a specially equipped piano. Grieg, Debussy, Saint-Saëns (above) and other composers have left rolls of this type, which give a good idea of how they wanted their piano pieces played.

Apart from duet arrangements which popularised orchestral works in the days before recordings, a vast amount of original music was written for piano duet. Schubert, the king of this style, was followed by later composers such as Bizet and Ravel. Many composers have written music for two pianos. Music of this kind has produced its own virtuosos, like the husband-and-wife duet of Cyril Smith and Phyllis Sellick (below). When Cyril Smith lost the use of one hand, the couple continued to play three-handed.

Early keyboard

THE STORY goes that when Handel was in Venice in 1708, he went to a masked ball in disguise, and sat down at the harpsichord to play. Hardly had he begun when Domenico Scarlatti, who was one of the guests, jumped up and shouted: 'That must either be the Saxon or the Devil himself!' Like many good musical stories, this one has had cold water poured on it by historians. But it brings the two master-harpsichordists of the age together, at a time when the harpsichord was the ruler of musical instruments, as the piano was to become in the 19th century. The harpsichord held its supremacy for at least three centuries, from about 1500 to about 1800. Now the pioneering revival work of Wanda Landowska and her successors have brought it back into general use, so that the keyboard accompaniments to the recitatives in Mozart's operas sound heavy on the piano, while no one would dream of using the piano for the keyboard part in Bach's Fifth 'Brandenburg' Concerto, as was common a generation ago.

The harpsichord developed about 1400 from the Oriental psaltery, which was brought back to Europe by the Crusaders. The psaltery is a trapeze-shaped instrument, usually held on the player's knees, with strings stretched over a resonating soundbox. The strings are plucked with a quill, producing a delicate lute-like sound. The harpsichord is basically a keyboard adaptation of the psaltery, with the strings at right-angles to the player instead of running parallel to his body, and plucked by tiny quills fitted into 'jacks' – small vertical pieces of wood which are raised by the keys, and activate the strings as the quills pass between them.

HARPSICHORD
During the 16th century the harpsichord evolved into a magnificent and sonorous instrument, capable of great carrying power. It was often sumptuously decorated, like the instrument (left), made in Paris in 1681 by the firm of J.A.Vaudry. This has two manuals (keyboards), and is an early example of the decorative technique called 'japanning'. The harpsichord's graceful bird's-wing shape was passed on later to the grand piano. This was the kind of instrument for which Couperin wrote his harpsichord suites or *ordres*, which had fanciful titles such as 'The Harvesters', 'The Sheepfold' and 'The Gnat'. By changing from one keyboard to the other, the harpsichordist could get a variety of effects.

Jean Philippe Rameau (left), the most important French composer of the 18th century, wrote many suites and other pieces for harpsichord.

Wanda Landowska (left), born in Warsaw in 1877, began her musical career as a pianist. But she had always been interested in old music. She went to Paris in 1900, and in 1903 played the harpsichord in public for the first time. In 1919 she played the accompaniment to Bach's 'St Matthew Passion' on the harpsichord instead of the piano – the first time this had been done for generations. She established the School of Ancient Music outside Paris in 1925, and there taught pupils how to play old instruments. In 1940 she settled in America, where she died in 1959. Among composers who were inspired by her were Falla and Poulenc.

Two of the finest harpsichord composers were Domenico Scarlatti, who wrote sonatas, and François Couperin, whose pieces were descriptive.

COUPERIN   SCARLATTI

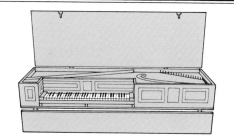

SPINET
Unlike the harpsichord, the spinet (left) never had more than one keyboard. It also lacked the stops with which a harpsichordist could vary the tone.

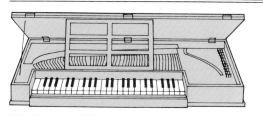

VIRGINALS
A kind of oblong spinet, the virginals (left) was a popular instrument among young girls in the 16th and 17th centuries. The 'Virgin Queen' Elizabeth prided herself on the virginals, and used to play before foreign ambassadors.

CLAVICHORD
The clavichord (left), a stringed instrument with a keyboard, was the predecessor of the piano. The strings are struck with small blades called 'tangents', not plucked like those of a spinet.

Like the grand piano, the harpsichord took up a great deal of room, so it was not long before an upright version was developed. Called the *clavicytherium*, it was a neat and space-saving instrument, like a harp with keyboard attached. But the commonest domestic rival to the harpsichord, at least until about 1650, was the virginals, oblong in shape, with the strings parallel to the keyboard like the psaltery.

Elizabethan composers poured out a stream of virginals music, mainly in the form of themes and variations (which they called 'airs with divisions'). One of the most famous collections is the 'Fitzwilliam Virginal Book', named after the Fitzwilliam Museum in Cambridge, and containing music by virtuoso composers such as Giles Farnaby and John Bull, as well as sets of variations by William Byrd and other Elizabethans. These were often based on popular tunes of the day, with names like 'The Carman's Whistle' and 'Goe from my Window'.

The commonest and cheapest of the plucked keyboard instruments was the spinet, really a small harpsichord, although quite different in shape. The strings of the spinet run diagonally from left to right of the player, and the right-hand side of the instrument juts out for a considerable distance. Apart from the difference in shape, the spinet was much simpler in construction than the harpsichord, with only one keyboard and no stops to vary the tone.

The heyday of composition for the harpsichord lasted for a century or so, from about 1650 to 1750. Almost every composer, from virtuosos like Purcell and Handel down to complete nonentities, produced harpsichord suites. Bach was also a master of the instrument, as he was of all other branches of music. Apart from many smaller works, he wrote six great suites or 'Partitas', the splendid 'Italian' Concerto for solo harpsichord, and the enormous set of 'Goldberg Variations', commissioned by a nobleman who suffered from insomnia and wanted some music to while away the night.

Superb harpsichords were still being made right up until the end of the 18th century, notably in London, where Jacob Kirkman and Burkat Shudi carried on the old tradition. But the harpsichord was doomed to vanish before the piano (see overleaf) for a century or more.

The piano was invented by an Italian, Bartolomeo Cristofori, about 1709. This instrument had the main elements of the modern piano: hammers to strike the strings instead of the plucking quills of the harpsichord, an escapement allowing the hammers to fall back so that a note could be repeated, and dampers that fell back on the strings as soon as the keys were released. Bach played an early piano when he visited Frederick the Great in 1747, but it was Bach's son Johann Christian (the 'English' Bach), who made the new instrument into a serious rival to the harpsichord.

Early pianos were in three different shapes: the harpsichord shape, which survives in the grand, and two domestic space-saving shapes, the upright and the square, with the strings running at right-angles to the keyboard. By Haydn's time the harpsichord had virtually lost the battle, although early pianos had a much thinner and more harpsichord-like tone than today's instruments. Their power was limited by the frame, which was made of wood, and could only stand strings of limited weight and tension. But in the 1850s the Americans introduced the iron frame, which could withstand a total 'pull' of as much as 30 tons, and enabled virtuoso works like those of Liszt to be played with the pianist's full strength unleashed. Iron-framed pianos also stayed in tune much longer than wooden-framed ones. Nowadays many players

are going back to the early types of piano for playing works of the classical and romantic periods. The sonatas of Mozart and Beethoven take on a new freshness when played on the instruments for which they were written, while Chopin's delicate figuration becomes as clear as a newly cleaned picture which has been covered for years in a coat of varnish.

Although all the music written for early keyboard instruments can be played on the piano, the result is never entirely satisfactory. The brilliant runs of virginals music sound heavy on the piano, while the lightning-fast ornaments of Couperin and Scarlatti become forced and laboured. But players and audiences have rediscovered the beauty of the plucked keyboard instruments, and composers are now writing for them again. Poulenc's 'Concert Champêtre' for harpsichord and orchestra and Falla's concerto for harpsichord and chamber orchestra re-established the tradition of Bach's concertos.

Elliott Carter's double concerto for harpsichord and piano reconciles the two great opponents, while Henze's 'Lucy Escott' variations is an important solo work. In 'HPSCHD' John Cage gives the instrument the full avant-garde treatment. This work consists of 58 amplified channels, each with its own loud-speaker; 51 of the channels give out computer-generated music, while the other seven transmit amplified music from seven harpsichords.

SQUARE PIANO, c. 1825

III

THE FORMS OF MUSIC

The symphony

EVERY FEW years someone declares that the symphony is dead, that it cannot be developed any further. Yet the symphony is the greatest achievement of Western music. It still offers a supreme challenge to composers, who constantly try to inject new life into the traditional form. Hans Werner Henze in Germany, and Michael Tippett in England, are just two of today's composers who find the symphony a spur to their creative imaginations.

The word 'symphony' comes from Ancient Greek and means simply 'a sounding together'. In other words, any combination of instruments can be a symphony. Stravinsky returned to this old meaning when, in 1920, he wrote his 'Symphonies of Wind Instruments' in memory of Debussy. But the symphony as we know it evolved from the 18th-century orchestral overture, which was normally divided into three parts: quick-slow-quick. This form was made tremendously popular by Europe's finest orchestra of the time, the Mannheim. The Mannheim players, conducted by Johann Stamitz, were the first to make delicate grades of volume from soft to loud, instead of sharply-defined 'terraces' of sound.

By the end of the 18th century, the symphony had achieved the sense of balance that is usually called 'classical'. It had expanded into four movements: a carefully-wrought, fast-moving first movement (generally the most complex in the symphony), sometimes provided with a slow introduction; a slow movement, lyrical or tragic in its general mood; a dance movement (minuet); then a light-hearted fast finale, to round off the work. The symphonies of Haydn and Mozart are based on such a balanced form. When Beethoven appeared on the scene, at the end of the 18th century, he blew this carefully-ordered system wide apart.

A classical symphony usually lasts from 15 to 20 minutes — this is the length of Haydn's various 'London' Symphonies, and of Mozart's passionate Symphony No. 40 in G minor. But Beethoven's Second Symphony is 30 minutes long and his Third, the 'Eroica', written in 1803, is a giant symphony that lasts almost an hour. It has a lengthy Funeral March as its slow movement and ends, not with a nimble finale, but with a huge set of variations. For his Ninth and final

GOETHE IN THE ROMAN COUNTRYSIDE

symphony, Beethoven felt that the orchestra alone could not express his ideas, so he added a chorus to sing Schiller's 'Ode to Joy' in the last triumphant movement.

The growing length and complexity of the symphony meant that successive composers wrote fewer and fewer. Haydn wrote 104 and Mozart 41, but composers after Beethoven found it difficult, if not impossible, to write more than nine. Brahms was so overawed by Beethoven's example that he did not produce his First Symphony until he was 43, largely because his contemporaries expected him to write 'Beethoven's Tenth'. His final total was four, the same number as Schumann.

Berlioz made an astonishing leap forward when he took the symphony into the realms of story-telling with his 'Fantastic' Symphony. It is only a short step from symphonies of this nature to symphonic poems. The master of such pieces was Richard Strauss. One of his symphonic poems, 'Zarathustra', portrays the German 'superman' ideals of the philosopher Friedrich Nietzsche. The opening bars of 'Zarathustra' have become familiar as the theme music of Stanley Kubrick's remarkable film, '2001'.

SYMPHONIC STYLES

JOSEPH HAYDN

The classical symphony reached its perfect form in the 104 symphonies of Joseph Haydn, often called the 'Father of the Symphony'. The poet Goethe (left) was the leading spirit of classicism in the arts. The years he spent in Rome (1786-88) mark the change from classical to romantic thought. Hector Berlioz broke away from the classical form by writing 'programme music', or music that tells a story. The 'Fantastic' Symphony was inspired by his love for Harriet Smithson (below), an actress whom he saw in Paris in 1827.

Berlioz's work reflects the feverish mental state Harriet produced in him. After seeing her act the parts of Ophelia and Juliet, the composer had wandered blindly through Paris and the nearby countryside, unable to eat or sleep. The result was a symphony that mingles reality and dream in a fantastic way. The symphony, first performed in 1830, tells of a young musician who, in the depths of despair because of a hopeless love, attempts to poison himself with opium. The drug does not kill him, but plunges him into a heavy sleep full of weird visions. Berlioz turns into musical images and ideas the sensations, emotions and memories that pass through the young man's mind.

The beloved becomes a recurring theme, at times distorted, as represented (above) by Ayrton. In 1833 Hector Berlioz and Harriet married, but the marriage was not a happy one. Far from being an ideal wife, Harriet grew jealous and finally took to drink. The couple separated in the 1840s. Harriet died in 1854, bedridden and alone – a pathetic end for the love of Berlioz's starry-eyed youth.

Debussy's three 'symphonic sketches', *'La Mer'*, depicting the sea, are a cross between symphonic poems and a full-scale symphony.

With Mahler, the symphony reached its greatest size, both in sheer length and in the number of instruments played. Most of Mahler's symphonies last well over an hour, while his Eighth, written for soloists, double chorus and boys' chorus, as well as orchestra, has been nicknamed the 'Symphony of a Thousand'. As a reaction against this over-writing, Sibelius tightened up the symphony. By the time he had written his Seventh, in 1924, he had compressed the traditional four separate movements into one continuous span of sound. His model was not the German and Austrian symphonists so much as Tchaikovsky, who was himself a great technical innovator. This is especially true of Tchaikovsky's Sixth Symphony, the *'Pathétique'*, which has an unusual second movement in five

DMITRI SHOSTAKOVICH   **PETER MAXWELL DAVIES**

beats to the bar, and ends with a very slow sad movement instead of the usual triumphant finale.

Later composers took advantage of these flexible ideas on what constitutes a symphony. Some, like Stravinsky with his 'Symphony of Psalms' and Britten with his 'Spring Symphony', have produced what are really choral works. Shostakovich wrote works of national propaganda: his 'Leningrad' Symphony celebrated Russia's struggle against the Germans, and his Thirteenth set Yevgeny Yevtushenko's poems to music. But after years of experiment, some modern composers still write traditional symphonies. Peter Maxwell Davies, with his only symphony so far, has returned brilliantly to the old four-movement form. Despite the prophets of doom, the symphony is alive and well.

The concerto

U NLIKE THE symphony, in which the musicians all work together towards a single end, the concerto is usually designed to show off the talents of one outstanding player. With a concerto there is always a slight element of risk: will the violinist fail to reach those ultra-high notes, or will the pianist come crashing down on the wrong chord? There is this sense of danger at the start of the last movement of Beethoven's glorious 'Emperor' Concerto: the pianist announces the theme quietly in two preliminary bars and then thunders into the mighty chords of the theme, like a mountaineer leaving a solid foothold and launching himself over a sheer cliff-edge into space.

Originally, the word 'concerto' meant simply a combined or concerted effort by a variety of different performers. The form was established at the end of the 17th century by the Italian composer, Arcangelo Corelli, whose concertos contrasted a small body of players (called the *concertante*) with a larger body (the *ripieno*). This type of concerto was also known as the *concerto grosso*, or 'large concerto', the 'large' referring to the fact that it was for a group of instrumentalists rather than for a solo player. Among the best known of such concertos are the 'Four Seasons' by Antonio Vivaldi, Handel's 12 string concertos, and Bach's six 'Brandenburg' Concertos – the most famous set of all. Each of the six is written for a different combination of soloists: thus No. 6 is for strings alone, while No. 5 is for flute and violin, dominated by a brilliant harpsichord part.

The competitive nature of the modern concerto, with a solo instrument contrasted with an orchestral group, is evident in this photograph. The solo flautist is James Galway and the orchestra is conducted by Pinchas Steinberg.

Antonio Vivaldi (1678-1741) was one of the first great concerto-writers. His most famous set, written entirely for strings, is known as the 'Four Seasons'. In 'Spring' the instruments evoke the sound of twittering birds. 'Summer' is a scene of unsettled weather, with more bird-song. 'Autumn' suggests a hunt, and 'Winter' ends the year in ice and snow. Vivaldi wrote numerous other concertos – about 400 in all – but these four are, in many ways, the ancestors of works by later composers inspired by nature, such as the beautiful 'Pastoral' Symphony by Beethoven.

The key figure in the evolution of the concerto was Mozart, whose 27 piano concertos represent perhaps the most important part of his work. They vary from the early light-hearted pieces to such tragically sombre works as the C minor Concerto, written late in his life. Mozart wrote many other concertos, including six for violin, four for horn, and one or two for combinations of instruments such as the flute and harp.

Beethoven, in expanding the concerto form, set himself such tremendous tasks that he wrote comparatively few concertos. There were five for piano, a solitary violin concerto and the Triple Concerto for violin, cello and piano – the usual instruments of the string trio. Beethoven's two final piano concertos, the Fourth in G major, and the 'Emperor' in E flat, show two entirely different approaches to the concerto. The Fourth is a quiet, restrained piece, whereas the 'Emperor' is a magnificent display-piece. Later piano concertos tended to be so difficult that only the composer himself could play them, at least to begin with. Chopin's two concertos, Liszt's two,

Bartók's three and Rachmaninov's four are typical examples.

For some unknown reason, the concerto evolved with only three movements, as opposed to the symphony's four. It lacks the lively minuet or scherzo that forms the dance element in the symphony, although Brahms's monumental Second Piano Concerto in B flat is a rare exception. Another feature unique to the concerto is the cadenza – the section towards the end of the first movement when the orchestra falls silent, the conductor lowers his baton, and the whole audience listens in astonishment to the soloist's skill.

In modern times, when every instrumentalist needs to be a virtuoso, the 'Concerto for orchestra' has developed. Bartók's, written in 1943, is a supreme example, while Britten's 'Young Person's Guide to the Orchestra' is a concerto for orchestra in all but name. Thus the concerto's wheel has turned full circle, back to an instrumental world that Bach and Corelli would recognise as not unlike their own.

BRAHMS AND HIS CONCERTO 'AGAINST THE VIOLIN'

One of the most popular of all concertos is Brahms's Violin Concerto in D major. It was first performed by Joseph Joachim, the Hungarian-born violinist who had championed Brahms 25 years earlier, when the composer was beginning to make his name. For a few years, this work was considered so difficult that it was called a concerto 'against the violin', rather than for it. But it was very much a collaboration between composer and soloist. Instead of writing out the cadenza at the end of the first movement, Brahms allowed his friend to compose it himself. In fact, the cadenza usually played today is Joachim's. The tender theme of the slow movement, played by the oboe, is based on Brahms's private musical motto: the notes F A F, standing for 'Frei aber Froh' ('Free but Happy'). The motto is another link with Joachim, since Brahms adopted it as a counterpart to Joachim's own motto, the notes F A E representing 'Frei aber Einsam' ('Free but Alone').

A musical medley

OVERTURE

Overtures introduce longer works, usually operas. Mozart's and Rossini's are the most frequently played overtures of this type. There are also a great many free-standing concert overtures. Some are descriptive – 'Fingal's Cave' by Mendelssohn depicts the Scottish natural scene; others are written for specific events – Brahms wrote the 'Academic Festival' overture when he took an honorary degree at a German university. Most spectacular of all is Tchaikovsky's '1812' overture, which calls for cannon-fire to gain its full effect. The composer himself called it 'very loud and noisy'. Written in 1882, it illustrates the defeat of Napoleon and the French army in 1812, and their disastrous retreat from Moscow.

PRELUDE

As its name indicates, the prelude was originally the introduction to a much larger work – a shorter kind of overture. Wagner's operas marked the change from overture to prelude. 'Tannhäuser' and 'The Mastersingers' have separate overtures, while 'Rhinegold' and 'Tristan' have preludes that lead straight into the main story without any break.

The free-standing kind of prelude is rare. The sole famous example is Debussy's '*Prélude à l'Après-midi d'un Faune*', based on a poem by Mallarmé. The music depicts the languor of a hot afternoon. The 'faun' of the title is a half-man, half-goat creature from classical Greek mythology.

SUITE

Today a suite can be any loosely-connected set of pieces. Originally, it was a succession of dances, for orchestra, chamber group or solo, always in the same key and creating contrasts with changes of pace.

The commonest kind of modern suite is made up of music written for ballets and plays, like Tchaikovsky's 'Sleeping Beauty', Ravel's 'Daphnis and Chloe', and the brilliant 'Midsummer Night's Dream' written by Mendelssohn.

This last work began as an overture, written in 1826 when the composer was only 17. In it he captures the magic of Shakespeare's moonlit forest scene. The first four wind chords evoke the atmosphere of fairyland, while later we hear the braying of Bottom after he has been changed into an ass. Seventeen years later, Mendelssohn enlarged the overture into a full-scale suite of incidental music. This includes the famous 'Wedding March', which has been played at almost every wedding for well over a century.

A GLANCE DOWN the list of a month's forthcoming programmes in any major concert hall will show an amazing variety in the works that are to be performed. True, nearly every orchestral concert includes a symphony – after all, large orchestras often have the word 'Symphony' as part of their name – and probably a concerto as well; but that is about as far as any positive statement about the content of programmes can go. The symphony and the concerto can be picked out and classified. But there are many 'fillers' in the programme: shorter works, often played at the beginning and end of concerts, which come in many disguises and are not always easily labelled.

'Portsmouth Point', a descriptive overture by Walton, is based on the scene drawn by Thomas Rowlandson (right).

SERENADE

'*Sera*' is Italian for 'evening'; a serenade is literally a song of the warm Italian night, sung under a girl's balcony by her lover. The term was taken over by composers and applied to a suite of light-hearted pieces – a type of music of which Mozart was a master. His 'Serenade for Thirteen Wind Instruments' is true out-of-doors music for elegant society strolling in a Viennese garden. Tchaikovsky and Elgar both wrote beautiful serenades for strings. Mozart did the same in his '*Eine Kleine Nachtmusik*' (meaning 'A Little Serenade'), written in 1787 for a small string orchestra. This work is a typical serenade in its cheerful ease and grace.

VARIATIONS

The variation form is found, not only in classical music, but in folk-music and jazz. It basically consists of a simple theme which is put through its paces in music of ever-growing complexity, usually ending with a variation of great brilliance. Most variations have been written for harpsichord or piano. But there are orchestral variations, of which Brahms's 'Variations on a Theme by Haydn' is probably the best-known example. Another masterpiece is the 'Enigma' variations, a set by Elgar (above). Elgar subtitled it 'To my Friends Pictured Within', and each variation is a portrait of someone he knew: his wife, his publisher – even a friend's dog makes an appearance. The enigma lies in an unplayed theme which has never been identified.

ARRANGEMENTS

Before the invention of the gramophone, the usual way for orchestral works to become known was through piano arrangements. Today, the reverse is likely to happen: a composer will orchestrate a keyboard work for the sheer love of altering and expanding the tone-colour of the music. A delightful example is Respighi's arrangement of piano pieces by Rossini for the ballet '*La Boutique Fantasque*'. Perhaps the greatest arranger of this kind was Ravel, who arranged some of his own piano music. His finest adaptation of all is the orchestration of Mussorgsky's piano suite, 'Pictures from an Exhibition', which he transformed into what is virtually a new work. Mussorgsky's suite consists of a number of musical 'tone-pictures' of paintings by his friend, Karl Amadeus Hartmann – a witch's hut, two Jews, and the final thunderous 'Great Gate of Kiev'. Ravel changed them from black-and-white to full colour.

HARTMANN'S 'GREAT GATE OF KIEV'

HARTMANN'S DRAWING OF A WITCH'S HUT

The programme planner's skill is shown by the way in which he varies the interest and pace of an evening's music. He may precede a difficult modern work with a well-known overture, or round off a concert with an orchestral show-piece like Ravel's 'Bolero'. There are many 'fillers' to choose from, apart from the most frequently played types (above). There is the *divertimento*, or 'diversion', a name which Mozart used as an alternative to 'serenade'. Bartók also used it for his 'Divertimento for Strings', an easy-to-listen-to work by an uncompromising composer. There are major works with purely descriptive titles, like Holst's 'The Planets', or Debussy's '*La Mer*', which is subtitled 'Three Symphonic Sketches' but is a symphony in all but name. There are shorter works that conjure up a mood or a place, such as Ravel's '*La Valse*' or Granados's 'The Maiden and the Nightingale'. Many extremely difficult modern works are almost unclassifiable: Stockhausen's *Gruppen* is one example. Finally, there is music for singers – oratorios and other choral works; near-symphonies with solo singers, like Mahler's 'Song of the Earth', and on a less exalted but equally enjoyable level, the rollicking sea shanties of the last night of the Henry Wood 'Proms', in which the audience is encouraged to drown the music of the orchestra by yelling itself hoarse.

Chamber music

CHAMBER MUSIC means literally 'room music'; it was originally played or sung in the private halls of royalty and the aristocracy. In its purest form, the string quartet, it is like four friends holding a private conversation. Each friend listens intently to what the others are saying, and the audience is almost like an eavesdropper. Whether playing in public or in private, a good quartet is so wrapped up in the music that its attention is entirely diverted away from the listening audience.

The soloist, on the other hand, has to be something of a showman. Far and away the most favoured instrument for solo concerts, or 'recitals', as they are called, is the piano. Most piano recitals contain elements of all kinds of music: from the fiery display of a 'Hungarian Rhapsody' by Liszt, to the quiet introspection of a Chopin nocturne, or from the towering structure of a piano sonata by Beethoven to a group of Debussy's descriptive preludes. Different soloists specialise in different forms of music, but the most popular have always been pianists like Rubinstein and Horowitz, who can win over audiences by the sheer exhilaration of their playing. The only instruments to compete with the piano for recitals are the violin and, in recent years, the guitar.

The sonata is the most extended and complex form of solo music. Originally, the term 'sonata' did not have its present meaning of a work in several movements, normally for one instrument. It was used for a work that was played, as opposed to a work that was sung ('cantata'). The earliest sonatas, such as those written about 1700 by the Italian violinist and composer, Arcangelo Corelli, were called *a tre* ('for three instruments'). The trio consisted of two violins and cello, together with a harpsichord to accompany and fill in the harmony. The harpsichordist normally played from the cello part, which had figures written below or above to indicate the harmony, just as a jazz pianist today fills in and improvises from a basic harmony. In Mozart's day, what we know as the 'violin sonata' was thought of as a piano sonata with violin accompaniment. But Mozart, in his later violin sonatas, gave both instruments equal importance. This idea of equal partnership was consolidated by Beethoven in his stormy C minor Sonata.

In the 17th century a distinction had been made between the *sonata da chiesa* ('church sonata'), played on religious occasions, and the *sonata da camera* ('room sonata'), written for private indoor performance. Chamber music derived from the 'room sonata' and, although it has been played in public for at least 200 years, it still retains this flavour of a private performance. It is most often written for a trio or quartet of instruments.

The pedigree of the string quartet goes right back to the beginning of the 17th century. But the quartet as we know it today is largely due to Haydn, who wrote his first four works for four string instruments early in his career, in 1755. Mozart's 27 quartets include some of his finest works, while Beethoven used the quartet for his deepest and most personal music, culminating in the five great quartets of his final period. Since Beethoven's time, most composers have tried their hand at writing a quartet, although several (Verdi, Sibelius, Debussy, Ravel) only made one attempt at the form. Few 20th-century composers have taken naturally to the string quartet, apart from Bartók and Shostakovich.

Early chamber music often took the form of a trio or quartet for strings and wind, accompanied by a harpsichord. (The viola da gamba, held by the central figure, was normally played pointing downwards, held between the knees.) The harpsichordist in the original engraving is said to be Domenico Scarlatti. The string quartet of two violins, viola and cello evolved in the work of Haydn, and is nowadays regarded as the purest form of chamber music.

Niccolò Paganini (left) was an Italian violinist who raised solo playing to brilliant technical heights. During the 1830s, Paganini's reputation was immense, but his appearance, as much as his actual playing, made him famous. People shuddered when the skeletal, hollow-cheeked figure walked on to the concert platform. One of his specialities was to remove the upper three strings of his violin and play on the G string alone. This string, it was said, had been made from the intestines of his murdered wife or mistress. Although all this was good publicity, Paganini did not deserve his sinister reputation. As well as playing the violin and viola, he was a serious composer. His 24 'Caprices' for solo violin are standard works for players today.

The combinations of instruments that have been used for chamber music are almost infinite. Brahms loved combining piano with strings, and wrote piano trios, quartets and a magnificent piano quintet. Among 20th-century sonata-writers, Francis Poulenc and Darius Milhaud produced an amazing diversity, both for wind instruments alone and for accompanied instruments, while Paul Hindemith's output included sonatas for virtually every instrument, among them the viola, cello, harp and trombone. The maximum number of instruments for a chamber music ensemble seems to be eight, beyond which the group grows unwieldy. One of the best-known of all chamber music works is Schubert's octet, which adds double bass, clarinet, horn and bassoon to the string quartet. Mendelssohn's octet for strings, written in 1825, is among the best things he composed. Stravinsky's octet written a century later, is for a typically pungent wind group of flute, clarinet, and two each of bassoons, trumpets and trombones. As the number rises beyond eight or nine, chamber music needs a conductor – and then it is no longer chamber music.

The singer and the song

BOY SOPRANO
The treble, or boy soprano, is the highest male voice. The upper line of music in church choir scores is almost always sung by trebles, although today, when boys' voices are breaking earlier than they did in the past, choirs are beginning to use girl sopranos. Until the 19th century the Papal choir in Rome employed adult male sopranos, known as *castrati*, whose voices had been prolonged from boyhood by castration.

SOPRANO
The highest of women's voices, the soprano, may be either lyrical, with voices suited to gently-flowing, smooth music, or *coloratura*, with the ability to sing runs and ornaments with great speed and power. This is the kind of voice that belongs to the best-known operatic sopranos, such as Maria Callas, Joan Sutherland and Kiri Te Kanawa (below). The main soprano roles in operas by Donizetti and Bellini were written for such voices.

CONTRALTO
The lowest female voice, in range about a fifth lower than the soprano, is rich and warm in quality. An intermediate voice is called a mezzo-soprano. The most outstanding contralto of recent times, Kathleen Ferrier, was superb in all kinds of singing, from opera to solo folksong. Janet Baker (above) has a mezzo voice of great beauty and power.

Singing is by far the most personal and immediate form of music. Everyone has a voice, although not everyone is equally efficient at controlling it. And everyone has a unique 'voiceprint', as distinctive as a fingerprint, which can be identified from a mere scrap of speech. This kind of vocal identity is particularly recognisable in the trained singer. For sheer personality and magnetism there is nothing in music to match the appeal of singers such as Melba, at the end of the last century, or Callas, among recent stars. Today almost every great singer of the past can be heard on record.

Solo singing of a professional kind implies an audience, and is thus a later development than the work songs and religious incantations in which a whole family or tribe sang together. When any untrained collection of people sings as a group, the voices are bound to separate out.

Men and women will sing an octave or so apart, and will subdivide further into high and low, male or female, voices. These four natural voices have become stylised into our soprano, alto, tenor and bass.

There is now an increasing interest in new approaches to voice production, challenging the traditional smooth-flowing vocal tones. The rediscovery of medieval music has led to experiments with the kind of nasal singing still found in Arab countries. Schoenberg pointed the way to an entirely new style when, in 1912, he wrote his song sequence '*Pierrot Lunaire*', which calls for a technique of voice production known as 'speech-song'. His successors extended the concept of song to include almost all the means of expelling air from lungs via the vocal chords, so that singers, even in choral works, may be called on to shout, hum or explode clusters of consonants. In

For over a hundred years enthusiastic amateurs have formed themselves into choirs. Here, an Oxford choir sings carols from the top of Magdalen College Tower.

TENOR

The most dramatic of all voices, whether male or female, is the tenor. Music written for tenors is vast in scope, from heroic operatic roles like Wagner's Siegfried, to the solemn Narrator in Bach's Passion music. Probably the most famous tenor of all was the Italian, Enrico Caruso (below). He was especially popular in Gounod's 'Faust' and Puccini's 'La Bohème'.

BASS

The deepest variety of voice is suited to slow, dignified music, such as the part of Sarastro, the high priest of Isis, in the 'Magic Flute' by Mozart. In choral music the bass part is often divided into First and Second Bass. A leading American bass in the 1930s was Paul Robeson (above). He established himself by singing negro spirituals, but later sang important roles in operas like George Gershwin's 'Porgy and Bess'. Most male voices are neither tenor nor bass, but baritone – half-way between the two.

COUNTERTENOR

'Male alto' is another name for this voice. Its range is much the same as the female contralto. Like boy trebles, male altos are used in church choirs. A countertenor voice is produced when a singer trains the high 'falsetto' part of his voice. Alfred Deller, in the 1950s, was the first to revive the lost art of solo countertenor singing. He has led the way to a revival of the counter-tenor voice, in opera and church music.

Luciano Berio's 'Sinfonia' the singers have to chant political slogans, and in his 'Visage' the solo soprano has a vocal display-piece ranging from low moaning to wild shrieking.

Stockhausen has carried vocal technique to extremes in his 'Stimmung' for six solo voices, first performed in 1968. To sing this work the performers have virtually to unlearn their previous training. Each voice sings on one note only throughout the whole piece, forming a continuous single six-part chord. But, within the pitch of that single note, the singer has to use every vowel sound there is, punctuated by shouted invocations of sacred names and short texts – a far cry from the traditions of opera or song recital. 'Stimmung' is a ritual as well as a piece of music. Such singing is for professionals. Amateur singing (see overleaf) has followed a different course.

Placido Domingo, José Carreras and Luciano Pavarotti (above) have three of the finest tenor voices performing today.

Side by side with increasing professionalism in singing, there has always been a flourishing amateur tradition, perhaps stronger than in any other field of music. When William Byrd published his first book of madrigals in 1588, he headed it with the little verse: 'Since singing is so good a thinge, I wish all men would learn to singe.' He gives several reasons for this wish: singing is good for the health, it prevents stammering and teaches pronunciation and, finally, 'the better the voyce is, the meeter it is to honour and serve God thereby.' Byrd wrote his madrigals (unaccompanied songs, usually in four or five parts) for amateurs. At the end of the 16th century any educated man was expected to be able to sing a madrigal part at sight. This ability lingered on into the 17th century, when Purcell and his friends entertained one another with their glees and catches, often to fairly obscene words – like today's Rugby songs, although composed and sung with far more skill.

Today the amateur singer may well sing madrigals by Byrd, Weelkes or Morley; but it is far more likely that, in the close-packed ranks of a choir, he or she will sing the choruses in Handel's 'Messiah' or Britten's 'War Requiem'. The growth of amateur choirs was one of the features of 19th-century music-making. As instrumental music grew steadily more difficult to play, amateurs became discouraged and turned to singing instead. Choral singing was a northern European phenomenon and was strongest of all in England. In Germany, Brahms wrote a large number of part songs for all sorts of choirs – female, male and mixed – often with a folksong base. The Italians were not so attracted to choral music of this type, although the madrigal was originally an Italian form. The earliest examples were written in the 14th century by the blind Italian composer, Francesco Landini, and the greatest of all Italian composers, Monteverdi, wrote his superb madrigals in the early 1600s.

Where solo songs are concerned, there is no real distinction between songs written for amateurs and those for professionals. The medieval troubadours of southern France were professionals, but their songs were taken up and sung all over Europe, as pop songs are today. The Elizabethan solo lute songs, written at the same time as the best of the madrigals, are often extremely difficult and have complex accompaniments. So do many of the 19th-century songs of Schubert, Brahms and Hugo Wolf. Yet few of them are beyond the reach of a skilled amateur.

The longest-lived of all amateur songs is surely the round, 'Sumer is Icumen In', composed about 1225. Used by Britten in the choral finale of his 'Spring Symphony', it is still being joyfully bellowed out today, as it was by the monks of Reading Abbey who first sang it six-and-a-half centuries ago.

AMATEUR SINGERS BY HOGARTH

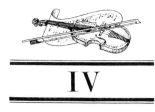

IV

CLASSICAL AND ROMANTIC

Haydn the pathfinder

**HAYDN
(1732–1809)**

MAIN WORKS

symphonies
(104)

cello concertos
(2)

trumpet
concerto

string quartets
(83) including
'The Seven Last
Words'

piano trios (32)

trios for
baryton, viola,
cello (126)

piano sonatas
(62)

operas (24)

masses (12)
including
'Maria Theresa',
'In Time of
War' and
'Nelson'

oratorios (4)
including 'The
Creation' and
'The Seasons'

WHEN THE 77-year-old Haydn lay dying in Vienna in May 1809, Napoleon, who had just conquered the city, posted a guard outside the composer's house to make sure that he was undisturbed. There is no better illustration of Haydn's status as the Grand Old Man of classical music. By the time of his death his symphonies were being played as far afield as America, and his beautiful oratorio, 'The Creation', had taken a permanent place alongside Handel's 'Messiah'.

Joseph Haydn was unique among composers for the high regard in which he was held from the start of his career. His first adult years in Vienna, where he studied theory and began to make his name as a composer, were a struggle. But at the age of 26 he was given his first salaried post, with an aristocrat, Count Morzin, and for the rest of his life he never needed to worry about money.

In 1761 he was employed by the Esterházy family as assistant conductor at Eisenstadt, outside Vienna, and remained there until he resigned as an old man, in 1804. The Esterházys, the wealthiest landowners in Hungary, were also lavish patrons of the arts. Under the terms of his contract, Haydn had to train the singers and orchestra and write compositions for the exclusive enjoyment of the Prince. Although he had to wear livery, like the other court servants and officials, Haydn was quite happy with a situation that Mozart came to regard as little better than slavery. He contentedly turned out symphonies, string quartets, and operas, first for Prince Pál Antal Esterházy, and then for Prince Miklós, known as 'The Magnificent'.

In the early 1760s Miklós built Esterháza, a palace that rivalled Versailles in splendour. It included a theatre with seating for 400 people, for which Haydn wrote many of his operas. Prince Miklós not only appreciated music: he played it as well. His favourite instrument was the baryton, an extinct string instrument, for which Haydn wrote over 120 works. The year that Esterháza was completed, Haydn became the Prince's *Kapellmeister*, or musical director. The help and encouragement which the composer gave the court musicians quickly won him the affectionate nickname, 'Papa', by which he was known for the rest of his life.

JOSEPH HAYDN

THE 'FAREWELL' SYMPHONY

Prince Esterházy did not allow the families of his musicians to live at Esterháza, his palace in the country, because it was too small for them all. But in 1772, the Prince stayed at Esterháza longer than usual, and the players were missing their families. Although Haydn was exempt from this ruling, he sympathised with the musicians. As a gesture of solidarity with them, he wrote the 'Farewell' Symphony. The orchestra played it in the winter of 1772.

After the four movements of a conventional symphony, the Prince must have been surprised to hear the beginning of yet another movement, and a slow one at that. As the movement went on, the musicians snuffed out their candles one by one, and walked quietly off the platform: first, the wind instruments, then the strings, until only two violins remained to complete the movement. Playing with their mutes on to soften the tone, they ended the symphony pianissimo, and walked off, leaving the platform completely empty. Fortunately, the Prince took the hint. The next day the court packed up and returned to Vienna, where the musicians were able to rejoin their waiting families.

Such a gesture explains the high esteem in which Prince Esterházy's musicians held their 'Papa' Haydn. To the composer, this particular work was simply the Symphony in F sharp minor. The title of 'Farewell' is a nickname. Many of Haydn's other works have been given nicknames, although it is not always easy to know which ones were approved by the composer himself.

When Haydn first met Mozart (left) in 1781, he commented: 'More than a century will pass before such a talent will be found again'.

Prince Miklós's palace of Esterháza (below) was among the most magnificent in Europe. It is still one of Hungary's tourist show-places.

Haydn's capacity for kindness, and his ability to recognise genius in others, is shown by his friendship with Mozart. Haydn praised Mozart's music on every occasion, and Mozart responded by dedicating six of his finest string quartets to Haydn. The two men met for the last time in 1790, shortly before Haydn went abroad. His symphonies had begun to be published in England in the 1780s, and in 1791 he went to London. He stayed for 18 months, writing the 'London' symphonies and being fêted wherever he went. This London visit, and another one in 1794-95, were the Indian summer of his career, when he completed his grand total of 104 symphonies. In a final burst of creativity in Vienna, between 1796 and 1801, Haydn wrote his oratorios, 'The Creation' and 'The Seasons'.

Haydn's work displays that feeling for objective balance and poise that is usually called 'classical' as opposed to the more subjective, 'romantic' approach, foreshadowed by Mozart and carried further by Beethoven and his successors. Much of Haydn's music is as sunny and uncomplicated as his life. The system of princely patronage, which Beethoven despised, had given Haydn near-perfect working conditions for more than 40 years of his life.

Molto Adagio

Hin ist alle meine Kraft,

alt und schwach bin ich

Joseph Haydn.

In the early 1800s, Haydn had this visiting card printed (left) to explain why he could not go out. The words mean: 'All my strength is gone, I am old and weak.'

Mozart and independence

MOZART (1756–1791)
MAIN WORKS
symphonies (41)
concertos: for piano (27) for violin (6) for flute (2) for clarinet for bassoon for horn (4) for flute and harp
'Sinfonia Concertante' for violin and viola
'Serenade for Thirteen Wind Instruments'
quintets: for strings (6) for clarinet and strings
quartets: for strings (27) for piano and strings (2) for oboe and strings
trios: for piano and strings (8)
sonatas: for violin and piano (28) for piano (19)
operas (23)
masses (19)

WOLFGANG AMADEUS MOZART was born in 1756 into an ordered and settled society. But by the time he died 35 years later, the world had been shaken, first by the American War of Independence in the 1770s, and then by the shattering upheaval of the French Revolution. During his lifetime, the intellectual movement known as *Sturm und Drang* ('Storm and Stress') provided the mental background for those who, like Mozart, questioned the fossilised social framework into which they had been born.

His father, Leopold, was one of the leading violinists of his day, and made sure that his son met and learned from the most talented people in Europe. As a young man in the service of the Archbishop of Salzburg, Mozart became increasingly critical of the system of patronage under which he and his father lived. He despised his colleagues, whom he described as 'those coarse, slovenly, dissolute court musicians', and commented bitterly that, although he sat below the valets at table, he 'had the honour of being placed above the cooks'. His headstrong character led to his dismissal in 1781. From then on, Mozart was on his own.

At first, things went well. As the finest pianist in Vienna, he filled the concert halls. But he found, to his cost, that the day of true independence for composers had not yet dawned. Mozart's blunt speaking cannot have done much for his popularity, but he was so aware of his own genius that he had little

MOZART'S JOURNEYS

Leopold Mozart, knowing that his five-year-old son Wolfgang was a genius, took him on short tours to Munich and Vienna. The first Grand Tour began in June 1763 and continued for over three years. In Paris, Mozart met Mme de Pompadour (above). At this time, his first sonatas were already being published.

In London, he played for the King and Queen and, under the influence of Johann Christian Bach (below), he wrote his first symphonies.
During his great Italian Tour, 1769-71, Mozart received the Order of the Golden Spur from the Pope, and was elected a member of the Bologna Philharmonic Society.

As a young man, on his last Grand Tour in 1777, Mozart met his cousin, Maria Thekla (above). Later, they poured out their high spirits in letters to each other. But Mozart's gaiety was short lived. While in Paris, in 1778, his mother fell ill and died in his arms. Overcome with grief, he returned to Salzburg to become the Archbishop's organist.

Mozart, at the age of six, sitting between his father, Leopold, and the Archbishop of Salzburg (below) during a visit to Vienna in 1762.

Mozart's works are noted by 'Köchel numbers' ('K' for short). Ludwig von Köchel (left) was an Austrian who studied the chronology of Mozart's works and systematically catalogued them. As nearly as possible, he put them in the order in which they were written.

Beethoven the revolutionary

**BEETHOVEN
(1770–1827)**

MAIN WORKS

symphonies (9)

overtures (11)

piano concertos
(5)

violin concerto

quintet for
strings

quintet for
piano and wind

string quartets
(17)

piano trios (7)

violin sonatas
(10)

cello sonatas (5)

piano sonatas
(32)

'Diabelli
Variations'

'Fidelio' (opera)

mass in C major

'*Missa
Solemnis*'

ninth symphony
(choral)

'Choral
Fantasia'

O F ALL THE great composers, Beethoven alone can fill the world's concert halls unaided. This has been true almost since the day of his death, and the reason for it lies in the universal quality of his music. Mozart has more ease and grace, and Bach more intellectual power, but Beethoven's music has a toughness that no amount of hammering can spoil. Mozart, played badly, is no longer Mozart; but Beethoven remains recognisably himself, however badly orchestras or soloists treat his music. Beethoven's music comes from the turmoil of battle – not a battle with an external enemy, but with the inner enemy of deafness.

Ludwig van Beethoven was born in Bonn in 1770, the year after Napoleon's birth. In his early years he was a fanatical admirer of the French Revolution and all its ideals. His gigantic '*Eroica*' Symphony, completed in 1803, was originally dedicated to Napoleon. Beethoven's own ideals, which he copied into a friend's album, were: 'To help wherever one can; love liberty above all things; never deny the truth even at the foot of the throne.'

Beethoven's early music was in the direct tradition of Haydn and Mozart. When he first arrived in Vienna, in 1792, he even took a few lessons from Haydn, although he later said they were of no use. The quartets, sonatas and symphonies of the years up to about 1800 continue the classical tradition. In them, Beethoven was

flexing his musical muscles, before the tremendous expansion of the so-called 'middle period' of his creative life.

Shortly before writing the '*Eroica*', Beethoven realised that he was going deaf. He poured out his despair in the 'Heiligenstadt Testament', written in 1802 at a country spa outside Vienna. Addressed to his brothers, Karl and Johann, it begins with an appeal for understanding from 'men who believe or declare that I am malevolent, stubborn or misanthropic'. It ends with a heartbroken postscript: 'as the leaves of autumn fall and are withered, so, too, my hope has dried up'. Yet Beethoven roused himself to compose his master works: the mighty Fifth Symphony (whose opening four notes made the Victory V rhythm, dot-dot-dot-dash, broadcast by the BBC during the Second World War), the three 'Rasoumovsky' string quartets and the 'Emperor' Piano Concerto.

If defiance of deafness gave these works their impetus, the revolutionary works of Beethoven's later life were only begun after an exhausting three-year lawsuit, in which he gained custody of his wayward nephew Karl. His renewed creativity produced the great works of his 'third period', some of which have only recently begun to be understood. Toughest of all is the 'Great Fugue', written as the last movement of the String Quartet in B flat, which for many years was thought to be virtually unplayable.

BEETHOVEN'S DEAFNESS

By 1800, Beethoven's ears buzzed constantly. He pounded his piano until the strings broke in his effort to hear them.

Beethoven was only 26 when his hearing began to go. Carl Czerny, who became his pupil in 1799, noticed that Beethoven's ears were stuffed with cottonwool, although his hearing seemed normal.

His grief found its most moving outlet in the 'Heiligenstadt Testament' (right), in which the composer expresses his sense of loneliness, cut off from his friends and from his music.

Beethoven, inspired by the democratic ideals of Napoleon (left), dedicated his Third Symphony (the '*Eroica*'), to him. But when, in 1804, news reached Vienna that Napoleon had crowned himself Emperor, Beethoven felt betrayed. He flew into a rage and cursed the new ruler as a 'tyrant'. He scratched Napoleon's name off the '*Eroica*' score (below).

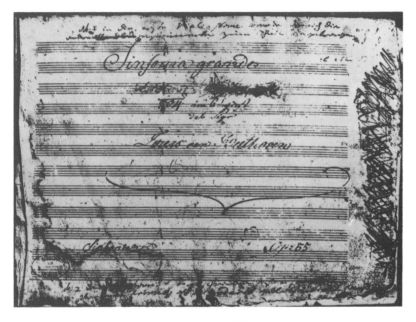

Beethoven's deafness increased at an alarming rate. At first, he used an ear trumpet, but soon this was useless. When he conducted his Seventh Symphony, in 1814, he could not hear the soft passages and ended several bars ahead of the orchestra. Eventually, he had to use 'conversation books' (above), in which his friends wrote down their questions and remarks for him.

In May 1824, he conducted the very first performance of his Ninth Symphony. His deafness was so bad that he could not tell when the work had finished, or hear the audience's applause.

The last five quartets still require complete concentration on the part of the listener. The same is true of Beethoven's final piano sonatas, especially the enormous '*Hammerklavier*' Sonata, which lasts the best part of an hour and ends with a fugue that remains one of the most difficult pieces ever written for the keyboard. The title of this sonata, which means simply 'keyboard', reflects Beethoven's growing interest in the establishment of German music. But he did not spend all his time on such lofty creative heights. The boisterous side of his nature was also reflected in his music, which is full of rough good humour. His letters to his publishers display the same qualities of earthy common sense. In fact, Beethoven was the first composer to make publishers run after him, instead of the other way round as was usual.

Although as a young man Beethoven had been something of a dandy, with increasing deafness and isolation from the world he neglected his appearance. Weber visited him in 1823 and described the sordid conditions in which the great man lived: 'The room was in the greatest disorder: music, money, clothes, lay on the floor, linen in a heap on the unclean bed, the open grand piano was covered in thick dust, and broken coffee-cups lay on the table'.

Beethoven shared his love of the country with Wordsworth, and spent much of every summer going for long rambles through the countryside, with a notebook at the ready to jot down thoughts that occurred to him. The best-loved of all music depicting nature is his 'Pastoral' Symphony, which is true scene-painting. But all Beethoven's greatest works reflect his belief in the beauty and goodness of nature. Alongside this belief went a faith in the eventual brotherhood of all mankind, expressed in the last movement of the Ninth Symphony, a choral setting of Schiller's 'Ode to Joy'. 'All mankind will be brothers' is the message of the work, which Beethoven passed on to future generations as no other composer has done before or since.

Beethoven's early works were largely a continuation of the formal classical tradition, in the style of Haydn and Mozart. Yet, with regard to the way in which he expressed his innermost feelings in his later works, he is a forerunner of the later, romantic composers.

The romantic composers

THE MOVEMENT known as 'Romanticism', which swept across Europe in the early 19th century, was largely a reaction against the formality and artificiality of the old aristocratic world. All kinds of ideas flowed together: the philosophy of Voltaire, whose satires mocked the archaic forms of religion and monarchy; the poetry of Goethe, who studied the inner world of his emotions; the theories of Jean-Jacques Rousseau, whose 'Social Contract', written in 1762, praised democracy and inspired the leaders of the French Revolution.

Romanticism came to music a good deal later than it had to literature. Beethoven, who represents a link between the classical and romantic periods, was more than 20 years younger than Goethe. The composers usually grouped together as the 'romantics' were nearly all born after 1800. Unlike the classical composers, who were relatively unaffected by developments outside the sphere of music, the romantics absorbed influences from literature, art and the natural scene.

Whereas Vienna had been the natural focus for musicians in the 18th century, by the 1830s the centre had shifted to Paris. Of the romantic composers, Hector Berlioz, born in 1803, corresponds most closely to the popular image of the passionate and unstable musician. As a young man he lived in a constant turmoil of exaltation and depression. He composed his 'Fantastic' Symphony as the outcome of a frenzied love affair, fought a running battle with the Paris musical establishment, and found inspiration in the plays of Shakespeare, Goethe's '*Faust*' and Virgil's '*Aeneid*'.

Berlioz was one of the few composers not to have been a pianist, which may be the reason for the originality of his orchestration. Franz Liszt, on the other hand, born in Hungary in 1811, was the greatest pianist of his age, and was already a virtuoso when he played for Beethoven in 1823.

The bust of Beethoven, representing the link between classicism and romanticism, overlooks the romantic writers and musicians (from left to right): Dumas the elder, Hugo, George Sand; then Paganini, Rossini and Liszt. Marie d'Agoult, Liszt's mistress, sits at his feet.

FRANZ LISZT

Liszt, the greatest and most flamboyant pianist of his age, vowed to do as much for the piano as Paganini had for the violin. He poured out a stream of concert studies, transcriptions of operas

and descriptive piano pieces, which made his reputation as great as that of any pop star performing today.

Liszt was the first musician to give solo recitals (he called them 'musical soliloquies'), which he ended with hair-raising acrobatics on the key-

board. Women in the audience mobbed him and, when on tour, Liszt was frequently carried through the streets in triumph, scattering gold pieces to the crowd. After the age of 35 or so, Liszt almost gave up solo concert playing to concentrate on composi-

tion and teaching. He was unfailingly generous to younger composers such as Wagner and Grieg (whose famous piano concerto Liszt read at sight when shown it by Grieg). Wagner married Liszt's illegitimate daughter, Cosima (below), in 1870.

FRANZ SCHUBERT

ROBERT AND CLARA SCHUMANN

HECTOR BERLIOZ

FREDERIC CHOPIN

Liszt's life was even more eventful and spectacular than that of Berlioz. In middle age, however, he turned to religion, becoming an *abbé* in the Roman Catholic Church – a remarkable contrast to his stormy youth.

Like Liszt, Frederic Chopin was a brilliant pianist who made his career in Paris. But while Liszt was an extrovert, Chopin was a fastidious introvert, shying away from the glare of publicity and preferring to make his money by giving expensive and sought-after piano lessons. He left his native Poland in 1830, aged 20, and never returned; yet all his finest music is filled with nostalgia for his country. Chopin died young from consumption, made worse by a disastrous winter holiday spent with his mistress, Baroness Dudevant (who wrote under the name George Sand). Yet during this time he completed his 'Preludes', a series of 24 exquisite miniatures for piano.

Berlioz, Liszt and Chopin, who knew each other during the 1830s and '40s in Paris and whose careers took them far afield, were truly 'international romantics', by choice as much as by circumstance. In complete contrast, the German romantics (see overleaf), were 'domestic': they centred their lives and their music on their immediate surroundings.

The German romantics tended to be content with the approval of a small group of friends or family, and had little interest in international publicity. Apart from Carl Maria von Weber, whose life was devoted to establishing German national opera, the earliest of these composers was Franz Schubert, born in Vienna in 1797. Schubert found his main creative outlet in the *Lied*, or solo song. He composed the first of his great songs as early as 1814 and by the end of his short life had produced over 600, including two extended song cycles.

These songs were first sung at private meetings of friends, nicknamed 'Schubertiads'. They were made known to a wider public by singers such as Schubert's friend, Johann Michael Vogl; but this was a slow process and, until the end of his life, Schubert made hardly any money from his music. He also wrote vast quantities of piano music, nine symphonies, string quartets and church music, with an ease as miraculous as that of Mozart in a previous generation.

Schubert's outpouring of song was matched by only one other of the romantics, Robert Schumann, who was born, like Chopin, in 1810. Schumann spent the best part of his life in Leipzig, and most of his songs and piano music were inspired by his wife Clara. Schumann loved musical puzzles and riddles. The first of his published works, the 'Abegg Variations', which was named after a girl he is said to have met at a dance, begins with the notes A B E G G.

Schumann was a brilliant journalist and founded his own music magazine. In it he brought unknown composers to the attention of the world – including Brahms, who was described in an article by Schumann as 'a young man over whose cradle Graces and Heroes stood watch'. This was in 1853, when Brahms was 20; three years later, Schumann died insane. Brahms looked after Clara Schumann at this terrible time, and it is probable that he fell in love with her. Brahms's music moved from the passion of his early piano sonatas and songs, and his First Piano Concerto, to the restraint of his symphonies and other later works. This change has been thought to reflect a similar restraint in his personal life, after he had abandoned the idea of marrying Clara. In fact, Brahms's career represents a reverse swing from romanticism back to classicism.

Of the romantics, only Felix Mendelssohn combined wide experience of the world with a domestic attitude to music. Typical of his fluency and charm are his piano pieces called 'Songs Without Words' which set the style for dozens of minor composers after him. Throughout the 19th century his oratorio, 'Elijah', first performed at the Birmingham Festival in 1846, held its own with the 'Messiah', and is still a mainstay of choral societies. His early death in 1847 meant that the musical world lost the one composer who bridged the gulf between the 'international' and 'domestic' romantics.

THE 'ERL-KING', SUBJECT OF SCHUBERT'S SONG

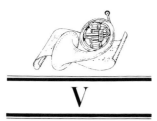

V

CHURCH MUSIC

Singing to the Lord

A GOTHIC CATHEDRAL, with its soaring nave, intricate roof-vaulting and glowing stained glass, is one of the world's noblest spiritual creations. Musicians have built their own cathedrals in sound: the Masses and other religious works in which timeless words are set in ways that reflect the constant changes in musical taste in the outside world. From the Notre Dame masters in the 13th century to Stravinsky and Vaughan Williams in the 20th, composers of every shade of religious belief have put all their feeling and skill into setting to music the solemn pleading of the *Kyrie* that begins the Mass, the exultant *Sanctus* at its centre, and the quiet *Agnus Dei* with which it ends.

The greatest composer of church music for unaccompanied choir, Giovanni Palestrina (left) led a prosperous and happy life among many friends. Born about 1525, he became choirmaster of the Julian Chapel at the Vatican in Rome when he was about 25 years of age. There he met St Philip Neri, a pioneer of the oratorio.

Many of these settings have been based on plainsong, the ancient single-line chants of the Christian Church, which have been shaped by countless generations of anonymous musicians into flowing, effortless melodies. Probably many of them go back beyond the beginning of Christianity. In their present form they are at least 1400 years old, as they were collected by Pope Gregory around 600AD – hence the name 'Gregorian' which is often applied to them.

Plainsong chants are not organised into a regular rhythmic pattern that can be split up into bars of a constant length. But music based on plainsong gradually acquired a rhythmic pulse. The Middle Ages brought religion and philosophy into everything, including the rhythm of music. Music in three-time was called *musica perfecta* ('perfect music'), because three is the number of the Holy Trinity, and has a beginning, a middle and an end. Two-time, on the other hand, was felt to be incomplete in some way and was called 'imperfect'.

MONKS SINGING THE DIVINE OFFICE c.1430

Single-line plainsong gradually evolved into music sung in two parallel lines a fourth or a fifth apart, corresponding to the difference between bass and tenor voices. This type of music is known as *organum*. From *organum* it was a short step to the three-part motet, which consisted of an underlying plainsong, a hymn with its own words, and a third part which was often a popular song. The Middle Ages saw nothing irreverent in this, any more than they did when a stone-mason carved a gargoyle among the saints and angels. Eventually full-scale Masses were based on popular songs. The great Flemish composer, Ockeghem, based a Mass on a love song called '*Ma Maîtresse*' ('My Mistress'), while another song, '*L'Homme Armé*' ('The Armed Man'), was used for 30 or more Masses by different composers, from Dufay in the 15th century to Carissimi in the 17th.

Church authorities down the ages have been concerned that beautiful music might distract the minds of the faithful from higher things.

By the mid-16th century, the Catholic Church was so worried about the degenerate state of church services and the music that went with them that it convened the Council of Trent in 1545, which discussed the matter on and off for nearly 20 years. 'Impure melodies' and 'scandalous noises' were banned, and only music of unruffled clarity was allowed. The master of this pure style was Palestrina, whose Masses, written for unaccompanied choir, had a great influence on most later church composers.

Twenty years before the Council of Trent, the Protestant, Martin Luther, published his 'Wittenberg Songbook', a collection of hymns which embodied his own musical reforms.

Martin Luther (left) was the first to make the famous statement that the devil should not have all the good tunes. Although he approved of choirs, he believed that the 'common man' should also be allowed to sing in church. By the time he died in 1546, aged 62, his tuneful hymns were being sung with great fervour all over Germany.

The songbook was produced, says Luther, 'so that the young might have something to rid them of their love ditties and wanton songs, and might instead of these learn wholesome things.' These Lutheran hymns reached their final flowering in the chorales of Bach, 200 years later. Bach not only summed up the whole Lutheran tradition: although a fervent Protestant, in his Mass in B minor he produced the supreme setting of the Catholic liturgy. The only Mass of comparable grandeur written since then is Beethoven's Mass in D, the 'Solemn' Mass, into which he put his most personal thoughts.

Entirely different is the music of the Eastern Churches, which draws on the Oriental (Jewish) tradition. Although highly ornamental, it lacks the interwoven voices normal in settings of the Catholic Mass. Rachmaninov wrote a noble setting of the 'Vigil' liturgy of the Orthodox Church, which is quite unlike any Catholic or Protestant religious music, and glows with the fervour of the earliest Christian chants.

GEORGE FRIDERIC HANDEL

MASTER OF THE ORATORIO

Most of the works by which Handel is remembered today were written in England. But his earliest triumphs belong to Rome (left), where his first oratorio, based on the Resurrection, was written and performed in 1708. Two years later he visited England for the first time, and finally settled there for good, as the leading opera composer of his age.

As time went by the public demand for Italian opera fell off. Handel (right) turned increasingly to oratorio. In 1741 his friend Charles Jennens (left) wrote the words of the 'Messiah'. Handel set them in a white heat of inspiration, composing the whole enormous work in only three weeks, and hardly crossing out or altering a single note.

The first performance of the 'Messiah', conducted by Handel from the harpsichord, was given in Dublin in 1742. A year later in London, George II (right) was so moved by the opening bars of the 'Hallelujah' Chorus that he leapt to his feet. The audience rose too, so beginning a tradition of standing to show respect while the chorus is being sung.

With the 'Messiah', the oratorio took deeper root in England than in any other country. But its great fame and popularity date from 1784, when it was performed in Westminster Abbey (left) to celebrate the centenary of Handel's birth (he was in fact born in 1685). Since then the 'Messiah' has remained the best-loved oratorio.

The genius of Bach

HANS
(GREAT GRANDFATHER)

JOHANN CHRISTOPH
(UNCLE)

JOHANN AMBROSIUS
(FATHER)

JOHANN
SEBASTIAN

J. S. Bach was the most famous member of a musical dynasty. His father taught him the violin and viola; his uncle probably taught him the clavier. One very early Bach was Hans, born c. 1570.

Bach's organ music, much of which was composed at Weimar in 1708-17, still forms the basis of the organist's repertory. His attitude to his church music is shown by the initials with which he began and ended his works: J.J., standing for *Jesu, Juva* ('Jesus help me') at the beginning, and S.D.G., *'Soli Deo Gloria'* ('Glory to God Alone') at the end of a piece.

Bach spent the years 1717-23 working for the Prince of Anhalt-Cöthen, writing orchestral and chamber music, and his first set of 24 keyboard Preludes and Fugues. From Cöthen he moved to Leipzig. where he composed his greatest choral works, among them the Mass in B minor.

Wilhelm Friedemann was J.S. Bach's eldest son. Although an extremely able musician, in later life he took to drink and died in poverty.

Johann Christian, J.S. Bach's eleventh son, is usually known as 'the English Bach'. Mozart, aged eight, played with him in London in 1764.

Carl Philipp Emanuel, J.S. Bach's third son, was court composer to Frederick the Great of Prussia. The King, who was ahead of his time in having pianos instead of harpsichords, was delighted when J.S. Bach came to play for him.

Almost 80 years after Bach's death, Felix Mendelssohn (left) revived the 'St Matthew Passion', and began the rediscovery of Bach.

WHEN FELIX MENDELSSOHN conducted Bach's 'St Matthew Passion' in Berlin on March 11, 1829, he brought into the light of day a masterpiece that had been forgotten for a century. The rediscovery of Bach was under way. Bach is now so much a part of everyday musical life – played straight, jazzed up, computerised or turned into pop – that it seems incredible that he had to be 'rediscovered' at all. Until Mendelssohn's epoch-making performance, Bach had been known almost entirely as a writer of learned preludes and fugues for keyboard. This was the way he was known to Haydn, Mozart and Beethoven.

Johann Sebastian Bach was born in 1685 – a vintage year for composers, as Handel and Scarlatti were both born in the same year. They went on to international fame and fortune, but Bach stayed in the restricted area of northern Germany. The opera composer, Handel, and the brilliant harpsichordist, Scarlatti, looked towards the future, while Bach was rooted in the past. His attitude to music was that of a medieval craftsman, working in a long-established family tradition. 'I have had to work hard,' he said, adding, 'anyone who works just as hard will get just as far.' His portraits show a solid, respectable citizen, which is exactly what he was. From 1723 until his death in 1750, he was *Cantor* (head of music) at St Thomas's School in Leipzig, responsible for training the boys and for providing the music for church services. Apart from his quarrels with the headmaster of St Thomas's and battles with the Leipzig Town Council, Bach's life was uneventful – ideal conditions for an enormous musical output that has been described as more like an industrial concern than the work of a single man.

Bach's steady attitude to his work was paralleled by a steady family life unique among the great composers. He married twice and had 20 children, three of whom grew up to become the most famous composers of their day, driving their father's memory into the shade. One of the most delightful aspects of Bach's character is shown by the 'Little Clavier Books', which he wrote for his son Wilhelm Friedemann, and his second wife Anna Magdalena. They contain simple pieces still taught today.

He combined his down-to-earth approach to composition with a deep religious faith. Bach was a Lutheran Protestant, brought up in the strong religious traditions of northern Germany. Apart from his five settings of the Passion story, of which only two (the 'St John' and 'St Matthew Passion') survive, he wrote sets of church cantatas for every Sunday in the calendar.

Before his final move to Leipzig, Bach had a varied musical career. At the age of 18 he was appointed organist at Arnstadt, where he gained his mastery of church music and, on one occasion, was reproved by the authorities for inviting a 'strange maiden' into the organ loft. He spent nine years as court organist at Weimar, and at the end of his time there was gaoled for a month for 'stubbornly forcing the issue of his dismissal'. He spent six happy years at Cöthen as *Kapellmeister* (musical director), writing the six masterly 'Brandenburg' Concertos and the first of his two books of keyboard Preludes and Fugues that make up the 'Well-tempered Clavier' ('clavier' means simply 'keyboard').

His amazing skill as an improviser was shown most vividly towards the end of his life, in 1747, when he visited King Frederick the Great of Prussia. Frederick was a keen flute-player and amateur composer. When Bach arrived at the court in Potsdam he was given no time to change his clothes, but was asked by Frederick to sit down at one of his pianos and improvise on a theme the King himself had written. Bach obliged with a three-part fugue straight out of his head. On his return to Leipzig, he composed a set of canons and fugues on the royal theme, together with a sonata for flute, violin and keyboard, which he sent off to Frederick as his 'Musical Offering'. In this work learning and grace go hand in hand. Bach's 'last will and testament', musically speaking, was the gigantic 'Art of Fugue', in which he summed up a lifetime's mastery of counterpoint (the skill of combining horizontal lines of music). He died before the work was finished.

Bach's sons composed in a new, light-hearted style known as the *galant*, and their father's learning went underground for a while. But it soon burst forth again. 'Johann Sebastian, mighty Bach', as the poet Dylan Thomas called him, now rules unchallenged as the most all-embracing intellect in musical history.

Organ loft to belfry

SIX HUNDRED years ago the French composer Guillaume de Machaut described the organ as 'the king of instruments'. At that time there were no less than three types of organ – the cumbersome church organ used for accompanying services, and the organs for secular use: the 'portative', so-called because it could be carried round by the player, and the 'positive', which was fixed in one position.

Today every church has its organ, ranging from harmonium-sized instruments in remote parishes to gigantic cathedral organs, with ranks of tall pipes towering above the choir, and an organ loft perched precariously against a pillar or inner wall. But it is not exclusively a church instrument, any more than it was in the Middle Ages. It is played in concert halls such as London's Royal Festival and Queen Elizabeth Halls, and portative organs appear in performances of Baroque music.

The organ is by far the oldest surviving keyboard instrument. The Greek water organ or *hydraulos*, invented in Alexandria in the 3rd century BC, had a wind chest, pipes and keys, like a modern organ. Water under pressure ensured that a constant supply of air was maintained in the wind chest. A large *hydraulos* was loud enough to fill a Roman amphitheatre with its sound. It was played at gladiatorial shows, no doubt while Christians were being thrown to the lions, which perhaps explains why organs did not appear in church until Christianity was several centuries old.

By the 9th century organs were becoming fairly common. About 850AD there was a famous organ at Winchester in England, which had 400 pipes and needed 70 men to pump the bellows. It made such a noise that listeners had to block their ears to stop themselves being deafened – as may be advisable today, when a huge organ like the one in London's Albert Hall is playing at full blast. These large church organs did not have proper keyboards; the notes were worked by levers which had to be struck with the fist, so the music must have been extremely ponderous – almost as slow as the bells that hung in every church tower, and were eventually mechanised by being connected to a keyboard to form a carillon – found in many European towns – which could play a variety of simple tunes.

CHURCH BELLS

For centuries the loudest sounds most people heard in their lifetime came from the bells in the church tower, ringing out joyfully for weddings and victories in battle, tolling solemnly for a death, or pealing urgently to give warning of dangers, such as the Great Fire of London (above). In a medieval town, bells were also the only means of telling the time. In Europe, most small churches had only a few bells, with a limited number of 'tunes' that could be played on them. The art of bell-ringing was developed almost entirely in England where, from the Middle Ages on, parish churches tried to have at least six bells, with cathedrals and large churches having as many as 12. The number of bells in a tower is called a 'ring', and the number of possible combinations or 'changes' can be worked out mathematically. For instance, with four bells there are 24 possible changes; but with eight bells the number rises to over 40,000, while with 12 bells it would take 30 years to ring all the different changes. The rules of change-ringing were laid down in 1668 by Fabian Stedman in his book '*Tintinnalogia*'. England's oldest bell-foundry, at Whitechapel in London, has been operating since 1570. The famous 'Big Ben' bell of Westminster (below) was cast at Whitechapel in 1858, and bells are still

being made there in the time-honoured tradition of hand craftsmanship. Methods of 19th-century bell-makers (below) are still much in evidence at Whitechapel today.

The portative, or portable organ (left), was a popular instrument from the 12th to the mid-17th century. The bellows, operated by the player's left hand, pumped air into the pipes. The keyboard was played with the right hand. Portative organs were sometimes carried in processions, suspended from the player's neck, and were also used in the chamber music of the time.

The leading organists of the time, such as Landini, the blind 14th-century composer, played the positive or portative organ, rather than the still-clumsy church instrument. Towards the end of the Middle Ages, as the clavichord and then the harpsichord evolved, keyboard-players began to have alternatives to the organ, although until well into the 16th century or even later the various keyboard instruments were more or less interchangeable.

The portative organ's sweet, clear sound was unlike the muddy tone of later organs, and was just as suitable as the harpsichord for a good deal of Renaissance keyboard music. The leading 15th-century organ composers, such as Hofhaimer and Paumann, are little more than names today. Yet in their lifetimes they were known throughout Europe, and Paumann's playing at Nuremberg was as famous as Bach's at Leipzig in a later century.

By 1500 organs had much their present form: two or more manuals (keyboards) and a pedal board, each controlling separate sets of pipes. A modern organ console (right) has an enormous variety of 'stops' or knobs to control tone quality. The pipes of modern organs like this German one (below) are opened and closed by electrical action.

The works of the 20th-century French composer Olivier Messiaen (left) reflect his strong sense of religious mysticism. Appointed organist of the church of the Holy Trinity in Paris in 1931, his influence on younger contemporary composers such as Stockhausen has been extensive.

Technical developments in organ building and advances in playing went hand in hand. Gradually two main schools developed: the French, with light, clear-sounding organs suitable for the brilliant music of Couperin, and the German, solid and substantial, like the more intellectual works of Reinken, Buxtehude and Bach himself. Bach learnt his all-round mastery of the organ from studying its construction as well as actually playing it. Yet the organ at Arnstadt, for which he composed his first preludes and fugues, is a modest little instrument, with only two manuals, a short pedal board and a limited number of stops. After Bach's unrivalled series of works, the great era of organ composition came to an abrupt end (see overleaf).

Bach's contemporary, Handel, wrote some splendid organ concertos for the concert platform, but classical and romantic composers fought shy of the organ, although they composed plenty of choral church music. Among composers famous in other fields Mendelssohn, Liszt, Brahms and Franck wrote a handful of organ works between them. The main supply of new works came from specialists like the French composer Vierne and the German Karg-Elert. The only recent composer to have produced majestic organ pieces comparable with those of Bach is Messiaen, whose large-scale works such as 'L'Ascension' and 'Les Corps Glorieux' combine intense religious mysticism with a totally new and original use of organ sonorities.

Although the organ is now the only instrument normally heard in church, this is very much a 19th-century development. In earlier times, despite the fact that it was still the main church instrument, it was not the only one. The noble Masses written by Guillaume Dufay and other composers of the 15th century were often accompanied by sackbuts (trombones) and drums, at least at their climaxes. All sorts of instruments were used by Renaissance composers of church music, as we can see from paintings of the time which show angelic choirs playing harps, rebecs (violins), recorders and other contemporary instruments. Around 1600 Andrea and Giovanni Gabrieli were writing magnificent music for trombones and other instruments, to be played in St Mark's in Venice.

Bach himself was just as happy making use of orchestral instruments in church as he was playing the organ. His finest works, like the Mass in B minor, the 'St Matthew Passion' and the church cantatas, make brilliant use of every instrument to accompany voices. An engraving of the 1730s shows an organist, who might possibly be Bach, playing with a mixed group of strings and brass.

Church bands of this nature were often made up mainly of amateurs, with a few professionals to play the difficult parts – rather like the average local orchestra today. In England one of the features of country churches in the 18th and early 19th centuries was the local church band, which accompanied the hymns with a few string instruments, and perhaps a clarinet and a serpent to provide the wind section. All these amateurs found their occupation gone as each church was provided with an organ in an attempt to bring the music up to date – a process described by Thomas Hardy in his comedy of village life, 'Under the Greenwood Tree'. Today many villages have lost their organist, and the organ is returning to its original status as one instrument among many, although still the grandest of them all.

THE VILLAGE CHOIR

VI

OPERA AND BALLET

The origins of opera

No one knows who composed the first symphony or the first concerto. These major forms evolved gradually during the 17th and 18th centuries. But the first of all operas was written by the Italian composer, Jacopo Peri. It was called 'Dafne', and was performed in Florence in 1597. It was an attempt by a group of Italian artists, scholars and noblemen to return to the simplicity of Ancient Greek drama. These men, the *Camerata* ('Society'), felt that the interweaving of complex lines of sound in medieval church music and secular madrigals was too complicated, and that emotion had become entangled in a thicket of notes. Their leader, Giovanni de' Bardi, put their beliefs in a simple way: 'In composing, you will make it your chief aim to arrange the verse well and to declaim the words as intelligibly as you can.'

Although the music of 'Dafne' is now lost, this new type of composition soon established itself. Its earliest beginnings coincided with the creative life of Claudio Monteverdi, the greatest Italian composer of his day, who wrote his first opera, 'Orfeo', in 1607 and his last, 'The Coronation of Poppaea', in 1642. Monteverdi and his contemporaries established a general operatic formula which has lasted ever since. The main divisions are: formal sung solo arias, duets and larger groupings, through which the characters display their emotions; irregular recitatives (half-way between song and speech) which explain what is happening and carry the action forward; solid block choruses, derived from the choruses in Greek plays, to provide grand choral effects; instrumental overtures, which were originally included to allow the audience time to settle down; and interludes, which accompany changes in scenery.

Naturally enough, opera took deepest root in Italy, where it began, and where the spoken language is song-like in its rhythm and lilt. But it soon spread to the rest of Europe, especially to France, where Louis XIV appreciated the opportunities it gave for splendid scenery and dancing, in addition to the purely musical side. His composer was Jean-Baptiste Lully, an Italian by birth, who had worked his way up from kitchen-boy to undisputed ruler of French music. Lully made a fortune by buying the monopoly of every opera performed in French.

HOW OPERA BEGAN

Opera began life as an attempt to recreate the elegance and simple power of Ancient Greek tragedy, in which the stories of gods and heroes were told in strongly dramatic form, with a chorus acting as commentator. In the late 16th century, a group of Italian noblemen wished to free music from medieval complexity and to restore the spirit of purity found in the Greek plays. So they combined the art of song with the drama of story-telling, and the first opera was born. Since then, Greek drama and legend have inspired many composers, including Gluck, Rameau, Berlioz and Stravinsky.

Early Christian mystery, miracle and morality plays are also ancestors of the opera. These were designed to teach Bible stories, to depict the lives of the saints, and to present the conflict between good and evil. Some, particularly the Christmas plays, included singing and dancing as well as acting.

The most temperamental of Handel's opera stars were Senesino, Cuzzoni and Berenstadt (below). When Cuzzoni objected to the way Handel wanted an aria sung, he seized her by the waist and threatened to throw her out of the window. Needless to say, she sang it as he wished.

Henry Purcell (left) was the greatest English composer of the 17th century. His opera 'Dido and Aeneas', written in 1689, is still performed.

English opera descended directly from the court masque, or mask, and the forms are very similar. The masque, a ceremonial entertainment, consisted of acting, dancing and music. The subjects were mythical or heroic, and the scenery and costumes were very elaborate. The English masque reached its perfection during the early 17th century. By their use of recitative, masque composers brought the form even closer to that of opera.

In Germany small courts also had their opera composers. In England, however, the Civil War in the 1640s, followed by Cromwell's Puritan régime, prevented the growth of operatic talent. The exception was Henry Purcell, whose 'Dido and Aeneas', written in 1689 for a girls' school in Chelsea, was the only opera of stature by an English-born composer until Britten's 'Peter Grimes' more than 250 years later.

Purcell's early death in 1695 left the way clear for Handel's domination of the English musical scene. Born in Halle in Germany in 1685, the same year as Bach, George Frideric Handel was an internationalist who had a brief but successful career as a composer in Italy, before settling in England in 1712. The previous year he had triumphed in London with his opera 'Rinaldo', which he followed with one opera after another for 30 years. Handel threw himself into the cut-and-thrust of London operatic life, scouring Europe for singers, hiring theatres and constantly finding himself at loggerheads with rival composers, notably the Italian Giovanni Battista Bononcini.

By about 1740 Italian opera in London was in decline. Apart from the natural wish for a change, the public was growing tired of incessant squabbling among the singers, both *castrati* (adult male sopranos) and female sopranos. The pomposity of Italian opera never quite recovered from the blow dealt by 'The Beggar's Opera', a collaboration between the composer Dr Pepusch and the poet John Gay, first performed in 1728. After this opera – about the adventures of a highwayman, his mistress and a whole cast of villains – it became almost impossible to take the posturings of gods and heroes seriously. Handel fought back by founding another Italian opera company, but the venture was doomed.

No such break in continuity occurred on the continent of Europe. After Monteverdi, Italy produced opera composers in an unbroken line, among them Cavalli, Alessandro Scarlatti (father of Domenico Scarlatti, the greatest of harpsichord composers), Vivaldi and Pergolesi. In France, Rameau took over from Lully and reigned supreme for the first half of the 18th century. Although Germany was less opera-minded, Handel's friend Telemann wrote no fewer than 40 operas.

Mozart and his times

At the age of 14 Mozart was awarded the Order of the Golden Spur by the Pope. He wore it when he posed for this unusually good likeness, painted seven years later.

B<small>Y THE</small> late 18th century, when Mozart reached maturity, opera in Vienna had separated into three main strands. The chief form was the serious Italian opera (*opera seria*), whose characters were classical gods or heroes, living and dying in an atmosphere of high tragedy. A less formal counterpart was the comic opera (*opera buffa*), based on the Harlequin and Columbine characters of Italian comedy (*commedia dell'arte*), with a cast of impudent servants, senile masters and assorted rogues. Alongside these Italian forms ran the native German *Singspiel*, whose appeal lay in the fact that, sung and spoken in German, it could be understood by the whole audience. Shortly before Mozart's operatic career began, Gluck favoured a return to the simplicity of the 17th-century opera, before plots became obscured by long solo arias which delayed the action and were mere excuses for singers to show off the acrobatic qualities of their voices.

Mozart gathered these three strands together, and transformed them through the power of his music and his unrivalled dramatic skill. By his early teens he had composed an example of all three types. As a mature composer he continued to write all three kinds, although the tradition of *opera seria* was almost at its last gasp. Of his two 'grand operas' 'Idomeneo' (1781), set in legendary Crete, is full of passion and fire and is still played today. But '*La Clemenza di Tito*' (1791) is rarely heard.

Mozart's three examples of *opera buffa*, 'The Marriage of Figaro', 'Don Giovanni' and '*Così fan Tutte*' ('This is the way all women behave'), are operatic masterpieces. They so widened and deepened the concept of the comic opera that, as with Shakespeare's comedies, we do not know whether we are meant to laugh or cry. Each has love in some form or another as its theme. Briefly, 'Figaro' deals with the ways in which a servant (Figaro) foils the attempts of his master to seduce the girl he is about to marry. 'Don Giovanni' is concerned with the adventures of a woman-chaser who is finally dragged down to Hell by the statue of a man he has murdered. (This does not sound like a comic opera, but Mozart rounds it off with a chorus telling the audience that it is not meant to be taken seriously.) '*Così fan Tutte*' is about two young

couples who vow to be faithful, change partners, and find that faithfulness is not as easy as they had originally thought.

To Beethoven, whose single opera, 'Fidelio', was of high-minded seriousness, these plots seemed immoral. For the words of all three works Mozart had the same libretto-writer, the brilliant and eccentric Lorenzo da Ponte. Both men were out of sympathy with the rigid social code of their day. For the first of their collaborations, 'The Marriage of Figaro', they used a play by the French author, Beaumarchais, which not only showed two servants getting the better of their master, but won the audience round to the servants' viewpoint. 'Figaro', written in 1786, marked the peak of Mozart's fame. The tenor Michael Kelly, who sang in the first production, wrote an account of it which brings Mozart vividly before us: 'I shall never forget his little animated countenance, when lighted up with the glowing rays of genius – it is as impossible to describe it as it would be to paint sun-beams.' During the dress rehearsal, after Figaro's war-like aria, '*Non piu andrai*', everybody shouted: '*Bravo! Bravo! Maestro! Viva, viva, grande Mozart!*' 'Figaro' became the rage of Vienna, and errand boys whistled the tunes in the streets.

David Hockney's design for Act I, Scene i of 'The Magic Flute' (left): a rocky garden from which Prince Tamino sets out in search of Pamina, the Queen of the Night's daughter. Tamino has a magic flute for protection and is accompanied by Papageno, a bird-catcher (above), with a chime of magic bells.

LORENZO DA PONTE

'MARRIAGE OF FIGARO'   'DON GIOVANNI'   'COSÍ FAN TUTTE'

Poet, adventurer, friend of Casanova, Lorenzo da Ponte is only remembered today because he wrote the words for three of Mozart's operas. He was born near Venice in 1749 and became a priest in 1773. Despite his religious vows, he lived a dissolute life. In Vienna, in 1783, he met Mozart. The composer considered all Italians unreliable, but their meeting led eventually to 'The Marriage of Figaro' (1786), 'Don Giovanni' (1787) and 'Cosi fan Tutte' (1790). Early in 1790 da Ponte

LORENZO DA PONTE

went to Trieste, where he married an English girl, although he was still a priest. Then he moved to London and became poet to the Italian Opera. In 1805, to evade his creditors, he went to America. There he ran various businesses, then a school in New York for teaching Italian, and finally became Professor of Italian Literature. In 1833 he persuaded the New Yorkers to build an opera house which, however, ran for only two seasons. Da Ponte died in New York in 1838, aged 89.

The same spirit of delight fills Mozart's two German-language operas, 'The Abduction from the Seraglio' and 'The Magic Flute'. 'The Seraglio', written in 1781, has a lightweight plot concerning the rescue of a girl from a sultan's harem, and is set to some of Mozart's most sparkling music. The plot of 'The Magic Flute' is absurd from many points of view, but it has an underlying seriousness. Written in 1791, the last year of Mozart's life, it is both a fairy-tale and a work filled with a deep belief in the ultimate triumph of right over wrong. Apart from two idealised lovers, who pass through various ordeals protected by the soft music of a flute, the cast includes a wicked queen, a noble high priest and a comic bird-catcher, who provides light relief. The librettist, a theatre director called Emanuel Schikaneder, was a Freemason, as was Mozart himself.

As the composer lay dying, 'The Magic Flute' was playing to a packed theatre and he followed the performance in his mind, with his watch beside him. Apart from the 'Requiem', left unfinished, it was his last major work. In its mixture of magic and tenderness, vulgarity and fantasy, 'The Magic Flute' sums up Mozart's universal human understanding.

The age of Rossini

ITALIAN OPERA in the first half of the 19th century was dominated by three great names: Rossini, Donizetti and Bellini. All three had the true Italian mastery of graceful, flowing melody – the art of *bel canto* or 'beautiful song', which had been cultivated in Italy since the early days of opera, and which demanded perfect vocal control, often at the expense of acting technique. The great singers of the age, like Isabella Colbran, who was Rossini's first wife, could sing runs, trills and leaps with an ease that few more recent singers have been able to manage. Italian audiences of the day went wild over their favourite opera stars, and composers vied with one another to produce opera after opera in which the plot was of far less importance than the opportunities for display given to brilliantly spectacular voices.

Gioacchino Rossini was the oldest of the three, and acted as father-figure to the others, encouraging and helping them with a generosity rare among composers in any age. He was born in Pesaro in northern Italy, in 1792. His father combined the unlikely talents of town trumpeter and inspector of slaughterhouses, and his mother was a competent singer. After a short time as a blacksmith's apprentice, Rossini found his true vocation in the opera house. His first real success came in 1812, with a comic opera called '*La Pietra del Paragone*' ('The Touchstone'). The next year he scored a double triumph in Venice with a comic opera, 'The Italian Girl in Algiers', and a tragic opera, 'Tancredi'.

Although Rossini produced comedies and tragedies with equal fluency, his genius was for the humorous side of life. One of his biographers wrote of 'the great laugh that Rossini brought into music', and Rossini said of himself, referring to the ease with which he composed: 'Give me a laundry list and I will set it to music.' His career was an uninterrupted success, first in Italy and then in Paris. One of the few black spots was the first night of 'The Barber of Seville', the most famous and most frequently performed of all his operas. Written in Rome in 1816, in the incredibly short time of 13 days, it was booed and hissed on the first night by a group of demonstrators. Rossini was so discouraged that he did not come to the theatre for the second night. He need not have worried: the opera was a triumph, and has remained so ever since.

In 1829 his opera 'William Tell' – which includes the famous scene when Tell shoots the apple off his son's head – was performed with great success in Paris. Rossini was 37, with nearly 40 operas behind him and the promise of an equally dazzling career ahead. Yet after 'William Tell' he never composed another note of opera, and very little other music. Perhaps Rossini felt he could no longer compete, as audiences began to turn away from comedy to the solemn grand operas of Giacomo Meyerbeer. He spent his final years as a man-about-town in Paris, holding regular dinner parties packed with celebrities. His love of food is recalled by a kind of steak known as *Tournedos Rossini*.

THE BARBER OF SEVILLE

Rossini (far left) sets the first scene of 'The Barber of Seville' outside Doctor Bartolo's house. Count Almaviva is there serenading Rosina, Doctor Bartolo's ward (left). (Bartolo actually wants to marry her himself.) Figaro, the barber of the story, appears and says he will help Almaviva win Rosina's love.
Act II takes place inside Bartolo's house (right), where Figaro is about to give the doctor a shave. Almaviva, disguised as a music-master, has already talked his way in. He says he has come in place of Basilio, the usual music teacher, to give Rosina her lesson.

Suddenly, Basilio turns up, but Almaviva bribes him to keep the secret (below). When Doctor Bartolo catches Count Almaviva kissing Rosina, he throws him out, and decides to marry Rosina as quickly as possible.

Donizetti (left) wrote operas at such speed that a contemporary cartoonist depicted him composing with both hands.

The Australian soprano Joan Sutherland (below) made her reputation in the tragic title role of Donizetti's 'Lucia di Lammermoor'. The 'Mad Scene' gives great scope for her superb voice.

Although composition for Bellini (left) was slow and painful, his operatic arias are effortless and flowing. Typical is 'Casta Diva', sung by the high priestess Norma in the opera of that name.

Among Rossini's protégés was Gaetano Donizetti, born in 1797. Although towards the end of his life Donizetti was ravaged by paralysis (he died insane), at the height of his career he wrote operas with an ease as great as that of Rossini. Apart from this operatic profusion he wrote quantities of chamber music and an enormous number of songs for solo voice. He was at his happiest with comedies such as 'Don Pasquale', which tells of the misadventures of a crusty old bachelor, but he also wrote a large number of dramatic works on historical themes. His tragic opera 'Lucia di Lammermoor', based on a novel by Sir Walter Scott, has been restored to popularity in recent years by the remarkable talents of singers such as Callas and Sutherland, who have revived *bel canto* singing.

The third member of the *bel canto* trio, Vincenzo Bellini, was the youngest although he died first, from a sudden attack of dysentery, aged only 33. He lacked the fluency of Rossini and Donizetti, but had the ability to write flowing, graceful melodies much admired by his friend Chopin, whose nocturnes have a Bellini-like melodic flow. Bellini's letters reveal him as a waspish, cantankerous character, always suspicious of his well-wishers, even of Rossini. His 11 operas are mainly tragic, dealing with the ill-starred love of a Druid high priestess in 'Norma', and with the conflict of Cavalier versus Roundhead in 'I Puritani' ('The Puritans'). First performed in 1835, a few weeks before Bellini's death, 'The Puritans' owed its success partly to Rossini, who went through it page by page, making suggestions for improvements to the orchestral accompaniment.

Of the three composers, only Rossini lived to see the new operatic worlds of Verdi and Wagner. Verdi continued the Italian operatic line, and no doubt Rossini approved. But Wagner's long-windedness could never have appealed to Rossini, who once remarked that Wagner had 'good moments, but bad quarters of an hour'.

artolo then summons a wyer. Meanwhile, he rsuades Rosina that lmaviva, whom she ows only as 'Lindoro', a traitor and that he d Figaro plan to kid-p her that night. While rtolo goes to warn the tch, Almaviva and garo climb up on to sina's balcony and

explain 'Lindoro's' true identity to her. When the lawyer arrives, Almaviva and Rosina sign the marriage contract which he has brought (below). Doctor Bartolo (right), realising that he has been outwitted, has to make the best of a bad job. He has won Rosina's dowry, if not her love.

Mighty Wagner

WAGNER
(1813-1883)

OPERAS

'Rienzi'

'The Flying
Dutchman'

'Tannhaüser'

'Lohengrin'

'Tristan and
Isolde'

'The Master-
singers'

'The Ring of
the Nibelungs'
cycle:
'Rhinegold'
'The Valkyrie'
'Siegfried'
'The Twilight
of the Gods'

'Parsifal'

Fᴏʀ ᴏᴠᴇʀ a century musical pilgrims have walked up the hill outside the little Bavarian town of Bayreuth, to soak themselves in the operas of the most dynamic and single-minded of all composers. Wagner's music, Wagner's words and Wagner's opera house still form a unique lure. They are a monument to an extraordinary man, whose colossal willpower dominated his friends and enemies alike. Wagner can still, through the sheer force of his genius, compel an audience to sit for four evenings through the 16 hours of his 'Ring of the Nibelungs' – probably the greatest single-handed creative effort in the history of Western art.

Richard Wagner's life was a long succession of adventures and misadventures. Born in Leipzig in 1813, he grew up at a time when the tide of nationalism was rising over Europe. Apart from a few minor compositions, the whole of his artistic energy went into the creation and establishment of German opera – serious and uplifting in style, as opposed to the frivolities of Italian opera. After a few early works, Wagner wrote the first of his masterpieces, 'The Flying Dutchman', during 1840 and 1841. It tells the story of a sea captain, doomed to sail the world for ever unless he can find a woman to give up her life for him, and it unites two of Wagner's constant themes: the use of an ancient legend, and the idea of salvation reached through self-sacrificing love.

The opera's magnificently descriptive sea music was inspired by a voyage Wagner made in 1839. At the time he was working in Riga, on the Baltic. To escape his creditors, he boarded a ship making for England. It was blown off course and the journey took three weeks instead of the expected eight days. In his autobiography Wagner described the origins of the boisterous sailors' chorus in the 'Dutchman'. The ship took refuge in a Norwegian fjord and, says Wagner, 'a feeling of indescribable content came over me when the enormous granite walls echoed the hail of the crew as they cast anchor and furled the sails. The sharp rhythm of this call clung to me like an omen of good cheer, and shaped itself presently into the theme of the seamen's song.'

This journey was the first of many. Under threat of arrest for his support of the 1848 Revolution, he fled from Dresden to Switzerland.

LUDWIG OF BAVARIA

In April 1864, Wagner wrote to a friend: 'You know that the young King of Bavaria sought me out...He wants me to stay with him always, to work, to rest, to produce.' The King was Ludwig II (above), who succeeded his father at the age of 18. Obsessed with Wagner's early operas, especially 'Lohengrin', he summoned the composer to him and promised him all the money he needed to carry out his projects. This impetuous behaviour was typical of Ludwig who, although not mad at this stage, was certainly unstable. His infatuation with Wagner lasted until the end of 1865 when Wagner, under political pressure and heavily in debt, was forced to leave Bavaria. Ludwig, however, remained passionately devoted to the composer. He put up a large sum of money to help build the opera house at Bayreuth (below), completed in 1876. In August the whole cycle of the 'Ring' was first performed. Less than seven years later, Ludwig heard that Wagner had died in Venice, and insisted that the body be brought to Bayreuth for burial. Ludwig is also remembered for his 'dream palaces', especially the fabulous castle of Neuschwanstein which contains murals of scenes from 'Tannhaüser' and 'Parsifal' – like a stage set for a Wagner opera.

Wagner wrote the most passionate of his operas, 'Tristan and Isolde', in the intervals of producing his gigantic 'Ring' cycle of four operas. The costumes (below) for the first performance in 1865, were designed by Franz Seitz.

Tristan (above) is the nephew of King Mark of Cornwall. Sent to bring Isolde (below), who is to marry King Mark, Tristan falls in love with her. The drawing shows Isolde holding a cup containing a love potion that both she and Tristan drink. The opera tells the story of their tragic passion, which ends when they die together in the *Liebestod* ('Love in Death') scene, a supreme operatic moment.

In Switzerland, he began work in earnest on his 'Ring' cycle of four vast operas. This gigantic undertaking was to last for the best part of 25 years – with a gap between 1857 and 1865, when Wagner abandoned the third of the sequence, 'Siegfried', and turned to the tragic love story of 'Tristan and Isolde' and the earthy good humour of 'The Mastersingers of Nuremberg'.

The 'Ring' is set in the mist-filled past of German mythology – a twilight world of gods and heroes, dwarfs and giants. The gods' downfall stems from a struggle to possess a hoard of gold hidden in the depths of the Rhine. Like the gods and goddesses of the Ancient Greeks, Wagner's characters are both timeless mythical beings and recognisable people, quarrelling, eager for power, falling in love and dying. In the 'Ring' operas Wagner made the fullest use of his musical innovation, the *leitmotiv* or 'leading motive' – a short theme, symbolising a character, an inanimate object or a feeling, from the gold in the Rhine to the spear of the god Wotan. Wagner's use of these motives means, for example, that a character can be singing about one thing while the orchestral accompaniment reveals some contrasting thought or event.

Wagner was able to finish the 'Ring' and to build his own opera house at Bayreuth through the generosity of Ludwig II, the 'Mad King' of Bavaria. But Ludwig was only one of the many friends exploited by Wagner. The conductor and pianist Hans von Bülow, who was married to Cosima, Liszt's daughter, was a champion of Wagner's works, but this did not prevent Wagner from making Cosima his mistress. He finally married her in 1870, and they remained together until his death in 1883.

In his last opera, the massively slow and stately 'Parsifal', Wagner returned to the world of medieval knighthood and Christianity, which had inspired two of his earlier operas, 'Tannhäuser' and 'Lohengrin'. 'Parsifal' deals with the quest for the Holy Grail. It would be hard to imagine a less operatic subject, in the normal sense of the word, and its intense seriousness and solemnity make it a work for convinced Wagnerians only. But it ended Wagner's career on a lofty note, summing up his ideas of a work of art in which words, music, costumes and sets combine in perfect unity.

84

Verdi the patriot

IN MARCH 1842 Giuseppe Verdi suddenly found himself famous. His opera 'Nabucco', first performed that month at the Scala opera house in Milan, was an instant success. 'Nabucco' (Italian for Nebuchadnezzar) tells the story of the Jewish captivity in Babylon; and the Italians, under the domination of Austria, immediately identified themselves with the exiled and persecuted Jewish people. The opera's stirring chorus, *'Va, pensiero, sull' ali dorate'* ('Fly, thought, on golden wings'), became the theme song of Italian patriots longing for independence. From then on Verdi took his place as the musical spokesman of Italy.

Before 'Nabucco', Verdi had written a couple of unsuccessful operas, as Wagner had done before the success of his 'Flying Dutchman' in 1843. The career of the two giants of 19th-century opera show striking similarities and contrasts. Both were born in 1813, both were deeply involved in the political upheavals of their day, and both wrote masterpieces towards the end of their lives (Wagner's 'Parsifal' and Verdi's 'Falstaff'). But whereas Wagner made his own operatic rules, Verdi built on the foundations of the Italian operas of Rossini, Bellini and Donizetti. Wagner, like Weber, approached opera through the orchestra rather than the voice. Verdi, far more instinctive in approach, begins and ends with the voice, using the orchestra in its traditional operatic role as accompaniment and support, rather than as commentator on the story.

Verdi was born in the small town of Roncole, near Parma, the son of an illiterate innkeeper. He might have become just another struggling musician but for the tremendous natural resilience and toughness inherited from his peasant family. The personal tragedies that struck him between 1838 and 1840, when his two children and then his young wife died, seem to have given him inner strength rather than discouragement. He certainly needed all his energy to write the 13 operas that separated 'Nabucco' from his first masterpiece, 'Rigoletto', performed in 1851. Verdi referred to this nine-year period as his 'years of the galley slave'. Most of these operas have a nationalistic theme and, although seldom heard today, they established Verdi's reputation as an Italian patriot.

VERDI AND POLITICS

The 1840s saw the rise in Italy of the movement called the *Risorgimento* ('Resurrection'). Its aim was to unify the separate states of Italy under one ruler. Verdi, who based many operas on patriotic themes, was associated with the movement. After a successful first performance of a Verdi opera, the audience used to shout *'Viva Verdi!'*, partly to show how they honoured him, and also because Verdi's name spelt the initials of the monarch who eventually became ruler of a newly-united Italy, *Vittorio Emanuele, Re d'Italia* ('Victor Emmanuel, King of Italy').

The thinking behind the *Risorgimento* was evolved by the theorist, Giuseppe Mazzini (above). He spent much of his early career in exile, but organised a patriotic movement called 'Young Italy' and master-minded risings in various Italian towns and cities.
The third leader was the statesman, Count Cavour (below), whose diplomatic skills helped bring about Italian unity. In 1861 he set up Italy's first elected government, in which Verdi was a deputy. Although the composer was a patriot, he was not a politician, and hardly ever attended after the first session.

Verdi admired the three very different men who led the *Risorgimento*. The most flamboyant of them was Giuseppe Garibaldi, the activist (above). In 1860 he led one of the most brilliant campaigns in military history. At the head of 1,000 red-shirted volunteers, he defeated vastly superior forces in Sicily, and finally took Naples for the Kingdom of Italy.

Verdi's opera 'Nabucco' (below) included a chorus that became the unofficial 'national anthem' of Italians longing for liberation from the rule of Austria.

Verdi's opera 'Nabucco' (below) included a chorus that became the unofficial 'national anthem' of Italians longing for liberation from the rule of Austria.

Unlike Wagner, who insisted on writing his own librettos, Verdi tended to look round for some existing plot to set to music. There is an amazing variety in the subjects he chose. In 'Rigoletto' the tragic hero of the title is a hunchbacked dwarf. *'La Traviata'* ('The Woman Led Astray'), written two years later, portrays the love story and death of a famous courtesan. 'Don Carlos' is about a Spanish prince who comes into conflict with the authority of the Inquisition. All Verdi's operas are full of vivid human incident, and many of his melodies are so famous that they have passed into the realm of super-classics. Typical of such tunes is the Grand March from 'Aida', played by military and brass bands, and the even more famous *'La donna è mobile'* ('Woman is Fickle') from 'Rigoletto'. Verdi himself finally became so tired of the popularity of this catchy tune that he would actually pay organ grinders not to play it in the streets.

As a great musical dramatist, Verdi worshipped Shakespeare, but apart from his early opera, 'Macbeth' (1847), he kept clear of setting the plays until near the end of his life. About 1880 he met Arrigo Boito, who was himself an opera composer and, more important, a poet who had the same love of Shakespeare. In Boito he found the ideal librettist, and their collaboration perfectly rounded off Verdi's life-work. 'Otello' brilliantly recreates Shakespeare's tragedy of love and jealousy, while in 'Falstaff' Verdi says farewell to the world of opera in a bubbling and joyful comedy about Shakespeare's scheming knight. The opera, which is based on 'The Merry Wives of Windsor', ends with the words: 'All the world's a joke' – the 80-year-old composer's last message to his audience.

Although Verdi was almost entirely an opera composer, he wrote one non-operatic masterpiece, the gigantic 'Requiem', first performed in 1874 in memory of the novelist and poet Alessandro Manzoni, who had died the previous year. Verdi lived on until 1901, as a revered master. He once remarked of himself: 'I am not a learned composer, but I am a very experienced one.' More than 200,000 people lined the Milan streets for his funeral. As the cortège rolled by, the vast crowd softly hummed the chorus from 'Nabucco' that had electrified their grandparents almost 60 years before.

Giuseppe Verdi (left) at the time of writing his patriotic operas. Verdi's spirit was with the revolution but, when he was not writing, he preferred peace on his farm at Sant' Agata to the turmoil of politics.

This cartoon (above) shows Verdi conducting his 'Requiem' in 1874. The death's-head figures are an allusion to the *'Dies Irae'* ('Day of Wrath') movement.

Realism and fantasy

EXOTIC DRAMA

Georges Bizet is the classic example of a composer who is mainly remembered for a single masterpiece, his opera 'Carmen'. His earlier works, like 'The Pearl Fishers' and 'The Fair Maid of Perth', are sometimes heard today, although they have never become popular. But with 'Carmen', Bizet brought something entirely new to opera: a combination of sultry passion and Mediterranean clarity of musical expression. It is the most successful Spanish music by a non-Spaniard. 'Carmen' centres round a Spanish gypsy girl, a corporal in the army, and a successful bullfighter. The rest of the characters include soldiers, smugglers and girls from the cigarette factory. The role of Carmen gives marvellous scope for a singer who combines personality and a superb voice. The corporal, Don José, who gives up his army career to flee with Carmen and finally murders her, provides a brilliant contrast to the bullfighter, Escamillo. The first performance of 'Carmen' was not a success, as the passionate music and story upset the audience. Just three months later, Bizet died, aged only 37. He never saw the triumph of 'Carmen', which soon became the most popular of all operas. The lively 'Toreador's Song', sung by Escamillo, is among the most famous of any opera aria ever written.

TRUTH TO LIFE

It took only eight years for Giacomo Puccini to write three operas that are the mainstays of the world's opera houses: 'La Bohème', 'Tosca' and 'Madam Butterfly'. All the ingredients for success are contained in 'La Bohème'. It mixes the pathos of the lovely Mimi, dying of consumption, and the cheerful high spirits of a 'Bohemian' group of young artists who can laugh at poverty. The setting is Paris in the 1830s, with its garrets and cafés. The music is a constant delight, full of dramatic moments and subtle use of the orchestra. 'Your tiny hand is frozen', sung by the poet Rodolfo to Mimi, is the best known aria from 'La Bohème'.

But there are many other notable highlights, such as the sad farewell the poor young philosopher sings to his overcoat before he sells it to buy food for the dying Mimi. This combination of simple, memorable melody and a strong sense of drama is Puccini's special gift. He was, perhaps, the most naturally operatic composer who ever lived. Puccini once described his life as a perpetual search for 'wildfowl, beautiful women and good libretti'. Certainly he was a good shot, he had plenty of mistresses, and his librettists never let him down. The settings of Puccini's other operas range from the Wild West to Japan and legendary China.

AFTER THE larger-than-life heroic worlds of Wagner and Verdi, it was natural for composers to react against grand gestures and look for themes closer to reality. This motive lay behind the operatic movement called *verismo* or 'truth to life' – a movement already begun by novelists like Dickens and artists like Millet. Bizet's 'Carmen', composed in 1875, is close to pure realism, but *verismo* as a definite style began in Italy about 15 years later, when two young composers each wrote a short opera marked by an unromantic approach to human drama: Pietro Mascagni's *'Cavalleria Rusticana'* ('Rustic Chivalry') and Ruggiero Leoncavallo's *'I Pagliacci'* ('The Strolling Players'), both of which have jealousy and murder as their themes.

LOVE IDEALISED

Richard Strauss, the greatest German opera composer after Wagner, won his first successes in the operatic world with two savage dramas: 'Salome', based on the Biblical story of Salome's passion for St John the Baptist, and 'Elektra', an Ancient Greek tragedy of murder and revenge. In these two operas Strauss unleashed the violent side of his nature. Yet his next opera was quite different: the sensuous and lyrical opera '*Der Rosenkavalier*' looks back beyond Wagner to the world of Mozart's light-hearted masterpieces.

First produced in 1911, '*Der Rosenkavalier*' is both a frothy Viennese fantasy and a tender love story. The part of the young lover, Octavian (above) is written for a soprano, in the tradition of operatic roles like that of Cherubino in Mozart's 'Marriage of Figaro', and also in the tradition of pantomime, where the 'principal boy' is, in fact, always a girl. The main emotional seriousness of the opera is given to the Marschallin, a princess no longer in her youth, who knows that sooner or later she will lose Octavian's love to a younger woman. The conceited Baron Ochs (above) is a magnificent comic creation, while the fourth main character, Sophie, is the innocent young girl for whom everything comes right in the end. The opera is permeated by the rhythm and lilt of the Viennese waltz, and breathes a spirit that goes right back to Schubert, and to the Strauss waltz kings.

FANTASY WORLD

The Czech composer, Leos Janáček, based his highly original music on the folksong of his homeland. His short, repetitious, rhythmic tunes are nearer to Bartók's than to those of his contemporaries. Allied to this melodic gift is a superb orchestral sense and dramatic flair that made Janáček very much at home in the opera house. His two most frequently heard operas, 'Jenufa' and 'Katya Kabanova', are powerful tragedies, but he was equally capable of light-hearted fantasy. 'The Cunning Little Vixen', first performed in 1924, is a fairy-tale opera in which humans and animals meet each other on equal terms. It must be the only opera based on a strip cartoon – a series of animal drawings, like comic versions of Beatrix Potter, which Janáček saw in a Czech daily paper. In the opera the human characters, like the Parson (right), drink, smoke and play cards, while the animals get on with their lives in the sun-dappled glades of the forest. Although Sharpears, the Vixen of the title, is shot by a poacher, this is not the end of the story. In the final scene a new vixen-cub, the very image of Sharpears, gives promise of nature's rebirth.

These two operas are nearly always played as a double bill, known familiarly as 'Cav and Pag'.

In operas such as '*La Bohème*' and 'Madam Butterfly', Puccini mixed *verismo* and romanticism into an operatic brew very much his own. But it was not long before 'truth to life' was reacted against in its turn. Opera can never be true to life except in a very general sense – after all, nobody in real life bursts into song at the moment of death – and the element of fantasy and playfulness has always been one of opera's strongest appeals. In his old age, after the sombre tragedies of his earlier operas, Janáček turned to pure fantasy in 'The Cunning Little Vixen'. Strauss showed a similar progression away from the fierce passions of his first operas to the light-hearted, lyrical '*Der Rosenkavalier*' ('The Knight of the Rose'), set in the idealised 18th-century Vienna of his imagination.

Debussy's solitary operatic masterpiece, '*Pelléas et Mélisande*', abandons realism of any sort for a shimmering dream-like world, where nothing is ever explained, and where the characters live, love and die like ghosts moving under water. Utterly different again is the colourful nationalism of Russian composers like Borodin and Mussorgsky, who continued the old tradition. Mussorgsky's vast historical panorama, 'Boris Godunov', is a highly-charged tragedy full of pageantry and drama – the musical equivalent of sprawling Russian novels such as Tolstoy's 'War and Peace'.

Puccini's 'Madam Butterfly' tells the tragic love story of Cho-Cho-San ('Butterfly') and an American naval officer.

The twentieth century

Peter Pears in the title role of Britten's opera 'Peter Grimes', in the BBC television production. Grimes is a fisherman whose apprentice dies mysteriously and who is himself hounded to his death by the local inhabitants. 'Peter Grimes' (1945) was Britten's first success.

Hans Werner Henze
(below) has written many
highly original operas;
among them are 'Elegy
for Young Lovers' and
'The Bassarids'. He has
also written for radio.

The operas of Gian-Carlo
Menotti (left) range from
the political drama of
'The Consul' to the gentle
fantasy of 'Amahl and
the Night Visitors'.

O PERA TODAY is what it has always been – a
combination of art, stagecraft and big business. Opera houses are dominated by financial
problems, ranging from the size of the government subsidy to demands by unions for higher
wages. This means that their musical directors
are unwilling to venture on new works that may
leave half the seats empty. In addition, opera-
goers are the most traditional of music lovers,
and will always prefer an old and well-tried
favourite to something new and disturbing.

However, a few modern operas are now in the
world's repertory, notably several by Britten,
and in particular 'Wozzeck', by Alban Berg. This
opera is far more revolutionary in its musical
idiom than any work of Britten's, even though
the first performance was given as long ago as
1925. It is written in an atonal technique, combined with traditional musical forms. Based on
a play by Georg Büchner, 'Wozzeck' tells of the
misfortunes of a down-trodden soldier who is
finally driven to murder his wife. The orchestral
sounds range from shattering discords to a gentle
lullaby accompaniment, and the voices similarly
have to cope with shouts, straightforward singing, and 'speech-song'. Although at first it met
with hostility, 'Wozzeck' is now almost an
operatic favourite, and never fails to grip the
audience, who come to share Berg's compassion
for his unhappy hero.

'Wozzeck' is a melodrama, and modern
musical techniques are ideally suited to lurid
tales of horror. Recent operas with highly
melodramatic subjects include Penderecki's 'The
Devils', a story of demonic possession and
torture, and Ginastera's 'Bomarzo', whose anti-
hero is a deformed and sadistic Renaissance

Prince. Penderecki is a Pole and Ginastera an
Argentinian, and they typify the way in which
most opera composers no longer come from
traditionally operatic countries. Apart from
Gian-Carlo Menotti, who has spent all his
working life in America, few Italian composers of
recent years have written operas. Among German
composers, Hans Werner Henze is the most
successful writer of operas. 'The Bassarids' retells
the Greek legend of Pentheus, the repressed
puritan who tries in vain to fight the god
Dionysus, while 'We Come to the River' is a
political satire in which many musical styles are
cleverly interwoven.

Of all the 20th-century opera composers, the
most prolific and naturally gifted was an
Englishman, Benjamin Britten. Born in 1913, he
did not attempt to write an opera until he was
in his 30s. Then in 1945 he burst on the operatic
scene with the magnificent 'Peter Grimes', the
tragic story of a fierce and solitary fisherman on
the Suffolk coast. Britten's later operas were all
highly original. 'Billy Budd', a stormy tragedy
set in the Navy of Nelson's day, is remarkable
for having an all-male cast, while 'Owen
Wingrave', first performed in 1971, made
operatic history by being shown first on television before moving to the opera house.

The capacity of even the largest opera house
is insignificant compared with the millions who
now watch opera on television. Modern technology is used in the opera house itself, both in the
form of back-projection and other scenic effects,
and in the means of sound production. Tippett's
'The Ice Break', for example, is set in an airport
lounge, with broadcast announcements and jet
aircraft screams added to the musical score.

The rich musical imagin-
ation of Michael Tippett
(right) is evident in 'The
Midsummer Marriage'
and 'The Ice Break'.

Benjamin Britten
(above) wrote several
'chamber operas'. Among
them, 'The Turn of the
Screw' is as compelling
as any grand opera.

Stravinsky, lord of the dance

**STRAVINSKY
1882-1971**

MAIN WORKS

BALLETS

'The Firebird'
'Petrushka'
'The Rite of
Spring'
'Pulcinella'
'The Wedding'
'Apollo Leader
of the Muses'
'The Fairy's
Kiss'
'Card Game'
'Orpheus'
'*Agon*'

OPERAS

'The
Nightingale'
'The Rake's
Progress'

FOR VOICE

'The Soldier's
Tale'
'*Renard*'
'*Oedipus Rex*'
'Symphony of
Psalms'
'*Canticum
Sacrum*'
Mass

INSTRUMENTAL

'Ragtime'
'Symphonies of
Wind
Instruments'
Octet
Symphony in C
'Symphony in
Three
Movements'
Concerto for
piano and wind
Violin Concerto

I N THE early 1900s the Russian Ballet blew like a gale of fresh air into the stuffy theatres of western Europe. Led by the wealthy impresario, Serge Diaghilev, with brilliant dancers such as Karsavina, Fokine and Nijinsky, the Russians dazzled audiences with the novelty of their dance techniques and the splendour of their stage sets. For their second Paris season, in 1910, they included a new score by an unknown composer, Igor Stravinsky. Called 'The Firebird', its combination of Oriental glitter and sensuous orchestration enchanted the Paris audiences and catapulted Stravinsky to instant fame. Ever since, the special magic of 'The Firebird' has never failed to excite the imagination, whether in the theatre or as an orchestral piece in the concert hall.

Stravinsky was the son of a leading bass singer of the Imperial Opera Company at St Petersburg, and had studied law before devoting himself full-time to music. He was a pupil of Rimsky-Korsakov, and learnt much of his brilliant orchestral writing from his teacher, who is best known for his symphonic suite, 'Scheherezade'. When Diaghilev commissioned 'The Firebird' he had heard only one or two of Stravinsky's orchestral works. But he was a great gambler, and in backing Stravinsky he had instinctively chosen a winner.

'The Firebird' was followed by two more ballet classics. In 1911 Stravinsky turned from Oriental fantasy to Russian everyday life in 'Petrushka', full of fairground bustle and folk

The sheer energy which Stravinsky put into his work is captured by Jean Cocteau in this drawing of a rehearsal for 'The Rite of Spring'.

melody. Then in 1913 came the most revolutionary of all his ballet scores, 'The Rite of Spring', subtitled 'Scenes of Pagan Russia'. With its powerful, dissonant harmony and dislocated rhythms, it upset the Paris audience who expected another 'Firebird'. On the first night the violence of the music spread to the audience, who came to blows and made so much noise that at times the orchestra could not be heard at all.

The 'Rite' still makes an overwhelming impact in the concert hall, and it marked a turning-point in Stravinsky's career. During the First World War, which he spent in Switzerland, he turned away from the massive orchestra of the 'Rite'. The most typical work from these years is 'The Soldier's Tale'. Written for a unique combination of narrator, a small group of players and a couple of dancers, it tells the age-old story of a soldier who bargains with the Devil for his soul, and loses it.

After the war Stravinsky returned to writing full-scale ballets, often in the form of parodies or re-workings of other composers' music. In 'Pulcinella' he turned to the early 18th century and the music of Pergolesi, and in 'The Fairy's Kiss', to Tchaikovsky, whose music he greatly admired. In such works, usually described as 'neo-classical', Stravinsky deliberately turned his back on the innovations of his contemporaries, Schoenberg and Bartók. Instead, he took refuge in an imaginary world of clarity and grace, summed up by the ballet 'Apollo Leader of the Muses', performed in 1928.

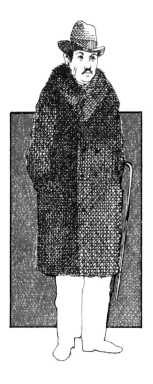

THE 'BALLETS RUSSES'

Serge Diaghilev took over Russian ballet at the beginning of the 20th century and injected into it a new vitality. He selected a group of dancers, choreographers and designers who learnt to combine the style of classical ballet with Isadora Duncan's new ideas of free expression. Perhaps the greatest among Diaghilev's dancers was Nijinsky, the first Petrushka (left). His most famous role was the Faun in Debussy's sensuous 'L'Après-midi d'un Faune'.
Diaghilev first brought his *Ballets Russes* to Paris in 1909 and, until his death in 1929, he dominated international ballet. Stravinsky was only one of the composers whom Diaghilev encouraged. He also commissioned ballets from Poulenc, Ravel, Satie and Falla. Picasso and Matisse were among the artists who designed his sets. His most famous costume designer was Léon Bakst.

Serge Diaghilev (left) was a key figure in the development, not only of ballet, but of the visual arts in general. He was born in 1872, and used his wealth and position to make St Petersburg a leading centre of the arts. Diaghilev was most interested in painting and the theatre, and he edited a magazine called 'The World of Art'. In ballet, he saw the chance to fuse the skill of his dancers with the talents of composers and artists into an art form that could rival opera in its own right.

'The Rake's Progress' (above) was Stravinsky's only full-scale opera. It is based on a series of drawings of the same name by William Hogarth.

Picasso sketched this portrait of Stravinsky (left) in 1920.

Stravinsky had always been attracted to America and to jazz (as early as 1919 he had written his 'Ragtime' for 11 instruments), and in 1939 he settled in Hollywood. When he took American citizenship in 1945, he broke finally with his Russian past, only making a visit to his native country to mark his 80th birthday, in 1962. By coincidence, Schoenberg, another exile from Europe, lived only a few miles from Stravinsky in California. In his earlier years Stravinsky had no sympathy with Schoenberg's 12-tone system of composition, which gives equal status to all 12 notes of the chromatic scale and rigidly controls them. But when he was in his 70s Stravinsky made a profound study of it. His last works, such as the ballet *'Agon'*, were nearly all written in the new technique. Yet even through this transformation the authentic voice of Stravinsky is clearly heard, pungent and terse, with the same disjointed rhythms and unerring instrumental writing that distinguished his early ballet scores.

Stravinsky's restless intellect was always looking for something original to say and nearly always succeeded in finding it. Born 35 years before the Russian Revolution, he lived long enough to write an elegy on the death of President Kennedy. He wrote a concerto for the jazz clarinettist Woody Herman and a 'Circus Polka' for the dancing elephants of the Barnum and Bailey circus. His philosophy was that of the craftsman. 'I compose,' he said, 'because I am made for that and cannot do otherwise.'

Ballet: classical to modern

FAMOUS BALLET COMPOSERS

1650-1750

LULLY
'Le Triomphe de l'Amour'

RAMEAU
'Les Indes Galantes'

1750-1850

HÉROLD
'La Fille Mal Gardée'

BEETHOVEN
'The Creatures of Prometheus'

ADAM
'Giselle'

1850-1900

TCHAIKOVSKY
'Swan Lake'
'Sleeping Beauty'
'Nutcracker'

DELIBES
'Coppélia'

SINCE 1900

DEBUSSY
'L'Après-midi d'un Faune'

STRAVINSKY
'The Firebird'
'Agon'

FALLA
'The Three-Cornered Hat'

BARTÓK
'The Miraculous Mandarin'

PROKOFIEV
'Romeo and Juliet'

SATIE
'Parade'

POULENC
'Les Biches'

COPLAND
'Billy the Kid'

KHACHATURIAN
'Spartacus'

The modern art of ballet grew out of dances such as the galliard, popular in England during the 16th century. William Byrd and other English composers wrote a great many galliards for the keyboard. The earliest ballets as we know them today were performed in France a hundred years later. At that time, when only men danced, Louis XIV was acknowledged to be the best dancer at the French court. He took his nickname of *Le Roi Soleil* (the 'Sun King') from a ballet in which he danced the leading part of the Sun. In 1661 he founded a Royal Academy of Dancing, and for the rest of his long reign, until his death in 1715, he actively encouraged the ballet. The King's favourite composer, Jean-Baptiste Lully, was also a keen dancer and evolved a type of entertainment called 'opera-ballet'. By the end of Louis XIV's reign ballet had become a profession, and women began to dance on the stage. Famous dancers such as Marie Camargo shortened their skirts above the ankle, which enabled them to perform country dances like the *Rigaudon*, and artistic ballets such as 'The Return of Spring-time'. In the mid-18th century the dancer Jean-Georges Noverre codified the theory and practice of ballet. 'Dancers,' he wrote, 'must speak and express their thoughts through the medium of gestures and facial expression.' In the 19th century his teachings were generally adopted. Ballerinas wore shorter dresses and danced on the points of their toes. Ballets like 'Coppélia' brought realism into the form, and set the stage for modern ballet.

GALLIARD DANCERS

THE 'SUN KING'

THE 'RIGAUDON'

'RETURN OF SPRINGTIME'

'COPPÉLI

BALLERINA, 1900

Ɪɴ PRIMITIVE times, when the whole community took part in religious or ceremonial dances, some people must have danced better than others and been considered worth watching. That is, presumably, the remote origin of ballet. In its modern form – that of a dance spectacular with music, costume and stage décor – it comes, like opera, from Renaissance Italy. The fashion for court ballets spread to France in the 16th century. Indeed, ballet is basically a French art, as composed music is an Italian art. While the vocabulary of music is in Italian, that of the ballet (including the word itself) is in French. Ballet as we know it today was largely created at the court of Louis XIV in the 17th century. By the end of his reign professional dancers had taken over from aristocratic amateurs, and the 18th century saw a tremendous expansion of dancing technique.

Yet in spite of such advances, the classical composers such as Haydn and Mozart seem to have taken little interest in it – at least, they wrote no major ballet scores. An exception was Beethoven, who in 1800 was commissioned by the choreographer Salvatore Vigano to provide the music for a ballet. This was a large two-act work; the subject was the story of Prometheus who risked the anger of the gods to bring civilisation and knowledge to mankind.

Early in the 19th century ballet, like music, took on the shades of the Romantic movement, with mystery rather than classical clarity as the goal. The first genuinely romantic ballet was 'La Sylphide', dating from 1832 (not to be confused with 'Les Sylphides', a Diaghilev ballet to music by Chopin). The part of the Sylphide – a supernatural elf-like being – was danced by Marie Taglioni, the queen of 19th-century ballerinas. After an early training of unheard-of discipline and practice, she took Europe by storm. She was Queen Victoria's favourite dancer, and was so adored in Russia that when she toured there a group of ballet fanatics cooked and ate one of her dancing shoes. Taglioni had her rivals, such as Carlotta Grisi who danced Giselle when the ballet of that name with music by Adolphe Adam, was performed for the first time at the Paris Opera in 1841. 'Giselle' begins the list of large-scale 19th-century ballets (see overleaf) still danced today.

The classical ballets of the 19th century culminated in Tchaikovsky's great threesome, 'Swan Lake' (1876), 'Sleeping Beauty' (1889) and 'Nutcracker' (1892). These works are free from any connection with opera. But for much of the 19th century there was a constant tug-of-war between opera and ballet. This conflict was strongest in Paris, where every opera was obliged to include a ballet, preferably in the second act. This gave the gilded youth of Paris the chance to admire the girls of the *corps de ballet,* and it also meant that they did not need to turn up until the second act. Wagner clashed head-on with this antiquated tradition when he staged 'Tannhaüser' in Paris in 1861. In this opera the ballet occurs in Act I, and Wagner refused to move it. The outcome was a disaster. On the opening night the music was drowned by whistling and hooting, and the opera was withdrawn after only three performances.

In Russia, the Imperial Ballet had been set up in St Petersburg (Leningrad) in the 18th century. Visits of dancers like Taglioni showed the Russians what the West had achieved; but the greatest influence was that of Marius Petipa, a Frenchman. Born in 1818, he went to Russia in 1847, became ballet master at the Imperial Ballet, and lived on until 1910. He was followed by Diaghilev's choreographers Fokine, Massine and Balanchine. Like so many emigrés after the Russian Revolution, Balanchine ended up in America, where he transplanted the great Russian traditions to the New World. The Russian political background still has an incalculable effect on ballet outside Russia. Since the flight of Rudolf Nureyev to the West in 1961, followed by Mikhail Barishnikov in 1974, western dancing has had an infusion of the classical Russian tradition, symbolised by the partnership of Nureyev and Margot Fonteyn.

Fonteyn and Nureyev represent the classical side of modern dancing. But there is another side, the contemporary dance, stemming largely from America. Beginning with the free-expression dancing of Loie Fuller and Isadora Duncan at the turn of the century, these new ideas now form an alternative to the pure classical technique. Martha Graham, also American, took the lead in this style of dancing from the 1940s on. She has been followed by dancer-choreographers such as Merce Cunningham, who dances to music by John Cage and other contemporary composers.

When choosing music for their ballets, recent choreographers such as Frederick Ashton have tended to rely on the music of the past, rather than commission fresh scores. Ballets have been danced to Elgar's 'Enigma Variations' and Czerny's piano studies. Such new music as is composed for today's ballets is mainly electronic, to accompany dances by groups such as the Netherlands Dance Theatre. Sooner or later, no doubt, some inspired composer will produce an electronic 'Swan Lake' or 'Rite of Spring' to open a new age in the evolution of ballet.

'MONOTONES NO. 2': MUSIC BY SATIE

VII

The open air

EXCEPT FOR carol singers who appear on every street corner at Christmas, and military bands which perform in city parks or on parade, the open spaces of our towns and cities are virtually without live music. Yet until the early years of this century there was always some music to be heard, although it was not always of professional quality. Organ grinders turned the handles of their mechanical pianos and clattered out the Grand March from 'Aida', knife-grinders and muffin sellers advertised themselves with different musical cries, and on the street corner the thudding bass drum and plaintive cornets of the Salvation Army band drowned the rattle of carriage wheels.

In earlier days still, when most work was physical rather than mechanical, there were work songs to go with the endlessly repetitious tasks of agriculture and hand crafts. Different kinds of song developed for different kinds of toil: in the cotton fields of the southern United States the Negro slaves sang their spirituals, while on ships all over the world sailors tramping round and round the capstan gained fresh energy from their shanty songs. On a more sophisticated level, many towns had their bands of musicians who played at public functions and often doubled as church musicians.

Composers were surrounded from childhood by such music, and brought it into their compositions. As early as the 16th century the French composer Jannequin was fascinated by the street cries of the capital and set them one against the other in his choral piece 'Les Cris de Paris'. In much the same way Charles Ives, at the end of the 19th century, listened to the military bands in his New England home town and reproduced them in his orchestral work 'The Fourth of July', in which several bands approach, get their tunes muddled up, and then go their separate ways again.

Pieces like this bring outdoor music into the concert hall. But far more music has been composed for outdoor use. Most famous of all such works are Handel's spectacular orchestral suites, the 'Water Music' and the 'Royal Fireworks Music', one written for George I to listen to on the River Thames, the other celebrating a peace treaty and written to accompany the fireworks in London's Green Park.

Aristocrats of the 18th and 19th centuries were enthusiastic about listening to music as they strolled in the open air. The Vauxhall Gardens (right) in London, were famous for outdoor music and dancing.

Braving chilly winds, a consort of double bass-players (below) drive their music out over the hills and valleys of Snowdonia in Wales. Like them, an increasing number of amateurs who enrol in summer schools take part in such open-air performances.

The martial skirling of bagpipes is heard at events such as the Royal Highland Gathering at Braemar in Scotland.

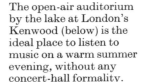

The open-air auditorium by the lake at London's Kenwood (below) is the ideal place to listen to music on a warm summer evening, without any concert-hall formality.

A military band (above) falls half-way between a brass band and an orchestra, as in addition to the brass instruments and drums, it has all the orchestral woodwind instruments as well as saxophones. A standard band has about 30 players, including nine clarinets, four cornets and three trombones. Although mainstream composers such as Berlioz and Walton wrote successful marches, the king of the march was John Philip Sousa (right).

The son of a Spanish trombone-player, Sousa was born in America in 1854. In 1892 he founded 'Sousa's Concert Band', introducing the sousaphone seven years later, to give more power to the brass. Sousa, who once said that a march 'should make a man with a wooden leg step out', began writing his loud, optimistic marches in the 1870s. By the time he died in 1932, he had written over 100, including 'The Stars and Stripes Forever'.

The grandest of all open-air music was composed by Berlioz, although he once remarked that 'music is not made for the street'. This is his *'Symphonie Funèbre et Triomphale'* ('Funeral and Triumphal' Symphony), written for a ceremony in the Place de la Bastille in 1840. With a gigantic wind band of over 200 players, plus percussion, it is one of his most impressive works. Filling huge open spaces with sound has appealed to other composers as well. Messiaen has described his *'Et Exspecto Resurrectionem Mortuorum'* as 'intended for vast spaces: churches, cathedrals and even performances in the open air and on mountain heights.'

Most open-air music is of a much simpler variety – band music for marching to, or for holiday-makers in deck chairs to enjoy as it booms out from a seaside bandstand. Then there is the carnival sound of the West Indian steel band, which began life out of doors and is only at home in the open, where it can transport a grey foreign city to the sun of Trinidad. In the same way the bagpipes only sound right in the open air, ideally on a cold and misty morning. The ultimate in open-air music has only become possible with the technology of the last few years: with a vast battery of loudspeakers, pop musicians can hurl their sound across the landscape to hundreds of thousands of listeners – surely the biggest live audiences that the world has ever seen.

Popular dance

UNTIL QUITE recent times music for dancing and music composed for more serious occasions constantly affected and enriched each other. Medieval carols, which were not only sung and played but also danced, found their way into Masses and motets written for church services. The vast number of instrumental suites written by composers from the Renaissance onwards were little more than strings of dances, with names that often indicated their country of origin, like the *allemande* from Germany, the *écossaise* from Scotland, and the polonaise from Poland. The most familiar example of the dance in classical music is the minuet, which forms the third movement in many symphonies by Haydn and Mozart. The name derives from the French *pas menus*, meaning 'little steps'.

Popular dancing has always been of two different kinds – chain or round dances, in which as many people as possible take part, and dances in which those taking part separate into couples.

One thing links dances of every age: new dances have always been attacked for their supposed immorality. The 'whirling dance' that preceded the waltz was not only said to be 'full of scandalous beastly gestures and immodest movements', but was also held responsible for murders and miscarriages. As for the waltz itself, no words were bad enough to describe it, and only 'women with iron characters' were thought to be immune from its harmful influence.

Apart from the difference between single-partner and community dances, early dances were either of walking or leaping type. None of these dances was particularly fast, as no one can dance fast in nailed boots on a barn floor. Even the upper-class dancers of the 17th and 18th centuries could only have moved at a moderate speed in their heavy clothes and powdered wigs. Speed came to the dance floor with the lighter clothes, greater informality and specially-built dance halls of the early 19th century.

The 16th-century pavan, a slow, majestic dance, was of Italian origin. On solemn occasions the pavan was often played by wind instruments.

Taking over from the minuet about 1800, the waltz was a combination of an ancient whirling dance and the *ländler*, a German peasant dance.

As the waltz had taken over from the minuet about 1800, so the polka and galop overshadowed the waltz in the 1840s and '50s. Finally all European dances were made to seem old-fashioned by the jazz rhythms from America, followed by the foxtrot, black bottom, Charleston and other dances of the 1920s. Composers such as Stravinsky, Milhaud and Constant Lambert seized on the rhythmic and instrumental possibilities of the new dance forms, bringing them into their music as Bach and Handel had done with the dances of their day.

Now all these dances have been retired, along with the minuet and the polka, and their place has been taken by the postwar succession of jitterbug, twist and other gyrations, down to the short-lived teenage dances of today. But old dances never really die: among today's composers, Peter Maxwell Davies has shown that the foxtrot is not yet dead, by his use of a 1920s tune in his 'L'Homme Armé' Mass.

As the most successful dance of all time, the waltz is linked for ever with the two Johann Strausses, father and son. The elder Strauss (above), who was born in 1804, while still in his teens joined the leading waltz band of Vienna, led by Joseph Lanner. In 1825 he set up his own dance band as a rival to Lanner and toured Europe with it.

When he died in 1849, a journalist described him as 'god of melody, hero of the waltz'. His son, Johann II (above), was even more successful. Born in 1825, he formed his own orchestra and made his public début in 1844. During his long career (he died in 1899) he produced over 500 works, including 'The Blue Danube' and 'Tales from the Vienna Woods'.

The lively and energetic polka took Europe by storm in the 19th century. It has two beats to the bar, as opposed to the three of a waltz.

Yet another dance mania erupted in the 1920s. As the craze for jazz swept across America, its rhythms were incorporated in dance music.

Operetta and musical

S IDE BY side with serious operas there have always been shows that treated life and love in a light-hearted and humorous way. Composers like Pergolesi had written comic operas as early as the beginning of the 18th century. But it was not until the mid-19th century that the form of comic opera called 'operetta' emerged, followed in the 20th century by the musical and its offshoot, rock opera.

During the 1850s and '60s Paris was the glittering centre of the entertainment world, and Jacques Offenbach touched the exact nerve that suited the frivolous and pleasure-loving French audiences. At the time he was running his own theatre, *Les Bouffes Parisiennes*, without much success. But in March 1858 he staged his own 'Orpheus in the Underworld' which was an instant triumph. 'Orpheus' went all over Europe, establishing a musical style that continued well into the 20th century.

In 'Orpheus' the main dance was the famous cancan. With its bevy of high-kicking girls in frilly underclothes it summed up French *joie de vivre*, and remained the typical French dance routine right into the 'Naughty Nineties' and beyond. The plot of this operetta was typical of Offenbach's lack of reverence for tradition. In their operas Monteverdi and Gluck had treated the myth of Orpheus and Eurydice, a loving husband and wife, with great seriousness. But in 'Orpheus in the Underworld' the couple dislike each other. Eurydice goes happily down to Hades with Pluto, and Orpheus only follows to fetch her back because he is dragged there by an elderly, disapproving aunt called Public Opinion.

Offenbach (left) won instant popularity with 'Orpheus in the Underworld' (below). He made Eurydice into a party-loving inhabitant of Hades, and Orpheus into a husband only too willing to get rid of her.

PLAYING THE HALLS

People have always loved to meet at free-and-easy kinds of entertainment. In France and Germany at the end of the 19th century artists, musicians and entertainers such as cabaret dancers (left) began to meet in bars and cafés. Performances by café artistes (right) were often savage and witty, with singers like Yvette Guilbert in the Paris of the 1890s and Lotte Lenya in Berlin in the early 1930s. English entertainment, less political and less subtle, appealed to a much wider audience, mainly working class.

The collaboration of W. S. Gilbert (left) and Arthur S. Sullivan (right) lasted from 1875 to 1896. During that time they made a unique contribution to the English musical stage with their light-hearted and tuneful operettas. Their quarrel and estrangement between 1890 and 1893 (allegedly over a carpet in their theatre) was regarded by audiences as a tragedy.

'Orpheus' is the best known of the 100-odd operettas Offenbach wrote, although '*La Belle Hélène*' ('The Beautiful Helen'), a skit on the Trojan War, was almost equally successful, and both are regularly revived today.

'Orpheus in the Underworld' was a triumph throughout Europe. In England it inspired the series of operettas by the comic verse-writer W. S. Gilbert and the composer Arthur Sullivan, beginning with 'Trial by Jury' in 1875. Although Sullivan thought of himself as a composer of serious operas, he is only remembered today for these 'Savoy Operas', named after the Savoy Theatre in London, which was specially built to stage them.

In London, the 'G and S' operettas had few distinguished successors, but in Vienna operetta took firm root. 'Orpheus' was first performed there in 1860, and soon had plenty of imitators. Although the Viennese were in many ways very similar to the Parisians in their easy-going attitude to life, Viennese operetta soon established a style of its own, quite distinct from the French variety. Where the French had sharp social satire, the Viennese preferred a tender fantasy world, and where the French had the vigorous two-in-a-bar cancan, the Viennese had the lyrical three-in-a-bar waltz. Johann Strauss's '*Die Fledermaus*' ('The Bat') was first performed in 1874. With its plot concerning mistaken identities, its highlight of a brilliant masked ball, its settings ranging from prison to ballroom, and above all its infectious music, it became the model for all later operettas, and the musicals and rock operas that succeeded them (see overleaf).

They were catered for in music halls (right), which had a heyday of a little over half a century, from the opening of the Surrey Music Hall in 1848. After the First World War they began to fade away in the face of competition from the gramophone, the cinema, and finally the radio. Star music hall singers had their own favourite songs, with choruses in which the audience loved to take part. They covered topical subjects, from the joys of drinking champagne (George Leybourne in 'Champagne Charlie') to riding one of the new 'sociable bicycles' (Katie Lawrence in 'Daisy Bell').

Some of the greatest and best known entertainers of recent times started 'on the halls'. Probably the most famous of all was Charlie Chaplin. His early silent films, and those of other popular actors like Buster Keaton (above), packed the cinemas in the early 1920s, and thus helped to kill off the tradition of the music halls.

Like Offenbach with his 'Orpheus', Strauss is mainly remembered for his single masterpiece, *'Die Fledermaus'*, although he had many other successes, notably 'The Gypsy Baron'. His most successful contemporary was Franz von Suppé, who is little played nowadays except for overtures like his 'Poet and Peasant'. The last major landmark in the history of the operetta was Franz Lehár's 'The Merry Widow', first performed in 1905. It has the best of both operetta worlds, as it is set in Paris and is based on the waltz.

Although the great days of operetta were over by the First World War, Lehár went on composing into the 1930s, with a whole series of operettas which provided star roles for the tenor, Richard Tauber. Lehár's long life spanned both the Viennese operetta and the American musical, as he was born in 1870 in the decade of *'Die Federmaus'*, and died in 1948 in the decade of 'Oklahoma!' and 'Guys and Dolls'. The musical is really the operetta transplanted from Europe to an American setting. Beginning with 'Show Boat', which dates from 1927 and is still remembered for the song 'Ol' Man River', the musical has turned increasingly to real life.

'Oklahoma!' opened in March 1943, at the height of the Second World War, and was an immense success, running for over 2000 nights on Broadway. It was a triple triumph, in which Oscar Hammerstein's lyrics, the music of Richard Rogers and Agnes de Mille's dance sequences were equally important. 'Oklahoma!' takes place among the pioneer farmers and cowboys of a mid-western state, and is an escapist story in the old operetta tradition. But one of the most memorable of all musicals, 'West Side Story', has as its background the gang warfare of the New York slums, which made a far greater impact on the audiences who first saw it in 1957. The dances, by the choreographer Jerome Robbins, were more closely integrated into the drama than they had been in earlier musicals, while the composer, Leonard Bernstein, and the Lyricist, Stephen Sondheim, both wrote in a much harsher way than had been heard before in musicals.

Later musicals, such as 'Hair' of 1967 and 'A Chorus Line' of 1975, did not make nearly as great a stir as 'West Side Story'. That was left to rock operas like 'Jesus Christ Superstar' (1972) and 'Evita' (1978). But operetta, musical and rock opera are all part of the same tradition of alternatives to grand opera, whether they are dealing frivolously with Helen of Troy in the 1860s, or in a more serious vein with Eva Perón a century later.

BERNSTEIN'S 'WEST SIDE STORY'

VIII

NATIONAL MUSIC

Music of the nations

THE LAST century was not only the age of railways, cast iron and the electric telegraph. It was an age when the powerful countries of Europe carved out empires for themselves in Africa and the East, while the smaller countries fought for their own separate identities, either physically by uprisings and rebellions, or more peacefully, by creating works of art with strong national characteristics. This was especially true of countries under foreign domination, such as Italy and Czechoslovakia, both ruled by Austria. But the general mood of self-assertion was shared by the Scandinavian countries and by Spain, where composers set out to create music that could give a feeling of national permanence in a changing world.

This normally took the form of going back to the folk songs and popular music of the country. In central Europe the lead was taken by the Czechs, who had three outstanding composers to give them a voice. The founder of their national music was Bedřich Smetana, born in Bohemia in 1824. Early in his career he took up the cause of nationalism in music. In 1848 he founded a music school in Prague, and in 1866 became principal conductor for Prague's new National Theatre, where his most famous opera, 'The Bartered Bride', was produced in the same year. With its cheerful music based on folksong and its down-to-earth rustic theme, it made Smetana's name. Just as successful was his portrait of his beloved country, painted in 'Má Vlast', a cycle of six symphonic poems.

The second father-figure of Czech music was Antonin Dvořák. Born in 1841, as a young man he played the viola under Smetana in Prague. Although towards the end of his life he became an international figure throughout Europe and America, in his symphonies and other works Dvořák never lost sight of his Czech background.

During his highly successful career, Dvořák (right) travelled far from Czechoslovakia. He spent three years in America, from 1892-95, as head of the National Conservatory of Music in New York. In his most famous work, the 'New World' Symphony, he combines his own Czech musical style with themes strongly influenced by the Negro spirituals he loved. Thus the flute theme in the first movement almost echoes the tune 'Swing Low, Sweet Chariot', and the beautiful cor anglais melody in the slow movement is a spiritual written by the composer himself. Finland's national composer, Jean Sibelius (right), unlike Dvořák, never ventured far from his native land of pine forests and lakes. Much of the brooding power of his music is drawn from the ancient Finnish legends of the 'Kalevala'. These formed the basis for works such as 'En Saga' and 'The Swan of Tuonela', which depicts the swan that floats and sings mournfully on the black river of death.

On an April evening in 1792, Rouget de Lisle, a young army officer fired by the ideals of the French Revolution, sat down to write a patriotic tune. By morning he had composed the '*Marseillaise*'. It was immediately taken up as an army marching song, then as the anthem of the Revolution. It became a rallying-call in the Revolution of 1830, depicted by Delacroix as 'Liberty Guiding the People' (left). Finally, it became the national anthem of France itself.

Leos Janáček, the third outstanding Czech composer, was born only 13 years after Dvořák, yet seems to belong far more to the 20th century than to the 19th. He worked tiny fragments of folk melody into his sombre operas 'Jenufa' and 'Katya Kabanova', and into the mosaic-like texture of the '*Sinfonietta*' and other works.

Another leading national composer, the Finnish Jean Sibelius, was born in 1865, when his country was under Russian domination. He came to fame in the 1890s with patriotic works such as the 'Karelia' Suite and 'Finlandia', before going on to his series of seven masterly symphonies. He lived on until 1957 as the embodiment of Finland's spirit of independence, although he wrote nothing during the last 30 years of his life.

The Danes had their own Sibelius in Carl Nielsen, born in the same year as Sibelius, and like him most famous today for his symphonies. On the north side of the Skagerrak an older composer, Edvard Grieg, born in 1843, had already begun to absorb the folk music of Norway, which later surfaced in his numerous works for piano, including the famous concerto, in his songs, and in the incidental music he wrote for 'Peer Gynt', the dramatic poem by the Norwegian playright Henrik Ibsen.

On the southern edge of Europe the Spanish composers Isaac Albéniz (1860-1909) and Enrique Granados (1867-1916) wrote brilliant piano music evoking the landscapes and dances of Spain. In England, patriotism was encouraged in a more generalised way by Elgar in his 'Pomp and Circumstance' marches, written as the First World War approached. One of them, sung to the words 'Land of Hope and Glory', is now almost an unofficial national anthem, although Elgar himself loathed having his tune treated in such a narrowly patriotic way.

Sibelius's seven symphonies were matched by the six of the Danish composer Carl Nielsen (right). As Denmark was not under foreign control, Nielsen did not share the revolutionary fervour of many nationalist composers. Largely self-taught, he began his musical career in a military band, and as a young man supported himself by playing in dance bands. In Denmark his fame rests on the hymns and songs he wrote for children, but in the wider world he is best known for the originality of his symphonies.

Albéniz (right) used the rhythms and melodies of his native Spain in such works as the piano suite 'Iberia'. A runaway at the age of nine, he had given piano recitals in Cuba, San Francisco and London by the time he was 13. Granados (far right) was another pianist-composer. His most famous pieces form the set called '*Goyescas*', named after the painter Goya. Granados drowned tragically in 1916, when his ship was torpedoed.

Saviours of folk music

MUSIC BASED
ON FOLKSONG

LISZT
'Hungarian
Rhapsodies'

BRAHMS
'Edward'
ballade

D'INDY
'Symphonie sur
un Chant
Montagnard
Français'

DELIUS
'Brigg Fair'

VAUGHAN
WILLIAMS
'English Folk-
songs Suite'
'Norfolk
Rhapsody'

HOLST
'Somerset
Rhapsody'

BARTÓK
'Rumanian
Dances'
'Bulgarian
Dances'

KODÁLY
'Dances of
Galanta'
'Dances of
Marosszék'

COPLAND
'Appalachian
Spring'

THE RELENTLESS march of civilisation kills off rare varieties of plants and animals. It also destroys fragile aspects of mental and spiritual life, from complete primitive cultures in the wild parts of the world, to folk art of all kinds in so-called advanced nations. Throughout the 19th century traditional folk music came under increasing attack from different directions: from the impact of the Industrial Revolution, which herded people into cities and cut them off from the countryside where folksong had its roots, and from town-produced music, which made the old rustic folk tunes seem quaint and antiquated by contrast.

A fuller appreciation of the wealth of folk music came with the rise of nationalism among composers in the 19th century. This did not apply just to local composers in emerging nations like Czechoslovakia. Brahms made settings of a large number of folk songs, while Liszt's 'Hungarian Rhapsodies' were based on what he believed to be genuine folk tunes, although they were of gypsy origin rather than truly Hungarian. But this tentative interest did not amount to a proper investigation and salvaging of folksong. It took an entirely new breed of collectors and classifiers to bring scientific method into a musical rescue operation.

One of the most enthusiastic and thorough of this new generation of folk tune collectors was also one of the greatest of all 20th-century composers – Béla Bartók. In 1937, although physically far from strong, he was rattling round the stony hills of southern Turkey in a cart, on the last of his journeys in search of songs that were fast becoming extinct. Protecting his primitive recording equipment on his knees, he jolted to a tented village of nomadic tribesmen and there, squatting on a mattress in a smoke-filled room, recorded a song sung by a 15-year-old boy. The boy was terrified that there was a devil

The Hungarian composer Zoltán Kodály (left) shared Bartók's enthusiasm for collecting folk songs. Between them they saved much of Hungary's vanishing folk culture. Born in 1882, Kodály, like Bartók, expressed a strong sense of nationalism in his music, in works like the 'Psalmus Hungaricus' ('Hungarian Psalm'). An inspired teacher, he evolved his own system of musical education.

inside the recording machine; nevertheless he sang his song, and Bartók recorded and later transcribed it. Three years later he left war-torn Europe for America, where he died in 1945, at the age of 64.

Bartók grew up in the last 20 years of the 19th century, when national awareness was at its height and found expression in music of all kinds. As a boy he was a piano prodigy, and started to compose at the age of nine. He lived in the Hungarian countryside, surrounded by peasant songs and instrumental music. When he was only four – so his mother tells us – he could pick out 40 different folk songs with one finger on the piano, and when he grew up this love of music with its roots in the countryside became an absorbing passion. Another strong early influence on him was the music of Richard Strauss. The two musical streams of Hungarian folksong and German romanticism joined together to produce the first of Bartók's major works, a patriotic symphonic poem entitled 'Kossuth', after the leader of the Hungarian revolt of 1848 against the Austrian empire.

Before Bartók (above) and his contemporaries, song-collecting lacked professional method. The Hungarian composer collected and classified in a scientific way. He used an old-fashioned hand-wound phonograph which required cartloads of recording cylinders. Travelling to villages all over the Balkans, he would invite peasants to sing into his recorder (left). When he returned from his trips, Bartók classified the tunes by rhythmic and melodic patterns, and published long essays about them. Between 1905 and 1918 he collected 3500 melodies from Rumania, 2700 from Hungary and 2500 from Slovakia.

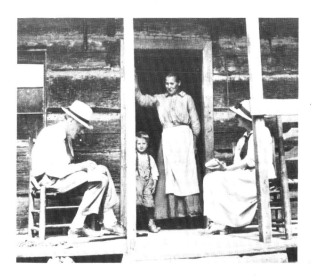

For generations the old English carols, ballads and songs, which came to America with the early settlers, had been kept alive in remote areas like the Appalachian Mountains. From 1916-18 the great English folk collector, Cecil Sharp, sought out this living tradition of folk songs. He and his companion, Maud Karpeles, noted down the words and music of more than 500 songs (above). Among them were the 'Cherry Tree Carol', dating to the Middle Ages and 'The Golden Vanity', a 16th-century sea ballad.

The folk songs collected by Cecil Sharp in the U.S.A. lived on as hill-billy music, and developed eventually into Country and Western. At the same time, a tradition of urban folksong was growing up in the American cities. During the Depression of the 1920s and '30s singers turned for their themes to the sufferings of people on the dole, and the modern protest song was born. Woody Guthrie was a leader of this trend. Born in 1912, he set up his own folksong group in 1940, with the singer Pete Seeger as one of its original members. But the protest movement really gathered force in the 1960s, with the Civil Rights movement and the Vietnam War. Singers like Joan Baez (right) and Bob Dylan won a vast following.

Bartók was not alone in realising that the traditions of folk music were in danger of dying out. His great friend and collaborator Zoltán Kodály, the English composers Ralph Vaughan Williams and Gustav Holst, and the Australian-born Percy Grainger were also pioneer collectors. They followed the lead set by Cecil Sharp, who began to collect English songs well before the end of the 19th century.

The folksong movement was strongest in countries which had no long tradition of composed music. Debussy mocked at the trend, noting how 'the tiniest villages have been ransacked, and simple tunes, plucked from the mouths of hoary peasants, find themselves trimmed with harmonic frills.' But Bartók used folksong in an entirely different way. His settings often have highly discordant harmony, while his major compositions, from the early piano pieces to late works like the 'Concerto for Orchestra', all stem from those thousands of tunes he noted down from peasant singers, absorbed into his own individual style, and transformed into great art by his genius.

Looking to the east

CUI

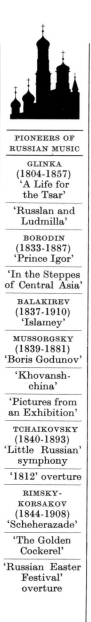

PIONEERS OF
RUSSIAN MUSIC

GLINKA
(1804-1857)
'A Life for
the Tsar'

'Russlan and
Ludmilla'

BORODIN
(1833-1887)
'Prince Igor'

'In the Steppes
of Central Asia'

BALAKIREV
(1837-1910)
'Islamey'

MUSSORGSKY
(1839-1881)
'Boris Godunov'

'Khovansh-
china'

'Pictures from
an Exhibition'

TCHAIKOVSKY
(1840-1893)
'Little Russian'
symphony

'1812' overture

RIMSKY-
KORSAKOV
(1844-1908)
'Scheherazade'

'The Golden
Cockerel'

'Russian Easter
Festival'
overture

WHATEVER kind of government it has had, Russia has always faced in two directions: east and west. Ever since the early 18th century, when Peter the Great imported fresh ideas from Europe to bring his medieval country up to date, the Russians have been both attracted by western attitudes and repelled by them. This comes out most clearly in the novels of their greatest writers, from Dostoevsky in the 19th century to Solzhenitsyn today.

The same sort of cultural split personality has occurred in Russian music, where the ancient chanting of the Orthodox Church first collided with the far more advanced techniques of the West. Such a cultural conflict continued through the time of the Soviet Union, under a different political guise. Music that was thought to show too much Western influence was condemned as 'decadent' or 'formalist', which was often another way of saying that it was not Russian enough in character.

Among the 18th-century imports to Russia was Italian opera, which was virtually the only music that interested the imperial court. At a time when leading instrumentalists were still serfs, who could be bought and sold by their masters, there was little chance of specifically Russian music developing, although a few collections of folk songs were made. The earliest use made of these tunes in serious music was not by a Russian composer at all but by Beethoven, who brought a different Russian folk melody into the first two of his three 'Rasoumovsky' string quartets, composed in 1806. Russia could also be a good place for a western composer to work, as the Irish pianist John Field discovered at much the same time. The composer of the earliest nocturnes, years before Chopin took up the form, Field settled in Russia early in the 19th century and died there in 1837, after a successful career.

The best known and most popular of all 19th-century Russian composers, Peter Tchaikovsky (above), stood aloof from the nationalism of his contemporaries, remaining in the European mainstream of music. His reputation mainly rests on his orchestral works, which are typically Russian in their contrasts of frantic gaiety and intense melancholy, and on his three ballets: 'Swan Lake' (right), 'Nutcracker' and 'The Sleeping Beauty'

BALAKIREV   MUSSORGSKY   BORODIN   RIMSKY-KORSAKOV

The 1830s also saw the appearance of the work that marks the start of purely Russian music – the opera, 'A Life for the Tsar', by Mikhail Glinka. An aristocrat brought up on a country estate where he heard nothing but folk music, Glinka had been a pupil of Field and also knew Bellini and Donizetti. The opera's hero is not some remote historical person but an old peasant called Ivan Susanin, whose self-sacrifice gives the work its title. In its powerful writing for the chorus and use of folk tunes, 'A Life for the Tsar' set the pattern for future Russian operas.

Glinka's use of folk music was taken up and expanded by his successors later in the 19th century – a group of nationalists known as 'The Five' or 'The Mighty Handful'. They were all amateurs by European standards and had careers outside music: Balakirev, Cui and Mussorgsky were all army officers, Rimsky-Korsakov was a naval cadet, and Borodin was a doctor and professor of chemistry. Cui rose to be a general and made little impact on the history of music. But the others laid down the lines most later Russian composers were to follow.

Balakirev is best known for his brilliant piano fantasy 'Islamey', based on Oriental folk themes, while Borodin's 'Prince Igor' makes effective use of Russian folk melodies, especially in the 'Polovtsian Dances', which have reached vast audiences in recent years in the musical 'Kismet'. Rimsky-Korsakov, a superb orchestrator and a great teacher, is mainly remembered for his symphonic suite, 'Scheherazade'. The genius among 'The Five' was Mussorgsky, whose gigantic opera 'Boris Godunov', is perhaps the most truly Russian musical work of all time, mixing sumptuous court ritual with scenes of low life, and contrasting the tormented life of the Tsar Boris with the massive vigour of the Russian people, expressed in the choruses.

Rimsky-Korsakov, one of 19th-century Russia's most prolific composers, lived long enough to hand on the nationalist traditions of 'The Five' to his pupil Stravinsky, and to fall a victim of Tsarist censorship in 1908, the year he died. The trouble occurred because his last opera, 'The Golden Cockerel', was thought to show disrespect to the ruling Tsar, Nicholas II. A stage set (above) shows the fantasy element of the opera, but the audience is also told that the tale has a moral. In the opera the lazy, greedy King Dodon, like the Tsar, is constantly threatened by invaders.

A wise Astrologer gives the King a golden cockerel which will crow if the King is in danger. In return he promises to fulfil any request the Astrologer may make. The King goes off to battle, meets the young Queen of Shemakhan (left), and marries her. When the Astrologer claims her in payment for the cockerel, the King kills him. The cockerel then pecks the King to death. The Russian censor thought that the opera was an attack on the corruption of the Tsar's court, and also on the conduct of the war with Japan in 1904-5, in which Russia was nearly defeated.

From the new world

CHARLES IVES AND HIS BROTHER MOSS

THE MILLIONAIRE GENIUS

Charles Ives, born in 1874, was both a musical pioneer and the founder of a multimillion dollar insurance agency. His father was a practical musician who had been a bandsman in the Civil War. He formed his own band and taught the young Charles (below) the rudiments of music by such unconventional methods as getting him to sing in one key while playing the accompaniment in a different one.

Charles Ives enjoyed a traditional musical training, but soon realised that there was no market for the kind of music he really wanted to write. So he decided to go into business. 'If a man has a nice wife and nice children,' he said,

'how can he let the children starve on his dissonances?' He married a girl named Harmony Twichell in 1908. From 1909 to the early 1920s Ives wrote music in his spare time. Then, ill and discouraged, he gave it up. But after the Second World War, when Ives (above) was over 70, his works began to be played, although orchestras still found them extremely difficult. By 1954, when he died, his originality had been recognised by Schoenberg, Stokowski and other leading musicians. Many of Ives's titles show his sense of national identity: 'Three Places in New England' and 'Central Park in the Dark', for instance.

WHEN THE Pilgrim Fathers set sail in the 'Mayflower' in 1620, they turned their backs not only on European social inequality and religious intolerance, but also on all the arts that went with them. Music especially was flourishing at this time, with the operas of Monteverdi in Italy and the great keyboard composers in England. But for pioneers struggling to live in a hostile country, sophisticated art was irrelevant. They had their hymns for church services and their folk songs and dances for merrymaking. When more settled times came in the 18th century, American audiences were satisfied with music and performers imported from Europe. English ballad operas like 'The Beggar's Opera' were popular in New England, while further south, French-controlled New Orleans had its own resident French opera company.

A Negro banjo-player and drummer set the pace for these early 19th-century slaves (below) who put their leisure-time energy into dancing.

In his short life (he died at 37), Stephen Foster (left) composed over 175 songs, many of which depict life in the American slave states.

In the 1920s many young composers from America went to Paris to study with the great French teacher Nadia Boulanger. Born in 1887, she taught that music should be light and clear in texture, in the tradition of Fauré, Debussy, Ravel and Stravinsky. Four of her pupils, shown here at her home in the mid-1920s, were (left to right): Virgil Thomson, Walter Piston, Herbert Elwell and Aaron Copland. Thomson, Piston and Copland later became the leading American composers of the 1930s and '40s, writing works combining American vigour with French clarity.

The first recognisably American music emerged among the congregations of New England. The leader here was the Boston hymn writer William Billings, who was born in 1746. His hymns, written with deliberate disregard for academic rules, set the pattern for later Americans like Charles Ives and John Cage, who forged their own musical language.

Throughout the 19th century American music lived largely on the European past. But side by side with symphony and opera in the big centres, an entirely different music was evolving among the Negro slaves of the southern states. Based on the powerful rhythms of the African countries from which their ancestors had been wrenched, on church hymns and on the work songs that lightened backbreaking toil in the cotton fields, their music gradually entered the general American consciousness. The authentic Negro music, which evolved into jazz towards the end of the 19th century, was being imitated as early as the 1830s by 'minstrel shows' – troupes of white men with blackened faces. A white composer strongly influenced by plantation songs and spirituals was Stephen Foster, who died in 1864, shortly before the slaves were liberated. He wrote over 150 songs, of which several have become classics, like 'The Old Folks at Home' and 'My Old Kentucky Home'. The Negro element was equally strong in the piano music of Louis Moreau Gottschalk, a contemporary of Foster. He was especially fond of the bouncing cakewalk dance rhythm and of banjo imitations, and in his time was a phenomenally successful touring pianist, giving concerts as far afield as the Caribbean and South America.

The German classical tradition in the States was carried on by Edward MacDowell, whose piano works are still sometimes played today. Another academic composer, Horatio Parker, who taught at Yale, had as his pupil Charles Ives – a man whose vast mental energies seized on every aspect of the American music of his time, tore it apart and reassembled it in a way that makes him the precursor of modern American music (see overleaf).

In the first two decades of the 20th century Charles Ives produced startlingly original music that has only recently begun to be appreciated. Born in 1874, the same year as Schoenberg, Ives was virtually cut off from modern developments in Europe, yet discovered for himself novel techniques such as writing in several keys at once (polytonality) or with several different rhythms (polyrhythm).

Ives's music incorporated everything that had gone before him, from hymns to ragtime. He wrote from a background of the American small town, not the vast city jungles of concrete and steel that were beginning to spring up all over the country. The first composer of skyscraper America was Edgar Varèse, who was born in France in 1883, studied in Paris, and settled in New York in 1916. His first large-scale work was inspired by the teeming and raw life of the city he saw all round him. Called '*Amériques*', it uses a huge orchestra of wind and percussion, including a steamboat whistle and a New York Fire Department hand siren. Towards the end of his long life (he died in 1965) Varèse, still a pioneer, had begun to experiment with electronic music, including his '*Poème Electronique*'.

Varèse was a French composer who crossed the Atlantic to America. The next generation of American composers – Walter Piston, Aaron Copland and Roy Harris – made the journey in the opposite direction and went to Paris to study composition under the famous teacher Nadia Boulanger, a pupil of Stravinsky. In this way Europe and America once more came together. The worlds of light and serious music were linked by George Gershwin, who also studied in Paris, and whose best known piece 'An American in Paris', written in 1928, is a portrait of 'a Yankee tourist adrift in the City of Light'. Gershwin was incredibly successful both with extended compositions such as this and with his popular songs. On one occasion he is said to have asked Stravinsky how much he charged for his composition lessons. Stravinsky in return asked Gershwin for his annual income, and when he learned that it was in six figures, said to the young American: 'How about my taking lessons from you?'

Gershwin's music is steeped in jazz. His 'Rhapsody in Blue', at its first performance in 1924, was played not by a symphony orchestra but by one of the leading jazz bands of the day, the Paul Whiteman Orchestra. The strongly rhythmic early type of jazz known as ragtime was adopted by composers such as Debussy and Stravinsky at a time when its leading American creator, Scott Joplin, was dying in poverty and neglect. The blues, the basis of all the finest jazz, gave its melancholy tinge to works by classically-trained composers, such as Ravel's violin sonata, which has a complete blues movement. Thus jazz contributed, if only slightly, to the main western tradition as well as to purely American music, and its influence still exists today.

LOUIS ARMSTRONG'S 'HOT FIVE'

IX

MUSIC TODAY

Debussy shows the way

IN DECEMBER 1894 a concert of new orchestral works was given in Paris. Among the pieces of music by Glazunov, Saint-Saëns, Franck and a number of composers forgotten today was a short piece by Debussy, the *'Prélude à l'Après-midi d'un Faune'*. The critics called it 'interesting', but otherwise took no notice of it. Based on a poem by Stéphane Mallarmé, it opens with a fluctuating, wayward tune played on the flute by the mythical faun of the title, leading into a short, delicately orchestrated movement, in which horn calls and swirls on the harp evoke the heat of a summer's afternoon. What was revolutionary about it was not the subject matter – atmospheric scene-painting was nothing new in music – but the way in which Debussy dissolved classical harmony into a fine haze and shimmer of sound.

Claude Debussy was born in 1862, and as a boy saw the horrors of the Franco-Prussian War of 1870-71 at first hand. His father was put in gaol for his part in the short-lived 'Commune' – the democratic uprising in Paris that followed France's defeat by Germany. Two years later, at the age of 11, Claude became a pupil at the Paris Conservatoire, where he stayed for a further 11 years. He was in constant trouble with his composition teachers for writing what seemed to them outrageously modern harmonies. On one occasion, when he was playing some wild progressions on the piano, a teacher asked him what rules of music he followed. *'Mon plaisir'* ('My pleasure'), answered Debussy. All the same, he could keep to the rules when he chose to do so. In 1884 he was awarded the top composition prize for a cantata on the theme of the Prodigal Son which Gounod, who was one of the panel of judges for that year, described as 'the work of a genius'.

During the next few years Debussy came under a vast number of influences, many of them non-musical ones. In the 1880s France was swept by a mania for Wagner, and he became enthusiastic about Wagner's operas. He made settings of poems by Verlaine and other leading poets; he studied the paintings of the pre-Raphaelites and of Whistler; he read the supernatural stories of Edgar Allen Poe. At the Great Exhibition in Paris in 1889, he listened to the strangely exotic sounds of *gamelan* music

Maurice Ravel (right) was the only French composer to rival Debussy during his lifetime. He wrote brilliant piano music, orchestral works, short operas, songs and chamber music.

Erik Satie (left) was a musical eccentric, who gave his pieces strange names, like 'Pieces in the shape of a Pear'. In recent years his music has been taken seriously by modern composers.

from Java. In the course of his travels, Debussy became the household pianist of Mme von Meck, who was Tchaikovsky's patron. More than any other composer before or since, he had an intense curiosity about all the other arts apart from music. He was also very much a man about town, and was at his happiest sitting in a Montmartre bar with a group of friends, listening to the latest witty café singer, or discussing theories of art and poetry far into the night.

Debussy has often been described as an Impressionist and, like the painters Monet and Renoir, he was more concerned with mood and atmosphere than with rigid structure. But he did not like being labelled, and when he was composing his orchestral 'Images' in the early 1900s, he told a friend: 'I am now writing something which the fools will refer to as Impressionism.' This was not long after he had reached the height of his fame with the opera *'Pelléas et Mélisande'*, which is a sombre love story full of half-lights and mystery, set in a twilight medieval world. First produced in 1902, *'Pelléas'* is Debussy's only completed opera, although he worked on and off at other possible themes, among them Shakespeare's 'As You Like It' and Poe's 'The Fall of the House of Usher'. Soon after *'Pelléas'* Debussy became involved in a tragic scandal, when his first wife tried to shoot herself after he had left her.

Debussy (left) outside his Paris home in 1910. At this period he was writing some of his finest works, such as the 24 piano preludes and the orchestral 'Images'.

The *gamelan* orchestra (below), played all over Indonesia, is a small percussion band which produces rhythmic patterns of great subtlety. It uses xylophones, celestes, gongs and drums. Debussy first heard a *gamelan* in 1889.

Edgar Allan Poe (above), the American writer of supernatural tales, was popular in France in the 19th century. Debussy left sketches for an opera based on Poe's 'Fall of the House of Usher'.

This time of emotional turmoil saw the creation of Debussy's finest orchestral work, the three symphonic sketches called '*La Mer*', which was completed in 1905. As the cover for '*La Mer*', Debussy chose a print by the Japanese artist Hokusai, which is sharp-cut and threatening in outline. Like the print, the music is all clarity and sparkle, with no Impressionistic woolliness or vagueness about it.

Most typical of all his works are the short piano preludes. Like Chopin, Debussy wrote 24 of them, but whereas Chopin's preludes are untitled, each of Debussy's creates a scene or a mood. The banjos of the café entertainers appear in 'Minstrels', and a Breton legend in '*La Cathédrale Engloutie*' ('The Submerged Cathedral'). Others depict fireworks, yachts becalmed on the sea, and even an ancient Greek vase. They form a kind of musical autobiography, in which many aspects of Debussy's character find a place.

Towards the end of his life he struck up a friendship with Stravinsky, who was in turn an enthusiast for Debussy's works. But his last years were made wretched by disease and by the outbreak of the First World War, which he saw as the end of civilisation. As a patriotic gesture, he added the words *musicien français* to the title page of his last works. He died in March 1918, as the Germans were bombarding Paris in their final gamble of the war.

Debussy's only opera, '*Pelléas et Mélisande*' (left), is a tragic love story with a legendary medieval setting.

Mahler's universe

MAHLER
(1860-1911)

MAIN WORKS

Symphonies (9)
(10th completed
in 1960s by
Deryck Cooke)
'The Song of the
Earth' (song-
symphony)
'Das Klagende
Lied' (cantata)

SONGS WITH
ORCHESTRA

'Lieder eines
fahrenden
Gesellen'
'Kindertoten-
lieder'
'Des Knaben
Wunderhorn'

The deeply religious com-
poser Anton Bruckner
(below) wrote the first of
his nine vast symphonies
in the 1860s. Although
rejected by Viennese
audiences, he was warm-
ly supported by Mahler
and his friends.

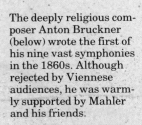

Mahler died in 1911 but
his wife, Alma (below),
lived until 1964, surviv-
ing him by more that 50
years. At first she lived
with the Austrian pain-
ter Oskar Kokoschka,
then she married Walter
Gropius, the German
architect. Her marriage
to Gropius is a link with
one of Mahler's most
enthusiastic disciples of
all, Alban Berg.

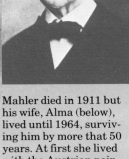

Berg wrote his haunting
violin concerto in mem-
ory of Manon Gropius,
Alma's daughter, and his
opera 'Wozzeck' was ded-
icated to Alma herself.

WITH THE exception of Beethoven, there are only two composers whose symphonies can guarantee a box-office success: Tchaikovsky and Mahler. Tchaikovsky has always been popular, but Mahler's symphonies were rarely played until the 1950s – 40 years after his death. This was partly due to their immense length and the demands they make on orchestras and conductors. But as they gradually became more familiar, audiences responded to their unique visionary power blended with world-weariness and humour, and to the sheer beauty of the sounds that Mahler drew from his players.

Gustav Mahler was born in 1860 in a small Czech town, the second of 14 children. He knew the misery of being poor and of seeing most of his brothers and sisters die. He also knew what it was like to be a Jew in the anti-Semitic Austro-Hungarian Empire. As he said about himself later in his life: 'I am thrice homeless, as a native of Bohemia in Austria, as an Austrian among Germans, and as a Jew throughout the world. Everywhere an intruder, never welcomed.'

Between 1875 and 1878 Mahler was a pupil at the Vienna Conservatory, where he became friendly with Hugo Wolf, who was to be the last great composer of the German *Lied* (solo song). He and his friends also championed the music of Bruckner, whose giant symphonies were received with jeers or indifference by the smart Viennese audiences. Mahler had already begun to compose, inspired mainly by the collections of folk poems '*Des Knaben Wunderhorn*' ('Magic Horn of Youth'), which mixed magic with the reality of the everyday world.

In 1881 Mahler suffered a major disappointment when his cantata, '*Das Klagende Lied*' ('The Song of Lamentation'), was rejected for the Beethoven prize by a jury which included Brahms. Rejection in one form or another was to be the fate of nearly all his compositions throughout his life; but the year before, in 1880, he had embarked on his highly successful career as a conductor. He found this work as stimulating as it was exhausting, and his absolute mastery of orchestral colour comes from his practical experience of instruments. His conducting career was a succession of increasingly important jobs – first at Leipzig in 1886, next at Budapest, then at Hamburg.

Finally, in 1897, he reached the pinnacle of every conductor's ambition – the Vienna Opera House, where he remained for ten years.

As an opera conductor, Mahler was famous for his brilliant interpretations of three works: Mozart's 'Don Giovanni', Beethoven's 'Fidelio' and Wagner's 'Tristan and Isolde'. He had a hypnotic power over orchestra and singers, one of whom said of him: 'The inspiration that radiates from the little man is fantastic.' In Vienna he treated audiences in a way that is universal now, but was disliked at the time, by dimming the house lights before the curtain rose and shutting out late-comers until the end of the act. Naturally enough, his strong and ruthless character made him many enemies, and his Jewish origins were held against him, even though he had diplomatically become a Roman Catholic before being appointed chief conductor of the Viennese Opera.

During these years his life fell into a regular pattern of conducting for most of the year and writing symphonies in the summer – a strenuous schedule, which may account for his death from heart failure at the age of 50. His First Symphony was played at Budapest in 1889, and the other eight followed at fairly regular intervals until his death in 1911. In 1902 he married Alma Schindler, who had studied composition and was an admirer of his music.

Mahler's life-work was an inspiration to Schoenberg and the other pioneers of modern music who lived in Vienna in the years before the Second World War. But in his symphonies he looked back to Brahms and Schubert, rather than towards the future. Mahler said that 'the symphony is the world, it must embrace everything', and in huge works like the Eighth Symphony (called the 'Symphony of a Thousand' from the size of the orchestra and choir) he came as near as any composer ever has to creating a musical universe. In his works the Holy Ghost and the Resurrection jostle with military marches and peasant dances, sleigh-bells jingle and mandolins twang, '*Frère Jacques*' becomes a funeral dirge, and Fate crashes out its hammer blows. From the child's dream of heaven to the grown man's fear of death, Mahler sets all his experience before us in ways which we can recognise and understand.

Schoenberg the lawgiver

SCHOENBERG
(1874-1951)

MAIN WORKS

ORCHESTRAL

'Chamber
Symphonies' (2)
'Five Pieces'
for orchestra
'Variations'
for orchestra
violin concerto
piano concerto

CHORAL

'Gurrelieder'
'Kol Nidre'
'A Survivor
from Warsaw'

OPERAS

'Die glückliche
Hand'
'Von Heute auf
Morgen'
'Moses and
Aaron'

OTHER WORKS
WITH VOICE

'Erwartung'
'Pierrot
Lunaire'
'Ode to
Napoleon'

string quartets
(4)
wind quartet
suite for piano
'Verklärte
Nacht' (string
sextet)

AT THE entrance to the citadel of modern music stands a formidable figure of powerful intellect and unswerving principles: Arnold Schoenberg. His 12-note system has been as influential in the musical world as Picasso and cubism in the field of painting. Like Picasso, Schoenberg was driven to his innovations by the feeling that art in the early 1900s had nothing new to offer. Born in Vienna in 1874, as a boy he played the violin and cello, and loved the music of both Brahms and Wagner, who had split the musical world into two camps. Brahms represented the spirit of classicism, going back to Beethoven and Bach, while Wagner embodied everything that was modern, especially by the way in which the ebb and flow of his music seemed to destroy all the firm landmarks of traditional harmony.

Schoenberg started his adult life in a bank, but in 1895 he gave it up and became a full-time musician. To begin with, he took any musical job that was going, conducting a metal workers' choral society, and scoring song hits and operettas. Meanwhile he was steadily composing his own works – songs, a string sextet, and the immense, two-hour-long 'Gurrelieder' for chorus,

soloists and orchestra, which was composed about 1900 but not completed until more than ten years later. Although these early works were romantic in feeling, Schoenberg's music was already moving towards 'atonality' – that is, it did not have a definite tonal centre or key, but used all 12 notes of the chromatic scale on an equal and democratic basis.

At the same time he was establishing himself as a teacher, and in 1904 began to teach his chief disciples, Alban Berg and Anton Webern. Schoenberg was also encouraged by two established composers, Richard Strauss (then at the height of his career) and Mahler, who was in charge of the Vienna Opera. As if all these activities were not enough, he began to paint in a highly dramatic 'expressionist' style, and had some of his works exhibited.

In 1911 he moved to Berlin. The following year he wrote 'Pierrot Lunaire', the work that marked him as a major figure on the musical scene. Even 80 years later, it is still an uncomfortable and disturbing work. With 'Pierrot' Schoenberg shocked the musical establishment, as Stravinsky was to do with 'The Rite of Spring' the following year.

In 1912, when 'Pierrot Lunaire' had its premiere in Berlin, a critic wrote: 'If this is music then I pray my Creator not to let me hear it again.' This work, the first-ever example of 'music-theatre', shocked audiences used to conventional musical forms. 'Pierrot', Schoenberg's setting of 21 poems by the Belgian poet Albert Giraud, is full of references to blood, skulls, corpses and crucifixes. The Pierrot of the title is the Italian commedia dell'arte figure with whitened face and white clothes. The main part is given to a female vocalist – here it is the soprano Mary Thomas (left) – who intones the verses in Sprechgesang ('speech-song'), to a constantly changing instrumental background.

Schoenberg used the 12-note technique in his opera 'Moses and Aaron' (below), begun in 1932. Only two acts were completed by the time the composer died in 1951.

Schoenberg enriched the lives of generations of students. He outlived his two greatest pupils, Webern (left) and Berg. Webern was accidentally shot by an American soldier in 1945.

Like Einstein brooding on the theory of relativity, or Freud working out the rudiments of psychoanalysis, Arnold Schoenberg (left) spent years evolving his private musical revolution. The result of his labour was the 12-note theory of composition, which he announced in 1922.

Throughout the First World War and for some years after, Schoenberg wrote virtually nothing. In 1922 he made public his 'law of non-repetition of notes' which stated that no note of the chromatic scale could be repeated before all the other 11 had been played in a fixed order. This sequence of 12 notes was called the 'note-row' or 'series', and was the basic building block from which Schoenberg began to construct his compositions, beginning with a set of piano pieces dating from 1923. The notes of the series could be played in reverse order ('retrograde'), upside-down ('inverted') or both together ('retrograde inversion') – exactly like the subject (theme) of a Bach fugue. Schoenberg said that the row was like a hat: whether you look at it from left to right, from above or below, it still remains a hat. In answer to critics who complained that the system was artificial, he replied that it had grown out of inner necessity. As Moses had codified the haphazard laws of the Jews in the Ten Commandments, so he had assembled the innovations of Wagner, Strauss, Debussy and others into one single all-embracing law. Yet when anyone came to Schoenberg to learn composition, he began with the foundations as laid down by Bach, Haydn, Mozart, Beethoven and other classical composers, saying that there was still plenty of good music to be written in the key of C major.

In 1925 Schoenberg took over the composition class at the Berlin Academy. But with the rise to power of Hitler in 1933 he was dismissed, because he was Jewish and because of the so-called 'decadence' of his music. He went into exile in America, where he remained until his death in 1951. As an old man he summed up his career by saying: 'I had the feeling that I had fallen into an ocean of boiling water, and not knowing how to swim or get out in any other manner, I tried with my legs and arms as best I could.' The turbulence of Schoenberg's heroic struggle in the water is still being felt today.

Alban Berg (left) was one of Schoenberg's most devoted followers. This portrait was painted by Schoenberg himself.

Parting of the ways

ENGLISH DREAMER
Frederick Delius (1862-1934) was the son of a Bradford merchant and was originally intended for the wool trade. As a young man he made his way to Florida, where he grew oranges, and came to know and love Negro music. From America he went to Leipzig, where he studied composition and became friendly with the Norwegian composer Grieg. He eventually settled in France, where he lived for most of his life. One of the first of his major orchestral pieces, 'Paris, the Song of a Great City', was written in 1898 and was inspired by his adopted country. The 'Mass of Life', his most important choral work, was based on Nietzsche's 'Zarathustra', which also inspired Strauss's symphonic poem 'Thus Spake Zarathustra'. Towards the end of his life Delius became blind and paralysed. His last works were written down with the help of Eric Fenby, who became the composer's biographer. The principle champion of Delius's music was the English conductor, Sir Thomas Beecham.

RUSSIAN MYSTIC
The Russian, Alexander Scriabin (1872-1915), was a brilliant pianist and a great harmonic experimenter, whose last orchestral pieces were among the most original of his period. After training as a military officer, Scriabin became a successful composer and concert pianist. He studied theosophy – the mystic philosophy of Madame Blavatsky, based on Indian teachings – and evolved a 'mystic chord', consisting of fourths one on top of the other, on which his final orchestral compositions were based. These were three symphonic poems, all with mystical overtones – 'The Divine Poem', 'The Poem of Ecstasy' and 'The Poem of Fire' (also called 'Prometheus', after the hero who defied the gods to bring fire to Man). 'The Poem of Fire' may have been the first true example of psychedelic music, as it contained a part for 'colour-organ', to throw lights of different colours on to a screen. When he died, Scriabin was writing a fourth symphonic poem, *'Mysterium'*, which was to be performed in a temple in the Himalayas and was to be an integration of all the arts – music, poetry, dance, light, even perfume.

THREE GREAT figures dominated music in the first half of the 20th century – Stravinsky, Bartók and Schoenberg. All of them wrote music that was far more dissonant and rhythmically disjointed than anything that had gone before, but they differed in their overall approach. Stravinsky led the return to poise and clarity known as the 'neo-classical' movement, Bartók went his lonely creative way as the last of the nationalists, while Schoenberg set up the intellectual system of 12-note music.

At the same time other composers were making their individual contributions to the general confusion. Free from the restraints of 19th-century harmony, composers like Milhaud wrote in several keys at once (polytonality) or used several different rhythms simultaneously.

BRAZIL'S BACH
The Brazilian Heitor Villa-Lobos (1887-1959) wrote an incredible total of 2000 works, most of which are unknown outside South America. Left an orphan at the age of only 12, he supported himself by playing the cello, wandering all over his country with the instrument slung on his back, and absorbing the music of the native Indians as well as that of the Portuguese settlers. In 1915 he met Milhaud in Brazil, and learned from him about the music of Debussy, Stravinsky and other composers. In the 1920s he spent some time in Paris, but for most of his life he worked in Rio de Janeiro. He is best known today for his '*Bachianas Brasilieras*', which treat Indian tunes in the style of Bach.

A GALLIC WIT
Born in the south of France, Darius Milhaud (1892-1974) was a true southerner in the sunny exuberance of his music. He was trained at the Paris Conservatory, and during the First World War was cultural attaché at the French embassy in Rio de Janeiro, where he met Villa-Lobos and became fascinated by the dance and folk music of Brazil. Back in Paris after the war, he had his first success with a ballet called '*Le Boeuf sur le Toit*' ('The Ox on the Roof'), based on Brazilian tunes. With five other composers he formed the group called *Les Six*, writing witty and deliberately superficial music, reacting against both Wagner and Debussy. For a time he was interested in jazz, which permeated the music he wrote in 1923 for the ballet '*La Création du Monde*' ('The Creation of the World'), based on African legends. Like Poulenc, another leading member of *Les Six*, Milhaud had his serious side and wrote quantities of symphonies, chamber music and large-scale operas.

GERMAN HUMANIST
A composer of great versatility and energy, Paul Hindemith (1895-1963) was also a leading viola-player. He soon came to the fore as a soloist, a teacher, and as an ultra-modern composer. Many of his early works were harshly discordant with a driving and relentless rhythm. He was also concerned with the value of music as a social activity, and wrote pieces for amateurs and children called *Gebrauchsmusik*, or 'music for everyday use'. In 1939 he settled in the United States, becoming Professor of Music at Yale. One of his last works was an opera based on the life of the astronomer Johannes Kepler, called '*Die Harmonie der Welt*' ('The Harmony of the World').

Yet others, such as Hindemith, felt that amateurs and schools had been cut off from new music by its increasing complexity, and wrote simple works for choirs and instrumentalists. Composers also experimented with the means of sound production, as well as with the sounds themselves. Around 1930 the first electrical sound-producing instruments appeared – the theremin, the *ondes martenot* and the trautonium, which were the remote ancestors of today's electronic instruments. Most curious of all instrumental novelties was the quarter-tone piano, for which the Czech composer Aloys Hába wrote experimental music.

The days of complete freedom for many composers, however, were numbered, as the 1920s and '30s saw the rise of dictatorships in Germany and Russia, which controlled artists as rigidly as everybody else. In Nazi Germany, Jewish composers were deprived of their jobs and went into exile. Even non-Jewish composers such as Hindemith found it impossible to work under Hitler's régime. In the 1930s his music was banned by the Nazis, who accused him of 'cultural Bolshevism'. The only composers in favour were those like Carl Orff, who wrote strongly rhythmic, tuneful music that everyone could appreciate. In Russia, the Communist authorities put similar pressures on their composers. The greatest of them all, Dmitri Shostakovich, subtitled his Fifth Symphony of 1937 'A Soviet artist's reply to just criticism', after his opera 'Lady Macbeth of Mtsensk' met with official disapproval.

Russian heroism during the siege of Leningrad in 1942 (left) inspired Shostakovich's patriotic Seventh Symphony.

Composers in control

Olivier Messiaen (left) has based many of his major works on birdsong, carefully notated in the field and then turned into music like the piano pieces called the 'Catalogue of the Birds'. Messiaen's experiments with rhythm inspired a number of younger composers, such as Pierre Boulez (right). Boulez now runs the centre for experimental music – IRCAM – in Paris.

WITH THE end of the Second World War in 1945, composers, like everyone else, had to pick up the pieces of a shattered world. Many of the greatest figures of the prewar period, such as Stravinsky, Schoenberg and Hindemith, were living in America, while Bartók died there only a few weeks after the war had ended. The playing of new music had almost stopped during the period of hostilities, and the 12-note musical innovations of Schoenberg and his pupils had virtually to be rediscovered.

The thin thread of musical continuity was maintained in the immediate postwar years by the French composer Olivier Messiaen, who had spent some time in a German prisoner-of-war camp before returning to teaching in Paris.

Born in 1908, Messiaen wrote music that was a rich mixture of Hindu rhythm, birdsong and a fervent Roman Catholic faith. In contrast, his teaching consisted not of vague mysticism, but of tough analysis of scores like Stravinsky's 'Rite of Spring', which inspired his brilliant pupils, Boulez and Stockhausen, to undertake their own musical experiments.

In their explorations of modern music, this new generation of composers discovered the scores of Schoenberg's leading disciple, Anton Webern. Until his career was disastrously cut short by an American bullet in 1945, Webern, while following in Schoenberg's footsteps, had developed his own individual form of 'serialism'. Webern's music is incredibly terse and brief, with whole movements lasting sometimes less than a minute. It is made up of tiny wisps of sound, sudden contrasts of volume, and chords that change from one group of instruments to another, giving the effect of a constantly varying prism of tone colour.

Boulez took these elements of Webern's music and combined them with the rhythmical experiments of Messiaen, who was fond of rhythms based on the primary numbers (5, 7, 11, 13, etc.), rather than on the regular pulse still found in the music of Schoenberg and Webern. Schoenberg had arranged one of the elements of music – pitch – in such a way that all the 12 semitones of the scale are organised in a definite sequence or series. But there were other elements that could be 'serialised' in a similar way – loudness or softness ('dynamics'), whether a note is played staccato or legato ('attack'), the length of each note of a given pitch ('duration'), and which instrument plays what note ('timbre').

Born in 1928, Karlheinz Stockhausen (left) has composed music in a wide variety of different styles. He has written for conventional instruments, composed purely electronic works, and combined human performers with electronics. He has also been greatly influenced by eastern attitudes to music, seeing it as a 'spiritual spiral' which affects composer, performer and audience alike. Another modern pioneer is Pierre Schaeffer (right), who composed some of the earliest examples of electronic *musique concrète* in Paris, about 1950.

Jean-Michel Jarre (above) is a composer of modern electronic music. His concerts are exciting visually as well as musically.

Most experiments in total control were confined to the piano, where in the early works of Boulez and Stockhausen the player may have to play a single chord made up of notes of different dynamics, attacks and durations.

While such works were being written in the early 1950s, the newly-invented tape recorder had for the first time given the composer complete control over his sound material, without any intervention on the part of a performer. There were two main methods of composition, at least in the beginning. First came *musique concrète*, which built up compositions from pre-recorded live sound, speeded up, slowed down, transformed and spliced together in a variety of ways. The pioneer here was Pierre Schaeffer, working in Paris. In opposition to *musique concrète*, musicians in the Cologne electronic studio, including Stockhausen, were experimenting with pure sounds produced from an electronic source rather than prerecorded and reassembled.

Composers soon came to realise that there is nothing more boring for an audience than watching loudspeakers. So from about 1960 on, the performer has been drawn into electronic music, sometimes in a highly dramatic way, as in Stockhausen's '*Kontakte*', composed in 1959-60. In this piece the electronic sounds, controlled from an instrument panel, are contrasted with the live sounds played by a pianist and a percussionist. As the name of the piece suggests, it is a true 'contact' between utterly different kinds of music, but it is also a symbolic contest between the machine and the live performer, reflecting the struggle between the human being and the latest discoveries of technology.

Return to freedom

CAGE
(b.1912)

MAIN WORKS

ORCHESTRAL

'Concert' for piano and orchestra
'Atlas Eclipticalis'

PERCUSSION AND ELECTRONICS

'First Construction in Metal'
'Imaginary Landscapes' (5)
'Radio Music'
'Cartridge Music'

MAGNETIC TAPE

'Williams Mix'
'Fontana Mix'

AUDIO-VISUAL

'Musicircus'
'HPSCHD'

PIANO

'4′ 33″'
'Music of Changes'
'Seven Haiku'
'Sonatas and Interludes'
'Winter Music'

VOICE

'The Wonderful Widow of Eighteen Springs'

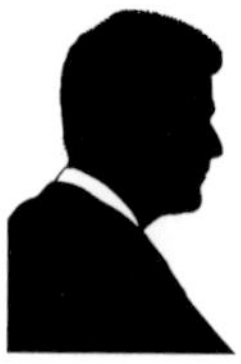

WHILE MANY composers in the years after the war were imposing total control over music, others were taking exactly the opposite course, and writing music that gave the performer far greater freedom than at any time since the days of improvisation in the 18th century. Leading this movement was the American John Cage, who was born in 1912 and is therefore a good deal older than Boulez, Stockhausen and their contemporaries. The son of an inventor, he studied architecture and painting before devoting himself to music in the early 1930s.

During this period he took lessons with Schoenberg, who had settled in California. His true musical ancestors, however, were Charles Ives, who tried to put every aspect of American life into his music, and Edgar Varèse, whose experiments with percussion astonished audiences in the 1920s and '30s. Even more important was Erik Satie, who brought his own brand of inspired nonsense into music, writing pieces with titles like *'Airs à faire fuir'* ('Tunes to make you run away'), *'Morceaux en forme de Poire'* ('Pieces in the shape of a Pear') and other works which poked fun at an over-reverent attitude to music. Well before the war Cage was experimenting with music for 'prepared piano', in which various objects were placed between the strings to alter the sound, and his first works for percussion alone date from the same period.

During the 1940s he was appointed musical director of Merce Cunningham's modern ballet company, and became known to a wider public. Like many other Americans at this time, he studied Zen Buddhist philosophy, with its emphasis on contemplation rather than western-style action. As a result of this interest, he became more concerned with the process of creating music than with the finished piece, sometimes writing down the score of a work after the performance rather than before it, and in this way standing the whole tradition of western music on its head. He also began to bring the element of randomness or chance into his works, using the ancient Chinese method of *I Ching* to decide on what course of action to pursue. In Cage's case, this took the form of tossing coins to determine the structure that his music would eventually take.

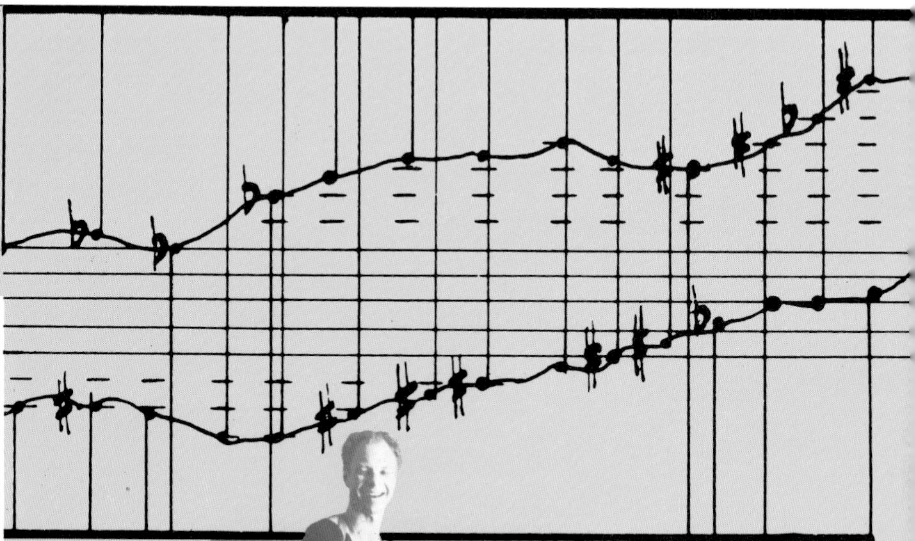

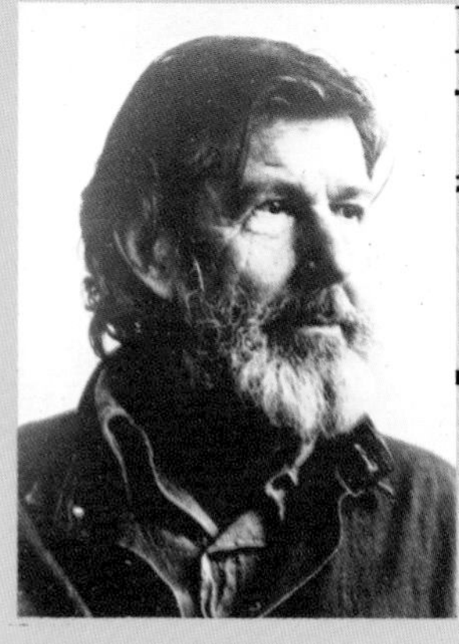

The American composer John Cage (below) was the prophet of indeterminate music – that is, music which is not fixed in a single form unchanged at each performance. A typical page (right) from his 'Concert for Piano and Orchestra' looks unconventional, although it uses a normal five-line stave. Cage says that the 'Concert' is 'presentable between minimum (nothing played) and maximum (everything played)'.

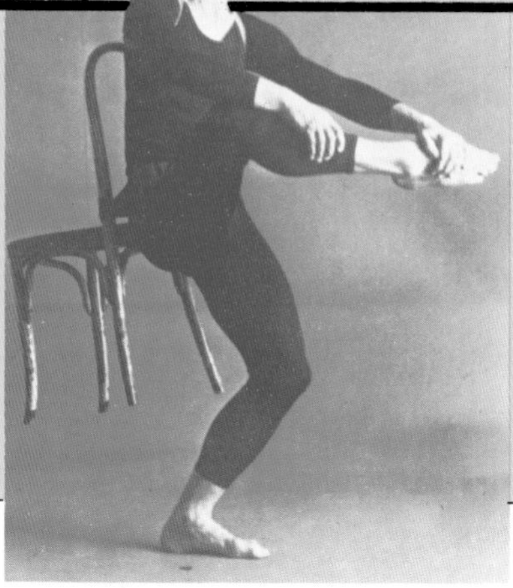

In 1943 Cage became the musical director of the ballet company run by Merce Cunningham (left), shown here dancing in his own 'Antic Meet' (1958). Born in 1919, Cunningham began his career in modern dance with Martha Graham. As well as music by Cage, his dances use music by other American composers, and by Erik Satie.

BRAKE DRUM

RICE BOWLS

ASS'S JAW

TIN CANS

Cage first came to prominence in the 1930s and '40s with works for unusual percussion instruments (left), which startled his audiences.

Cage's most original and eccentric piece dates from 1952. Called '4'33"', it is a completely silent piece for piano, during which the pianist sits at the keyboard for exactly four minues and 33 seconds, moving his hands at three widely spaced intervals to give the impression of three movements. Audiences felt that Cage was making fools of them – as he was, to a certain extent. But he also had a more serious purpose: to make people question why they were sitting at a concert at all, and above all, to make them think about the quality of silence, which is the negative image of sounded music.

This is obviously not the kind of 'music' that can have a successor, and Cage went on to a wide variety of different kinds of composition. His 'Imaginary Landscape No. 4' is a piece for 12 radios, which can never be the same on two different occasions, as the radios will pick up different stations and programmes. The 'Atlas Eclipticalis', composed in 1961, takes its name from a set of star charts. Cage laid a transparent template across the charts and marked off the stars as dots, which were then treated as notes to be played. The 'Atlas' is written for between one

and 98 orchestral players; the conductor moves his hands in circles to give the impression of the hands of a clock. It may be played either on its own or together with other Cage works, such as 'Winter Music', which can be played by any number of pianists between one and 20, and 'Cartridge Music', in which all the sounds are fed into the cartridges found in the pick-up heads of gramophones.

Cage's attitude to music is mirrored in the works of other composers who have turned to chance or 'aleatory' (from the Latin *alea*, meaning 'dice') methods in their compositions. The imprecision of his scores has been taken to extremes by Stockhausen, whose '*Aus den Sieben Tagen*' ('From the Seven Days'), described as 'intuitive music', has no notes at all, but consists of a succession of poetically phrased instructions. Cage's emphasis on silence as an element of music has been carried further by Morton Feldman, whose piano pieces are at the lowest limit of audibility. If he has achieved nothing else, John Cage has made both composers and audiences think deeply about the significance of music in the final years of the 20th century.

A Japanese philosopher, Daisetz Suzuki (left), shown here with Cage in the 1960s, had a great influence on the composer's music. Cage went to Suzuki's lectures on Zen Buddhism at Columbia University in the late 1940s, when he was already a mature composer. His studies of Zen led him to explore the use of chance in music.

Morton Feldman (left), born in 1926, is a follower of Cage and writes music of great subtlety, often at the lowest limit of audibility. In his early works he used the element of chance, but his later works are fully written out. He has composed pieces in which the players have identical parts played at different speeds, giving the effect of resonance from a single sound.

Greek composer Yannis Xenakis (left) studied music in Paris, and then worked for some years with the architect Le Corbusier before turning to full-time composing. After 1955 he introduced calculus and the theory of probabilities into 'stochastic music' (from a Greek word for 'goal' or 'target'), involving the use of computers to work out problems too complex for the brain.

Blending of opposites

In recent years players from the Far East have come to the fore in western music. One of the finest of them is the Korean violinist Kyung Wha Chung (left). In the same way western players such as Yehudi Menuhin have been attracted to the music of the East. Here Menuhin (right) is playing Indian *raga* music with Ravi Shankar, the most famous player of the sitar – an Indian lute.

MUSIC TODAY is more fluid than at any previous time in history. Now that anything from plainsong to electronic music can be heard at the flick of a switch, the divisions between different kinds of music have broken down. Not only is the entire spectrum of music immediately available: the whole of sound is now at our fingertips, as modern inventions like the Moog synthesiser and the computer produce sounds that never existed before.

Composers and performers have seized gladly on these new possibilities, rock and pop musicians more readily than 'serious' musicians. Today's audiences are growing used to seeing a symphony orchestra sitting on the same platform as a rock group, to play works by composers, such as David Bedford, who are at home in both worlds. In the same way orchestral players often provide the backing for pop groups. Some rock musicians have studied with 'conventional' composers, like the German group Can, who attended Stockhausen's classes.

Equally important is the increasing closeness of eastern and western music. The two have never been completely separate – after all, the shawm, lute and other instruments were brought back from the East many centuries ago by returning Crusaders. But in recent years, with the coming of jet travel and the reduction of the world to a 'global village', it has become possible for musicians to be equally at home all over the world. This new development is most obvious in the instrumental field. The Chinese pianist Fou Ts'ong, the Korean violinist Kyung Wha Chung and the Japanese conductor Seiji Ozawa, are typical of the trend.

Among today's composers, the Japanese Toru Takemitsu writes works such as 'November Steps' in which the classical Japanese court orchestra is combined and contrasted with a western symphony orchestra. Britten's church parables, 'Curlew River' and 'The Prodigal Son', were inspired by the music and acting of the ancient Japanese *Noh* plays. Stockhausen's music became much freer and more improvisational in the late 1960s, after a lengthy tour of the Far East. Western instrumentalists have been slower than western composers to appreciate eastern music, although Yehudi Menuhin has matched his violin with Ravi Shankar's sitar in the give-and-take of Indian *raga* music. The most versatile instrumentalist so far produced by this crossing of dividing lines is the phenomenal Japanese percussionist Stomu Yamash'ta.

For years it has been said that music is a universal language, and up to a point this is true. But there have always been obstacles to a genuinely universal music. National pride has meant that for much of the past 150 years music has been compartmentalised by countries. Eastern music has been almost a closed book until fairly recently, while popular and serious music have tended to go their own separate ways. The next few years are bound to see a new unification of the many strands of music, using conventional instruments, computers and synthesisers; chance compositions and rigidly determined ones; the familiar western 12-note scale and the far smaller intervals of eastern music. The 'harmony of the world' has been the dream of musicians down the ages. In the distant future it may be a sounding reality.

The brilliant Japanese percussionist Stomu Yamash'ta (left) has had pieces written specially for him by western composers. A revolutionary method of violin teaching was evolved by another Japanese, the teacher Shinichi Suzuki (right). His method is to teach children at a very early age – they may be as little as two years old. To begin with they learn by ear, without printed music.

The worlds of serious and popular music are no longer as rigidly separated as they once were. Symphony orchestras and rock musicians play on the same platform, and groups like the Electric Light Orchestra (above) use violin and cello, as well as the electric guitars of rock.

One hundred top composers

compiled by Hugo Cole

All the composers in this section have made a unique contribution to music, and are included for that reason. The unquestionably great composers – Bach, Mozart, Beethoven, Brahms – are here. But so, too, are the march king Sousa and the waltz king Strauss, because there were no others like them. Many worthwhile composers have been omitted – because they are so remote in time or because their music is so difficult as to be only of specialist interest. If all the composers who continue to stir our emotions or bring us delight were included, they would number thousands rather than hundreds.

Arnold, Malcolm (b.1921)
English composer who began his career as an orchestral trumpeter. He is best known for his film scores and works for light entertainment, in which his gifts as an inventor of catchy tunes and an inspired orchestrator find ample scope.

Bach, Johann Sebastian (1685-1750)
German composer and organist. He spent most of his life at Weimar and Leipzig, where he won fame as a keyboard-player, improvisor and indefatigable composer of music for the church and for the entertainment of noble patrons. Although most of the great composers who succeeded him were familiar with his 48 keyboard Preludes and Fugues, for many years after his death he was remembered only as a learned contrapuntal composer and as the father of C.P.E. Bach (1714-88), a great innovator but a minor composer. Today he is recognised as a universal genius and as a central figure in the development of western classical music.

Balakirev, Mily Alexeievich (1837-1910)
Russian composer, pianist and teacher, who founded the School of Music in St Petersburg, at which the works of many leading nationalist composers were played. Despite the fact that his own output was small, he lead the way in using traditional Russian themes, and in introducing exotic, near-Eastern elements into concert works.

Bartók, Béla (1881-1945)
Hungarian pianist and composer who evolved a national style based on the folk music of his country. His earliest works, which are colourful and picturesque, are tinged with romanticism. These were

succeeded by music that was generally harsher and more extreme in style. In the 1920s he emerged as a leading figure in European contemporary music, and in time he became one of the most powerful and individual composers of his age. In 1940 he settled in America, and lived there for the rest of his life. His graded piano pieces, called 'Mikrokosmos', form one of the best introductions to music of the 1920s and '30s.

Beethoven, Ludwig van (1770-1827)
Born in Germany, he spent most of his life in Vienna, where he quickly won fame – first as a remarkable pianist, then as a great composer. Revered by his contemporaries, he was also criticised for the obscurity, eccentricity or violence of his music. He broke through the conventions of his time to establish his own powerful individuality, and enlarged the boundaries of the symphony, sonata, quartet and concerto. Although he was as unsuccessful in love as he was as guardian to a much-loved nephew and, after the onset of deafness in 1801, became increasingly solitary and unhappy, he showed the same largeness of vision and generosity of spirit in life as in his music.

Bellini, Vincenzo (1801-35)
Italian opera composer who wrote three or four operas which remained in favour all over Europe throughout the 19th century and which are still revived to display the talents of great singers in the bel canto ('beautiful song') tradition.

Berg, Alban (1885-1935)
Austrian composer who was an early and devoted pupil of Schoenberg and the first of that composer's students to win world fame. His Violin Concerto and the operas 'Wozzeck' and 'Lulu' – all

complex, highly expressive and richly sensuous – are the last autumnal fruits of the romantic age. His later works, composed on strict 12-note principles, demonstrate the way in which 'serial' techniques can be made to serve many musical purposes.

Berio, Luciano (b.1925)
Italian composer who was among the first to experiment with unorthodox ways of producing sounds from voices and instruments in his series of 'Sequenzas' for solo instruments, he explored the latest avant-garde playing techniques, often introducing actions as well as sounds into his scores. He also experimented with electronic music at an early date. Despite this, many of his works are lyrical and easy to listen to, preserving typical Italian clarity and directness.

Berlioz, Hector (1803-69)
French composer whose picturesque, illustrative works outraged the musical establishment of his day, although they formed the basis of modern orchestral technique. He was also a virtuoso conductor, visiting all the great cities of Europe to direct his own works. He never won more than grudging acceptance in his native country, and died a disappointed man.

Bernstein, Leonard (1918-91)
One of the most versatile of all American musicians who had outstanding gifts of communication as pianist, conductor, educator and composer. His music is emotional, colourful and designed to make an immediate impact on mass audiences (and often suspect in 'highbrow' circles for precisely that reason). It owes

something to Stravinsky and Copland as well as to jazz, Broadway shows and traditional Jewish music.

Birtwistle, Harrison (b.1934)
English composer, one of the younger generation of composers who have brought a traditional sense of drama back into music. Two of his best-known works to date are the opera 'Punch and Judy' and the orchestral 'The Triumph of Time'

Bizet, Georges (1838-75)
French composer. A star pupil of the Paris conservatoire, whose earliest works show the same lightness of touch and genius for vivid orchestration that marks his great opera, 'Carmen'. His earliest operas contain arias and ensembles of great interest and beauty, but he only broke through the conventions of his time with 'Carmen' itself.

Borodin, Alexander (1833-87)
Russian composer who was also a doctor and a professor of chemistry. Perhaps the most gifted of the group of nationalist composers known as 'The Five', he remained an amateur all his life. His works include two symphonies, two quartets, many songs, and the unfinished opera, 'Prince Igor'.

Boulez, Pierre (b.1925)
French composer and conductor. A pupil of Messiaen, he became a leading experimenter in the total organisation of musical material. In his works he has created new types of ensemble-sound, characteristically sharp, clear and brittle. As a conductor, he has campaigned unceasingly for contemporary music.

Brahms, Johann (1833-97)
German composer who showed early talent as a pianist and for a time earned his living playing in taverns and dance halls. The violinist Joachim, having heard him play on a concert tour, introduced him to Liszt and to Robert and Clara Schumann, who became his close friends and encouraged him to compose. Although his early music is as romantic as that of Schumann, he became increasingly conscious of his role as upholder of the great tradition of the classical symphonists, and was apparently never tempted to write opera or 'programme' music. His abstract instrumental works show mastery of large-scale form and every sort of technical device. The tone of voice is grave, but the lyrical warmth of his themes and his fine sense of musical drama give life and impetus to even the most serious and complex of his major works.

Britten, Benjamin (1913-76)
The most versatile and resourceful English composer since Purcell. He was also a fine pianist and conductor, although in his last years the after-effects of a stroke restricted many of his activities. Much of his music was written for particular performers, as commissioned material, or for the Aldeburgh Festival, which he founded in 1948 and where many of his major works were first performed. His music for amateurs and children, like his operas and the 'War Requiem', is sung and played all over the world.

Bruckner, Anton (1824-96)
Austrian organist and composer of nine symphonies. In 1868 he was appointed professor at the Vienna Conservatory, but his enthusiasm for Wagner (which is reflected in his music) led leading Viennese critics and musicians to ignore or oppose him. It was only in his last years that his serious, romantic and noble symphonies began to win favour in Austria, and only since the Second World War that they have taken their place in the world repertory.

Byrd, William (1543-1623)
English composer of vocal and instrumental music, who wrote both for the Catholic and the Anglican Churches. He became organist of the Chapel Royal in London and, together with Thomas Tallis, was given an exclusive license to print music of all kinds in England.

Cage, John (1912-92)
American composer and a leading avant-gardist of his generation. He broke new ground with 'prepared pianos', in introducing experimental notations into music, and in his highly individual use of electronics. He also staged elaborate mixed-media events and became involved in Eastern philosophies.

Chabrier, Emmanuel (1814-94)
French composer. Although his full-scale, somewhat Wagnerian opera 'Gwendoline' had considerable success in the 1880s and '90s, his most individual works are the shorter orchestral pieces and songs. Their exuberance, colour and boldness in harmony and orchestration established a tradition for entertainment works in the high style – civilised, yet often with a touch of parody or irreverence.

Chopin, Frederic (1810-49)
One of the greatest of the pianist-composers. He was born in Poland but spent much of his working life in Paris, where he earned a living teaching, playing at aristocratic soirées, and giving occasional public concerts. He was a bold harmonic innovator and a fine melodist, owing something to Bellini. Although he was not a virtuoso performer in Liszt's class, he discovered a new, intimate and poetic character for the 19th century piano. Pianist-composers from Liszt down to Scriabin, Rachmaninov and Prokofiev have been

influenced by his far-reaching technical and musical inventions.

Copland, Aaron (1900-91)
American composer, trained in Paris, whose earlier works, often severe and dissonant, put him among the most advanced composers of the inter-war years. In the 1930s he adopted a plainer, more accessible style and reached a wider audience with his film, ballet and theatre scores which still provide the models for many concert works and film scores which have an 'American' flavour.

Couperin, François (1668-1733)
The most distinguished of a large family of French musicians. He became organist to Louis XIV and won fame as a composer for harpsichord-playing. The proper effect of his music for harpsichord depends largely on the elegant and idiomatic playing of ornaments and decorative passages.

Debussy, Claude-Achille (1862-1918)
French composer who was the most subtle harmonist of his age. He rebelled against tradition to create music in which timbre, texture, as well as the colour and 'taste' of sounds were all-important. His piano preludes, which greatly extend the technical range of the instrument, and his opera 'Pelléas et Mélisande', written throughout in a low-key conversational tone (deriving at a distance from Mussorgsky's 'Boris Godunov'), are among his most radical works.

Delius, Frederick (1862-1934)
English composer who spent some years as an orange painter in Florida before devoting himself to music. He studied in Leipzig where he came under the influence of Grieg. From 1889 until his death he lived in France, and in his last years suffered from paralysis and blindness. His operas and choral works, like his better known short orchestral pieces, are rich and subtle in harmony, romantic in mood and contemplative in spirit.

Donizetti, Gaetano (1797-1848)
After Rossini, the most versatile and brilliant Italian composer of his age. He wrote over 60 operas in a working life of 26 years. 'Don Pasquale', the last in a tradition of opera buffa, still holds the stage. Many of his other operas have also been revived in recent years.

Dvořák, Antonin (1841-1904)
The most versatile of the great Czech composers of the 19th

century. His colourful, genial and dramatic symphonies, concertos and chamber works reflect the character of Czech music. His gifts as a melodist and his masterly orchestration are unique and personal. His music quickly found favour in western Europe and also in America, where he spent three years teaching. He also visited England on nine occasions.

Elgar, Edward (1857-1934)
English composer, who was largely self-taught and spent many years as violinist and teacher in his native Worcestershire before his oratorios and orchestral works brought him national fame in the 1900s. Always a traditionalist, he used the idioms of late romanticism and the 19th-century orchestra with a skill that no other English composer had equalled. In later life he felt himself increasingly out of touch with the spirit of the new age, and wrote little music.

Falla, Manuel de (1876-1946)
Spanish composer who, while studying in Paris, acquired many of the characteristics of the leading French composers of his day. His best works, including the ballets 'Love the Magician' and 'The Three-Cornered Hat', are based on Spanish folk music and are rhythmical, passionate and pungent. A meticulous craftsman and a perfectionist, he wrote no more music after he emigrated to the Argentine in 1938.

Gershwin

Fauré, Gabriel (1854-1924)
French teacher and composer of many fine songs and chamber works. Most of his music is lyrical rather than dramatic – his serene and unspectacular 'Requiem' typically omits the 'Dies Irae' ('Day of Wrath') movement. He was a subtle and original harmonist, and a great teacher who became director of the Paris Conservatoire, where Ravel was among his pupils.

Franck, César (1822-90)
Belgian organist and composer who was educated in France. He was the first of a number of serious and idealistic composers of abstract music who shared an enthusiasm for the later works of Beethoven and Wagner and who experimented in 'cyclic forms', using short themes which recur throughout a work. His finest pieces are vigorous and fervent, very French in melody and sentiment.

Gabrieli, Giovanni (1557-1612)
Italian composer who was also organist of St Mark's in Venice for many years. In his numerous noble and brilliant motets and instrumental works, he often made use of independant groups of instrumental performers, sometimes widely separated in space and each with his specific musical role. In this he anticipated the later developments of the classical orchestra, with its contrasting groups of instruments.

Gershwin, George (1898-1937)
American composer of songs, revues and musical comedies. He

brought down the idioms of popular music into the concert hall and opera house with his 'Rhapsody in Blue', 'American in Paris' and the opera 'Porgy and Bess'

Gibbons, Orlando (1583-1625)
English composer who became organist of the Chapel Royal, London, and later of Westminster Abbey. He wrote a great deal of fine music for the church, 30 'Fantasies' for viols, and was one of the last great composers of madrigals. His motet 'Hosanna to the Son of David' and 'The Silver Swan' and 'What is our life?' are among the classics of the English choral repertory.

Glass, Philip (b.1937)
American composer and leading member of the so-called 'minimalist school', by which a composer uses a minimal number of notes or chords in a piece. Even so, Glass has written whole operas by such means, including 'Einstein on the Beach'.

Glinka, Mikhail Ivanovich (1804-57)
Known as 'The Father of Russian music', he may perhaps be more accurately described as 'the first great composer who happened to be a Russian'. He acknowledged his origins by basing his operas on national themes. He made some use of Russian folk music and of the near-Eastern scales and intervals much loved by later Russian composers. His music is vigorous, tuneful and brilliantly orchestrated, deriving from classical models, particularly from Italian opera.

Gluck, Christoph von (1714-87)
German composer who lived and worked mainly in Italy and France. His earliest operas were written in the conventional Italian manner, but in 'Orfeo' and 'Alcestis' he adopted a simpler style, subordinating the music to dramatic requirements. In Paris, he continued to write operas in both the new and old styles. Mozart, in composing 'Idomeneo', was much influenced by Gluck's classical operas, which also provided the models and inspiration for Berlioz's 'Les Troyens'.

Gounod, Charles (1818-93)
French composer whose fame rests mainly on 'Faust', for many years the most popular of all grand operas. His oratorios and cantatas, too lavish and emotional for modern tastes, were greatly admired in Victorian England. He was a skilled and individual harmonist, melodist and orchestrator.

Granados, Enrique (1867-1916)
Spanish pianist and composer. In the 'Goyescas' he used tunes and dance rhythms from many parts of Spain, brilliantly translating them into virtuoso piano studies about

Granados

losing the essential flavour of the original folk models. His songs include the beautiful 'Maiden and the Nightingale'.

Greig, Edvard (1843-1907)
The first Norwegian composer to win a world-wide reputation. Although folk influences shape and colour most of his music, he was also a harmonic innovator who prepared the way for later 20th-century musical impressionists. The Piano Concerto and the music for 'Peer Gynt' contain much of the essential Greig, but he was at

his best when working on a small scale: his many short piano pieces and songs are perfect of their kind.

Grieg

Handel, George Frideric (1685-1759)
German composer who made his name in Germany and Italy before he first visited England in 1710. He became an English citizen in 1726 and, until his death, dominated the English musical scene as performer, impresario and composer. For almost a hundred years after his death his oratorios formed the staple diet of English choral societies and provided the models against which the works of English composers were measured. In opera, oratorio and instrumental works the force of his genius was dramatic, immediate and direct. He exploited the virtuosity of performers to the full, yet often achieved the grandest effects by the simplest of methods.

Haydn, Joseph (1732-1809)
Austrian composer who spent most of his life in the service of noble households in Austria and Hungary, notably at Esterháza. There he composed for the use of the resident musicians, many of the symphonies and quartets that were to spread his fame across Europe and to form the basis of the classical repertory. Some of his finest symphonies were written for performance in Paris and London, which he visited twice in the 1790s. His oratorios, church music and opera are as genial, resourceful and full of human warmth as the rest of his music, but it is in the instrumental works that his musical character emerges most vividly and dramatically.

Henze, Hans Werner (b.1926)
One of the most brilliant and versatile of contemporary composers, he was born in Germany and now lives in Italy. His works range from fairly conventional operas and symphonies, which have gone the rounds of the world's major opera houses and concert halls, to experimental theatre pieces, electronic music, brass band music, and politically orientated works which use every sort of dramatic and musical means to convey a left-wing message.

Hindemith, Paul (1895-1963)
German viola-player and composer. In the 1920s he was a leader of the 'neo-classical' movement and a prolific producer of angular and energetic contrapuntal works, including 'utility music', of striking originality. His later music is less dissonant and less determinedly anti-romantic, although as resourceful in its use of compositional device. He settled in America in 1939 and remained active as composer, theorist and teacher.

Holst, Gustav (1874-1934)
English composer and teacher who began his career as a professional trombonist. Folk music, eastern philosophy and a life-long friendship with Vaughan Williams influenced his outlook and music. His works range from the brilliant orchestral suite 'The Planets', to the short chamber opera 'Savitri', and include many occasional pieces for amateurs.

Ives, Charles (1874-1954)
American composer whose early experiments with unorthodox intervals, rhythms and instruments, and use of popular material in 'serious' works outraged conventional musicians of the time. Discouraged by lack of understanding, he devoted himself increasingly to his successful insurance

business. He lived to see the beginning of a great interest in his music in the 1940s and '50s, but his works are still written about more frequently than they are performed.

Janáček, Leos (1854-1924)
Czech composer whose highly individual style grew out of the folk music and speech rhythms of his native land. His mosaic-like methods of construction owe nothing to classical models, and his genius was little appreciated in Czechoslovakia or elsewhere during his lifetime. But his choral works, chamber music, and above all his operas, have become increasingly popular in recent years.

Khachaturian, Aram (1903-78)
Russian composer in the traditionalist mould. His colourful and exuberant ballet scores and piano concertos, much influenced by the music of his native Armenia, have become popular with audiences in the West as well as in Russia.

Kodály, Zoltán (1882-1967)
Hungarian composer, collector of folk music and educationalist. A brilliant orchestrator and natural melodist, he was the first Hungarian of stature to compose in a recognisably national idiom. He also wrote much for children and amateurs and evolved a system of musical education for Hungarian schools which is used in many parts of the world.

Lassus, Roland de (1530-94)
One of the most versatile composers of his age who, although born in France, spent much of his working life in Italy and Bavaria. His church music and madrigals became widely known throughout Europe during his own lifetime. Only Palestrina among the 16th-century composers of church music equalled him in range and skill, although Lassus was bolder and more experimentally-inclined of the two.

Ligeti, György (b.1923)
Hungarian composer now living in Germany. He is the main creator of a new kind of music in which colour, timbre and atmosphere are all-important. He is also a specialist in the use of clusters of notes, very small intervals between notes, and intricate free-running parts which together produce ever-changing clouds of sound.

Liszt, Franz (1811-86)
Hungarian conductor and composer who was also the most famous pianist of his time. In middle age he renounced his career as a virtuoso and became musical director at Weimar, where he actively supported Berlioz, Wagner and other revolutionary composers of the day. In 1865 he took minor orders, becoming the Abbé Liszt. In later years he taught many piano pupils, and became honorary director of the Budapest Conservatory. His technical and harmonic innovations had a great influence on later 19th-century romantics, including Wagner and Franck.

Lully, Jean-Baptiste (1632-87)
Italian-born composer, violinist and dancer. He acquired a virtual monopoly on every opera performed in french as musical director at the court of Louis XIV. With his operas and dance music, he established conventions which remained unchallenged in France for almost a hundred years.

Mahler, Gustav (1860-1911)
Austrian conductor and composer. His song-cycles and nine symphonies were conceived on the grandest scale but are intensely personal in their expression of human emotions. As director of the Vienna State Opera he created new standards in opera production. He experimented boldly with unconventional instruments in his own works, and brought the subtle nuances of chamber music to the symphony orchestra. His latter years were mostly spent in America, as director of the New York Philharmonic Orchestra.

Maxwell Davies, Peter (b.1934)
English composer who was influenced by medieval techniques as well as by Stravinsky and Schoenberg. Much of his work has been written for the Fires of London, a chamber group which he directs himself. He now lives in the Orkney Islands, off the north coast of Scotland, where he directs the annual Music Festival which he founded in 1977.

Mendelssohn, Felix (1809-47)
German composer who combined a poetic imagination with classical purity of style. His music was often performed in England during the 19th century, when his oratorio, 'Elija', rivalled Handel's 'Messiah' in popoular favour. Today his fame rests mainly on his small piano pieces and the orchestral works, which include the 'Italian' Symphony, a violin concerto, several fine concert overtures and the music for 'A Midsummer night's Dream'.

Messiaen, Olivier (1908-92)
French organist, composer and one of the most influential teachers of his time. Much of his music is religious in inspiration, mystical and ecstatic in mood. But his later works are also highly organised according to his own system of controlling rhythms, pitches and durations. He made a deep study of birdsong and of eastern melodic and rhythmic techniques, and elements from both play a vital part in his music.

Milhaud, Darius (1892-1974)
French composer of almost 400 works ranging from light entertainment pieces to large-scale operas and opera-oratorios. One of the first neo-classicists, he experimented boldly with polytonality, with Latin American instruments and rhythms, and also with jazz, without losing his spontaneity and exuberant melodic invention.

Monteverdi, Claudio (1567-1643)
Italian composer who was active in Mantua and Venice as court and church composer. He was a master of both the older contrapuntal and the newer expressive manners. The modern revival of interest in early music has reinstated him as the first great composer in whose operas all available resources are made to serve the main dramatic purpose. His compositions include the 'Vespers' and many madrigals.

Mozart, Wolfgang Amadeus (1756-91)
Born in Austria, he spent much of his youth travelling round Europe with his sister and father, who exibited the children as musical prodigies. He spent some years unhappily in the service of the Archbishop of Salzburg, but after

1781 he earned a precarious living as a freelance performer and composer. He wrote his first symphonies when he was eight, and thereafter produced a continuous series of major and minor works (almost all written to commission or for immediate performance) until his death. Only a few of his masterpieces were hailed with enthusiasm during his lifetime, and he was constantly disappointed in his applications for steady employment. Many of his contemporaries found his music difficult and obscure, only a few fellow-composers (including Haydn) recognised the extent of his genius.

Mussorgsky, Modeste (1839-81)
Russian composer who was largely self-taught. After a career in the army followed by one as a civil servant, he devoted himself to music. His rugged and individual style was much admired by Debussy, but his work became known mainly through rearranged and polished versions made by Rimsky-Korsakov and other composers. Today his masterpiece, 'Boris Godunov', is recognised as one of the most original and completely Russian of all operas.

Nielsen, Carl (1865-1931)
Denmark's greatest and most influential composer. He was for some years a violinist in the Royal Orchestra, later its conductor and then director of the national Conservatory. His fame rests mainly on his six symphonies, which are epic works – plain, direct and vigorous – and more nearly related to those of Sibelius than to the central European tradition.

Offenbach, Jacques (1819-80)
Composer, named after his birthplace, Offenbach-am-Main in Germany. He came to Paris as a boy and established himself, first as a cellist, then as a prolific composer of songs and almost 100 operettas. Many of these were in one act and on the smallest scale, and almost all were light-hearted and satirical. In 1855 he became manager of his own theatre. His most ambitious opera, 'The tales of Hoffman', was completed after his death, and won instant and lasting success.

Palestrina, Giovanni (1525-94)
The most illustrious Italian composer of church music in his time. His many Masses, motets and madrigals, written in a pure euphonious style, formed the main basis from which the music of the Roman Catholic Church developed over three centuries or more.

Penderecki, Krzysztof (b.1933)
Polish composer who is a pioneer in the use of new sounds. He introduced clusters of notes, quarter-tones and sliding tones, as well as unorthodox methods of performing such as key-rattling (woodwind), playing on the wrong side of the bridge (strings), and blowing through mouthpieces (brass). His music, however, is generally simple in overall structure and strongly dramatic in effect, and is not too difficult for the ordinary listener.

Poulenc, Francis (1899-1963)
Traditionalist French composer who was an individual harmonist and worked most happily on a small scale. The sophisticated gaiety of his earlier works won him a reputation as a parodist. But his operas, church music, and particularly his songs and choral works, despite their unpretentious simplicity, reveal a serious and contemplative side to his character.

Prokofiev, Sergei (1891-1953)
Russian pianist and composer who between 1918 and 1932 lived mainly in France. There is brilliant, often satirical works earned him a reputation as one of the playboys of the musical world. After his return to his native Russia he softened his acid, angular style (although without losing his distinctive personality) and wrote many film scores, ballets, choral and instrumental works which were designed to appeal to a wider, non-specialist audience.

Puccini, Giacomo (1858-1924)
The most famous and successful of 20th-century Italian opera composers. He was a fine melodist and an original harmonist, although there were occasions when he borrowed tricks from his contemporaries. He was above all a great man of the theatre, who subordinated librettists and producers to his own will, and knew precisely how to obtain the dramatic effects he had in mind. Almost all his works have remained in the world repertory.

Purcell, Henry (1659-95)
The greatest and most versatile of all English composers. He became organist of Westminster Abbey and the main composer of ceremonial and state music, first for James II, then for William and Mary. He composed in the older contrapuntal manner as well as in the latest styles imported from France and Italy. He wrote much for the theatre and showed unrivalled skill in setting words to music.

Rachmaninov, Sergei (1873-1943)
Russian composer and pianist who won wide popularity with his first three piano concertos and a few solo works for piano. His music, in the romantic tradition and generally sombre in tone, also includes two symphonies, a rhapsody on Paganini's most famous theme and many fine songs. After 1918 he lived in exile, mainly in the United States of America.

Rameau, Jean Philippe (1683-1764)
The most distinguished French composer of his time. In his operas and opera-ballets he continued and developed further the formal and courtly style first evolved by Lully. He developed the theory of harmony that governed classical music.

Ravel, Maurice (1875-1937)
One of the most original French composers of the 20th century. He was a master of precise effects, whose works combine classical clarity of texture and structure with sensuous and often sumptuous harmony and orchestration. His output was small: after a car accident in 1935 he suffered from mental paralysis and wrote no more.

Rimsky-Korsakov, Nickolai (1844-1908)
One of the most distinguished and influential of the Russian nationalist composers, who turned to music after an early career in the navy. The individuality of his best works lies largely in their brilliant orchestration. He became Professor of Composition at St Petersburg, and edited or prepared for performance many of the unfinished scores of Mussorgsky and Borodin. His most famous pupil was Stravinsky.

Rossini, Gioacchino
(1792-1868)
Italian opera composer who, from 1812 to 1826, reigned supreme in Europe as provider of both comic and serious opera. He was honoured and fêted in London and Paris, where he lived after 1824. His last operas were written for the French stage. After the comparative failure of 'William Tell' (1829) he retired from the operatic scene. Although he composed little music of any kind thereafter, even the smallest pieces of later years show that his wit and mastery of musical technique never deserted him.

Saint-Saëns, Camille
(1835-1921)
French pianist who was one of the most skilled and prolific composers of his time. In his youth he was regarded as a musical revolutionary, but in later life he was thought of as among the main supporters of the French classical tradition. His best works have a classical clarity of texture and form and contain many memorable tunes and striking inventions of harmony or orchestral colour.

Satie, Erik (1866-1925)
French composer, humorist and eccentric who produced music of childlike simplicity, charm and innocence. He became the figurehead of younger French composers who reacted against the obscurity and pretentiousness of the musical establishment, and is still venerated for his attitudes as well as his music, by many of today's avant-garde composers.

Scarlatti, Domenico
(1685-1732)
Italian composer and harpsichordist who emigrated first to Portugal and then to Spain. In Spain he wrote most of the 550 one-movement sonatas on which his fame is based. Drawing on the rhythms, harmonies

and tunes of Spanish music, these display hitherto unknown varieties of keyboard virtuosity.

Schoenberg, Arnold (1874-1951)
Austrian teacher, theorist and composer, who worked mainly in Vienna and Berlin until forced by Nazi persecution to emigrate to America in 1933. His first works, romantic and planned on the grandest scale, established him early in the century as a notable composer. But he quickly abandoned traditional attitudes. His later works, incomprehensible to the majority, made a great impact on the contemporary musical world. In the 1920s he evolved the 12-note method of composition – 'with 12 notes related only to one another' – in which almost all his later works were written. After he settled in America he taught harmony and counterpoint. His music was little played or appreciated in his lifetime, and still poses difficulties for today's listeners.

Schubert, Franz (1797-1828)
Austrian composer, the son of a schoolmaster, who for many years taught in his father's school. He never held a permanent musical post, much of his music being written for his immediate friends, or for the amateur societies of Vienna. During his short and uneventful life, he produced masterpieces in every field except opera. He was virtually the inventor of 'romantic harmony' and of the *Lied*: the solo song with accompaniment, in which the piano comments on and illustrates the words and mood.

Schumann, Robert (1810-56)
German pianist and composer. He was a romantic, often inspired by extra-musical ideas, who nevertheless was much influenced by Bach, particularly in his keyboard works. He married the pianist Clara Wieck, who became famous as an interpreter of his music. After a serious mental breakdown in 1851, he composed little, and died insane.

Shostakovich, Dmitri (1906-75)
Russian composer who won early attention with his First Symphony, written while he was still a student. His first compositions are generally dissonant, angular and often satirical in tone. Although his more extreme work was condemned by the Soviet authorities in 1936, he was quickly reinstated in public

favour. Thereafter he showed ability to write both the big public works demanded of him by the state as well as introspective and personal music without compromising his musical character. This emerges in the 15 symphonies and 15 quartets, as one of the most powerful of the century.

Sibelius, Jean (1865-1957)
Finland's greatest composer. He was an independent, who evolved in his seven symphonies and many tone-poems an idiom and mode of construction which owed little to either his predecessors or contemporaries. His music, plain and generally serious in tone, has for long been particularly well-loved in England and America.

Smetana, Bedřich (1824-84)
The first major Czech composer to develop a distinctive national style. His descriptive tone-poems on national and patriotic themes, and his most popular opera, 'The Bartered Bride', which derives directly from folk material, form the basis of the national repertory. He actively campaigned for Czech music, and organised the first opera performances at the Prague National Theatre in the 1860s.

Sousa, John Philip (1854-1933)
American bandmaster who toured the world with his own virtuoso band (the ancestor of today's 'Symphonic Wind Bands'). Several of his operas were produced with some success, but he is remembered today for his exuberant and inventive marches.

Stockhausen, Karlheinz (b.1928)
German composer and teacher who travels widely, directing and organising performances of his own music. He was a pioneer of electronic music and the music of chance, and devised new

methods of sound production and plots for musical action. His works, and the inventive ideas behind them, have had a great influence on younger composers, particularly those in western Europe.

Strauss, Johann (II) (1825-99)
Son of the Austrian violinist-composer Johann Strauss (I). He followed in his father's footsteps as a prolific composer of waltzes, polkas and marches, and as director of his own orchestra. He developed the concert-waltz and later the Viennese operetta, delighting a musical élite as well as the general public with his elegant, aristocratic light music.

Strauss, Richard (1864-1949)
German composer. His earliest tone-poems and operas, much influenced by Wagner but more extreme in their structural ingenuity and free use of dissonance, marked him out as the leading rebel and modernist of the 1900s. His later works are less adventurous, although the operas still reveal his power as a musical illustrator of endless resource and as a creator of subtle complexities of sound.

Stravinsky, Igor (1882-1971)
Russian composer who was a pupil of Rimsky-Korsakov. With his three great ballet scores 'The Firebird', 'Petrushka' and 'The Rite of Spring', he established himself between 1910 and 1913 as a thoroughly Russian composer, and as a master of large-scale effects who had little respect for past traditions. From 1914 to 1939 he lived first in Switzerland, then in Paris, where he won a second reputation as an internationalist and entertainer of genius. He settled in America in 1939. After the Mozartian opera 'The Rake's Progress' (1951), he abandoned the 'neo-classical' manner of the 1920s. His last works, composed on strict 'serial' principles, again explore new ground.

Tallis, Thomas (c. 1505-85)
English organist who became, with Byrd, joint master of the Chapel Royal in London. He composed mainly church music, both in Latin and in English, much of which is still sung in Anglican cathedrals. His most famous work is a Mass written in 40 separate parts.

Tchaikovksy, Peter Ilyich
(1804-93)
Russian composer who was influenced as much by Bizet and Massenet as by Russian folk music, and whose idol was Mozart. Although his output was uneven, he wrote great works in almost every musical genre. He was a subtle and original melodist and harmonist, his music directly expressing his own passionate and often melancholy nature. He died of cholera just after the first performance of his greatest symphony, the *'Pathétique'*.

Tippett, Michael (b.1905)
English composer. After many years as a teacher and conductor of amateur choirs and orchestras, he produced a series of major works of power and imagination, beginning with the oratorio, 'A Child of Our Time' (1941). His earlier style, influenced by the Elizabethan madrigal composers, has undergone many transformations. His symphonies and operas, for which he is also the librettist, reflect a philosophical, visionary approach to music.

Varèse, Edgar (1885-1965)
French composer who settled in America in 1915, where he became a leading figure in the 'new music' movement, organising concerts at which contemporary works were performed. His own music is extreme in its avoidance of all traditional processes, creating virtually a new language founded on the use of tiny, often-repeated melodic or rhythmic fragments and using unconventional assemblies of instruments and sound-producing objects.

Vaughan Williams, Ralph
(1872-1958)
English composer and a pioneer of the folk music revival. His vocal and instrumental works alike tend to be written in a flowing, song-like idiom much

influenced by folk traditions. He wrote many works for amateurs, and was regarded by many as the father-figure of English music from the 1930s until the time of his death.

Verdi, Giuseppe (1813-1901)
Italian opera composer who wrote his first music for the local band of his home town, Bussetto. He studied privately at Milan, although not at the Conservatory, which refused him admission. His third opera, 'Nabucco' (1842), was a resounding success. In the following 23 operas, written over a period of 50 years, he refined the art of popular Italian opera. His later works are as vigorous and tuneful, and often as melodramatic, as the earlier works, but characters and their relationships are explored in music of wonderful variety and subtlety, while the orchestra comes to play an increasingly important role in the drama. Although he became a national hero, in later life he lived a secluded life on his farm at Sant' Agata.

Villa-Lobos, Heitor (1887-1959)
Brazilian composer, pianist, conductor and teacher who trained in Paris. For many years the leading figure in South American music, he made much use of native Indian instruments and rhythms, and was influenced by improvised folk music, and also by the spirit of Bach and 'neo-classicism'. In his music — which is as exuberant, picturesque and confident as he was himself — old and new, popular, traditional and classical, all meet and blend in new ways.

Vivaldi, Antonio (1678-1741)
Italian priest, violinist and composer who, for many years, taught music in a girls' orphanage in Venice. He wrote operas, church music, symphonies and concertos for strings, or strings and wind, mostly in a light and brilliant style. His string concertos exploit the technical possibilities of instruments with great skill and imagination, and are much performed today.

Wagner, Richard (1813-83)
German composer, largely self-taught, who wrote his first opera at the age of 19. He held conducting posts at various small opera houses and in 1843 became second conductor at Dresden, where his first mature opera, 'The Flying Dutchman', was produced. Forced to leave Dresden for political reasons, he

settled in Switzerland in 1849. From 1864 until his death he was largely supported by Ludwig II of Bavaria. In 1871 he moved to Bayreuth where he produced 'The Ring of the Nibelungs' (1876), in which he realised his vision of a new kind of music-drama that combined music, words, action and décor. He wrote his own librettos and many essays on musical subjects and showed genius as conductor and producer of his own works.

Weber, Carl Maria von
(1782-1826)
German composer, conductor and pianist. He created the German romantic opera, in which the orchestra plays a more important role than it had in any previous opera. Although his last two operas, 'Euryanthe' and 'Oberon', were hampered by inadequate librettos, they contain some of his finest music and pointed the direction that Wagner was later to follow.

Webern, Anton von (1883-1945)
Austrian composer who was one of Schoenberg's most distinguished pupils. He became conductor of 'workmen's symphony concerts' in Vienna, but in later years lived a secluded life, devoting himself to teaching and composition. He was accidentally shot during the allied occupation of Austria. In his very short works the timbre counts as much as the motifs, in which every note is often assigned to a different instrument. His precisely planned music has provided the inspiration for many 'serial' composers of the postwar years.

Weill, Kurt (1900-50)
German composer who distinguished himself in contemporary intellectual music circles before he won instant fame with 'The Threepenny Opera' in 1928. This was written in collaboration with Bertold Brecht, with whom he worked on several more operas. All of them were written in a direct and often harsh jazz-influenced idiom. In 1934 he emigrated to America where he made a second reputation as composer of musicals of a smooth and comparatively conventional type.

Wolf, Hugo (1860-1903)
Austrian composer. The last of the great writers of *Lieder* (solo songs with accompaniment) who went beyond Schubert and Schumann in matching music intimately to words and in using the piano as a vital partner in interpreting the texts. In his lifetime, he attained more fame as a ferocious critic, hostile to the music of Brahms and other traditionalists, than as a composer. He lived in great poverty and died insane.

Xenakis, Yannis (b.1922)
Composer, architect and mathematician of Greek parentage who works mainly in Paris. He is best known for his 'stochastic music', in which the detailed structure of a composition is decided by mathematical means, and sometimes by use of computer. He has also written music in the form of competitive games, and works in which natural sounds are imaginatively and remarkably transformed by electronics.

Musical terms

Compiled by Hugo Cole

This glossary of musical terms is not definitive, and is not intended as a substitute for a detailed dictionary of music. All the entries included here define terms used in the colour section of this book, and are designed to expand the information given there.

accidental: on a sheet of written music, any sharp, flat or natural that is not shown in the key signature (*see illustration*).

allegretto: fairly quick. A dynamic marking on a sheet of music (*see illustration*).

aria: literally 'an air'. Any operatic song that forms a self-contained unit.

atonal music: music without a definite key, as composed by Schoenberg and others in the early 1900s. It led directly to the more formalised serial or 12-note music.

bagatelle: literally 'a trifle' Short pieces, usually for piano.

ballade: a romantic piece (generally for piano), which is lyrical rather than dramatic in nature. Chopin's four piano ballades are the best known examples.

bar: time unit into which a piece of music is divided, corresponding to the metre (which is usually regular) of the piece.

bar lines: on a sheet of written music, the vertical lines marking the beginning and end of separate bars (*see illustration*).

baton: the stick used by a conductor to beat time and to show the performers where they should come in.

bel canto: literally 'beautiful song'. The Italian art of singing which aims at a smooth, sweet flow of sound and effortless execution of virtuoso passages.

canon: a piece of music (either vocal or instrumental) in two or more parts, in which the first part is always exactly echoed by the following part.

cantata: a word used at different periods, to describe almost every sort of work for voice (or voices) with instrumental accompaniment.

canzona: a word used mainly in the 16th and 17th centuries, to describe short pieces for voices, and later, for a keyboard or instrumental ensemble.

catches: 17th- and 18th-century songs sung in several parts. Often rounds or canons, they were mainly of English origin and were usually cheerful or even bawdy.

chorale: hymn tune of the German Protestant Church, to be sung by the congregation.

choreographer: a composer of dance movements. Balanchine and Ashton are among the best known of recent years.

chord: any combination of notes that is played or sung simultaneously.

classical: a word sometimes used (as in record catalogues) to describe 'highbrow' music; musicians use it to define only the period from Bach to Beethoven.

clef: on a sheet of written music, the sign at the beginning of a line, which indicates the pitch of the lines and spaces of the stave (*see illustration*).

concert studies: piano pieces, written for public performance rather than for practice purposes, which test or display some particular aspects of the player's technique. Franz Liszt was the master of this form.

consonance: a smooth combination of sounds; the opposite of 'dissonance'. Also called 'concord'.

consort: a term used in the 17th century to describe a group of instruments, generally of viols.

corps de ballet: the dancers who form the ensemble (corresponding to the chorus in an opera). While solo dancers have individual parts, the corps de ballet often carry out movements *en masse*.

counterpoint: (adjective, 'contrapuntal'). The interweaving of independent melodic strands (see also 'harmony' and 'fugue'). The fugue, of which Bach was the master, is the strictest form of counterpoint.

crotchet (or **quarter-note**): on a sheet of written music, the basic time unit of modern western music *(see illustration)*.

descriptive music: music written to illustrate some subject or idea, or to tell a story. Often called 'programme music', it is unlike abstract music which exists in its own right and has no reference outside itself.

dissonance: a combination of notes which sounds harsh to the the ear. Often called 'discord'.

dynamic markings: marks on a sheet of music which indicate softness or loudness; they normally range from *pp* (pianissimo), meaning 'very soft', to *ff* (fortissimo), 'very loud' (*see illustration*).

escapement: a mechanical device in the piano which releases the hammer to strike the string.

flat: on a sheet of written music, indicates that the pitch of a note is to be lowered by a semitone (*see illustration*).

fugue: a contrapuntal piece based on a short theme, known as the subject. Normally, the subject is given out at the beginning of the fugue by each voice or instrument in turn. Keyboard fugues are generally written in a fixed number of parts or 'voices' as though for an ensemble of instruments.

glees: part songs, popular with amateurs in 18th- and 19th-century England and America.

hammer: the hammer-shaped component of the piano mechanism which strikes the string when a key is depressed.

harmonic series: every musical sound is made up of a number of pure tones: the fundamental, corresponding to the main note, and the overtones, which appear on an ascending ladder at ever-diminishing intervals of pitch. Fundamental and overtones make up the 'harmonic series'.

harmony: everything that concerns chords and the relationships between them. Most music can be regarded in two ways: harmonically, in terms of chords, or contrapuntally, in terms of interweaving melodies (see also 'counterpoint').

impromptu: literally 'an extemporised piece of music'. The word is, however, most often used to describe short piano pieces, composed in advance of performance.

intermezzo: a piece of music performed between the acts of a play or opera. Occasionally, a short instrumental piece written for the concert hall.

key signature: on a sheet of written music, the group of sharps or flats at the beginning of each line showing which notes are to be 'sharpened' or 'flattened' throughout the section following (*see illustration*).

libretto: the 'book' of the opera, corresponding to the written script of a play.

Lied: (plural *Lieder*). German songs with piano accompaniment. The word is also used to describe songs written by non-German composers in the tradition established by Schubert and Schumann.

miniatures: short pieces of music, generally for piano.

Moog synthesiser: an electronic device invented by Robert Moog in the 1960s. As the name indicates, it produces sounds of every description entirely by electronic means. It is found almost exclusively in pop music.

motet: a short choral work, generally unaccompanied. Most motets are sacred, not secular, but the word has had many special meanings in different musical ages.

movement: a self-contained section of a larger piece of instrumental music. Generally, each movement progresses at its own speed and has its own distinct character.

musique concrète: the earliest form of electronic music, created in Paris in the late 1940s and early '50s. It was made up of pre-recorded natural sounds, rather than the electronically-generated sounds of later electronic music.

mute: any device which, by being attached to an instrument, damps down or subdues its normal tone.

natural: on a sheet of written music, indicates the cancellation of a sharp or flat which would otherwise be expected (*see illustration*).

neo-classical: a style of composition adopted in the 1920s and '30s by Hindemith, Stravinsky, Milhaud and other composers. Neo-classical music is generally anti-romantic in mood, formal and symmetrical in the 18th-century manner, but 'modern' in use of up-to-date harmonies. It also often imitates or caricatures the styles of earlier composers.

nocturne: a short, dreamy piano piece, often with much elaborate and decorative writing. It was developed in this form by John Field and later raised to high levels of romance by Chopin.

octave: the interval of an eighth. The notes making up an octave interval share the same letter-name and so many acoustic properties that we hear them as virtually the 'same' note (*see illustration*).

oratorio: any large-scale concert work based on a religious subject, written for soloists, chorus and orchestra.

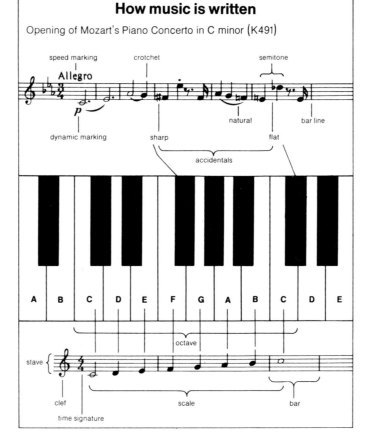

How music is written

Opening of Mozart's Piano Concerto in C minor (K491)

speed marking crotchet semitone

Allegro

dynamic marking sharp natural bar line flat

accidentals

A B C D E F G A B C D E

octave

stave

clef scale bar

time signature

orchestration: the process of setting out or arranging music so that it is playable by many instruments at the same time.

ornaments: decorative notes or passages in music constructed according to established conventions. Sometimes they are notated, sometimes added *ad lib* by the performer.

part songs: music written for several voices. The term is most often used to describe secular pieces, harmonic rather than contrapuntal, of the 19th or 20th centuries.

partita: a suite of short pieces, generally for solo instrument, which originated in the 18th century. Bach wrote partitas for keyboard and for unaccompanied violin.

pedal board: the keyboard on which the organist plays with his feet, used mainly for bass parts. The hand-keyboards of the organ are called 'manuals'.

pianissimo: very softly. A dynamic marking on a sheet of music (*pp* for short) (*see illustration*).

pitch: the 'height' of a note as registered by the human ear (to be distinguished from 'frequency', which is an objective description of vibration-rate).

polytonality: the simultaneous use of two or more distinct keys in a piece of music.

prepared piano: a piano which has been prepared in advance, or treated so that its normal action is modified to produce a variety of unorthodox percussive sounds.

programme music: music which tells a story or paints a picture (see also 'descriptive music').

proms: concerts at which the audience stands, walks or sits on the floor; especially applied to the London Proms, started by Henry Wood in 1895, and now promoted by the BBC at the Albert Hall.

quaver (or **eighth-note**): on a sheet of written music, a time unit having half the value of a crotchet.

recitative: passages for solo voice or voices in operas, cantatas or oratorios, in which the vocal line more or less follows the natural inflections and rhythms of speech. Typically, recitative is used for connecting sections between arias, and for the more prosaic conversations or explanations in operas. In music of the 18th-century and earlier, recitative is

generally lightly accompanied, the bass line and principal harmony alone being given.

reed: the vibrating tongue, made of cane, metal or plastic, used in organ pipes and in the mouthpieces of most woodwind instruments to set the air in the pipe in vibration. The clarinet and saxophone have a single reed which vibrates against the mouthpiece of the instrument. Oboes and bassoons have a double reed, in which the two parts of the reed vibrate against each other.

romantic: a word used to describe music of the post-classical period, starting with Schubert and Mendelssohn, and extending into the 1900s. Mahler, Elgar and Rachmaninov are ofter called 'late romantic' composers.

round: a short piece for voices in which the parts are identical and follow one another at regular intervals, each part starting again as soon as it ends.

sackbut: (French, *sacqueboute*.) The medieval and Renaissance ancestor of the modern trombone, narrower in bore, but essentially the same instrument.

scale: the sequence or ladder of neighbouring notes on which music is conventionally based. Western scales are generally made up of steps of a tone or a

semitone (*see illustration*). The octave's 12 semitones form the chromatic scale.

scherzo: literally 'a joke'. A light-hearted movement, nearly always in a quick tempo, found in Beethoven's sonatas and symphonies and in many later works. The scherzo succeeded the minuet of earlier times.

sea shanty: work song used in the days of sail to synchronise movement and keep up the spirits of sailors hauling on the ropes or turning the capstan.

semitone: the smallest interval of the conventional western scale (*see illustration*).

serial music: music composed in the method devised by Schoenberg, in which all 12 notes of the chromatic scale are given equal status. A 'row', consisting of the 12 notes arranged in a fixed order, provides the basic harmonic and melodic material for a movement, or for a whole work. Later composers have adapted the method, using rows of less than 12 notes, deriving other rows from the original row by semi-mathematical processes, using the row less systematically as a source of melody only, or extending the principle to cover rhythm, speed and timbre.

sharp: on a sheet of written music, indicates that the pitch of

a note is to be raised by a semitone (*see illustration*).

Singspiel: German opera, generally of a popular kind, with spoken dialogue between the musical numbers.

speech-song: (German, *Sprechgesang*). A declamation, halfway between speech and song. Sometimes (as in Schoenberg) it is carefully notated; at others it is only approximately indicated in the score.

speed markings: marks on a sheet of music which indicate the speed at which a piece should be played; they normally range from *largo*, meaning 'slow' to *prestissimo*, 'very fast' (*see illustration*).

spirituals, Negro: originally, religious songs sung by Negro slaves in the American cotton plantations; now also applied to imitation spirituals composed for professional entertainers and for domestic use.

stave (or **staff**): on a sheet of written music, the lines (five in modern western music) on which musical notes are indicated (*see illustration*).

subscription concert: one of a series of concerts for which the audience takes season tickets, generally at a special rate.

symphonic poem: also called a 'tone poem'. Extended orchestral work of the 19th and 20th centuries, which generally paints a picture, illustrates a story or describes a character.

timpani: tuned kettledrums used in orchestras and bands.

toccata: literally 'touch-piece'. Originally, the improvisation in which a keyboard-player would try out his instrument. Later, any brilliant display-piece with rapid passage-work and some massive chordal passages which show instrument and player to advantage.

tone poem: also called a 'tone picture' or 'symphonic poem'. A descriptive piece, almost always for large orchestra, based on a non-musical story or subject – 'Don Quixote' (Strauss) or '*La Mer*' (Debussy), for instance.

troubadours: wandering French musicians of medieval times who composed, sang and performed their own songs and dances.

twelve-note music: the first form of 'serial music'.

virtuoso: an outstandingly skilled player or singer who overcomes the greatest difficulties in music with apparent ease.

Further reading

As music reaches an ever wider public, a flood of new books pours out on composers' lives, on instruments and instrumental techniques, as well as on general musical history. Here the author gives a small selection of books; most are in print, while the rest can be found without much difficulty in libraries or second-hand bookshops.

General

The Number One musical dictionary is the 'Oxford Companion to Music' (OUP), by Percy A. Scholes, which was first published in 1938 and is being constantly brought up to date by experts. A smaller book is the 'Concise Oxford Dictionary of Music', also originally by Scholes. 'The Musical Companion' (Gollancz) first appeared in 1934 and has been similarly updated; it consists of long sections on various aspects of music. Otto Karolyi's 'Introducing Music' (Pelican) is a useful paperback giving basic information on how music is written and played, and Howard Sharet's 'Learn to Read Music' (Faber) explains the mysteries of musical literacy in a simple and straightforward way. 'The Music Yearbook' (A. and C. Black), edited by Arthur Jacobs, is an annual packed with statistics and background information. The most monumental book on music is Grove's 'Dictionary of Music and Musicians', published in 20 volumes.

Composers' lives

The most informative series is the Dent 'Master Musicians' series, which take the form of a biography followed by a discussion of the music. Two other series, which have shorter texts but are more heavily illustrated, are Faber's 'The Great Composers' and Midas books' 'Life and Times' series. The BBC's small 'Music Guides' are devoted to the music rather than the personalities. There are also a number of large biographical works to choose from. Some of the most interesting works are the earliest, like Anton Felix Schindler's 'Beethoven as I knew him' (Faber). Berlioz's 'Memoirs' (Gollancz), translated by David Cairns, casts a brilliant light on the French musical scene in the mid-19th century. Composers' letters always make fascinating reading, and there are various selections from the correspondence of Mozart, Beethoven, Verdi, Wagner and Schoenberg. Among 20th-century composers, Stravinsky's autobiography and conversations with Robert Craft reveal a brilliant mind, while in 'Stockhausen: Conversations with the Composer' (Picador), Jonathan Cott does the same for Stockhausen's enigmatic personality.

More books have been written about Wagner than about any other composer. Elaine Padmore's life in Faber's 'Great Composers' series is a good introduction; Ernest Newman's 'Wagner Nights' (Putnam) is a detailed analysis of the operas, while one of the most stimulating of all books is Robert Donington's 'Wagner's *Ring* and its Symbols' (Faber), which analyses Wagner's masterpiece in terms of Jungian and other symbolism.

Historical

Most historical books are aimed more at the specialist than the ordinary reader, but there are exceptions, such as Arthur Jacobs's 'A Short History of Western Music' (Pelican). 'Man and his music', by Alan Harman and Wilfrid Mellers, began life as a single-volume account in 1100 pages, and is now in four paperback volumes (Barrie and Jenkins). This whole field is surveyed in the ten volumes of the 'New Oxford History of Music'. For those who want to make a thorough study of early music, Gustave Reese's lucidly written 'Music in the Midle Ages' and 'Music in the Renaissance' (both Dent), usefully unravel the musical strands from Ancient Greece right through to the 16th-century composers of madrigals.

The last 80 years or so have seen vast musical changes which leave many people bewildered. Paul Griffiths's 'A concise History of Modern Music' (Thames and Hudson) carefully maps the main roads and byways, as does Tony Palmer's 'All You Need is Love' (Futura) for the very different worlds of jazz, pop and rock.

Instruments

A highly readable introduction, with plenty of social history and technical information, is provided by the paperback 'Musical Instruments through the Ages' (Pelican), edited by Anthony Baines. Mr Baines is also the author of two books that are unlikely to be superseded for many years to come: 'Brass Instruments' and 'Woodwind Instruments and their History' (both Faber). Even more exhaustive is 'Percussion Instruments and their History' (Faber) by James Blades. David Munrow's unique contribution to our understanding of early music lives on in his 'Instruments of the Middle Ages and Renaissance' (Oxford), which can be bought on its own, or with two illustrative records. There are a great many books on the history and workings of the piano, the most popular instrument of all time, but its players are a good deal more interesting. Their triumphs and disasters are the subject of Harold C. Schoenberg's 'The Great Pianists' (Gollancz).

Behind the notes

Practical insight into the way composers think is given in Deryck Cooke's 'The Language of Music' (Oxford) which is a study, with plenty of examples, of music as a means of communication. George Perle's 'Serial Composition and Atonality' (Faber) is a tough but rewarding guide to the music of Schoenberg and his successors. Donald Tovey was a musical thinker of an older school, but his 'Essays in Musical Analysis' (Oxford) still form an unsurpassed introduction to the standard classical repertory.

Antony Hopkins's 'talking about Music' radio programmes have been put together to form three deftly written books on sonatas, concertos and symphonies. All the various forms are gathered together and put under the microscope by Charles Rosen in 'The Classical Style' (Faber), a book full of original insights.

Opera and ballet

The name of Gustave Kobbé is to opera what Wisden is to cricket — in other words, Kobbé's 'Complete Opera Guide' (Putnam), which gives brief synopses of every major and most minor operas. E. J. Dent's 'Opera' (Pelican) is a very readable introduction, although it only takes the story up to 1940, the year it was written. 'A Concise History of Opera' (Thames and Hudson), by Leslie Orrey, treats all aspects of opera in detail.

For ballet enthusiasts there is 'The Encyclopedia of Dance and Ballet' (Putnam) edited by Mary Clarke and David Vaughan; Horst Koegler's 'Concise Oxford Dictionary of Ballet' (OUP) provides much the same information in more compressed form.

Musicians on music

Many composers have been fluent with words as well as with notes. Schumann ran his own musical magazine, and a good cross-section of his writing is included in 'The Musical World of Robert Schumann' (Gollancz), translated by Henry Pleasants. Berlioz and Debussy were highly outspoken music critics whose often eccentric views came out in book form: 'Evenings in the Orchestra', by Berlioz, and 'Monsieur Croche, Anti-Dilettante' by Debussy. In our own time, Boulez has set down his thoughts in 'Boulez on Music Today' (Faber). Other books in which composers record their ideals and beliefs are Ives's 'Essays before a Sonata' (Calder and Boyars), Busoni's 'The Essence of Music' (Rockliff), Copland's 'Music and Imagination' (Mentor) and Tippett's 'Moving into Aquarius' (Routledge).

Acknowledgements

The publishers wish to thank the following people who have helped in the preparation of this book:
Richard Merewether at
Paxman Instruments
116 Long Acre, London W.C.2
for assistance and advice on the process of making a French horn;
Martin Godleman at
Granston Musical Instrument Workshop
240 Portobello Road, London W.11
and
Peter Spicer
master-craftsman
Tunbridge Wells, Kent
for assistance and advice on the process of making a violin.

The publishers also wish to acknowledge sources of photographs and prints. Reading each column of the book from top to bottom, and from left to right:

Foreword: courtesy of Sir Robert Mayer
Contents page: Photographie Giraudon
page 7: SCALA
pages 10-11: The Bettman Archive, New York; Roger Vlitos; National Portrait Gallery; Mansell Collection; Capital Radio
pages 12-13: Frederico Arborió Mella; Ernst Eulenberg Ltd; Universal Edition
pages 14-15: Daily Telegraph; Henry Grant Photo Library; SCALA; BBC copyright photograph
pages 16-17: Mary Evans Picture Library; National Gallery
pages 18-19: Anthony Haas; Anthony Haas; Stanley Castle; Academy of St Martin-in-the-Fields
pages 20-21: EMI; The Bettman Archive, New York; BBC copyright photograph; BBC copyright photograph; ENI; CBS; EMI
pages 22-23: Erich Auerbach; David Redfern
page 25: photographs by Mike Laye
pages 26-27: David Redfern; BBC copyright photograph; courtesy BTA; David Redfern
page 29: French Government Tourist Office; photograph by Anglia Television
page 31: A. H. Leach and Co
page 33: photographs by Mike Laye
pages 34-35: BBC copyright photograph; The Rank Organisation; Greater London Council
pages 36-37: Horniman Museum; Keith Spence; BBC copyright photograph
page 39: David Redfern; The Bettman Archive, New York; The Bettman Archive, New York; The Bettman Archive, New York; David Redfern; Spectrum Colour Library
pages 40-41: David Redfern
pages 42-43: Victoria and Albert Museum; Popperfoto

pages 44-45: The Royal College of Music, London; Photographie Giraudon
pages 46-47: Edition Blauel; by permission of Mrs Elizabeth Ayrton; Novosti Press Agency; Dacca
page 48: BBC copyright photograph
pages 50-51: National Maritime Museum; Mansell Collection; The Bettman Archive, New York; The Bettman Archive, New York
page 53: Radio Times Hulton Picture Library
pages 54-55: Robert Harding Picture Library; Robert Harding; Courtesy BTA; Frank Spooner Pictures; The Bettman Archive, New York; photograph by Mike Laye
page 57: National Gallery
pages 58-59: The Royal College of Music, London; Erich Lessing; Magnum Photos; Berlin Staatsbibliothek Preussischer Kulturbesitz, Musicabteilung
pages 60-61: Kunsthistorisches Museum, Vienna; (lower) Westermann Verlag
pages 62-63: Mansell Collection; Staats und Universitätsbibliothek, Hamburg; SCALA; Mansell Collection
pages 64-65: Staatlicher Museen Preussischer Kulturbesitz, Berlin; The Bettman Archive, New York; Radio Times Hulton Picture Library; Robert Harding Associates; The Bettman Archive, New York; Bulloz
pages 66-67: The Bettman Archive, New York; Photographie Giraudon
page 68: by permission of the British Library
page 70: Archiv für Kunst und Geschichte, Berlin
pages 72-73: courtesy of the Whitechapel Bell Foundry; courtesy of the Whitechapel Bell Foundry; SPECTRUM; Guild Records; SPECTRUM; Decca
pages 74-75: Mary Evans Picture Library; John Webb for the Tate Gallery
page 77: National Portrait Gallery; Mansell Collection
pages 78-79: Civico Museo Bibliografico Musicale, Bologna; Daily Telegraph
page 81: The Bettman Archive, New York; Reg Wilson; SCALA
pages 82-83: Richard Wagner Gedenkstatte der Stadt Bayreuth; Bayer Verwaltung der Staatl Schlösser Garten und Seen, Munich; Bayer Verwaltung der Staatle Schlösser Garten und Seen, Munich
pages 84-85: Radio Times Hulton Picture Library; Syndication International; The Bettman Archive, New York; Biblioteca Nazionale Braidense, Milan
pages 86-87: Syndication International; Boosey and Hawkes Music Publishers Ltd and Fürstner Ltd; Boosey and Hawkes Music Publishers Ltd and Fürstner Ltd; Rosemary Vercoe
pages 88-89: BBC copyright photograph; Schott Music Publishers; Schirmer; Schott Music Publishers; BBC copyright photograph
pages 90-91: The Bettman Archive, New York;

The Raymond Mander and Joe Mitchenson Theatre Collection; Picture Index; Caboue
page 92: top to bottom all courtesy of Ballet for All
page 93: Anthony Crickmay; Radio Times Hulton Picture Library
pages 94-95: Anchony Crickmay; National Gallery
pages 96-97: TOPIX; SPECTRUM; Mary Evans Picture Library; courtesy BTA; SPECTRUM
pages 98-99: Mary Evans Picture Library; Mary Evans Picture Library
pages 100-01: Mary Evans Picture Library; Welsh Opera; Mary Evans Picture Library; Mary Evans Picture Library; John Baxter
pages 102-03: photograph by Fred Fehl; National Gallery
pages 104-05: Mansell Collection; Photographie Giraudon; Finnish Embassy; The Bettman Archive, New York; The Bettman Archive, New York; Radio Times Hulton Picture Library
pages 106-07: Hungarian Embassy; G. D. Hackett; Hungarian Embassy; CBS; courtesy of the English Folk Dance and Song Society
pages 108-09: Mary Evans Picture Library; from a print in the V & A Enthoven Collection; Robert Harding Associates for George Rainbird Ltd; Scottish Opera
pages 110-11: Abby Aldrich Rockefeller Folk Art Center, Williamsburg, Virginia; The Bettman Archive, New York
pages 112-13: The Bettman Archive, New York; Photographie Giraudon
page 115: Roger-Viollet; Syndication International; Robert Harding Associates
page 116: Radio Times Hulton Picture Library; Österreichische Nationalbibliothek
pages 118-19: Unicorn Records; Reg Wilson; The Bettman Archive, New York; Archives SNARK/Museen der Stadt, Wien
pages 120-21: Novosti Press Agency; Archives SNARK/Musée F. Leger
pages 122-23: Editions LEDUC of Paris; Frank Spooner Pictures; Frank Spooner
pages 124-25: James Klosty; copyright © 1960 by Henmar Press Inc, New York/reprint permission granted by the publisher; photograph by Richard Rutledge, courtesy of Cunningham Dance Foundation; Universal Edition; Boosey and Hawkes
pages 126-27: BBC copyright photograph; EMI; Camera Press; London Features International
page 128: SCALA

Index

Figures in bold type indicate that a subject is illustrated.
Figures in square brackets indicate an entry in the fact
panel on the left-hand side of the page.

THE NEW DECADE SERIES

SONGS OF THE 2010s

FOR ORGANS, PIANOS & ELECTRONIC KEYBOARDS

E-Z PLAY TODAY
371

ISBN 978-1-5400-9035-5

HAL•LEONARD®

E-Z Play® Today Music Notation © 1975 by HAL LEONARD LLC
E-Z PLAY and EASY ELECTRONIC KEYBOARD MUSIC are registered trademarks of HAL LEONARD LLC.

Visit Hal Leonard Online at
www.halleonard.com

World headquarters, contact:
Hal Leonard
7777 West Bluemound Road
Milwaukee, WI 53213
E-mail: info@halleonard.com

In Europe, contact:
Hal Leonard Europe Limited
1 Red Place
London, W1K 6PL
Email: info@halleonardeurope.com

In Australia, contact:
Hal Leonard A...
4 Lentara Cour...
Cheltenham, V...
Email: info@ha...

All About That Bass

Registration 2
Rhythm: Pop or Rock

Words and Music by Kevin Kadish
and Meghan Trainor

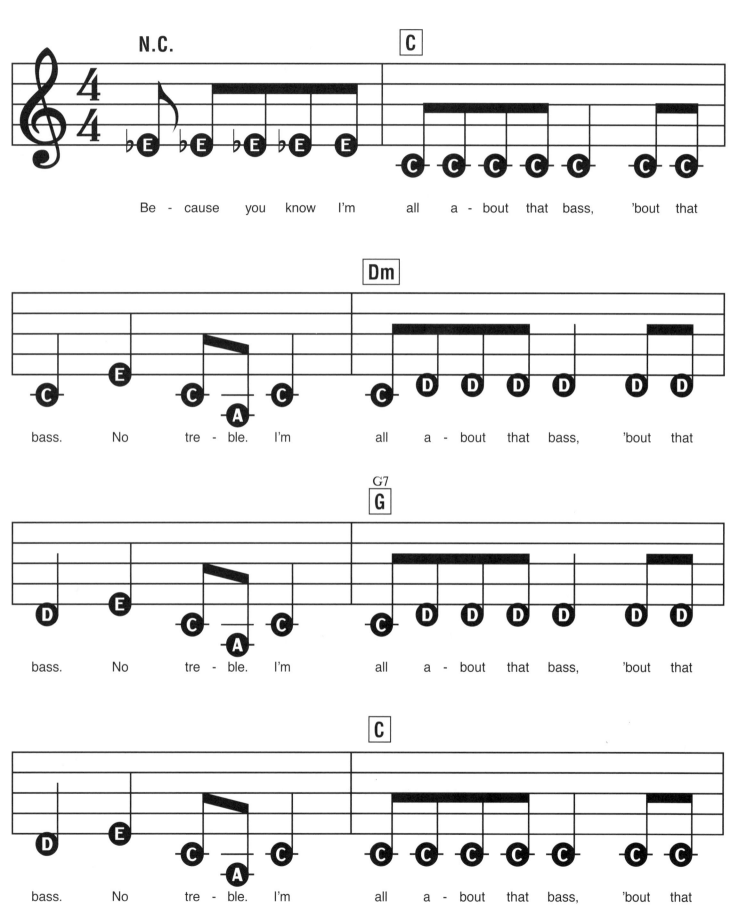

N.C.

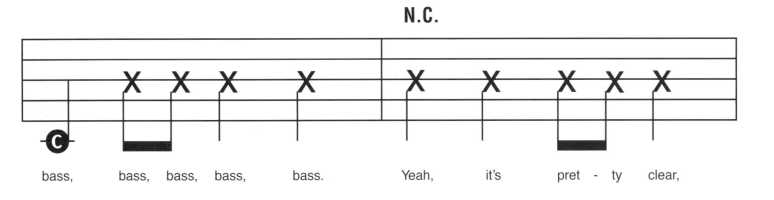

bass,   bass, bass, bass,   bass.   Yeah,   it's   pret - ty   clear,

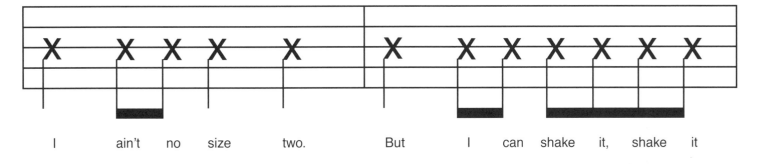

I   ain't   no   size   two.   But   I   can   shake   it,   shake   it

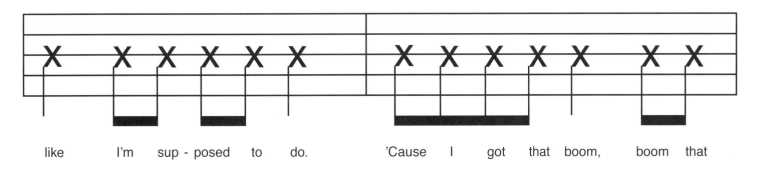

like   I'm   sup - posed   to   do.   'Cause   I   got   that   boom,   boom   that

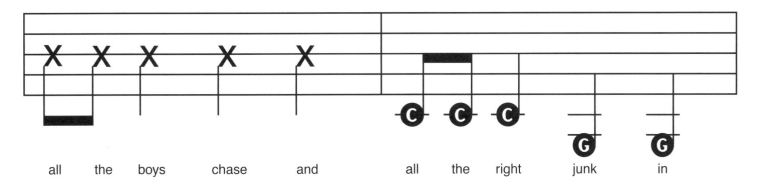

all   the   boys   chase   and   all   the   right   junk   in

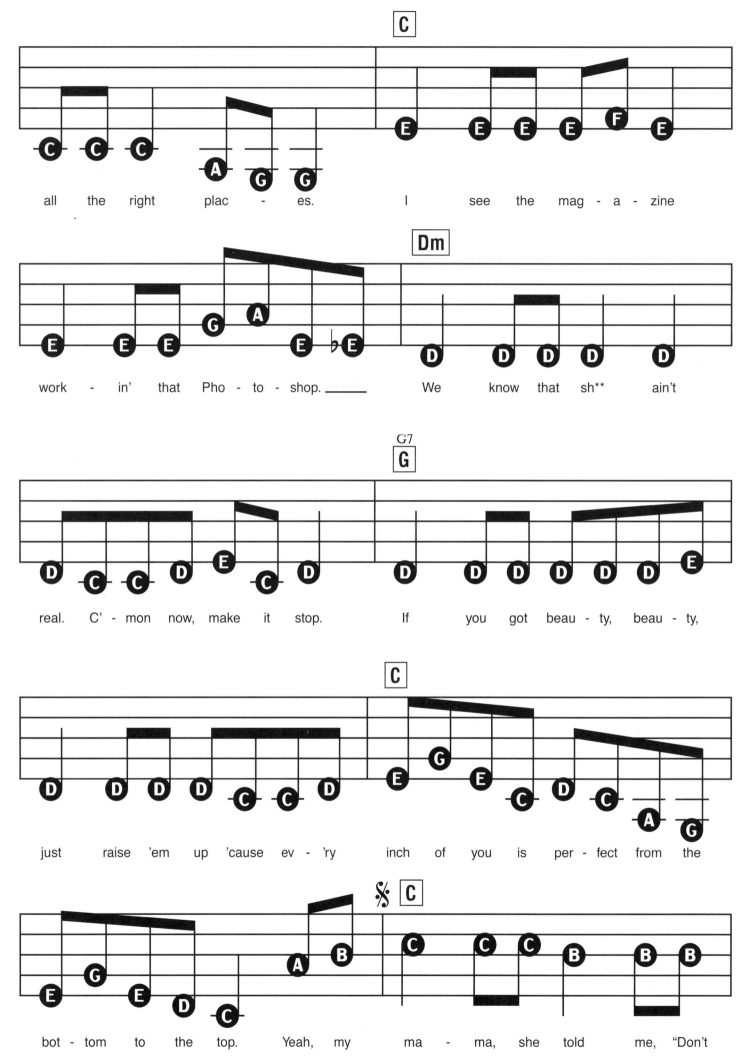

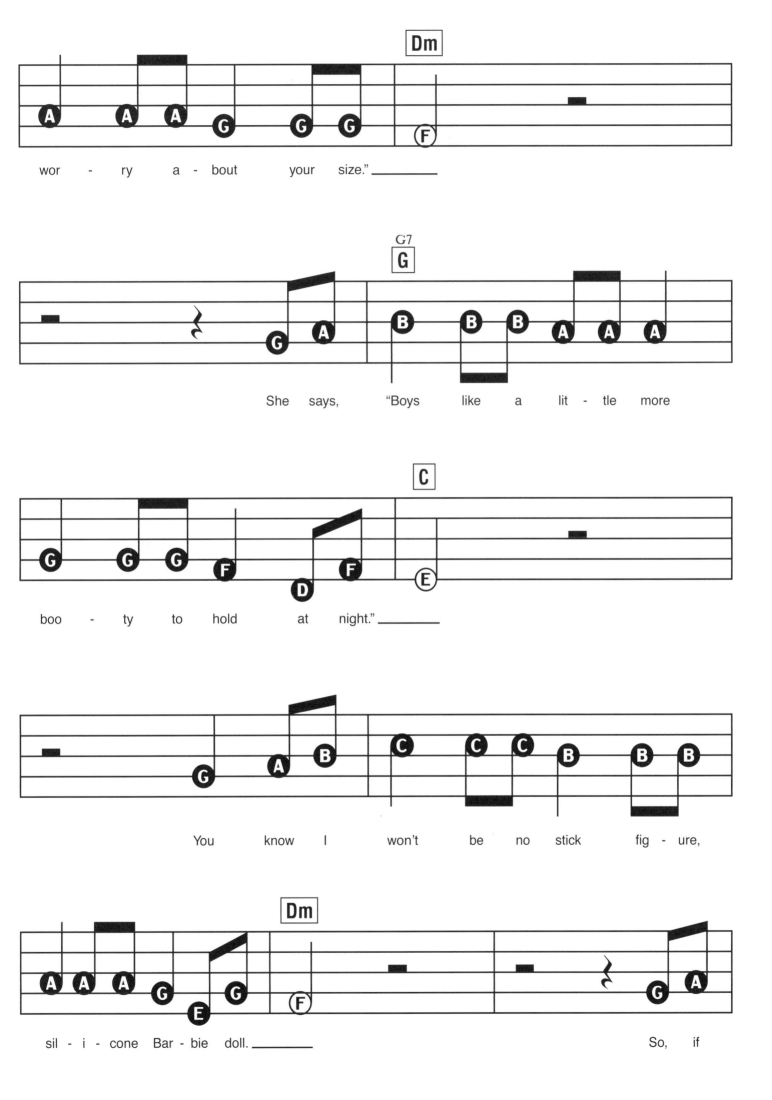

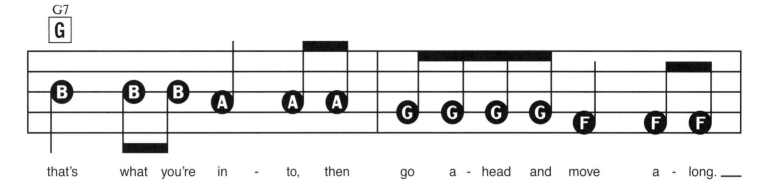

that's what you're in - to, then go a - head and move a - long. ___

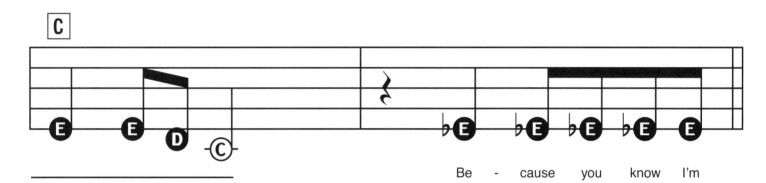

_____ Be - cause you know I'm

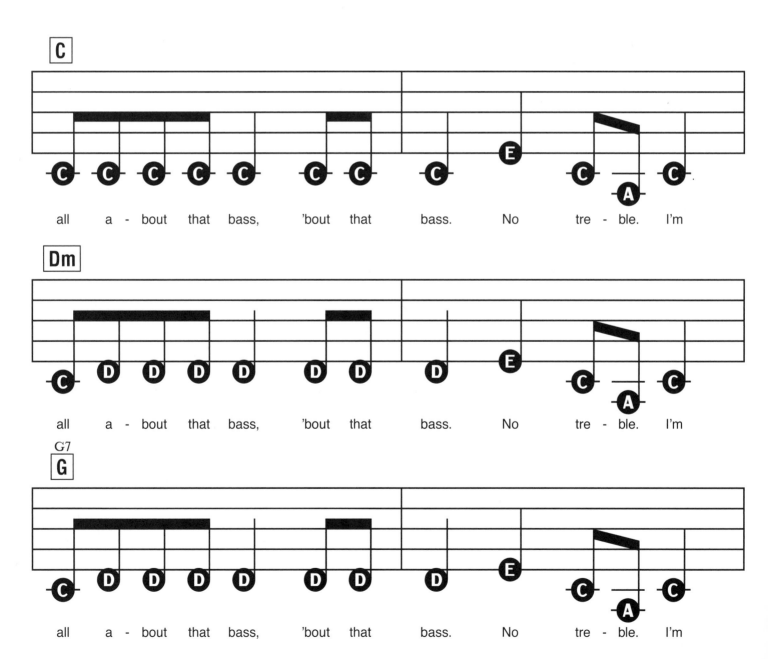

all a - bout that bass, 'bout that bass. No tre - ble. I'm

all a - bout that bass, 'bout that bass. No tre - ble. I'm

all a - bout that bass, 'bout that bass. No tre - ble. I'm

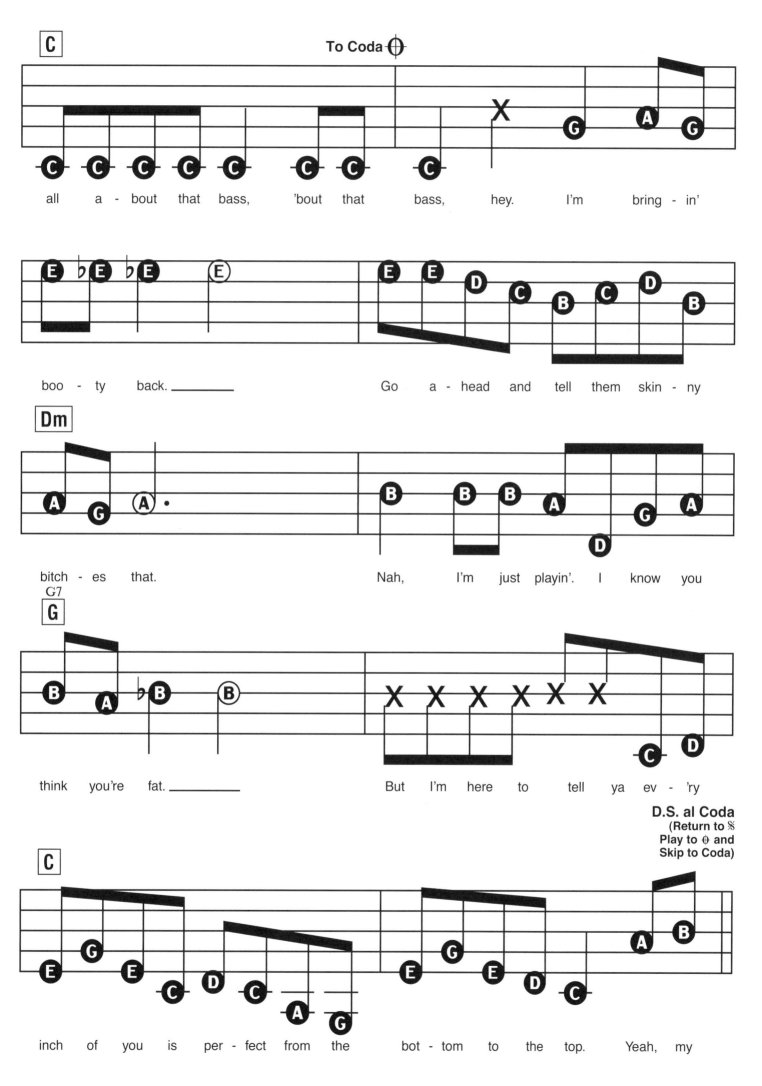

C

To Coda ⊕

all a - bout that bass, 'bout that bass, hey. I'm bring - in'

boo - ty back. _____ Go a - head and tell them skin - ny

Dm

bitch - es that. Nah, I'm just playin'. I know you

G7
G

think you're fat. _____ But I'm here to tell ya ev - 'ry

D.S. al Coda
(Return to 𝄋
Play to ⊕ and
Skip to Coda)

C

inch of you is per - fect from the bot - tom to the top. Yeah, my

10

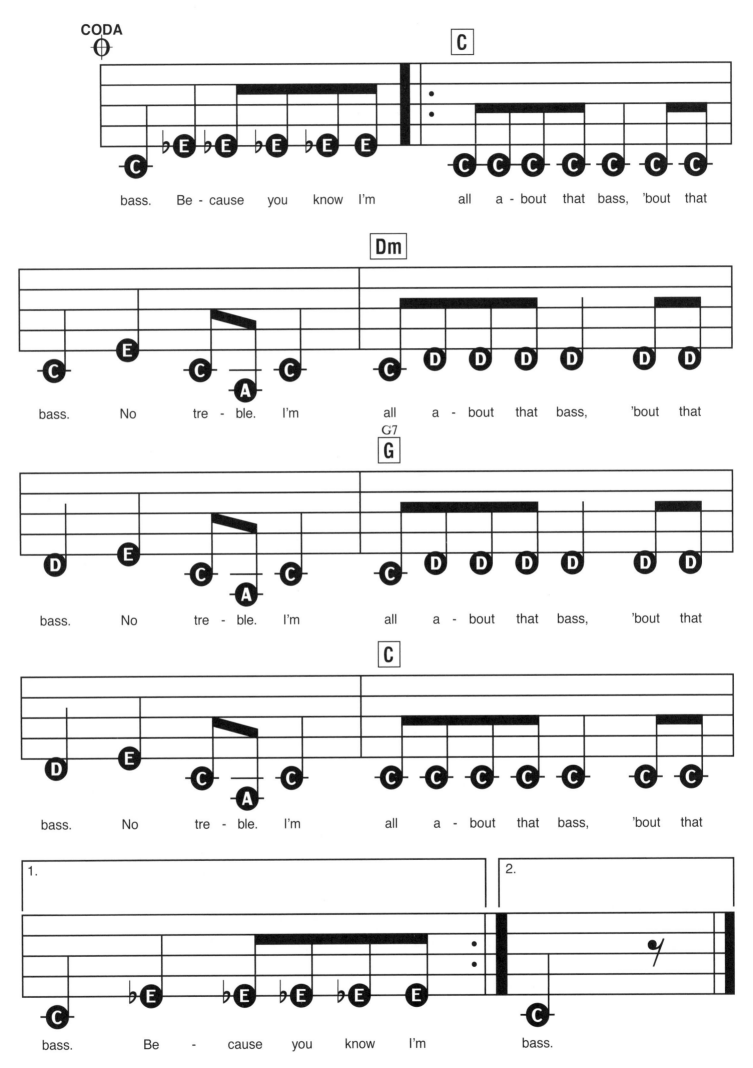

All of Me

Registration 8
Rhythm: Ballad

Words and Music by John Stephens
and Toby Gad

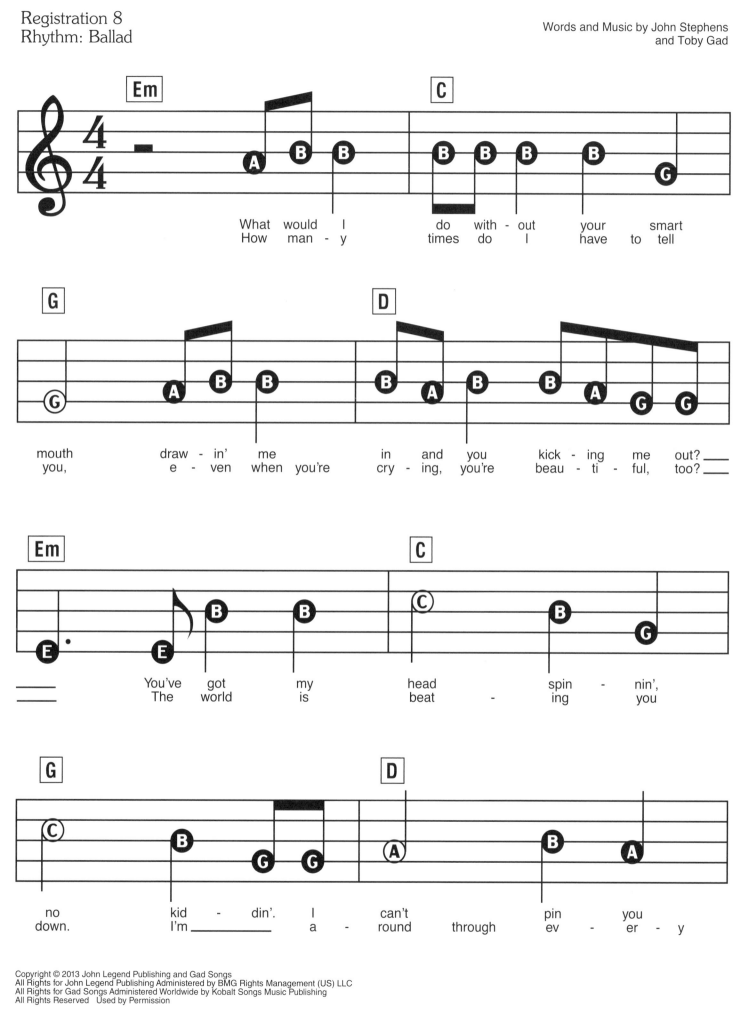

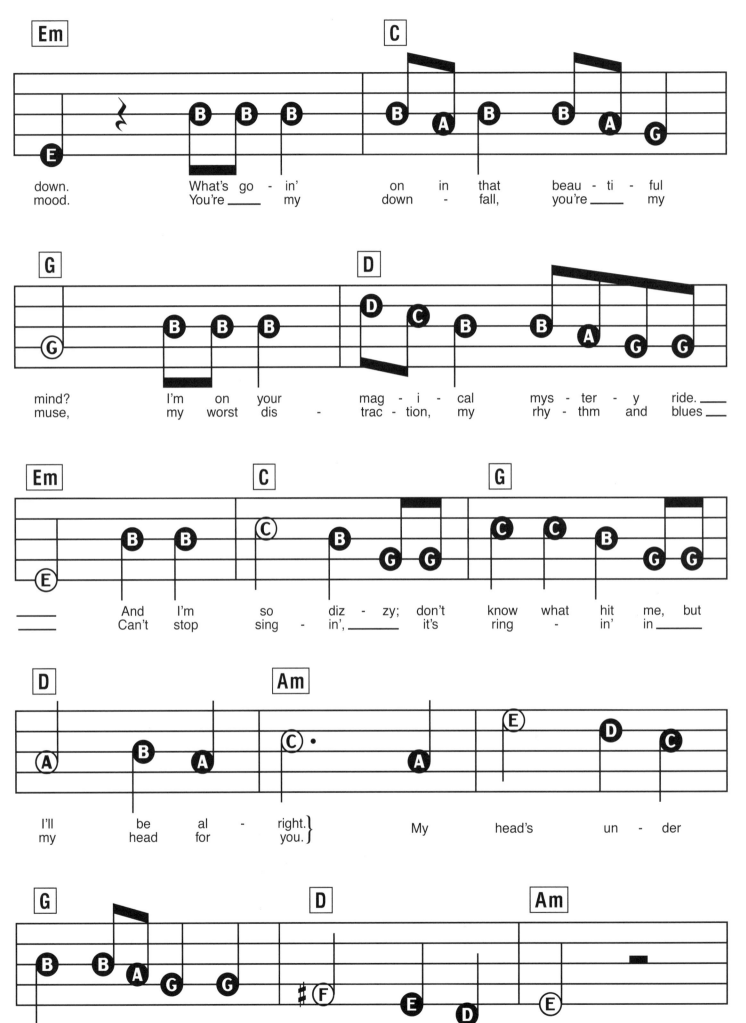

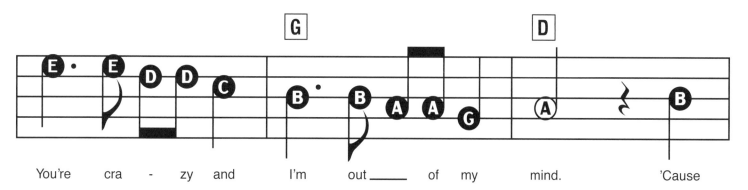

You're cra - zy and I'm out ____ of my mind. 'Cause

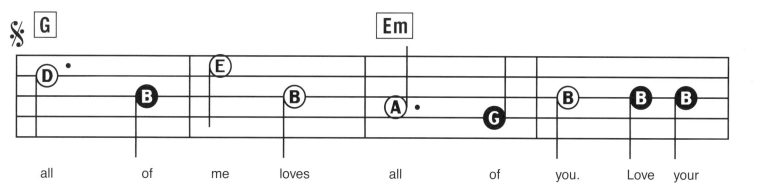

all of me loves all of you. Love your

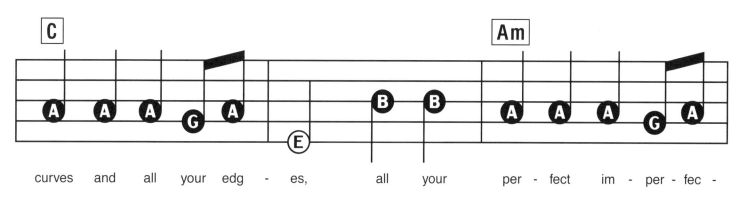

curves and all your edg - es, all your per - fect im - per - fec -

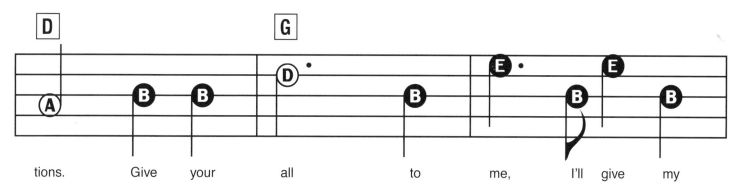

tions. Give your all to me, I'll give my

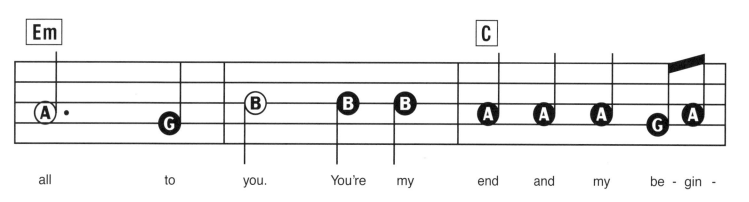

all to you. You're my end and my be - gin -

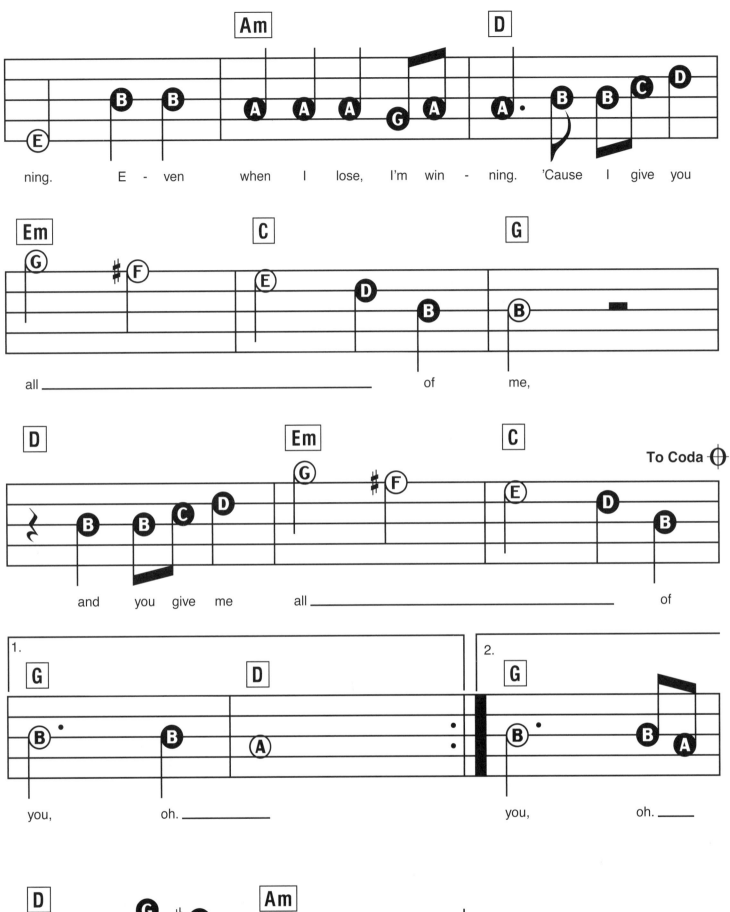

ning. E - ven when I lose, I'm win - ning. 'Cause I give you

all _____ of me,

and you give me all _____ of

1. you, oh. _____ 2. you, oh. _____

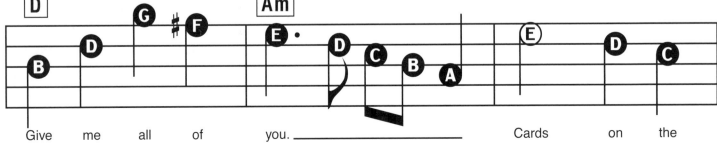

Give me all of you. _____ Cards on the

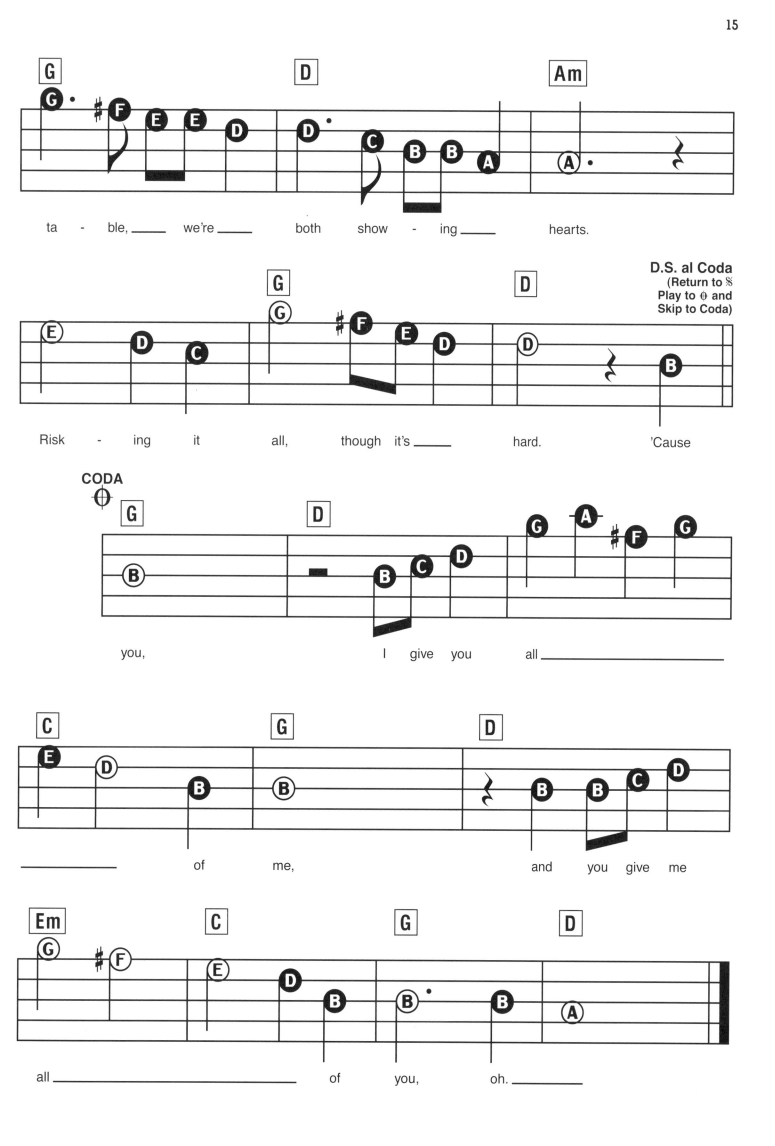

Bad Romance

Registration 4
Rhythm: Dance or Rock

Words and Music by Stefani Germanotta
and Nadir Khayat

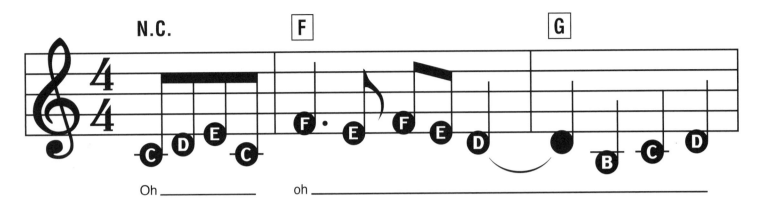

Oh _____ oh _____

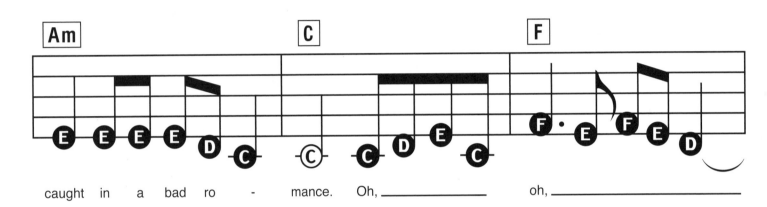

caught in a bad ro - mance. Oh, _____ oh, _____

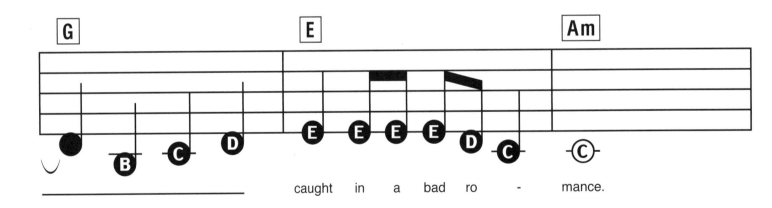

caught in a bad ro - mance.

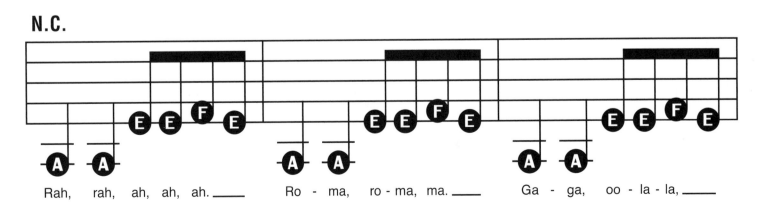

Rah, rah, ah, ah, ah. ____ Ro - ma, ro - ma, ma. ____ Ga - ga, oo - la - la, ____

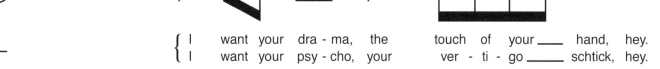

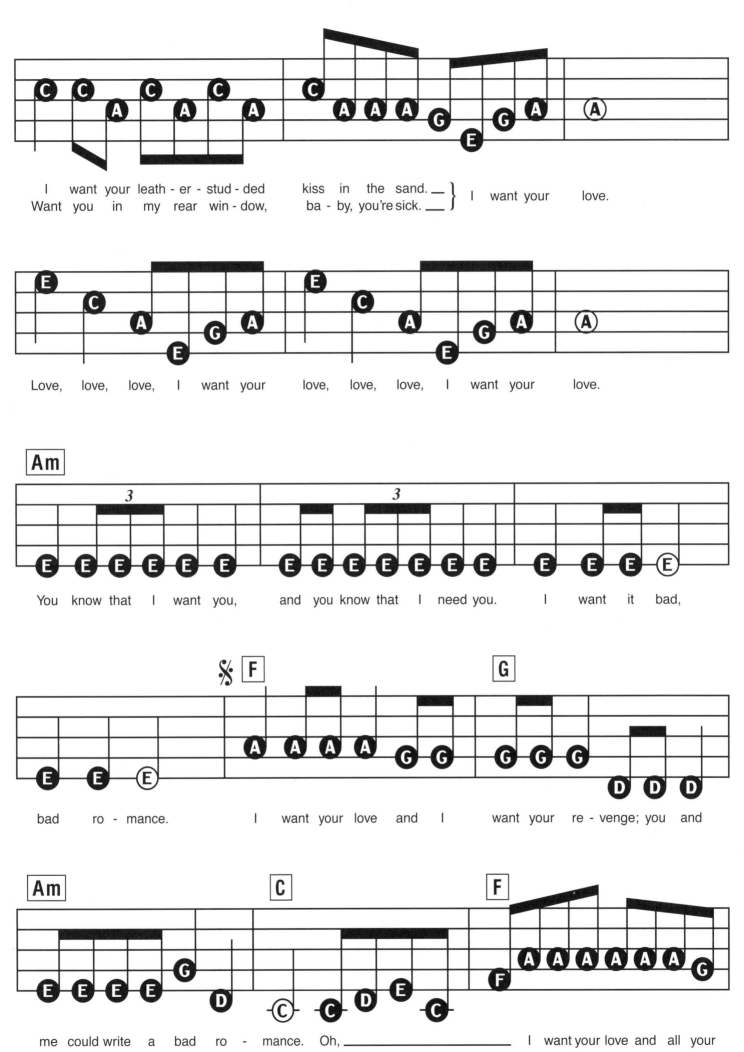

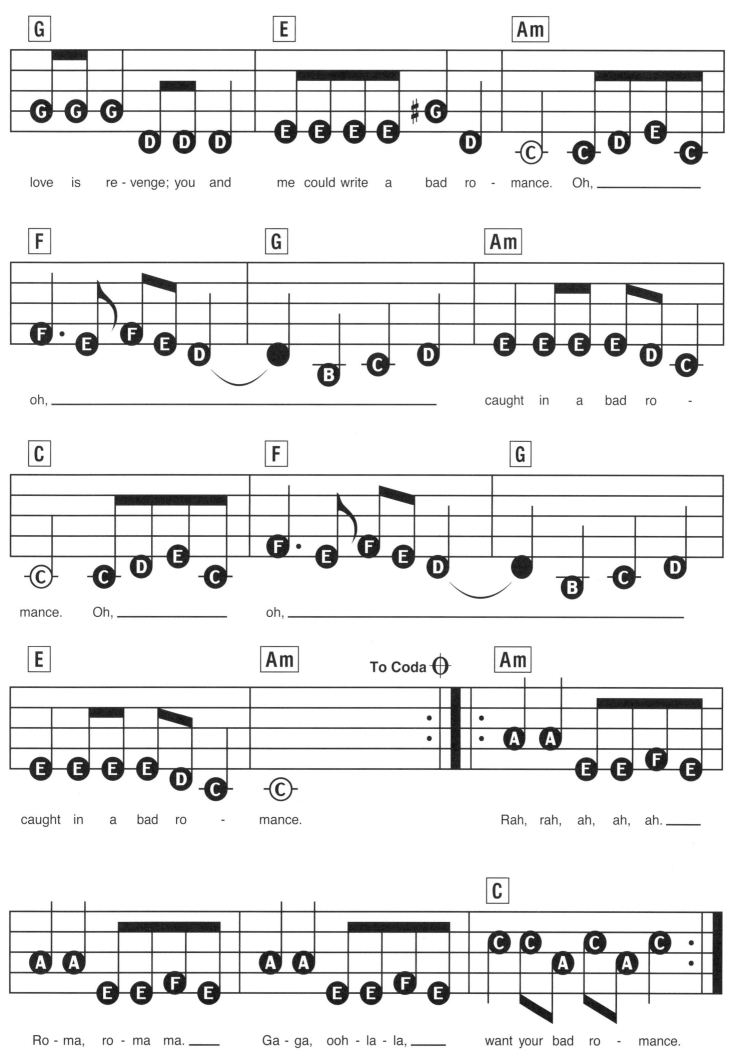

20

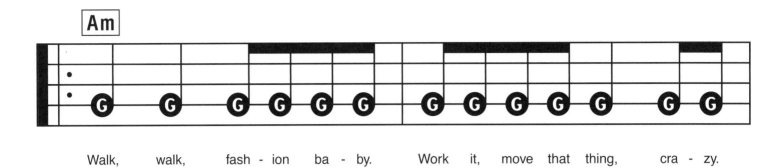

Walk, walk, fash - ion ba - by. Work it, move that thing, cra - zy.

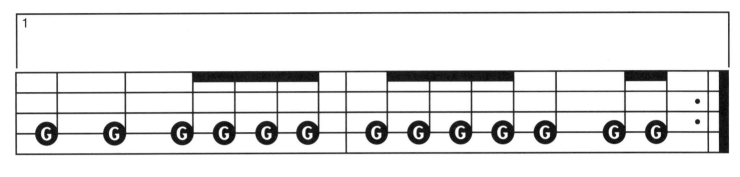

Walk, walk, fash - ion ba - by. Work it, move that thing, cra - zy.

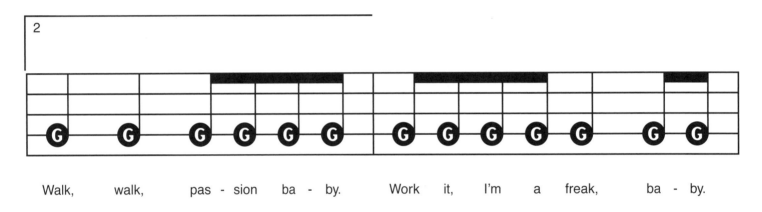

Walk, walk, pas - sion ba - by. Work it, I'm a freak, ba - by.

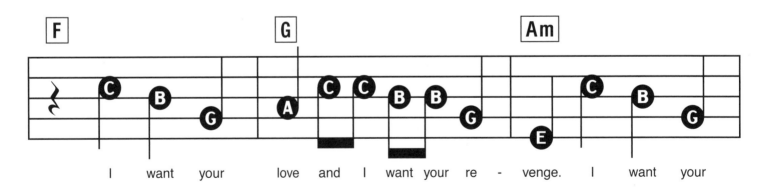

I want your love and I want your re - venge. I want your

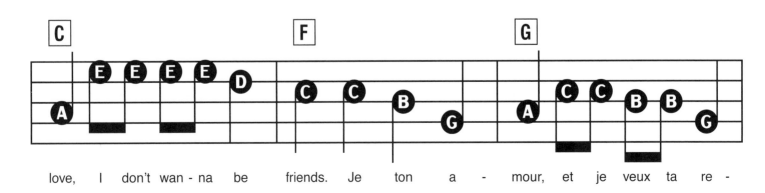

love, I don't wan - na be friends. Je ton a - mour, et je veux ta re -

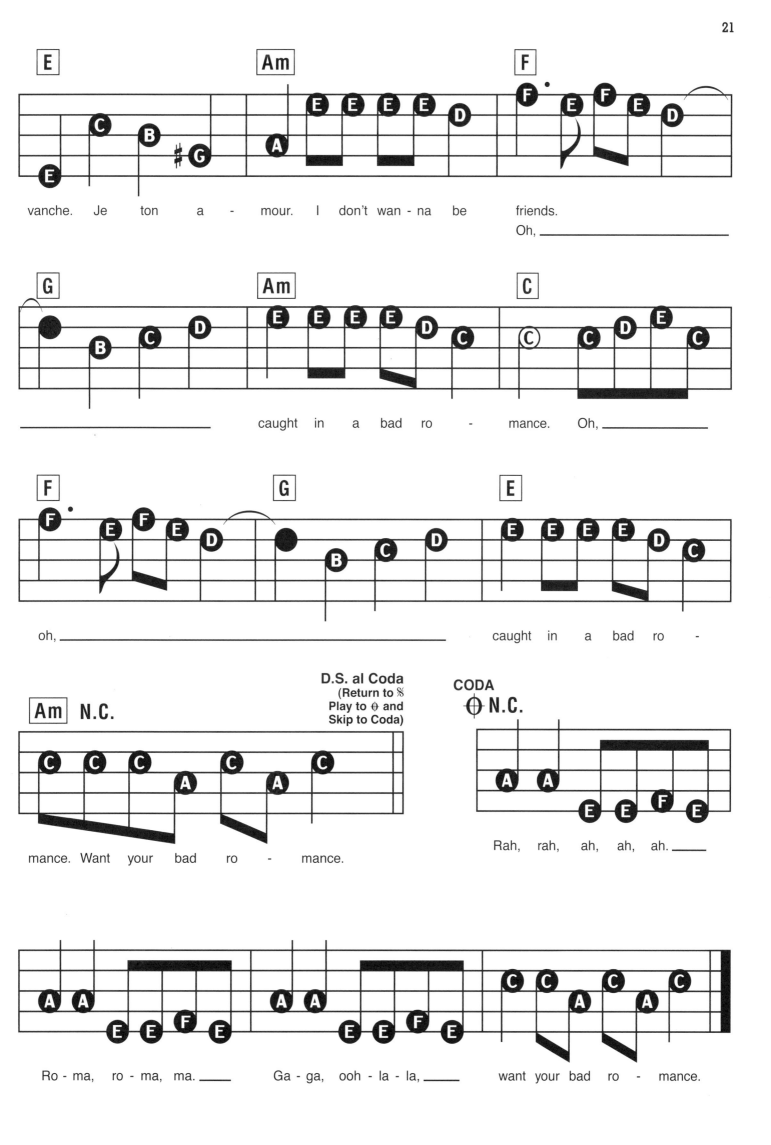

Best Day of My Life

Registration 8
Rhythm: Pop or Rock

Words and Music by Zachary Barnett, James
Adam Shelley, Matthew Sanchez,
David Rublin, Shep Goodman
and Aaron Accetta

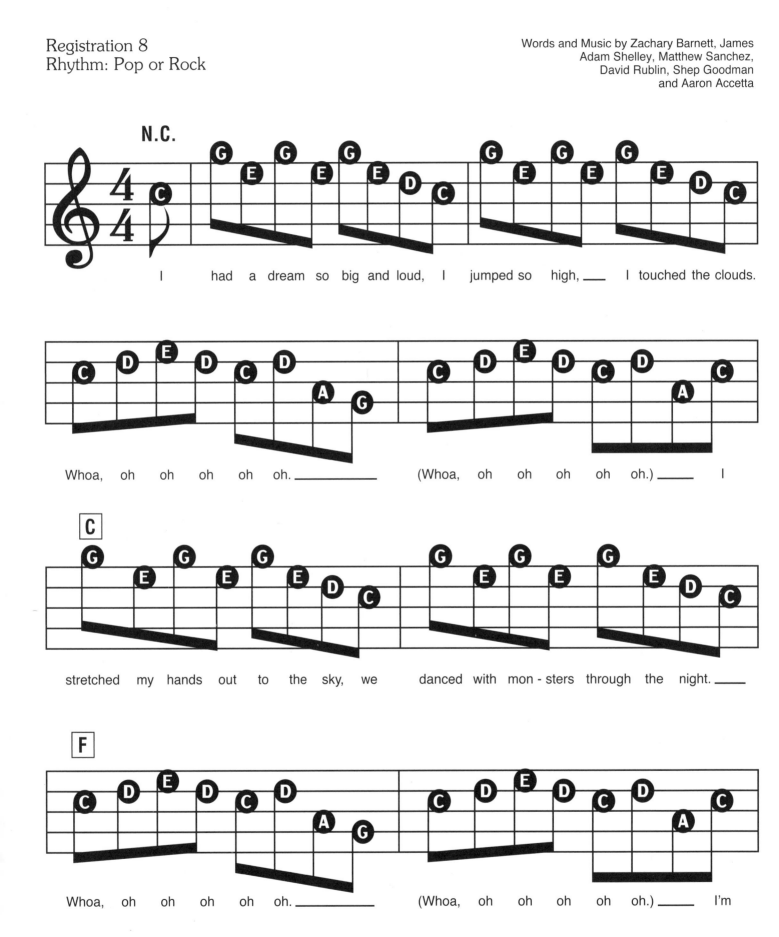

23

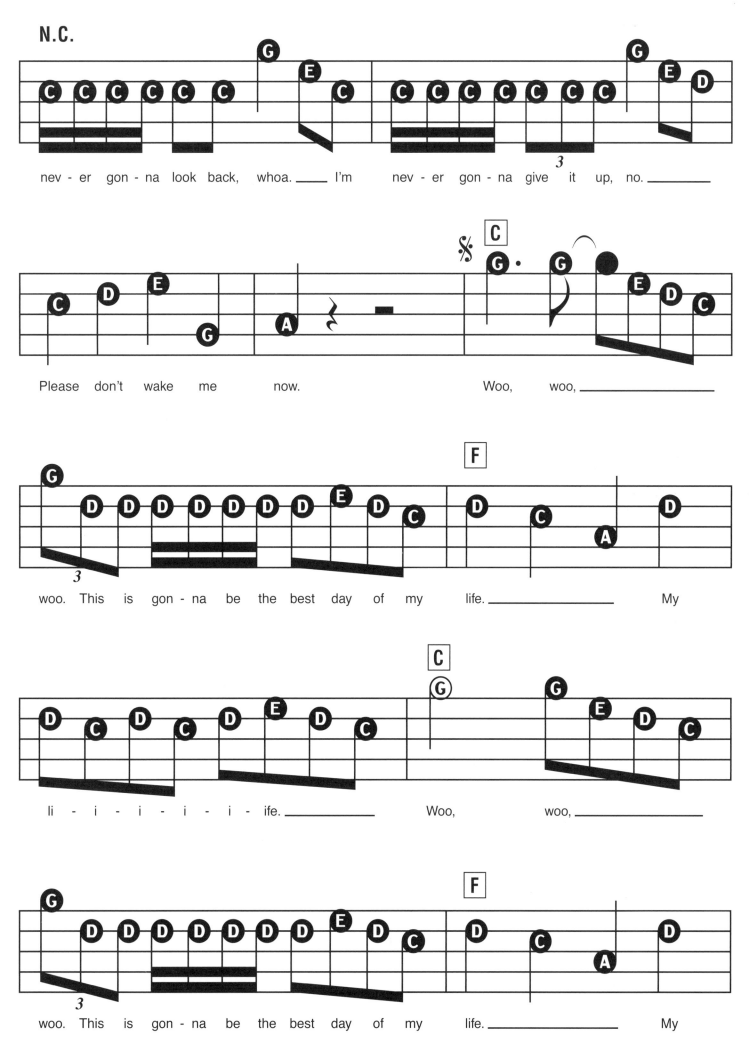

24

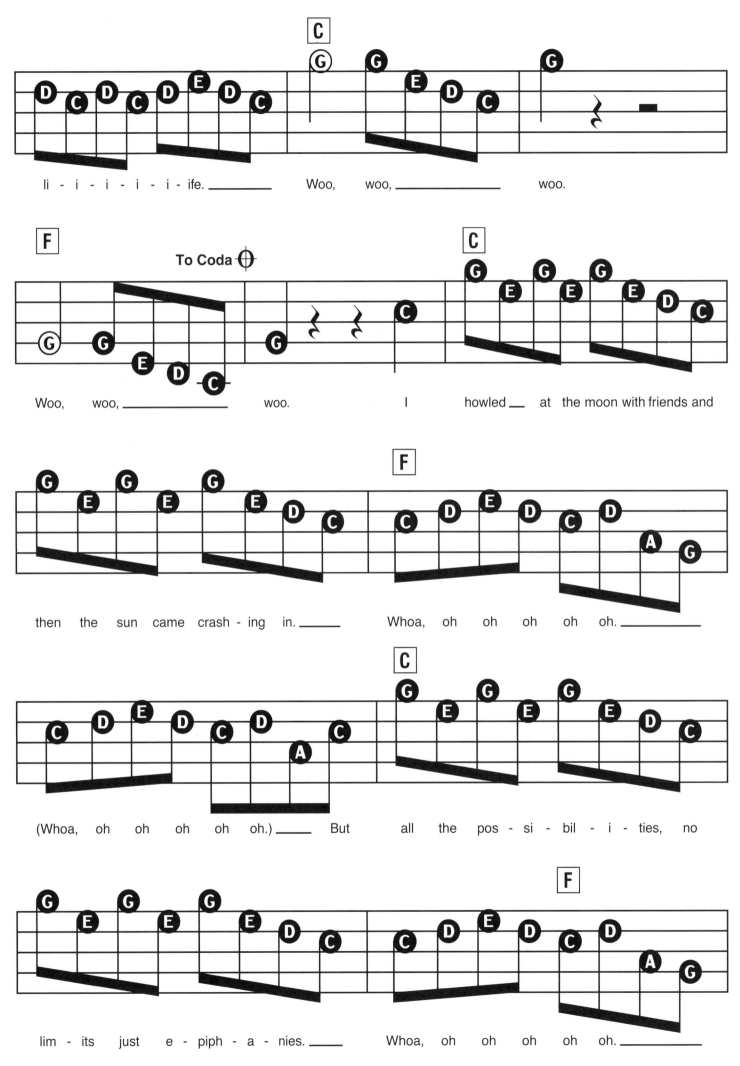

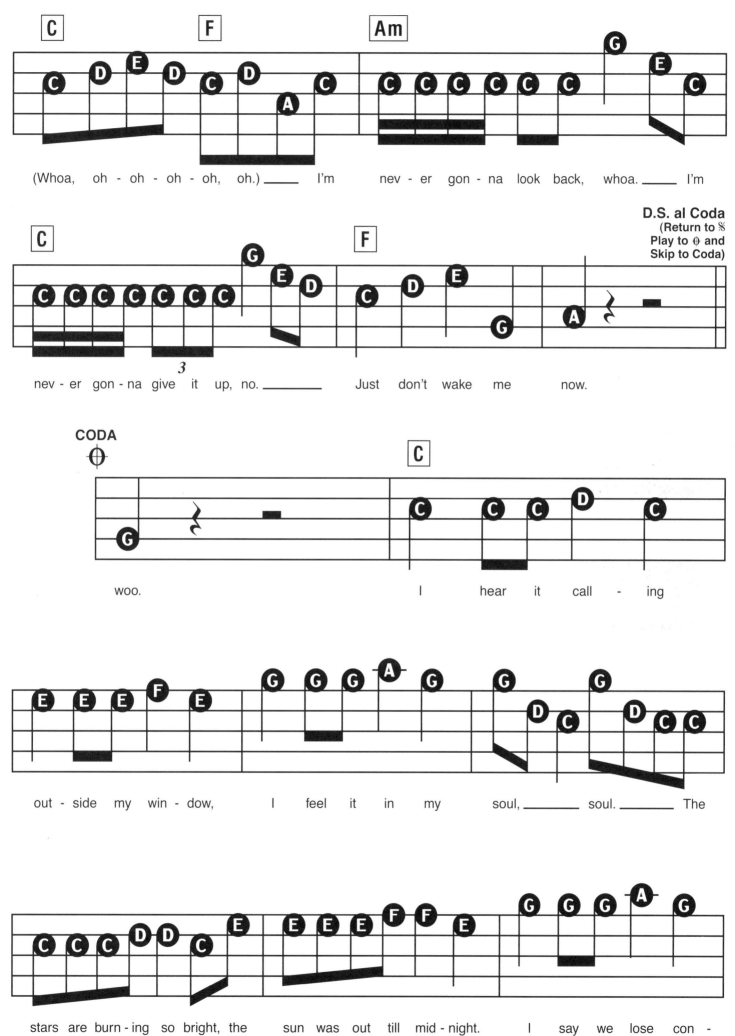

26

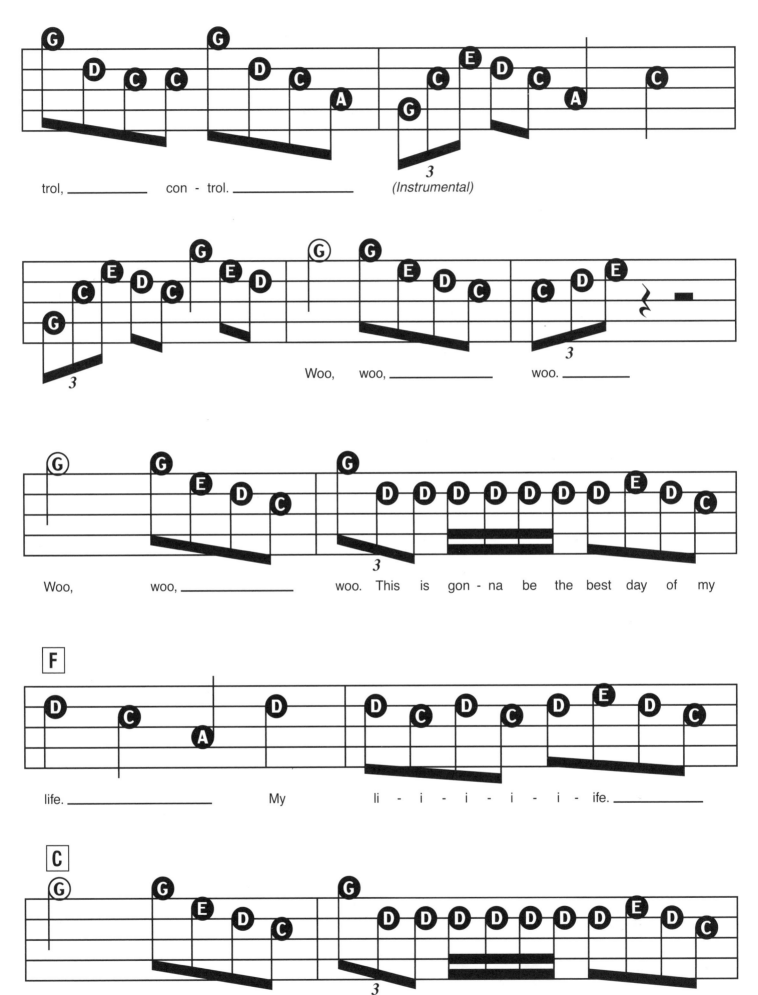

27

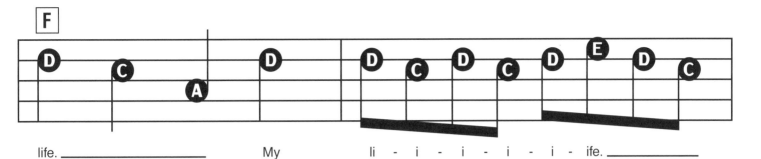

life. _____ My li - i - i - i - ife. _____

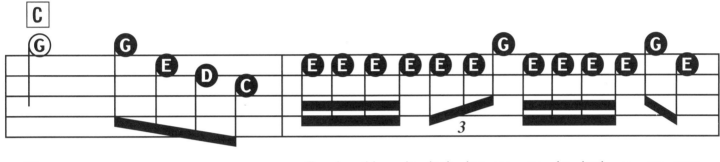

Woo, woo. _____ Ev - 'ry - thing is look - ing up, ev - 'ry - bod - y up now.

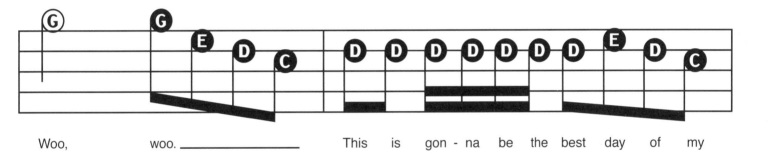

Woo, woo. _____ This is gon - na be the best day of my

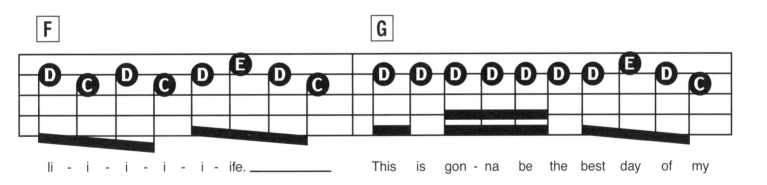

li - i - i - i - i - ife. _____ This is gon - na be the best day of my

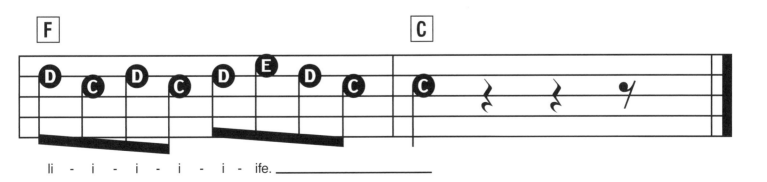

li - i - i - i - i - ife. _____

Call Me Maybe

Registration 1
Rhythm: Pop or Rock

Words and Music by Carly Rae Jepsen,
Joshua Ramsay and Tavish Crowe

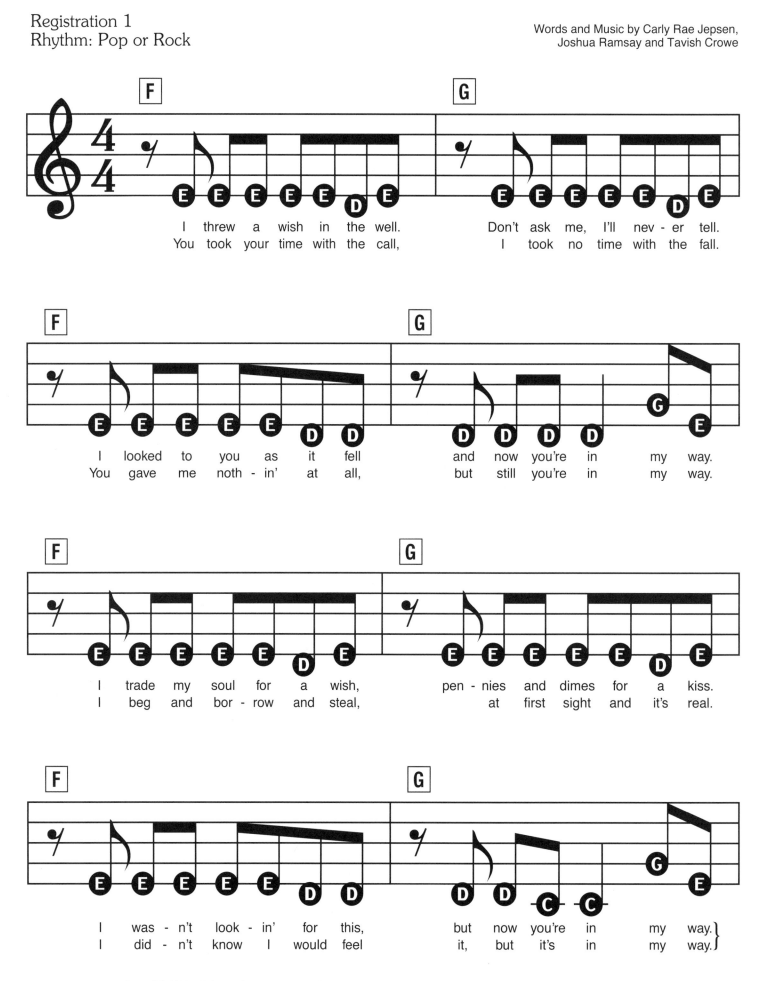

29

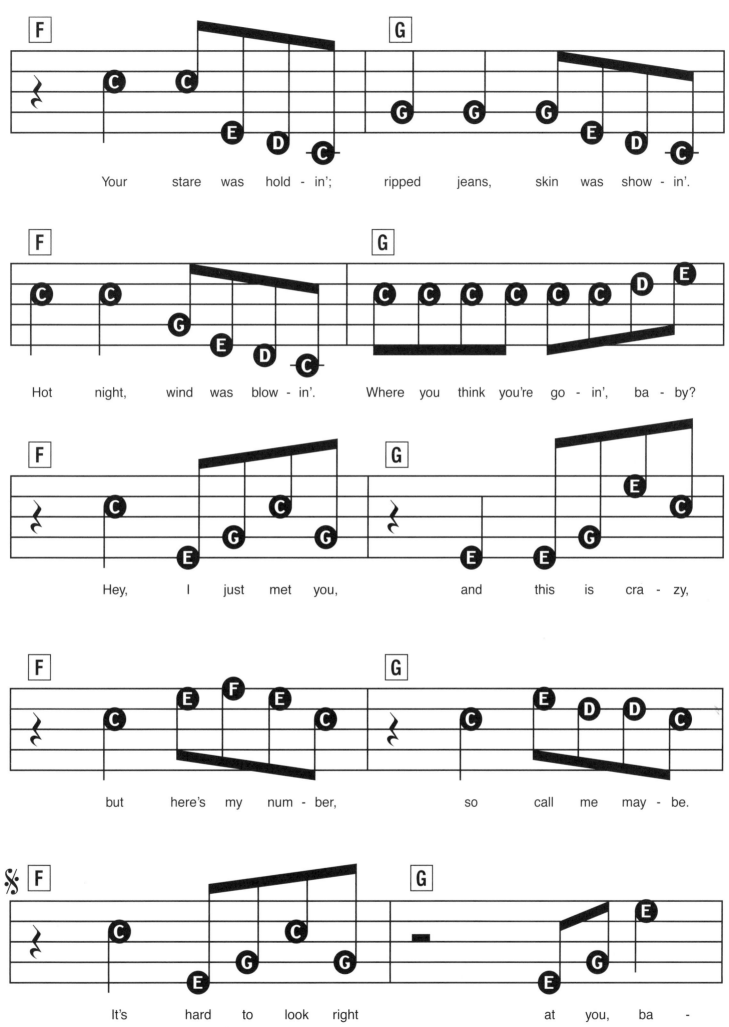

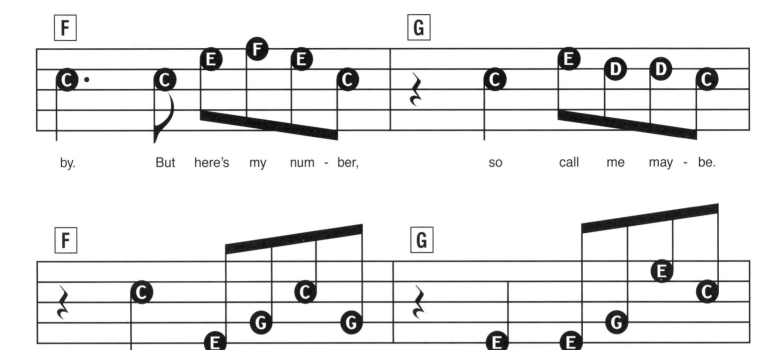

by.   But here's my num - ber,   so call me may - be.

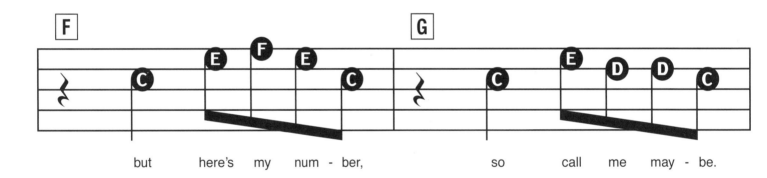

Hey,   I just met you,   and this is cra - zy,

but here's my num - ber,   so call me may - be.

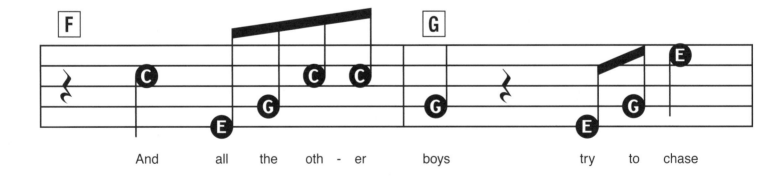

And all the oth - er boys   try to chase

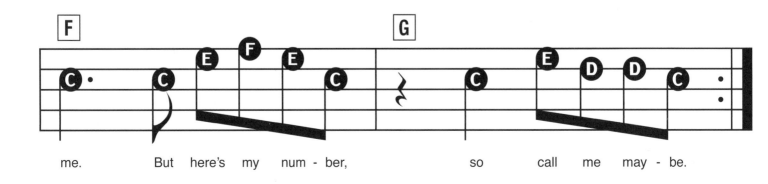

me. But here's my num - ber,   so call me may - be.

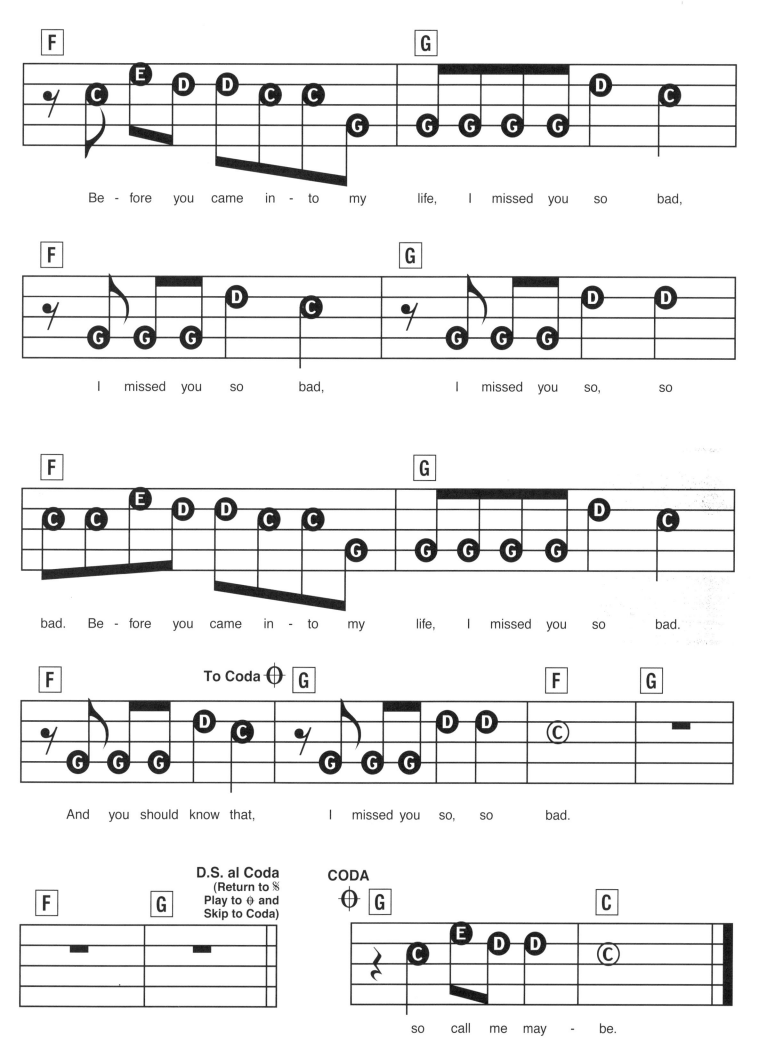

City of Stars
from LA LA LAND

Registration 8
Rhythm: Ballad

Music by Justin Hurwitz
Lyrics by Benj Pasek & Justin Paul

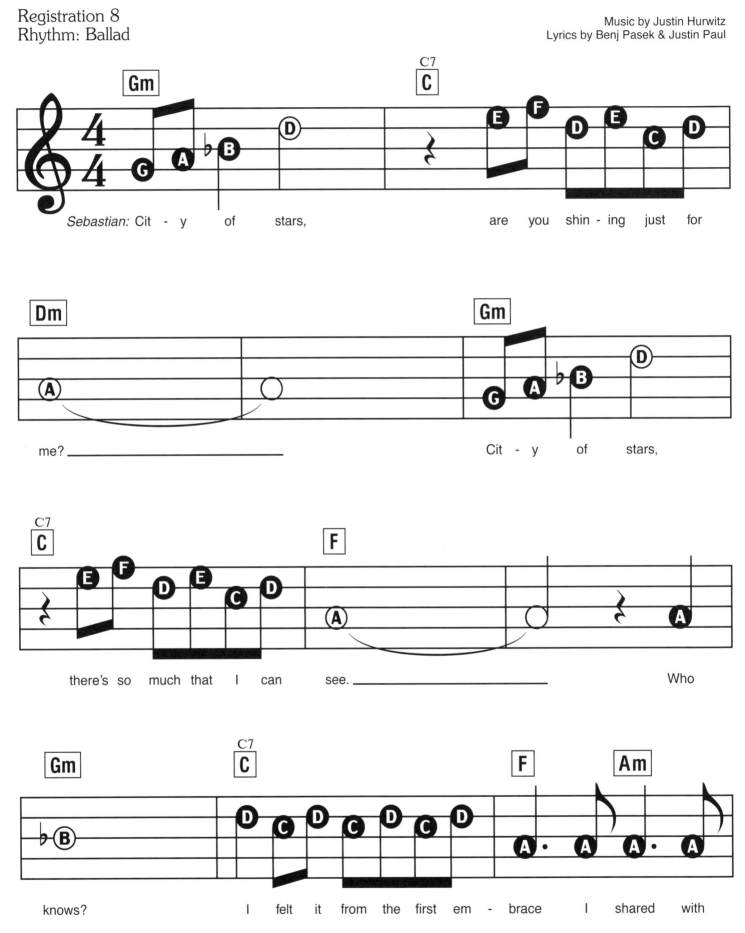

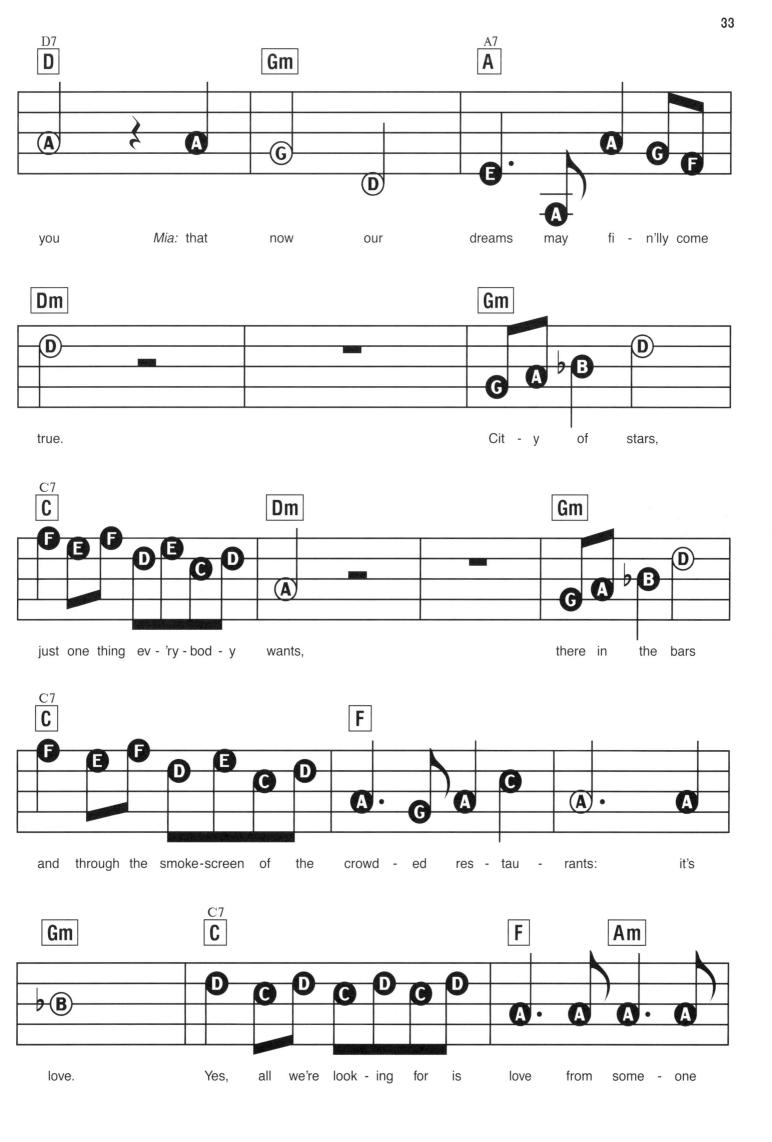

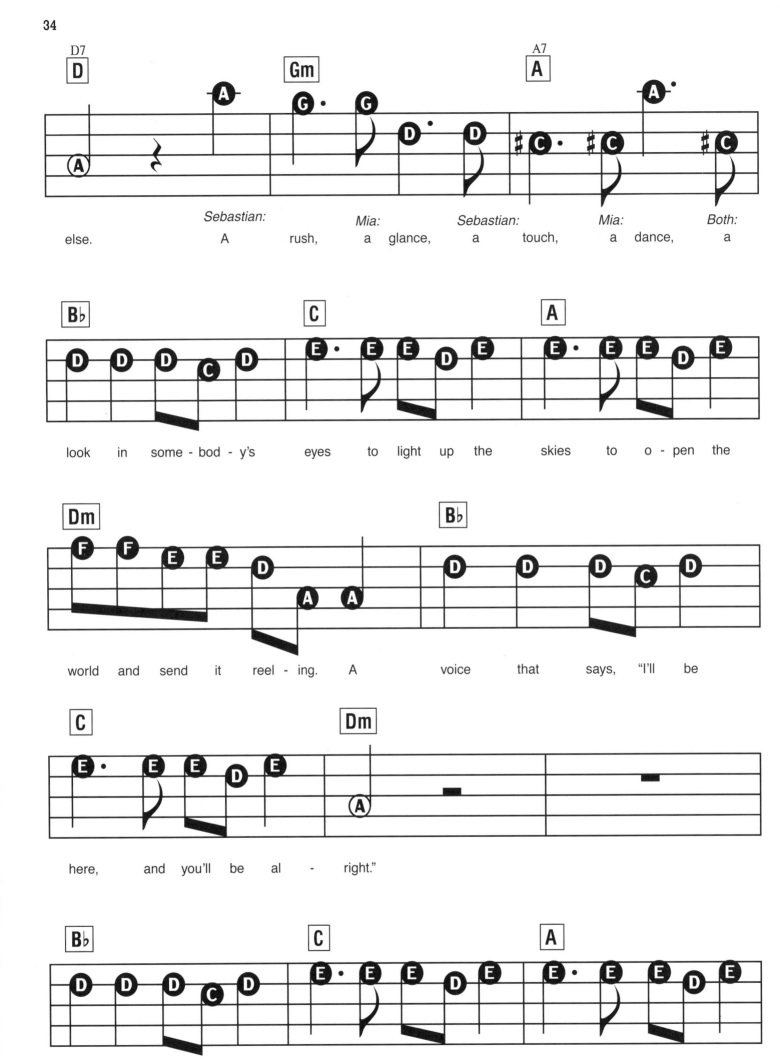

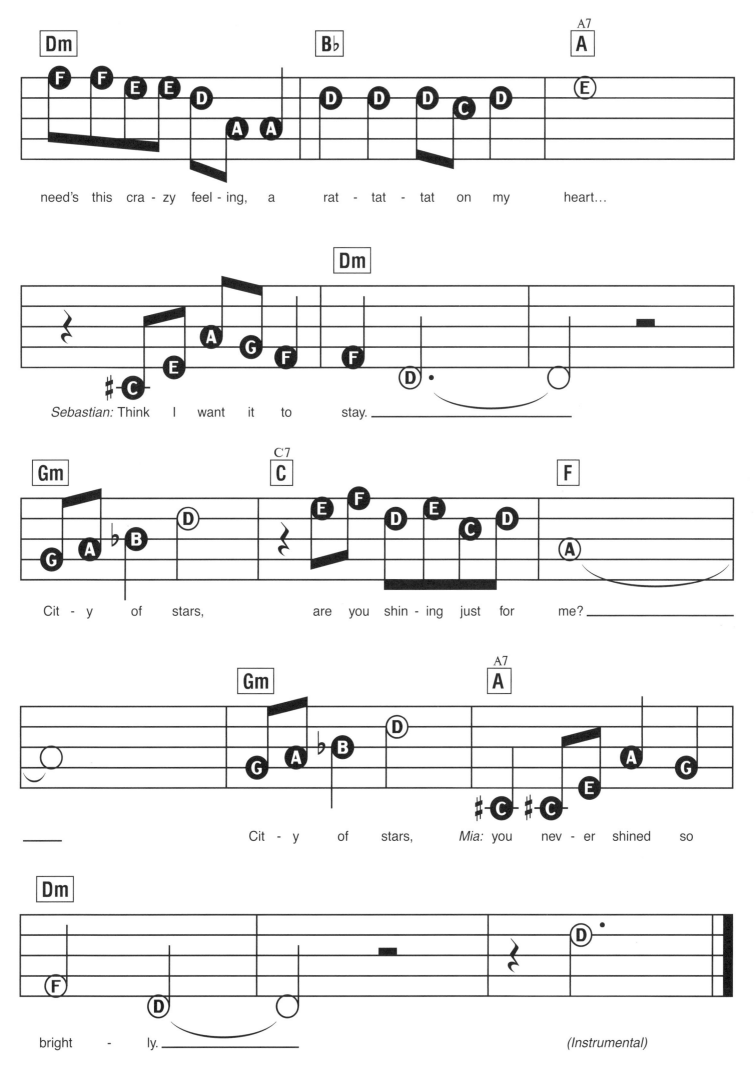

Happier

Registration 2
Rhythm: Pop or Rock

Words and Music by Marshmello,
Steve Mac and Dan Smith

37

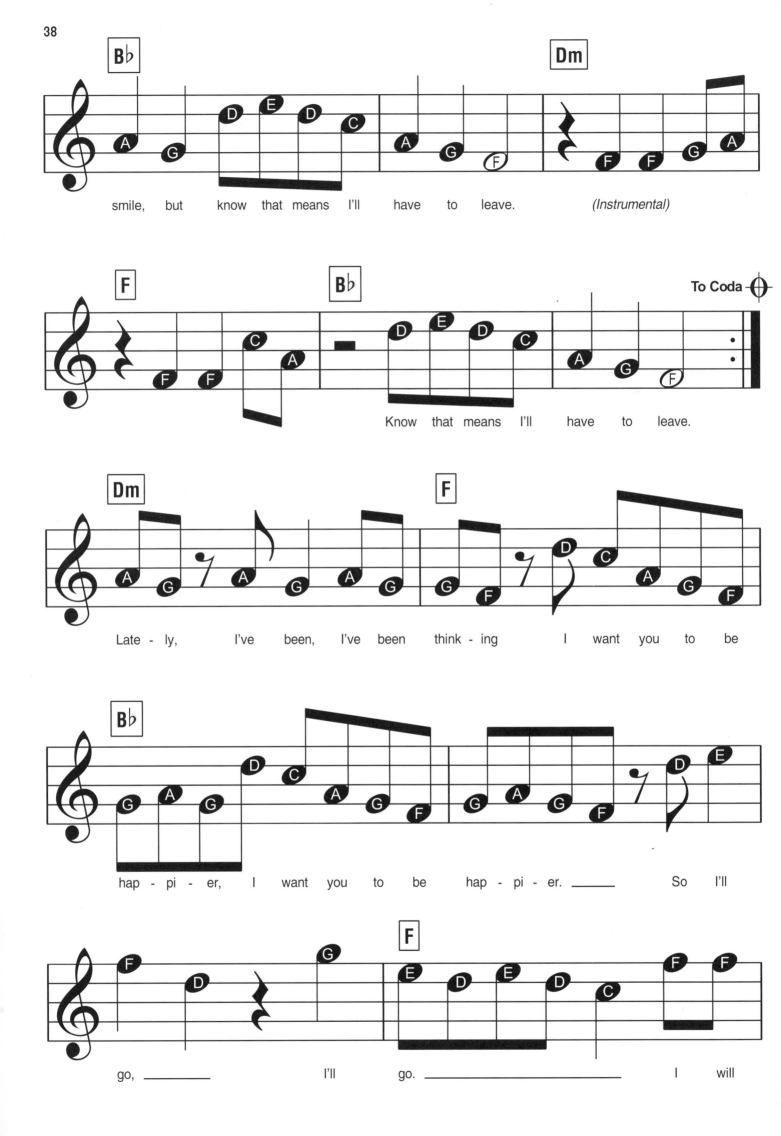

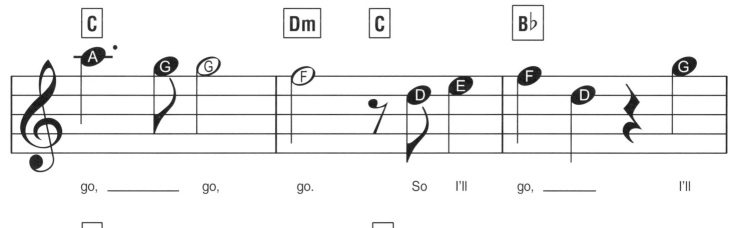

go, _____ go, go. So I'll go, _____ I'll

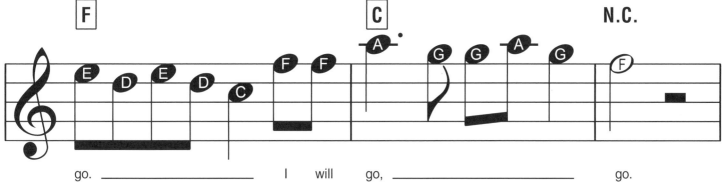

go. _____ I will go, _____ go.

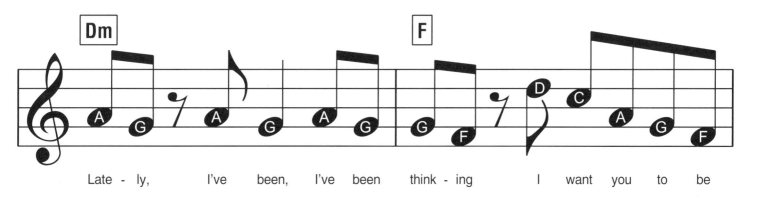

Late - ly, I've been, I've been think - ing I want you to be

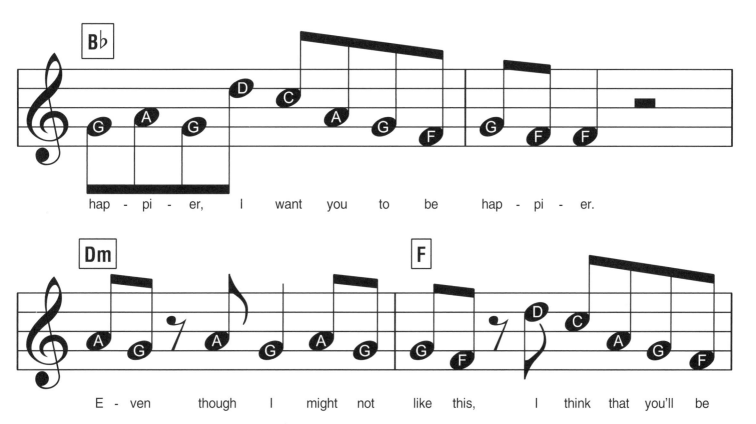

hap - pi - er, I want you to be hap - pi - er.

E - ven though I might not like this, I think that you'll be

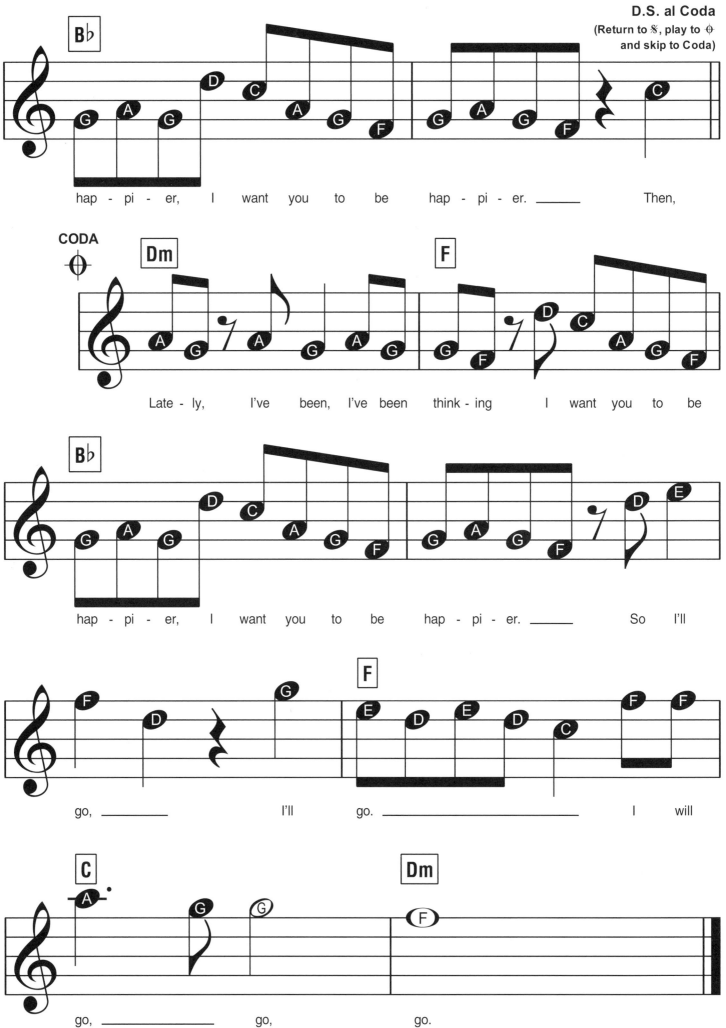

D.S. al Coda
(Return to 𝄋, play to ⊕
and skip to Coda)

Counting Stars

Registration 4
Rhythm: Pop or Rock

Words and Music by
Ryan Tedder

Late - ly I been, _____ I been los - in' sleep

dream - in' a - bout the things that we could be. But, ba - by, I been, _____

I been pray - in' hard. Said no more count - in' dol - lars, we'll be count - in' stars. _____

_____ Yeah, we'll be count - in' stars. _____ *(Instrumental)*

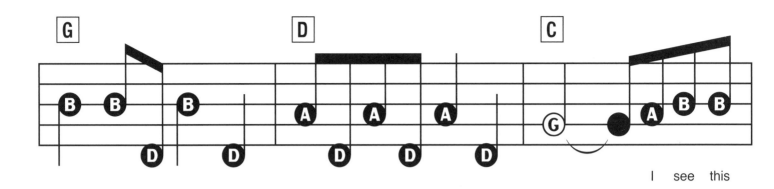

I see this

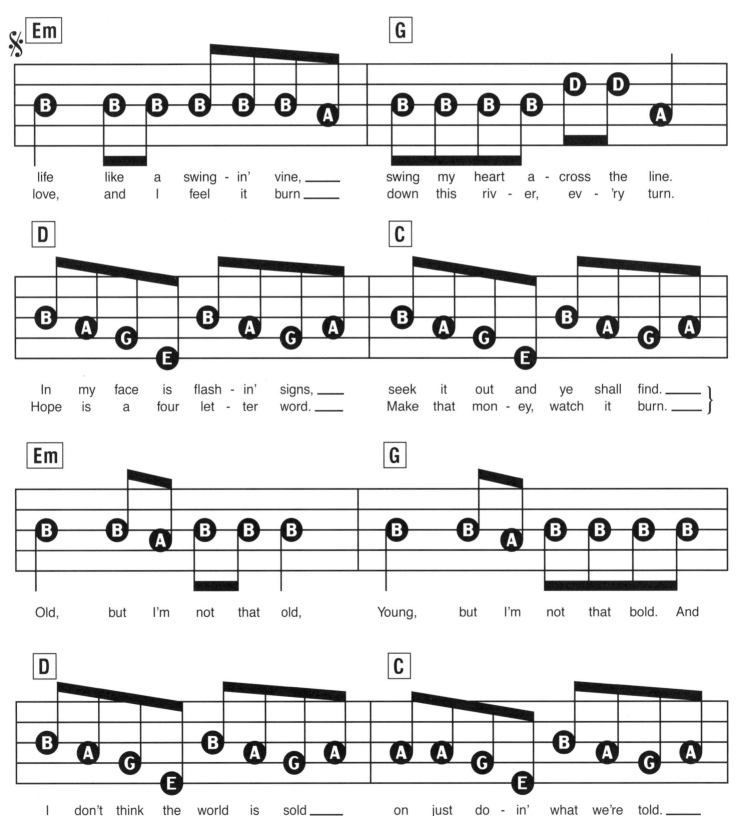

life   like   a   swing - in'   vine, ____   swing   my   heart   a - cross   the   line.
love,   and   I   feel   it   burn ____   down   this   riv - er,   ev - 'ry   turn.

In   my   face   is   flash - in'   signs, ___   seek   it   out   and   ye   shall   find. ____
Hope   is   a   four   let - ter   word. ____   Make   that   mon - ey,   watch   it   burn. ____ }

Old,   but   I'm   not   that   old,   Young,   but   I'm   not   that   bold.   And

I   don't   think   the   world   is   sold ____   on   just   do - in'   what   we're   told. ____

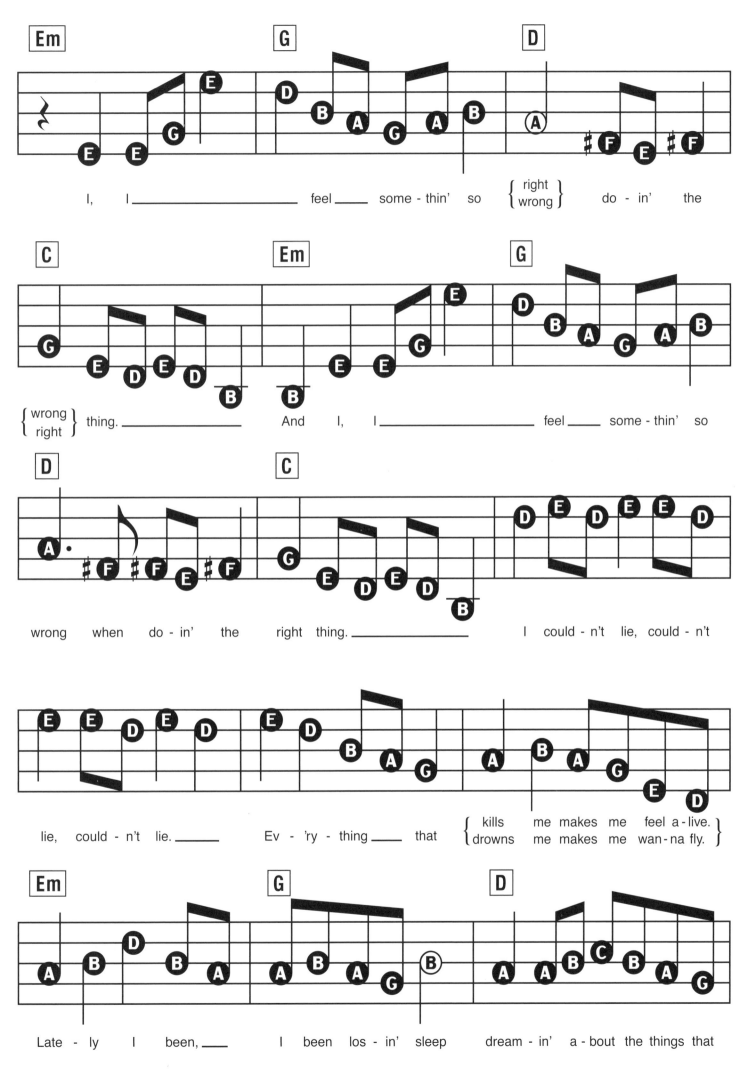

44

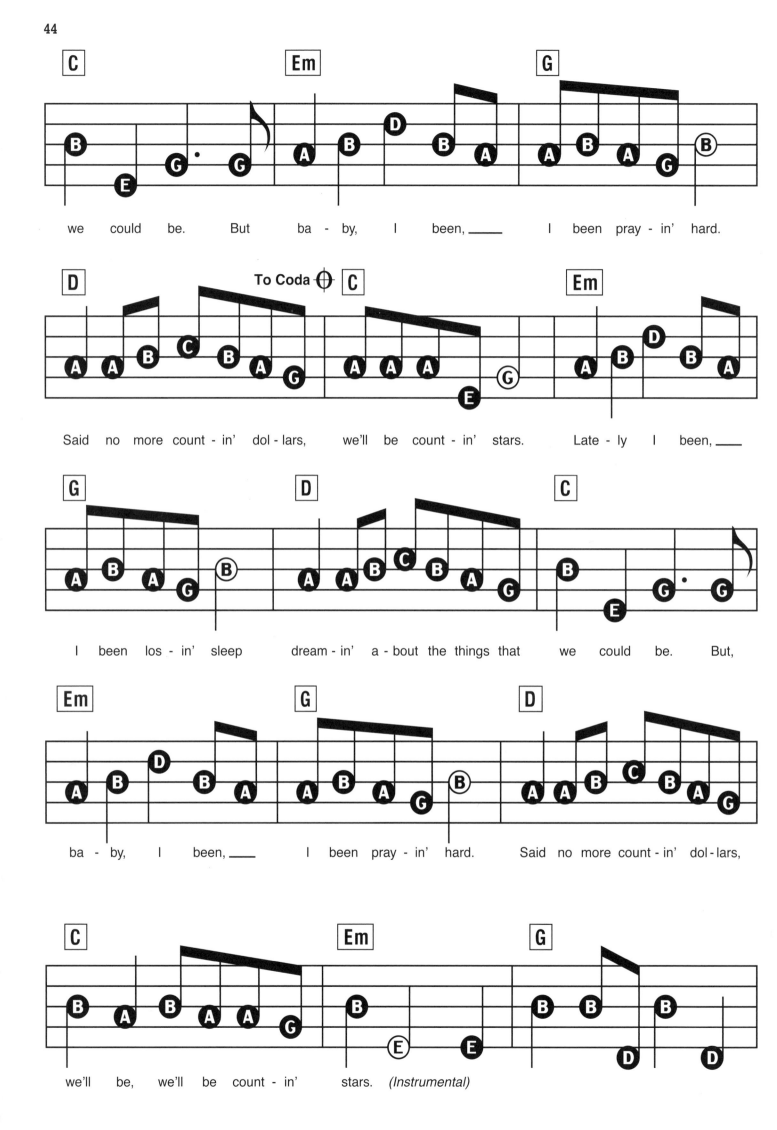

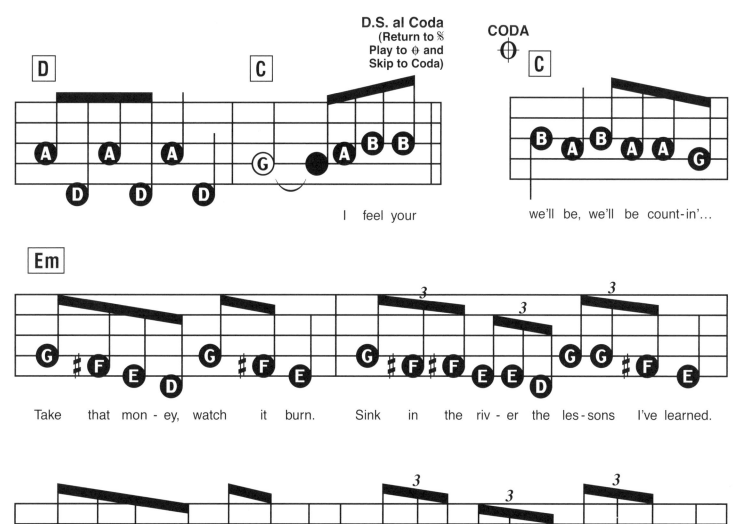

D.S. al Coda
(Return to %
Play to ⊕ and
Skip to Coda)

CODA
⊕

I feel your

we'll be, we'll be count-in'...

Em

Take that mon - ey, watch it burn. Sink in the riv - er the les - sons I've learned.

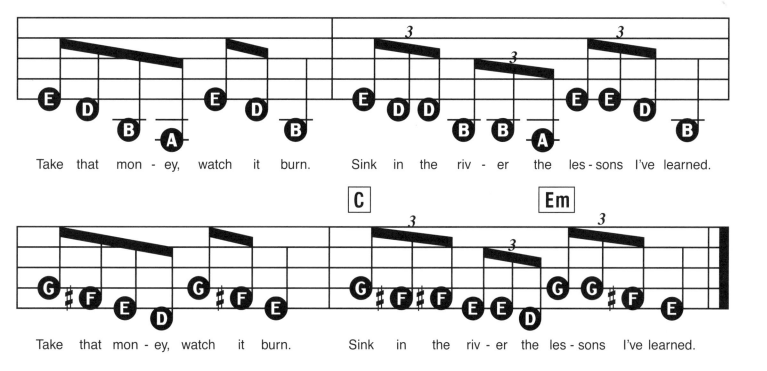

Take that mon - ey, watch it burn. Sink in the riv - er the les - sons I've learned.

Take that mon - ey, watch it burn. Sink in the riv - er the les - sons I've learned.

C   Em

Take that mon - ey, watch it burn. Sink in the riv - er the les - sons I've learned.

Get Lucky

Registration 4
Rhythm: Dance or Rock

Words and Music by Thomas Bangalter,
Guy Manuel Homem Christo,
Nile Rodgers and Pharrell Williams

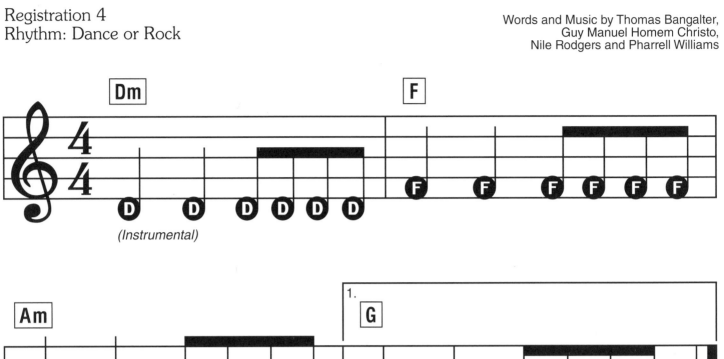

(Instrumental)

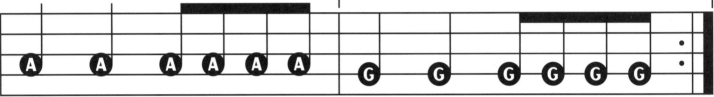

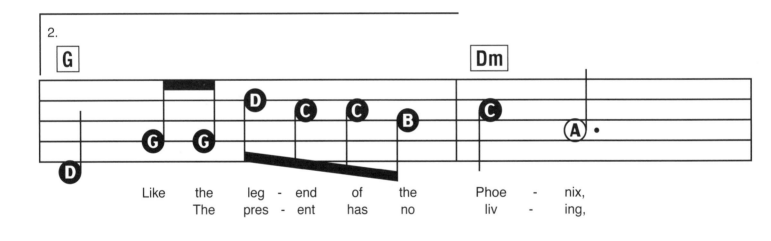

Like the leg - end of the Phoe - nix,
The pres - ent has no liv - ing,

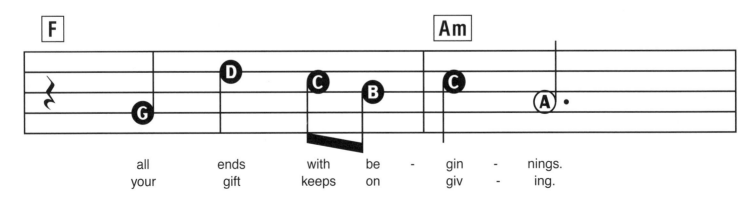

all ends with be - gin - nings.
your gift keeps on giv - ing.

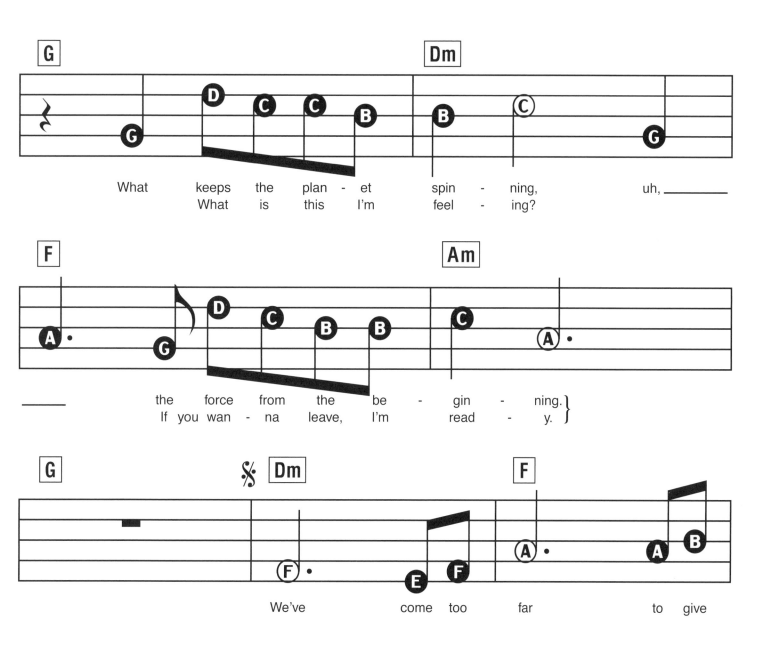

What keeps the plan - et spin - ning, uh, _____
What is this I'm feel - ing?

_____ the force from the be - gin - ning.
If you wan - na leave, I'm read - y.

We've come too far to give

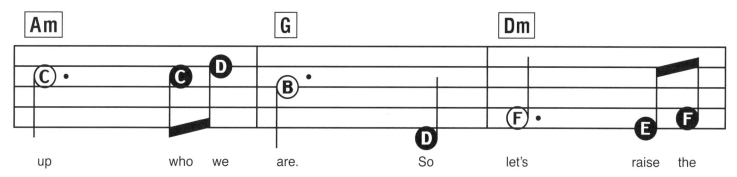

up who we are. So let's raise the

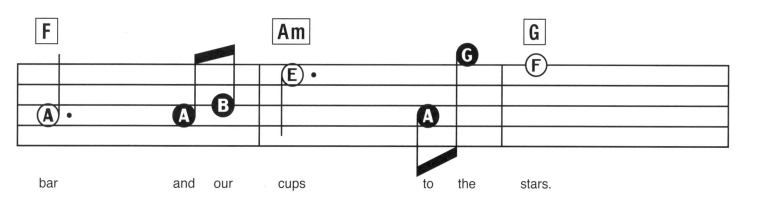

bar and our cups to the stars.

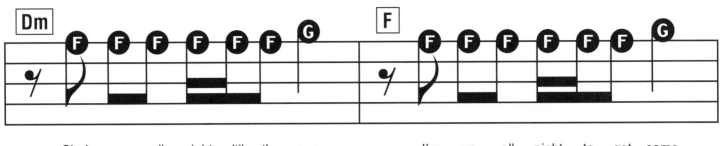

She's up all night 'til the sun.   I'm up all night to get some.

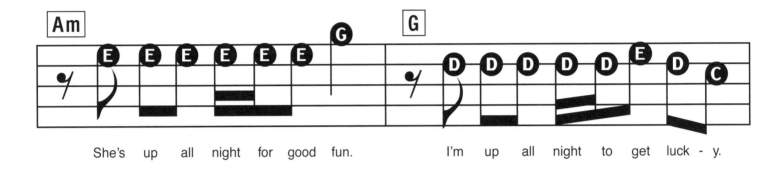

She's up all night for good fun.   I'm up all night to get luck - y.

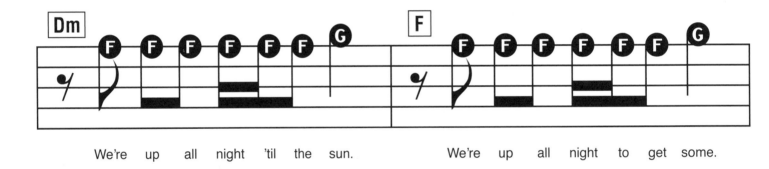

We're up all night 'til the sun.   We're up all night to get some.

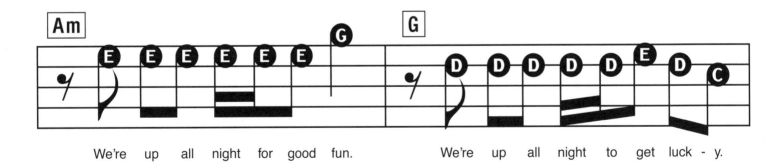

We're up all night for good fun.   We're up all night to get luck - y.

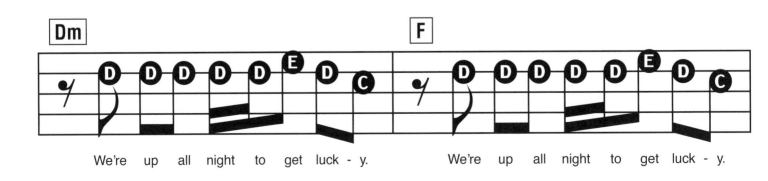

We're up all night to get luck - y.   We're up all night to get luck - y.

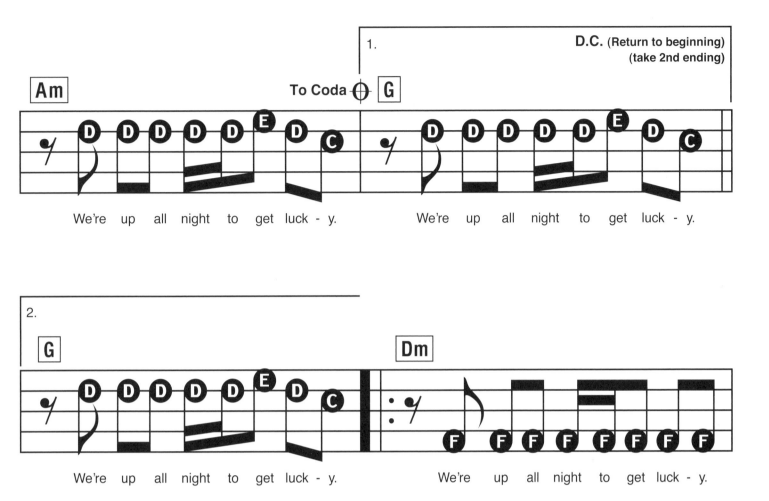

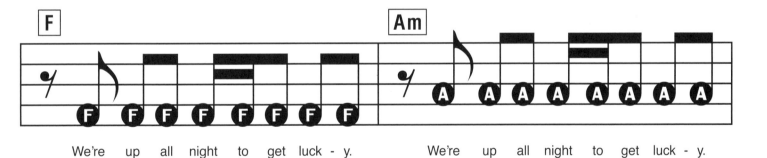

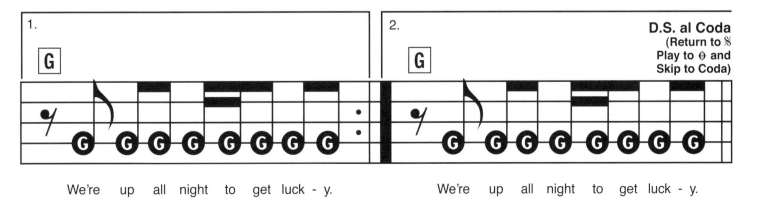

CODA

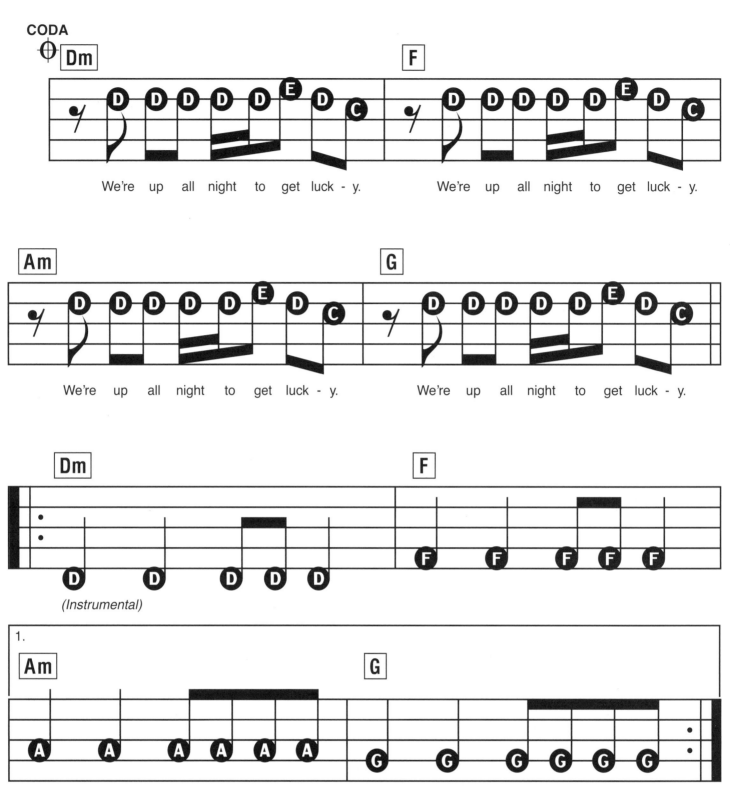

We're up all night to get luck - y.

We're up all night to get luck - y.

We're up all night to get luck - y.

We're up all night to get luck - y.

(Instrumental)

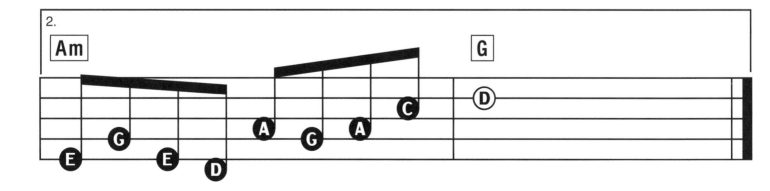

Cups
(When I'm Gone)
from the Motion Picture Soundtrack PITCH PERFECT

Registration 4
Rhythm: Folk

Words and Music by A.P. Carter,
Luisa Gerstein and Heloise Tunstall-Behrens

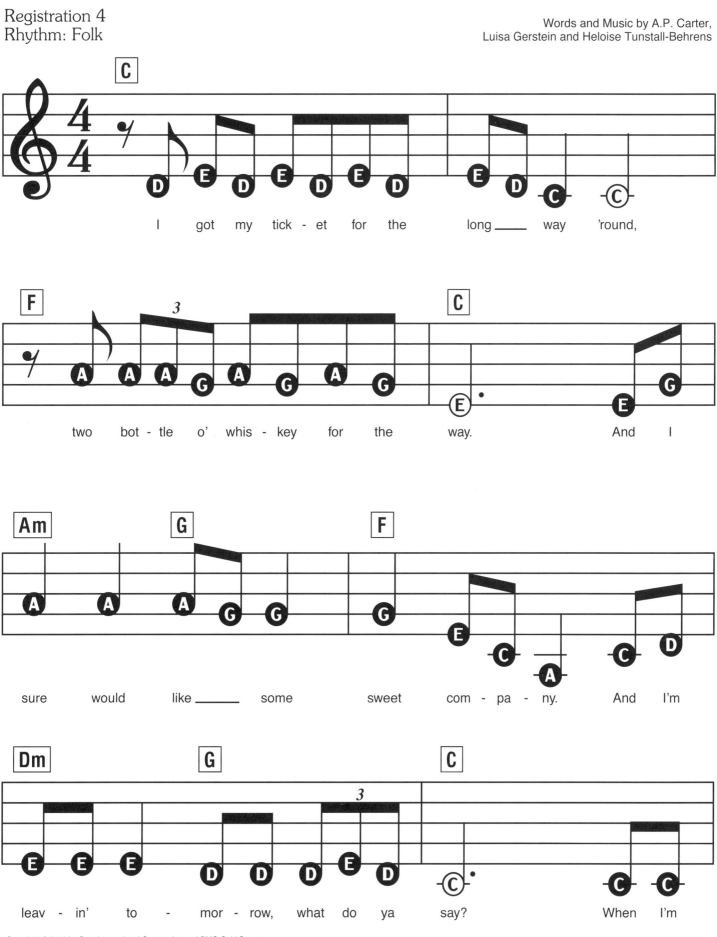

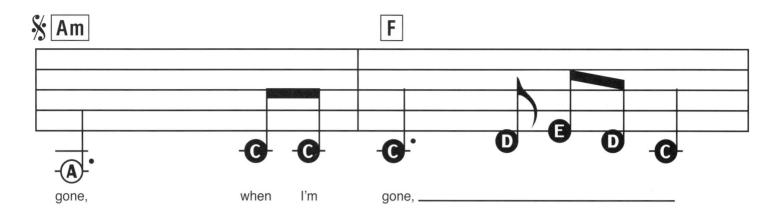

gone,   when I'm gone, _____

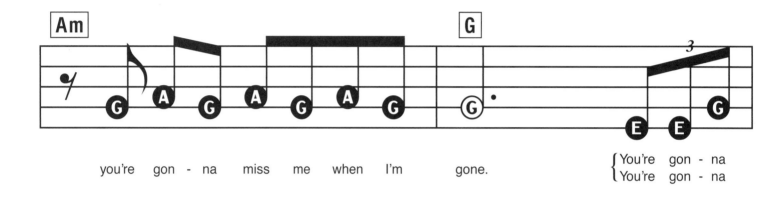

you're gon - na miss me when I'm gone. { You're gon - na / You're gon - na

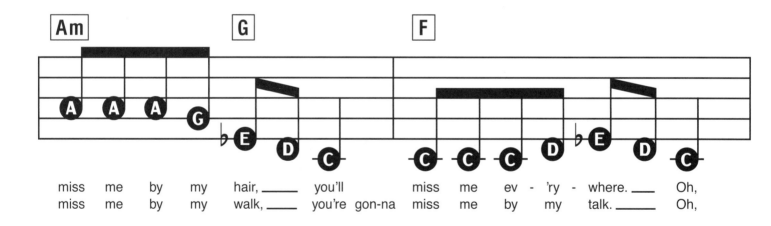

miss me by my hair, ____ you'll miss me ev - 'ry - where. ____ Oh,
miss me by my walk, ____ you're gon-na miss me by my talk. ____ Oh,

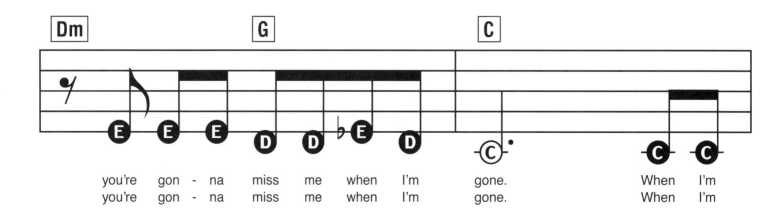

you're gon - na miss me when I'm gone. When I'm
you're gon - na miss me when I'm gone. When I'm

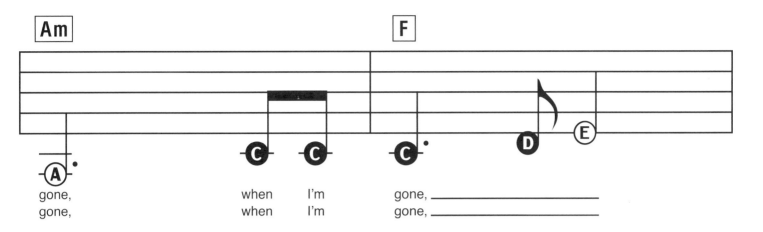

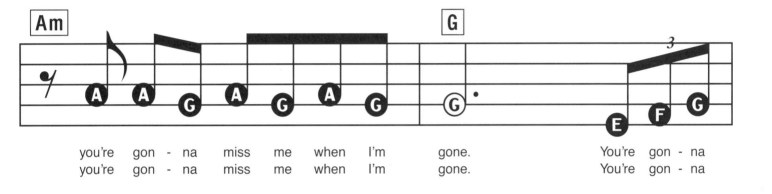

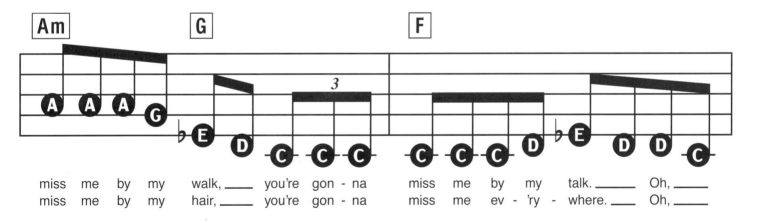

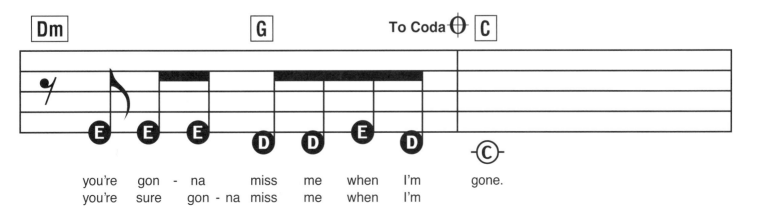

N.C.

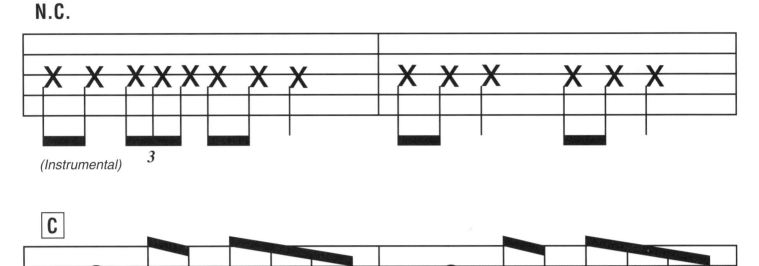

(Instrumental)

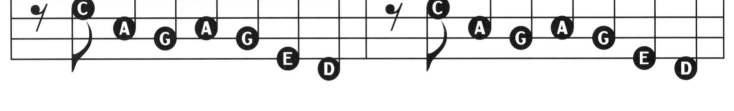

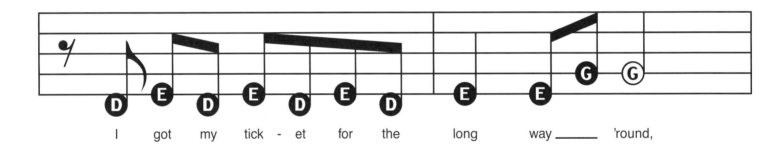

I got my tick - et for the long way _____ 'round,

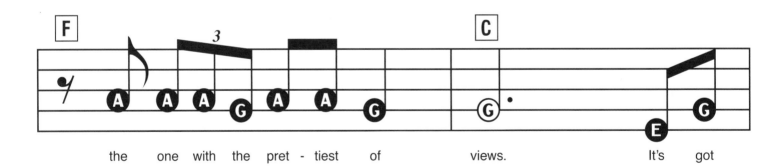

the one with the pret - tiest of views. It's got

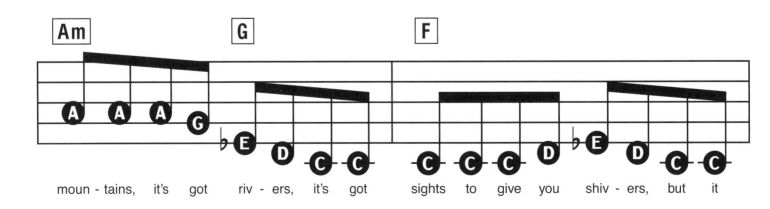

moun - tains, it's got riv - ers, it's got sights to give you shiv - ers, but it

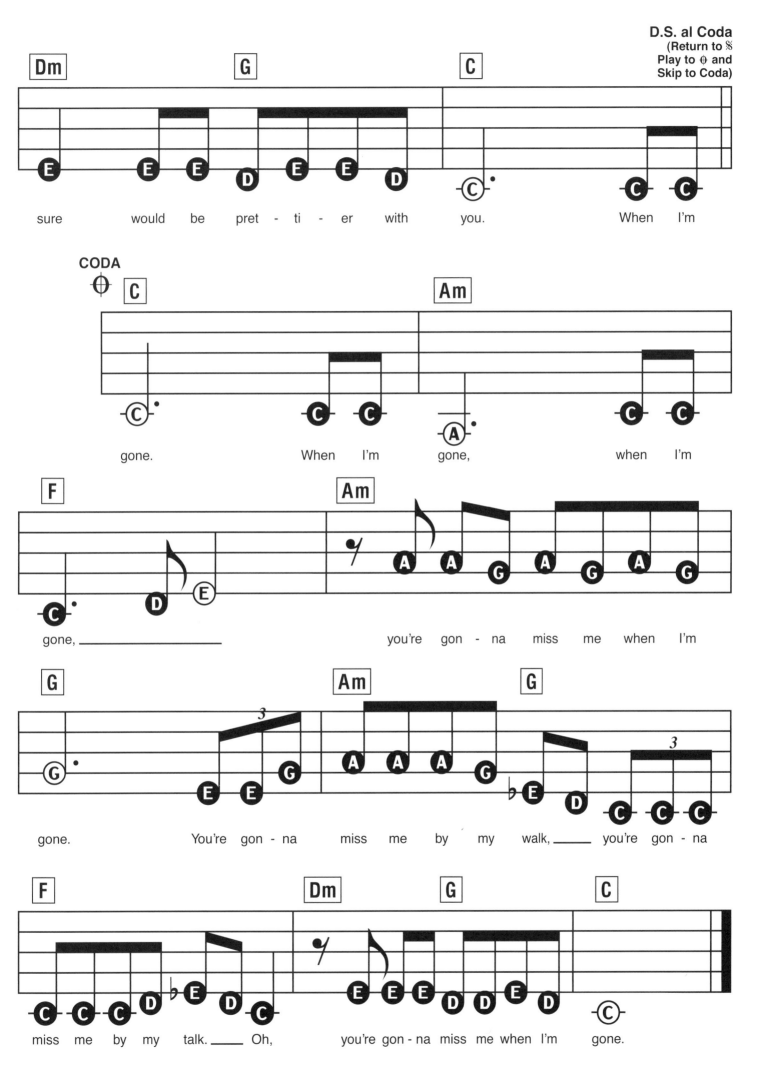

D.S. al Coda
(Return to %
Play to ϕ and
Skip to Coda)

Feel It Still

Registration 2
Rhythm: Rock

Words and Music by John Gourley, Zach Carothers,
Jason Sechrist, Eric Howk, Kyle O'Quin,
Brian Holland, Freddie Gorman, Georgia Dobbins,
Robert Bateman, William Garrett,
John Hill and Asa Taccone

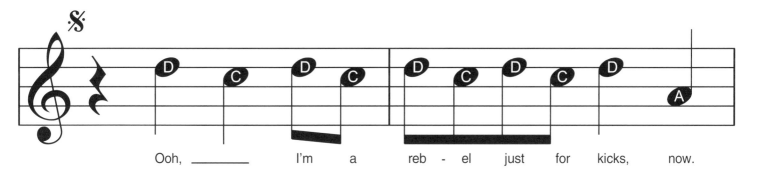

Ooh, _____ I'm a reb - el just for kicks, now.

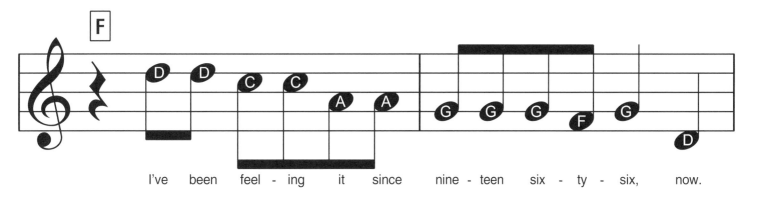

I've been feel - ing it since nine - teen six - ty - six, now.

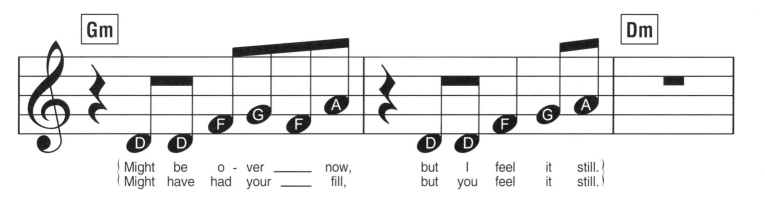

Might be o - ver _____ now, but I feel it still.
Might have had your _____ fill, but you feel it still.

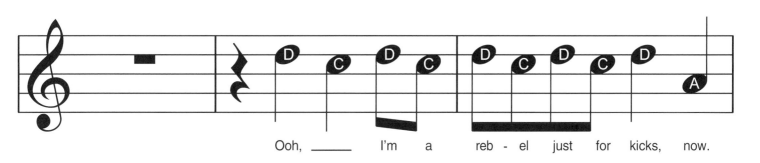

Ooh, _____ I'm a reb - el just for kicks, now.

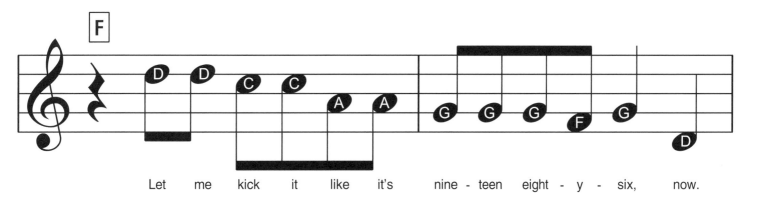

Let me kick it like it's nine - teen eight - y - six, now.

58

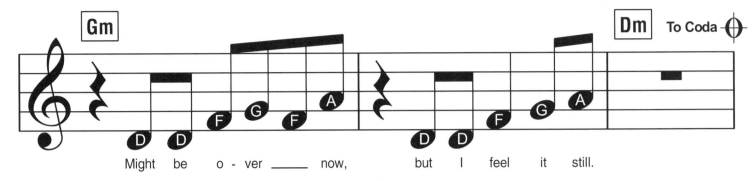

Might be o - ver ___ now, but I feel it still.

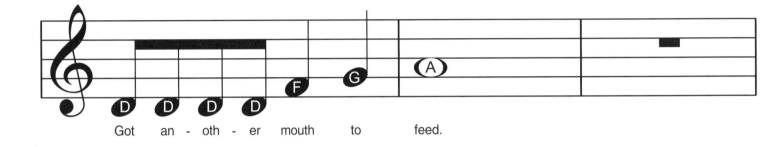

Got an - oth - er mouth to feed.

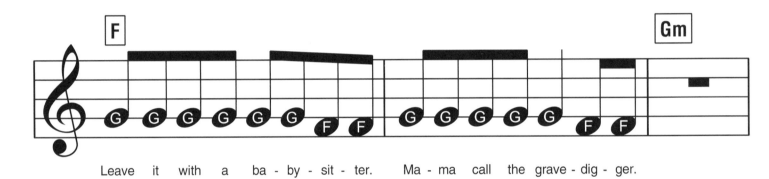

Leave it with a ba - by - sit - ter. Ma - ma call the grave - dig - ger.

D.S. al Coda
(Return to 𝄋, play to ⊕
and skip to Coda)

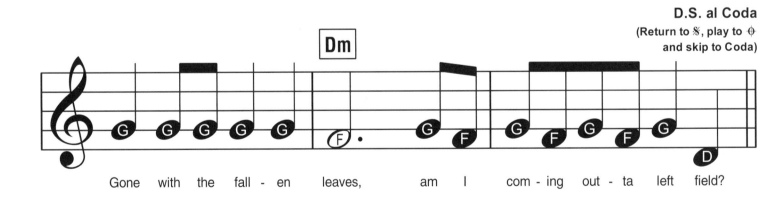

Gone with the fall - en leaves, am I com - ing out - ta left field?

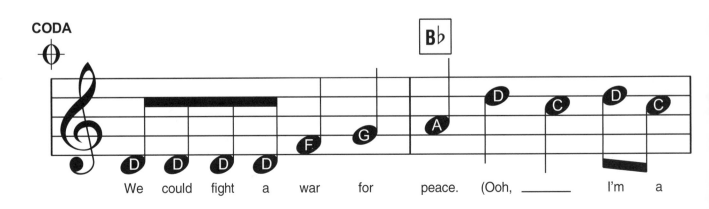

We could fight a war for peace. (Ooh, ___ I'm a

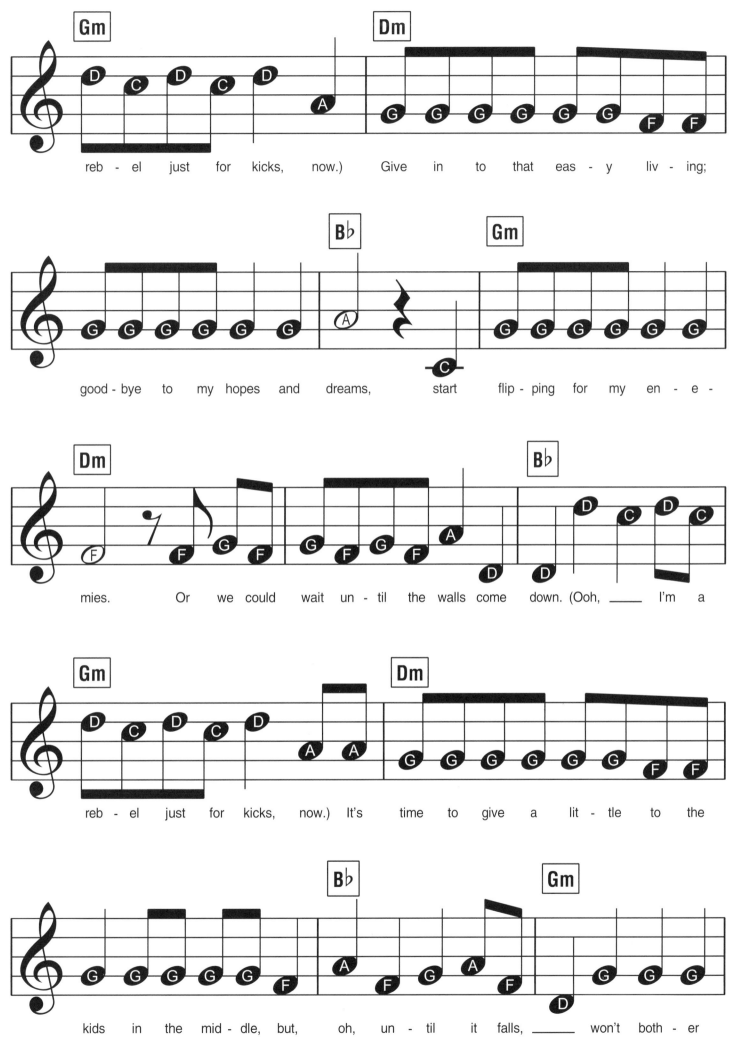

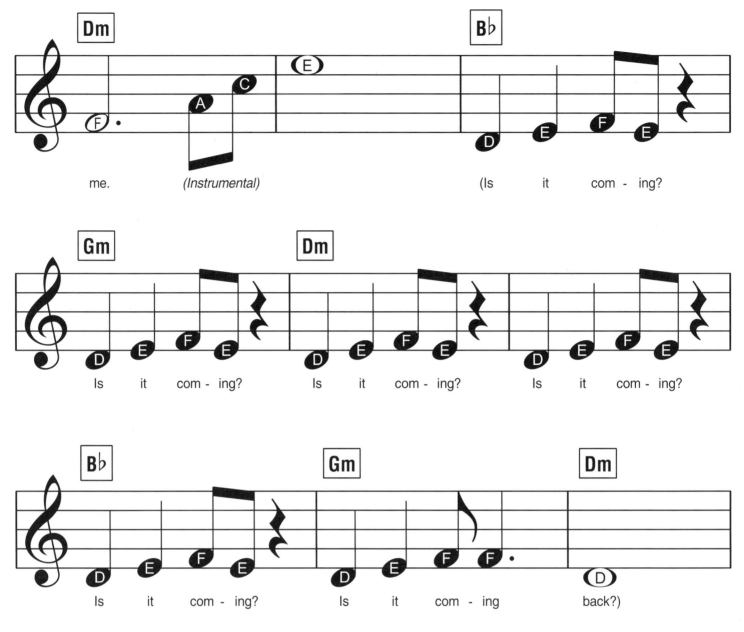

me. *(Instrumental)* (Is it com - ing?

Is it com - ing? Is it com - ing? Is it com - ing?

Is it com - ing? Is it com - ing back?)

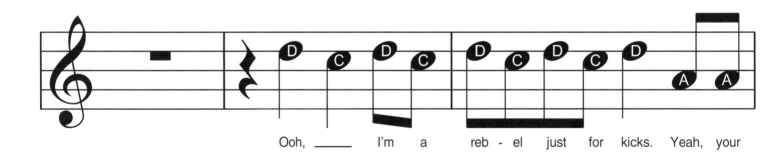

Ooh, _____ I'm a reb - el just for kicks. Yeah, your

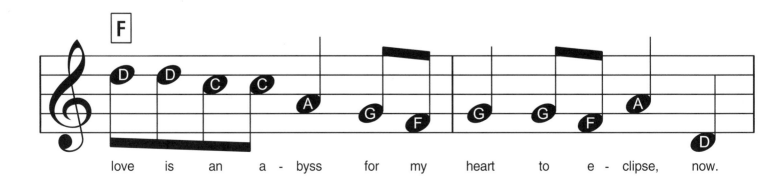

love is an a - byss for my heart to e - clipse, now.

61

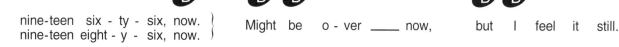

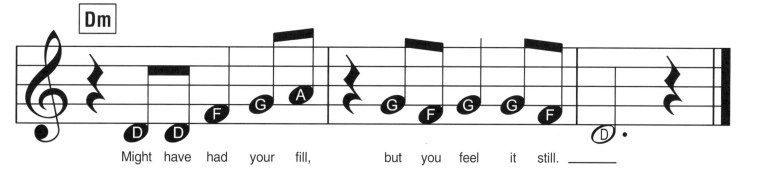

Firework

Registration 4
Rhythm: Dance or Rock

Words and Music by Katy Perry,
Mikkel Eriksen, Tor Erik Hermansen,
Esther Dean and Sandy Wilhelm

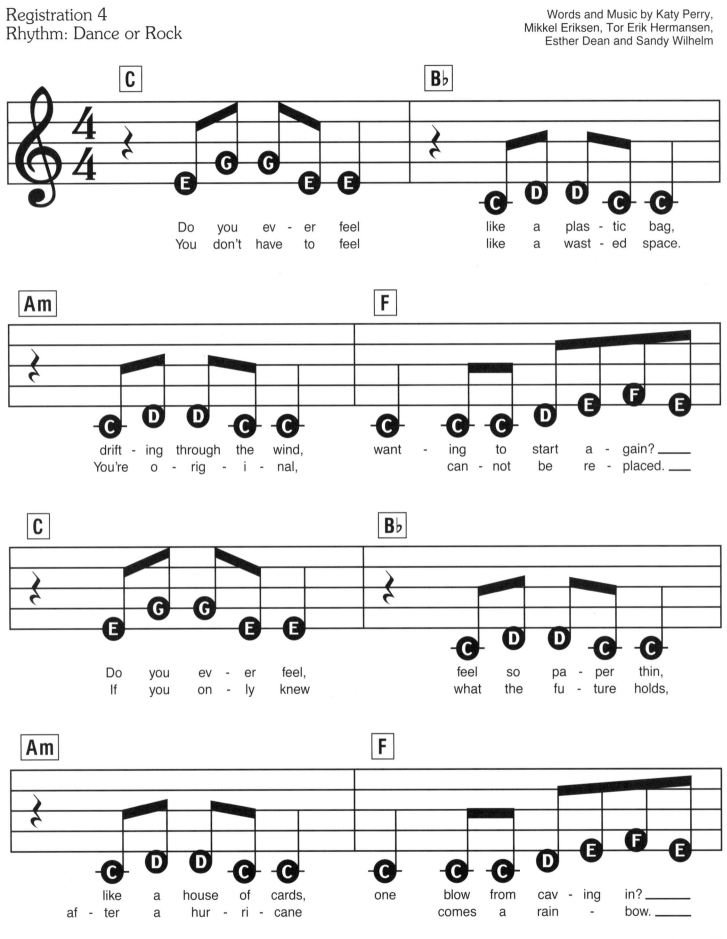

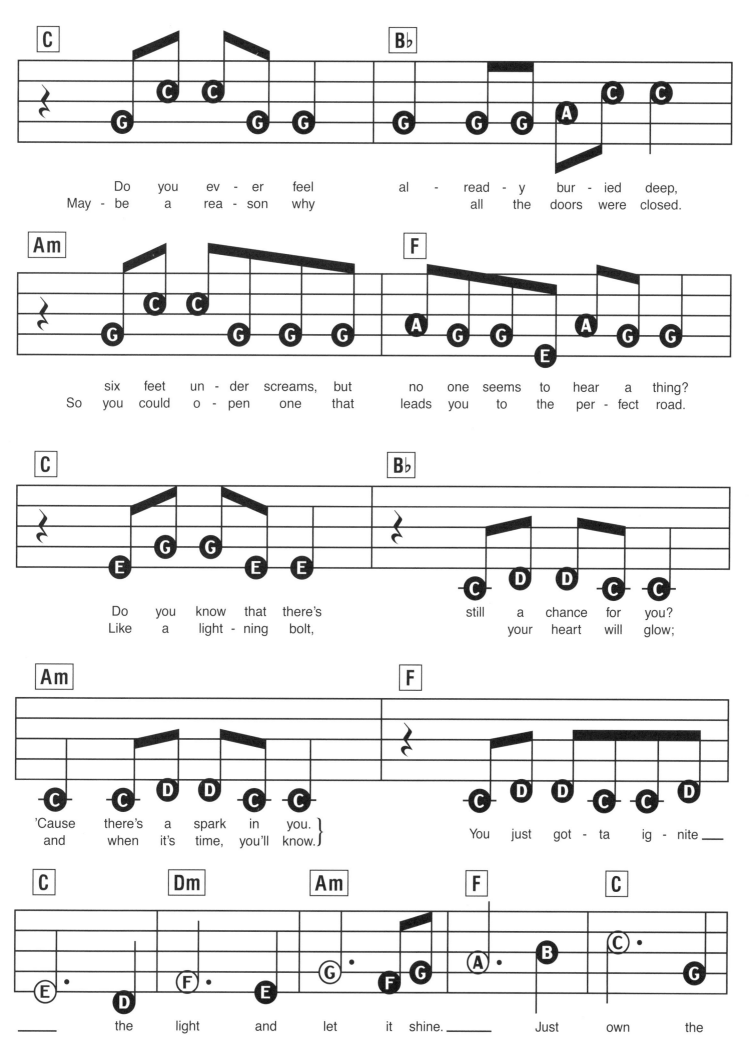

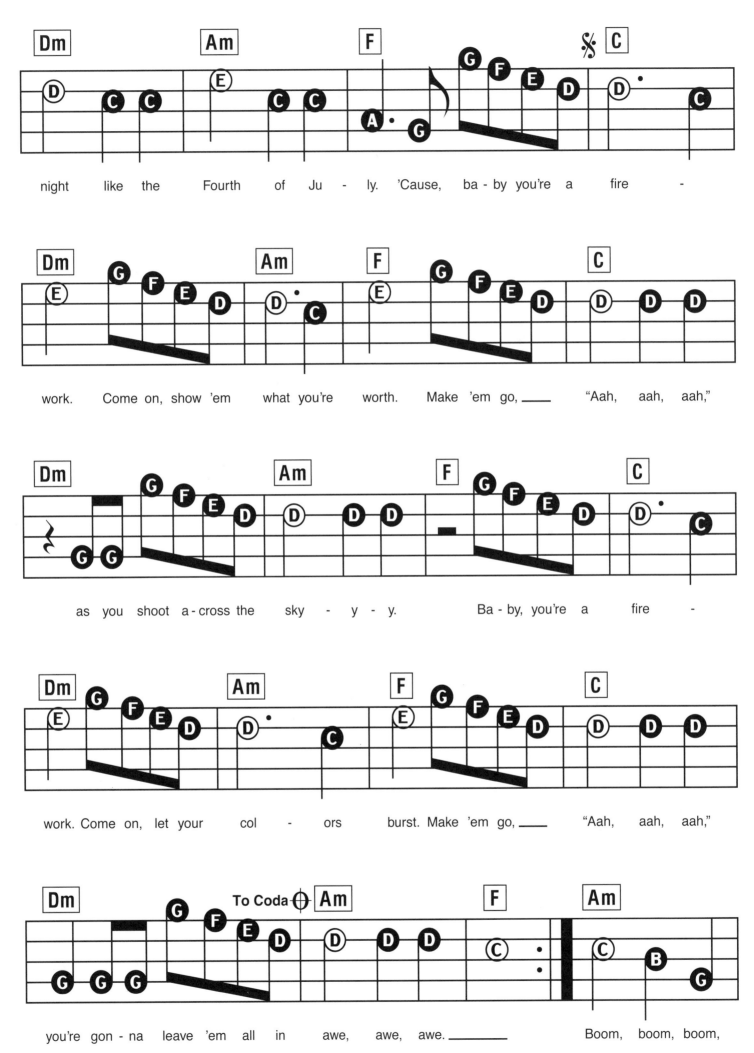

65

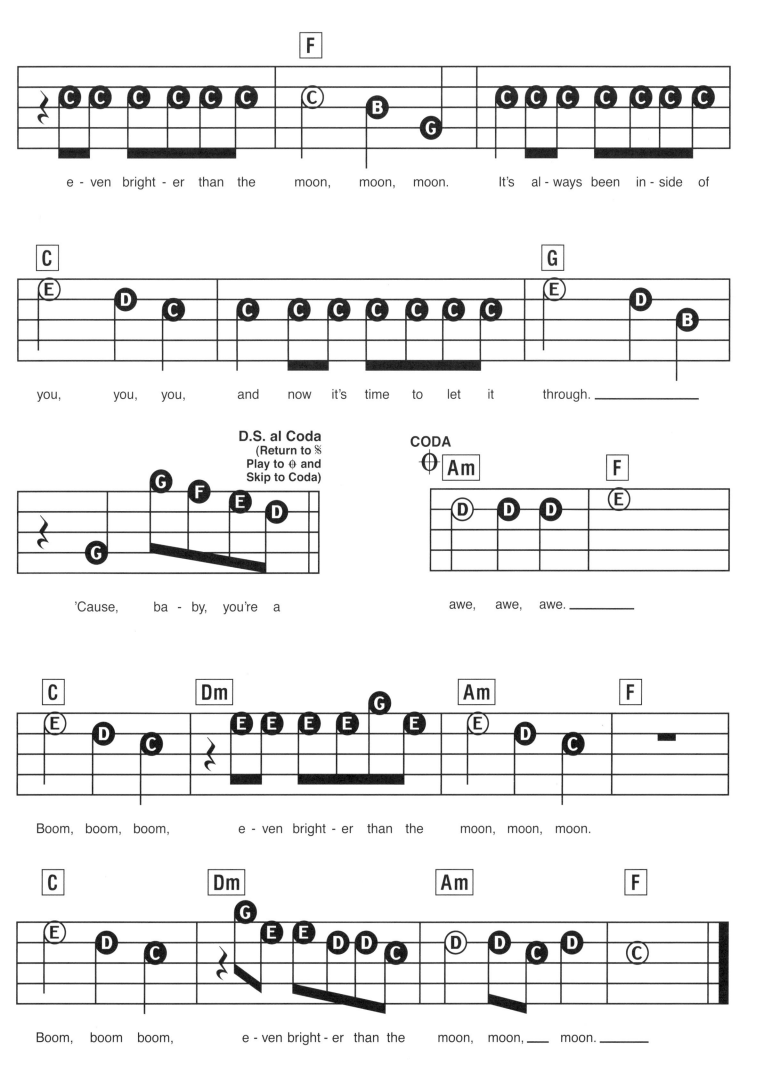

Girls Like You

Registration 4
Rhythm: Pop

Words and Music by Adam Levine,
Brittany Hazzard, Jason Evigan,
Gian Stone and Henry Walter

70

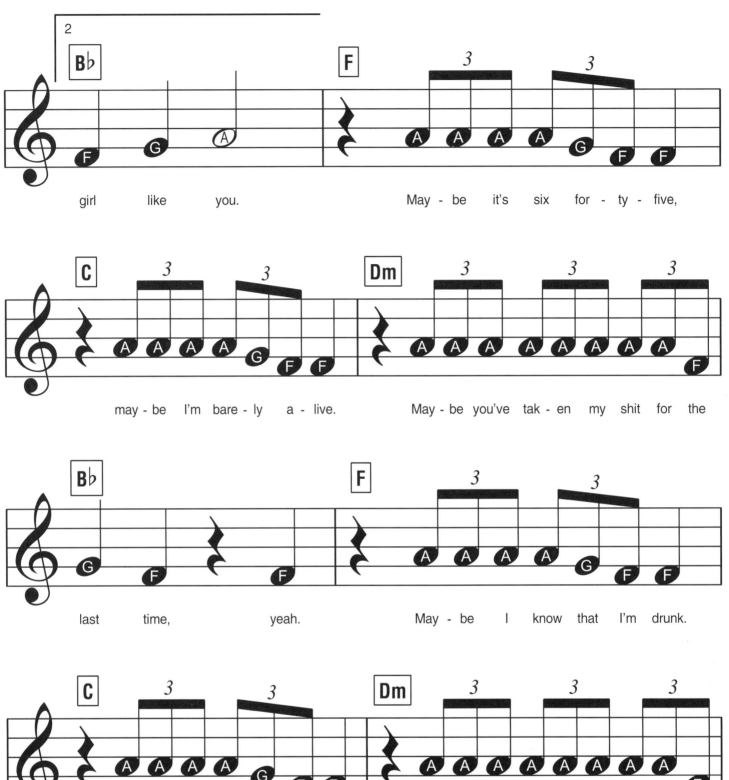

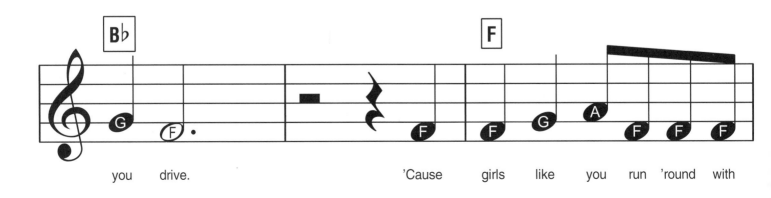

71

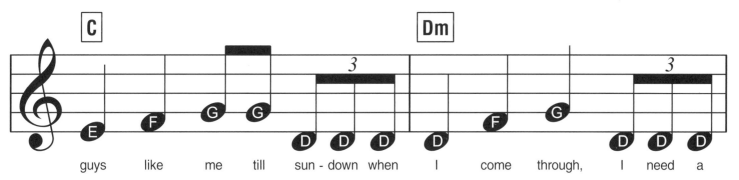

guys like me till sun - down when I come through, I need a

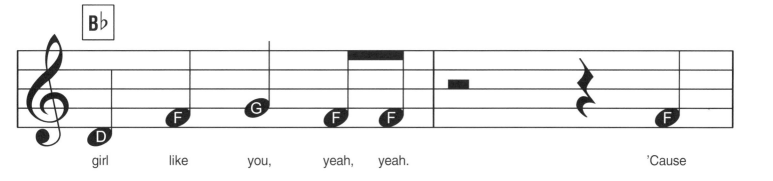

girl like you, yeah, yeah. 'Cause

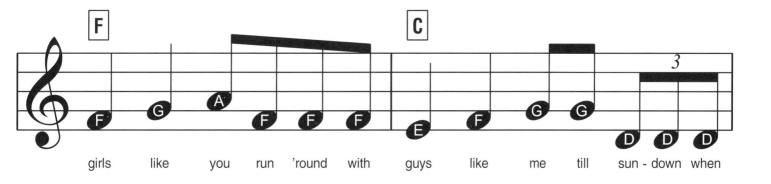

girls like you run 'round with guys like me till sun - down when

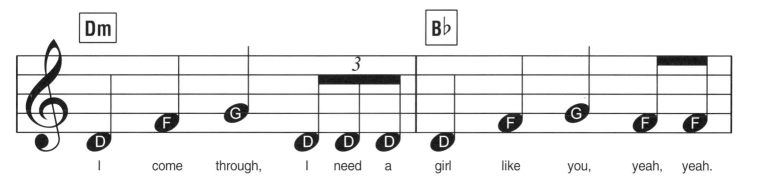

I come through, I need a girl like you, yeah, yeah.

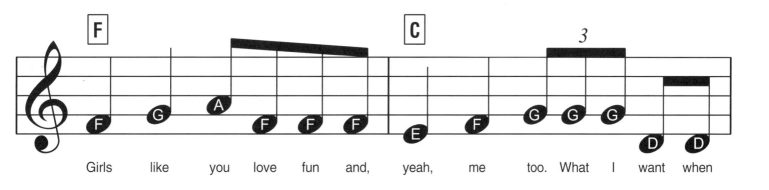

Girls like you love fun and, yeah, me too. What I want when

Happy
from DESPICABLE ME 2

Registration 8
Rhythm: Rock

Words and Music by
Pharrell Williams

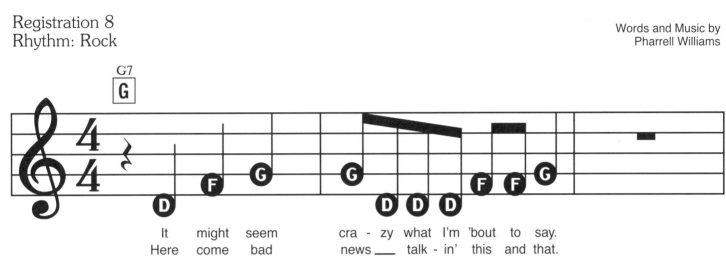

It might seem cra - zy what I'm 'bout to say.
Here come bad news ___ talk - in' this and that.

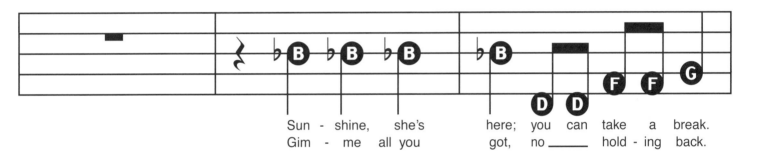

Sun - shine, she's here; you can take a break.
Gim - me all you got, no _____ hold - ing back.

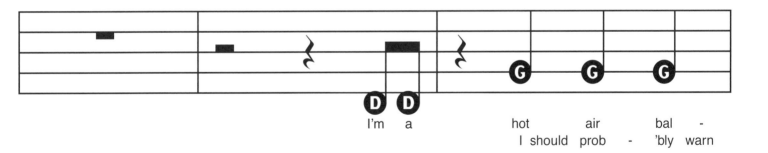

I'm a hot air bal -
I should prob - 'bly warn

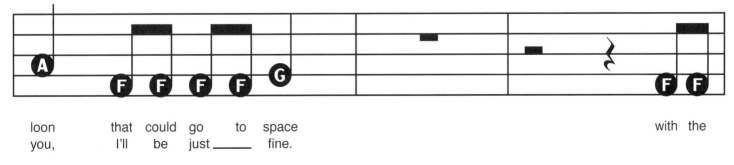

loon that could go to space
you, I'll be just _____ fine.

with the

74

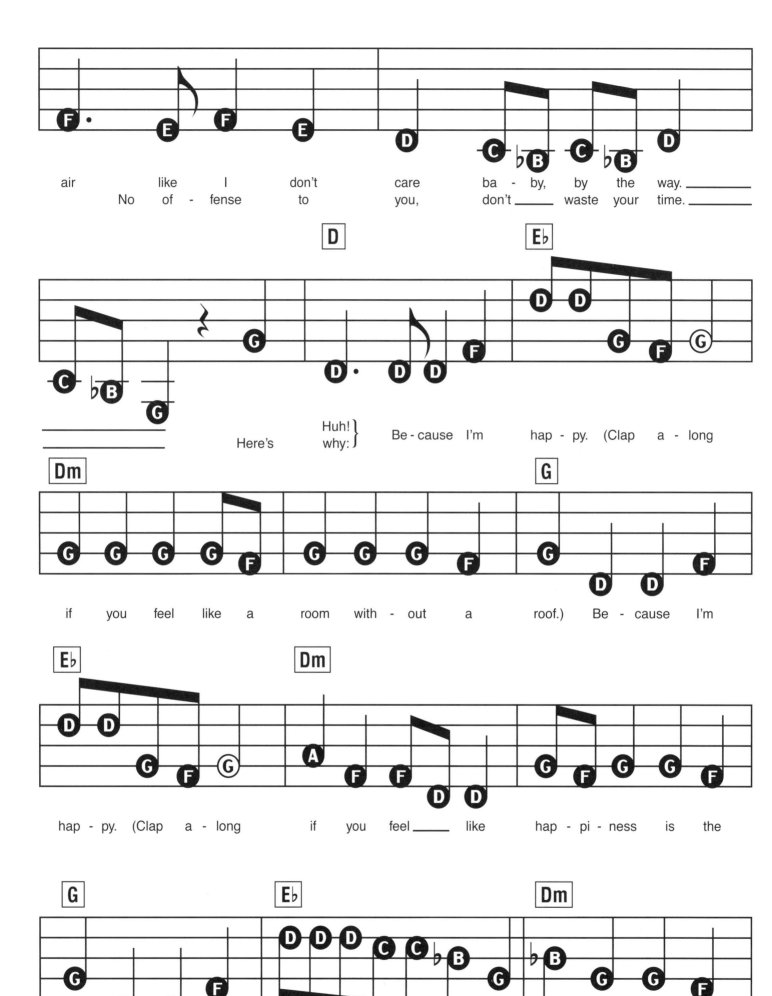

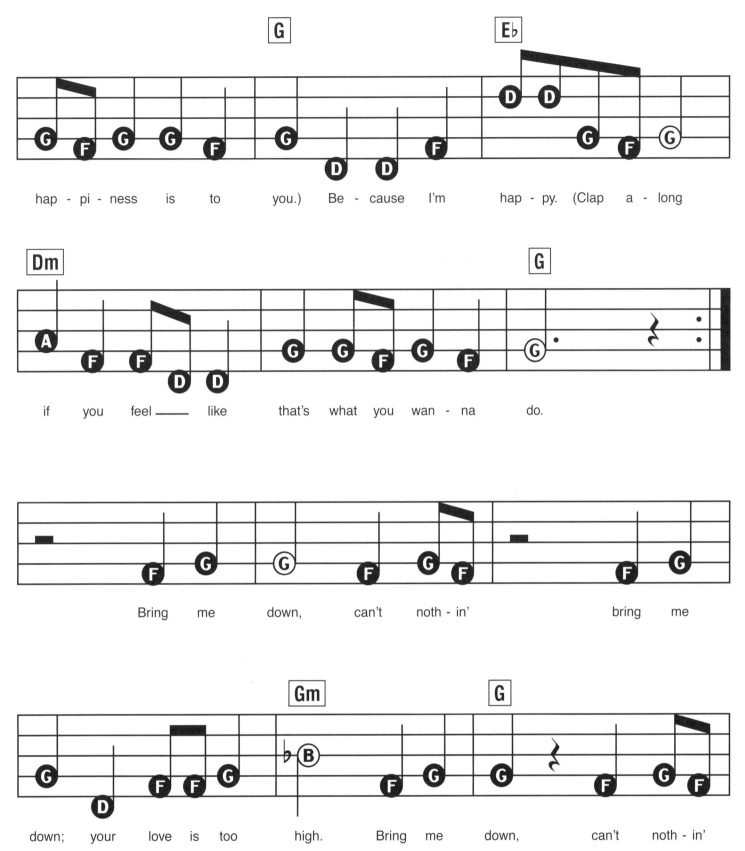

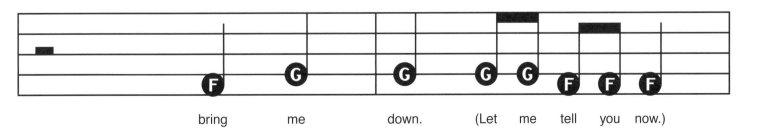

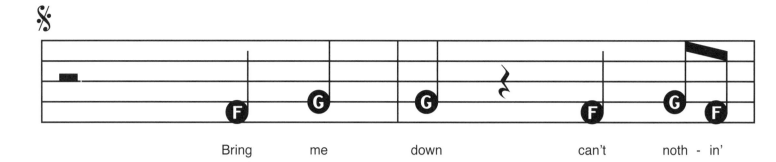

Bring   me   down   can't   noth - in'

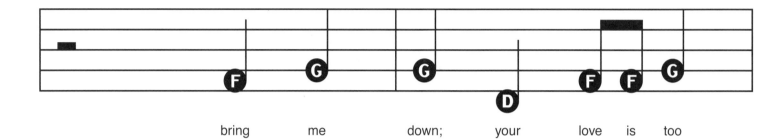

bring   me   down;   your   love   is   too

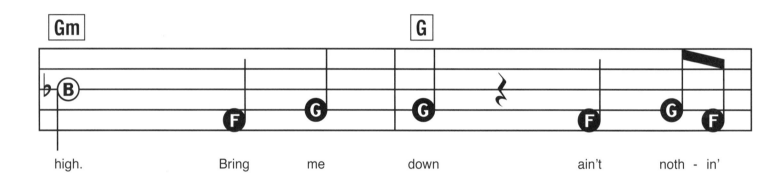

Gm   **G**

high.   Bring   me   down   ain't   noth - in'

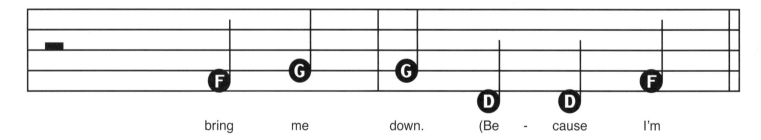

bring   me   down.   (Be - cause   I'm

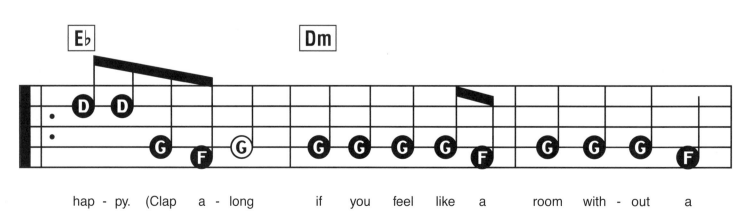

E♭   **Dm**

hap - py. (Clap   a - long   if   you   feel   like   a   room   with - out   a

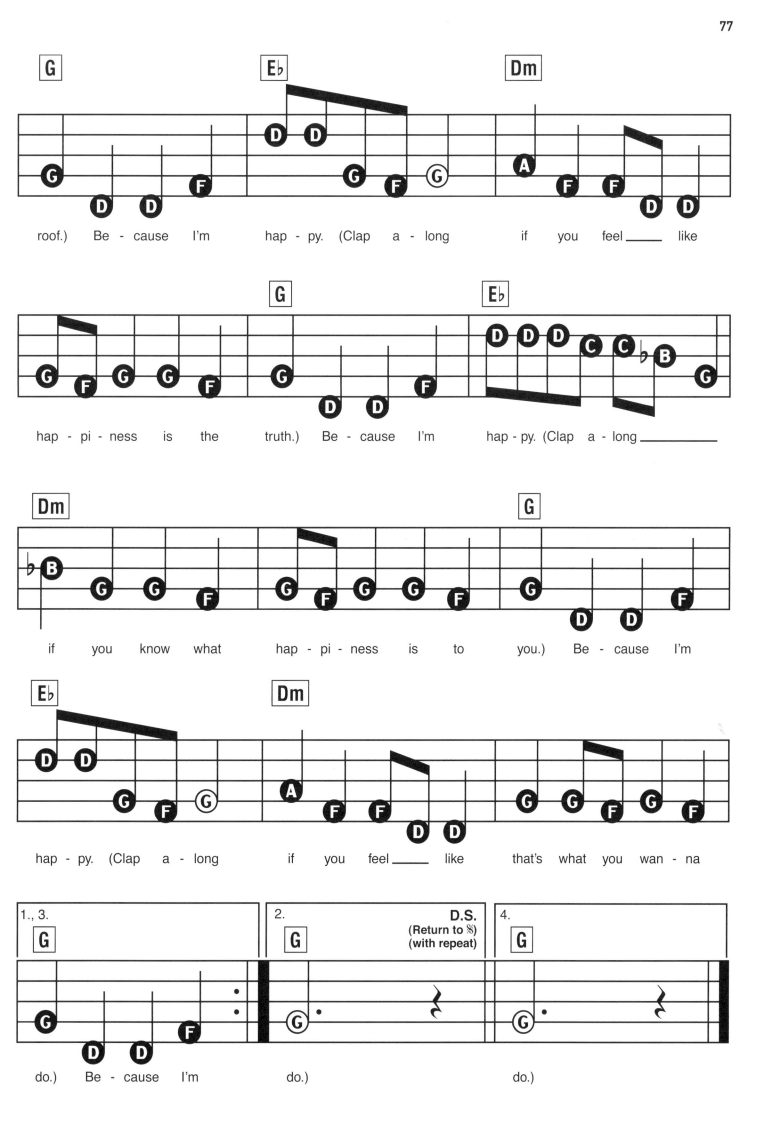

Havana

Registration 5
Rhythm: Latin or Pop

Words and Music by Camila Cabello, Louis Bell,
Pharrell Williams, Adam Feeney, Ali Tamposi,
Jeffery Lamar Williams, Brian Lee, Andrew Wotman,
Brittany Hazzard and Kaan Gunesberk

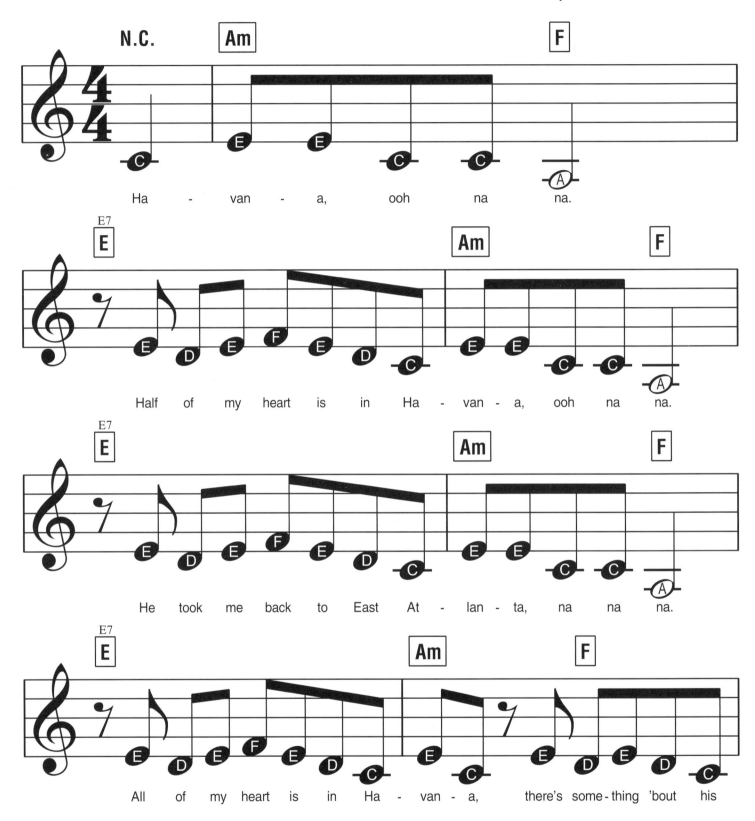

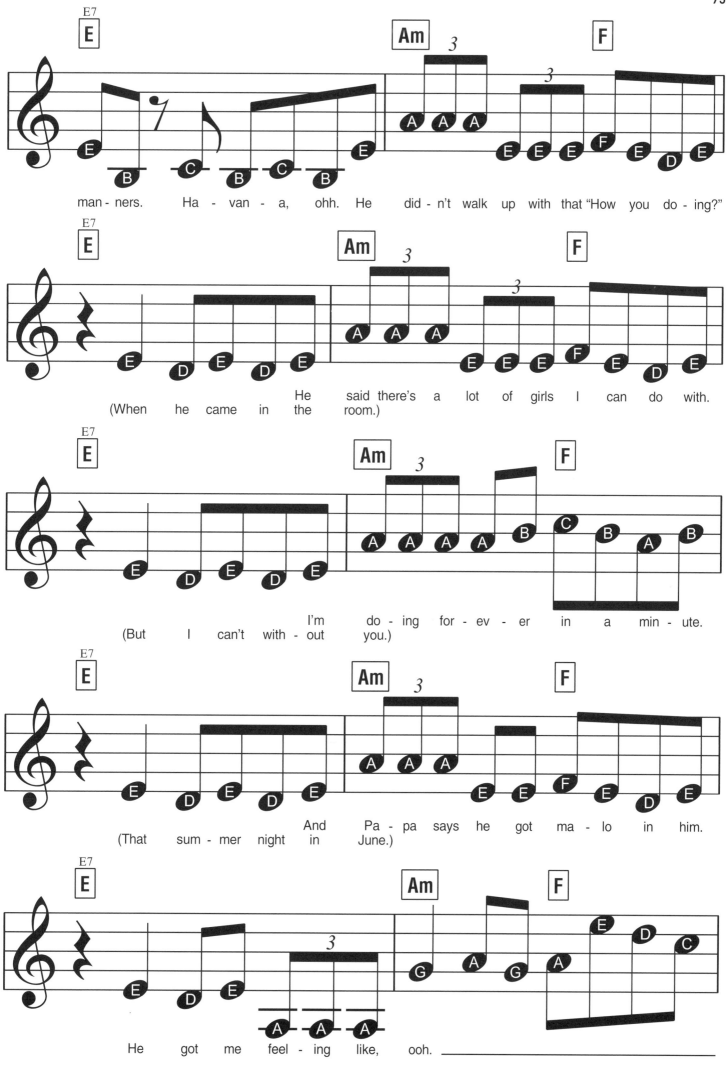

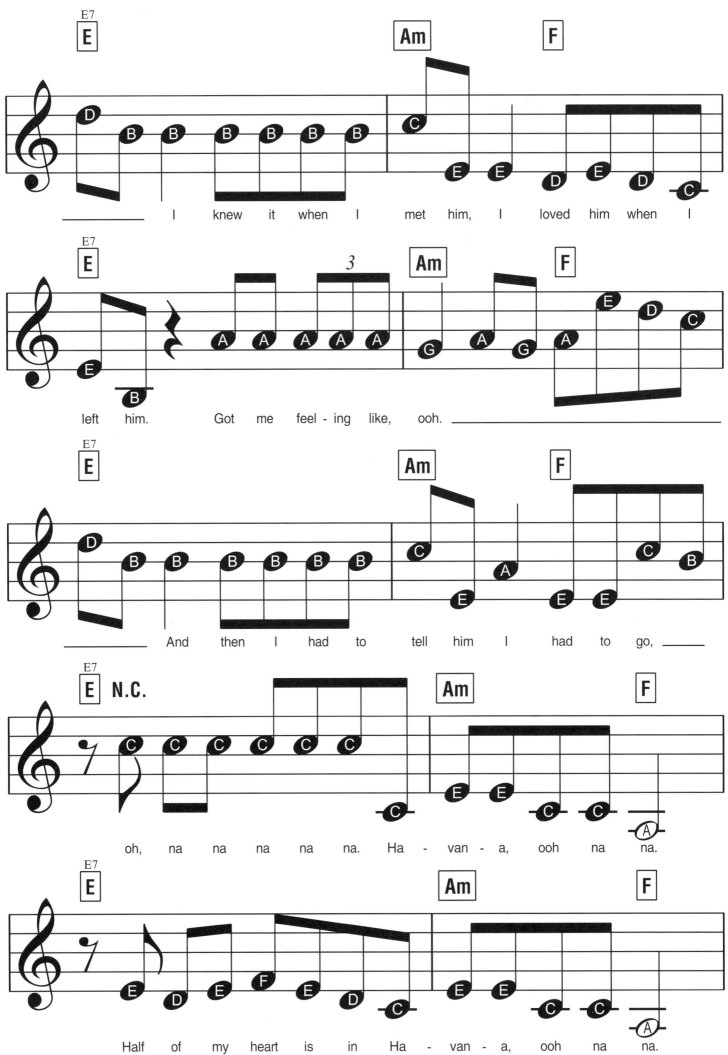

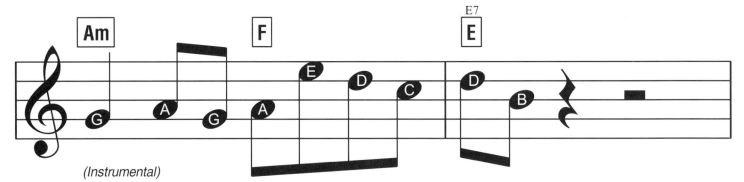

(Instrumental)

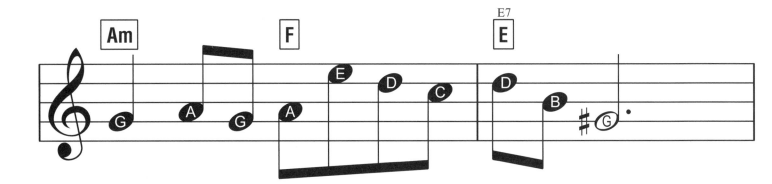

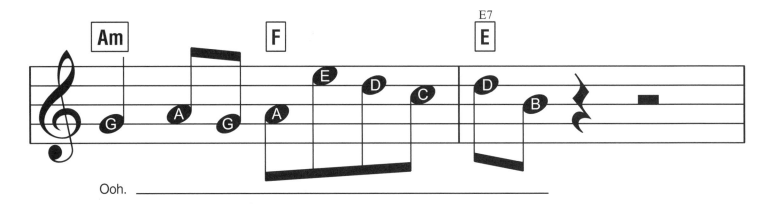

Ooh. _____

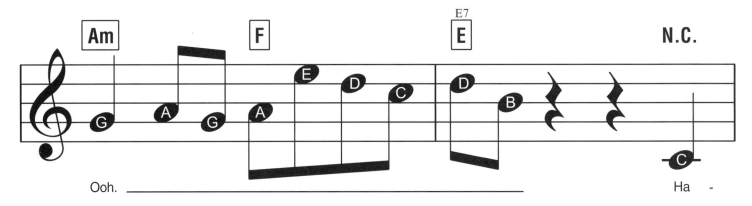

Ooh. _____   Ha -

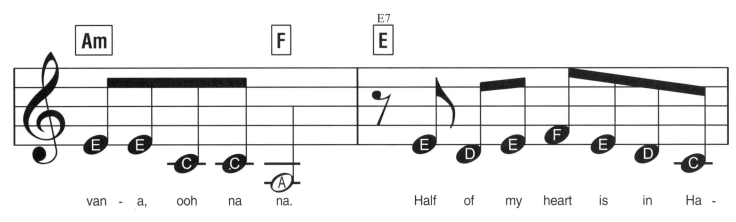

van - a, ooh na   na.   Half of my heart is in Ha -

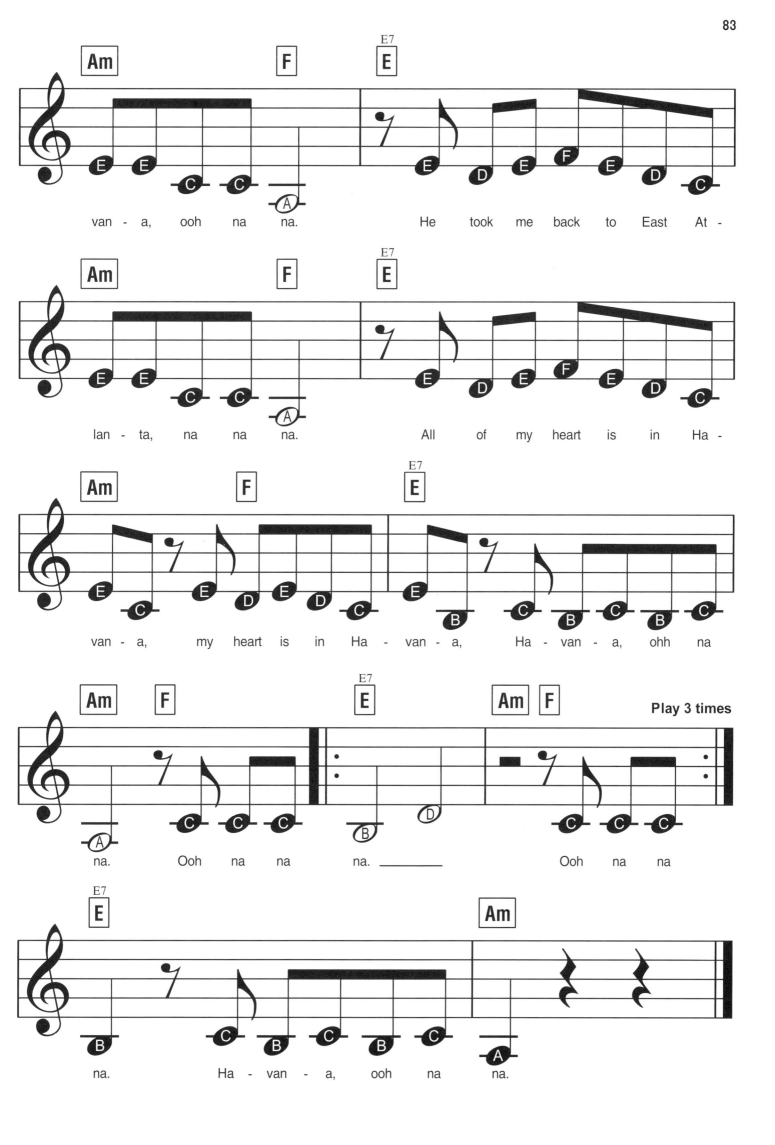

Ho Hey

Registration 4
Rhythm: Folk

Words and Music by Jeremy Fraites
and Wesley Schultz

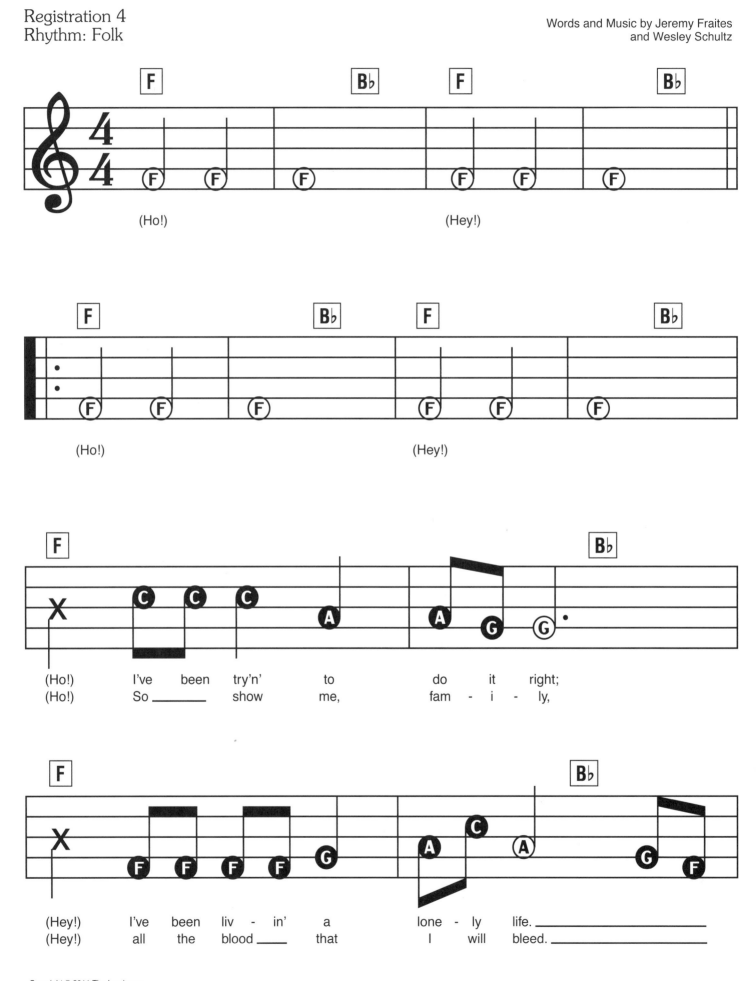

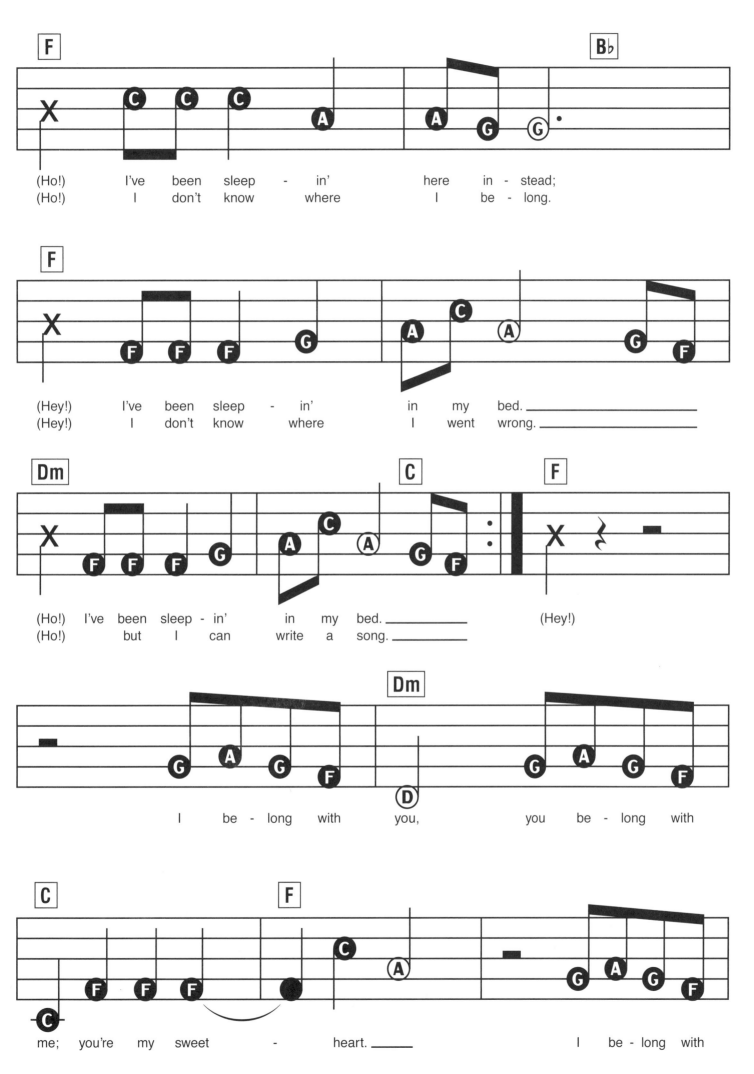

86

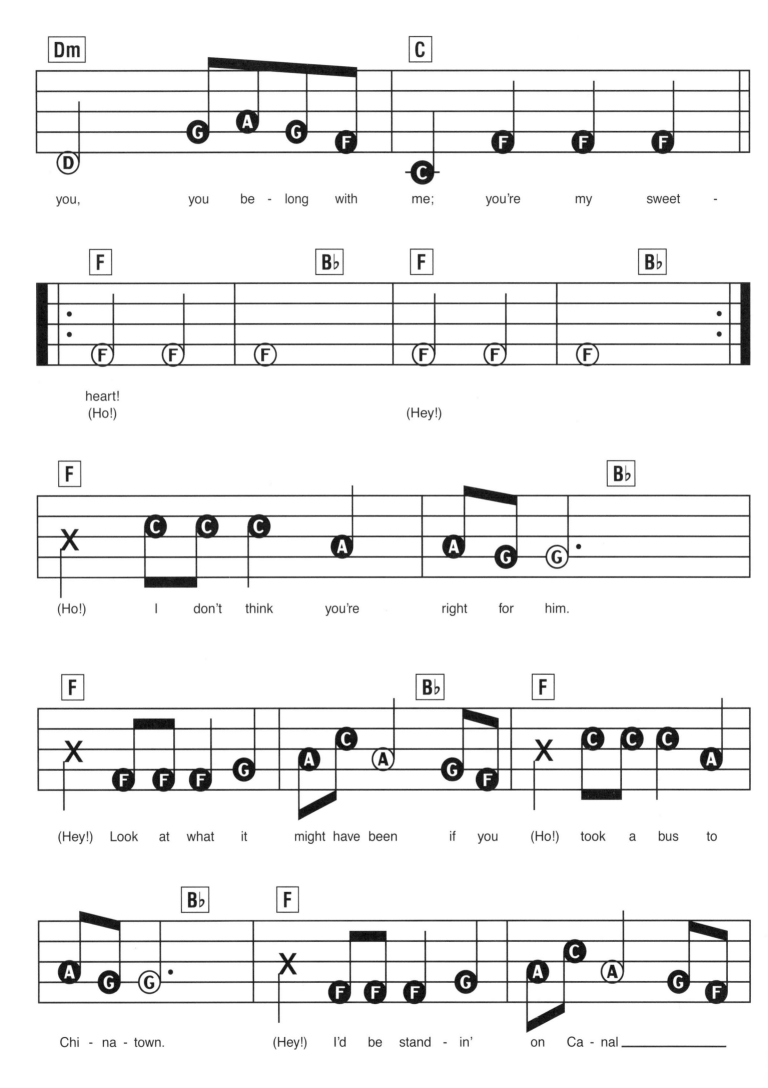

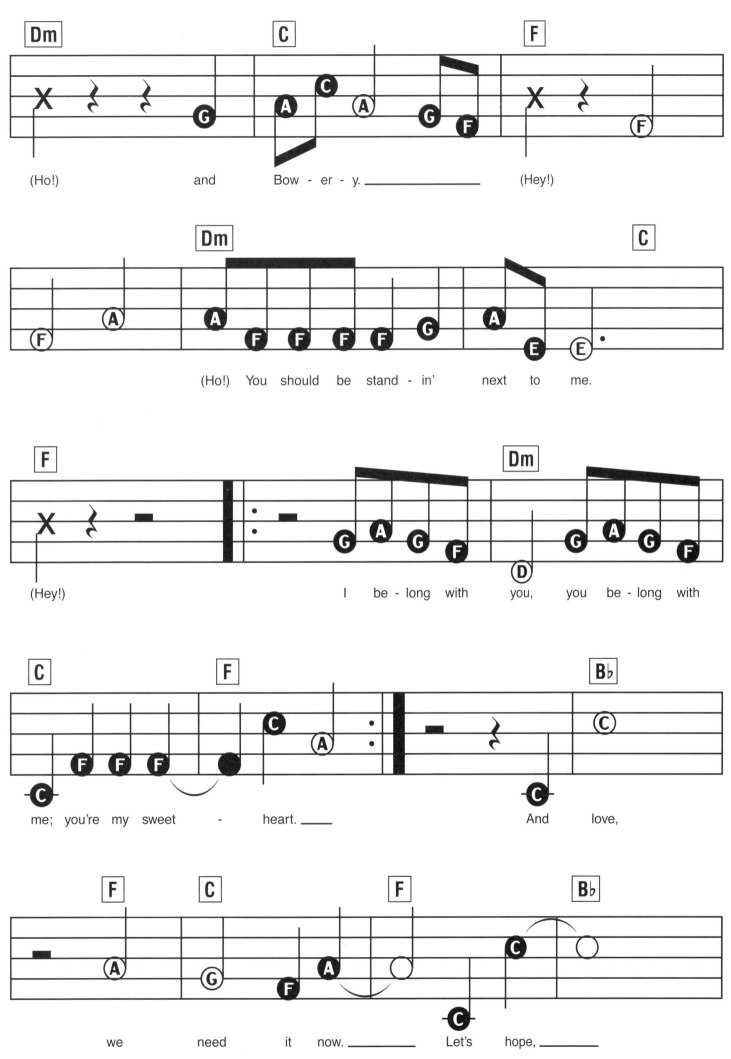

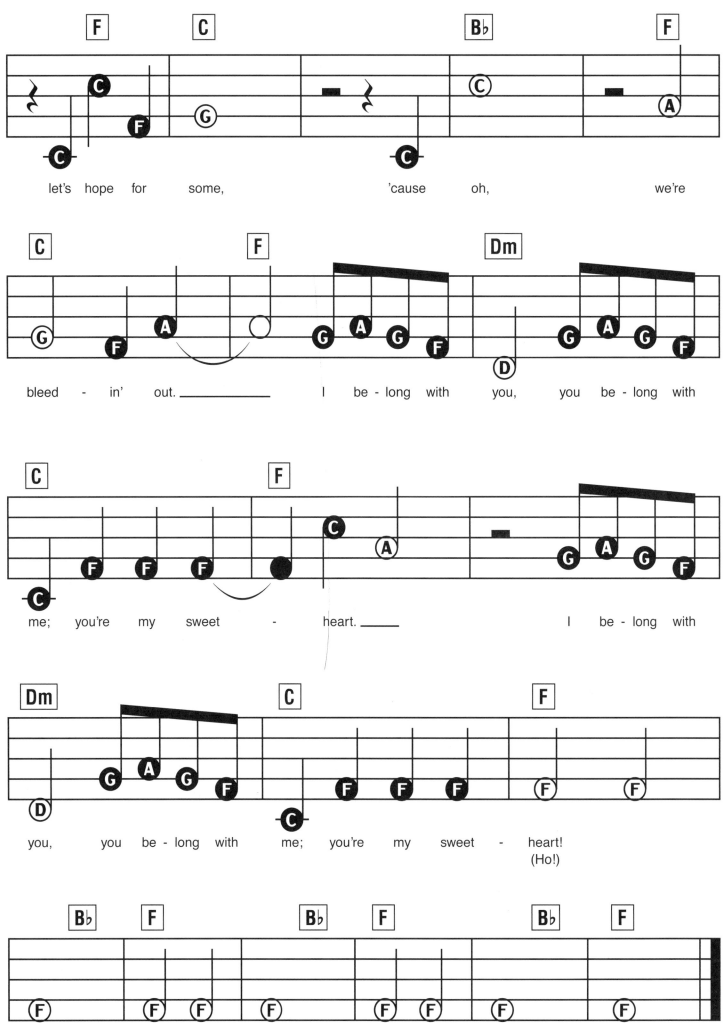

Hello

Registration 8
Rhythm: Ballad

Words and Music by Adele Adkins
and Greg Kurstin

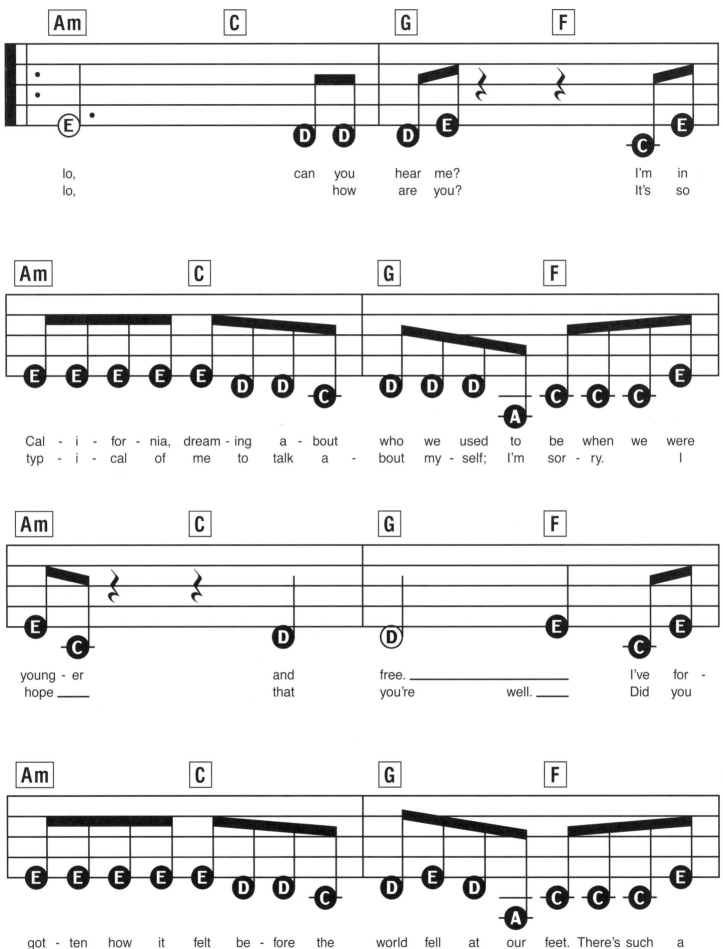

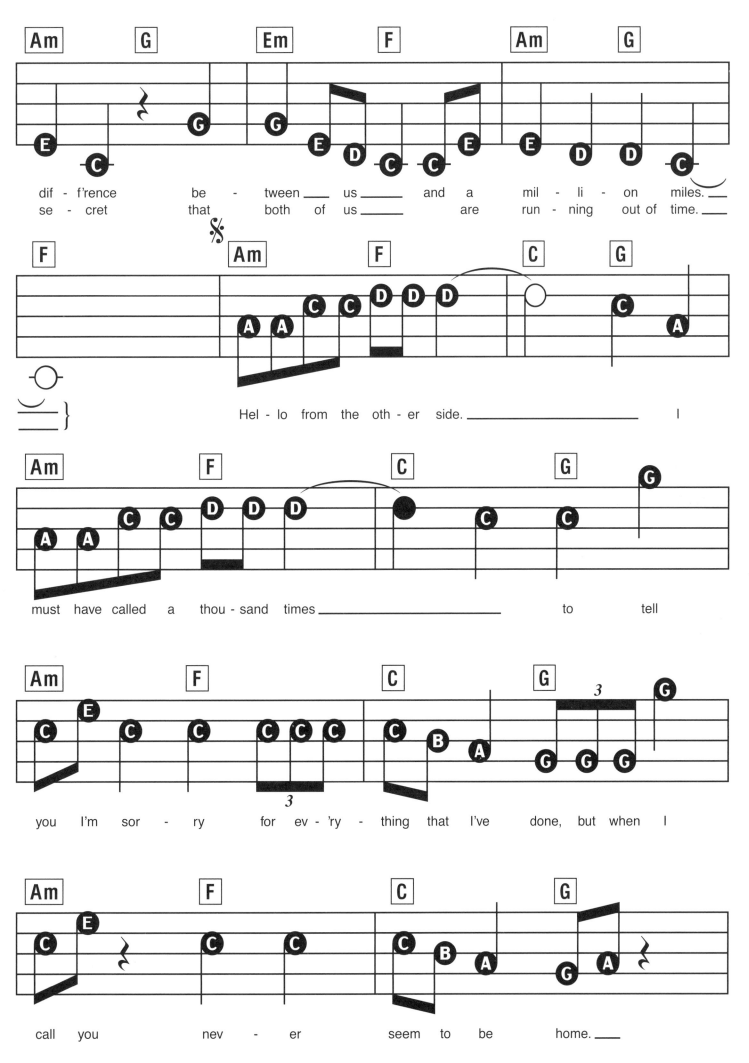

92

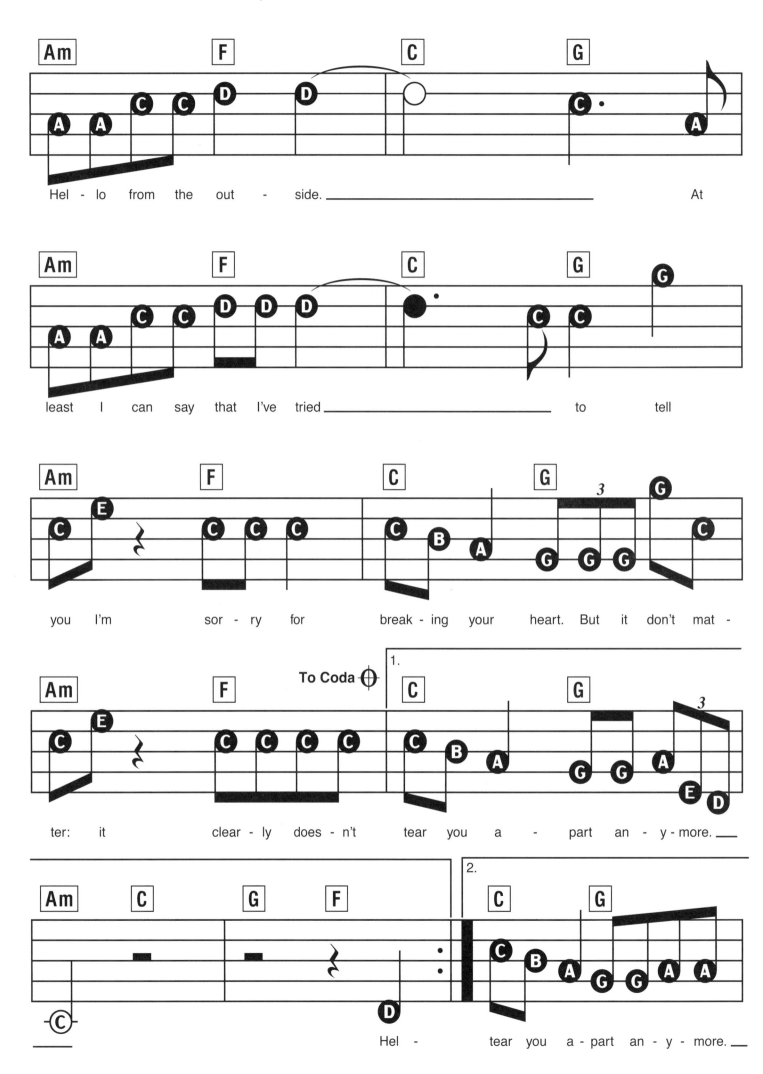

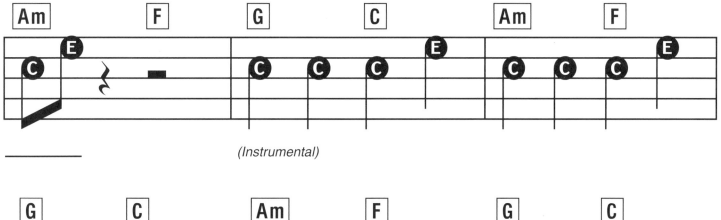

(Instrumental)

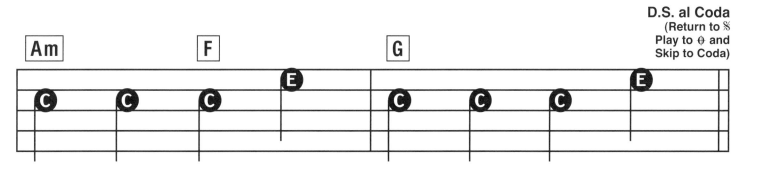

D.S. al Coda
(Return to 𝄋
Play to ⊕ and
Skip to Coda)

CODA

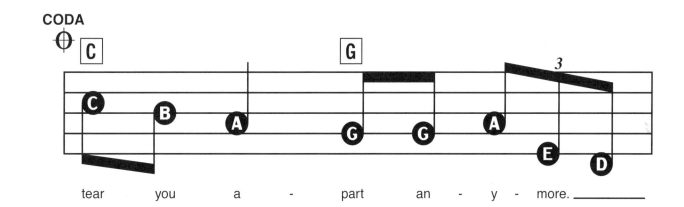

tear   you   a - part   an - y - more. _____

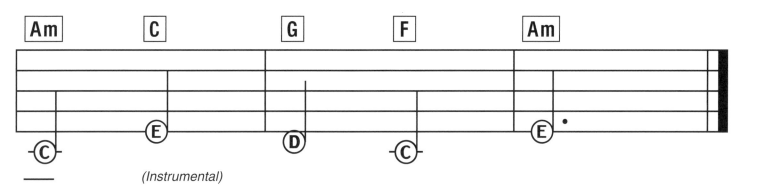

(Instrumental)

Hey, Soul Sister

Registration 4
Rhythm: Country Rock

Words and Music by Pat Monahan,
Espen Lind and Amund Bjorklund

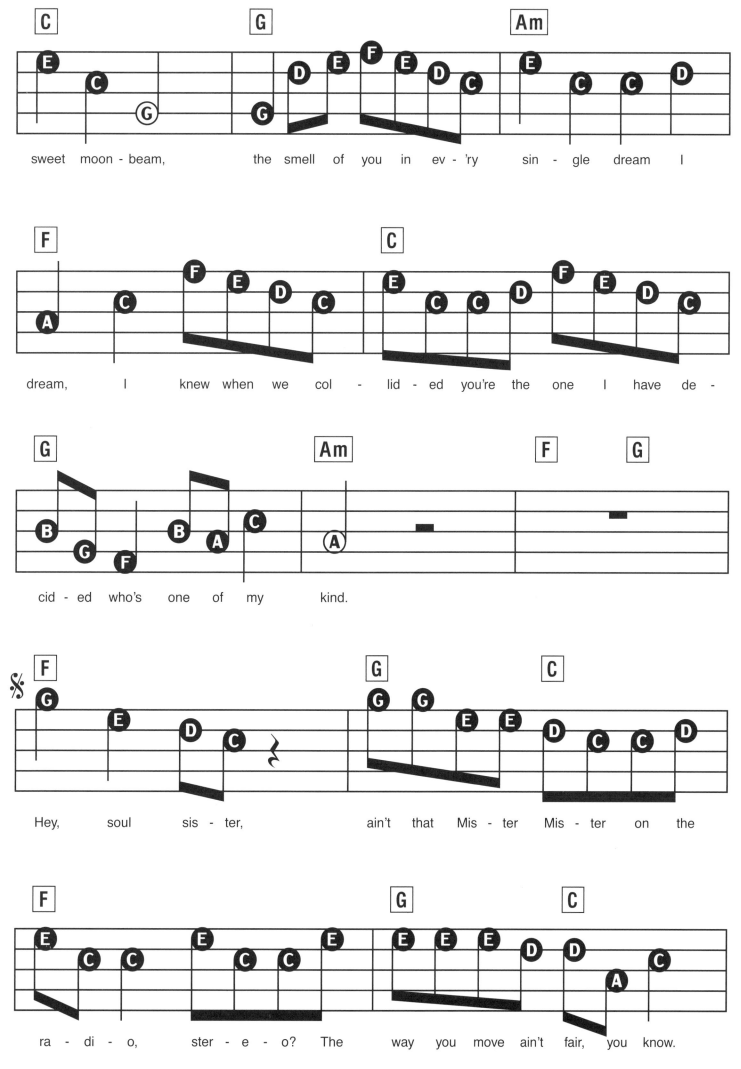

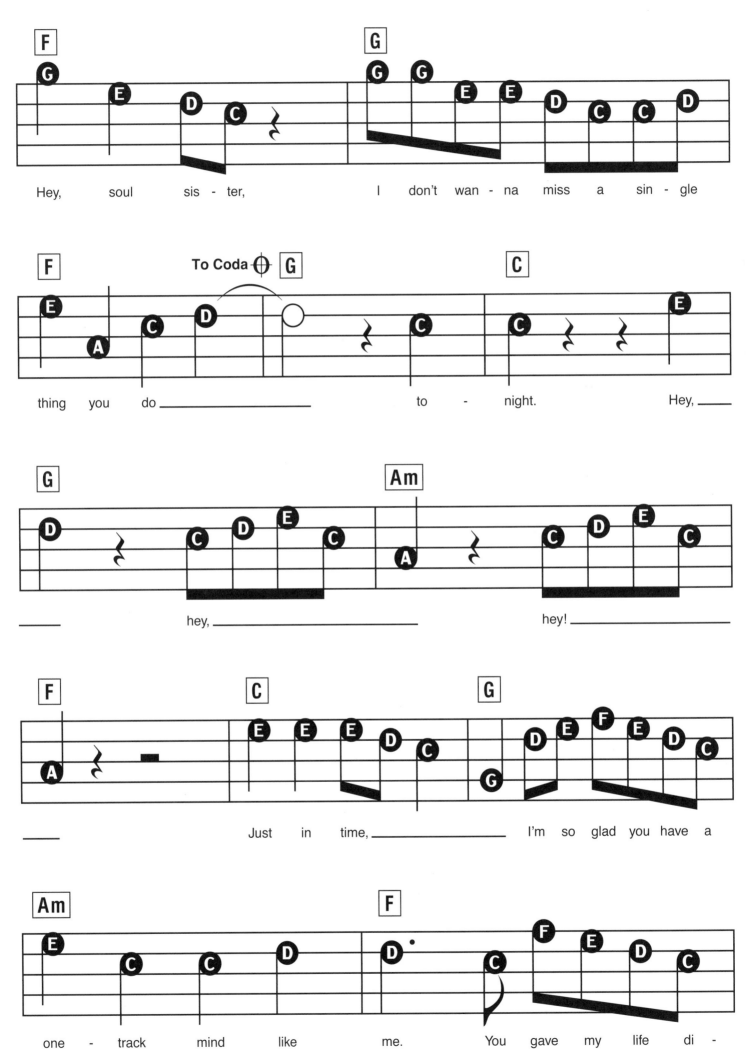

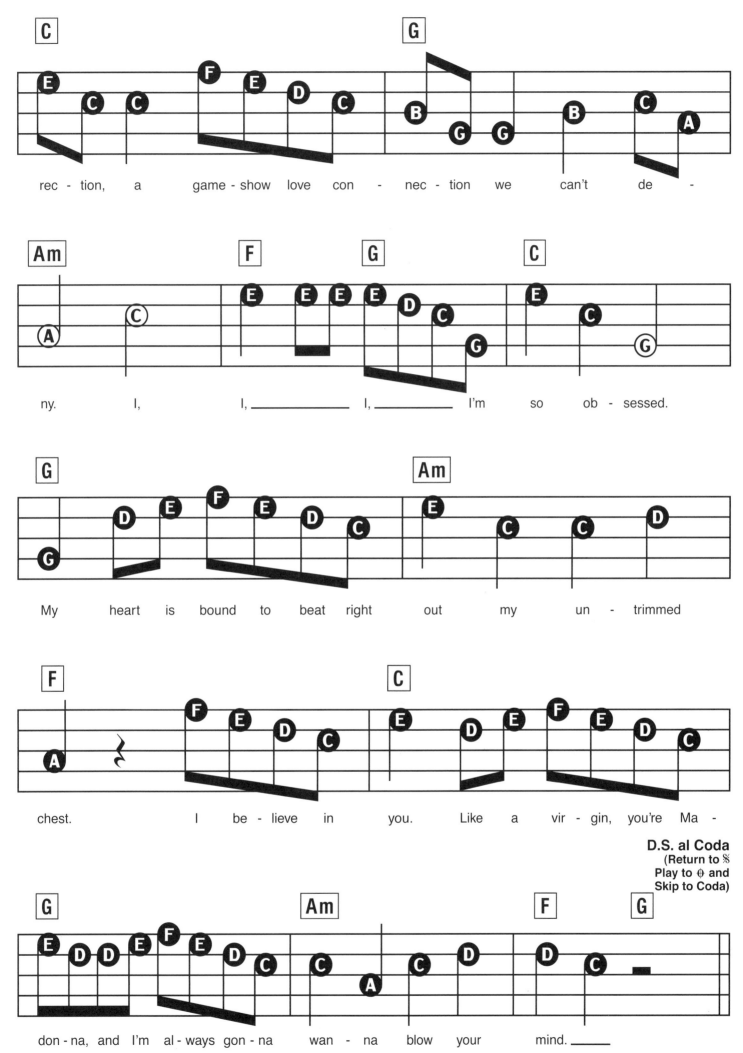

98

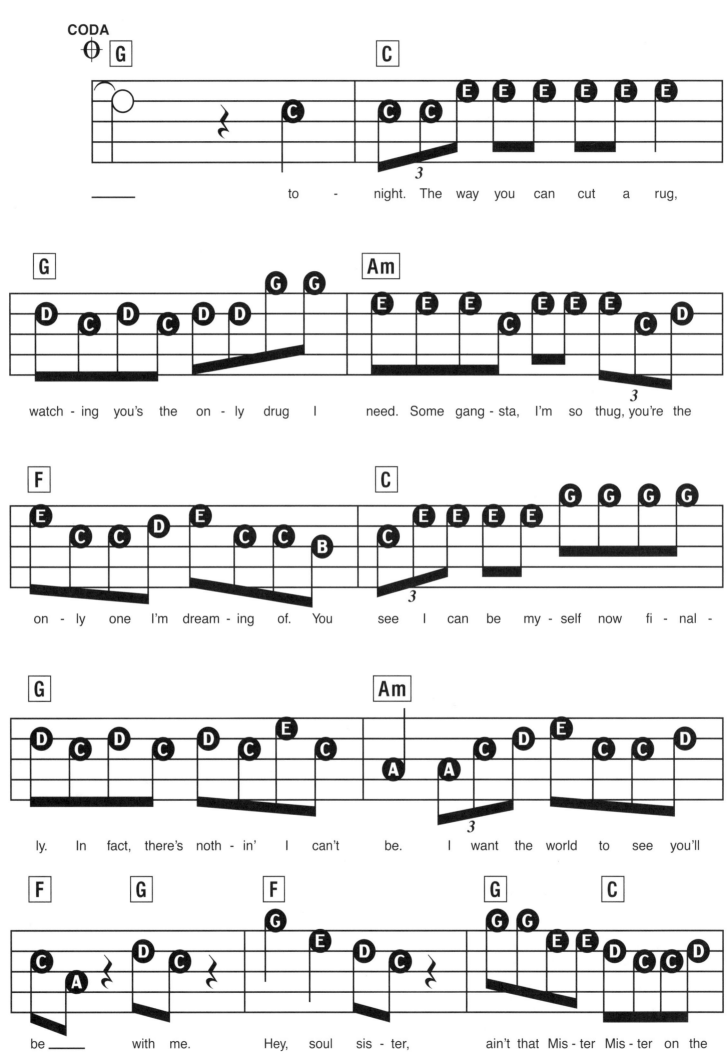

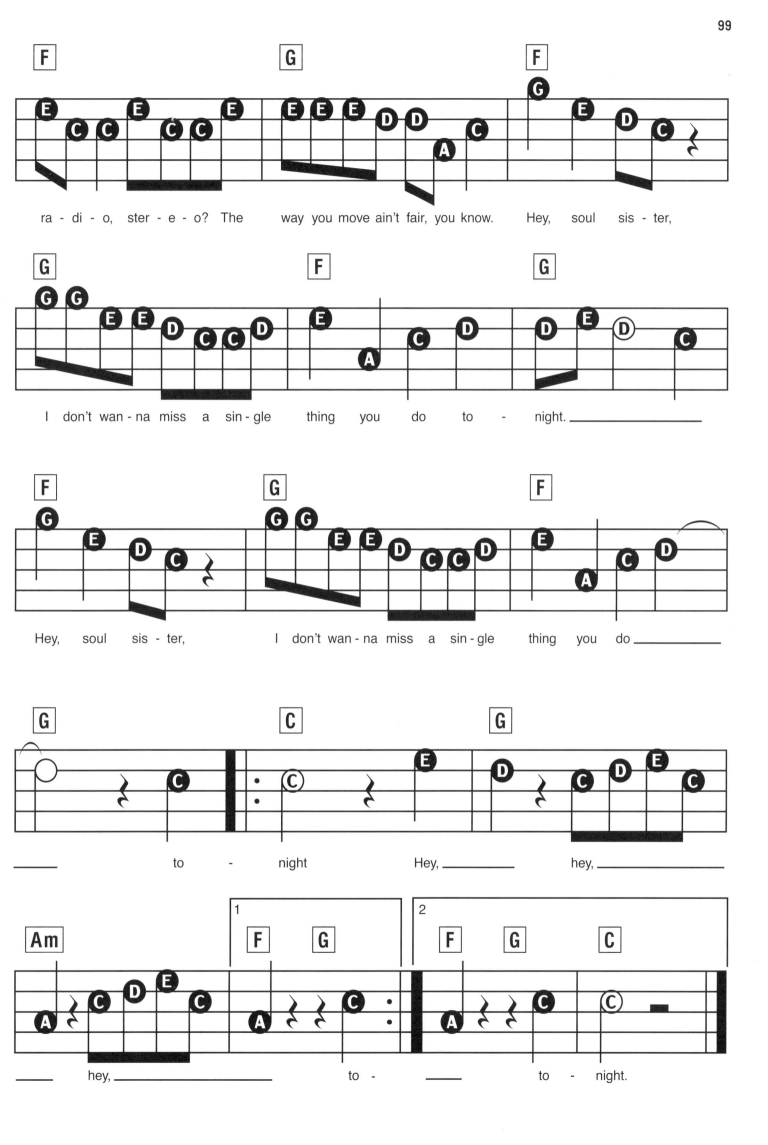

High Hopes

Registration 2
Rhythm: Fast Rock

Words and Music by Brendon Urie,
William Lobban Bean, Jonas Jeberg, Samuel Hollander,
Jacob Sinclair, Jenny Owen Youngs, Ilsey Juber,
Lauren Pritchard and Tayla Parx

(Instrumental)

D.S. al Coda
(Return to 𝄋, play to ⊕
and skip to Coda)

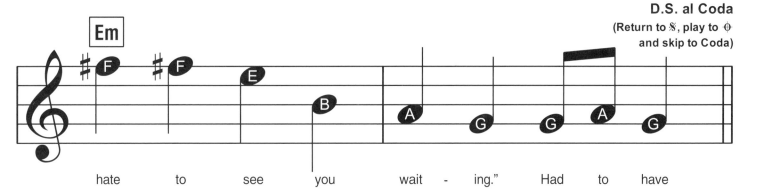

hate   to   see   you   wait - ing." Had   to   have

CODA

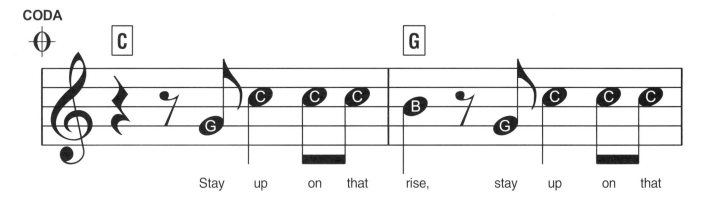

Stay   up   on   that   rise,   stay   up   on   that

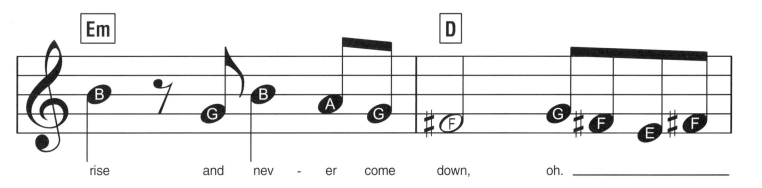

rise   and   nev - er   come   down,   oh. _____

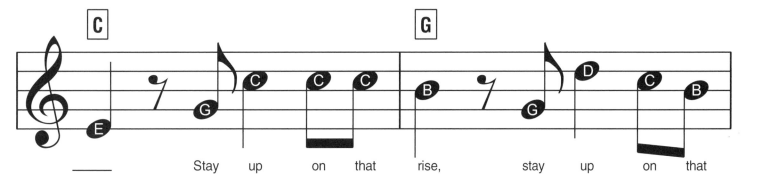

_____ Stay   up   on   that   rise,   stay   up   on   that

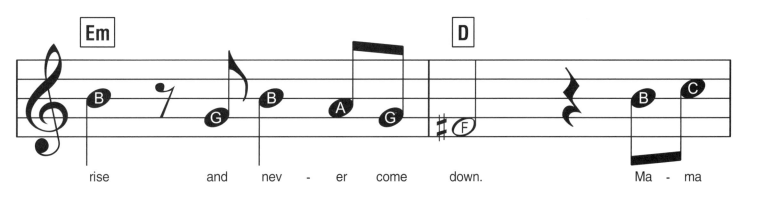

rise   and   nev - er   come   down.   Ma - ma

104

I Knew You Were Trouble

Registration 4
Rhythm: Country Pop or Rock

Words and Music by Taylor Swift,
Shellback and Max Martin

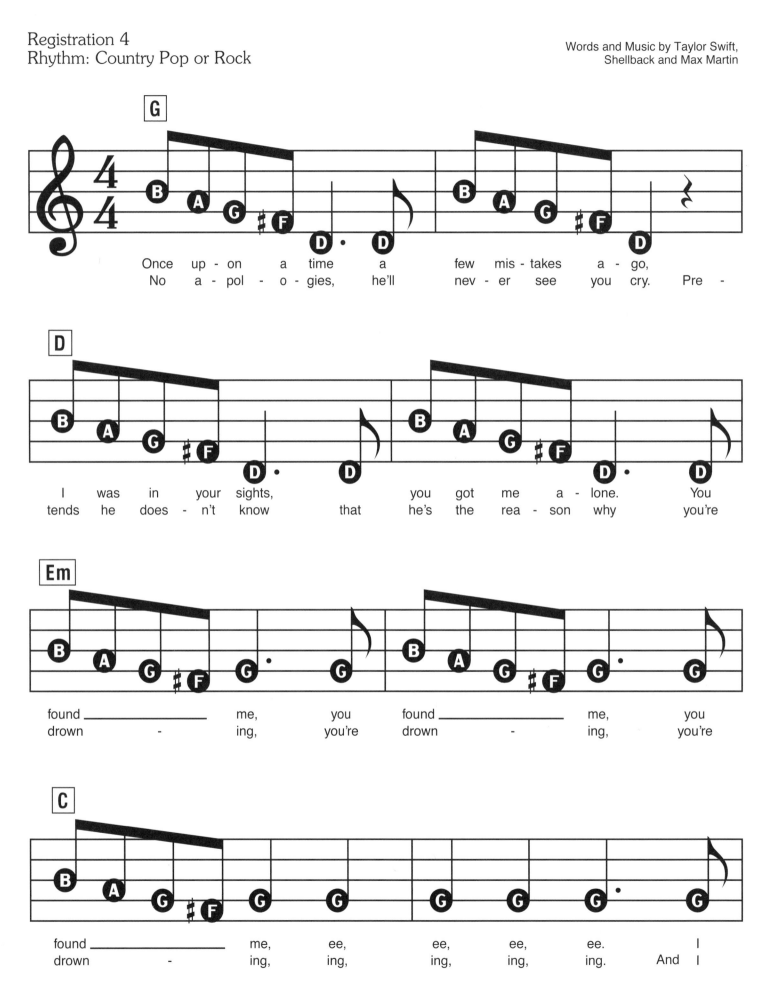

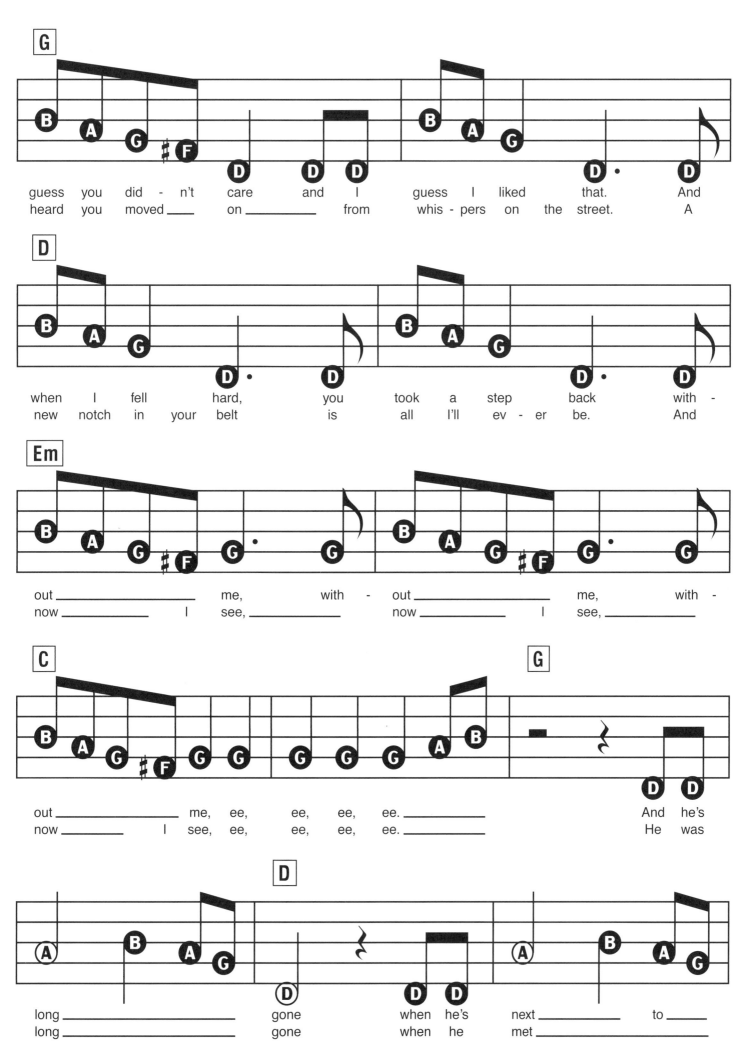

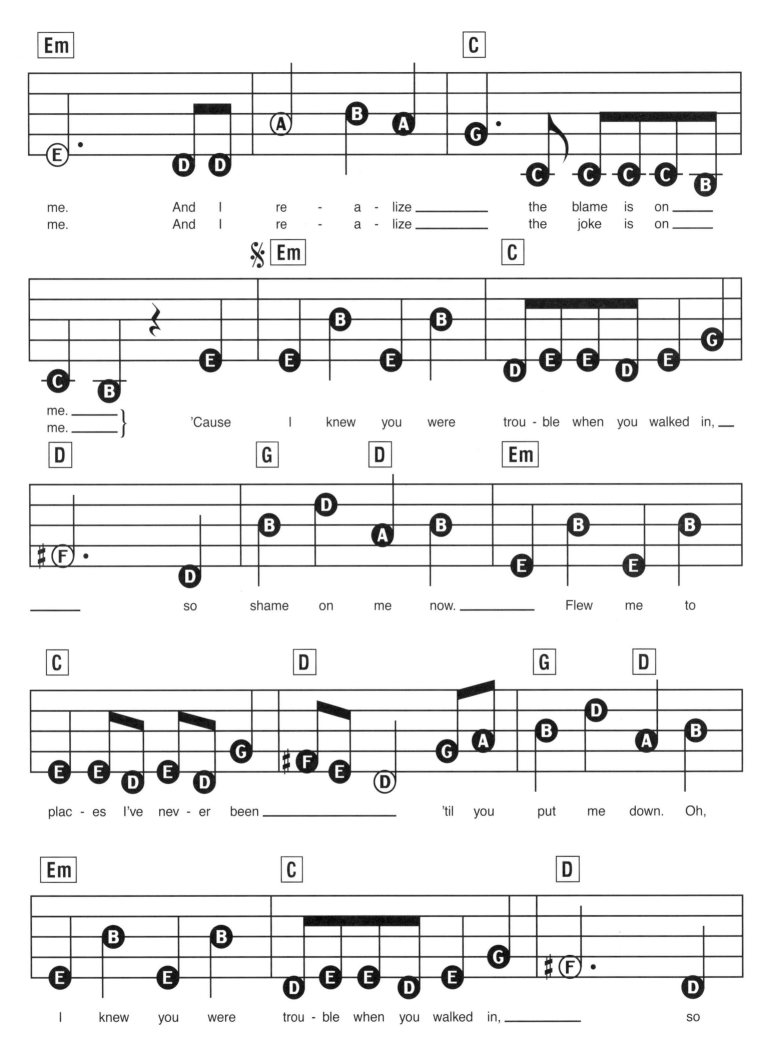

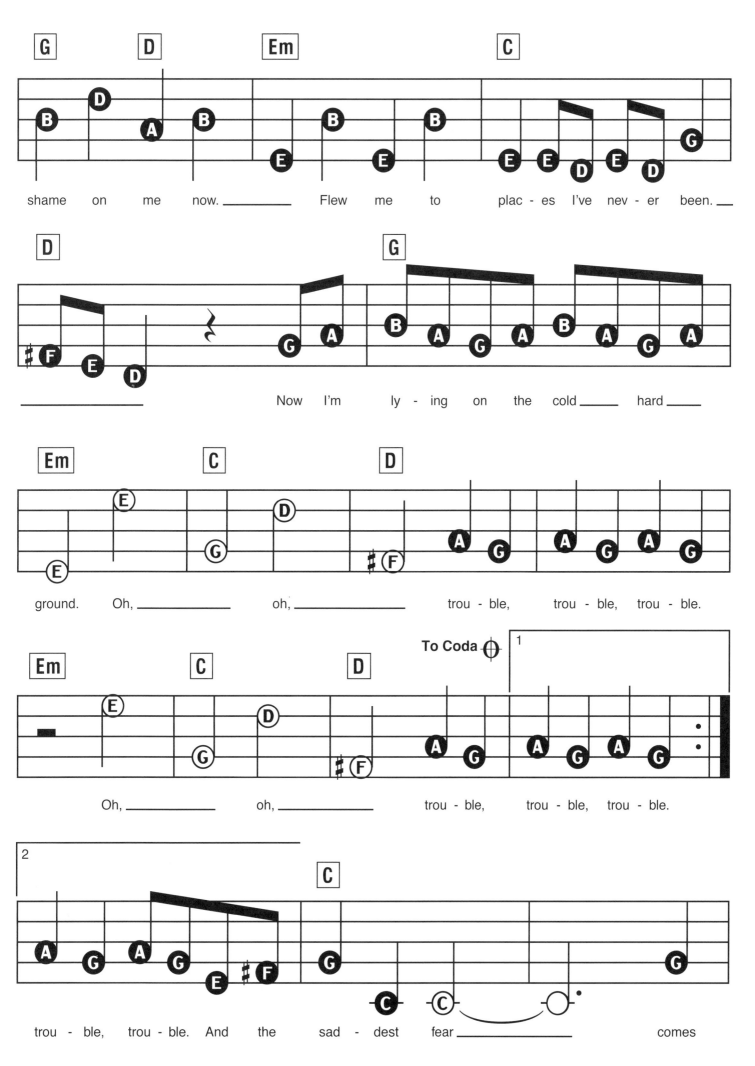

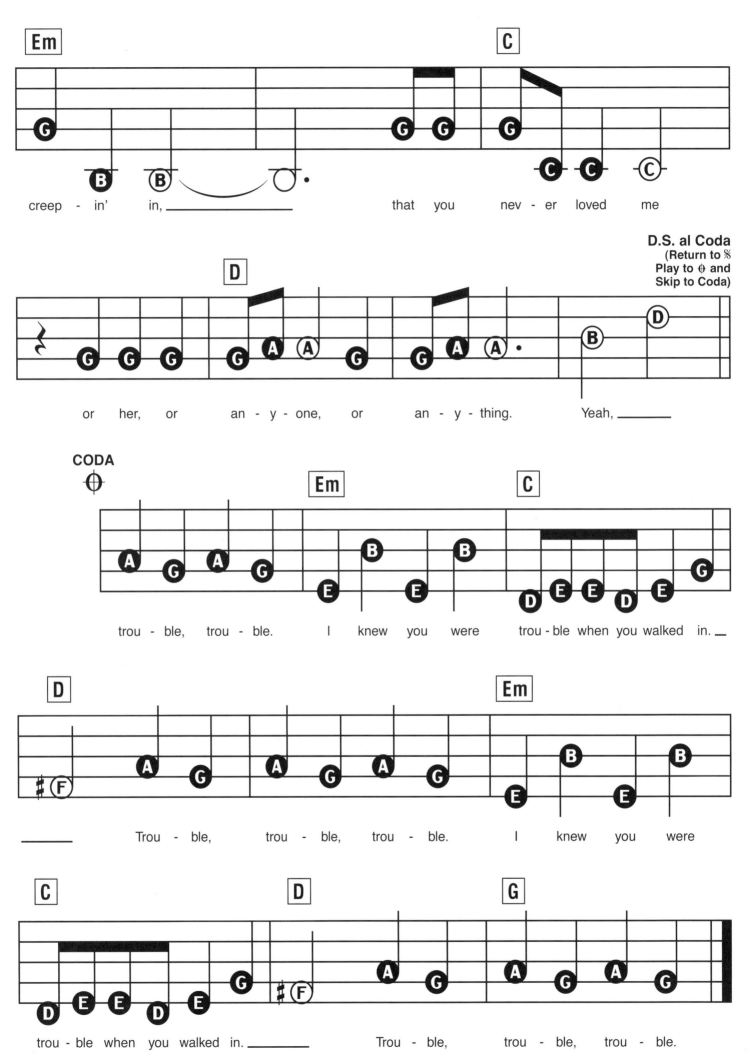

I Will Wait

Registration 4
Rhythm: Country Rock or Country Pop

Words and Music by
Mumford & Sons

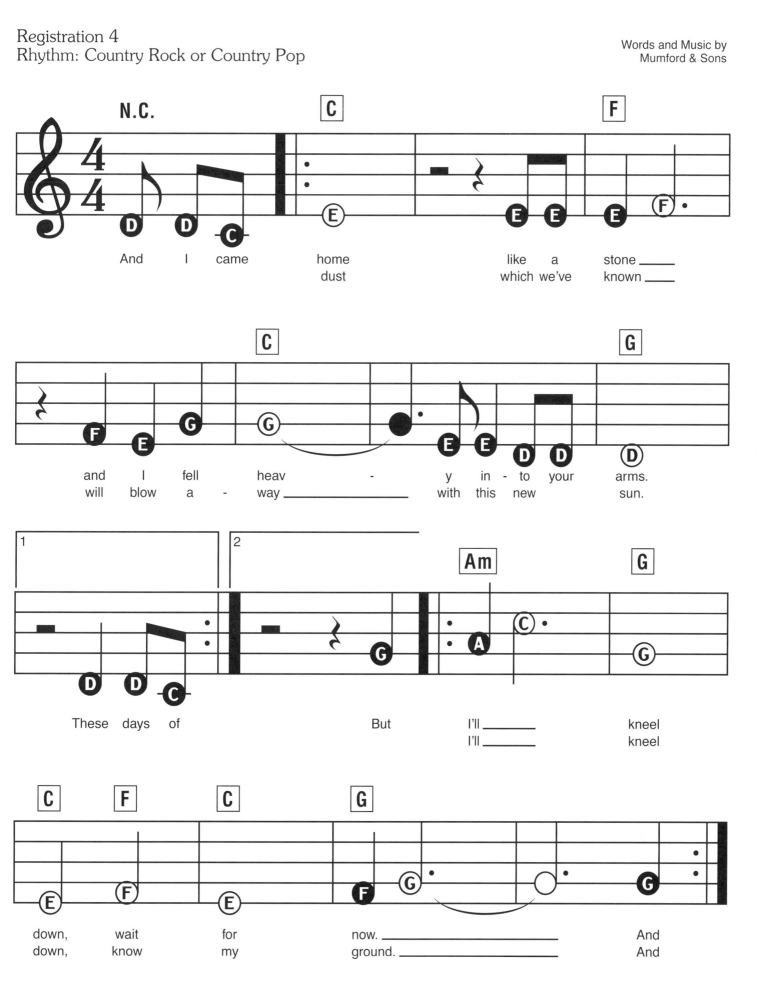

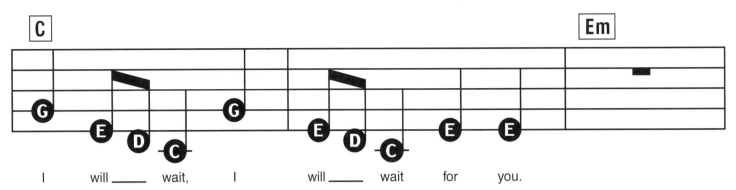

I will ___ wait, I will ___ wait for you.

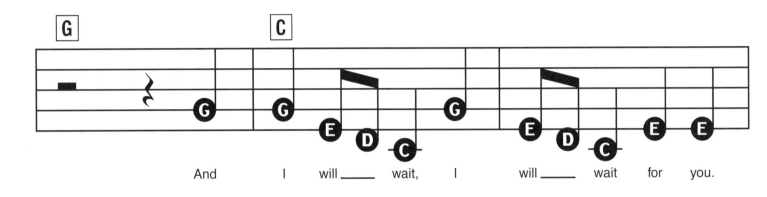

And I will ___ wait, I will ___ wait for you.

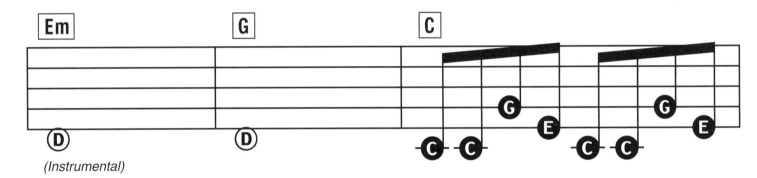

(Instrumental)

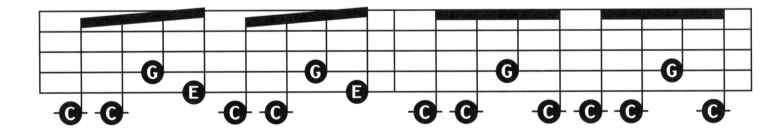

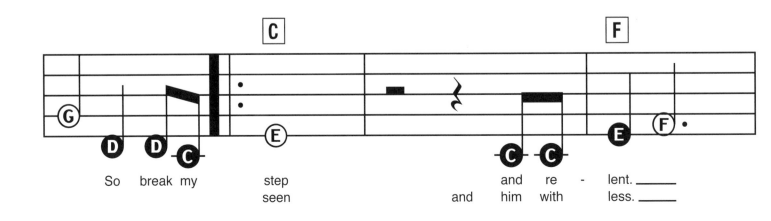

So break my step seen and him with and re - lent. ___ less. ___

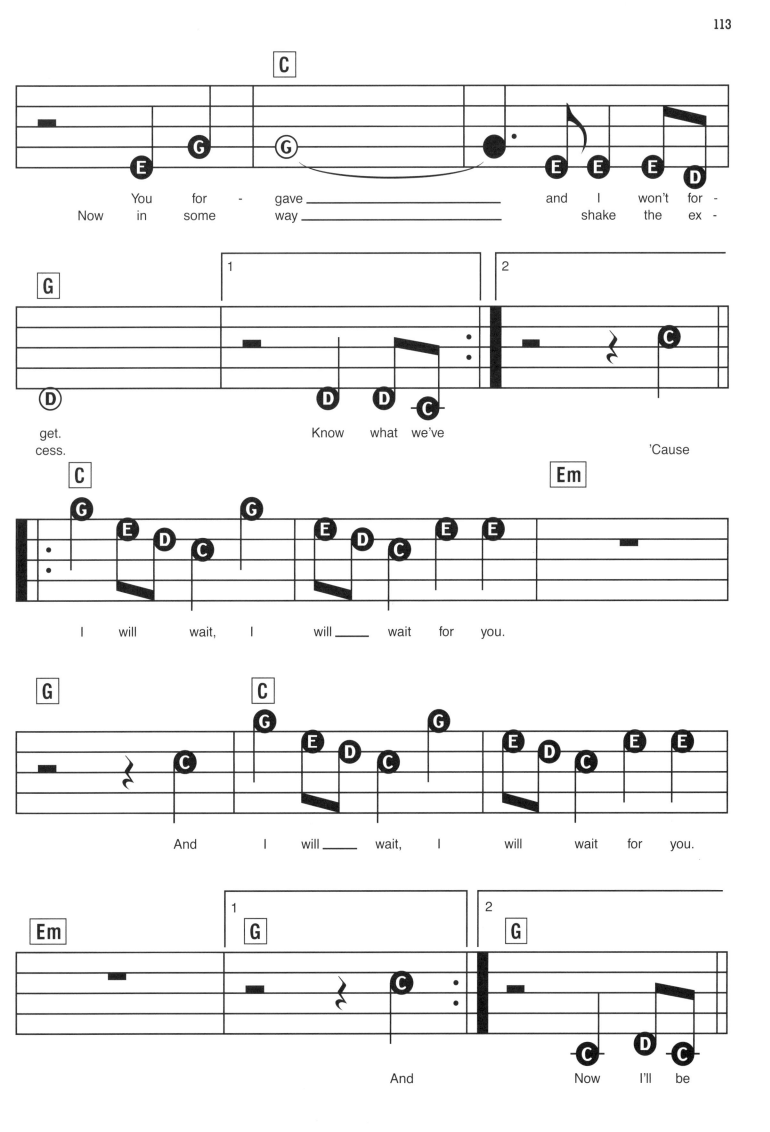

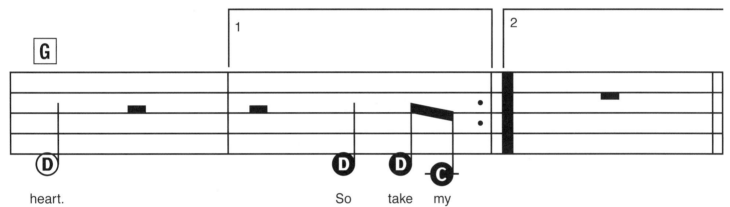
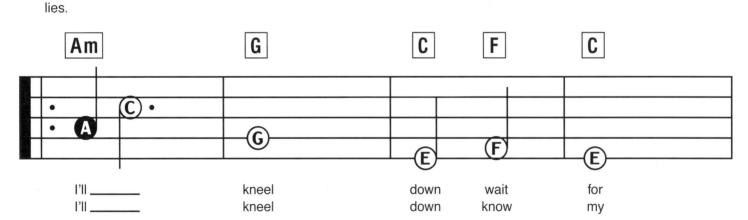
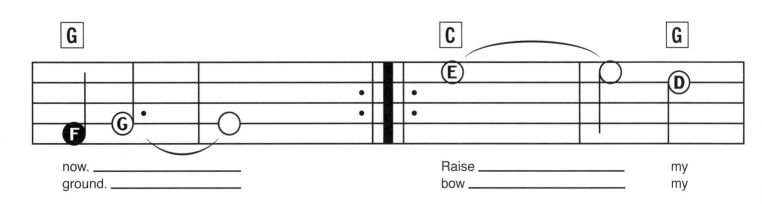

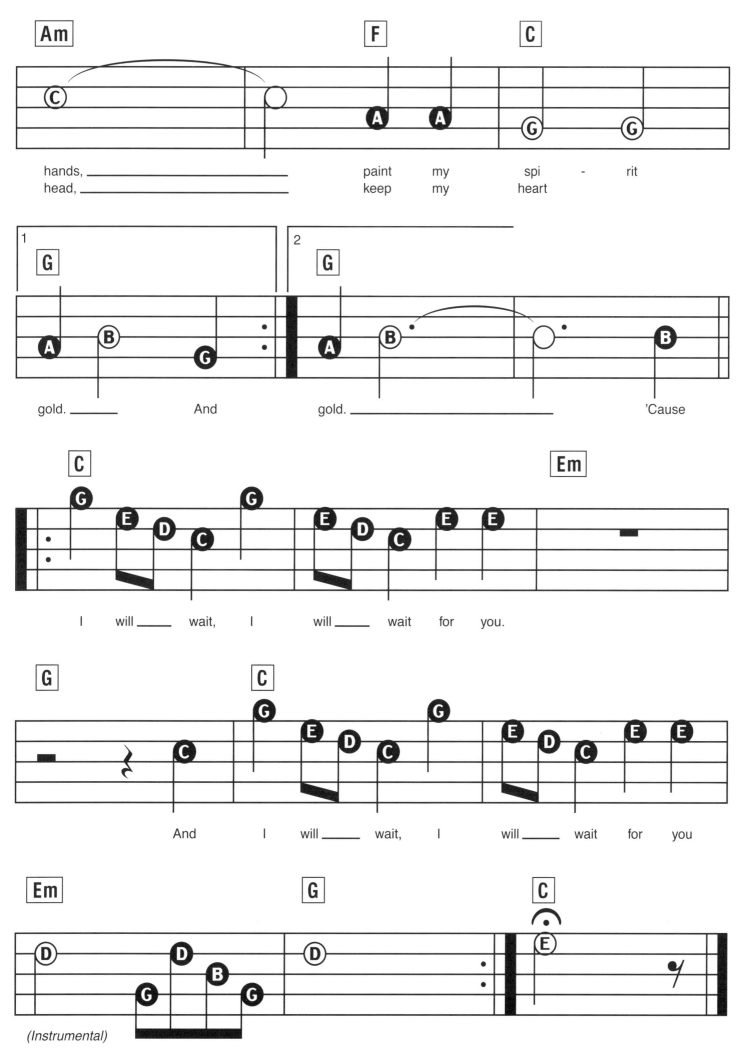

I Won't Give Up

Registration 4
Rhythm: 6/8 March

Words and Music by Jason Mraz
and Michael Natter

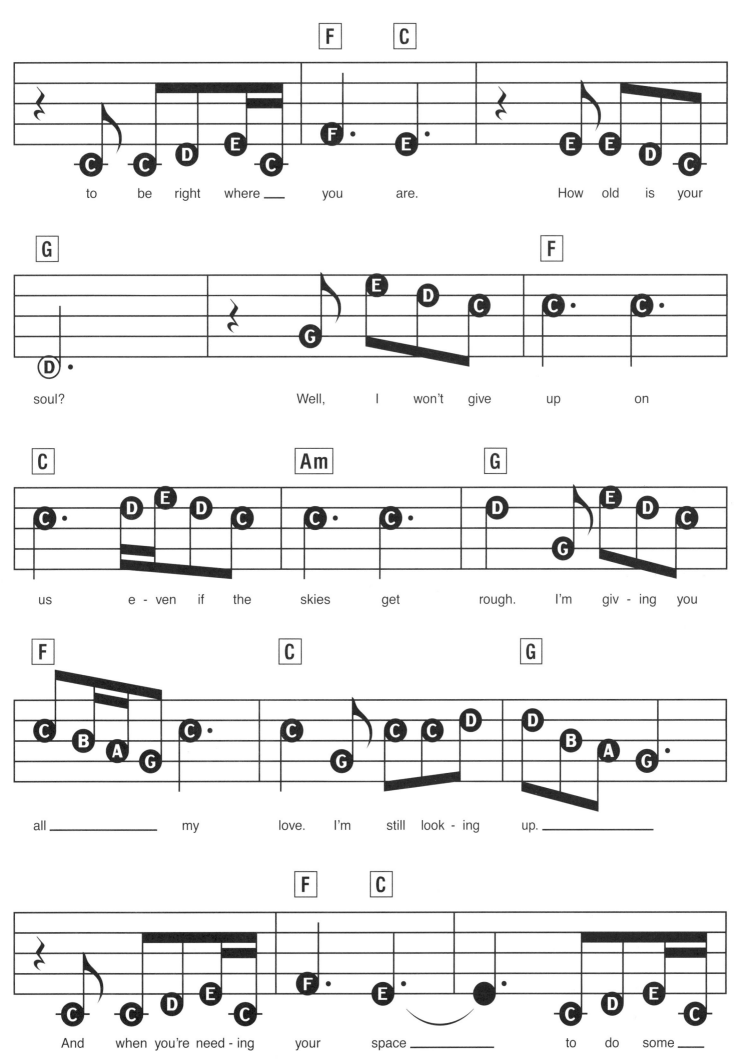

118

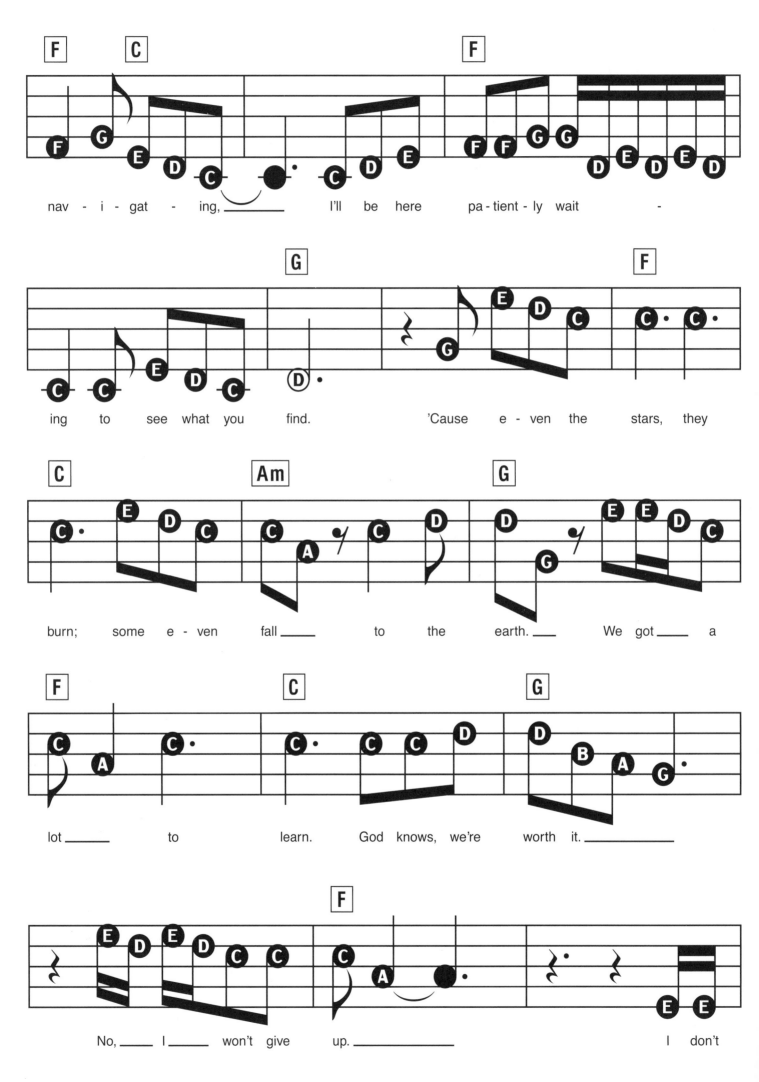

119

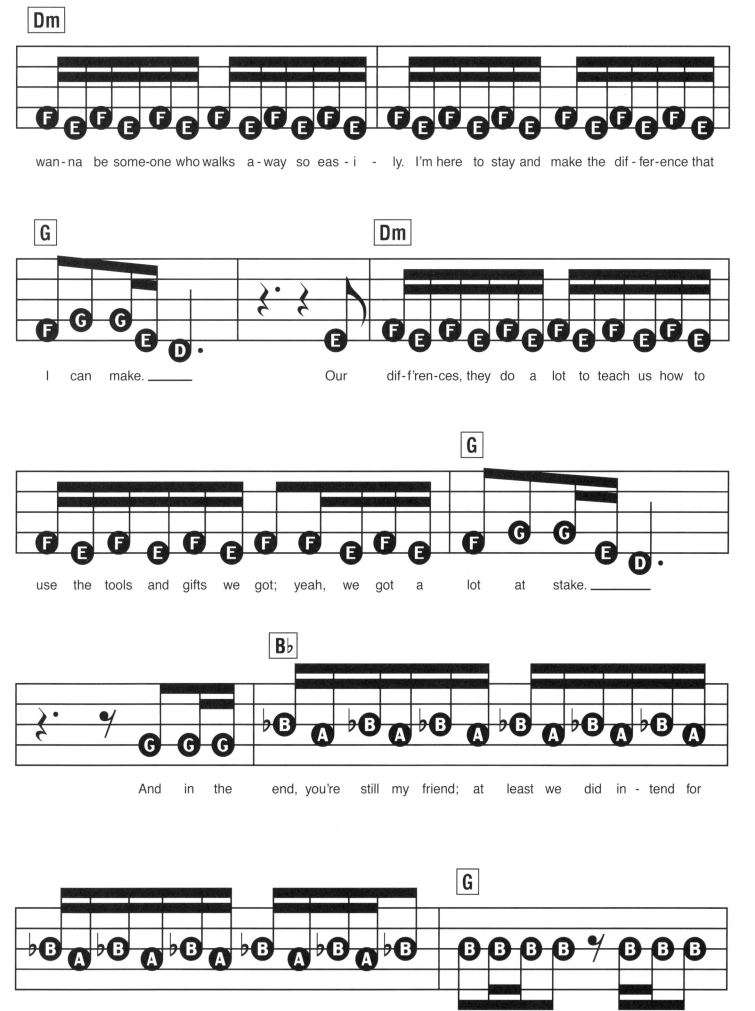

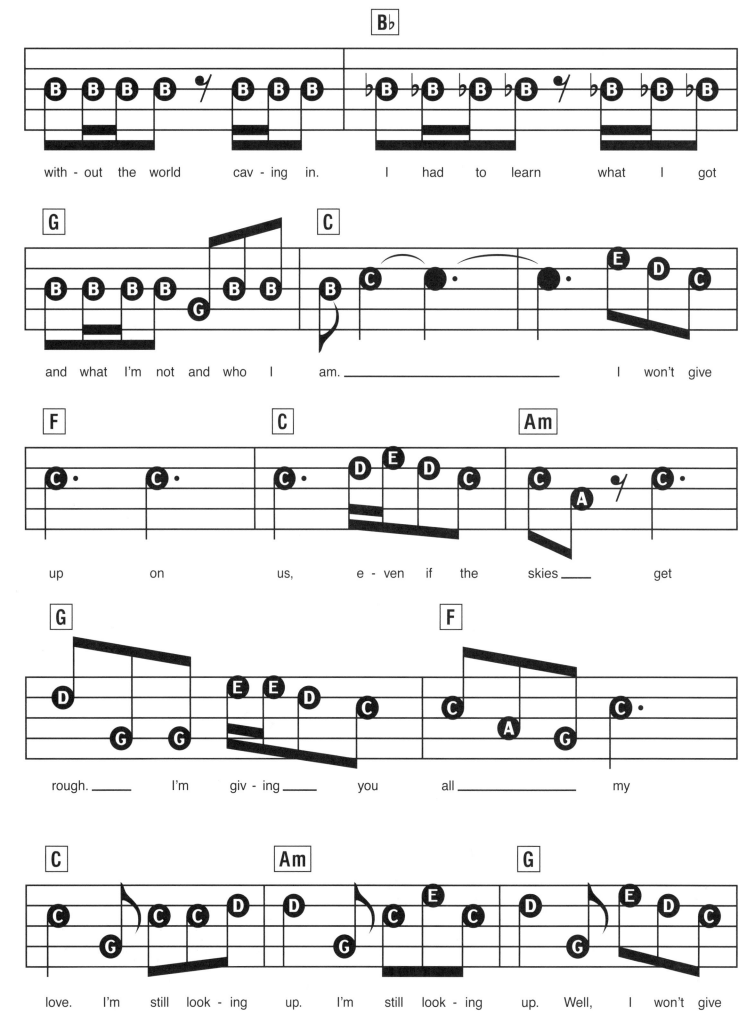

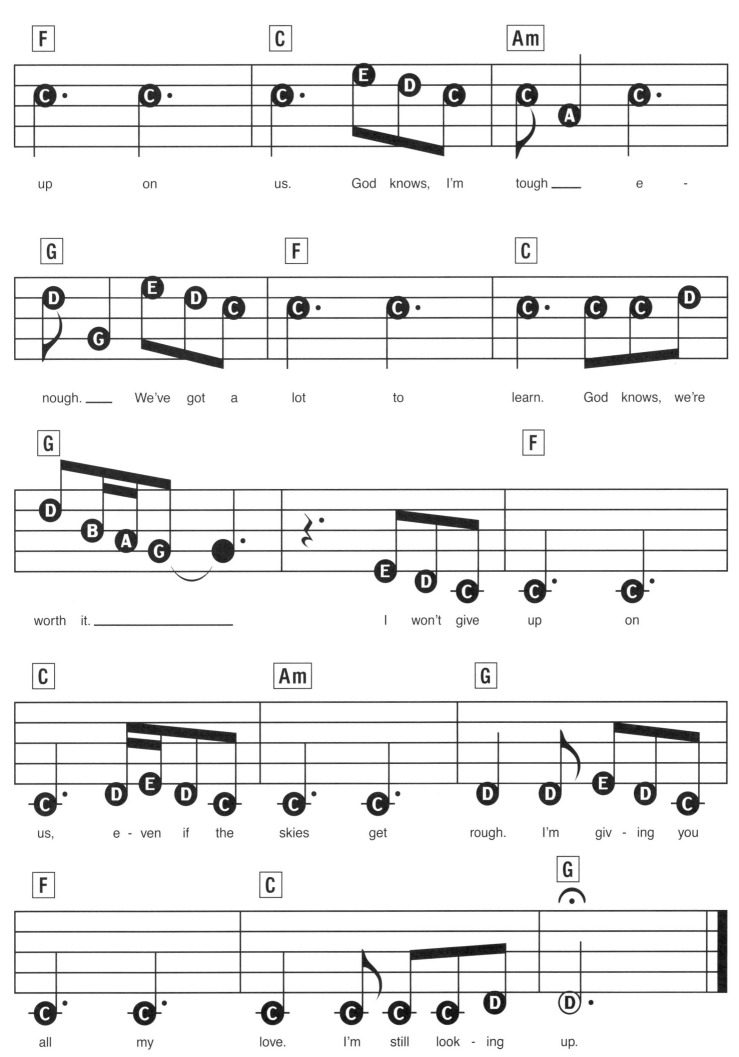

Little Talks

Registration 2
Rhythm: Pop or Rock

Words and Music by
Of Monsters and Men

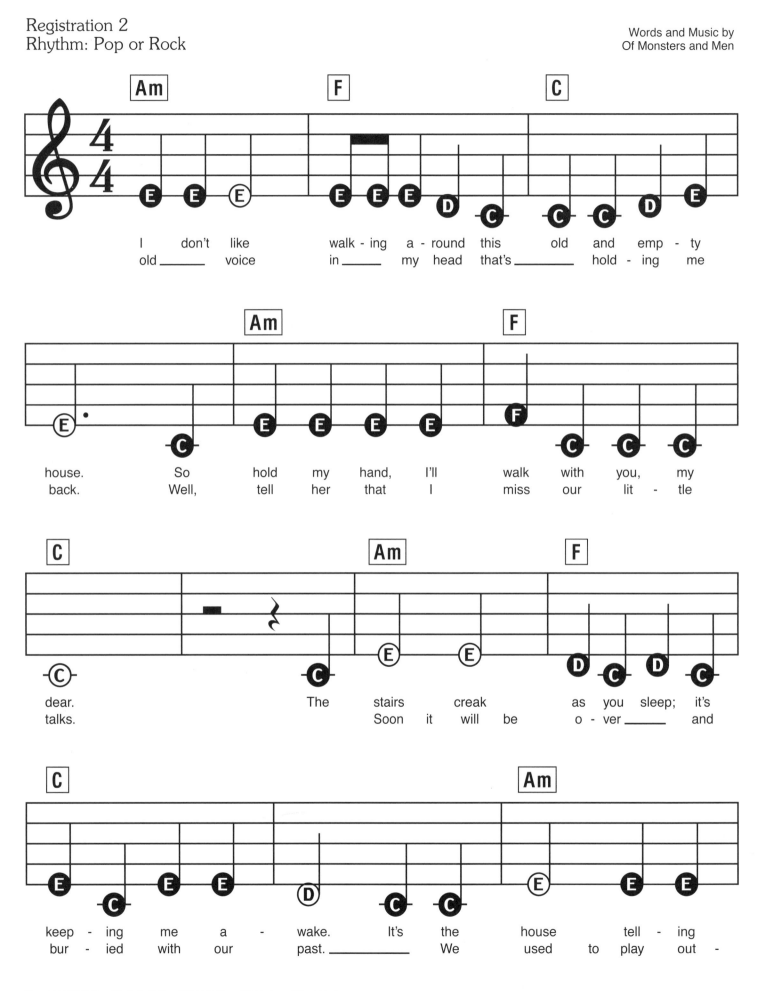

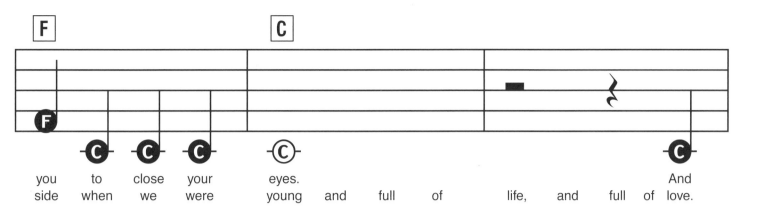

you   to   close   your   eyes.   And
side   when   we   were   young   and   full   of   life,   and   full   of   love.

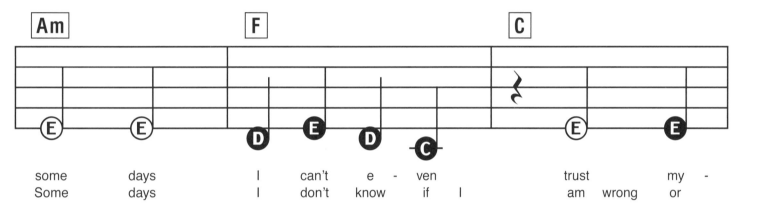

some   days   I   can't   e - ven   trust   my -
Some   days   I   don't   know   if   I   am   wrong   or

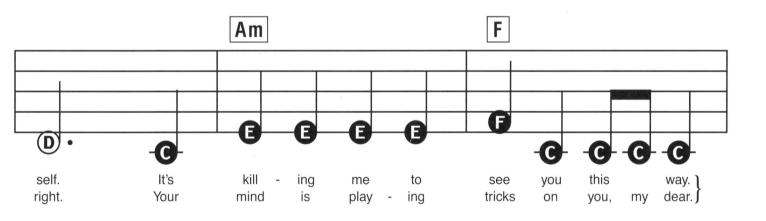

self.   It's   kill - ing   me   to   see   you   this   way.
right.   Your   mind   is   play - ing   tricks   on   you,   my   dear.

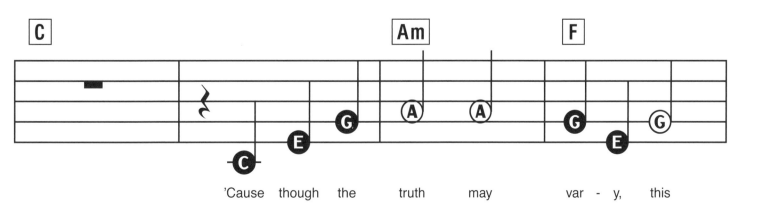

'Cause   though   the   truth   may   var - y,   this

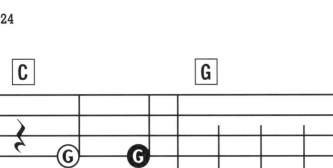

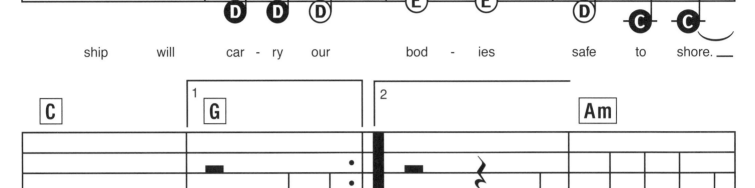

ship will car - ry our bod - ies safe to shore. ___

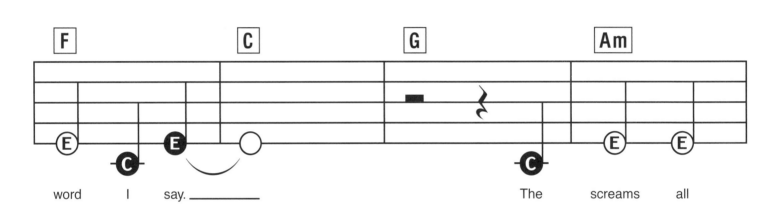

___ There's an Don't lis - ten to a

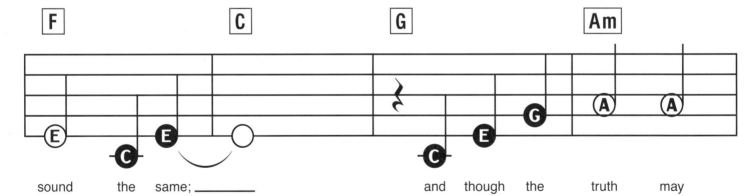

word I say. ___ The screams all

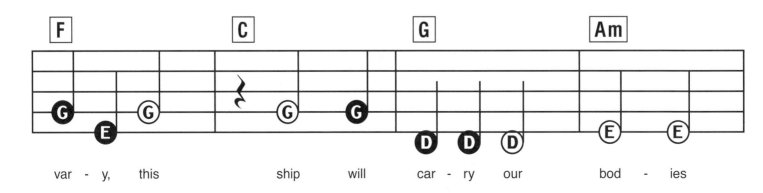

sound the same; ___ and though the truth may

var - y, this ship will car - ry our bod - ies

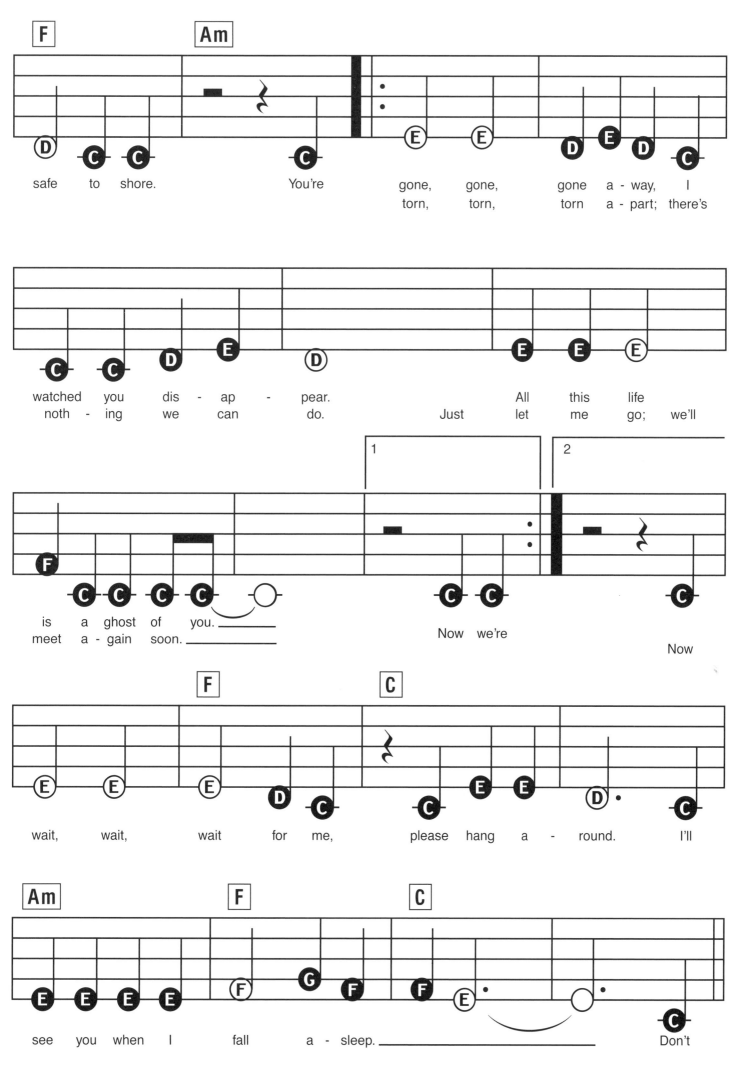

126

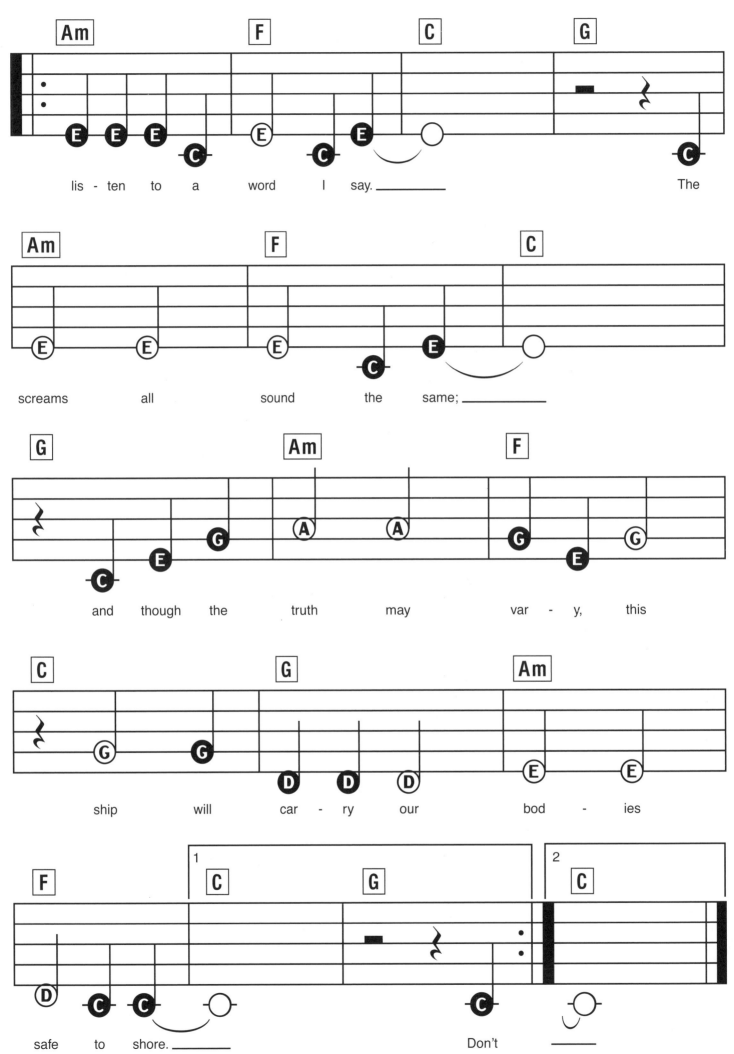

Jar of Hearts

Registration 8
Rhythm: 4/4 Ballad or Pop

Words and Music by Barrett Yeretsian,
Christina Perri and Drew Lawrence

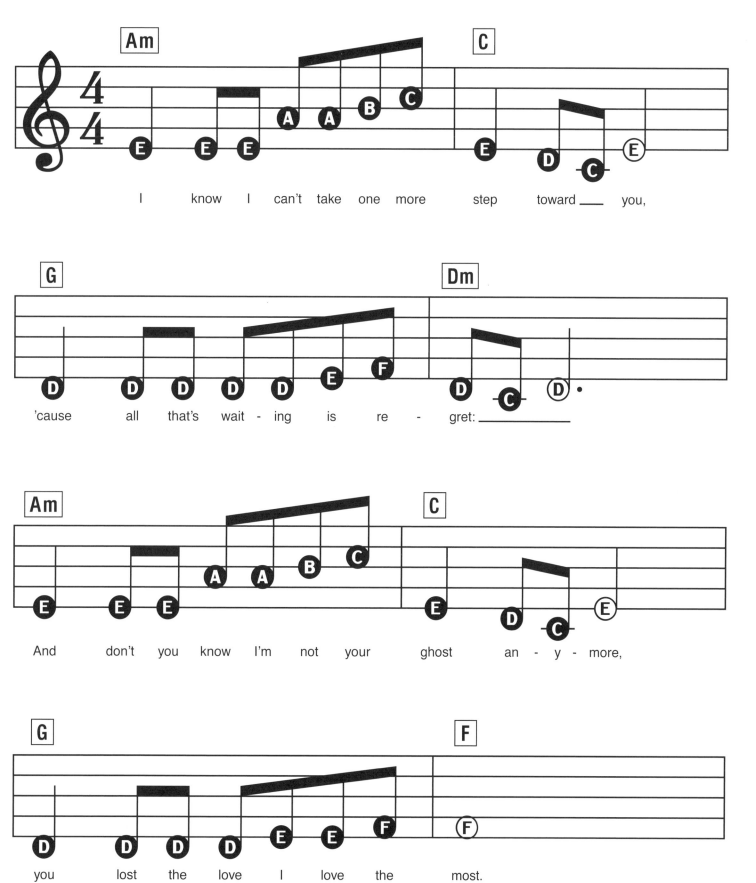

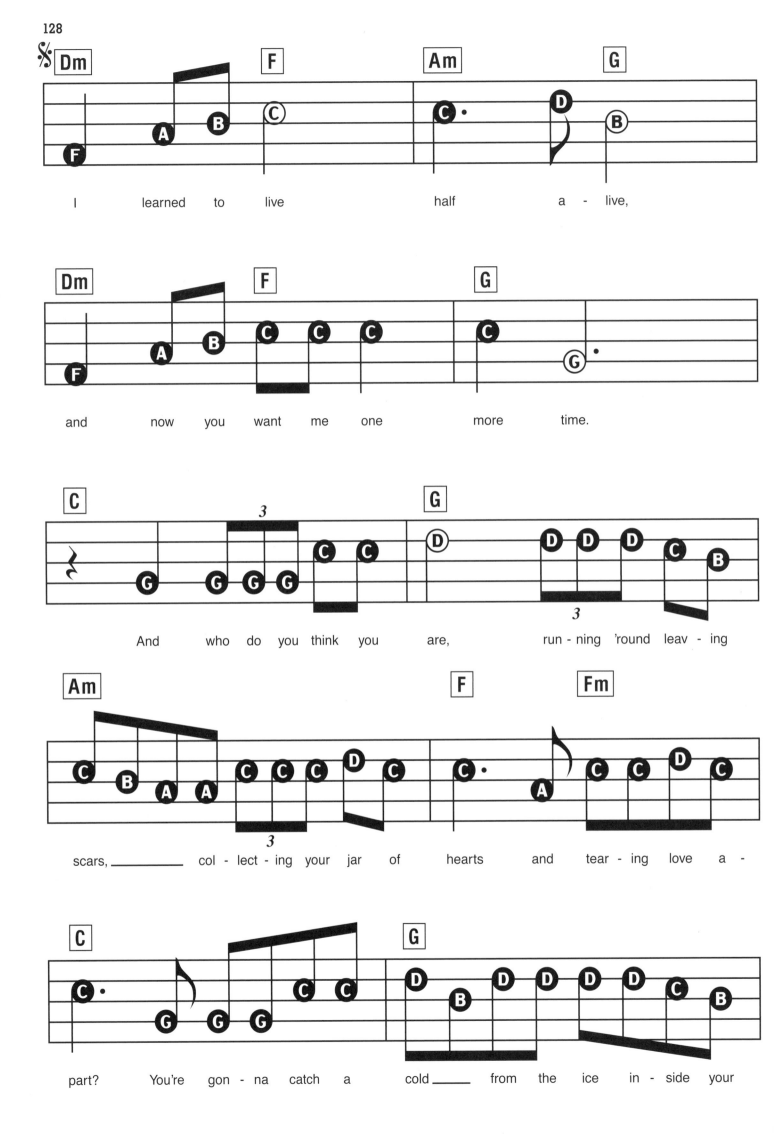

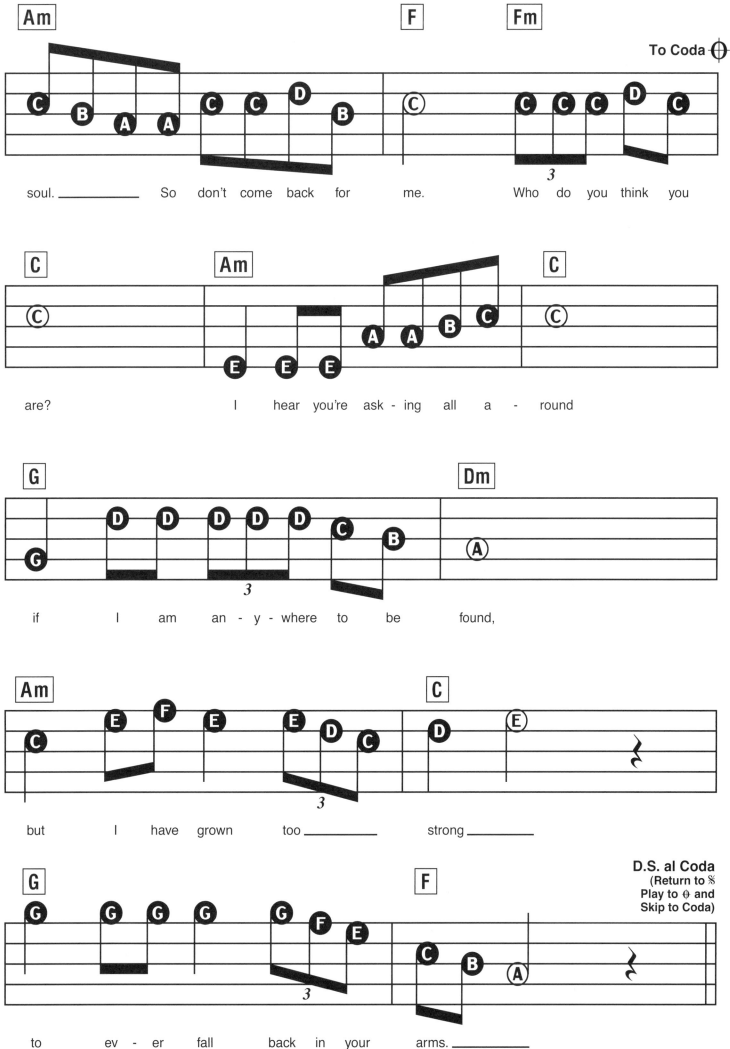

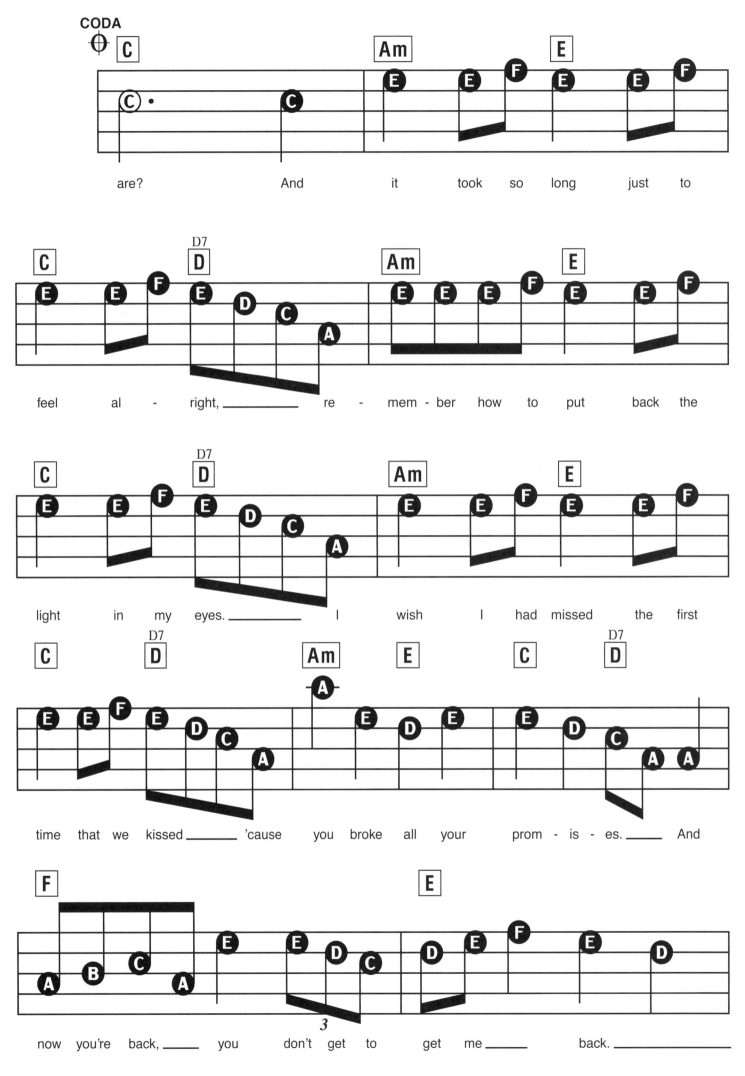

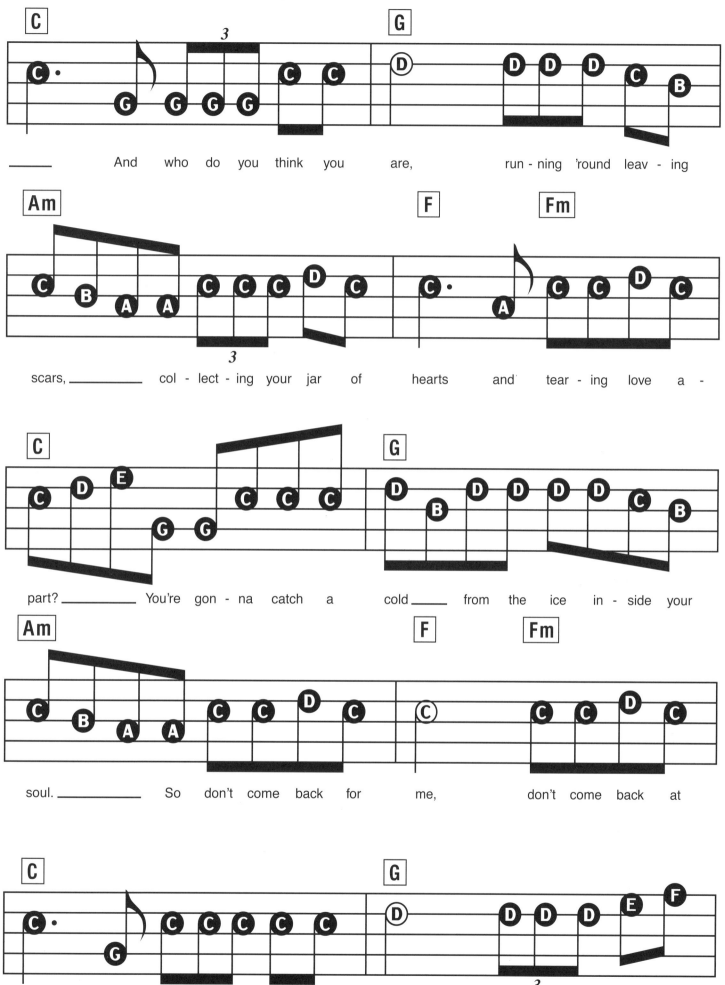

And who do you think you are, run-ning 'round leav-ing

scars, _____ col-lect-ing your jar of hearts and tear-ing love a-

part? _____ You're gon-na catch a cold ___ from the ice in-side your

soul. _____ So don't come back for me, don't come back at

all. And who do you think you are, run-ning 'round leav-ing

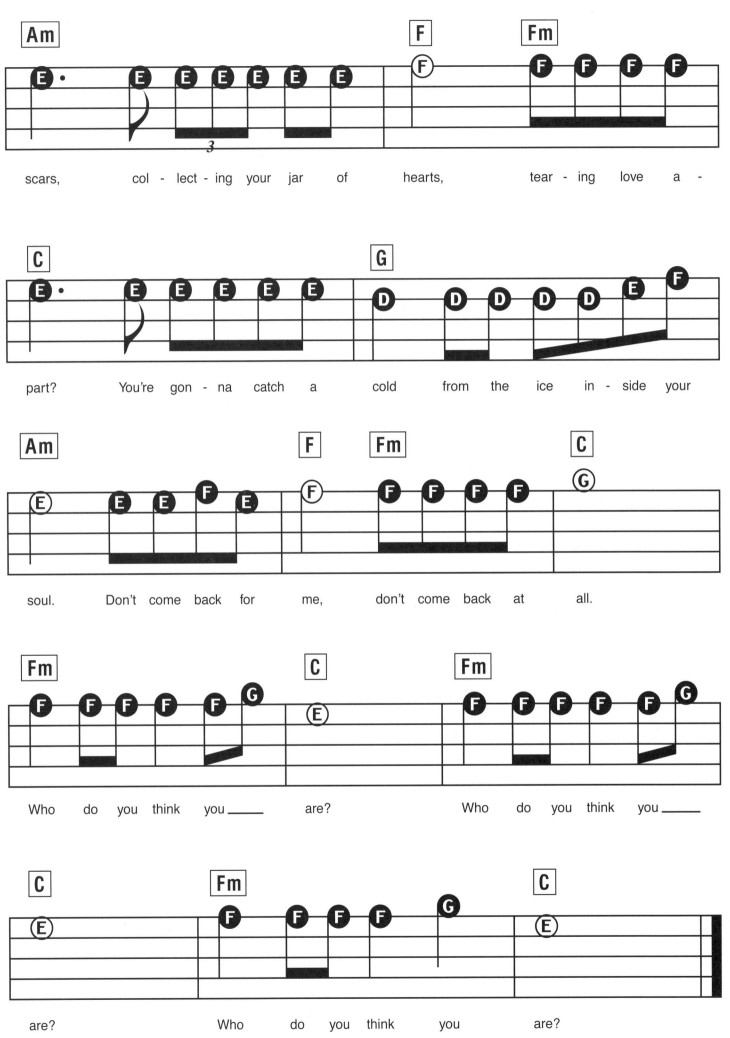

Let It Go
from FROZEN

Registration 8
Rhythm: Rock or Dance

Music and Lyrics by Kristen Anderson-Lopez
and Robert Lopez

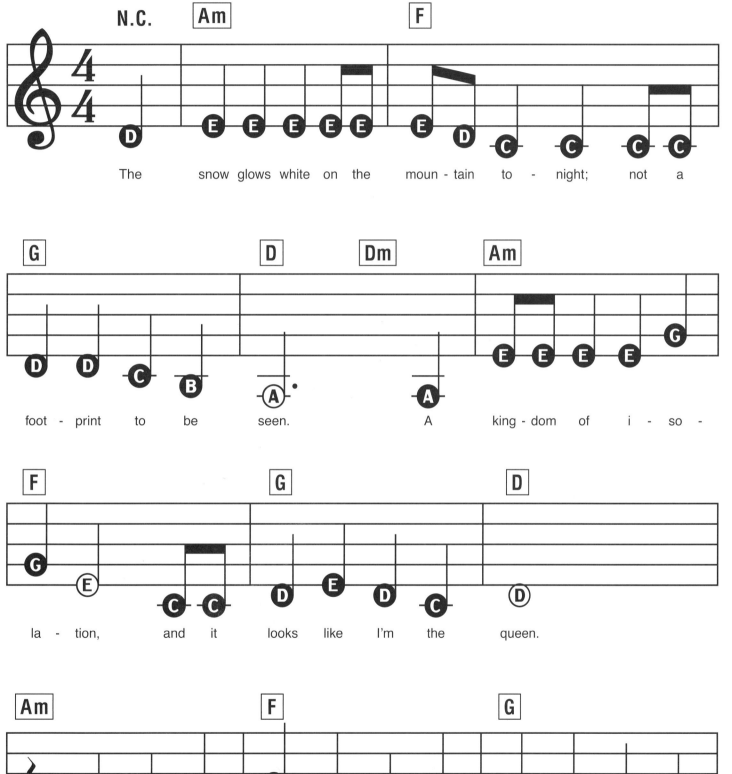

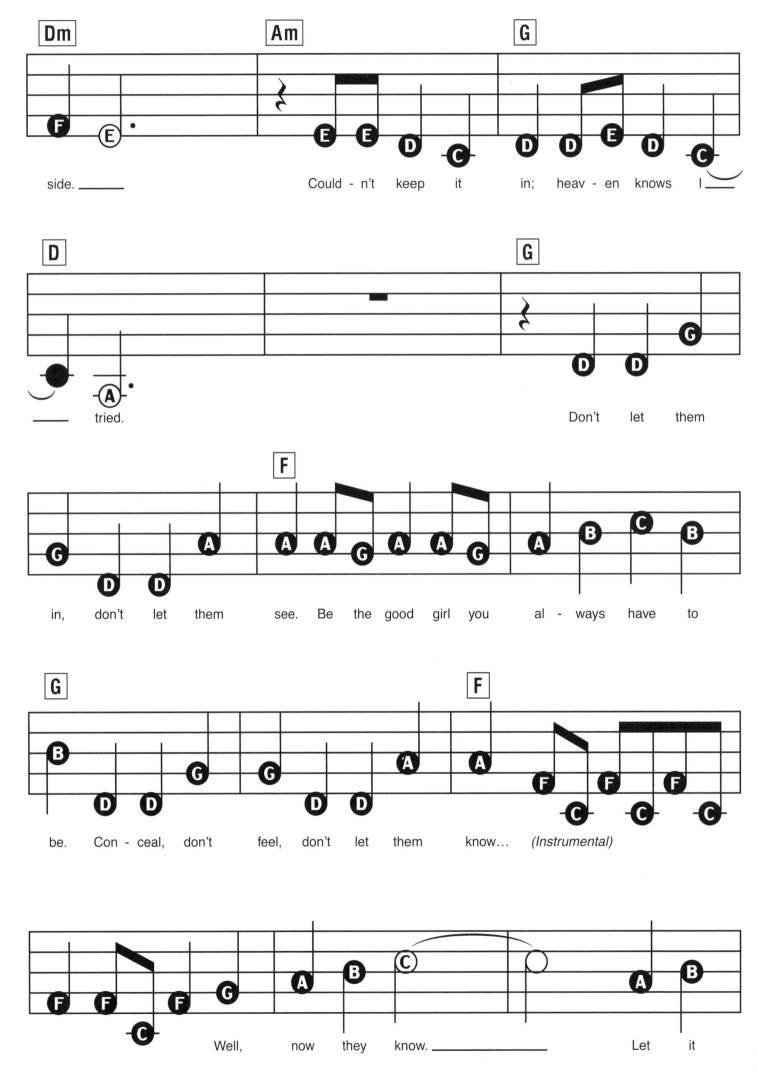

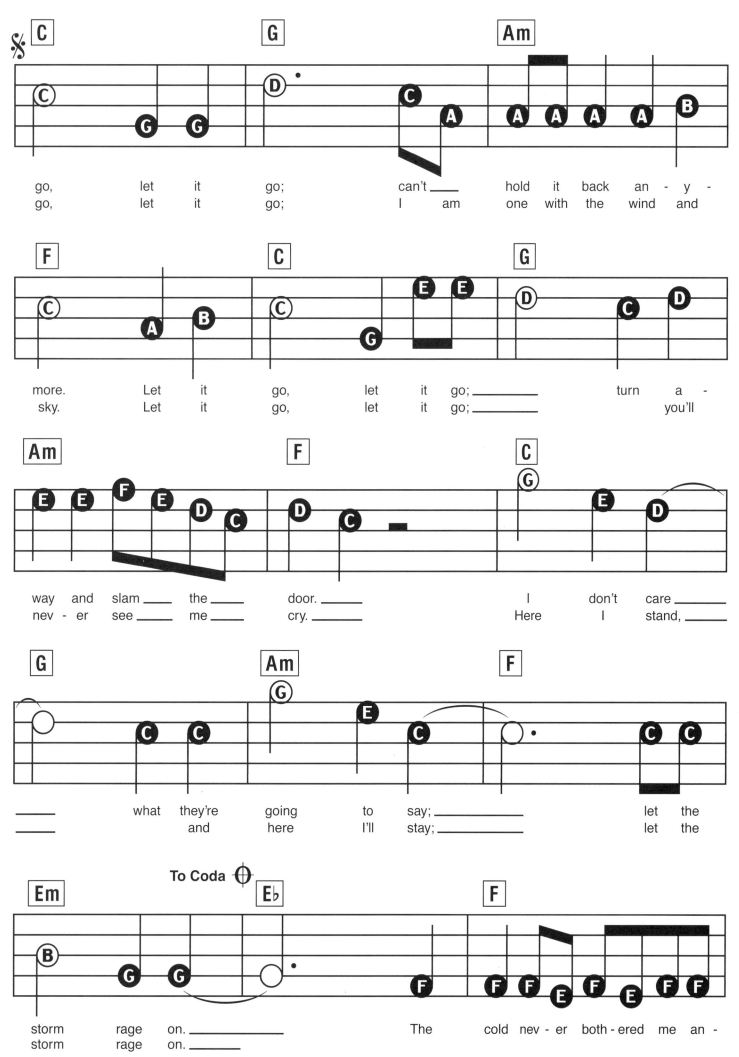

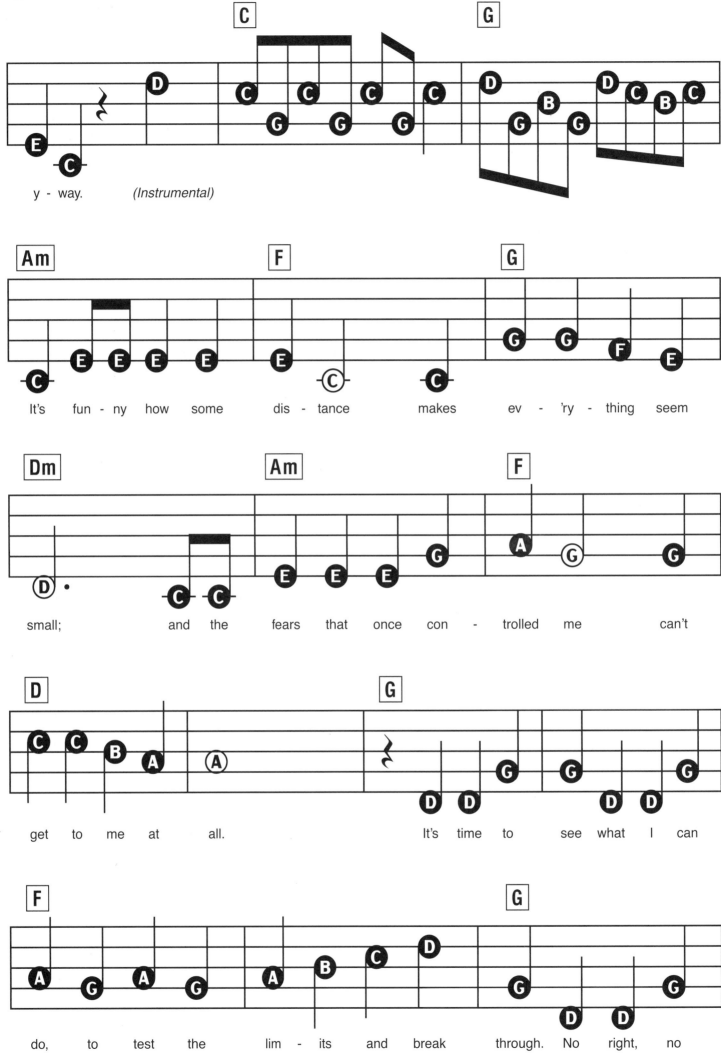

D.S. al Coda
(Return to 𝄋
Play to ⊕ and
Skip to Coda)

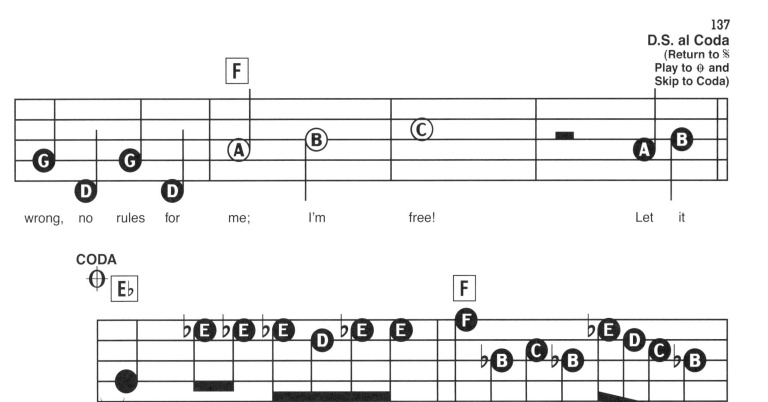

wrong, no rules for me; I'm free! Let it

CODA
E♭

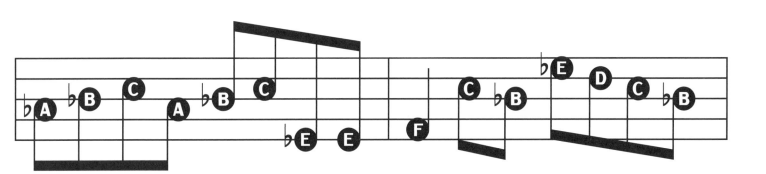

(Instrumental)

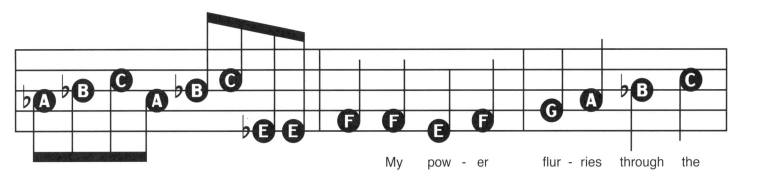

My pow - er flur - ries through the

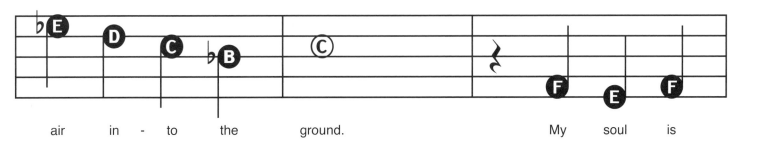

air in - to the ground. My soul is

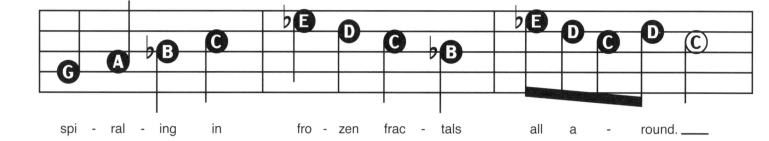

spi - ral - ing   in   fro - zen   frac - tals   all   a - round. ___

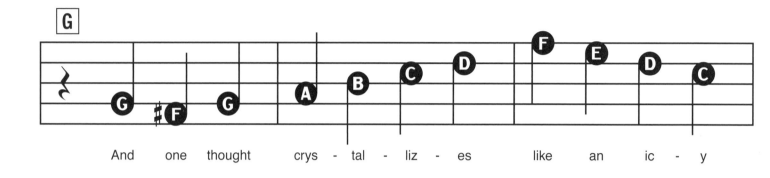

And   one   thought   crys - tal - liz - es   like   an   ic - y

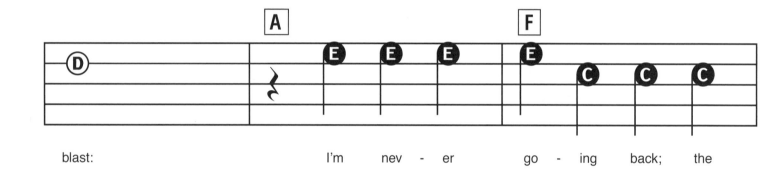

blast: I'm   nev - er   go - ing   back;   the

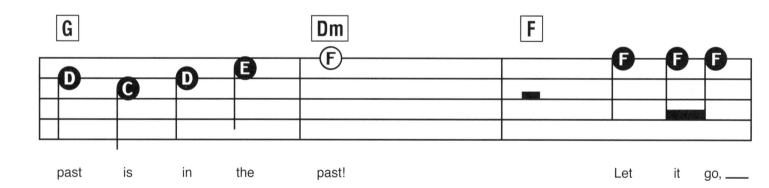

past   is   in   the   past!   Let   it   go, ___

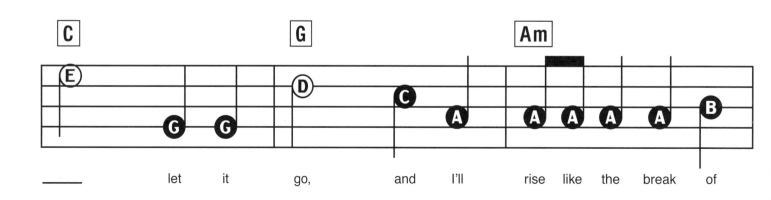

___   let   it   go,   and   I'll   rise   like   the   break   of

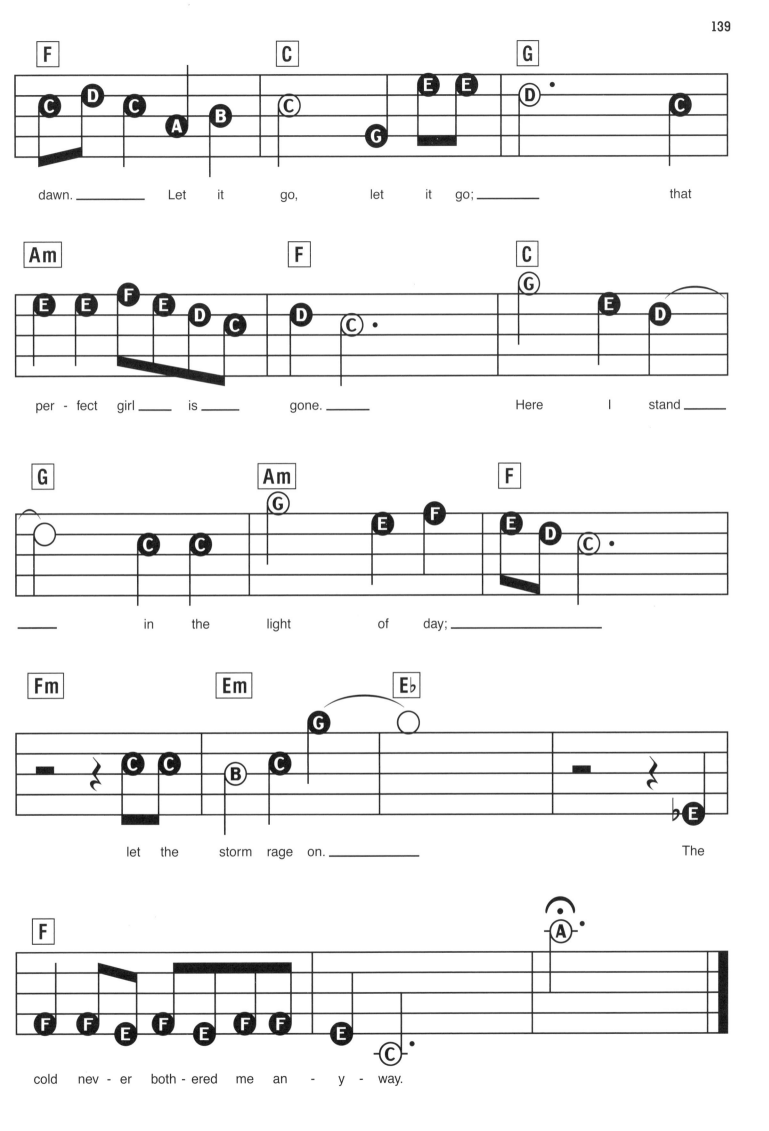

Just Give Me a Reason

Registration 8
Rhythm: 8-Beat or Rock

Words and Music by Alecia Moore,
Jeff Bhasker and Nate Ruess

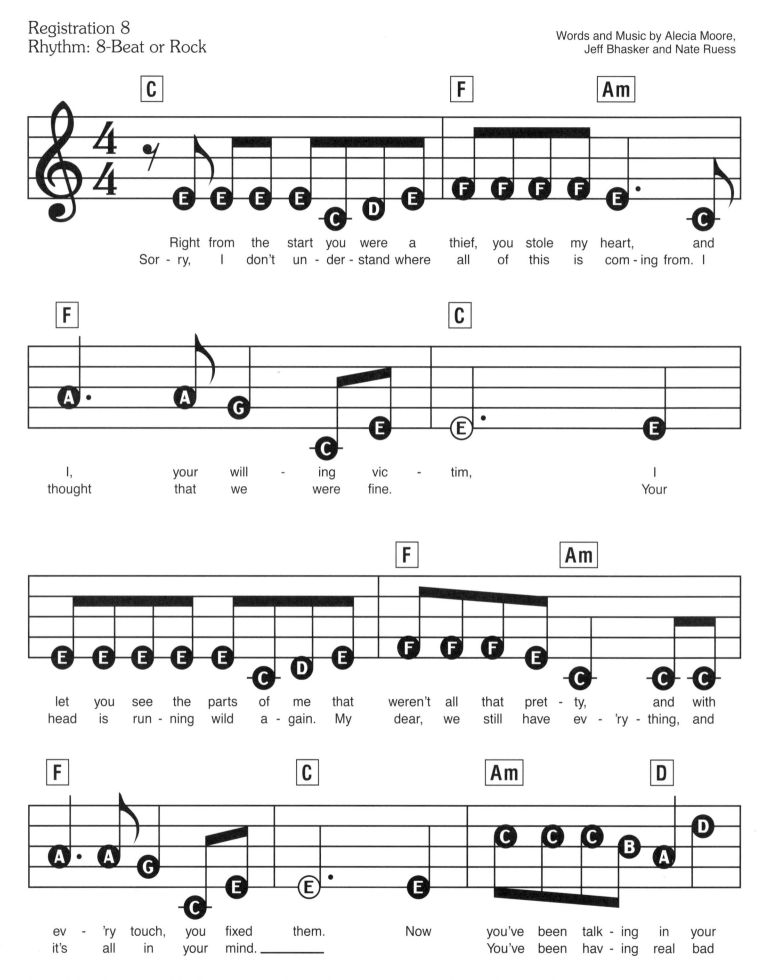

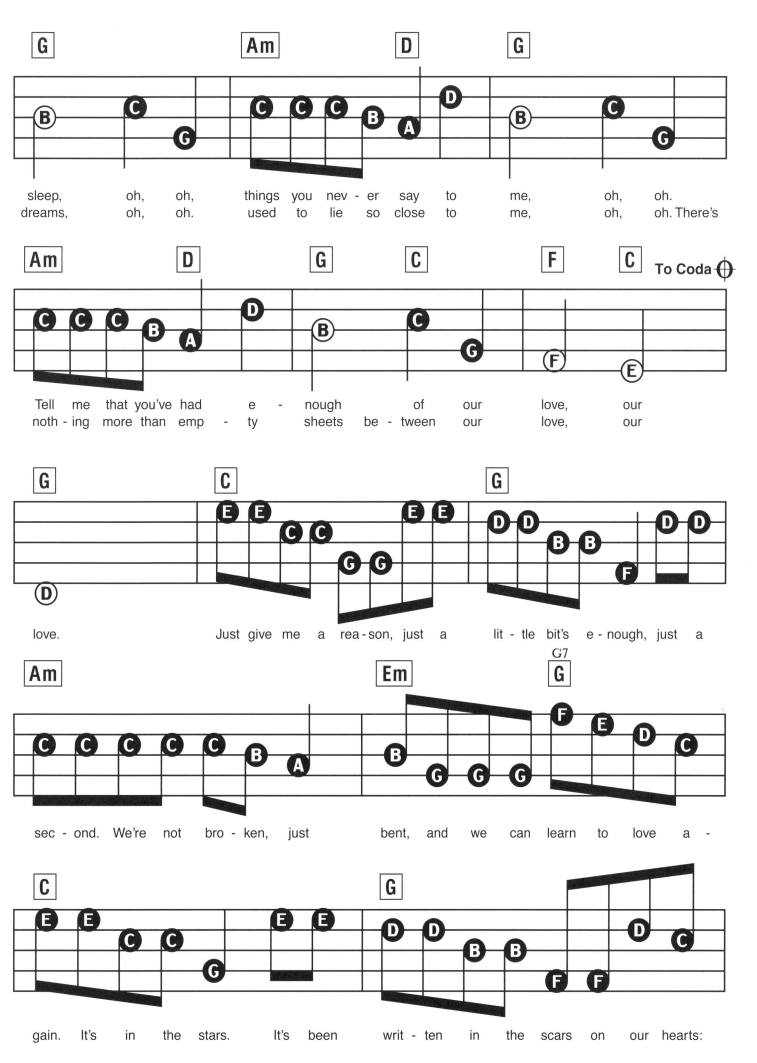

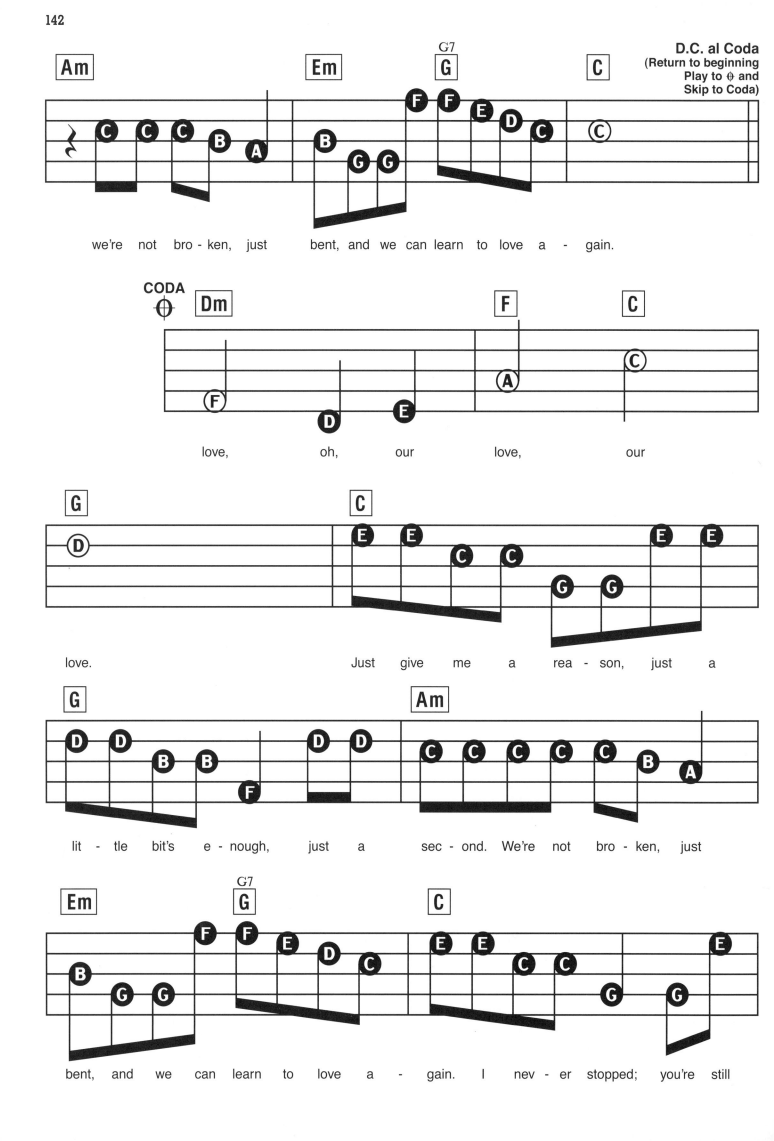

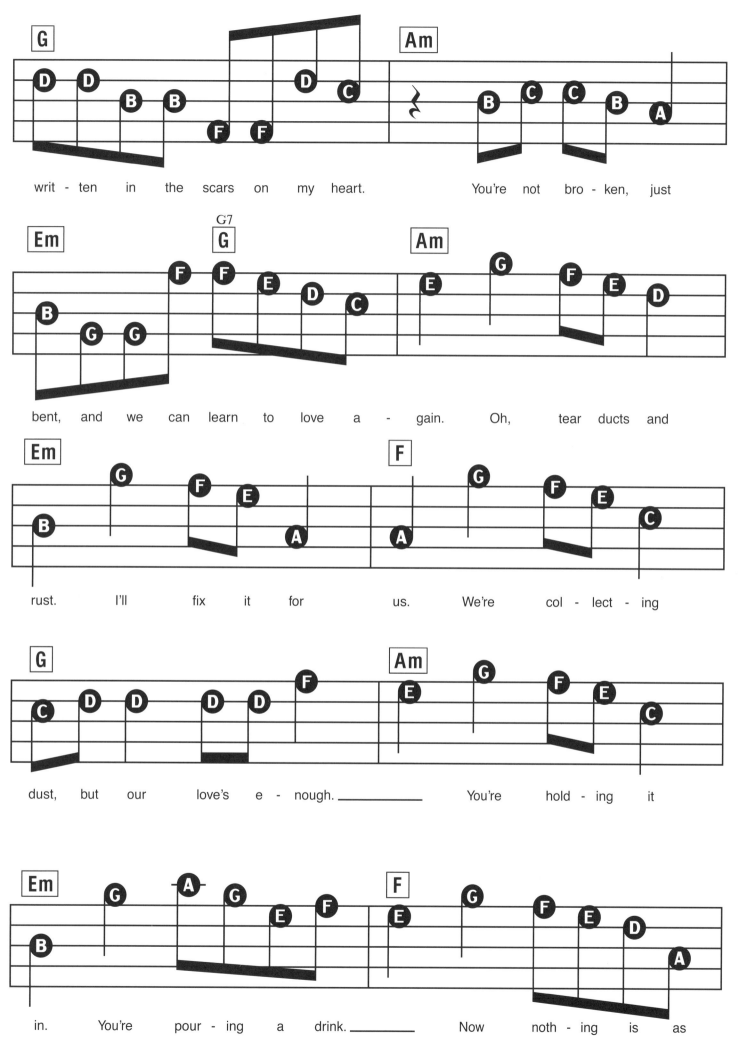

143

144

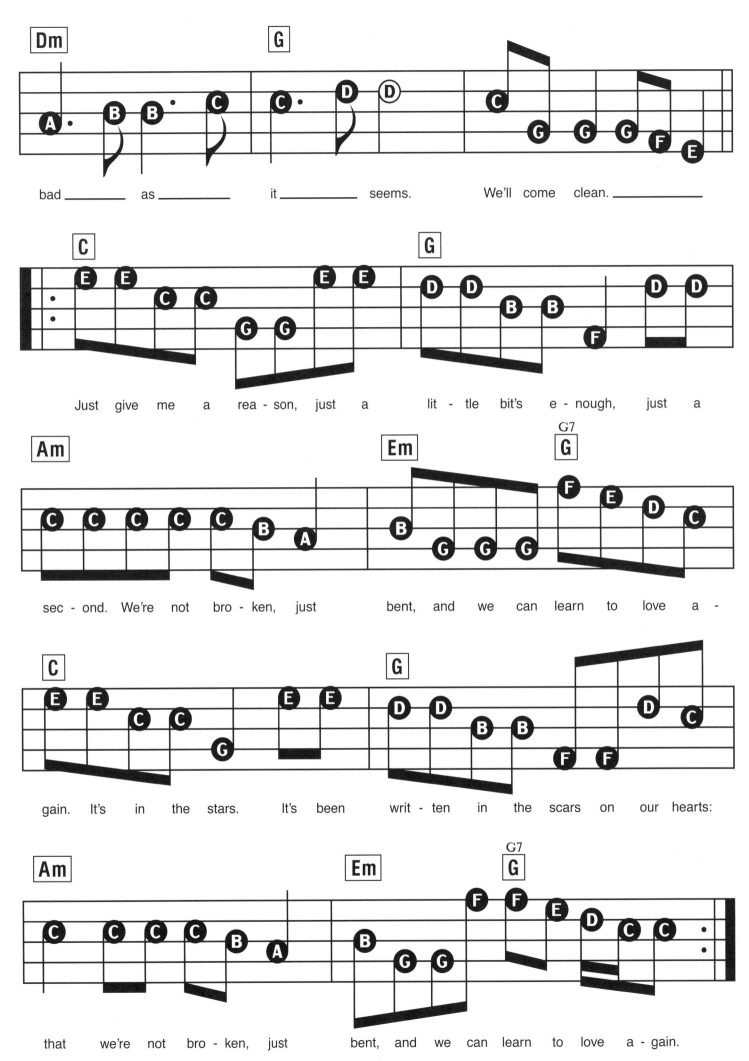

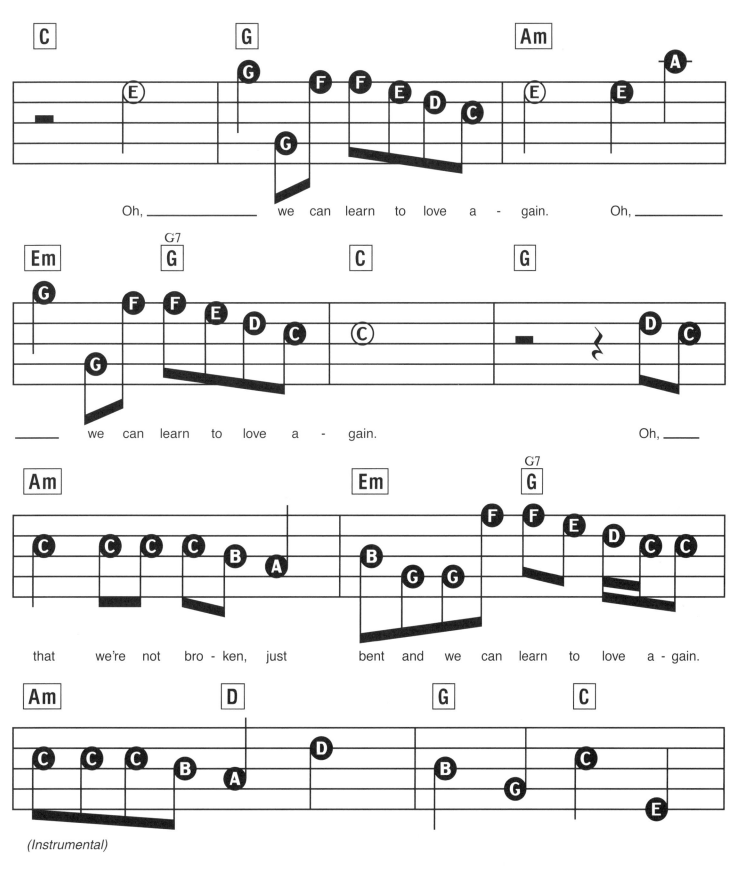

Oh, _____ we can learn to love a - gain. Oh, _____

_____ we can learn to love a - gain. Oh, _____

that we're not bro - ken, just bent and we can learn to love a - gain.

(Instrumental)

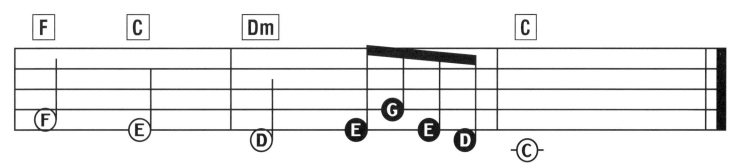

Just the Way You Are

Registration 4
Rhythm: 16-Beat or Rock

Words and Music by Bruno Mars,
Ari Levine, Khari Cain,
Philip Lawrence and Khalil Walton

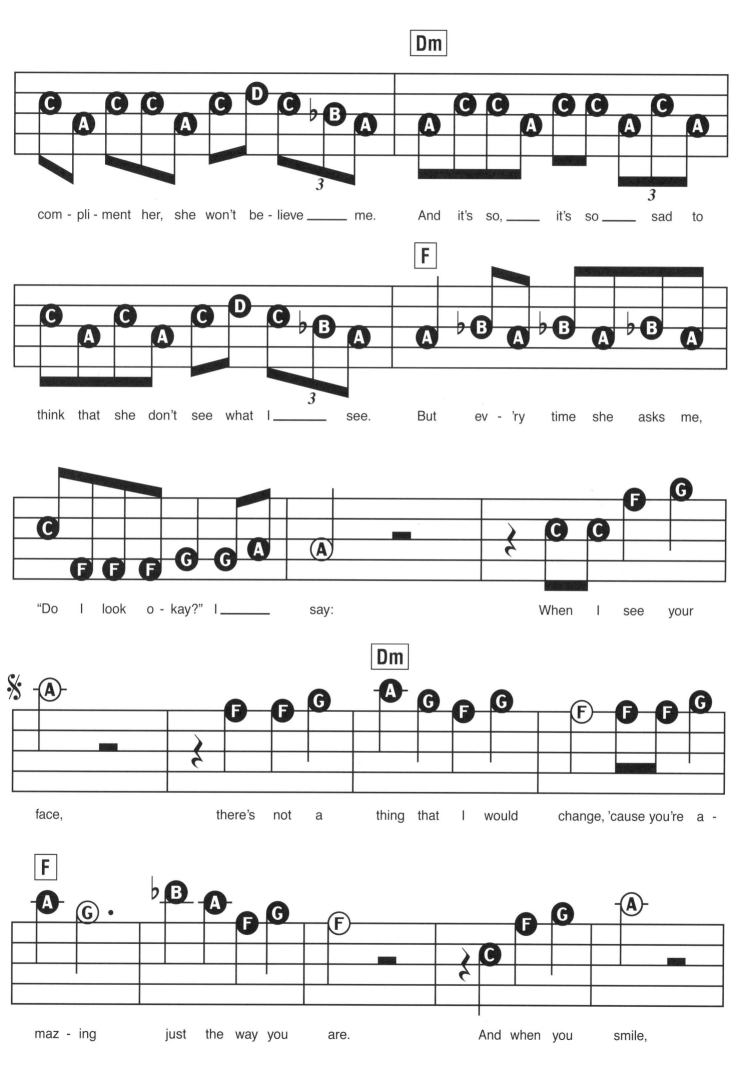

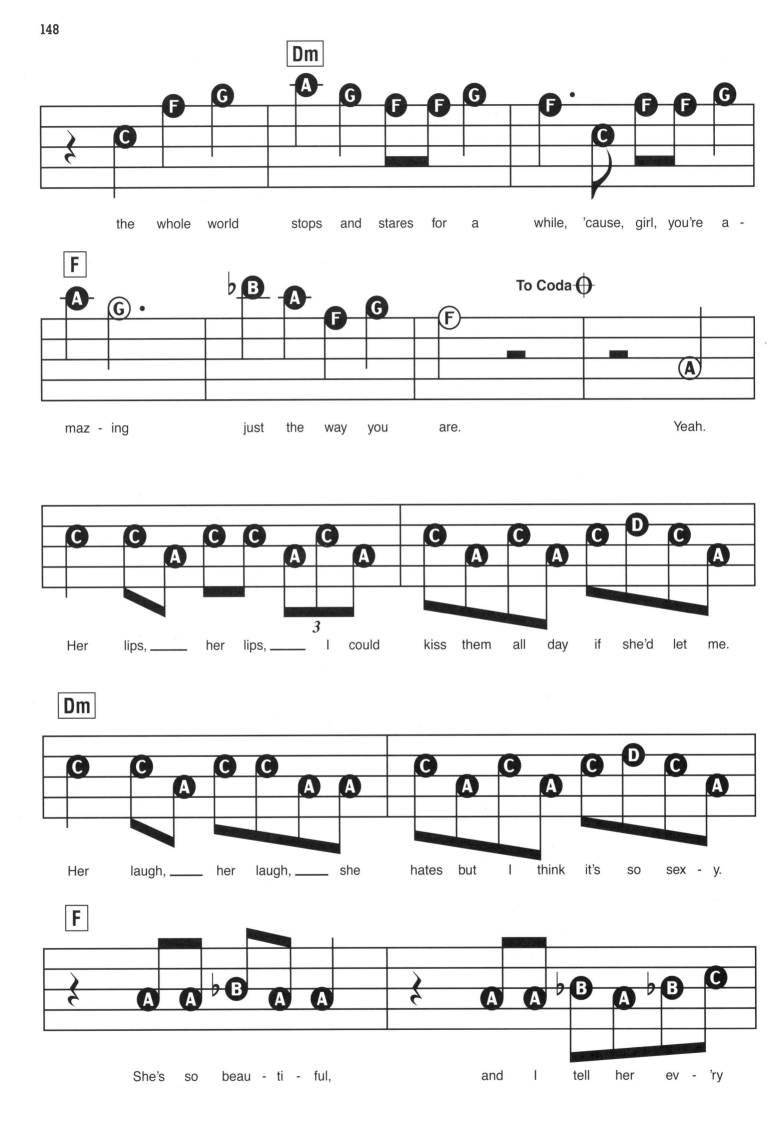

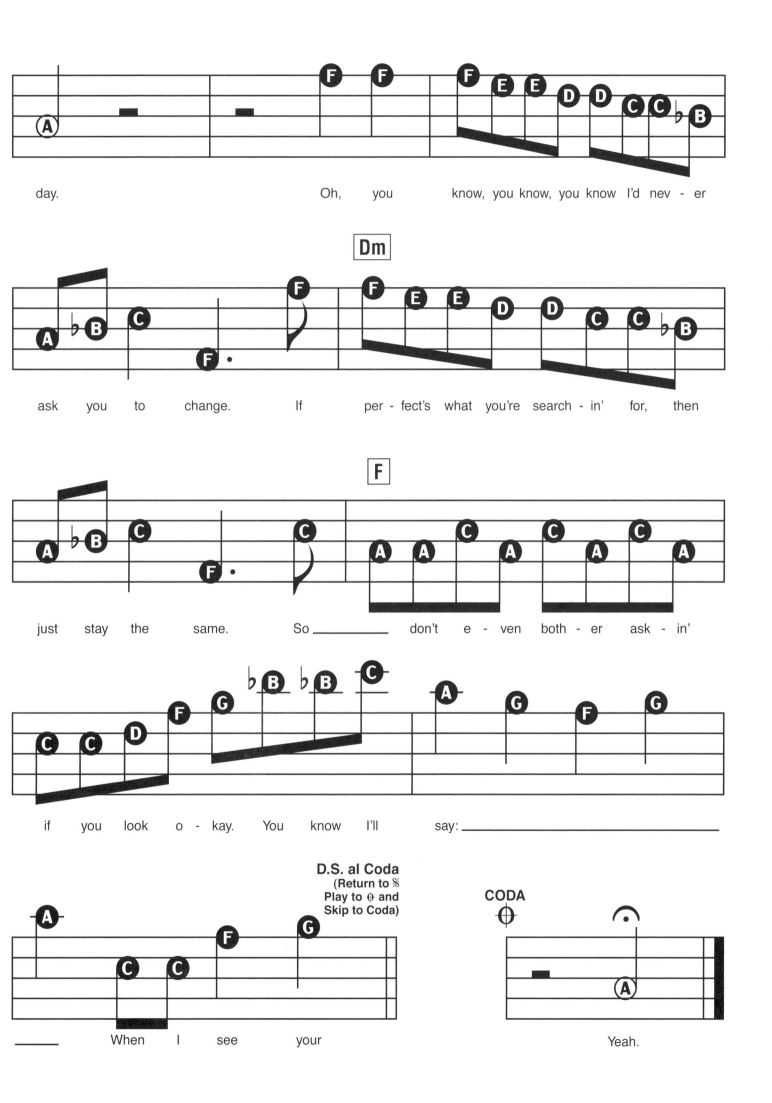

day.   Oh,   you   know, you know, you know I'd nev - er

ask   you   to   change.   If   per - fect's what you're search - in' for,   then

just   stay   the   same.   So _____ don't e - ven both - er ask - in'

if   you   look   o - kay.   You   know   I'll   say: _____

D.S. al Coda
(Return to 𝄋
Play to ⨁ and
Skip to Coda)

CODA

_____ When   I   see   your

Yeah.

Million Reasons

Registration 4
Rhythm: Rock or 8-Beat

Words and Music by Stefani Germanotta,
Mark Ronson and Hillary Lindsey

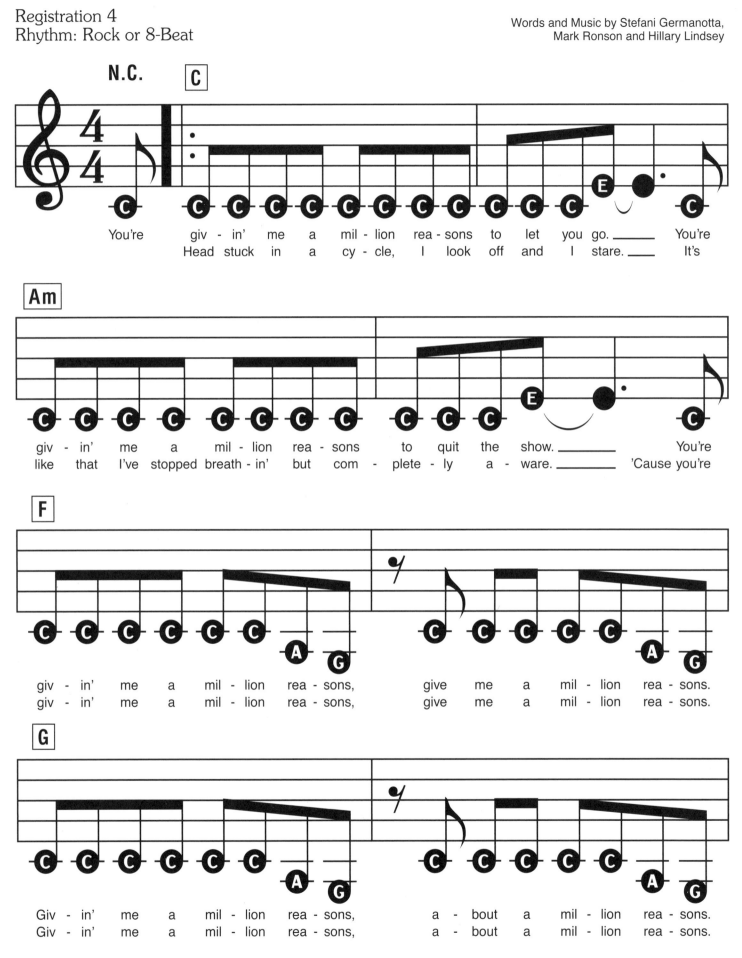

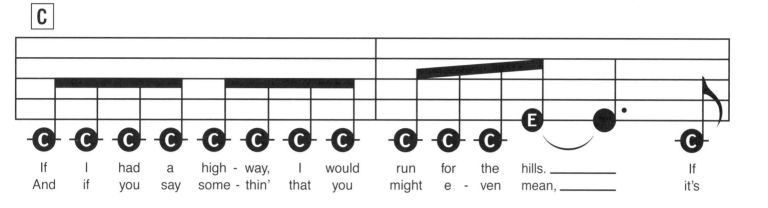

151

C

If I had a high-way, I would run for the hills. _____ If

And if you say some-thin' that you might e-ven mean, _____ it's

Am

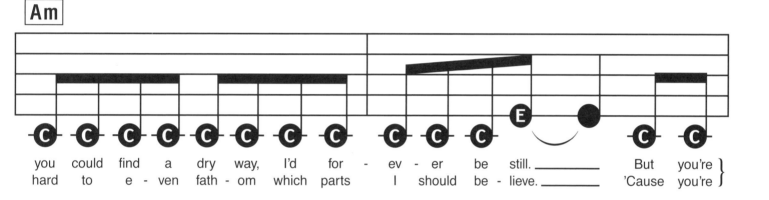

you could find a dry way, I'd for-ev-er be still. _____ But you're }

hard to e-ven fath-om which parts I should be-lieve. _____ 'Cause you're }

F

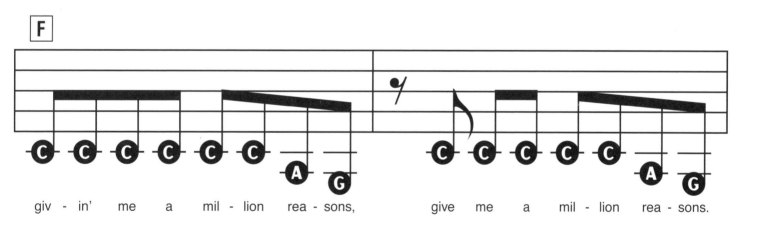

giv-in' me a mil-lion rea-sons, give me a mil-lion rea-sons.

G

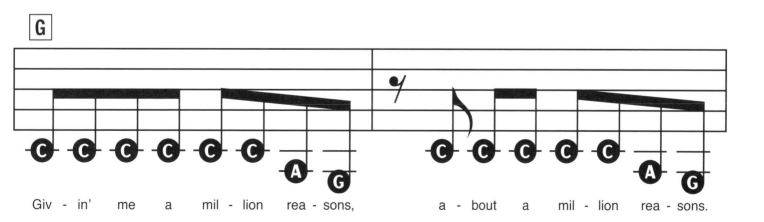

Giv-in' me a mil-lion rea-sons, a-bout a mil-lion rea-sons.

152

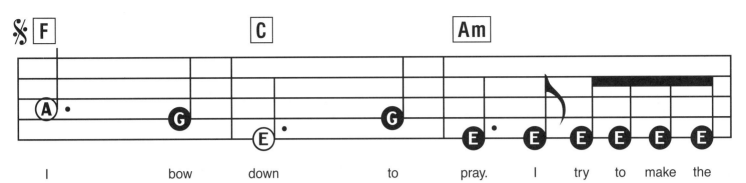

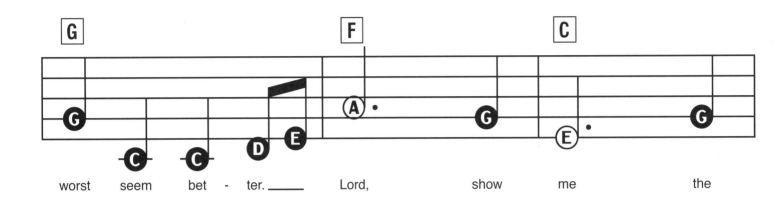

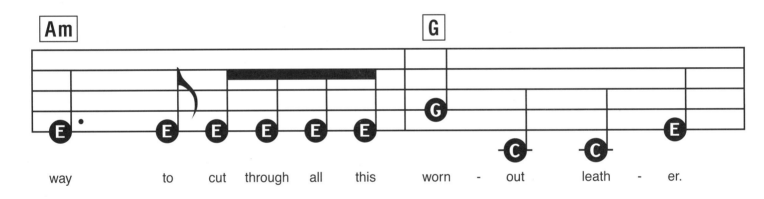

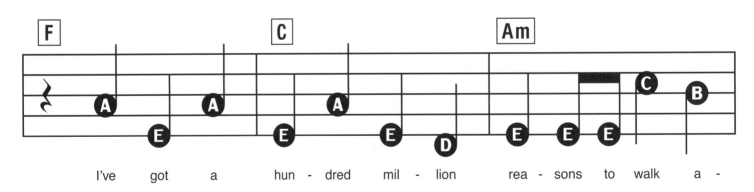

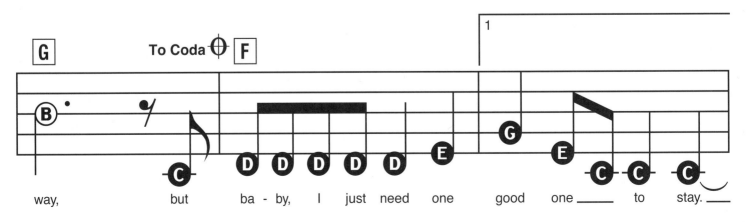

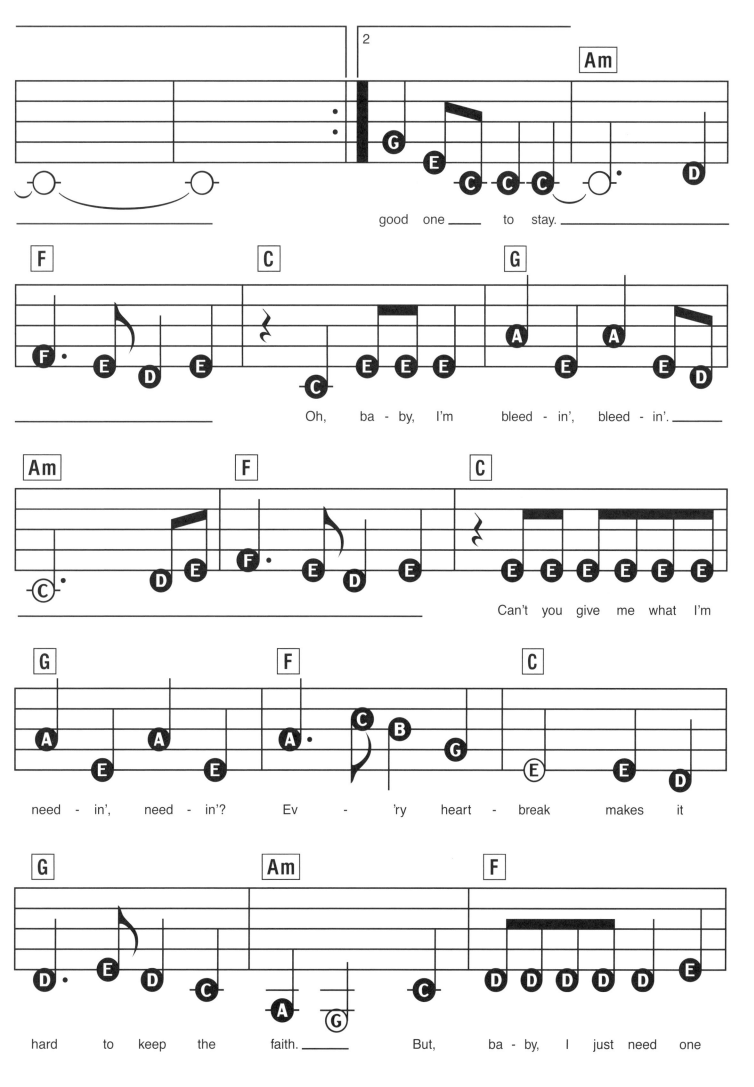

D.S. al Coda
(Return to %
Play to ⊕ and
Skip to Coda)

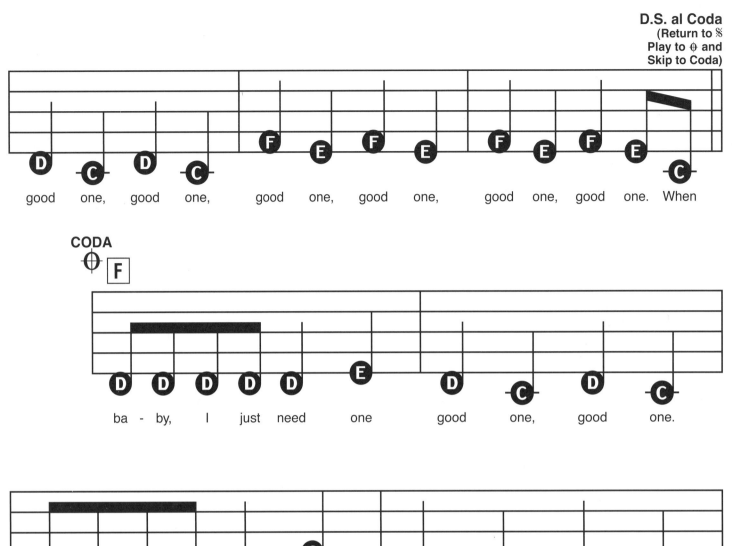

good one, good one, good one, good one, good one, good one. When

CODA

⊕ F

ba - by, I just need one good one, good one.

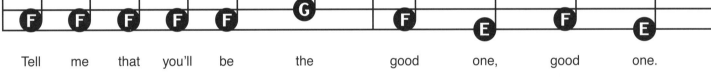

Tell me that you'll be the good one, good one.

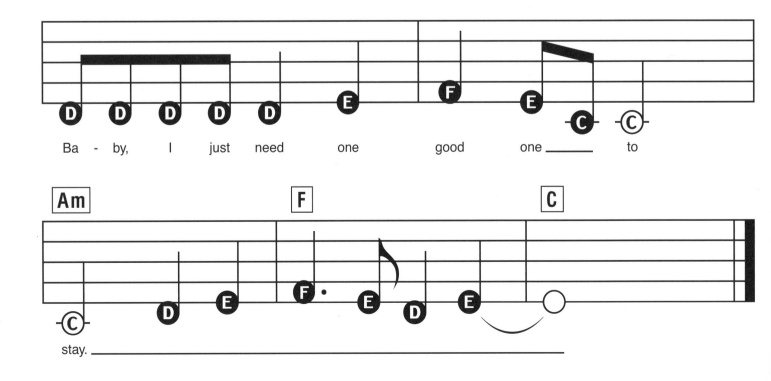

Ba - by, I just need one good one ____ to

Am **F** **C**

stay. ____

Look What You Made Me Do

Registration 3
Rhythm: Pop or Rock

Words and Music by Taylor Swift,
Jack Antonoff, Richard Fairbrass,
Fred Fairbrass and Rob Manzoli

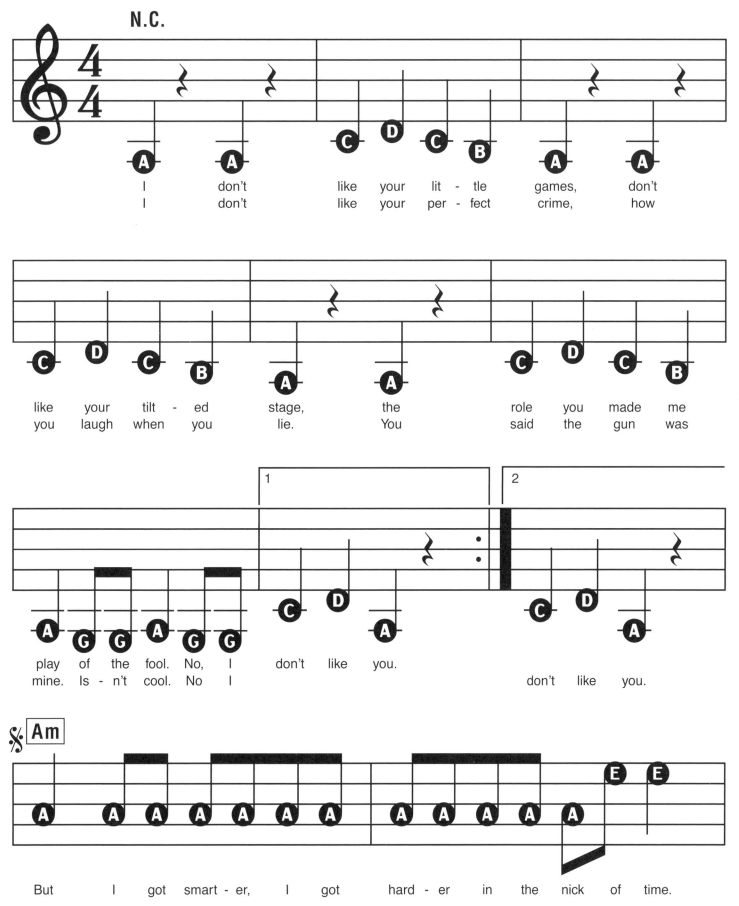

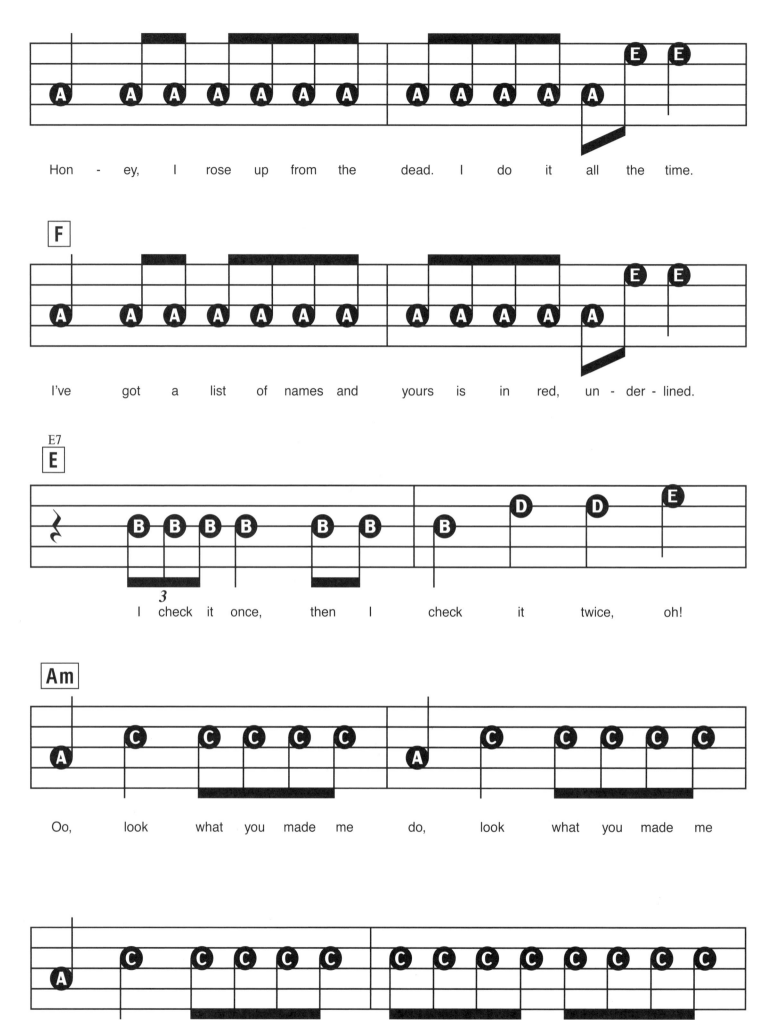

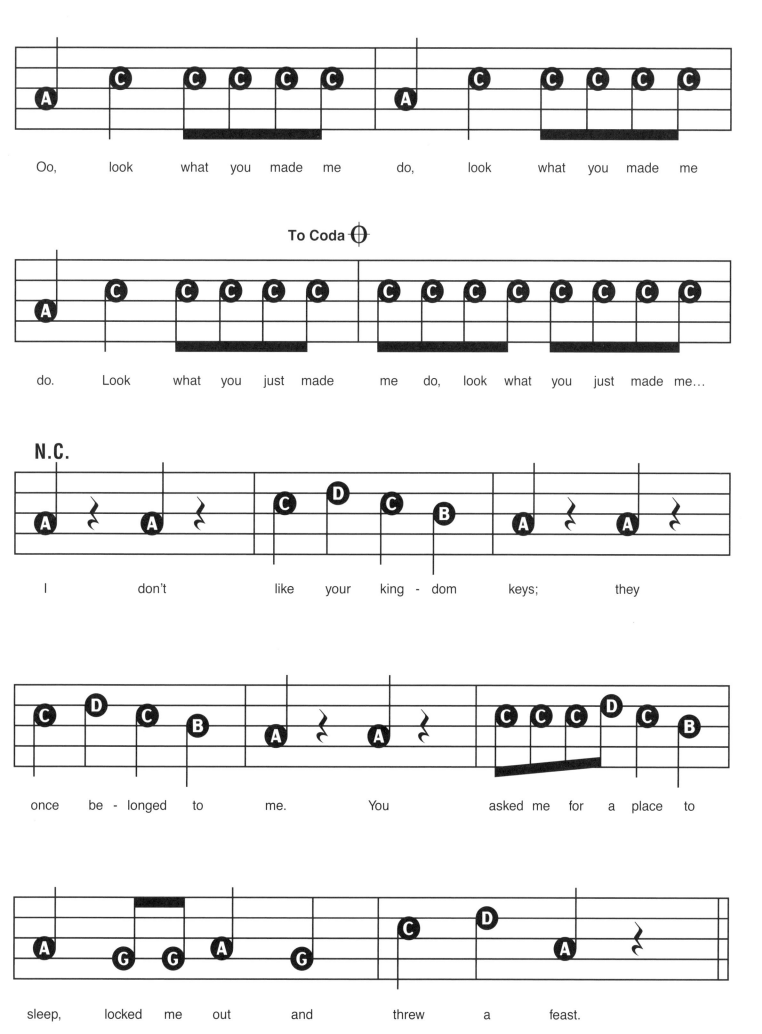

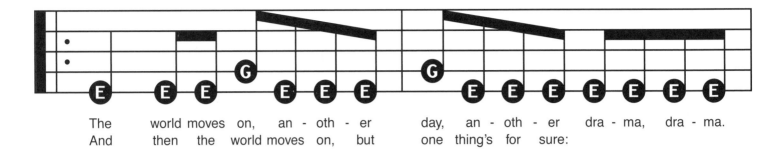

The world moves on, an - oth - er day, an - oth - er dra - ma, dra - ma.
And then the world moves on, but one thing's for sure:

1

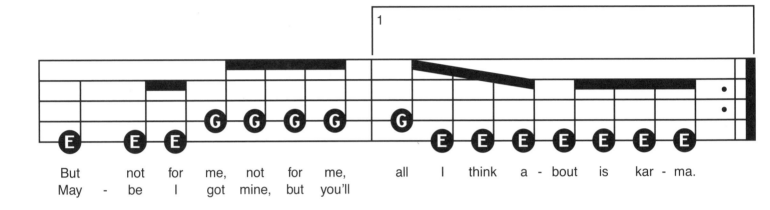

But not for me, not for me, all I think a - bout is kar - ma.
May - be I got mine, but you'll

2

D.S. al Coda
(Return to 𝄋
Play to ⊕ and
Skip to Coda)

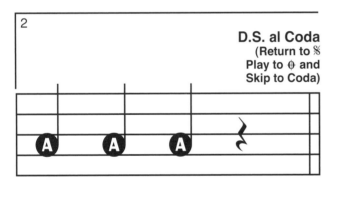

all get yours.

CODA
⊕

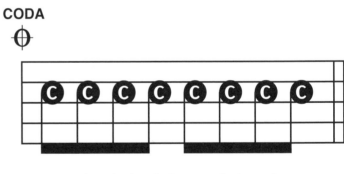

me do, look what you just made me...

Am

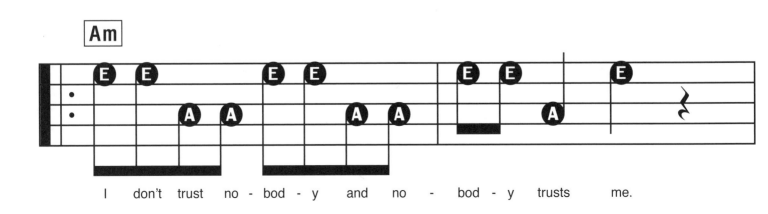

I don't trust no - bod - y and no - bod - y trusts me.

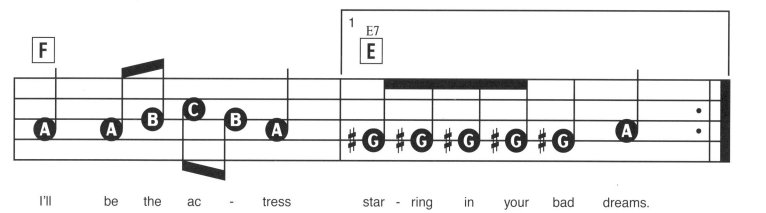

I'll be the ac - tress star - ring in your bad dreams.

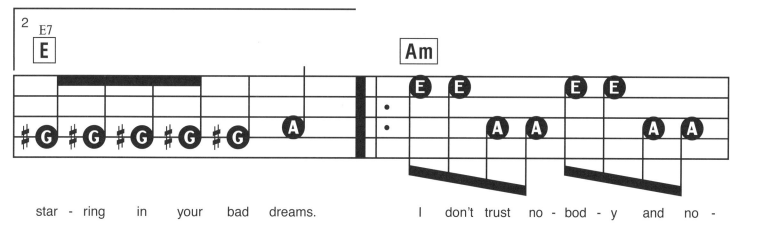

star - ring in your bad dreams. I don't trust no - bod - y and no -

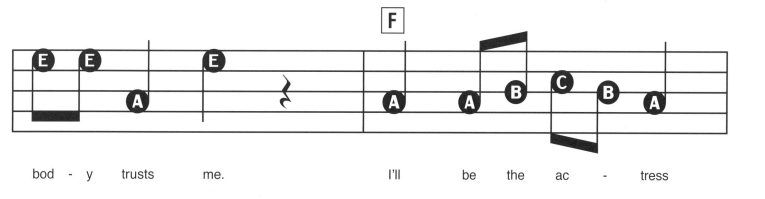

bod - y trusts me. I'll be the ac - tress

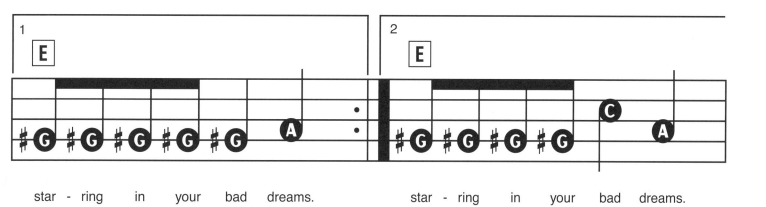

star - ring in your bad dreams. star - ring in your bad dreams.

160

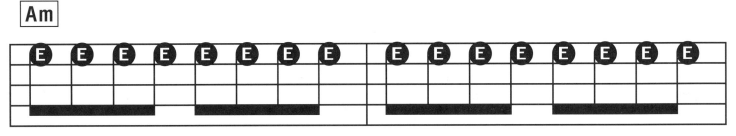

(Instrumental)

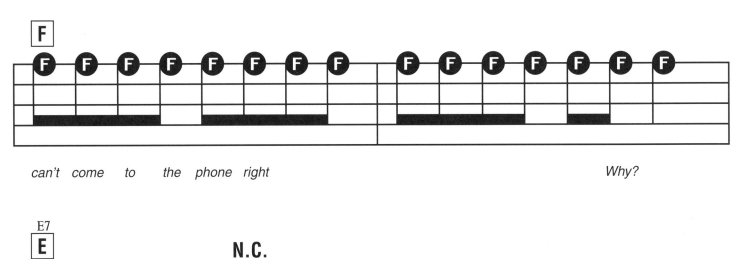

(Spoken:) "I'm sorry, the old Taylor

F

can't come to the phone right Why?

E7 / E   **N.C.**

Oh, *'cause she's dead!"* *(Sung:)* Oo, look what you made me

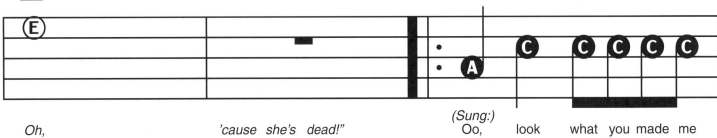

do, look what you made me do. Look what you just made

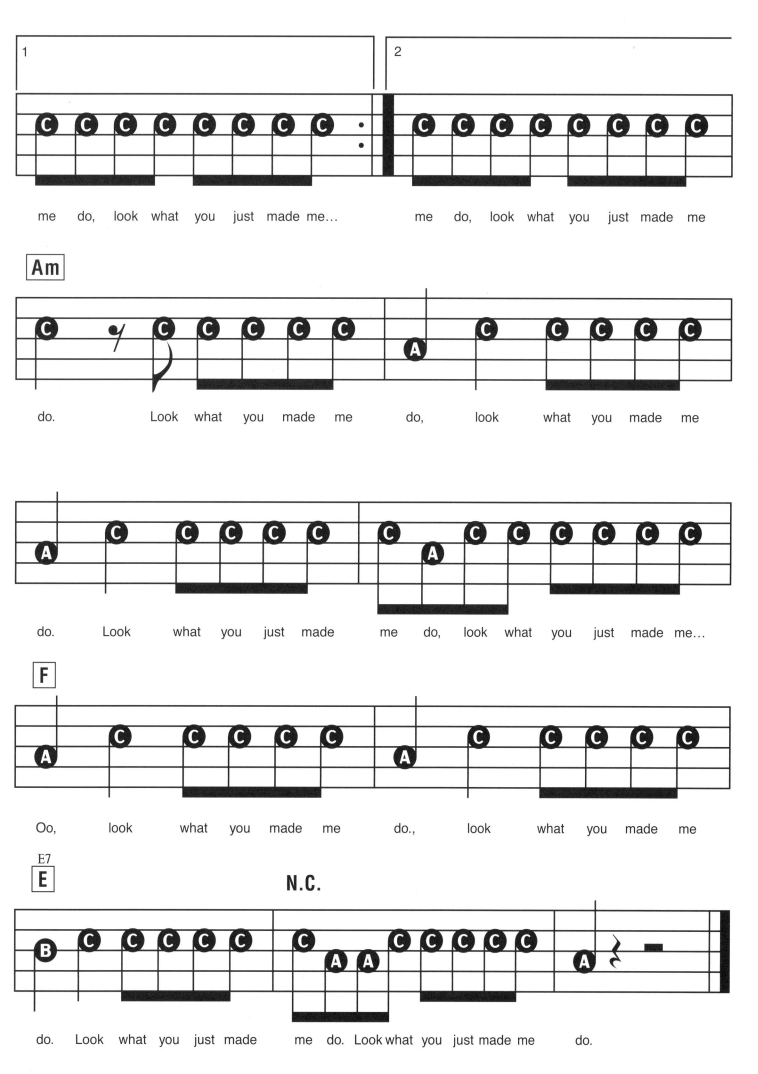

One Call Away

Registration 8
Rhythm: Rock or 8-Beat

Words and Music by Charlie Puth,
Justin Franks, Breyan Isaac, Matt Prime,
Blake Anthony Carter and Maureen McDonald

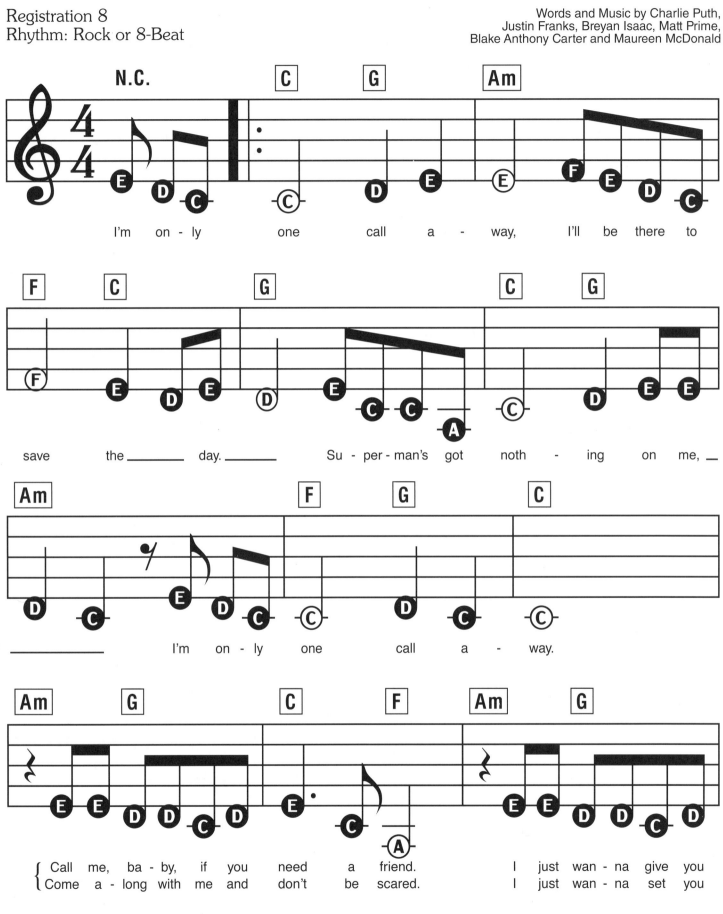

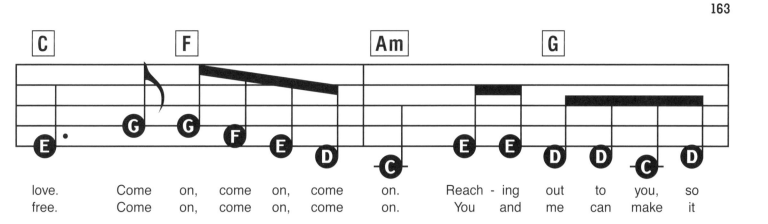

love. Come on, come on, come on. Reach - ing out to you, so
free. Come on, come on, come on. You and me can make it

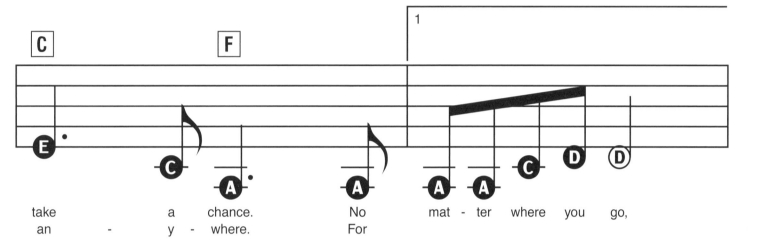

take a chance. No mat - ter where you go,
an - y - where. For

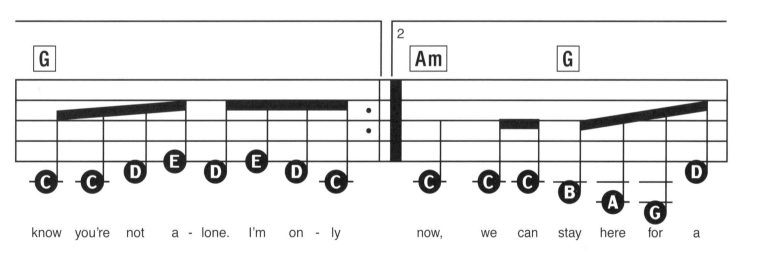

know you're not a - lone. I'm on - ly now, we can stay here for a

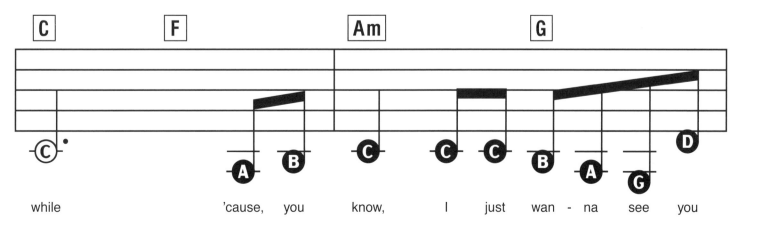

while 'cause, you know, I just wan - na see you

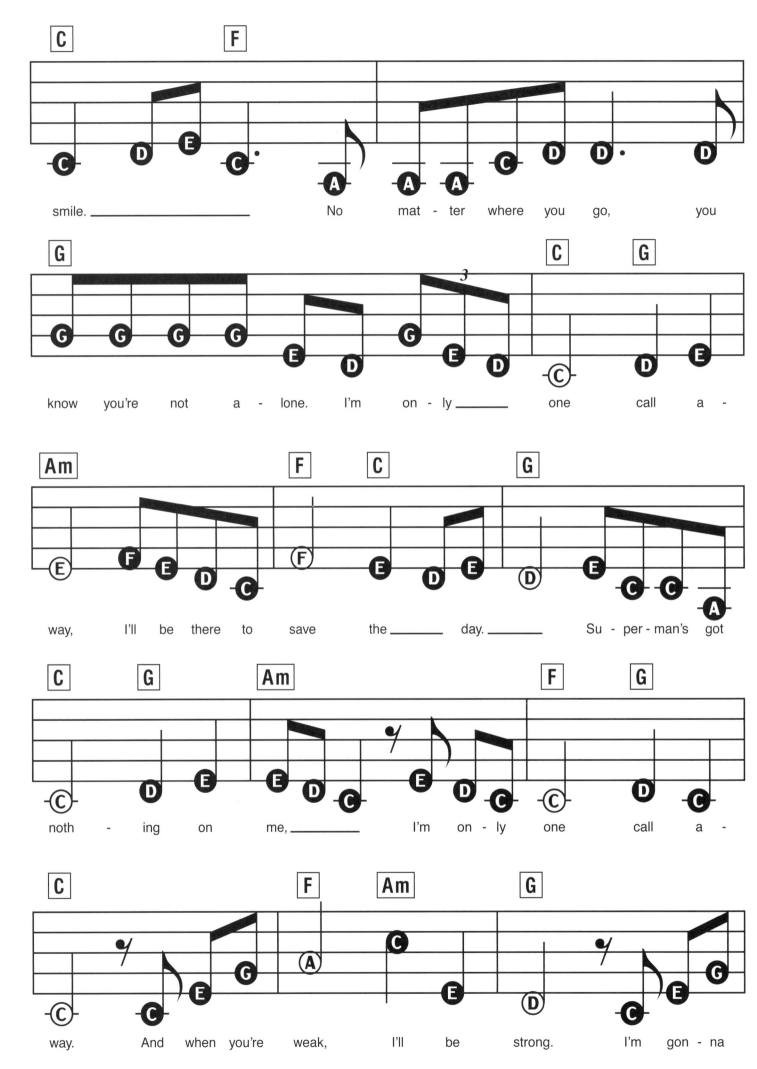

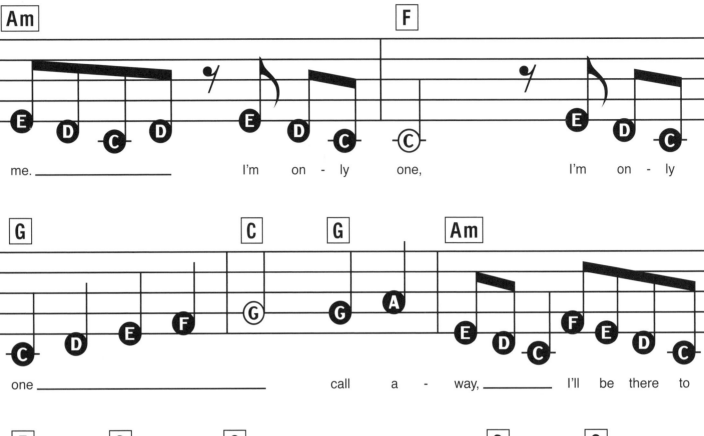

me. _____ I'm on - ly one, I'm on - ly

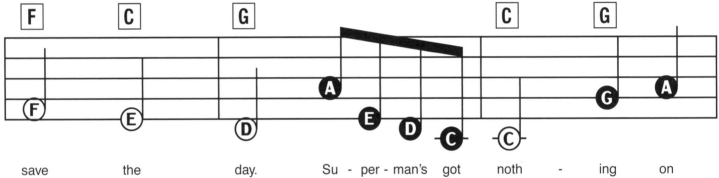

one _____ call a - way, _____ I'll be there to

save the day. Su - per - man's got noth - ing on

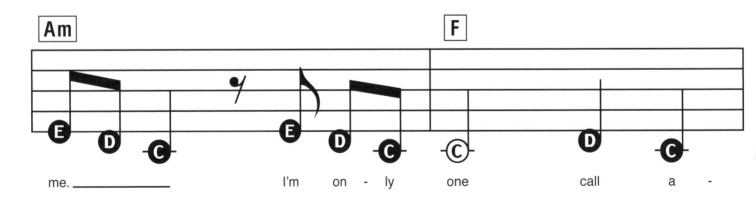

me. _____ I'm on - ly one call a -

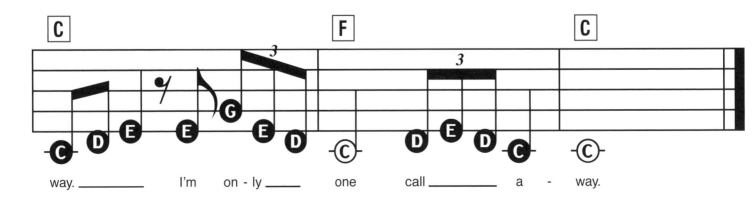

way. _____ I'm on - ly ____ one call _____ a - way.

Memories

Registration 10
Rhythm: Pop or Ballad

Words and Music by Adam Levine,
Jonathan Bellion, Jordan Johnson,
Jacob Hindlin, Stefan Johnson,
Michael Pollack and Vincent Ford

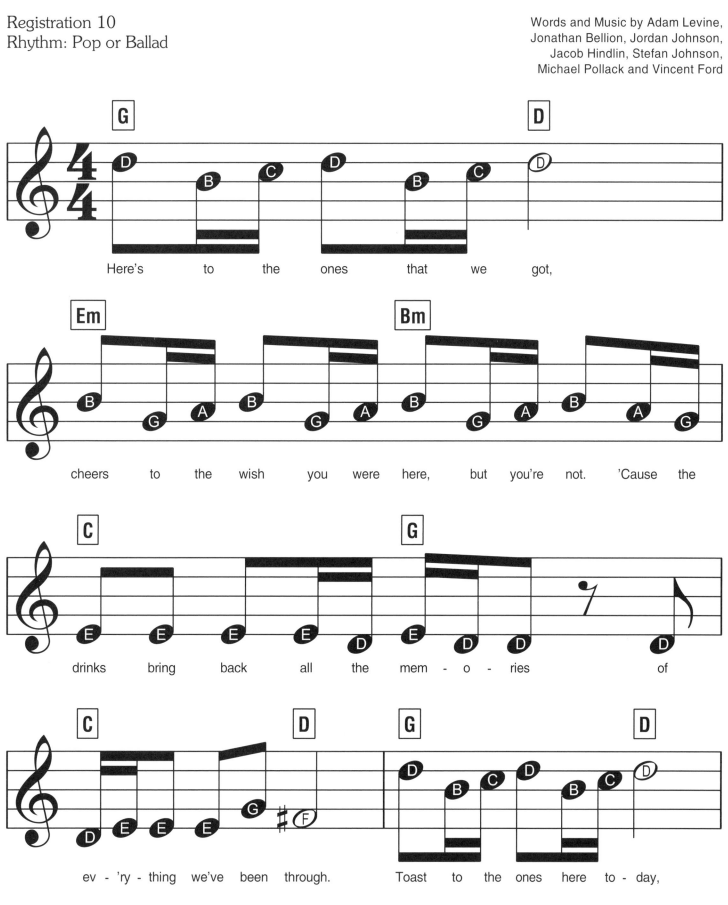

168

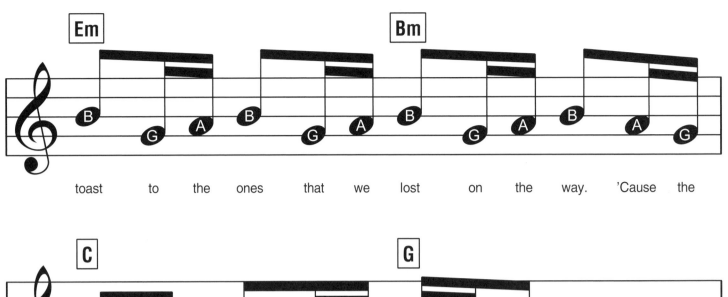

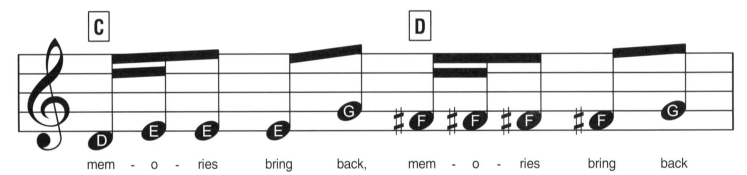

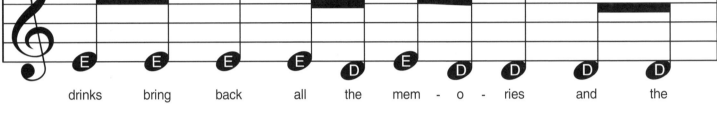

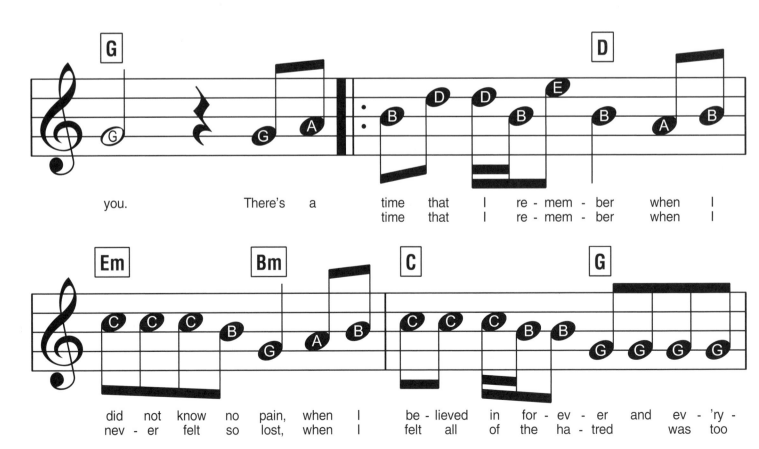

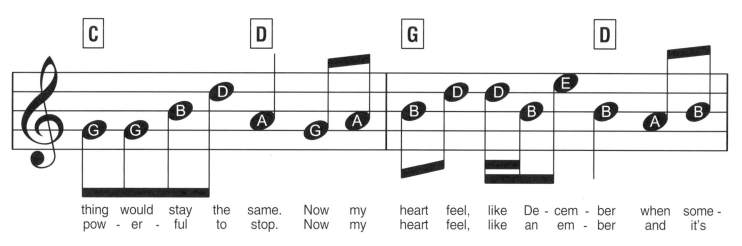

thing would stay the same. Now my heart feel, like De - cem - ber when some -
pow - er - ful to stop. Now my heart feel, like an em - ber and it's

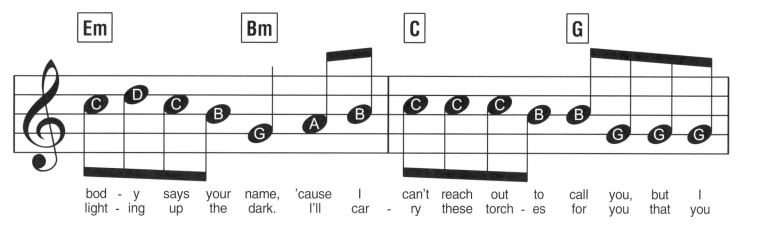

bod - y says your name, 'cause I can't reach out to call you, but I
light - ing up the dark. I'll car - ry these torch - es for you that you

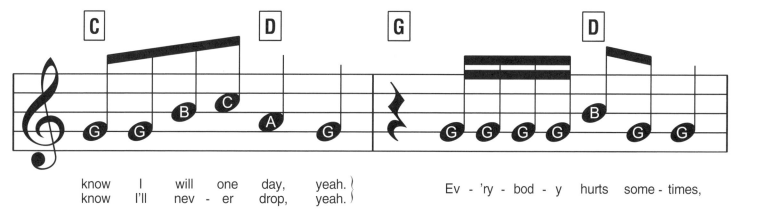

know I will one day, yeah.
know I'll nev - er drop, yeah.

Ev - 'ry - bod - y hurts some - times,

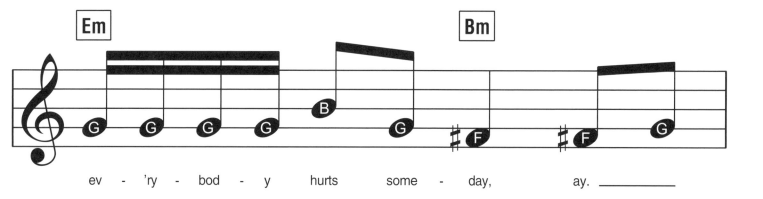

ev - 'ry - bod - y hurts some - day, ay. _____

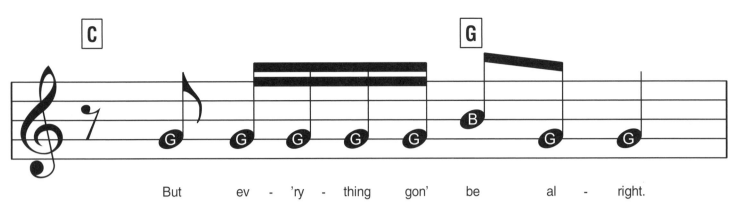

But ev - 'ry - thing gon' be al - right.

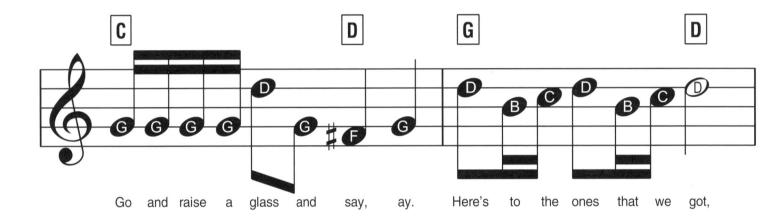

Go and raise a glass and say, ay. Here's to the ones that we got,

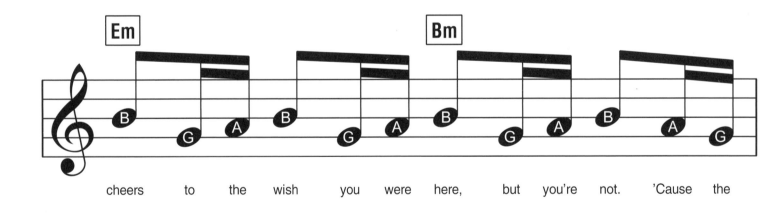

cheers to the wish you were here, but you're not. 'Cause the

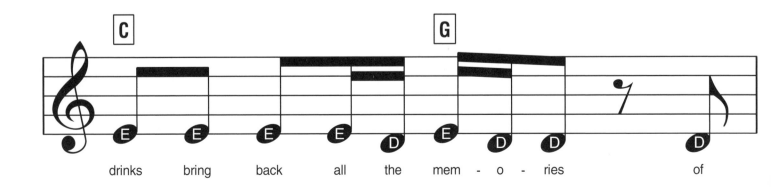

drinks bring back all the mem - o - ries of

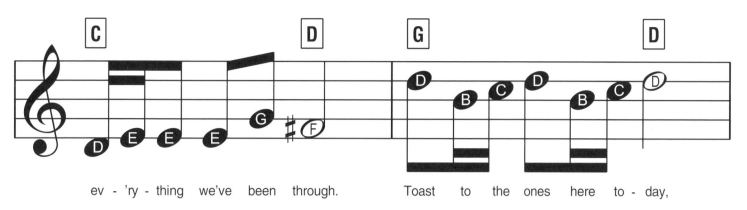

ev - 'ry - thing we've been through. Toast to the ones here to - day,

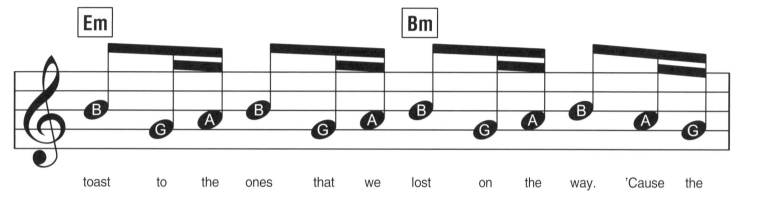

toast to the ones that we lost on the way. 'Cause the

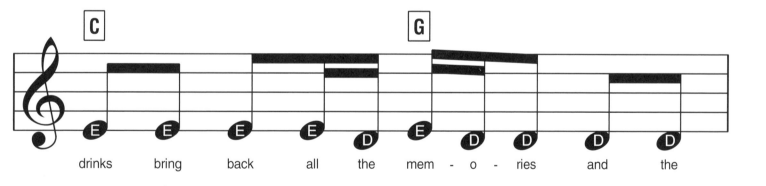

drinks bring back all the mem - o - ries and the

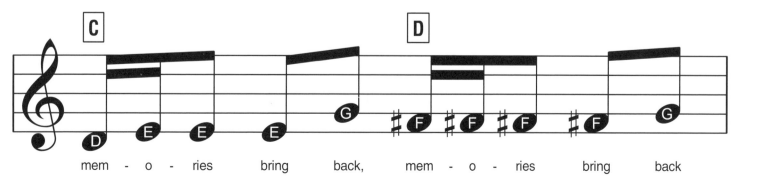

mem - o - ries bring back, mem - o - ries bring back

172

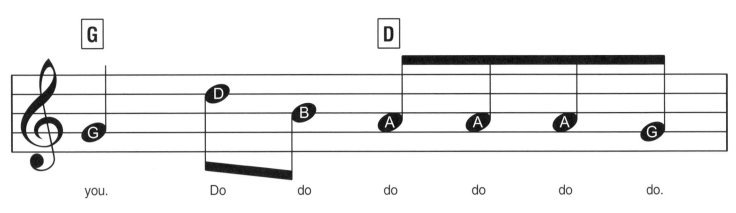

you. Do do do do do do.

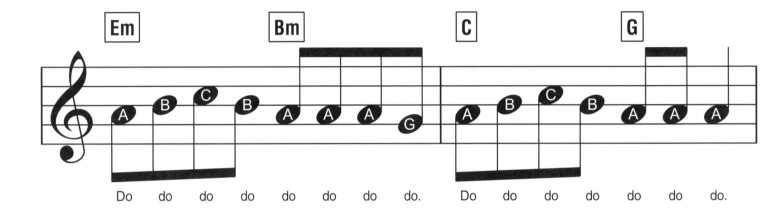

Do do do do do do do do. Do do do do do do do.

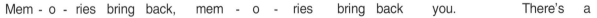
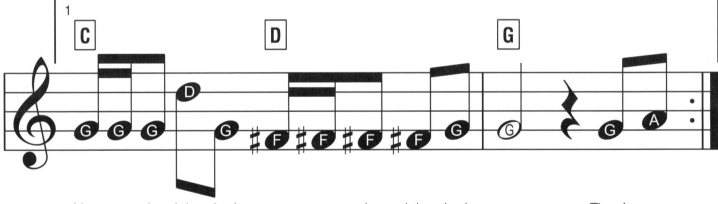

Mem - o - ries bring back, mem - o - ries bring back you. There's a

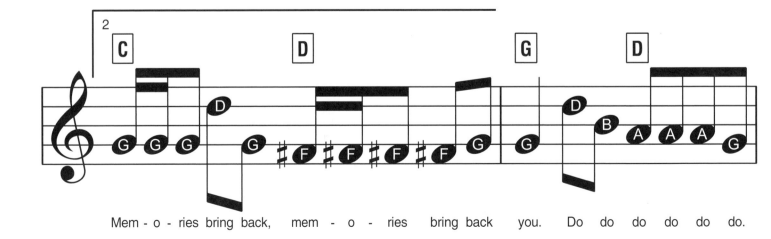

Mem - o - ries bring back, mem - o - ries bring back you. Do do do do do do.

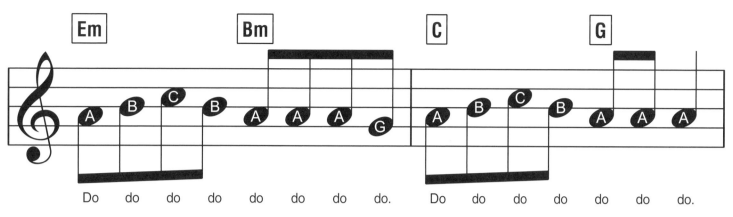

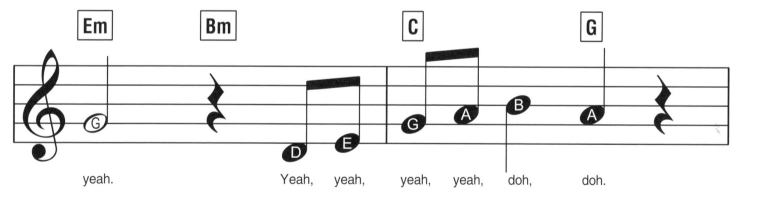

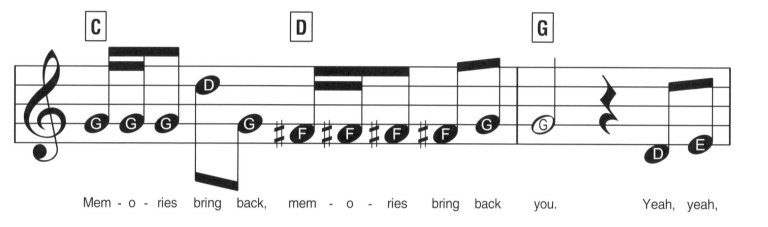

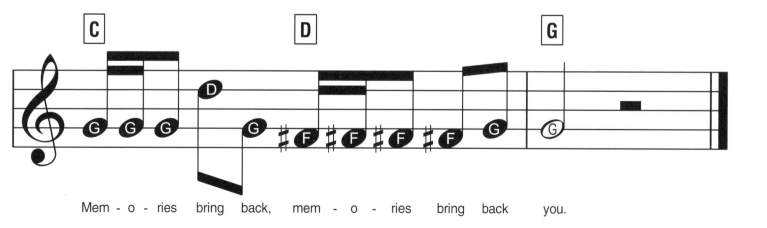

Lover

Registration 4
Rhythm: 6/8 Ballad

Words and Music by
Taylor Swift

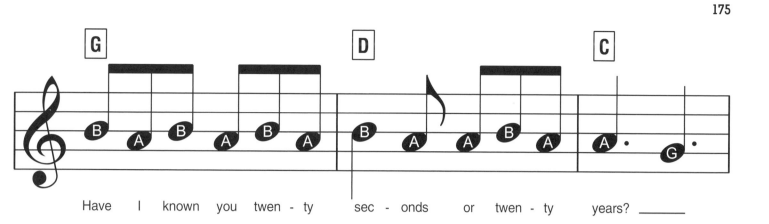

Have I known you twen - ty sec - onds or twen - ty years? _____

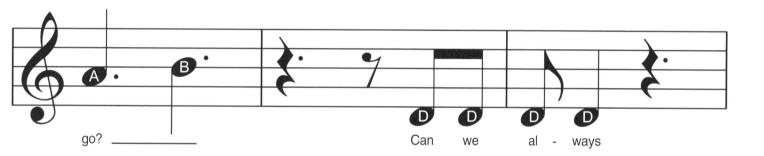

Can I go where you

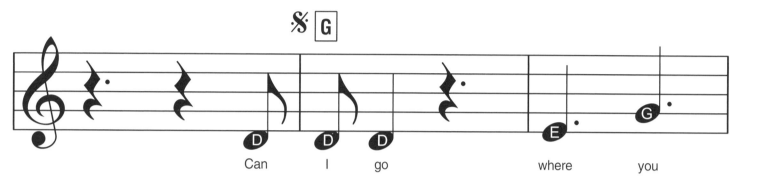

go? _____ Can we al - ways

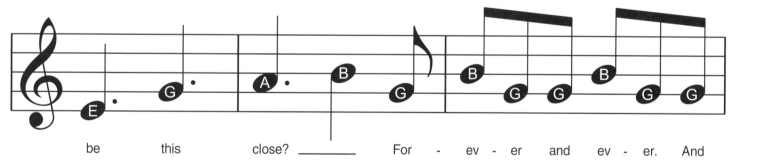

be this close? _____ For - ev - er and ev - er. And

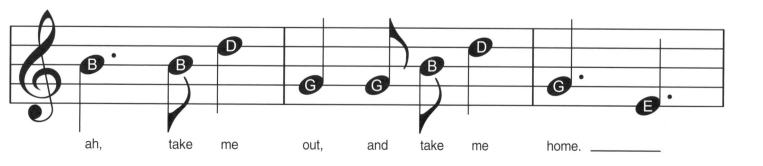

ah, take me out, and take me home. _____

178

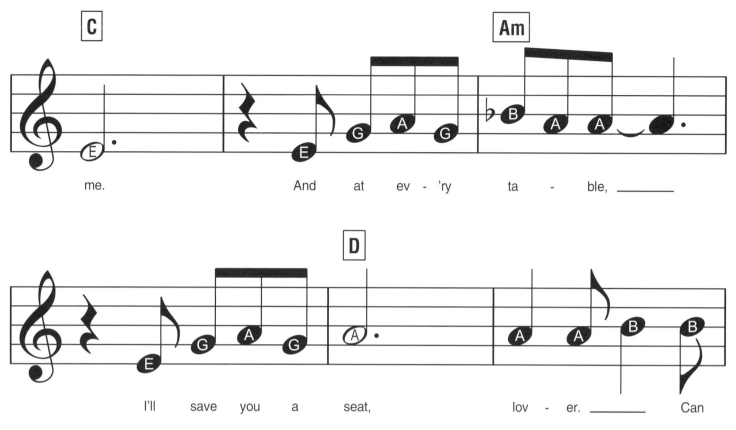

me. And at ev - 'ry ta - ble, _____

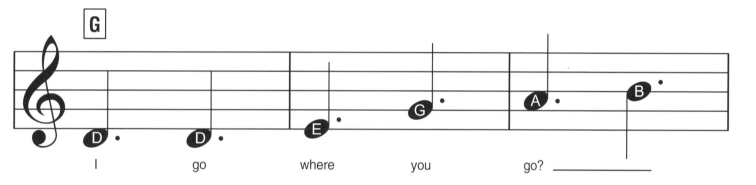

I'll save you a seat, lov - er. _____ Can

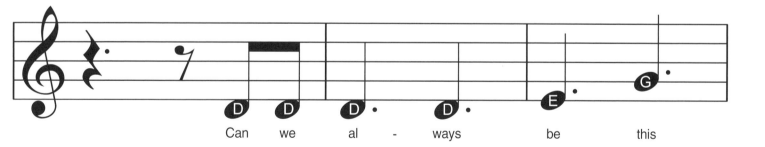

I go where you go? _____

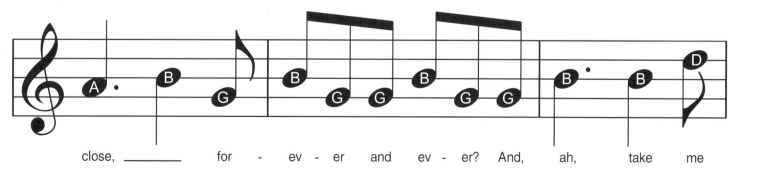

Can we al - ways be this

close, _____ for - ev - er and ev - er? And, ah, take me

No Tears Left to Cry

Registration 9
Rhythm: Ballad

Words and Music by Ariana Grande,
Savan Kotecha, Max Martin and Ilya

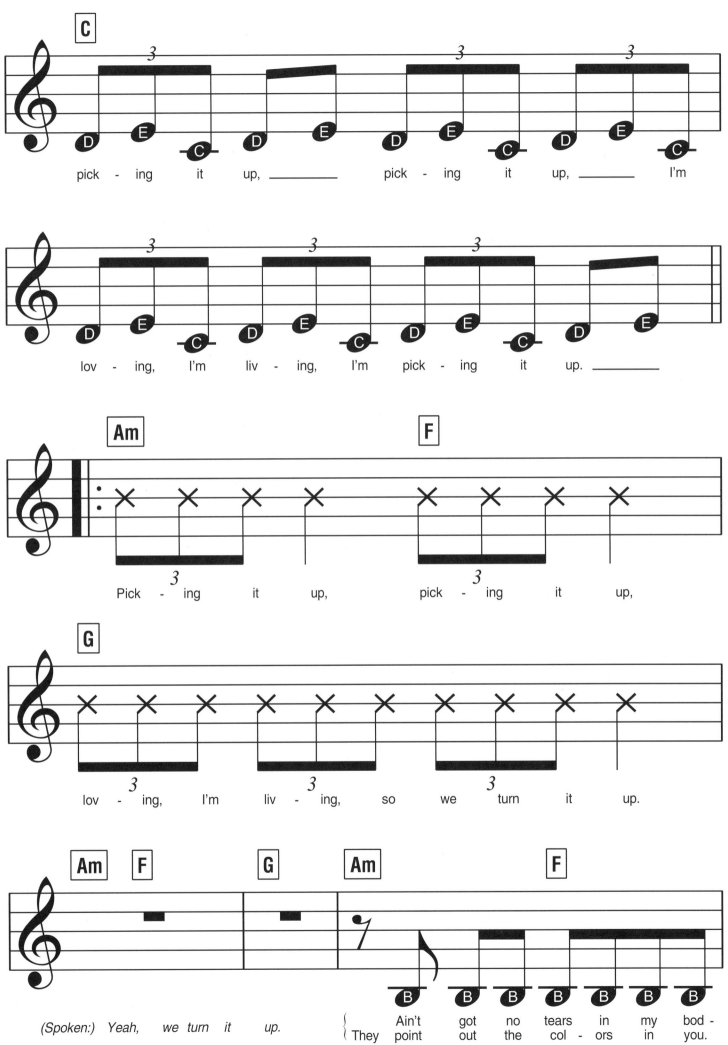

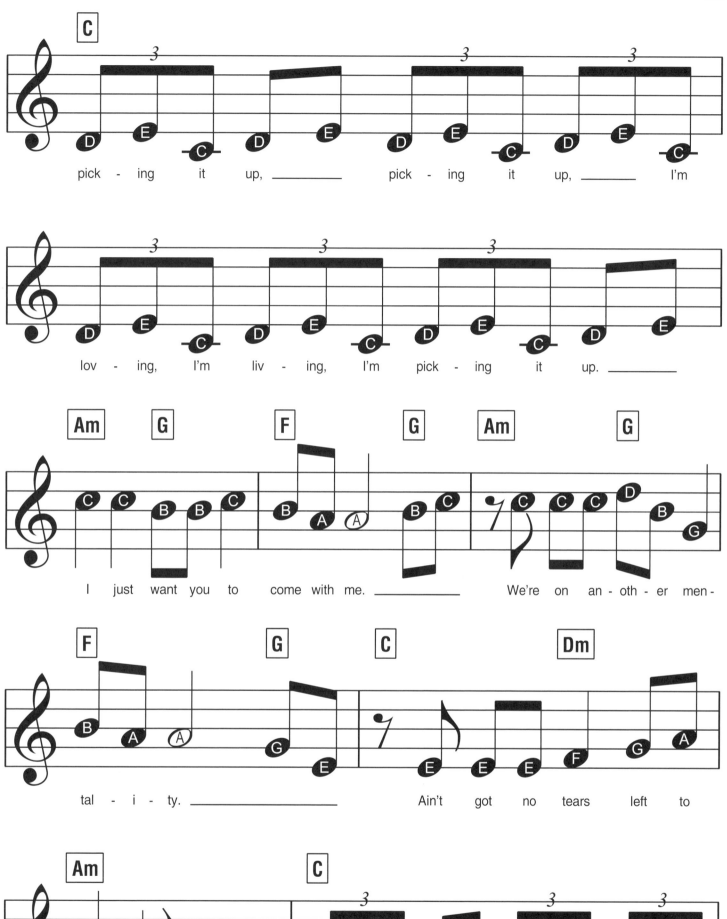

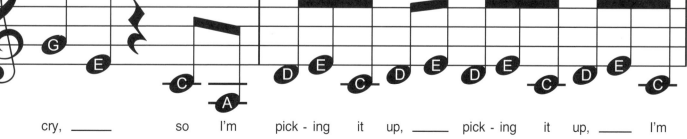

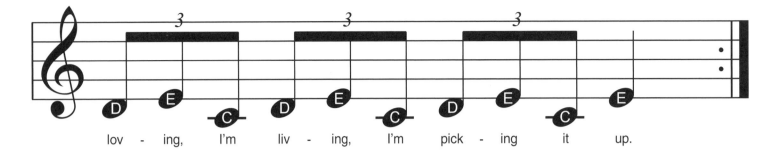

loving, I'm liv - ing, I'm pick - ing it up.

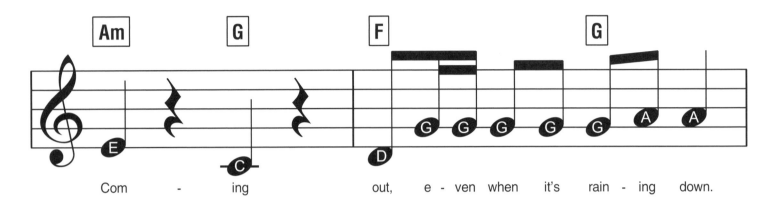

Com - ing out, e - ven when it's rain - ing down.

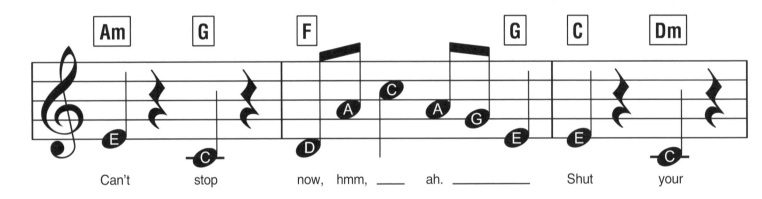

Can't stop now, hmm, ___ ah. _____ Shut your

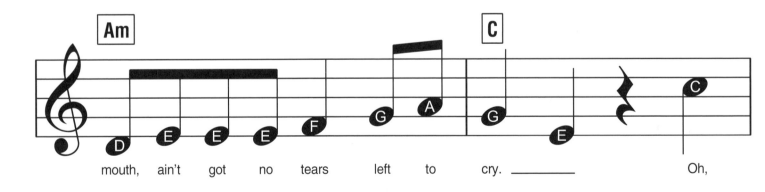

mouth, ain't got no tears left to cry. _____ Oh,

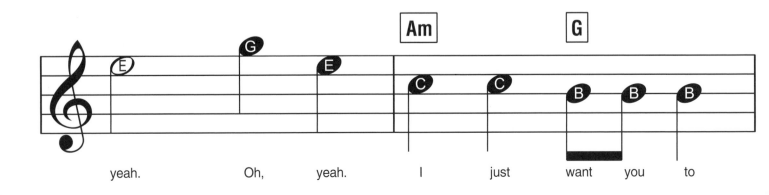

yeah. Oh, yeah. I just want you to

187

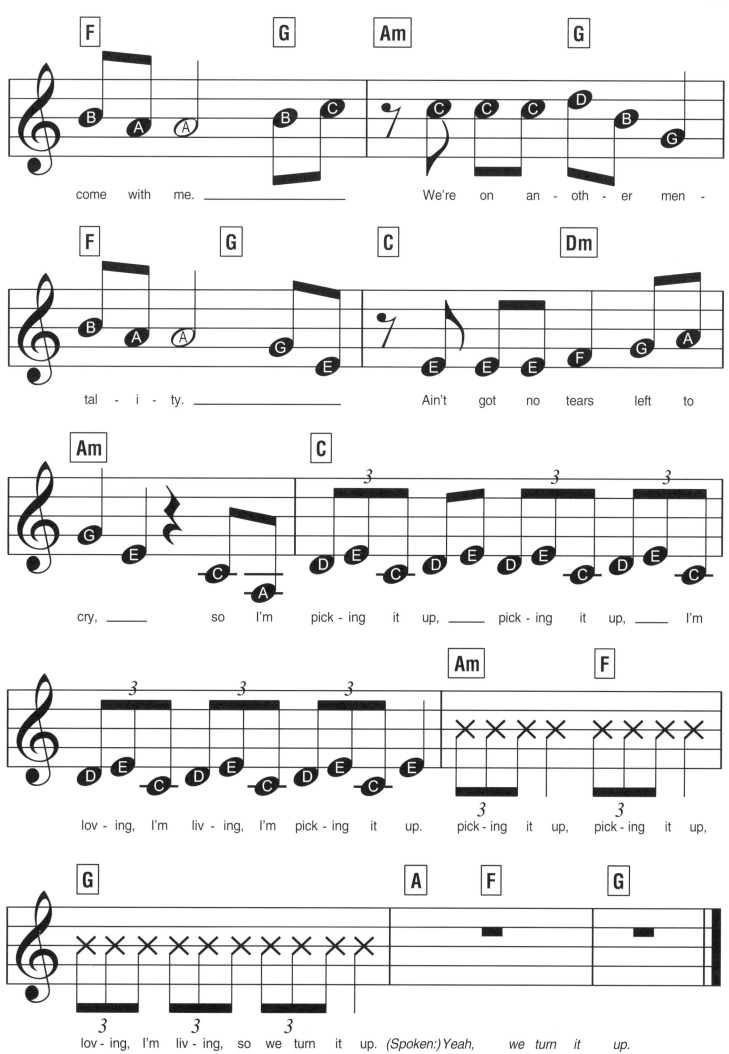

The Middle

Registration 9
Rhythm: Rock or Pop

Words and Music by Sarah Aarons,
Marcus Lomax, Jordan Johnson,
Anton Zaslavski, Kyle Trewartha,
Michael Trewartha and Stefan Johnson

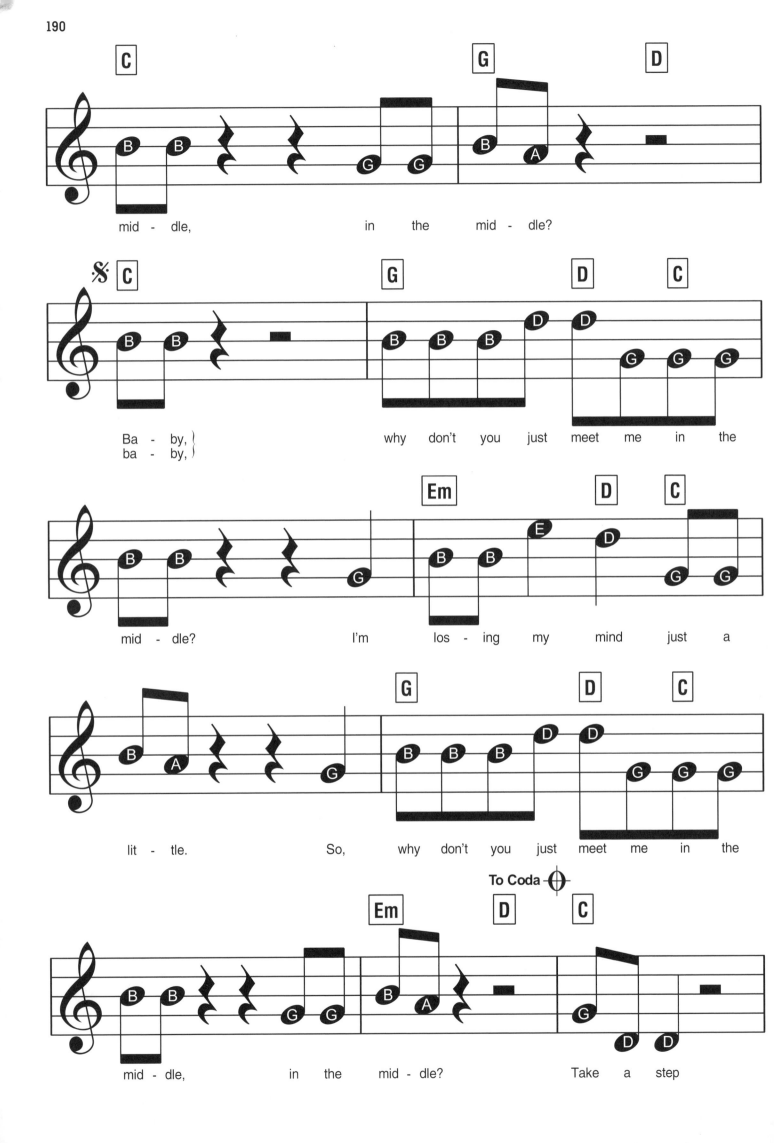

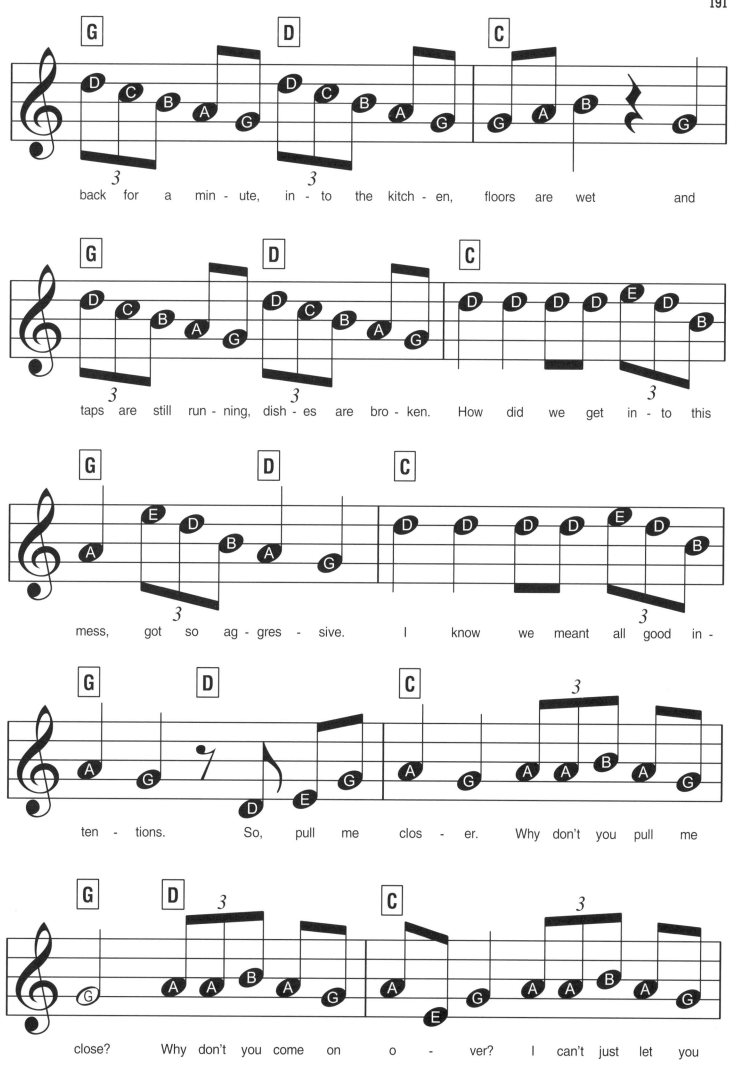

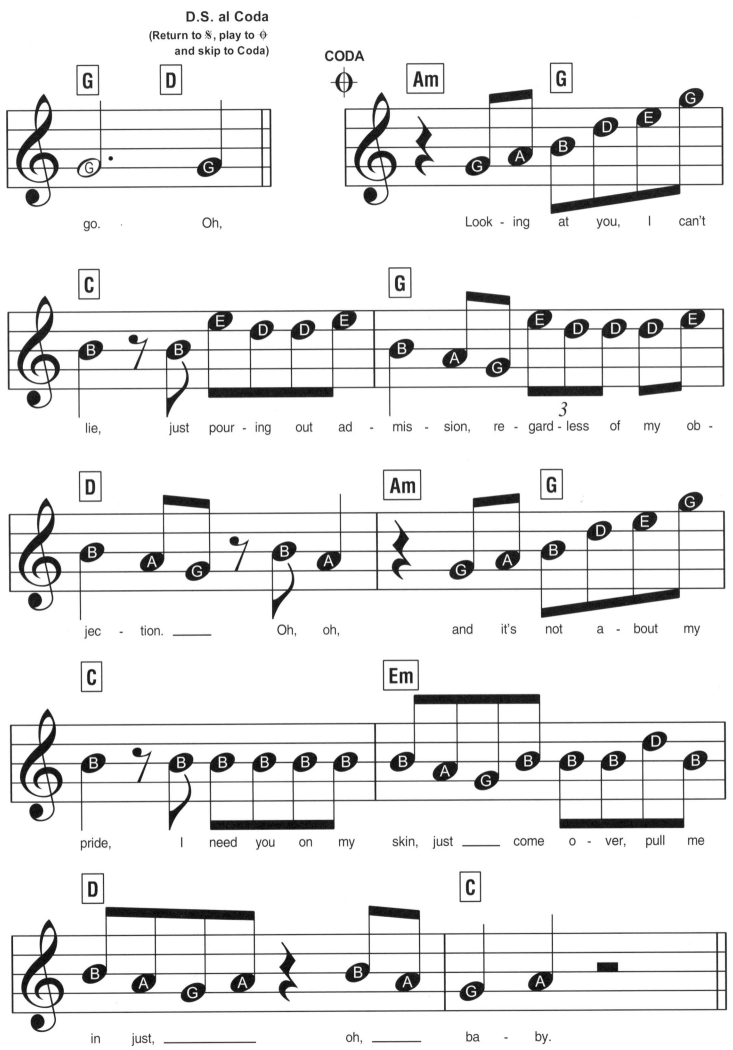

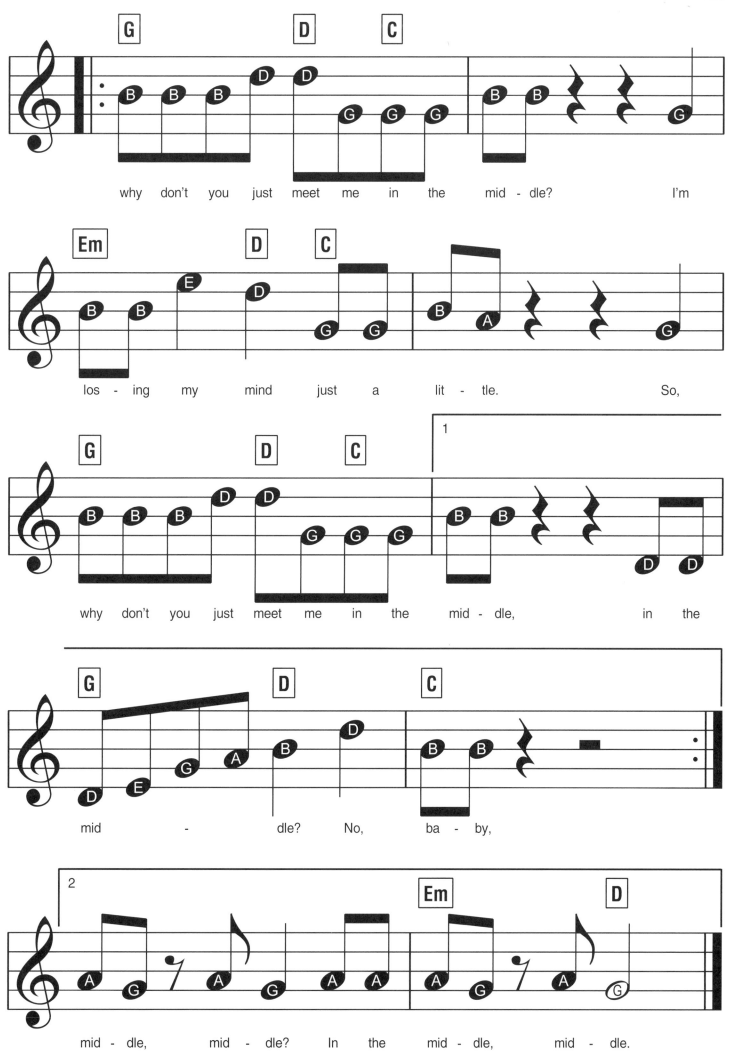

Love Me Like You Do
from FIFTY SHADES OF GREY

Registration 1
Rhythm: Pop or Rock

Words and Music by Max Martin,
Savan Kotecha, Ilya,
Ali Payami and Tove Lo

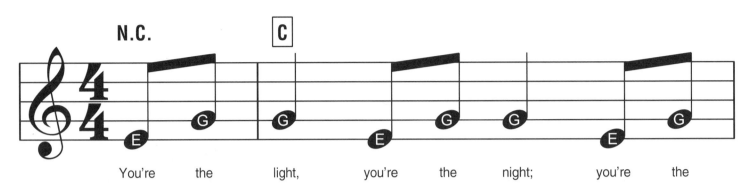

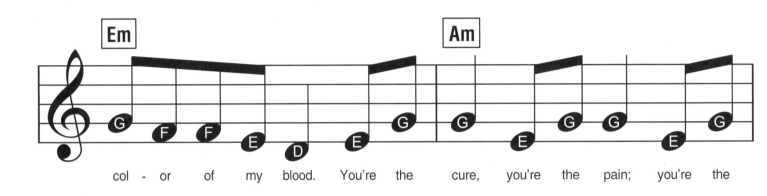

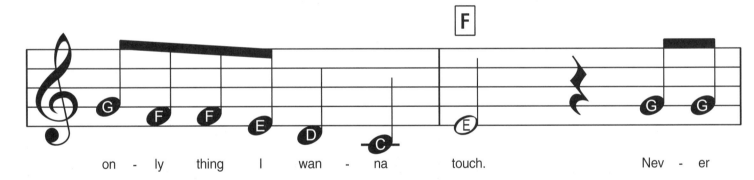

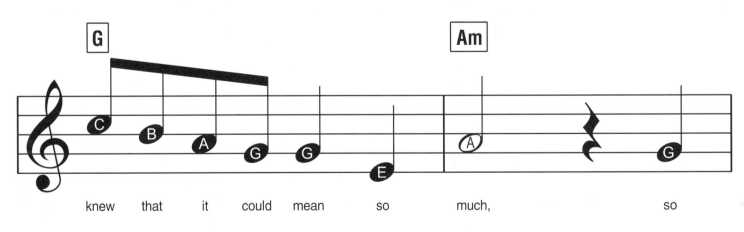

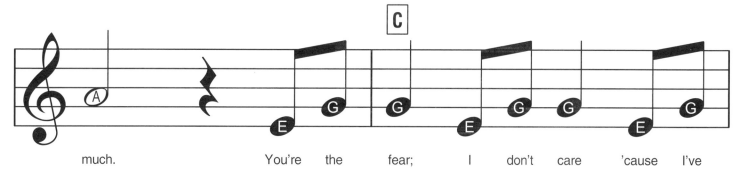

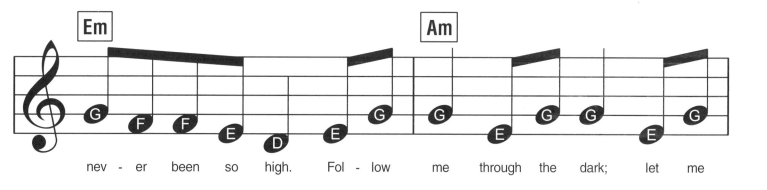

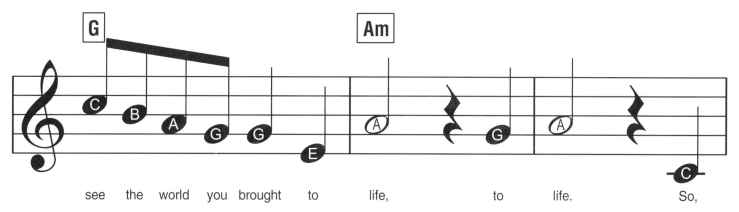

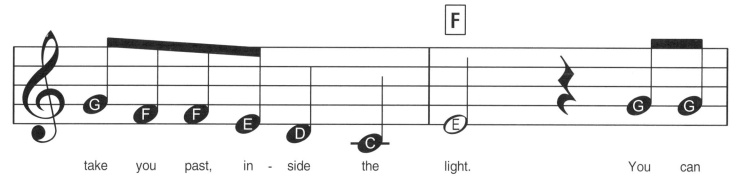

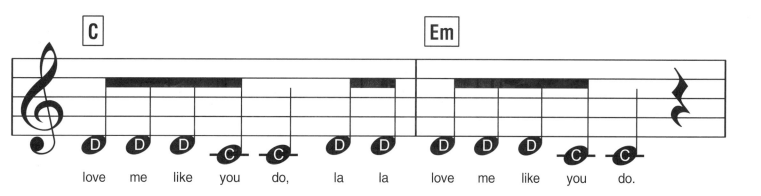

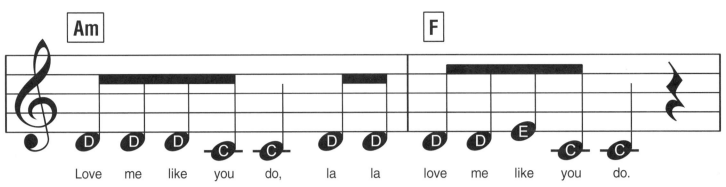

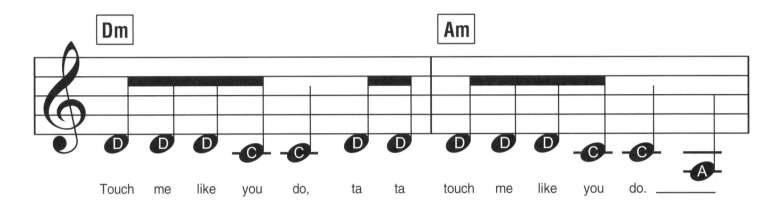

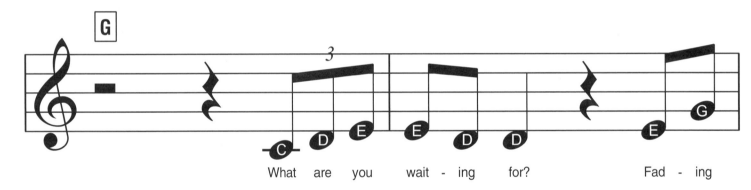

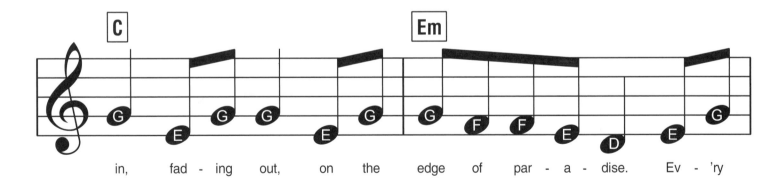

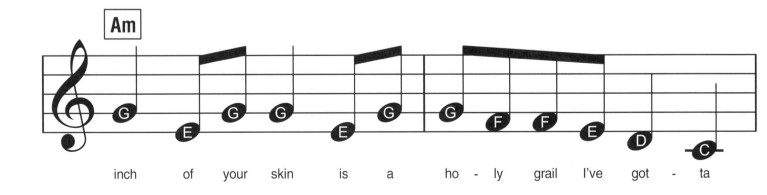

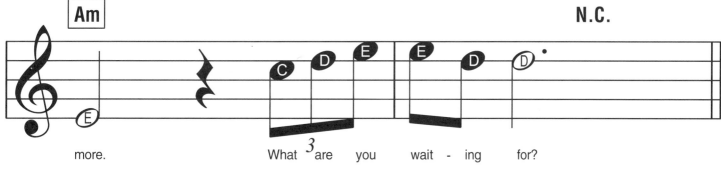

199

Love Yourself

Registration 4
Rhythm: Pop or Ballad

Words and Music by Justin Bieber,
Ed Sheeran and Benjamin Levin

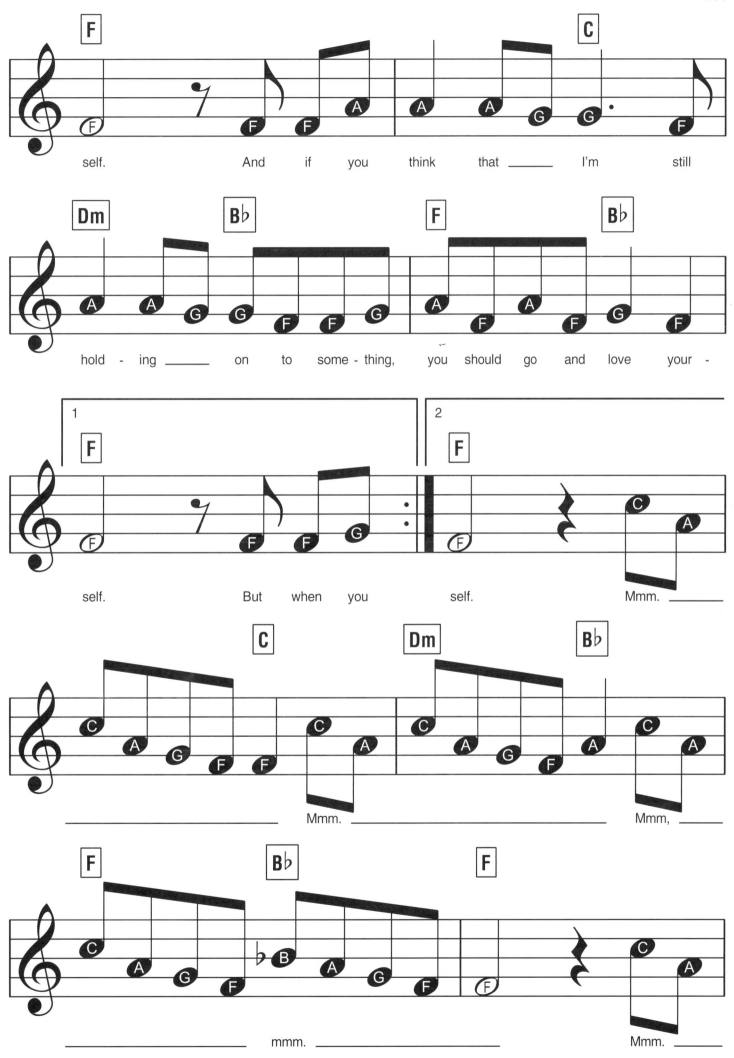

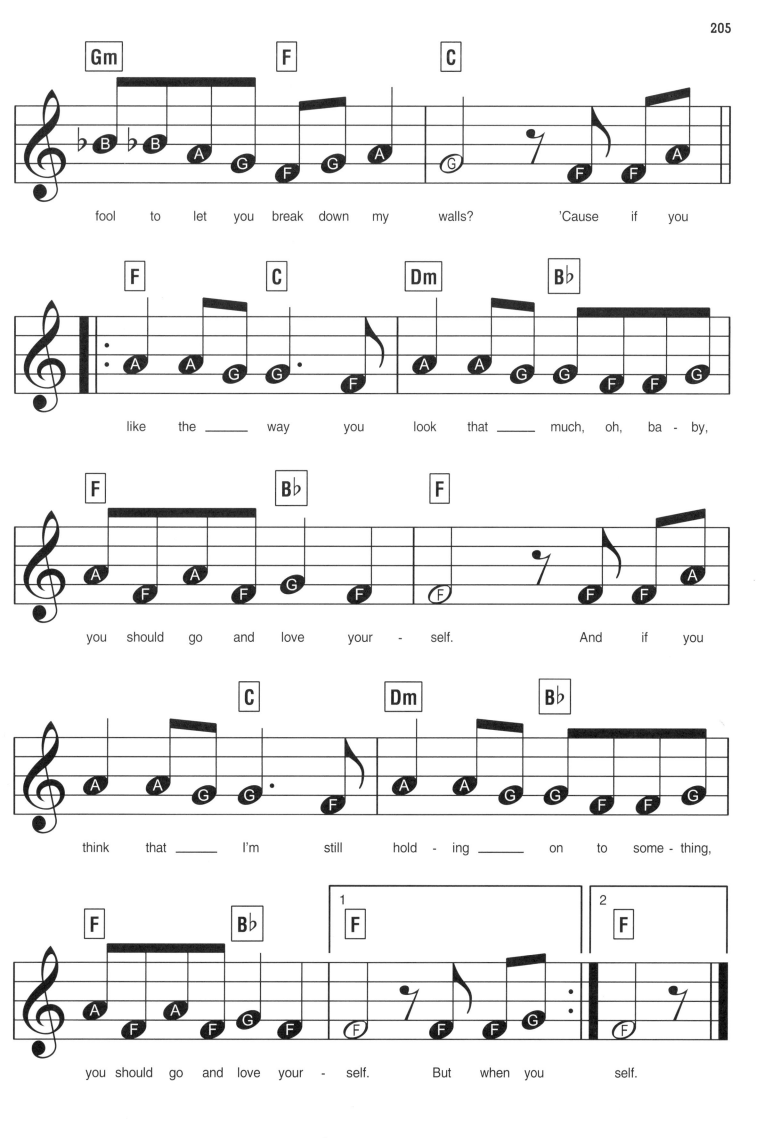

Radioactive

Registration 4
Rhythm: 8-Beat or Rock

Words and Music by Daniel Reynolds,
Benjamin McKee, Daniel Sermon,
Alexander Grant and Josh Mosser

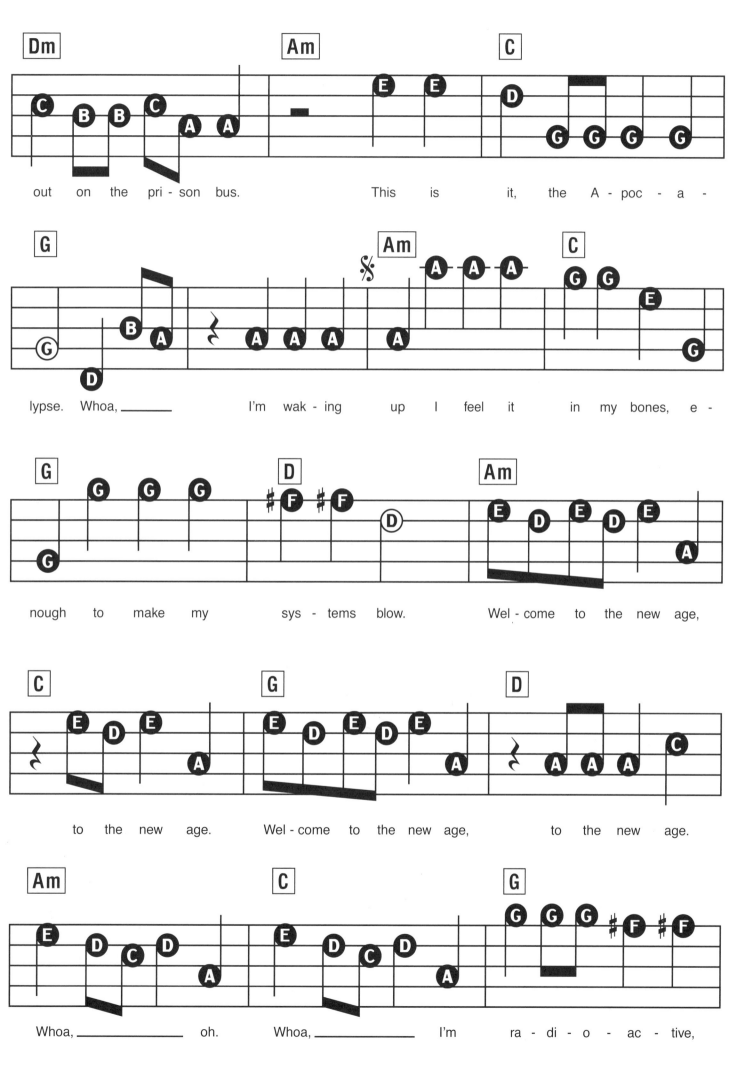

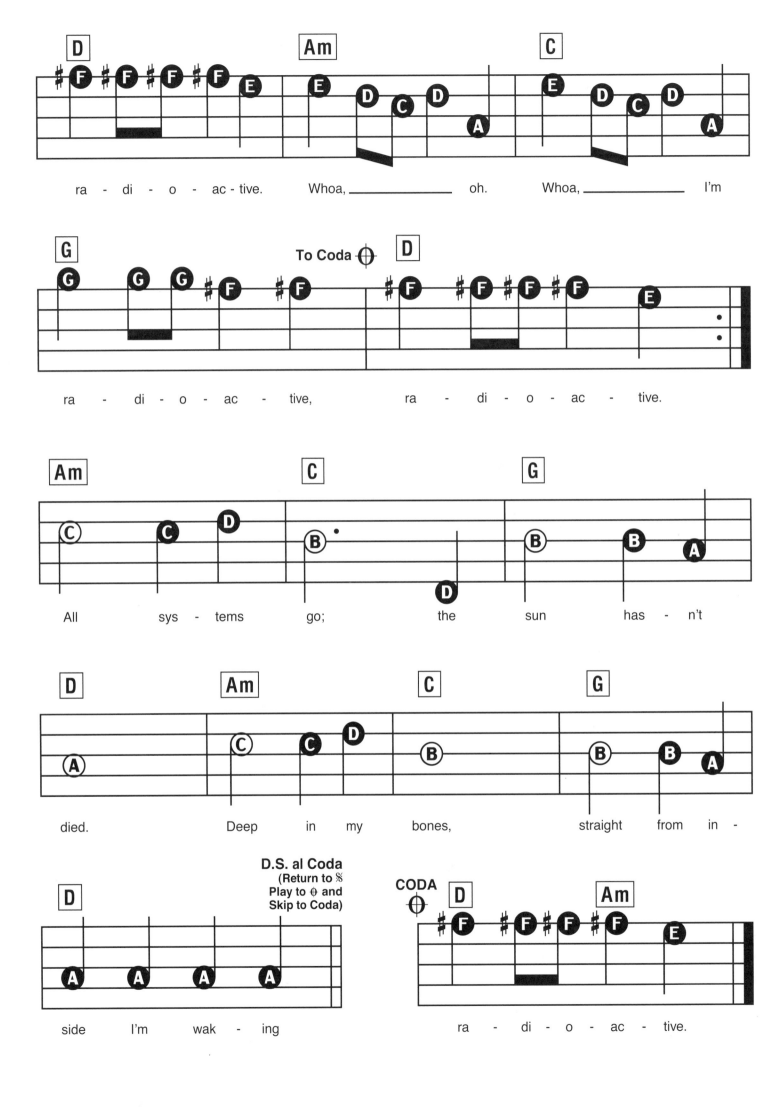

Perfect

Registration 4
Rhythm: Slow Rock or 6/8 March

Words and Music by
Ed Sheeran

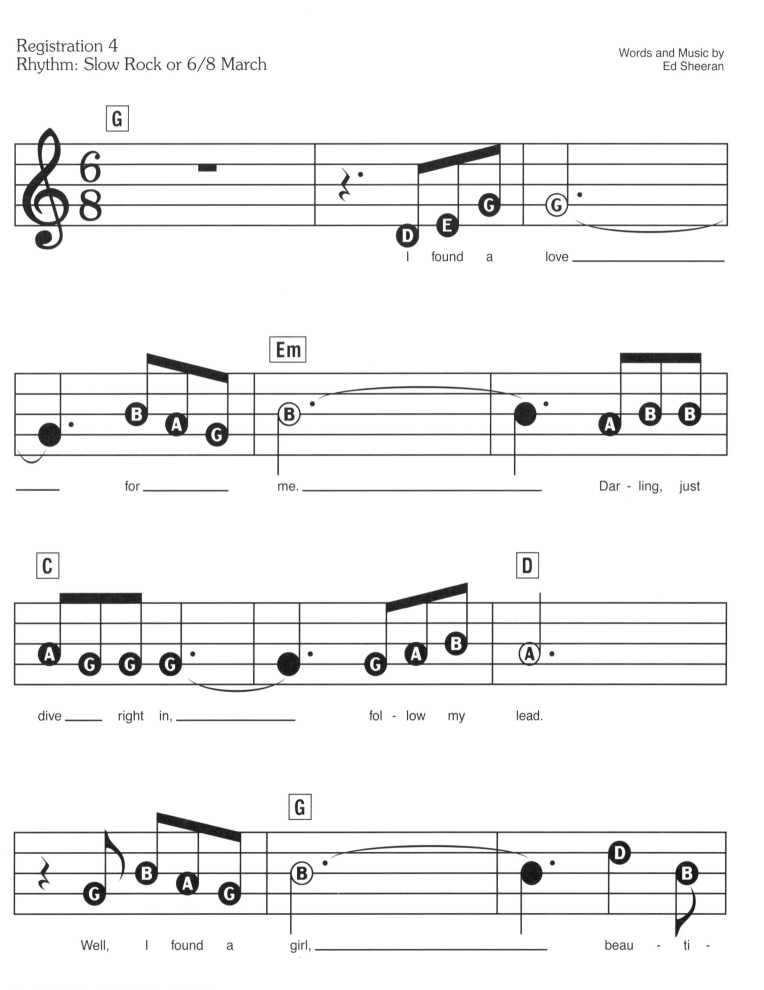

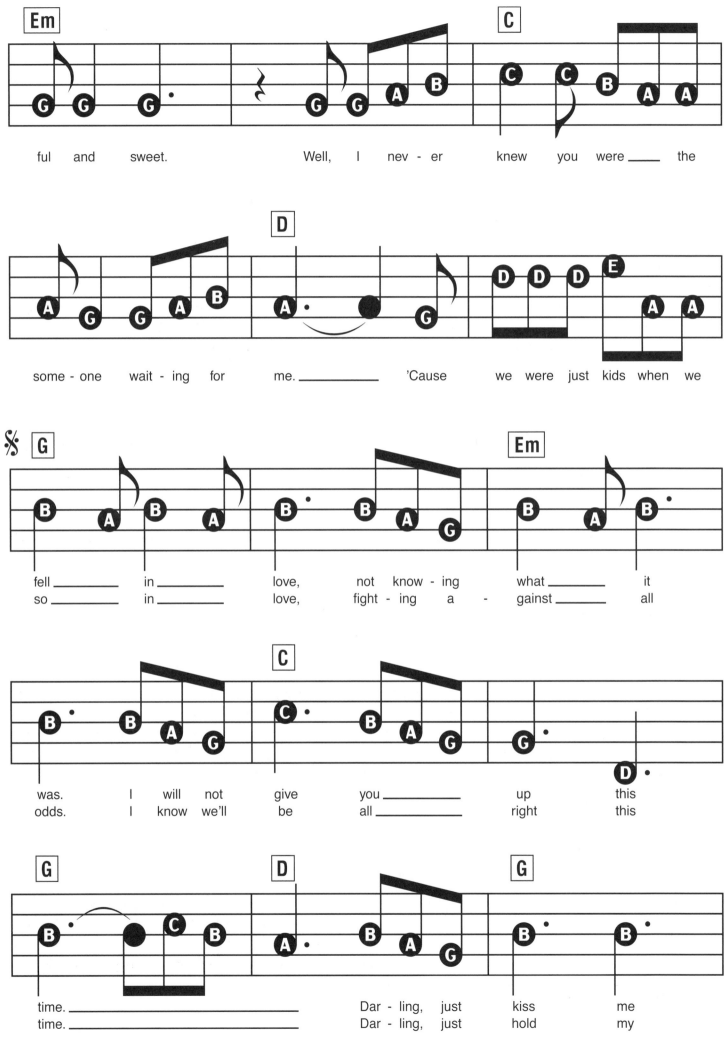

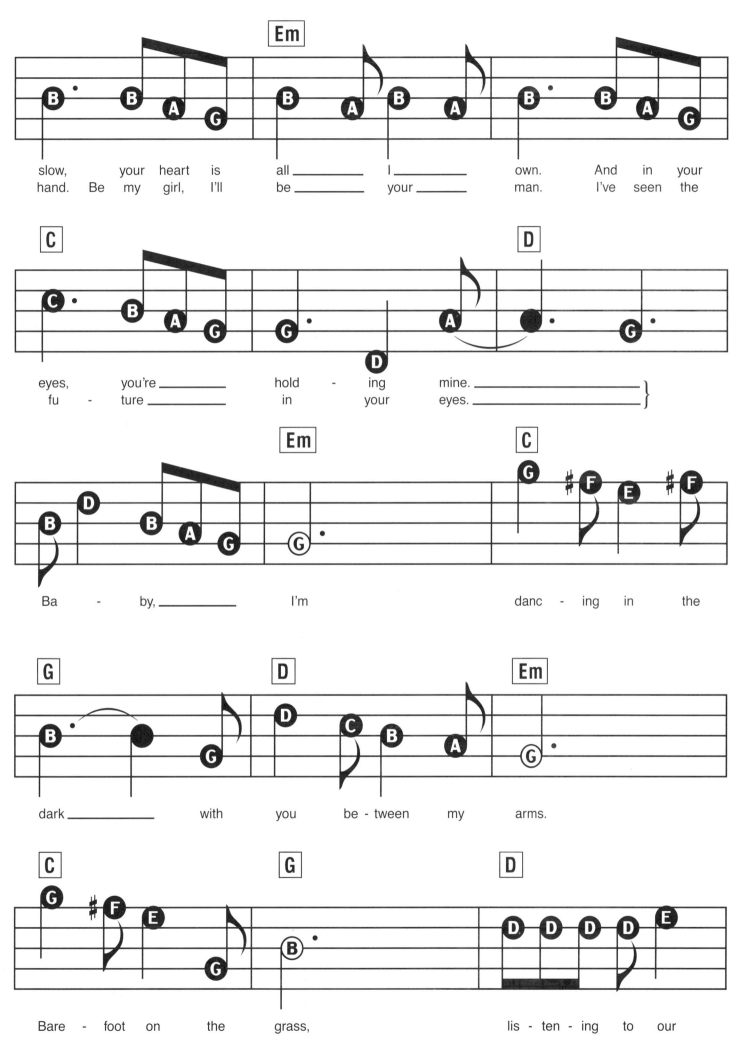

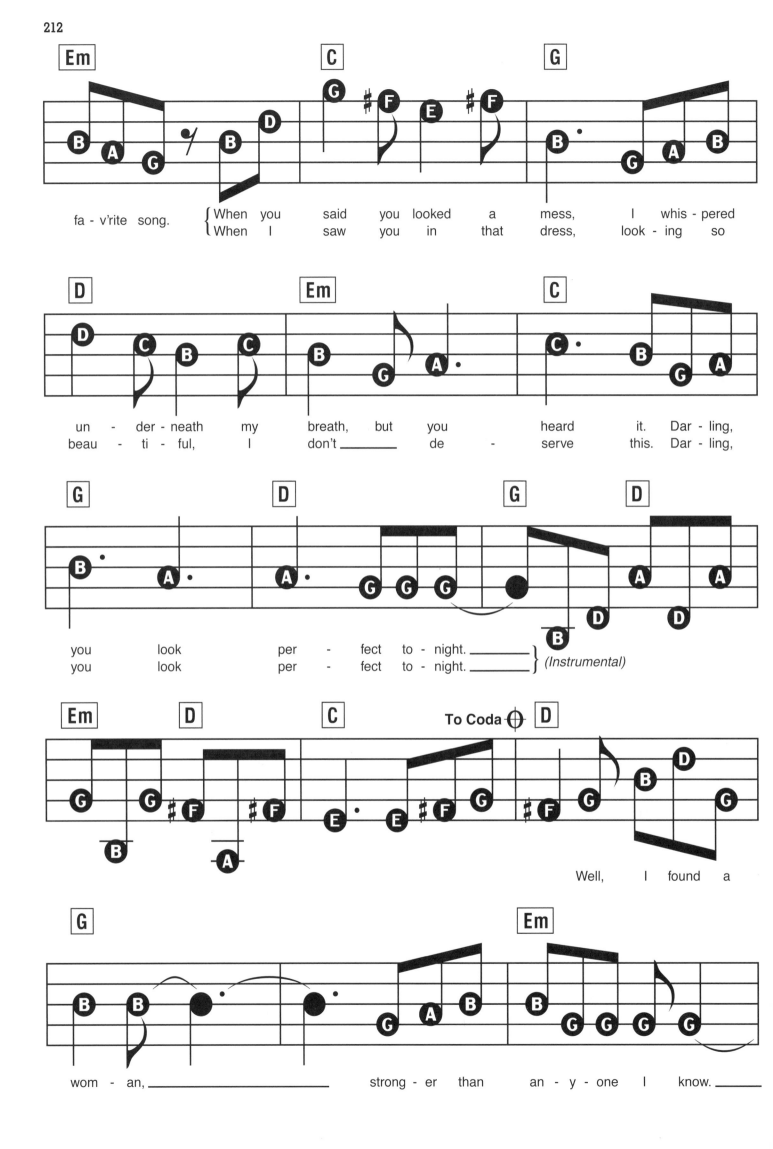

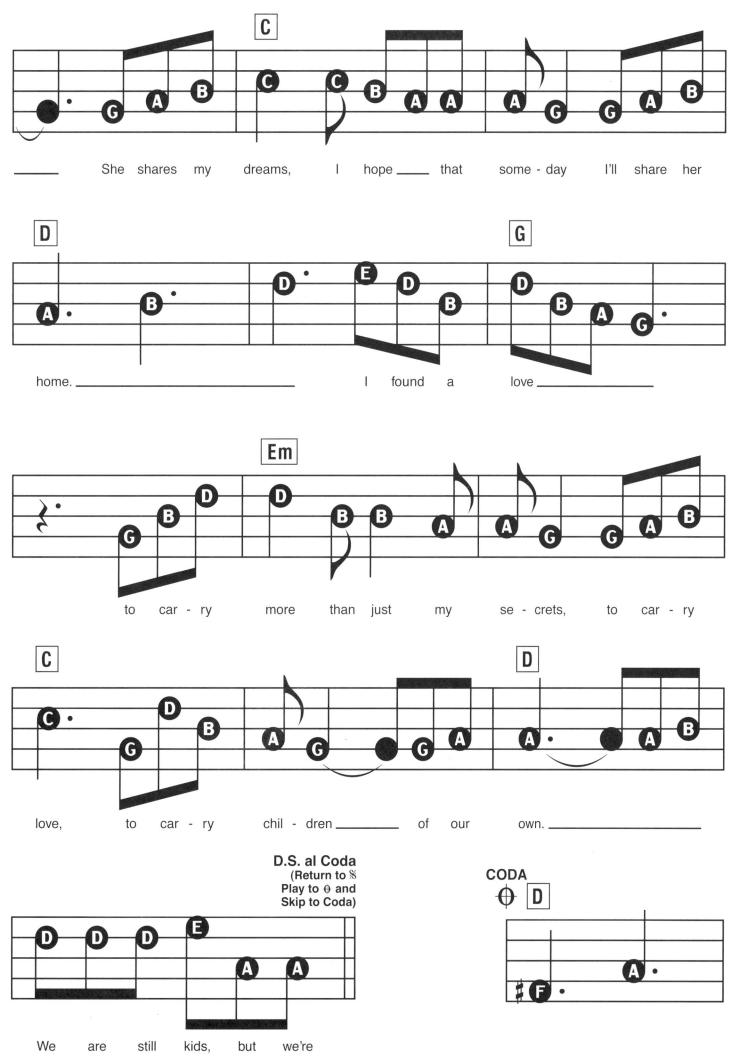

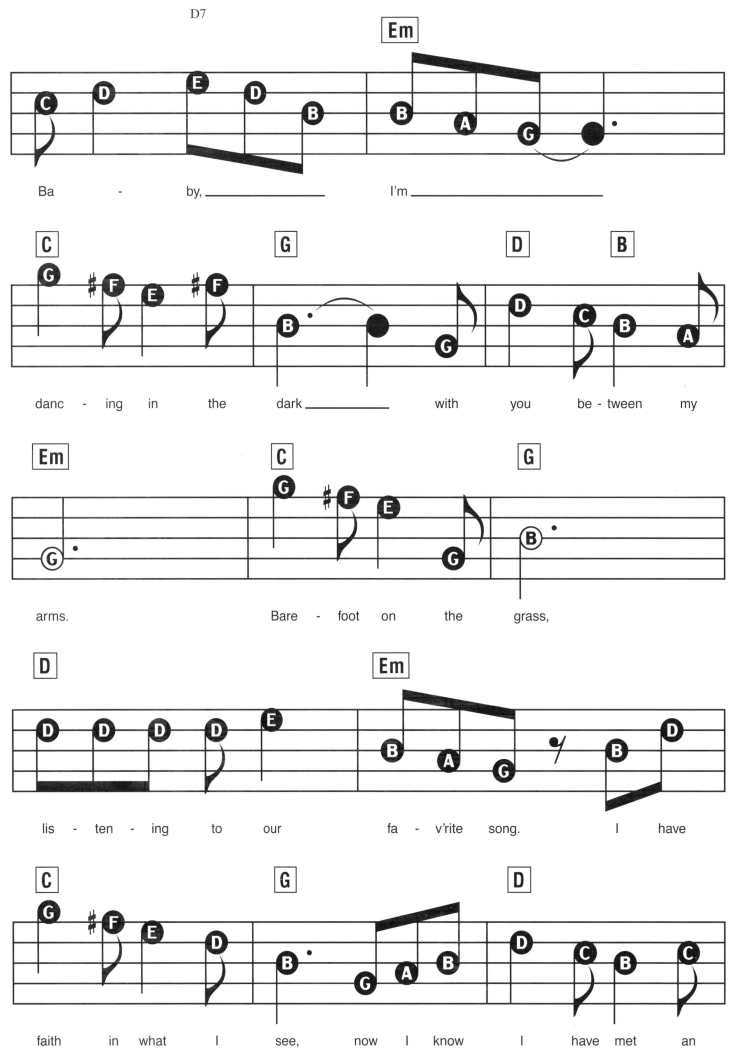

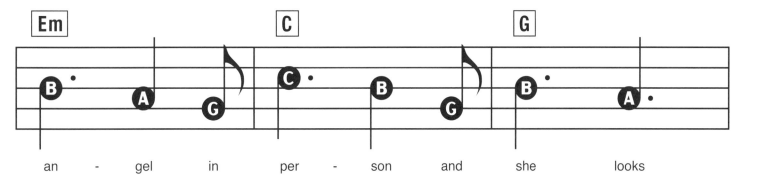

an - gel   in   per - son   and   she   looks

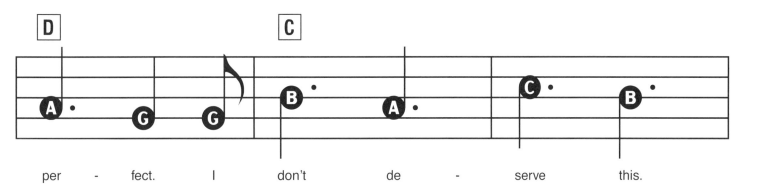

per - fect.   I   don't   de - serve   this.

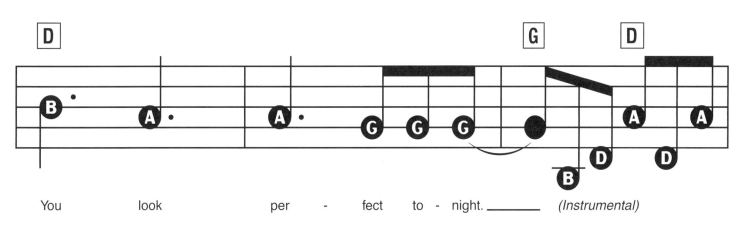

You   look   per - fect   to - night. _____ *(Instrumental)*

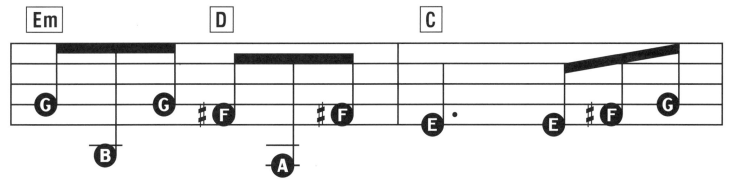

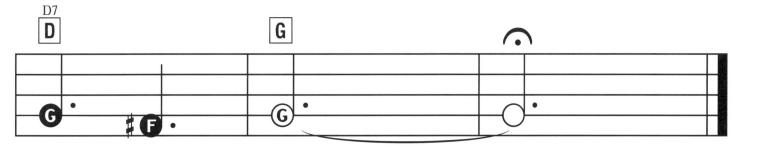

Rise Up

Registration 8
Rhythm: Ballad

Words and Music by Cassandra Batie
and Jennifer Decilveo

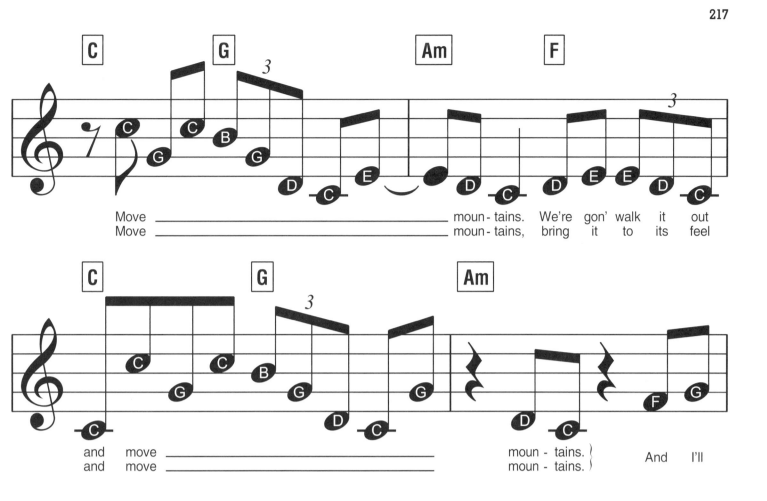

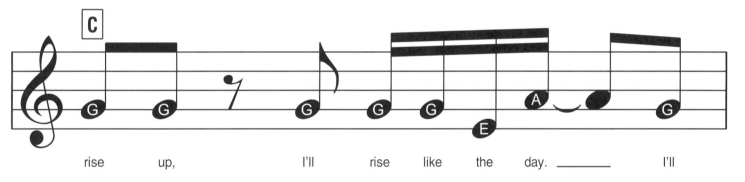

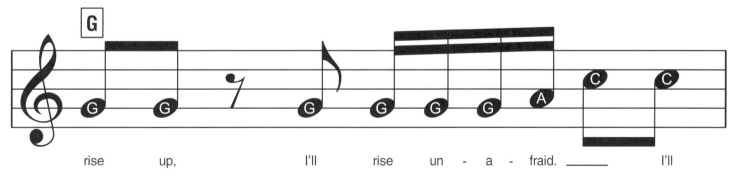

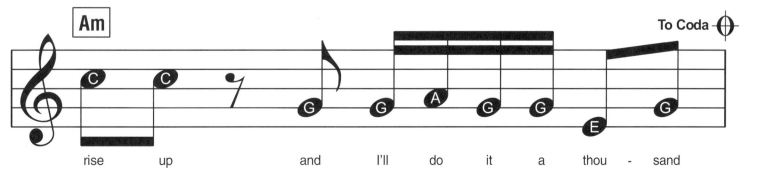

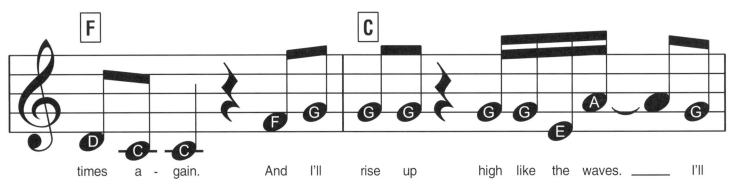

times a - gain. And I'll rise up high like the waves. _____ I'll

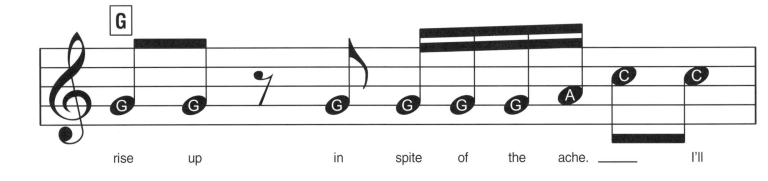

rise up in spite of the ache. _____ I'll

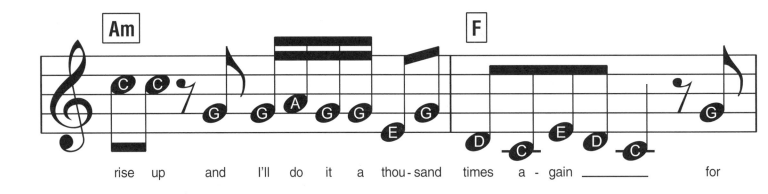

rise up and I'll do it a thou - sand times a - gain _____ for

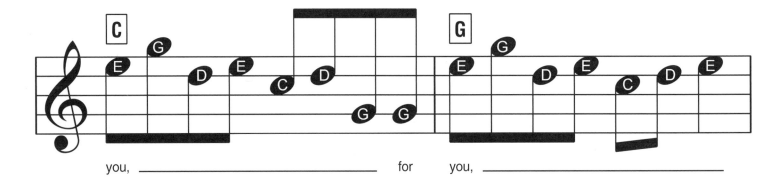

you, _____ for you, _____

D.C. al Coda
(Return to beginning,
play to ⨁ and skip to Coda)

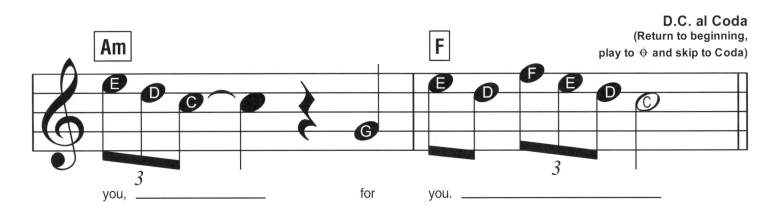

you, _____ for you. _____

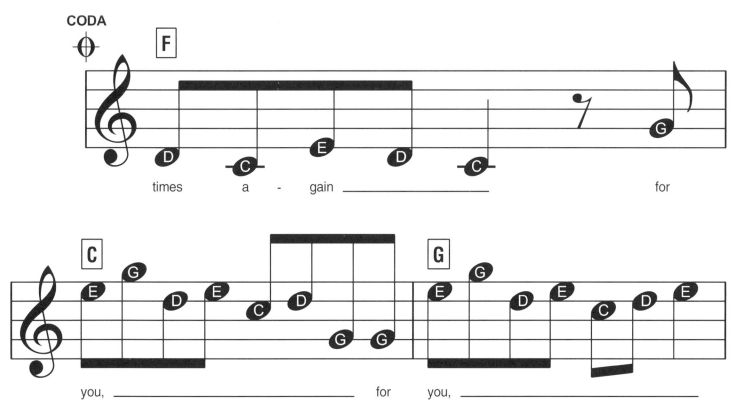

times a - gain _____ for

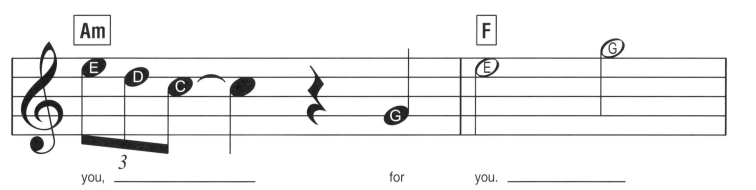

you, _____ for you, _____

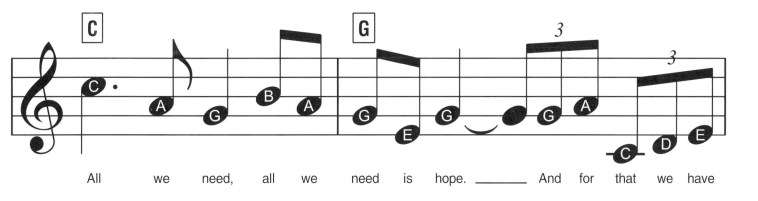

you, _____ for you. _____

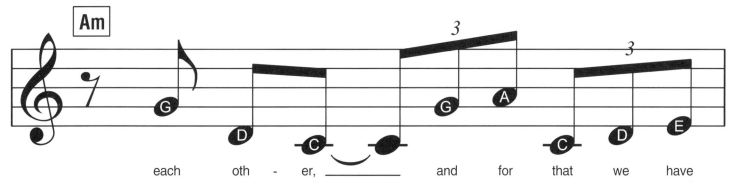

All we need, all we need is hope. _____ And for that we have

each oth - er, _____ and for that we have

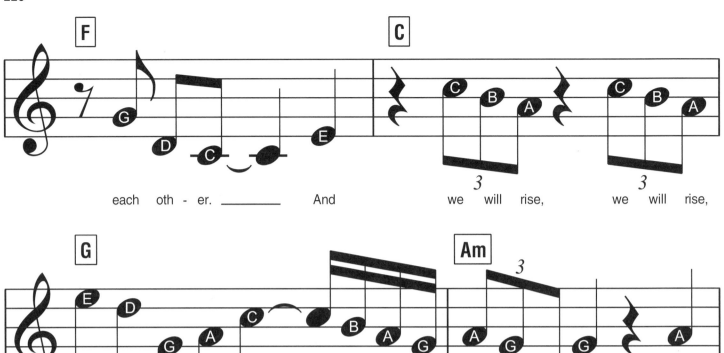

each oth - er. _____ And

we will rise, we will rise,

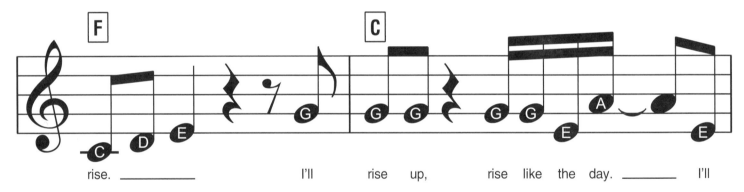

we'll ____ rise ____ up. _____ We'll

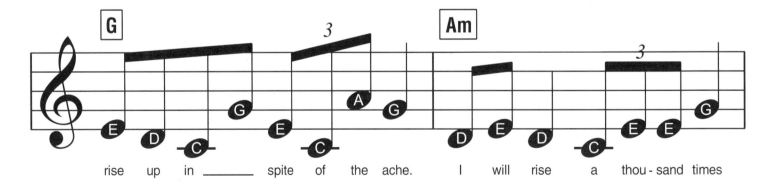

rise. _____ I'll rise up, rise like the day. _____ I'll

rise up in _____ spite of the ache. I will rise a thou - sand times

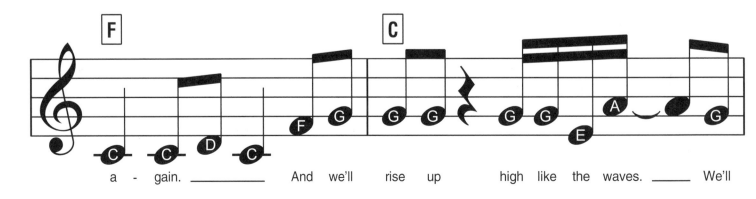

a - gain. _____ And we'll rise up high like the waves. _____ We'll

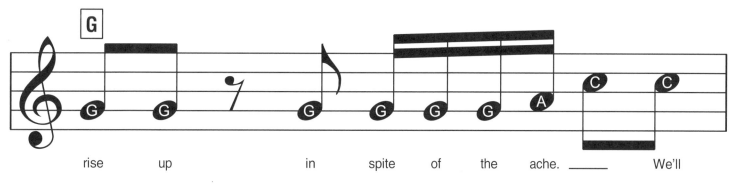

rise up in spite of the ache. _____ We'll

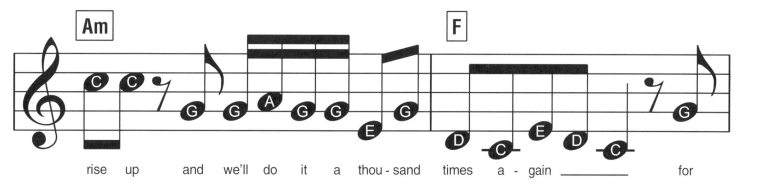

rise up and we'll do it a thou-sand times a-gain _____ for

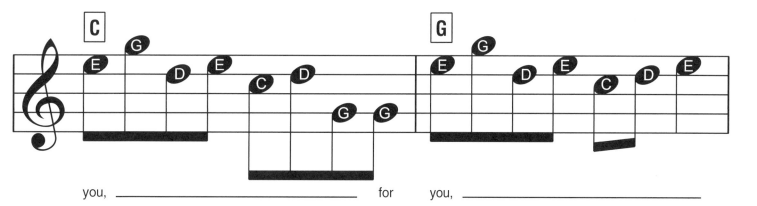

you, _____ for you, _____

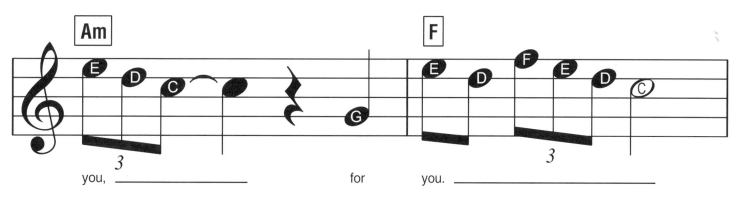

you, _____ for you. _____

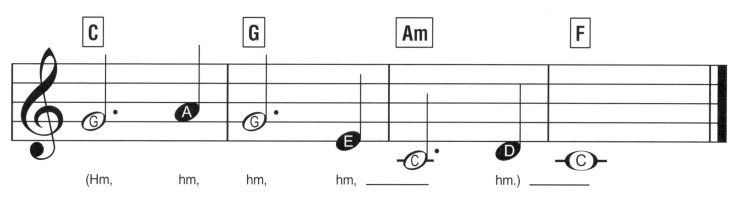

(Hm, hm, hm, hm, _____ hm.) _____

Shape of You

Registration 5
Rhythm: Pop or Techno

Words and Music by Ed Sheeran,
Kevin Briggs, Kandi Burruss, Tameka Cottle,
Steve Mac and Johnny McDaid

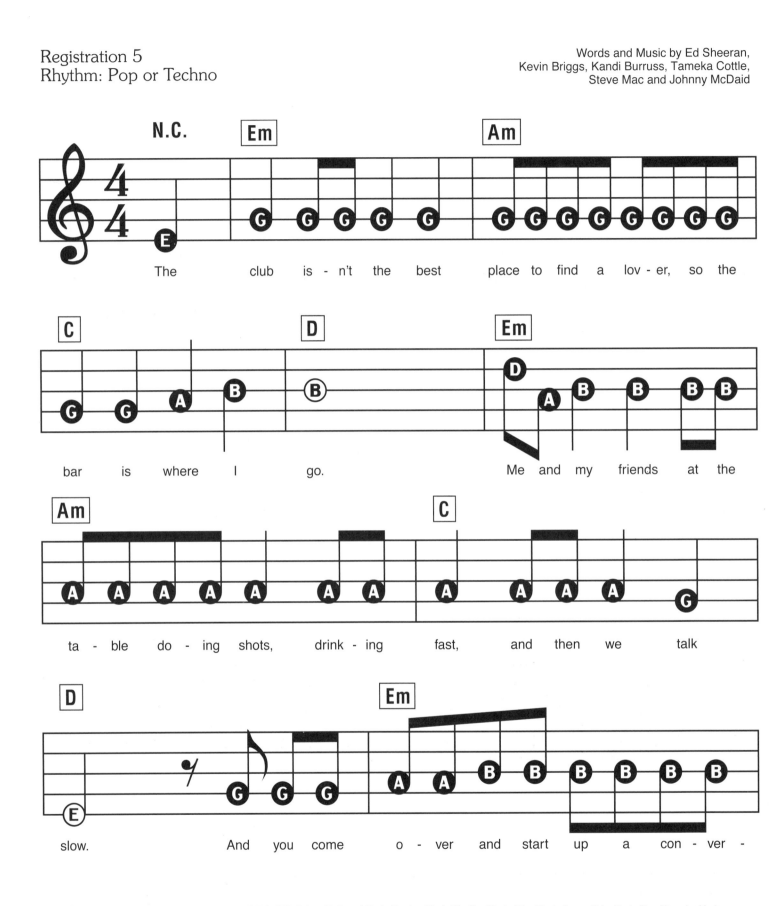

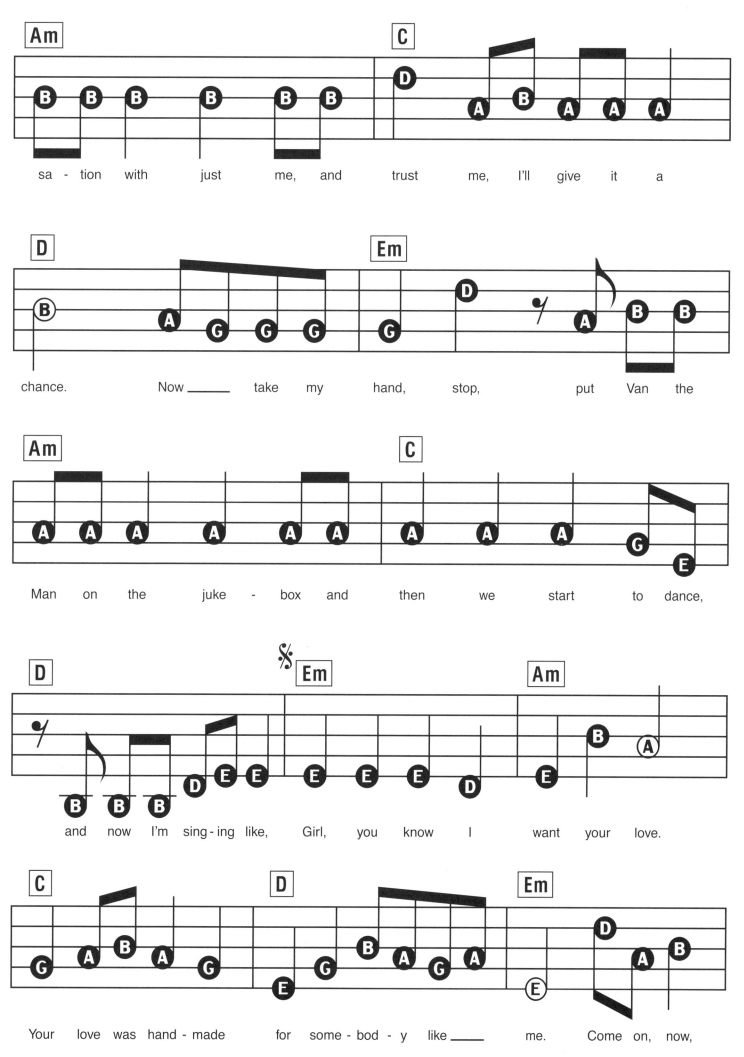

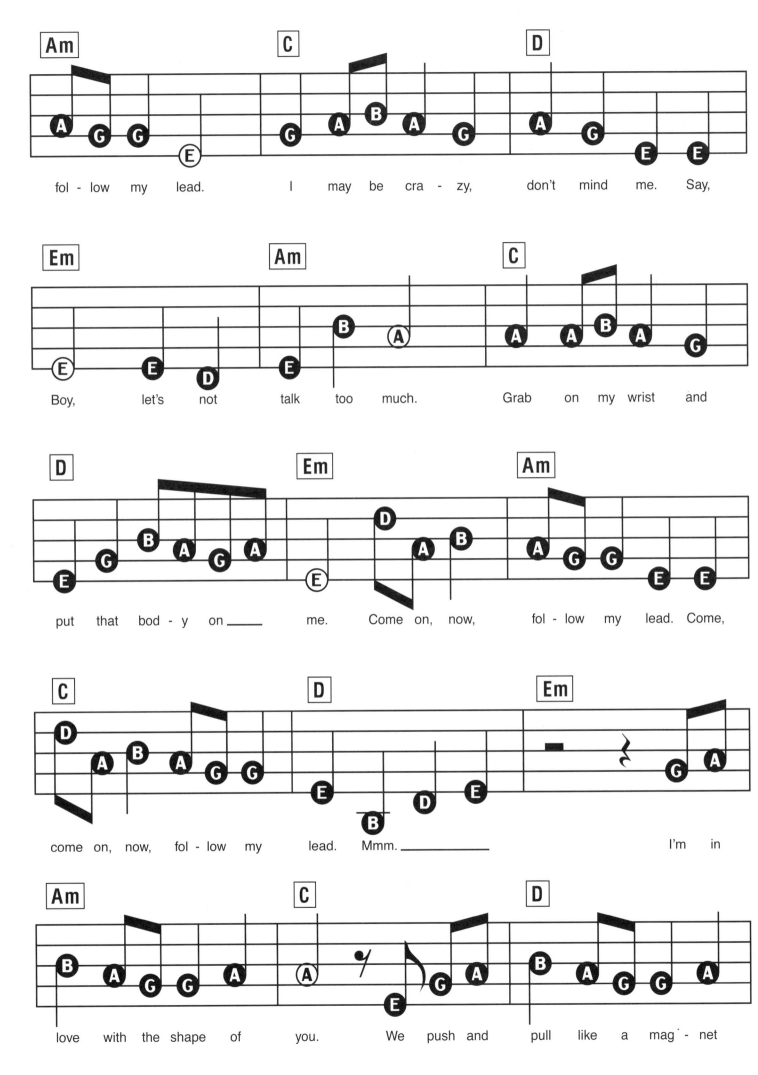

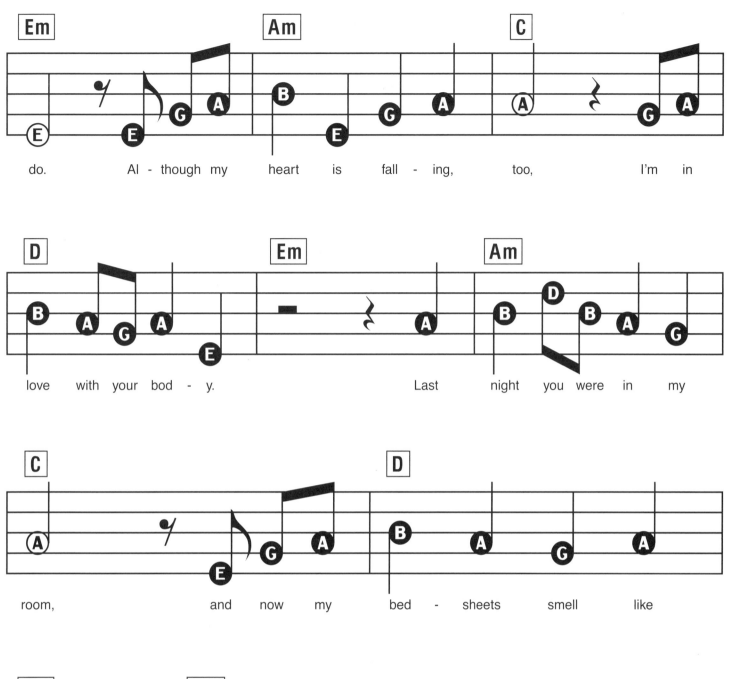

do. Al - though my heart is fall - ing, too, I'm in love with your bod - y. Last night you were in my

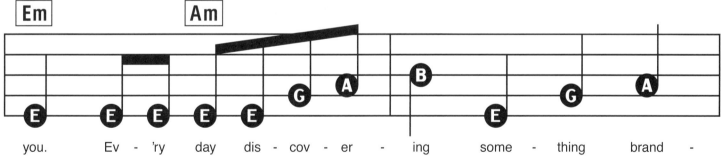

room, and now my bed - sheets smell like you. Ev - 'ry day dis - cov - er - ing some - thing brand -

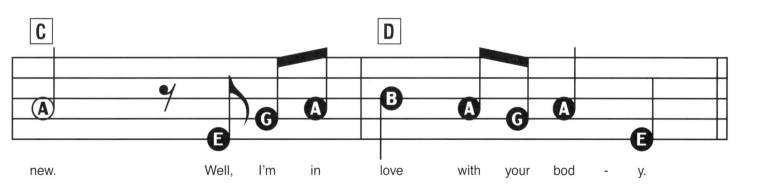

new. Well, I'm in love with your bod - y.

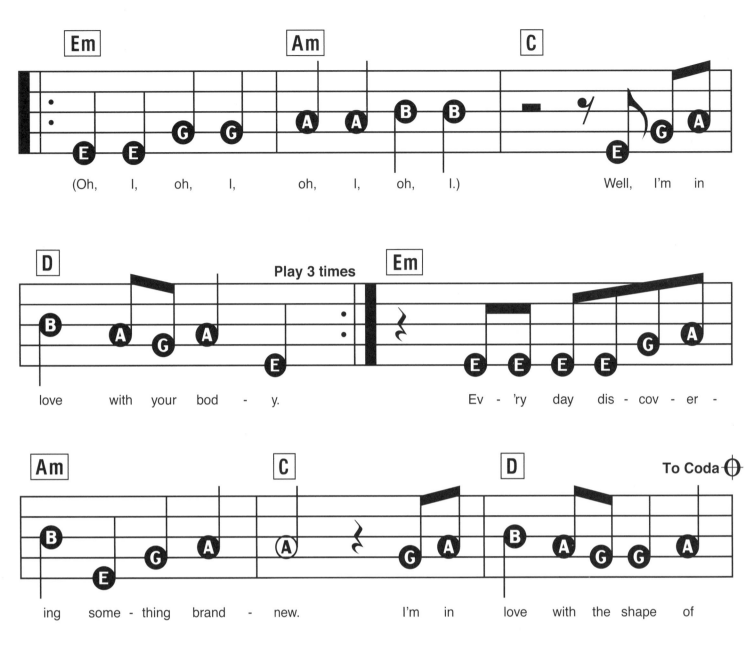

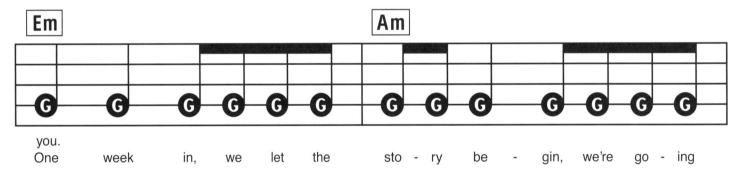

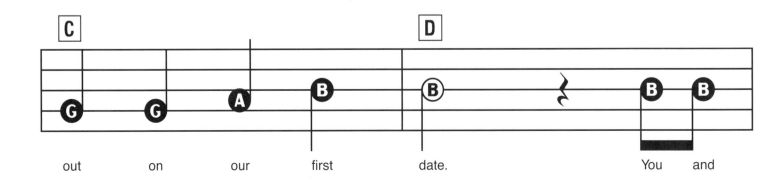

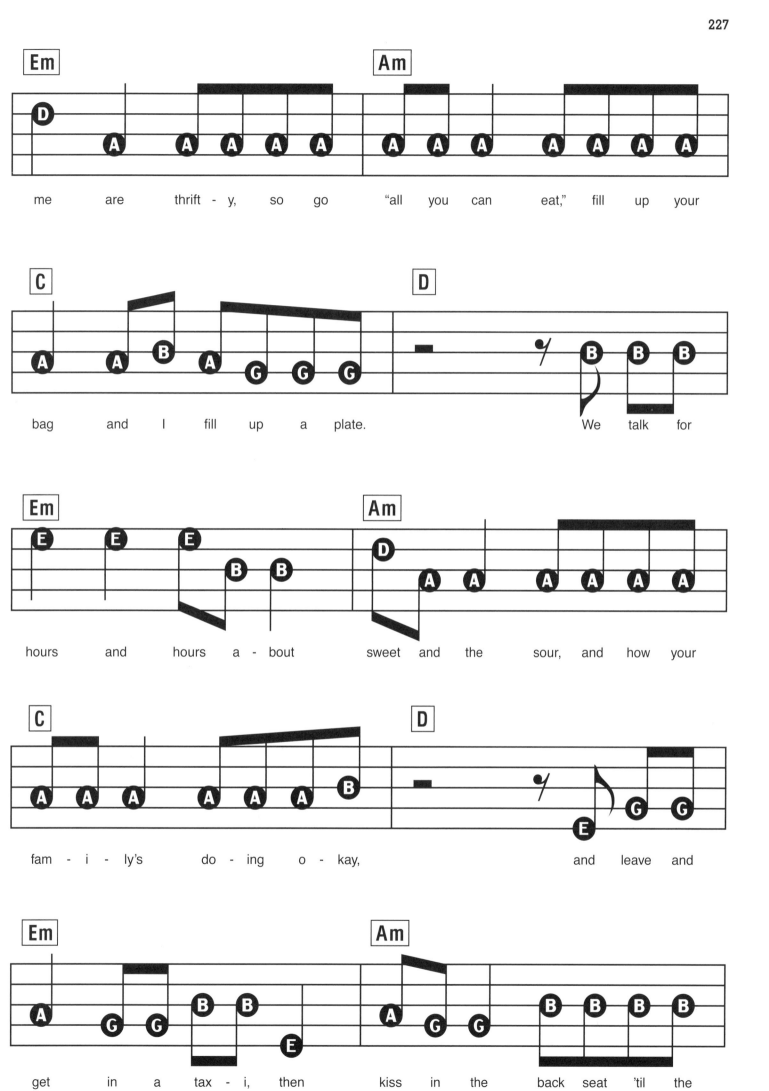

228

D.S. al Coda
(Return to ℅
Play to ⊕ and
Skip to Coda)

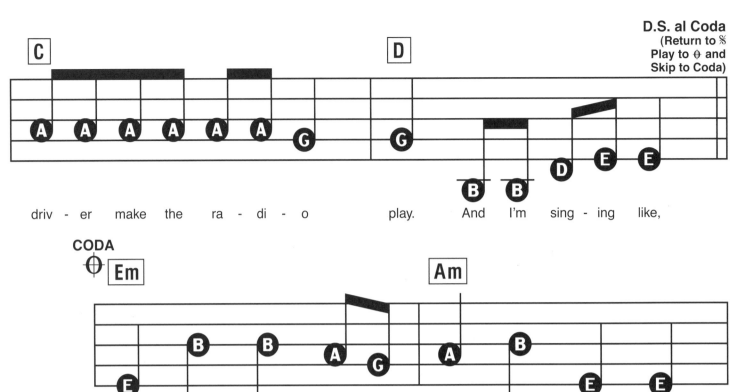

driv - er make the ra - di - o   play.   And I'm sing - ing like,

CODA

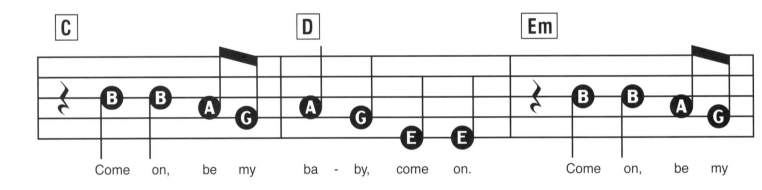

you.   Come   on,   be   my   ba - by,   come   on.

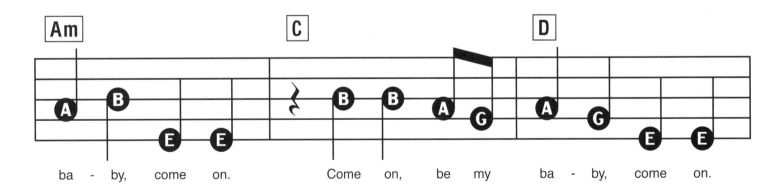

Come   on,   be   my   ba - by,   come   on.   Come   on,   be   my

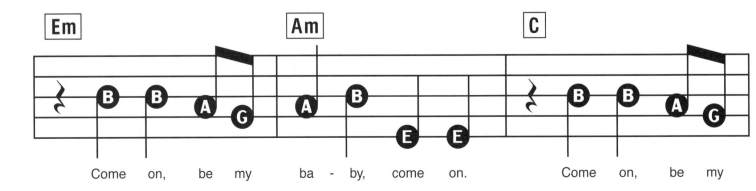

ba - by,   come   on.   Come   on,   be   my   ba - by,   come   on.

Come   on,   be   my   ba - by,   come   on.   Come   on,   be   my

229

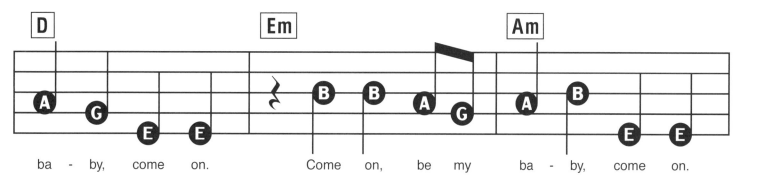

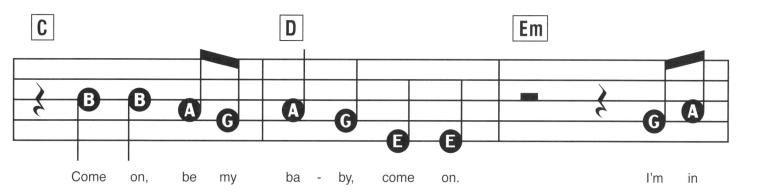

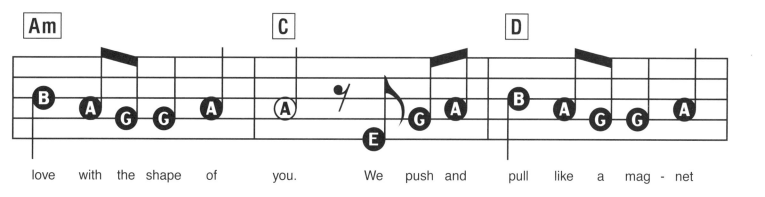

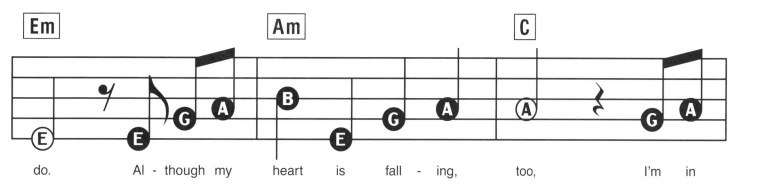

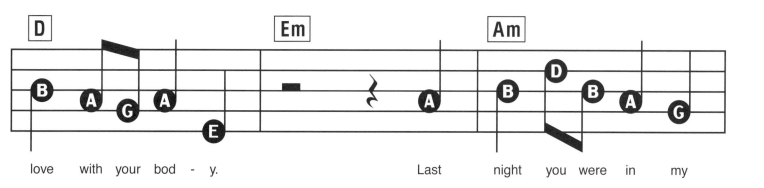

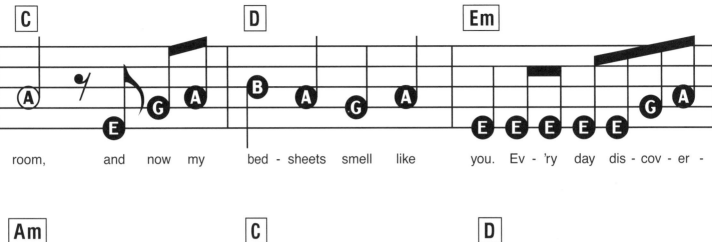

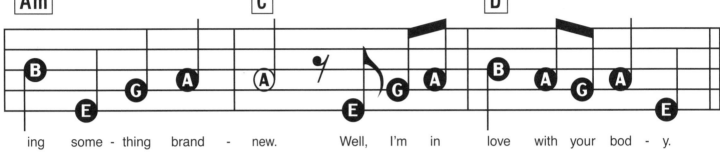

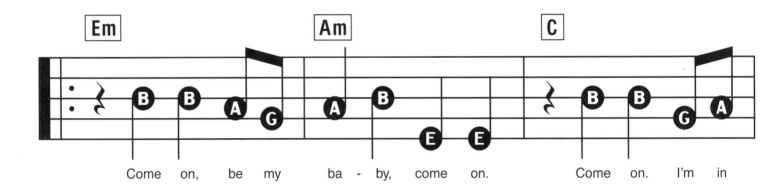

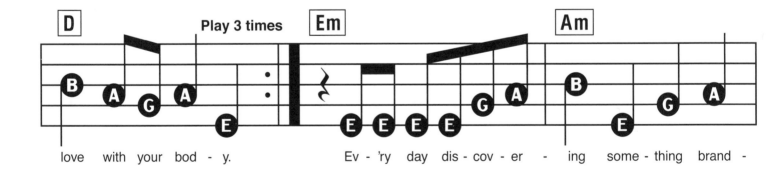

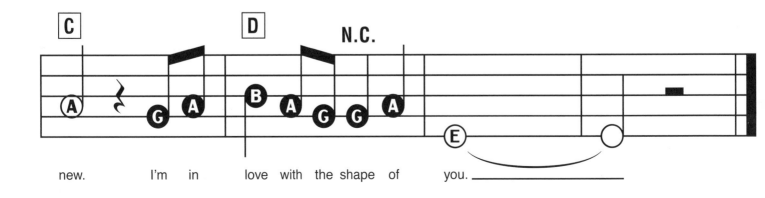

Rewrite the Stars
from THE GREATEST SHOWMAN

Registration 1
Rhythm: None

Words and Music by Benj Pasek
and Justin Paul

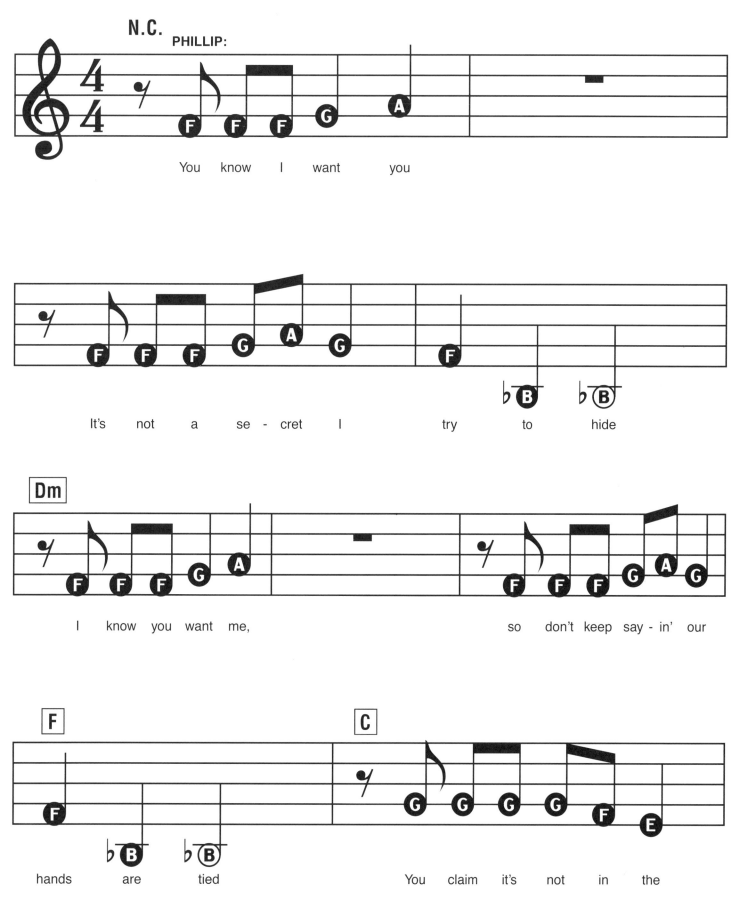

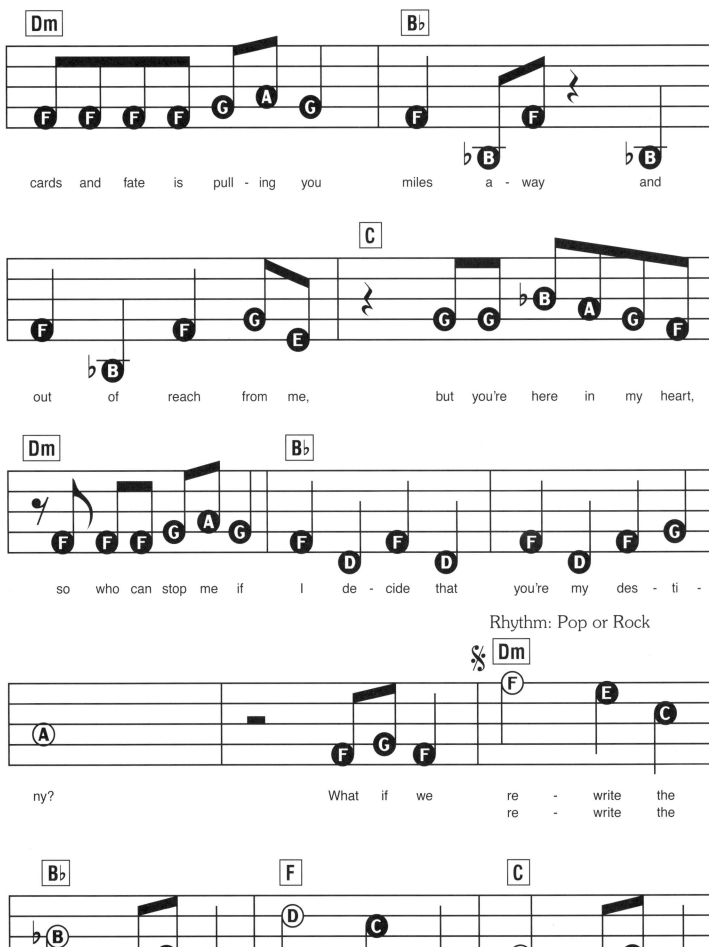

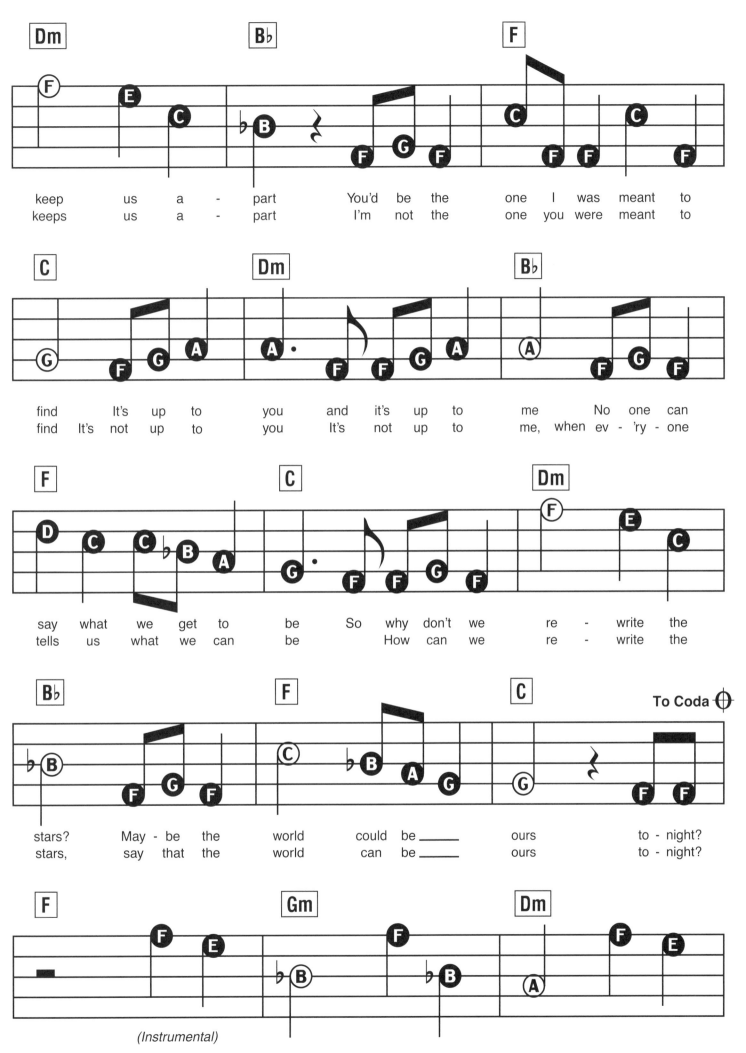

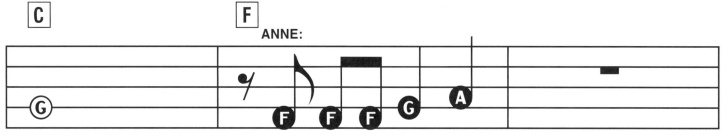

ANNE:

You think it's eas - y?

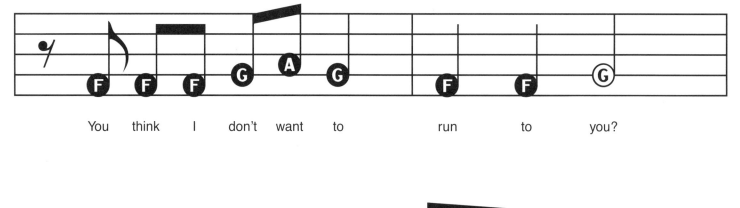

You think I don't want to run to you?

But there are moun - tains, _____

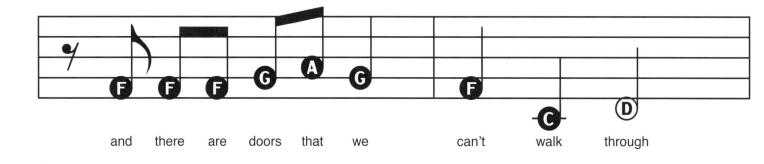

and there are doors that we can't walk through

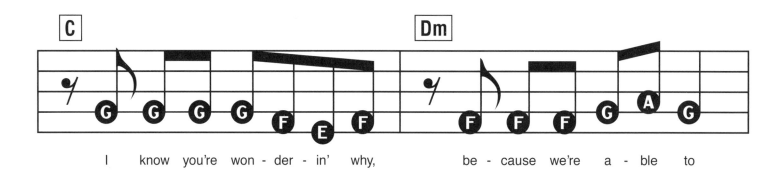

I know you're won - der - in' why, be - cause we're a - ble to

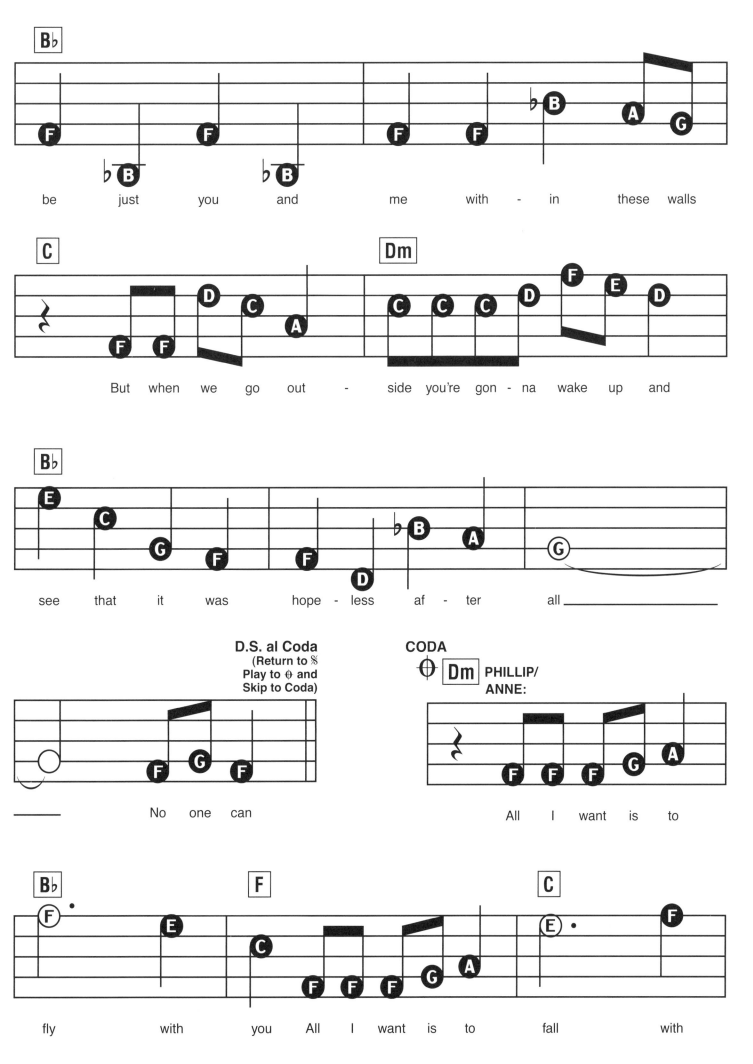

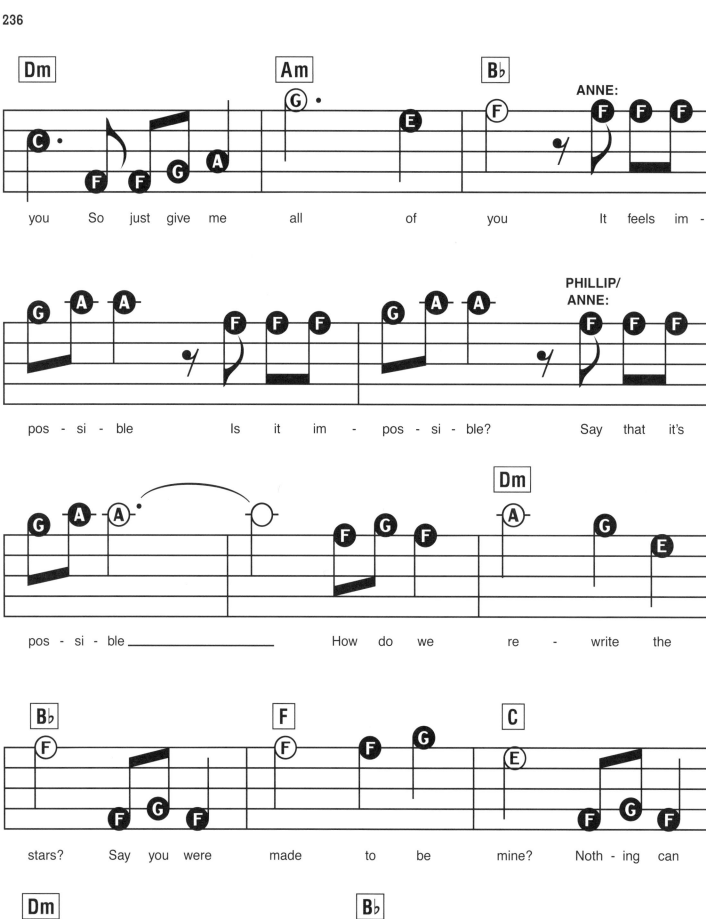

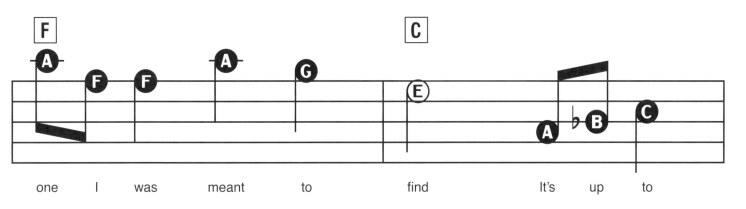

one I was meant to find It's up to

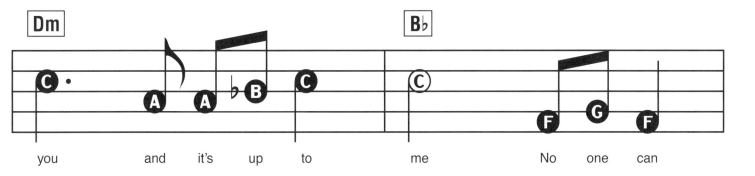

you and it's up to me No one can

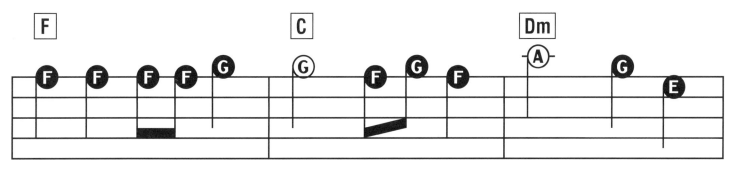

say what we get to be Why don't we re - write the

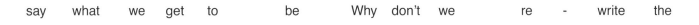

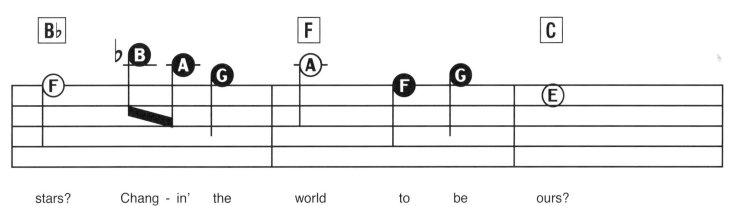

stars? Chang - in' the world to be ours?

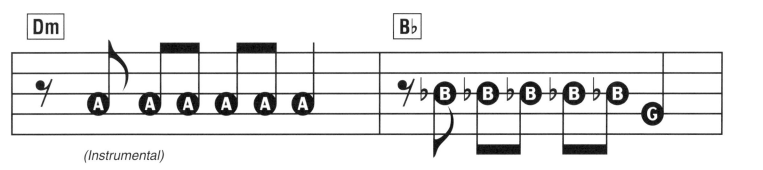

(Instrumental)

238

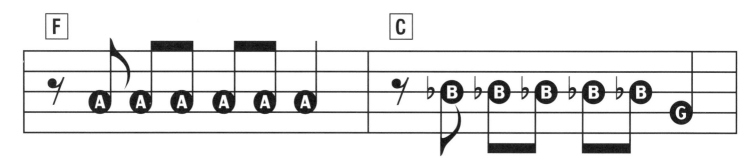

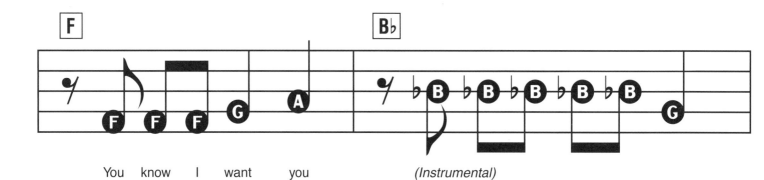

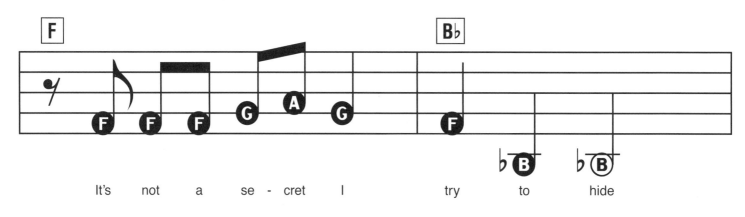

You know I want you   (Instrumental)

It's not a se - cret I   try   to   hide

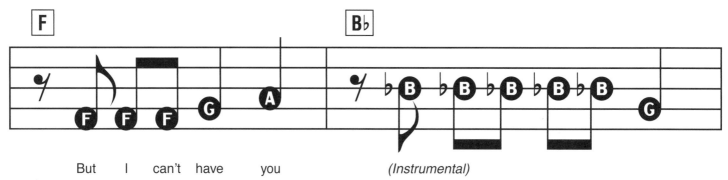

But I can't have you   (Instrumental)

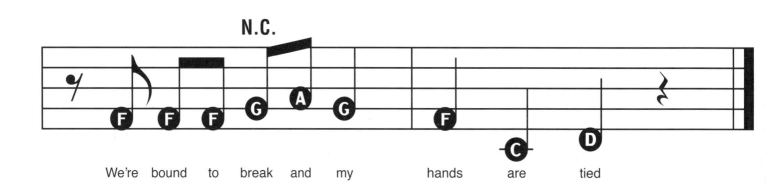

We're bound to break and my   hands   are   tied

Roar

Registration 1
Rhythm: 8-Beat or Rock

Words and Music by Katy Perry,
Max Martin, Dr. Luke,
Bonnie McKee and Henry Walter

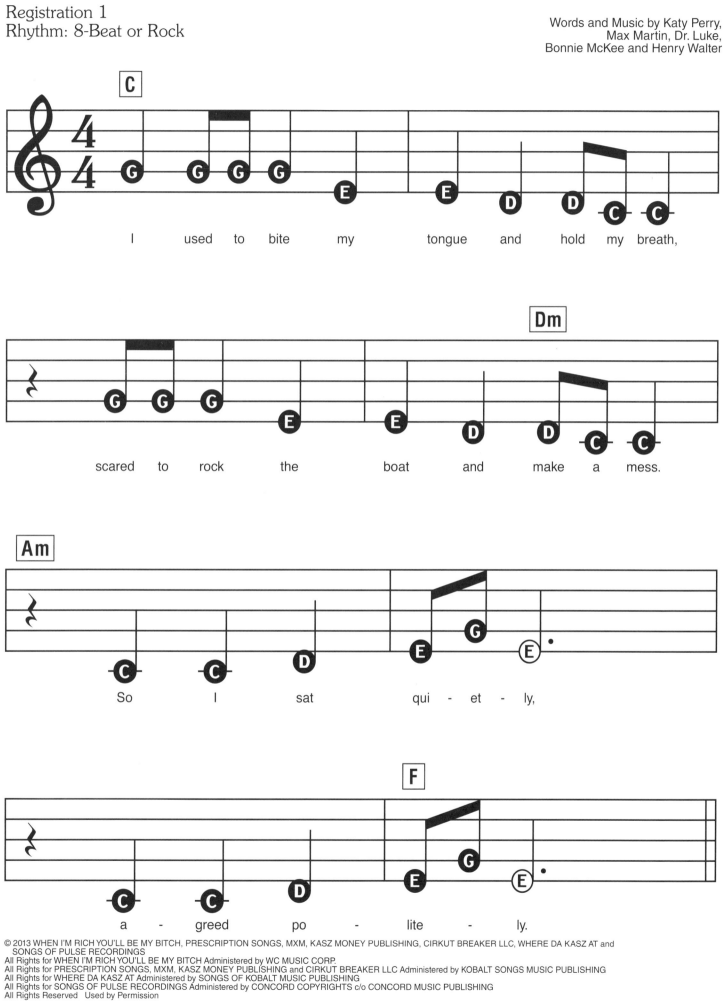

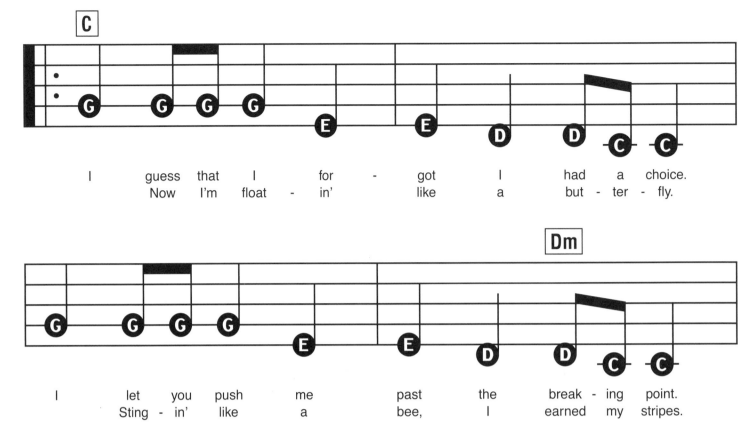

I guess that I for - got I had a choice.
Now I'm float - in' like a but - ter - fly.

I let you push me past the break - ing point.
Sting - in' like a bee, I earned my stripes.

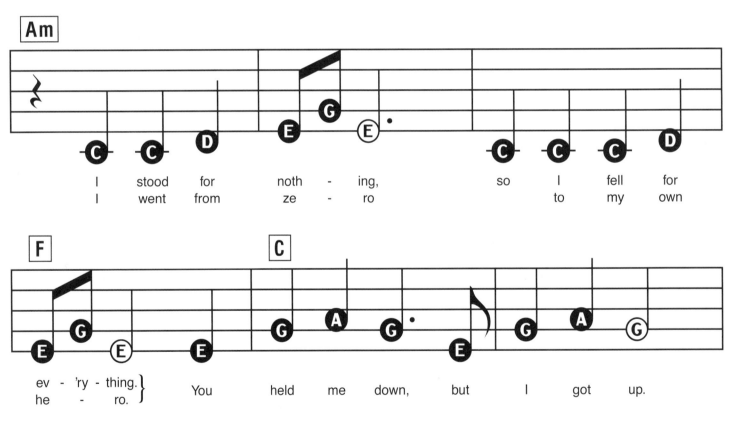

I stood for noth - ing, so I fell for
I went from ze - ro to my own

ev - 'ry - thing.
he - ro.

You held me down, but I got up.

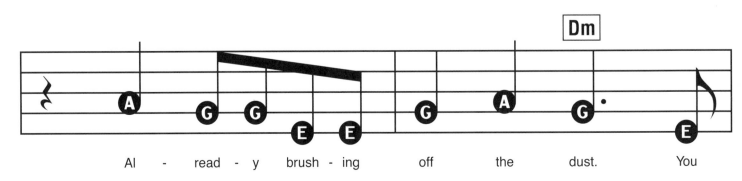

Al - read - y brush - ing off the dust. You

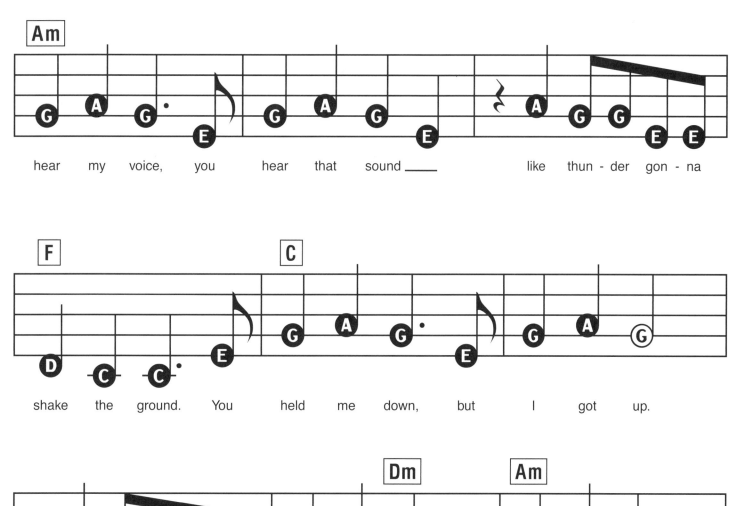

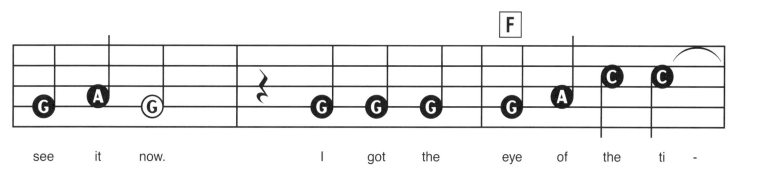

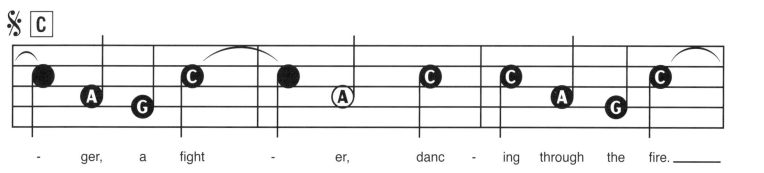

242

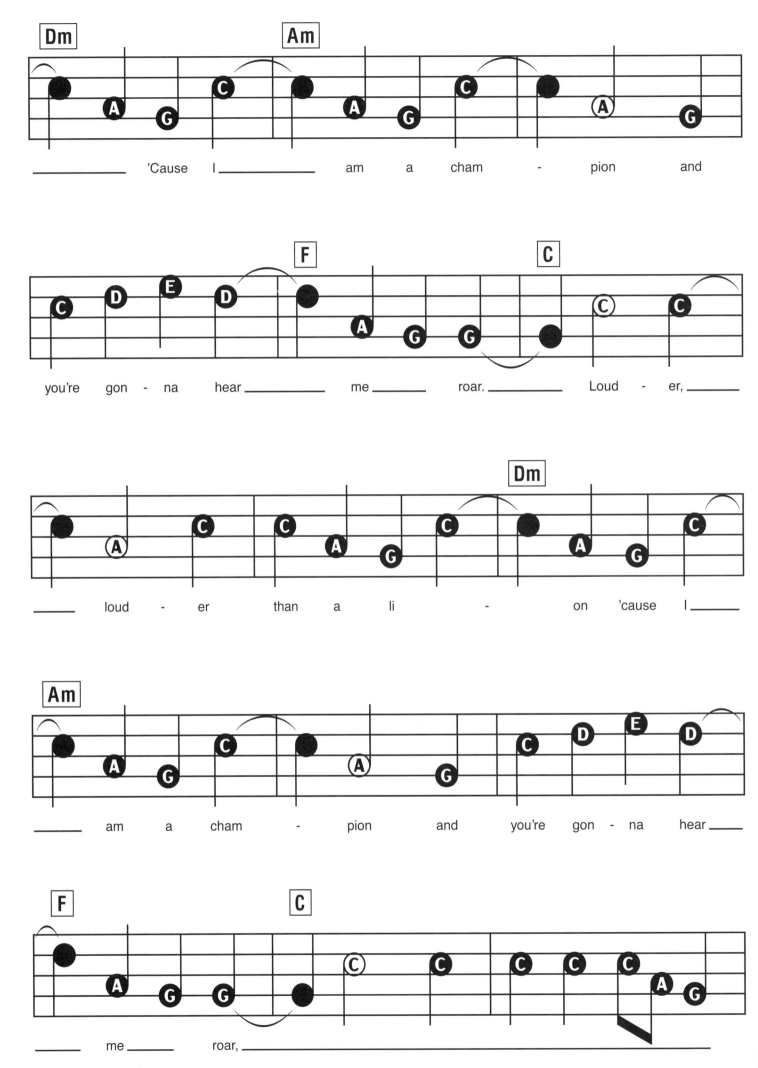

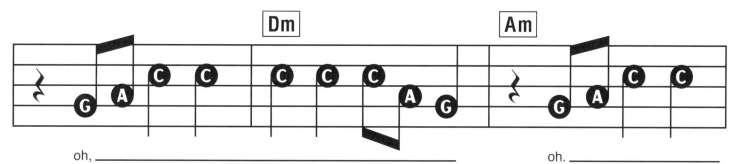

oh, _____ oh. _____

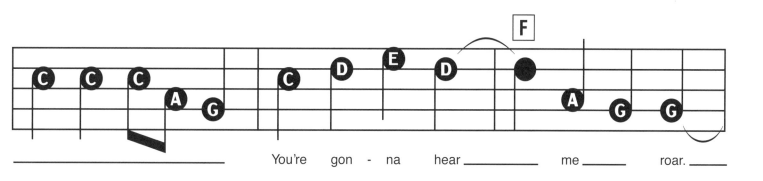

_____ You're gon - na hear _____ me _____ roar. _____

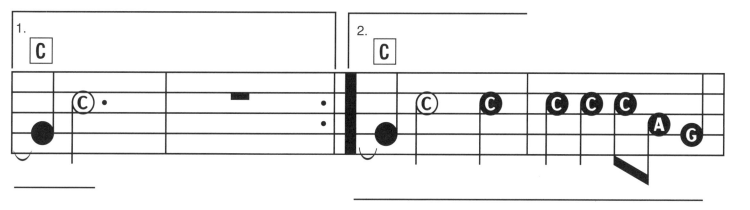

1.
C

2.
C

_____

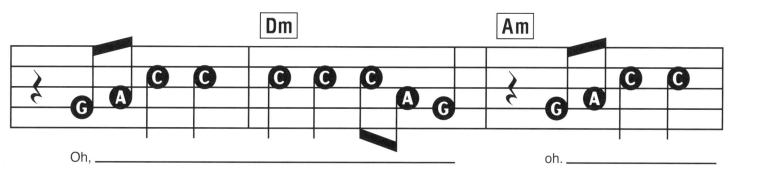

Oh, _____ oh. _____

To Coda ⊕

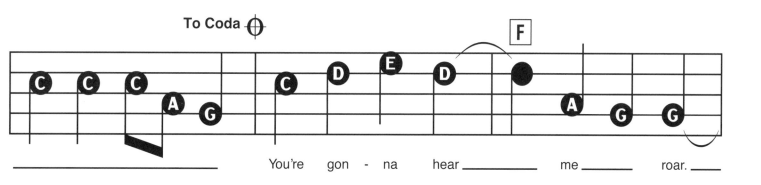

You're gon - na hear _____ me _____ roar. _____

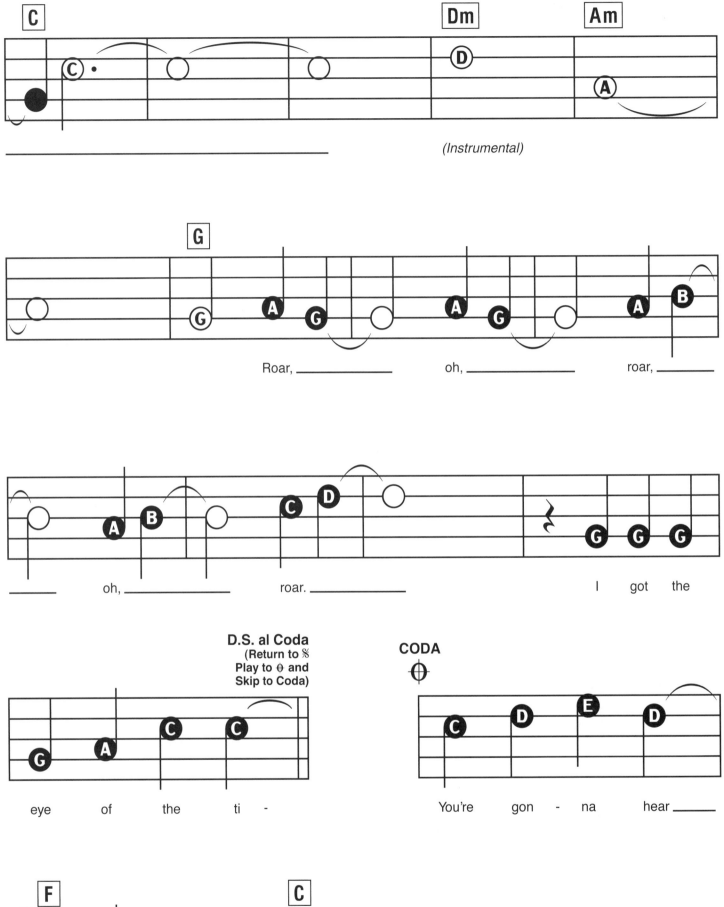

(Instrumental)

Roar, _____ oh, _____ roar, _____

_____ oh, _____ roar. _____ I got the

D.S. al Coda
(Return to 𝄋
Play to ⊕ and
Skip to Coda)

CODA
⊕

eye of the ti -

You're gon - na hear _____

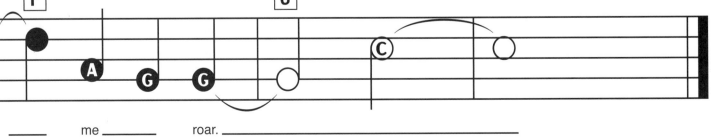

_____ me _____ roar. _____

Rolling in the Deep

Registration 4
Rhythm: Rock or Pop

Words and Music by Adele Adkins
and Paul Epworth

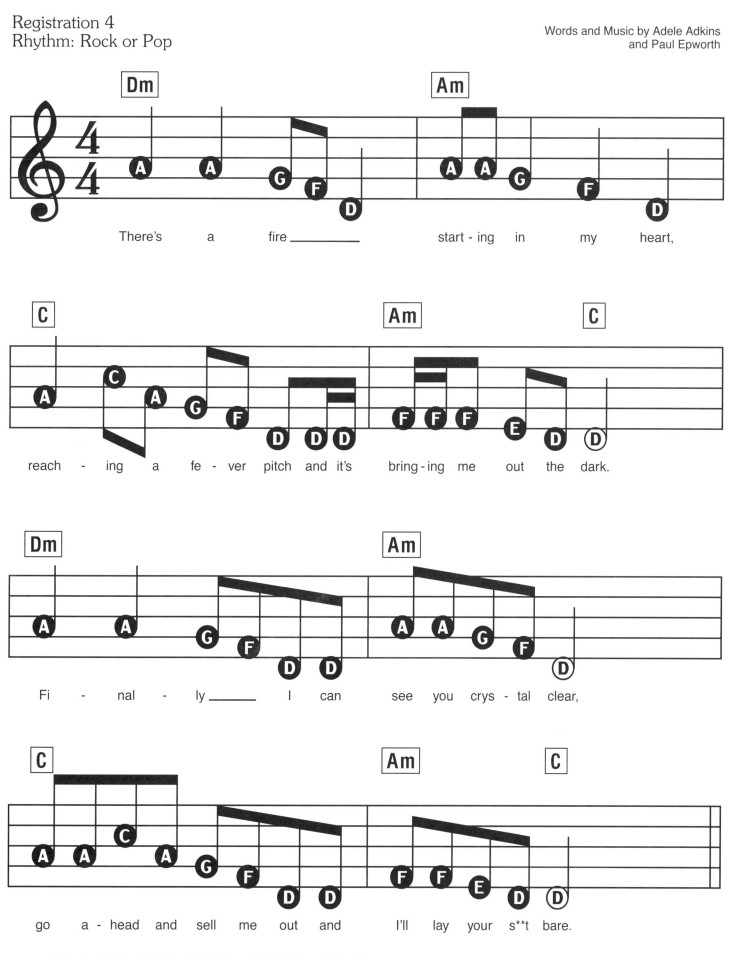

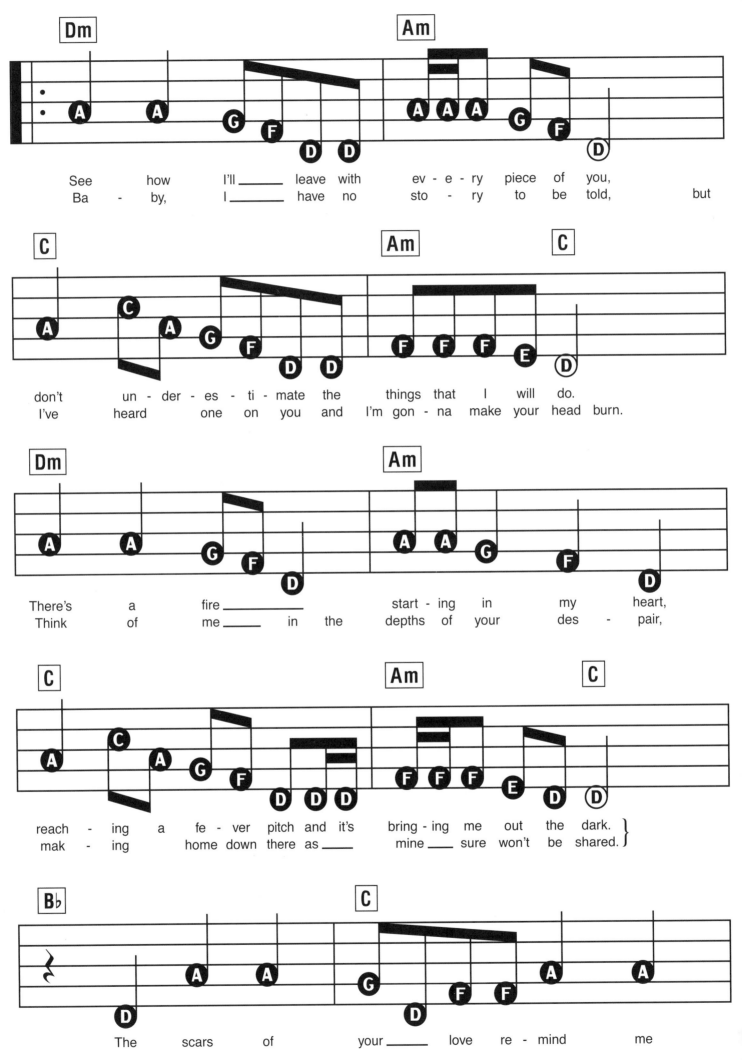

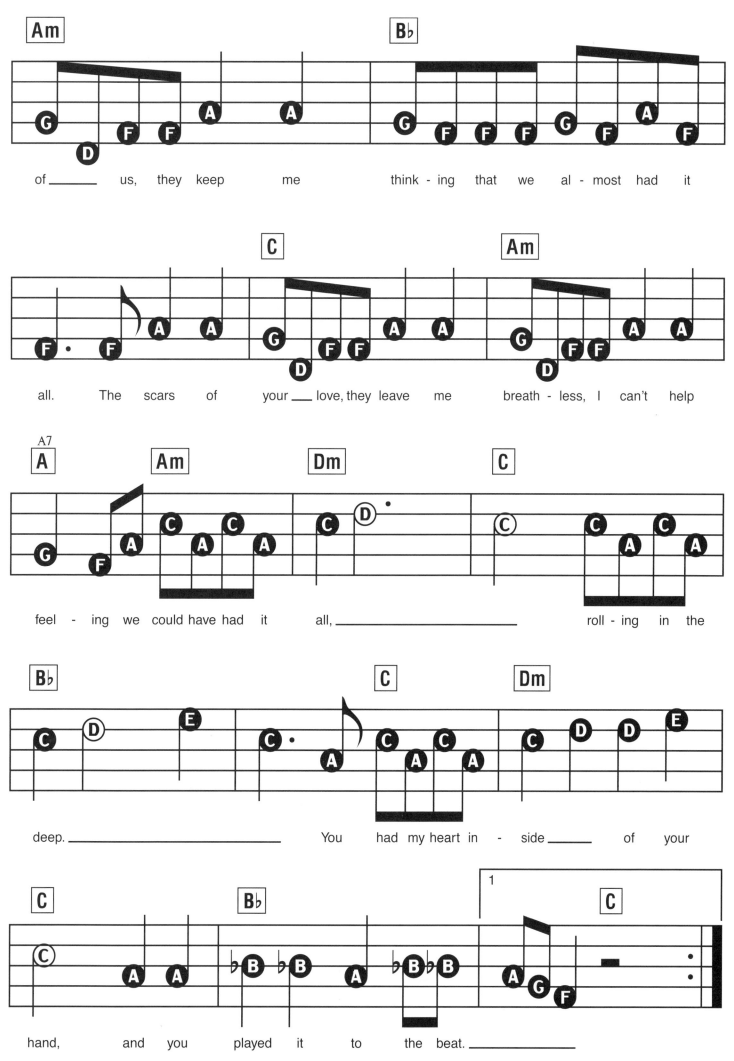

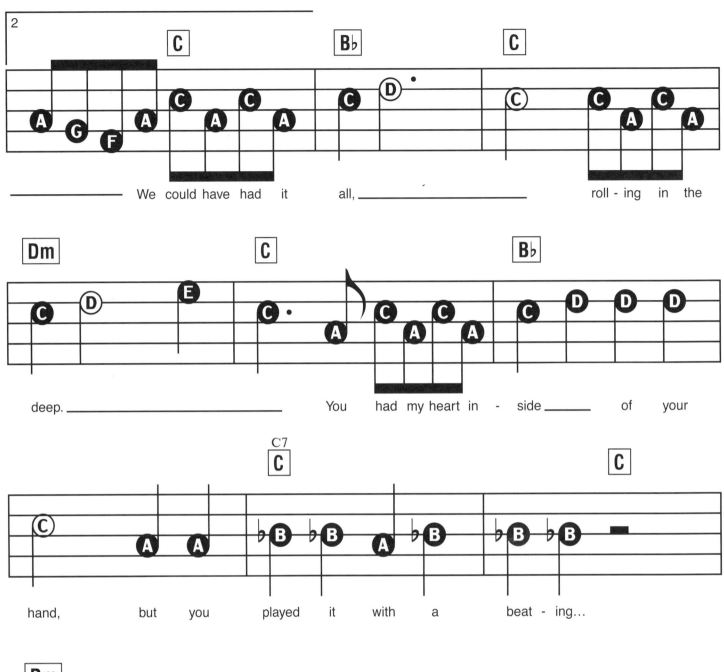

We could have had it all, _____ roll-ing in the

deep. _____ You had my heart in - side _____ of your

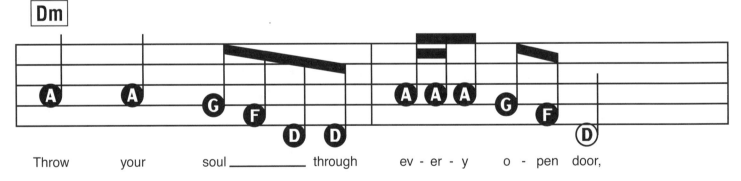

hand, but you played it with a beat - ing…

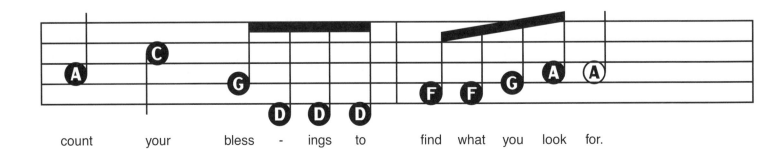

Throw your soul _____ through ev - er - y o - pen door,

count your bless - ings to find what you look for.

249

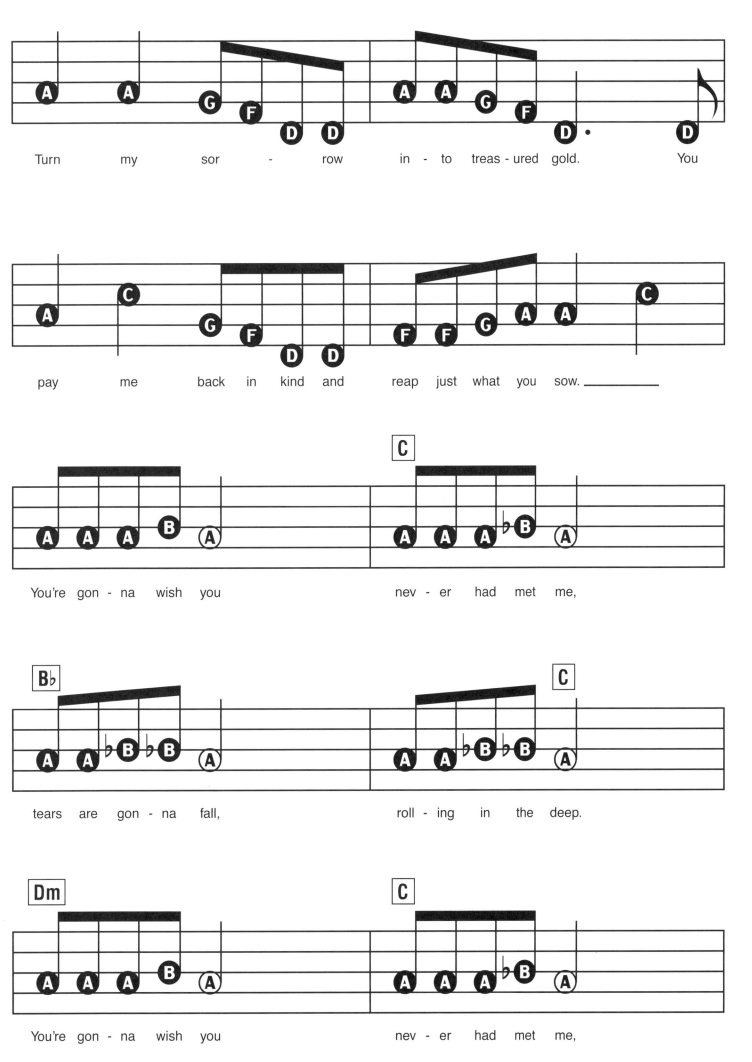

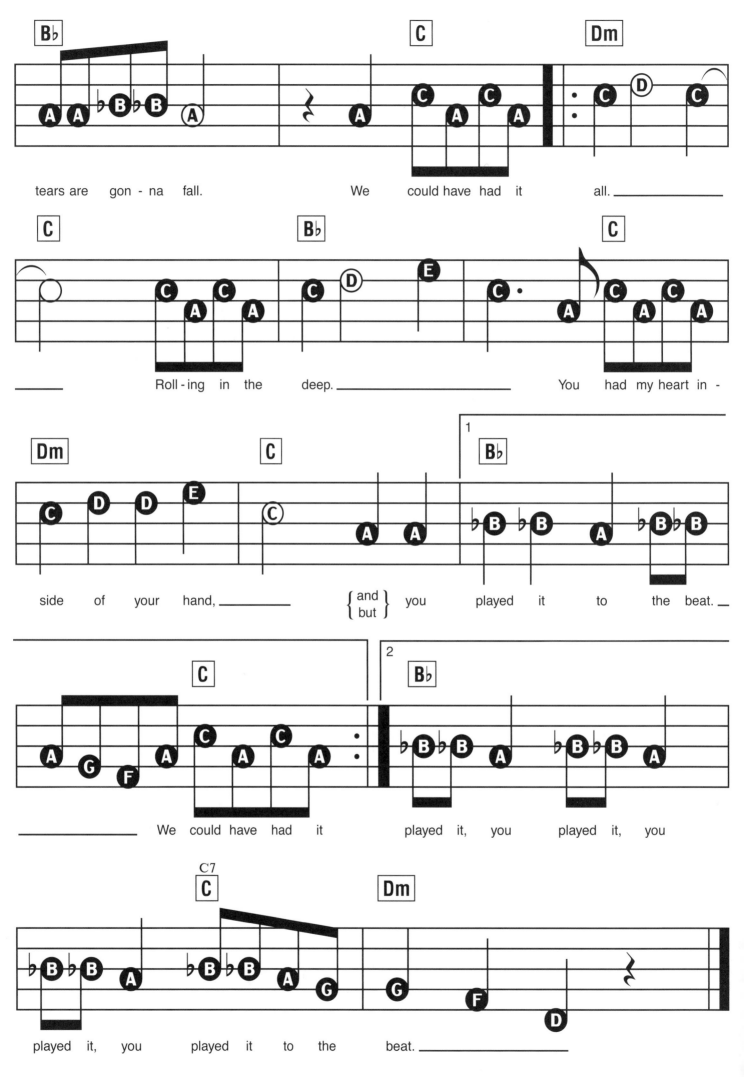

See You Again
from FURIOUS 7

Registration 8
Rhythm: Ballad

Words and Music by Cameron Thomaz,
Charlie Puth, Justin Franks, Andrew Cedar,
Dann Hume, Josh Hardy and Phoebe Cockburn

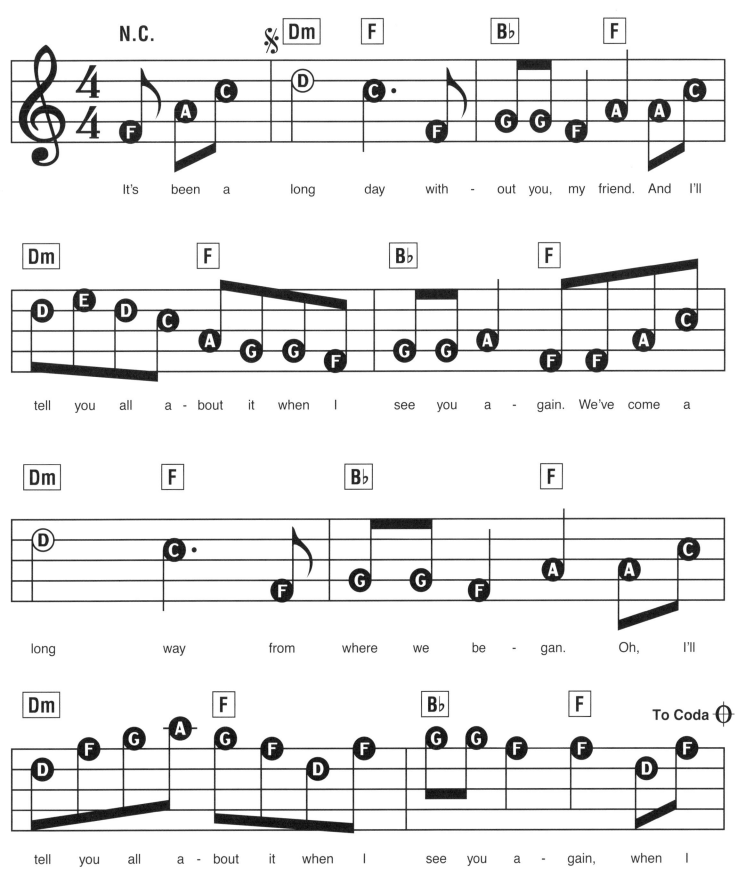

252

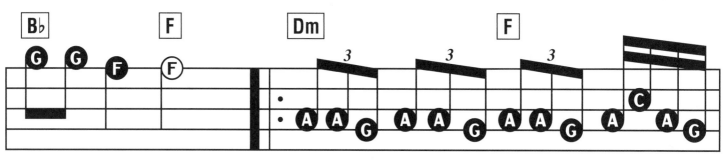

see you a - gain.   Rap 1: *(See additional lyrics)*

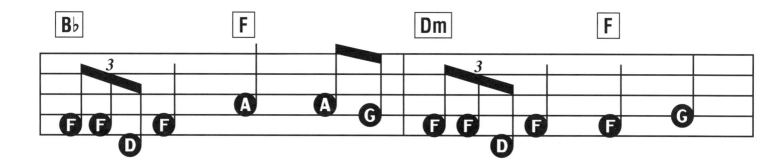

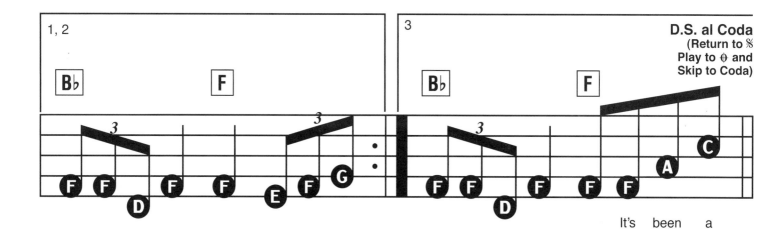

D.S. al Coda
(Return to ℅
Play to ⊕ and
Skip to Coda)

It's been a

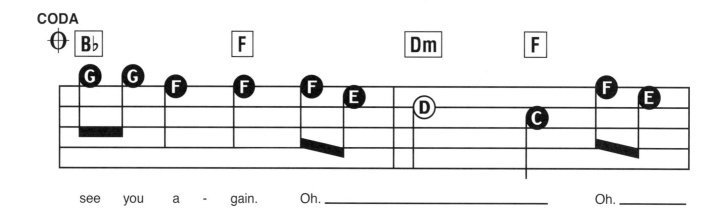

see you a - gain.   Oh. _____   Oh. _____

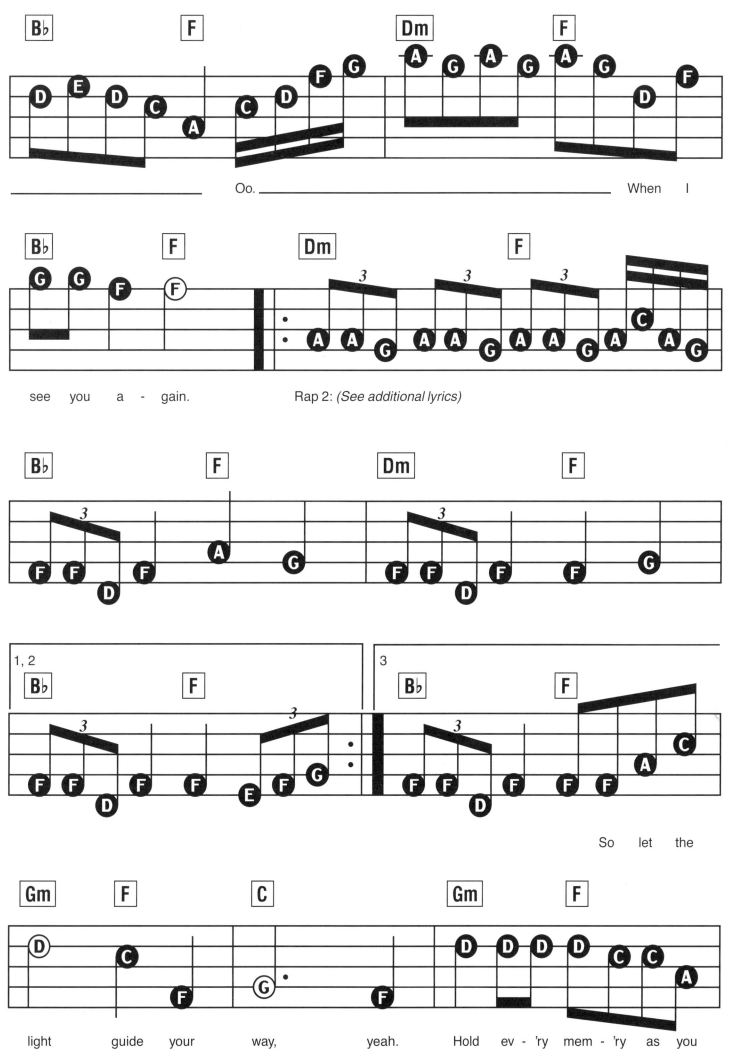

Oo. _____ When I

see you a - gain.   Rap 2: *(See additional lyrics)*

So let the

light guide your way, yeah. Hold ev - 'ry mem - 'ry as you

254

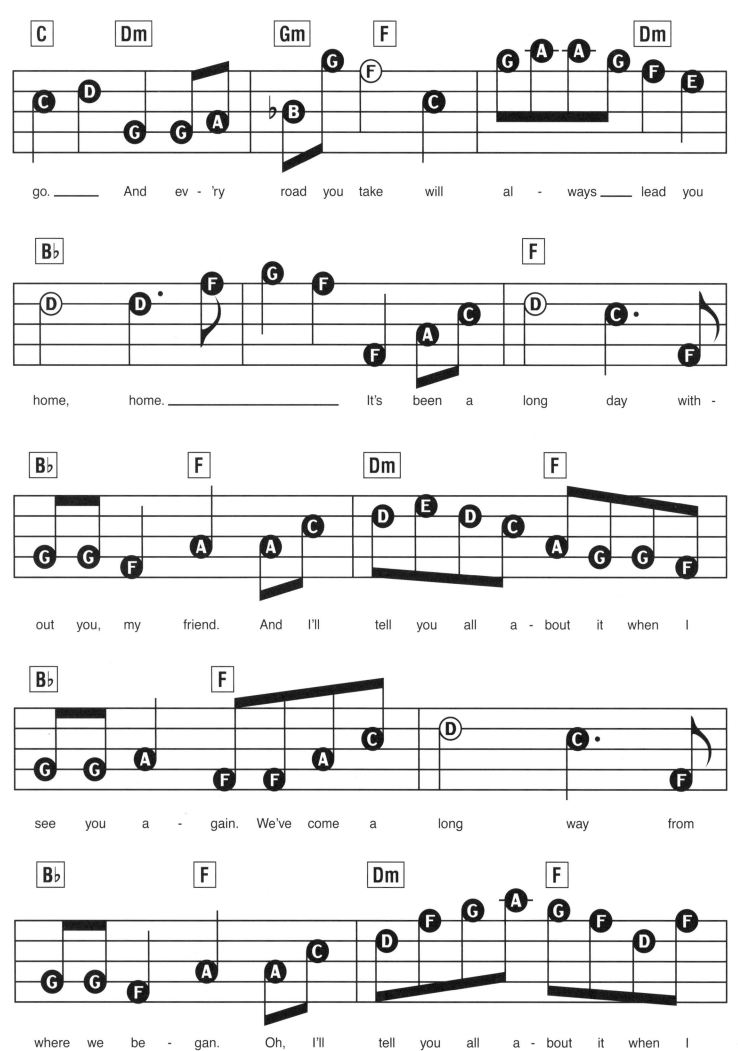

255

see you a - gain, when I see you a - gain. Oh. _____

_____ Oh. _____ Oo. _____

_____ When I see you a - gain. Oh ____ see you a - gain.

Additional Lyrics

Rap 1: Damn who knew all the planes we flew
Good things we've been through
That I'll be standing right here
Talking to you about another path I
Know we loved to hit the road and laugh
But something told me that it wouldn't last
Had to switch up look at things different see the bigger picture
Those were the days hard work forever pays now I see you in a better place.

How could we not talk about family when family's all that we got?
Everything I went through you were standing there by my side
And now you gonna be with me for the last ride.

Rap 2: First you both go out your way
And the vibe is feeling strong and what's
Small turn to a friendship, a friendship
Turn into a bond and that bond will never
Be broken and the love will never get lost
And when brotherhood come first then the line
Will never be crossed established it on our own
When that line had to be drawn and that line is what
We reach so remember me when I'm gone.

How could we not talk about family when family's all that we got?
Everything I went through you were standing there by my side
And now you gonna be with me for the last ride.

Royals

Registration 9
Rhythm: 8-Beat or Calypso

Words and Music by Ella Yelich-O'Connor
and Joel Little

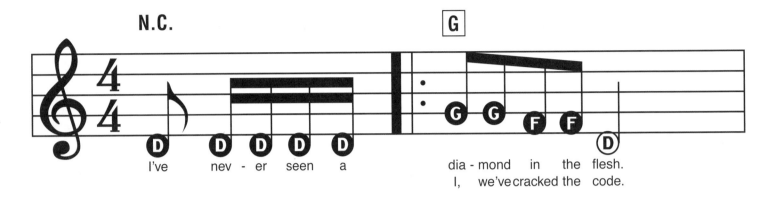

I've nev - er seen a dia - mond in the flesh.
I, we've cracked the code.

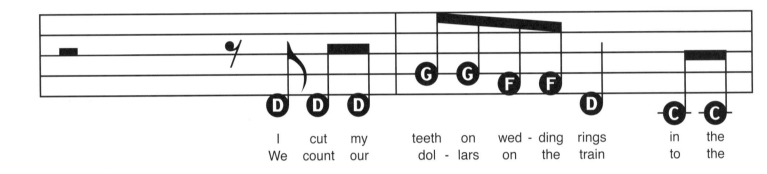

I cut my teeth on wed - ding rings in the
We count our dol - lars on the train to the

mov - ies. _____ And I'm not proud of my ad - dress. _____
par - ty. _____ And ev - 'ry - one who knows us knows _____

In the torn - up town this. no post - code
that we're fine with this. We did - n't come from

257

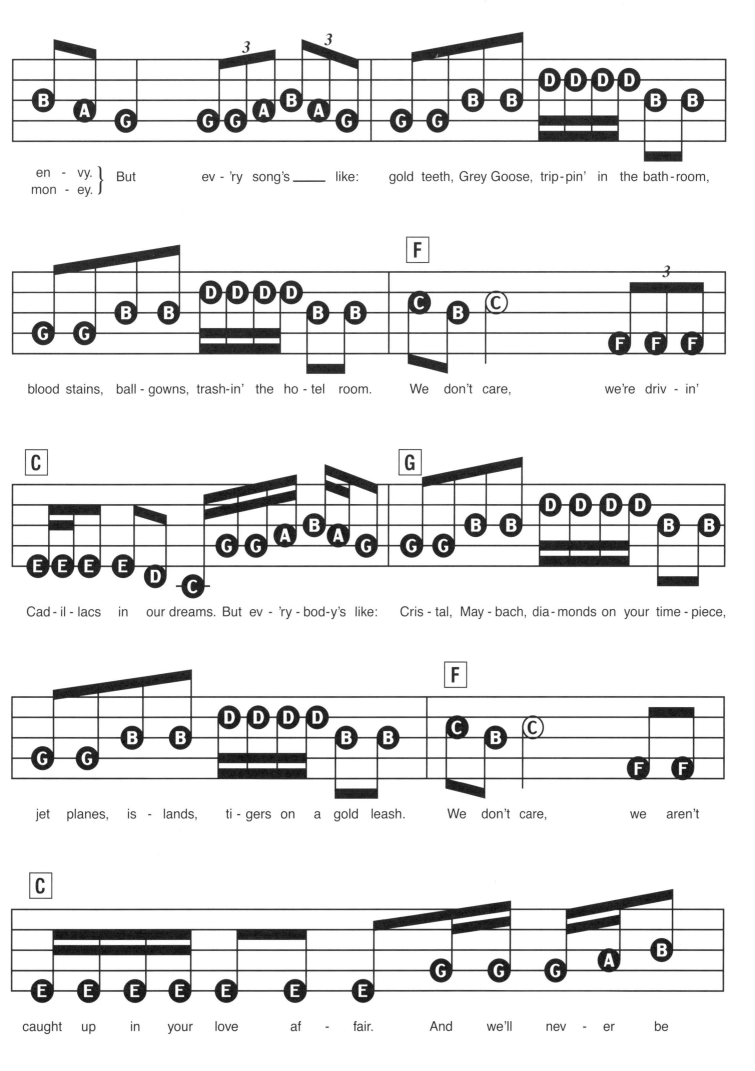

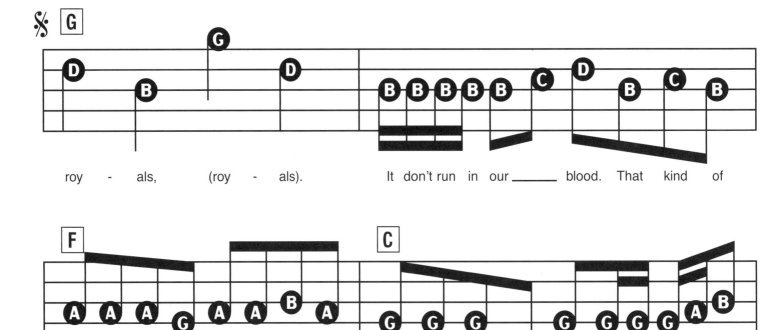

roy - als, (roy - als). It don't run in our _____ blood. That kind of

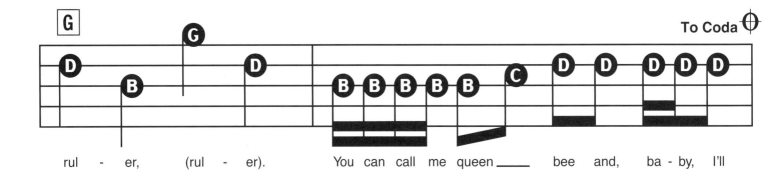

luxe just ain't for us. We crave a dif - f'rent kind of buzz. Let me be ___ your

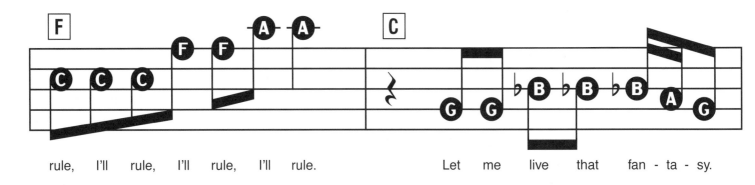

rul - er, (rul - er). You can call me queen _____ bee and, ba - by, I'll

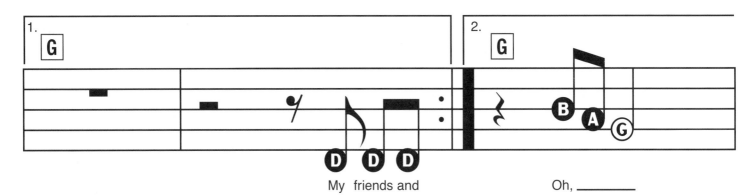

rule, I'll rule, I'll rule, I'll rule. Let me live that fan - ta - sy.

1.

My friends and

2.

Oh, _____

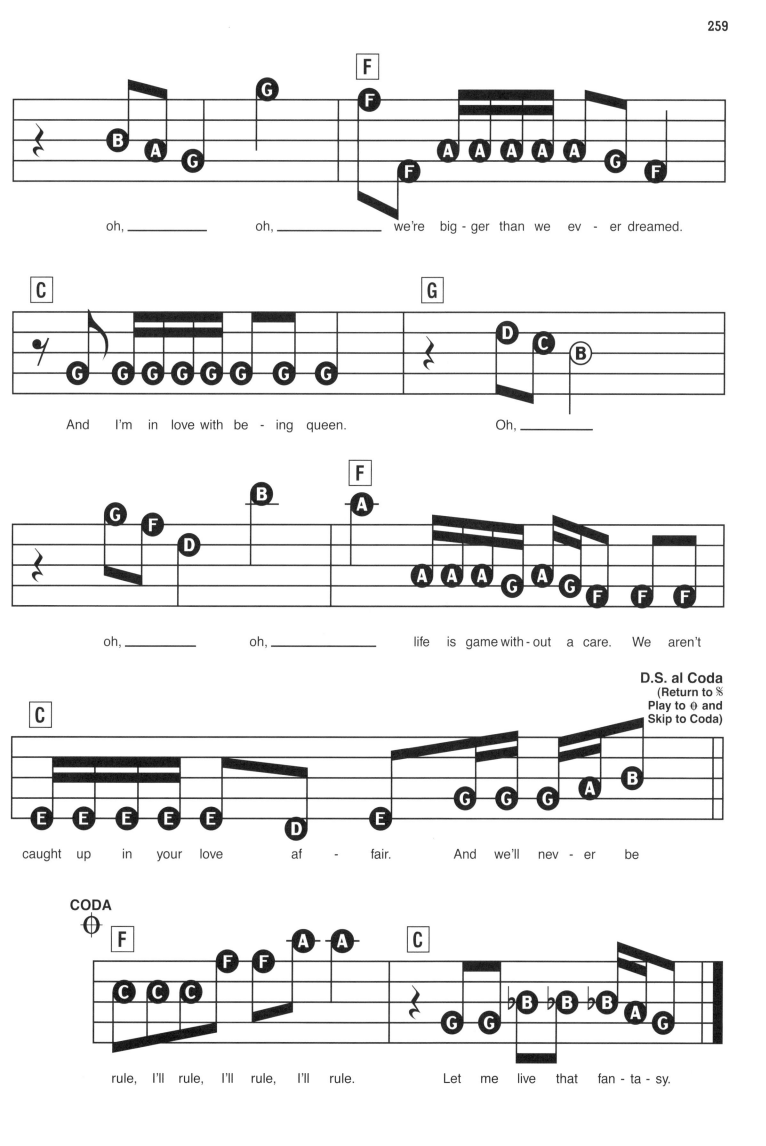

Say Something

Registration 8
Rhythm: Waltz

Words and Music by Ian Axel,
Chad Vaccarino and Mike Campbell

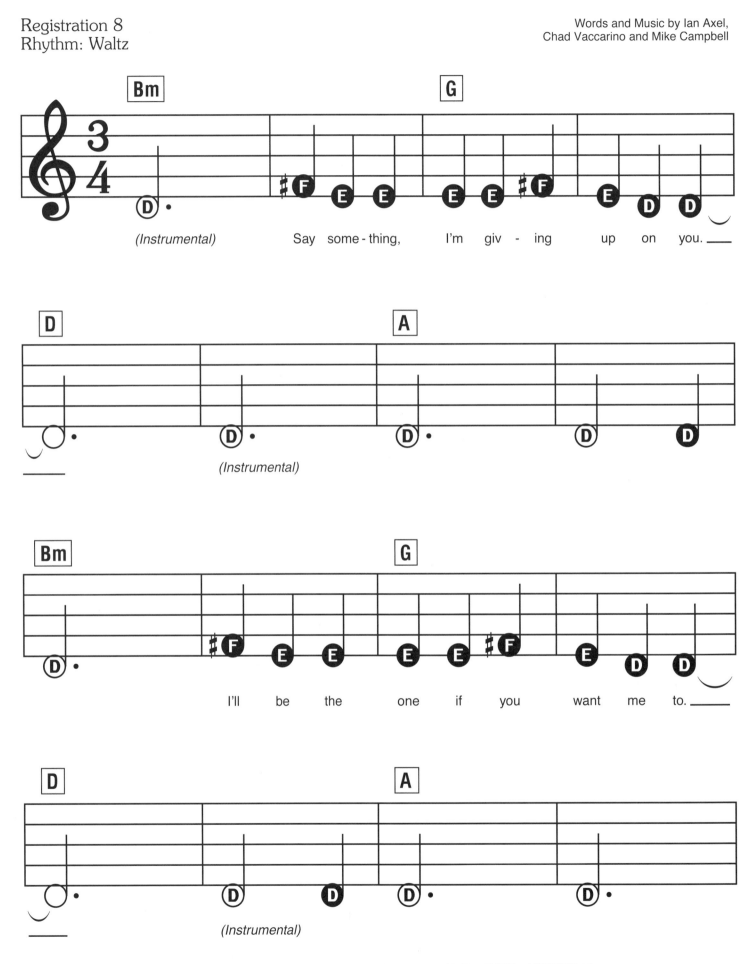

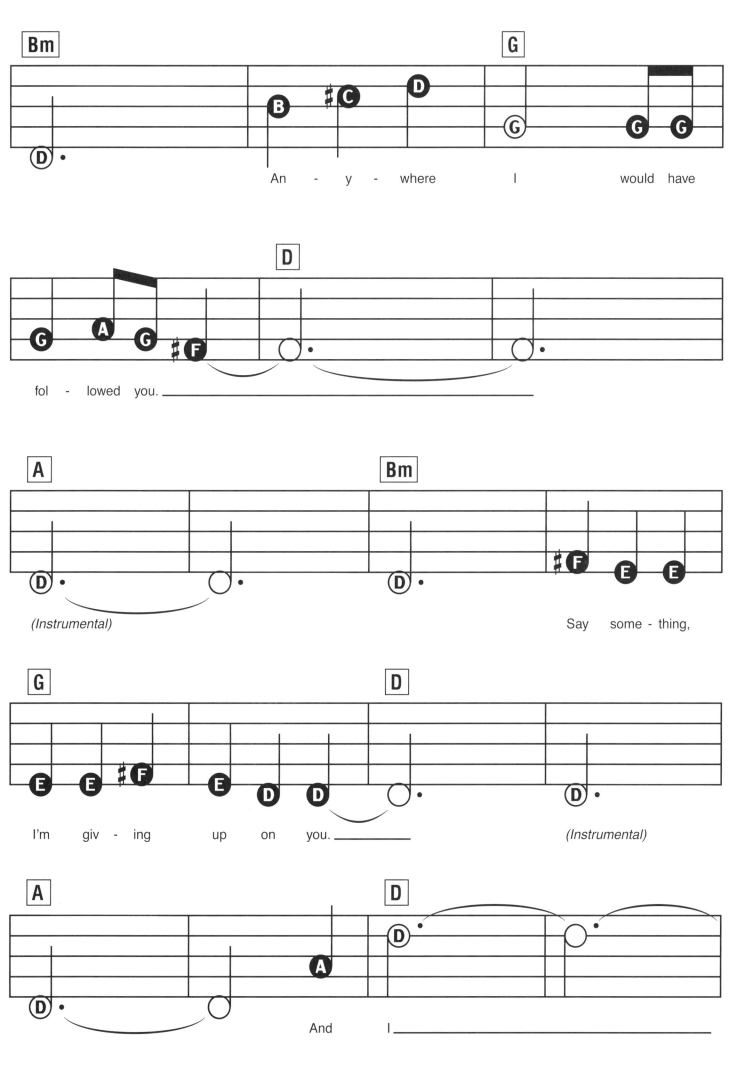

262

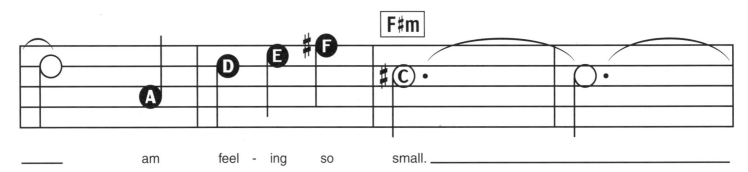

_____ am feel - ing so small. _____

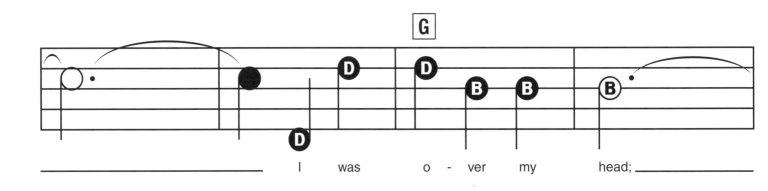

_____ I was o - ver my head; _____

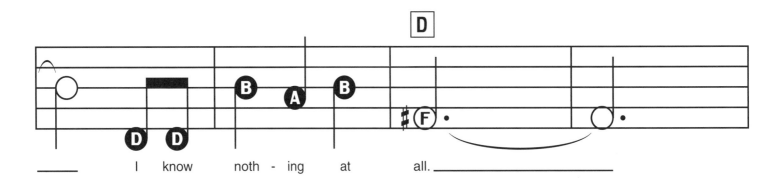

_____ I know noth - ing at all. _____

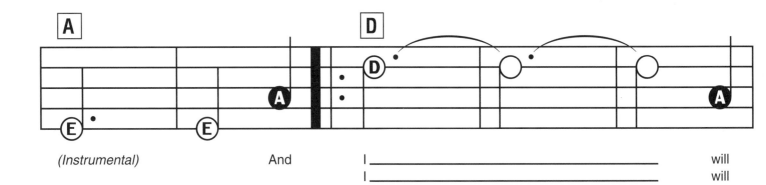

(Instrumental)   And   I _____ will
                                              I _____ will

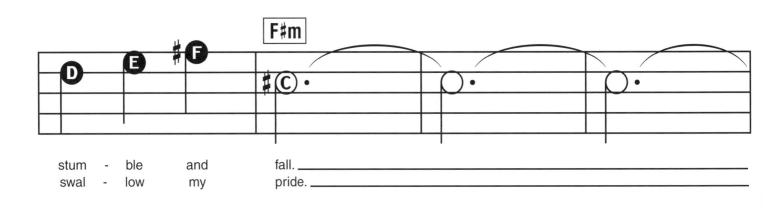

stum - ble and   fall. _____
swal - low my   pride. _____

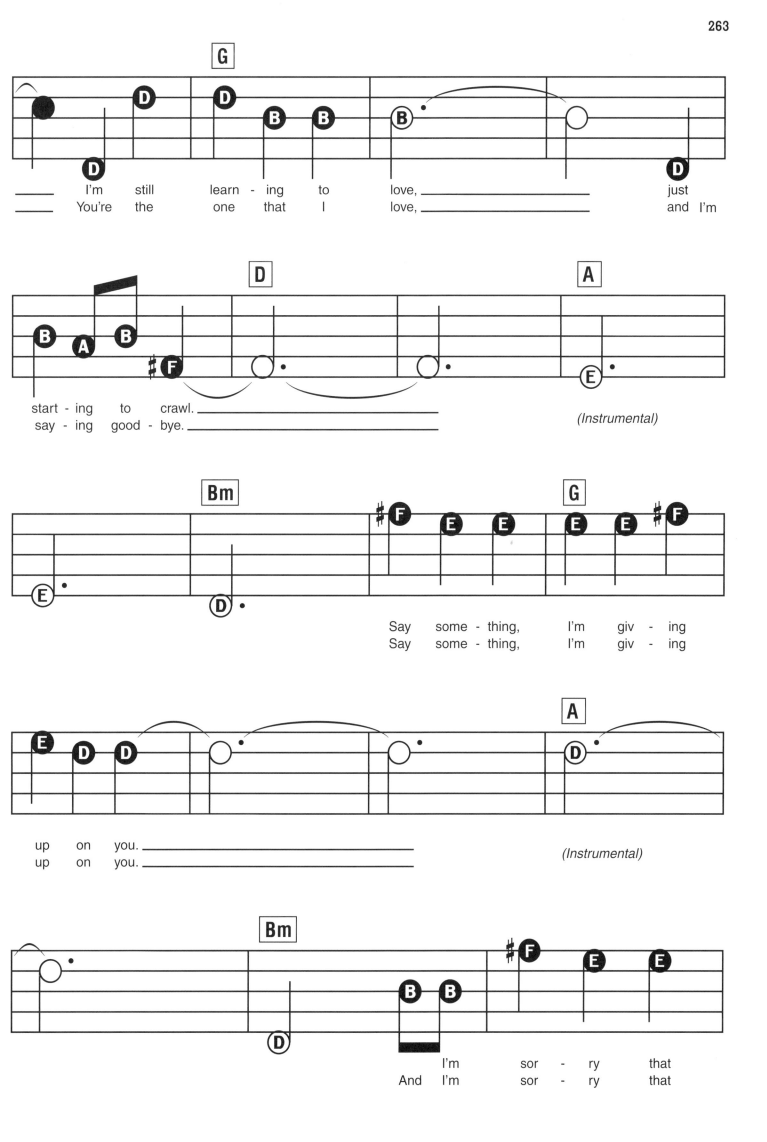

264

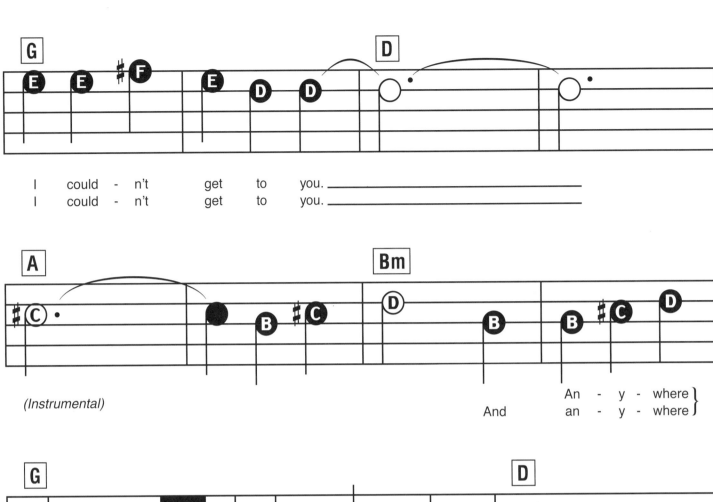

I could - n't   get   to   you.
I could - n't   get   to   you.

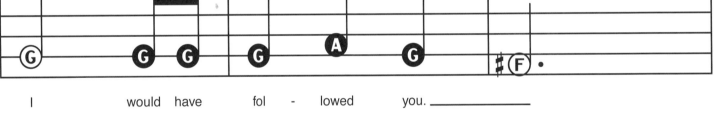

(Instrumental)

An - y - where
And   an - y - where

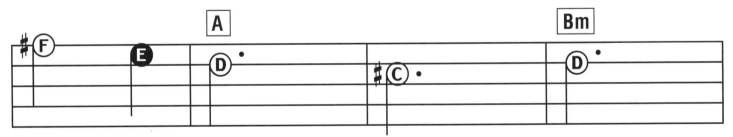

I   would have   fol - lowed   you.

(Instrumental)

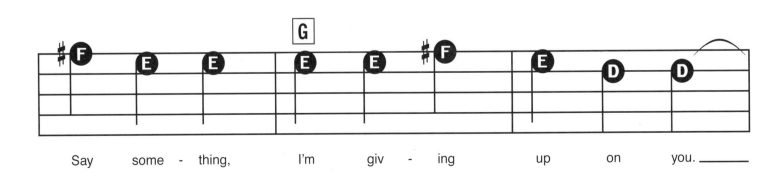

Say   some - thing,   I'm   giv - ing   up   on   you.

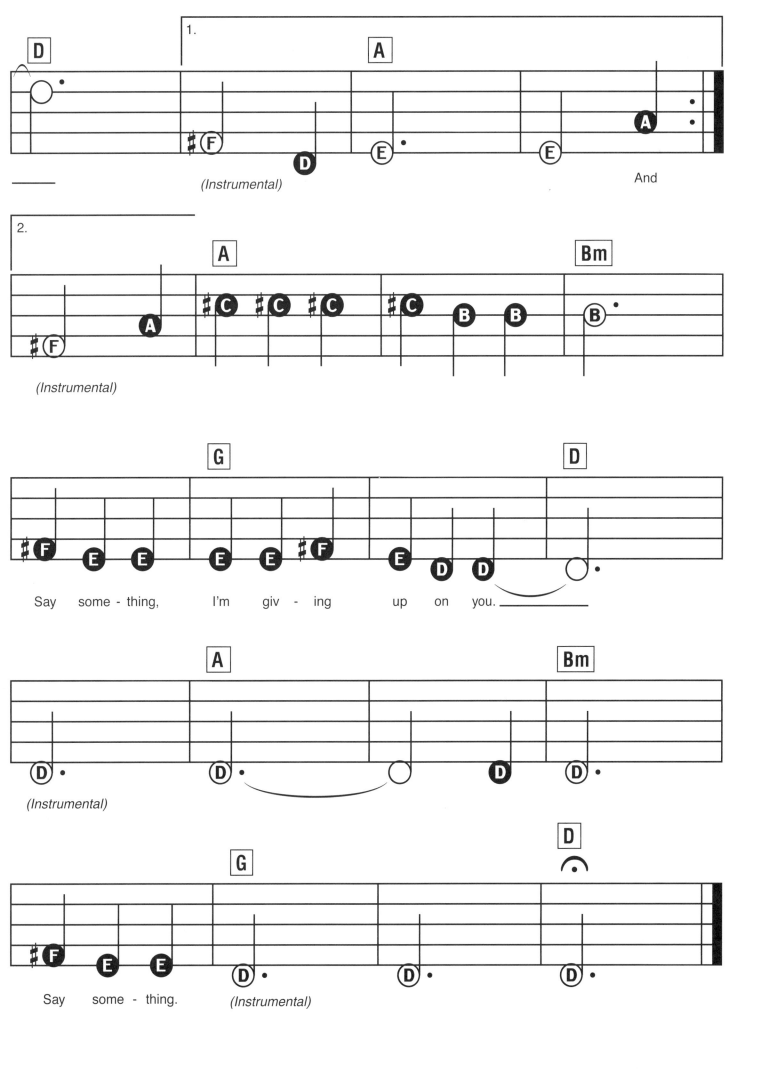

Scars to Your Beautiful

Registration 1
Rhythm: Pop

Words and Music by Alessia Caracciolo,
Warren Felder, Coleridge Tillman
and Andrew Wansel

She just wants to be beau-ti-ful. She

goes un-no-ticed, she knows no lim-its. She

craves at-ten-tion, she prais-es an im-age. She

prays to be sculp-ted by the sculp-tor. Oh, she don't

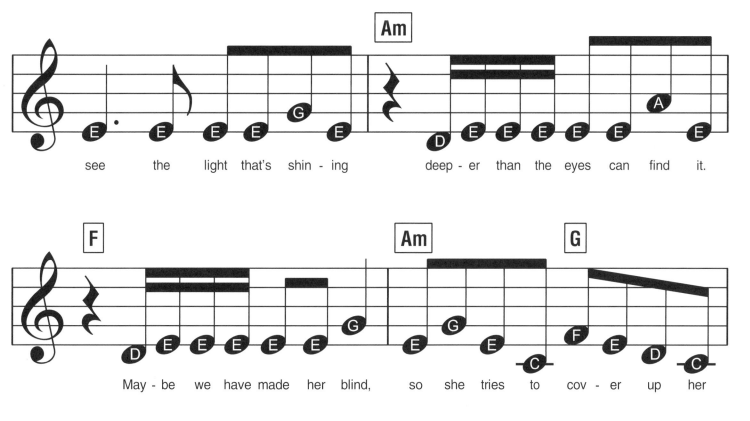

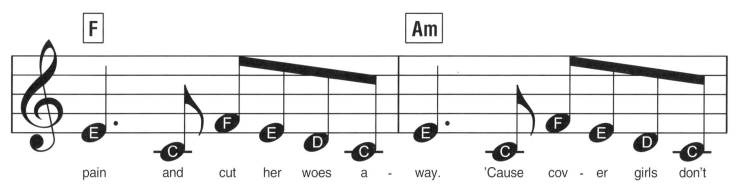

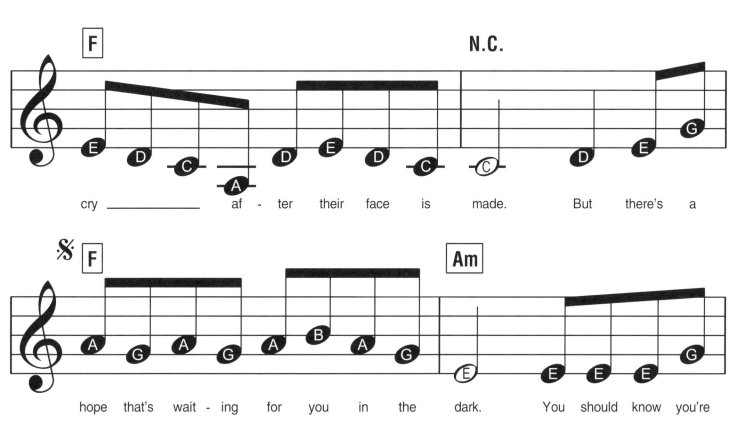

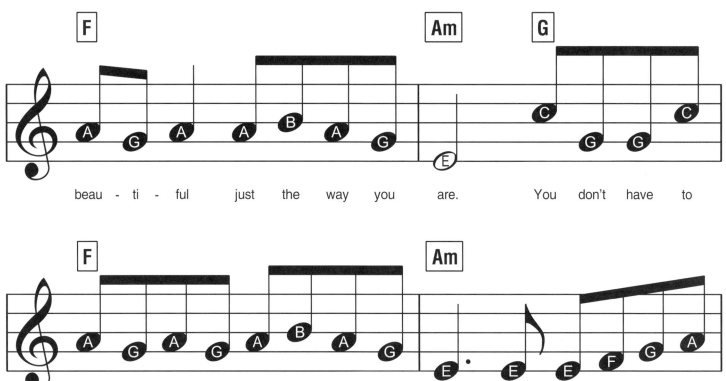

beau - ti - ful just the way you are. You don't have to

change a thing; the world could change its heart. No scars to your beau -

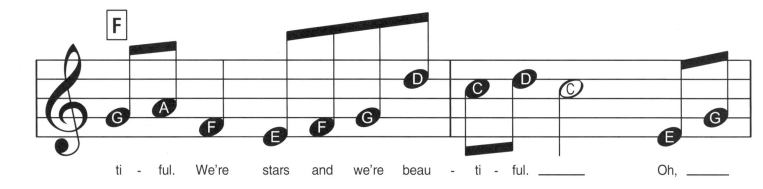

ti - ful. We're stars and we're beau - ti - ful. _____ Oh, _____

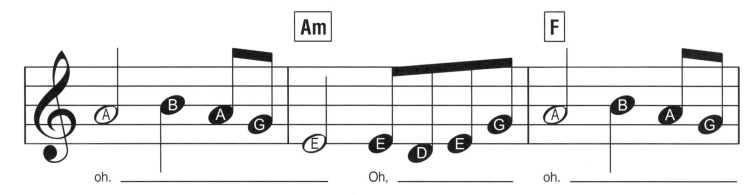

oh. _____ Oh, _____ oh. _____

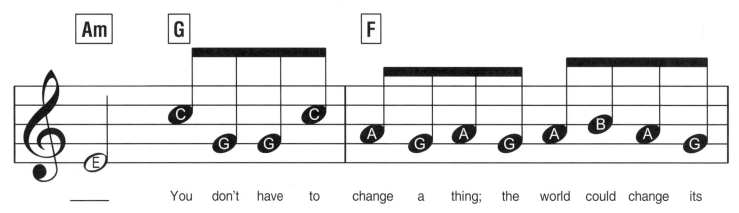

_____ You don't have to change a thing; the world could change its

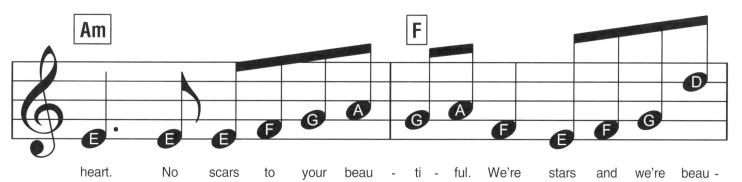

heart.   No   scars   to   your   beau - ti - ful.   We're   stars   and   we're   beau -

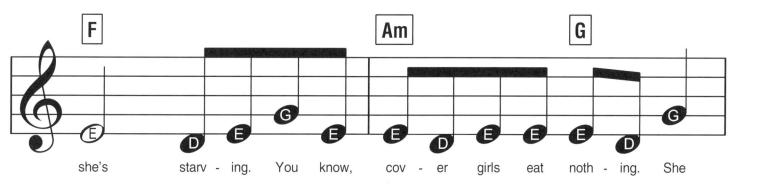

ti - ful. _____   She   has   dreams   to   be   an   en - vy,   so

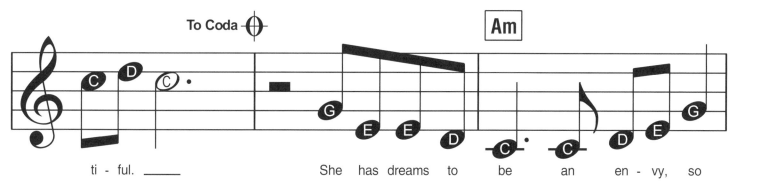

she's   starv - ing.   You   know,   cov - er   girls   eat   noth - ing.   She

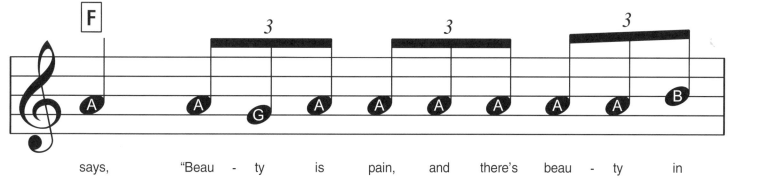

says,   "Beau - ty   is   pain,   and   there's   beau - ty   in

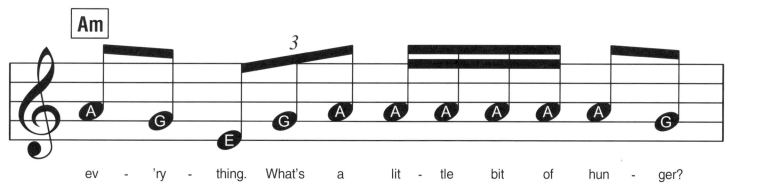

ev - 'ry - thing.   What's   a   lit - tle   bit   of   hun - ger?

CODA

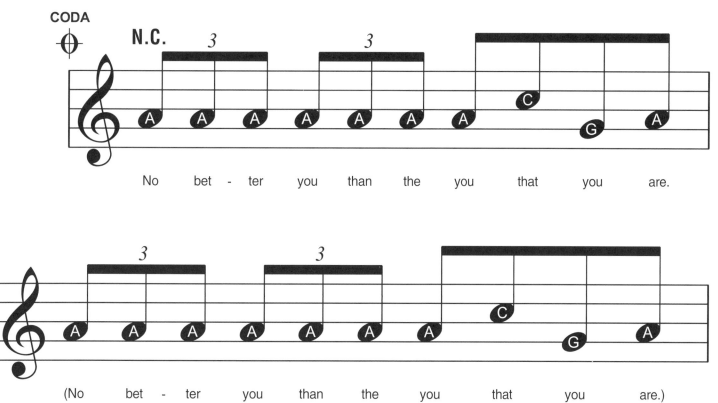

N.C.

No bet - ter you than the you that you are.

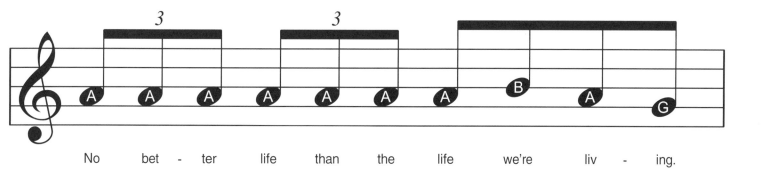

(No bet - ter you than the you that you are.)

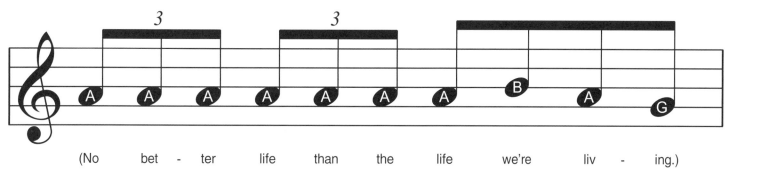

No bet - ter life than the life we're liv - ing.

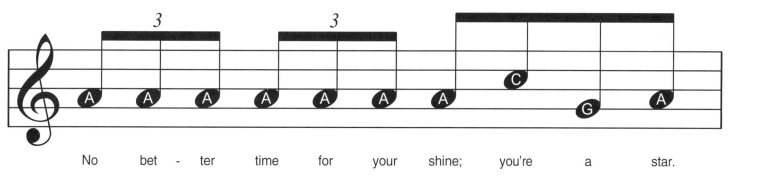

(No bet - ter life than the life we're liv - ing.)

No bet - ter time for your shine; you're a star.

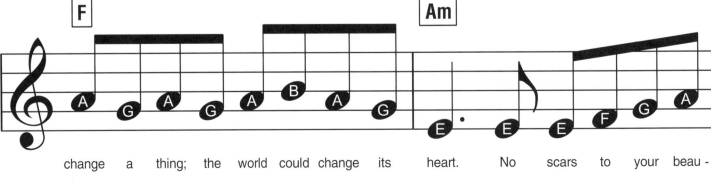

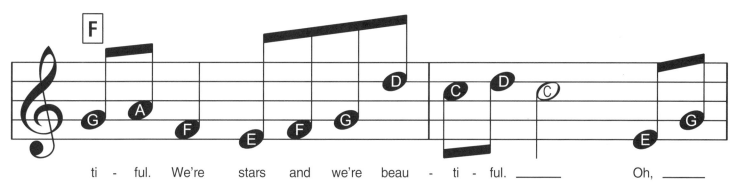

ti - ful. We're stars and we're beau - ti - ful. _____ Oh, _____

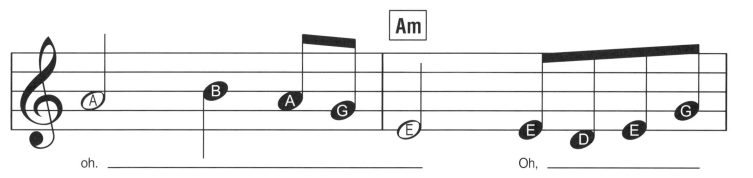

oh. _____ Oh, _____

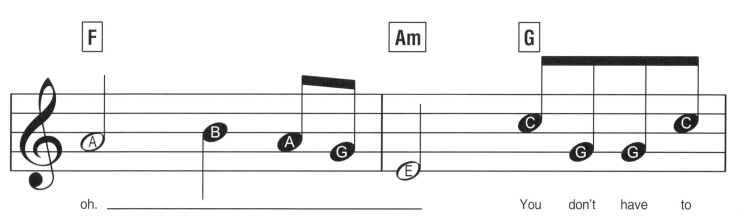

oh. _____ You don't have to

change a thing; the world could change its heart. No scars to your beau -

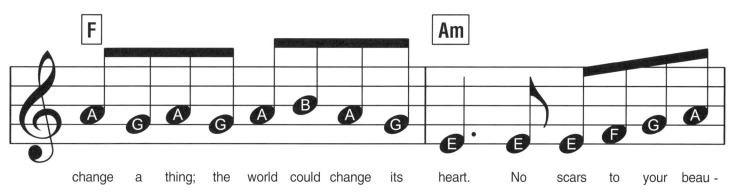

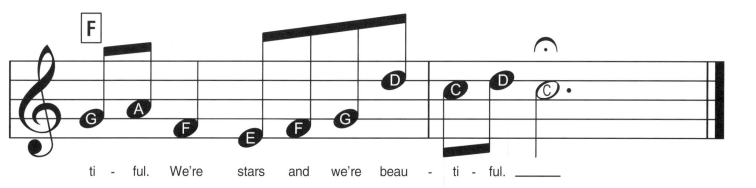

ti - ful. We're stars and we're beau - ti - ful. _____

Señorita

Registration 4
Rhythm: Latin or Pop

Words and Music by Camila Cabello,
Charlotte Aitchison, Jack Patterson,
Shawn Mendes, Magnus Hoiberg,
Benjamin Levin, Ali Tamposi
and Andrew Wotman

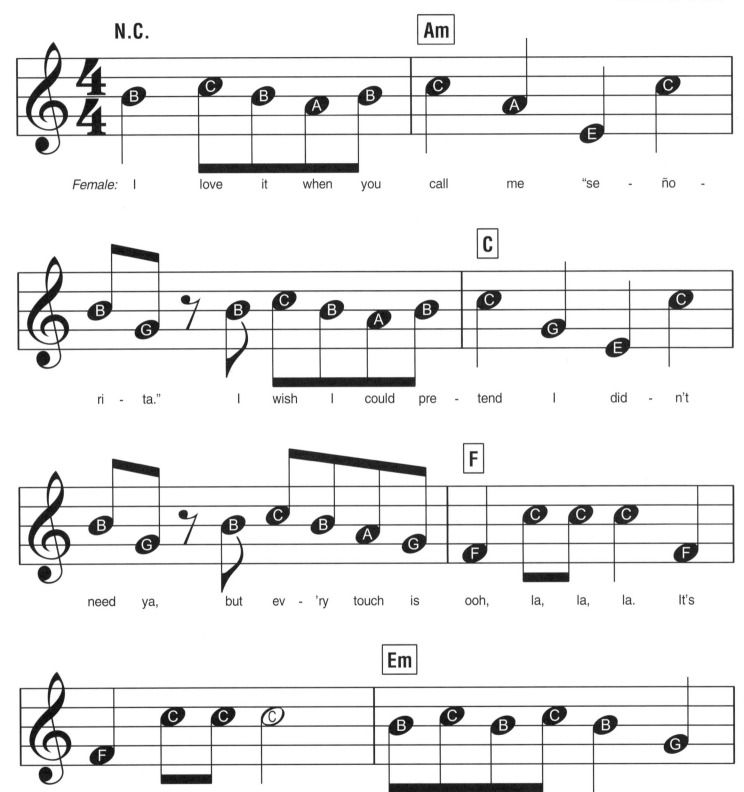

275

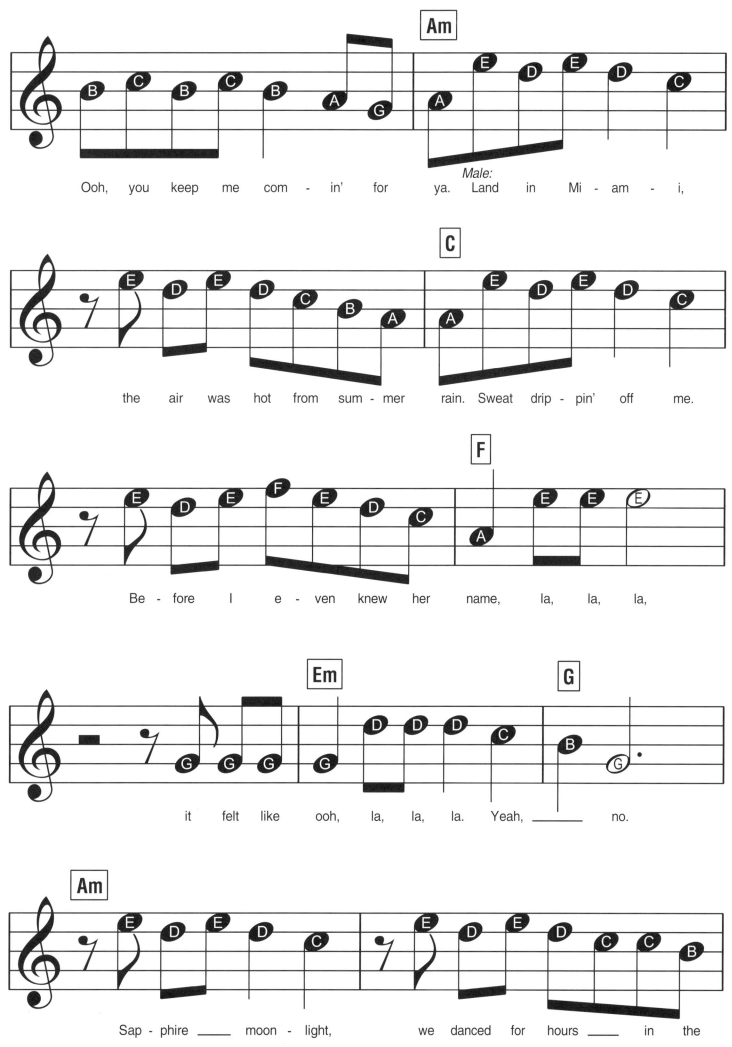

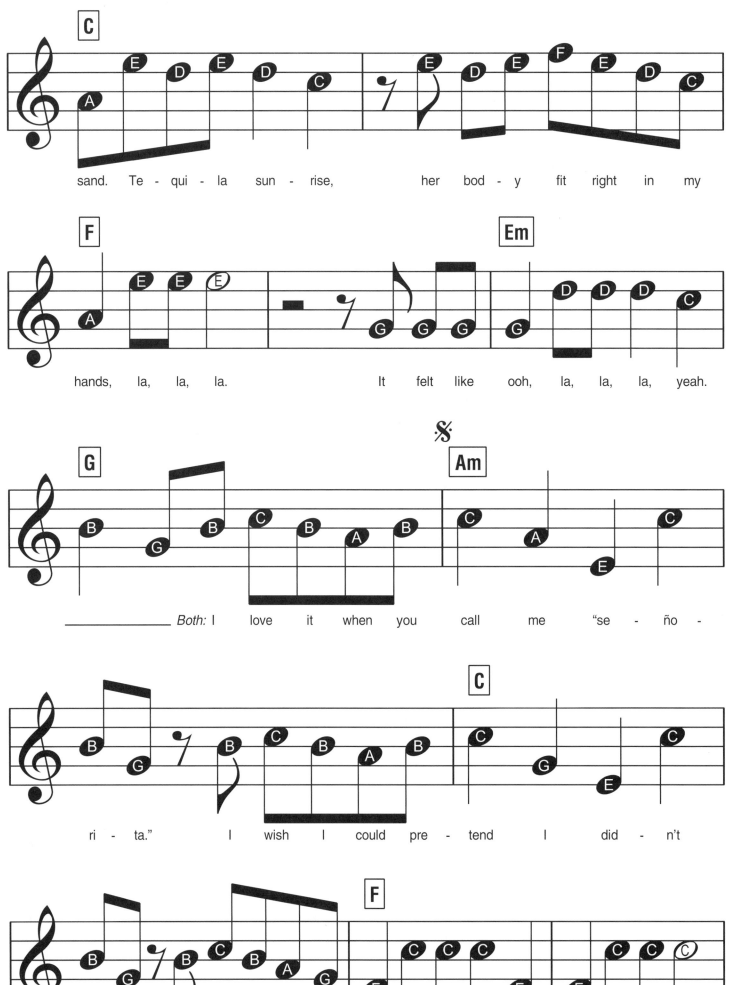

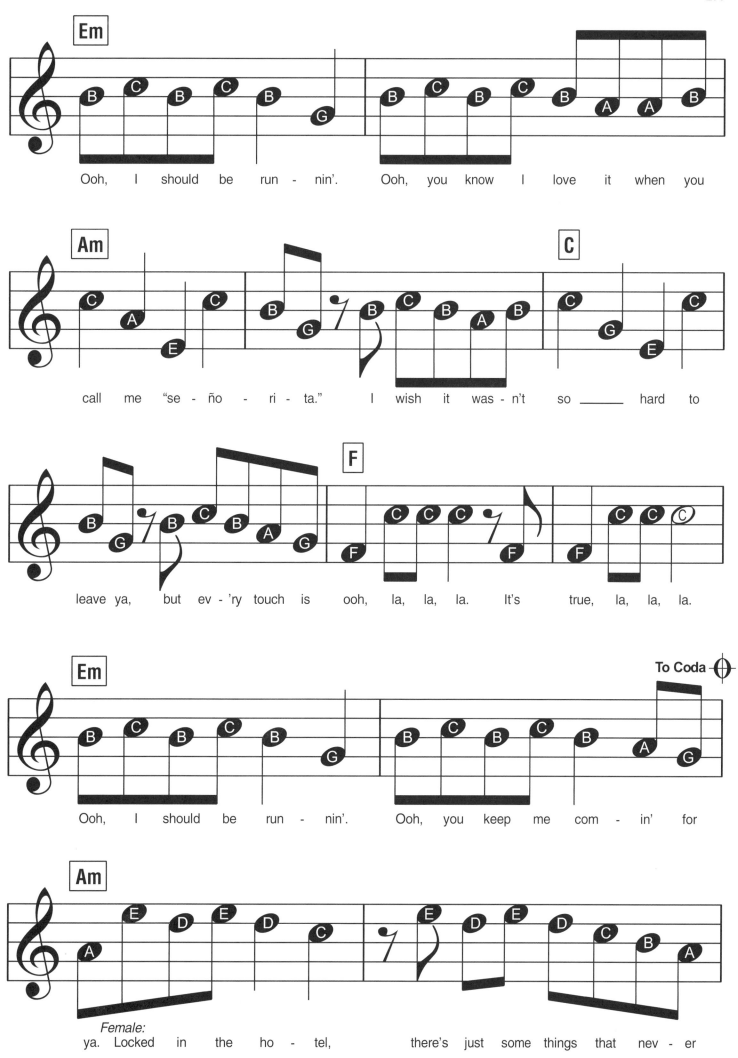

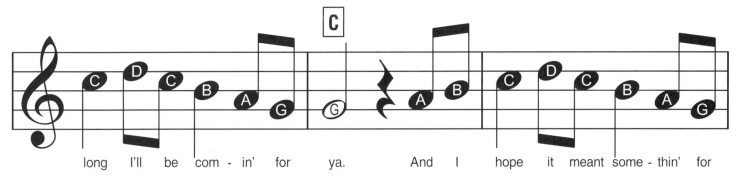

long I'll be com - in' for ya. And I hope it meant some - thin' for

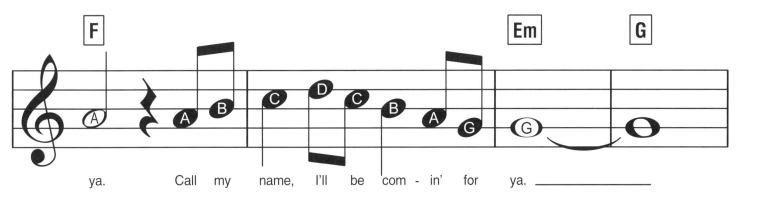

ya. Call my name, I'll be com - in' for ya. _____

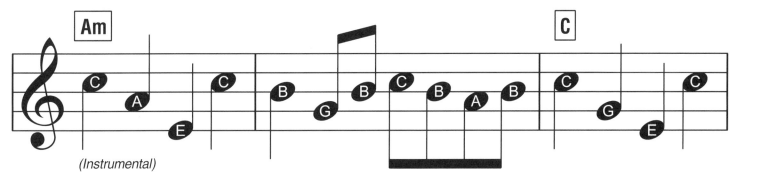

(Instrumental)

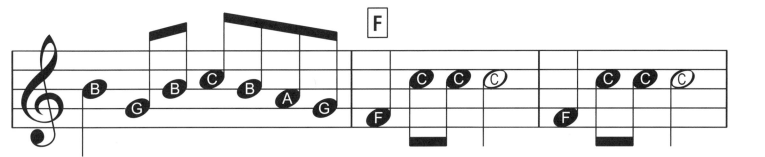

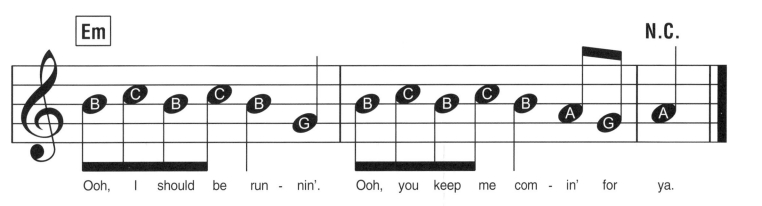

Ooh, I should be run - nin'. Ooh, you keep me com - in' for ya.

7 Years

Registration 2
Rhythm: Rock or 8-Beat

Words and Music by Lukas Forchhammer,
Morten Ristorp, Stefan Forrest,
David Labrel, Christopher Brown
and Morten Pilegaard

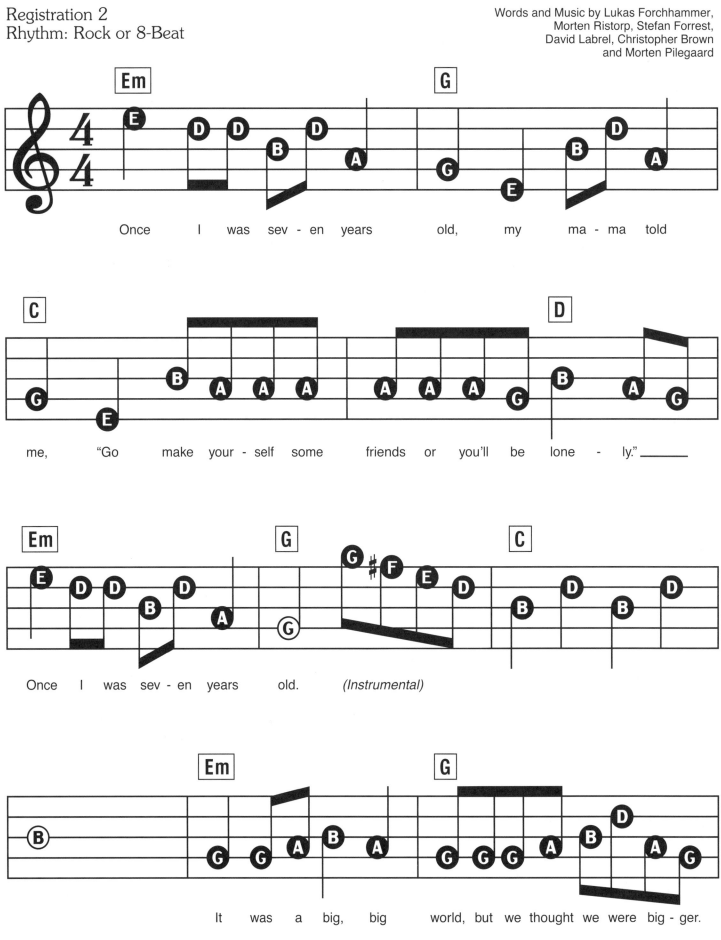

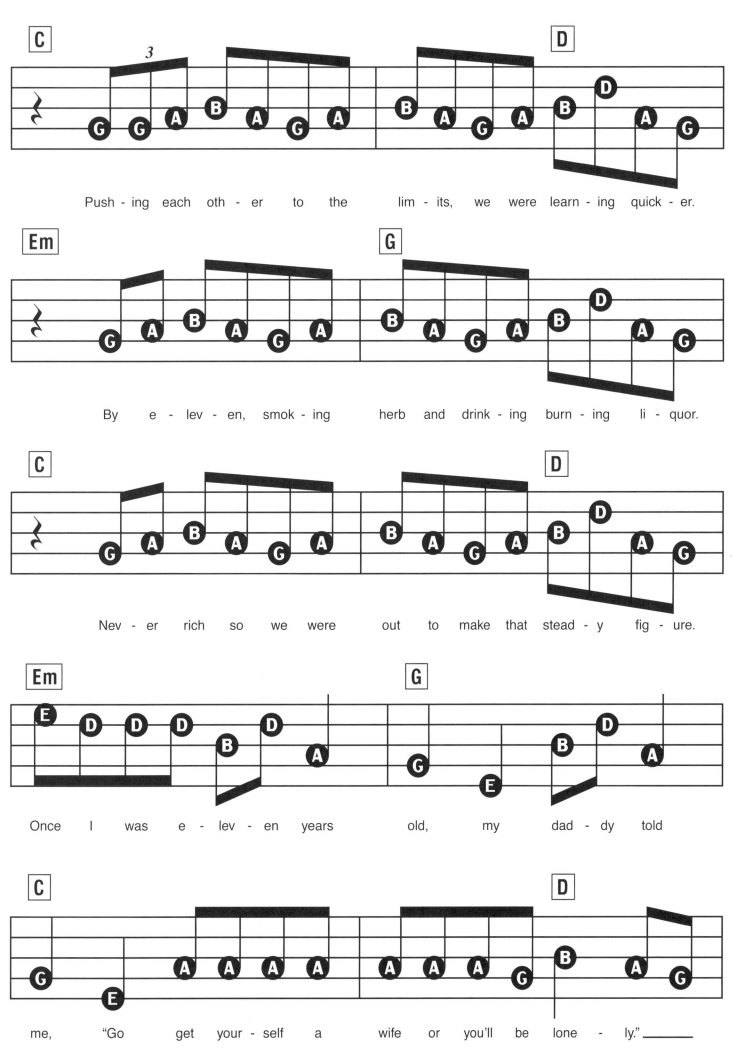

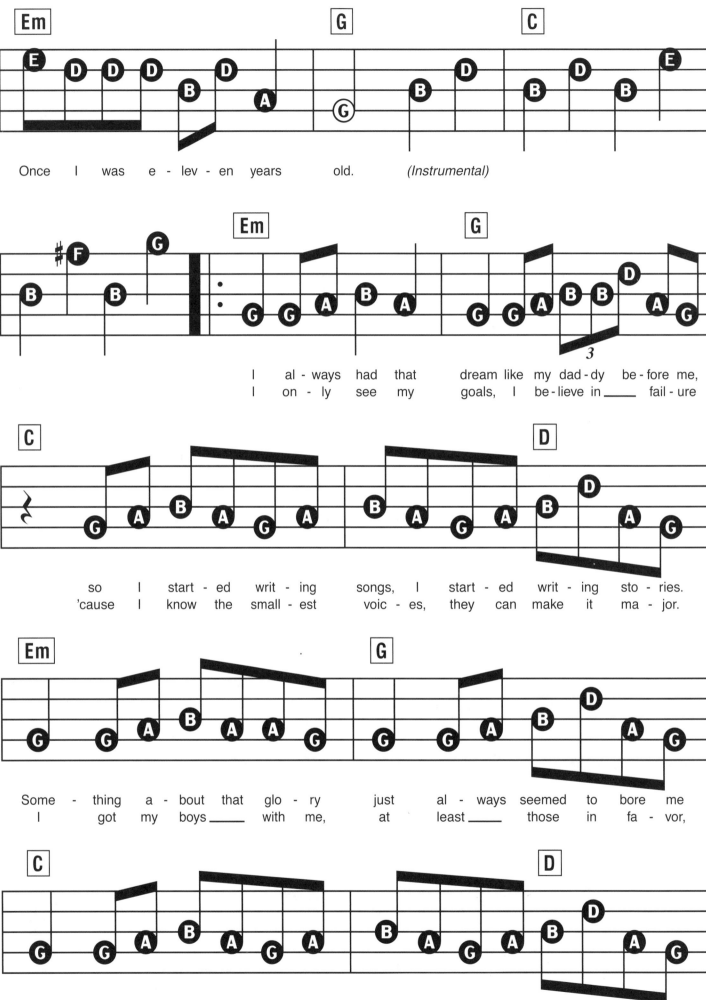

283

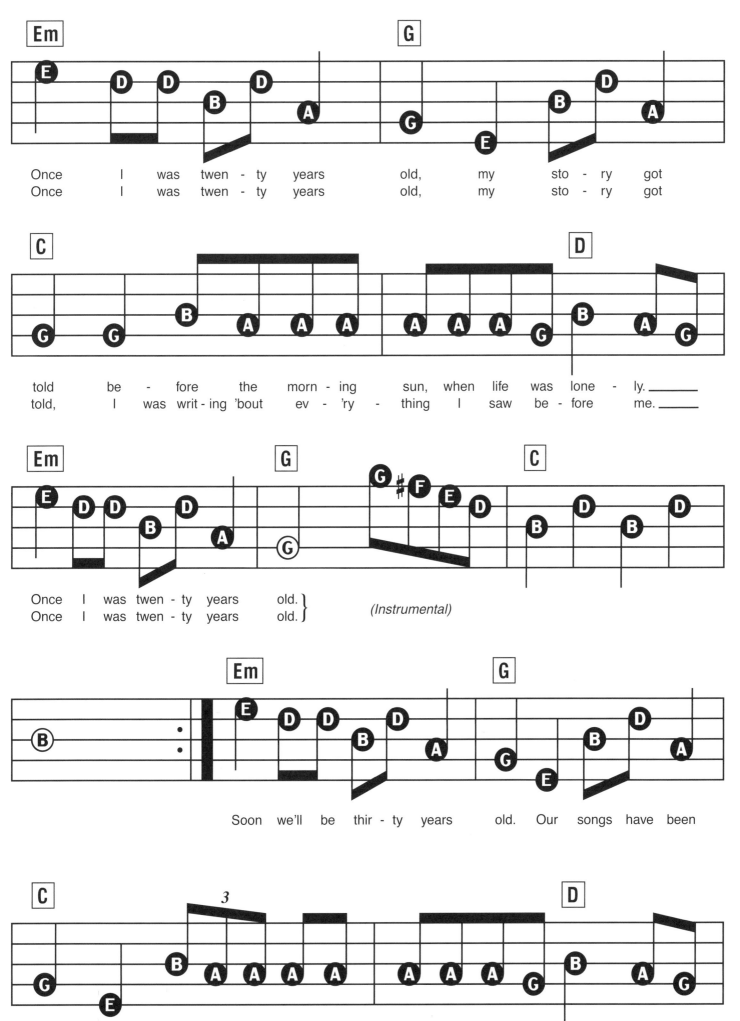

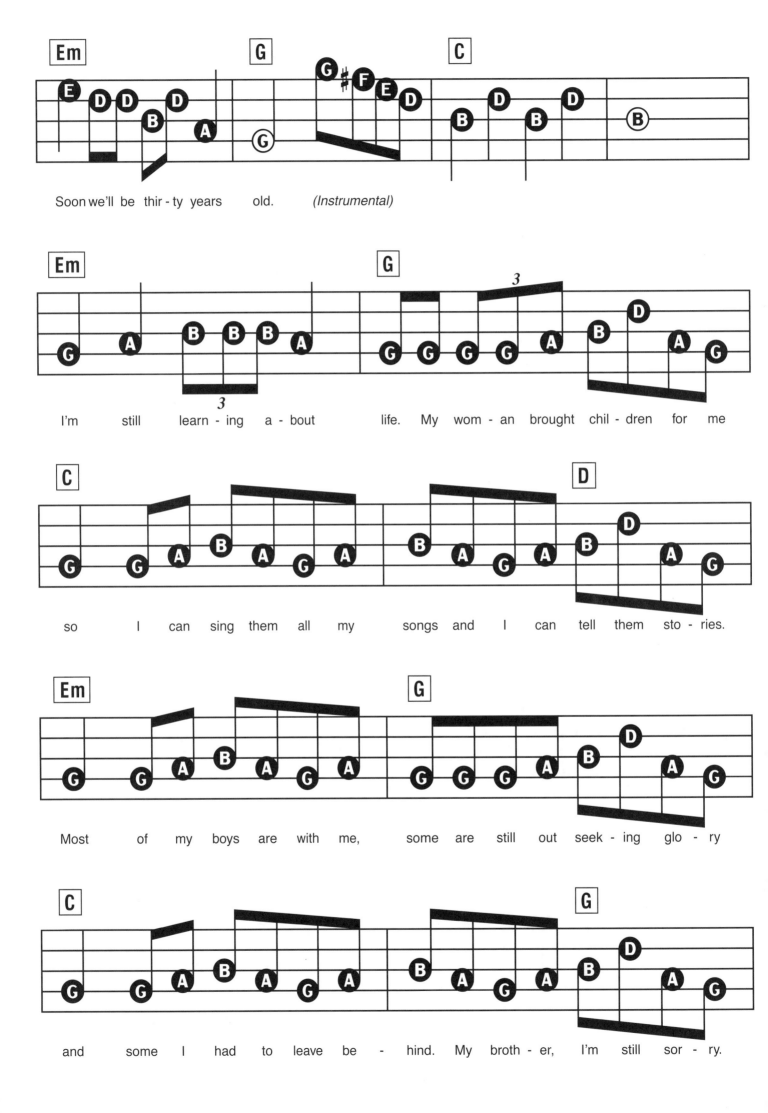

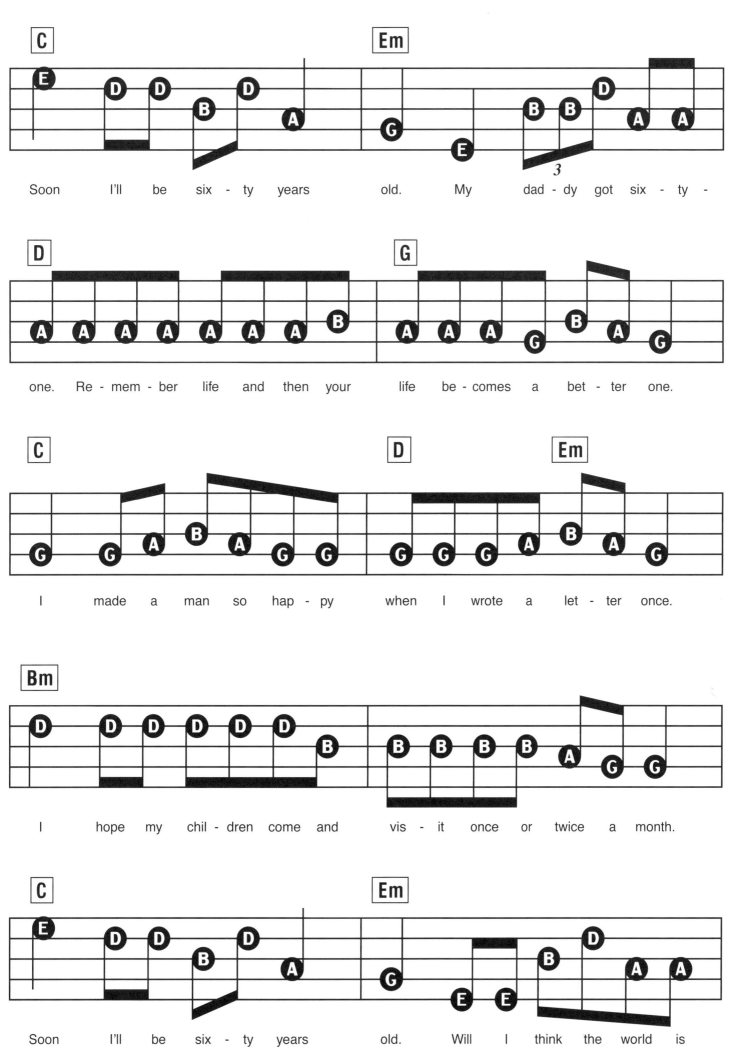

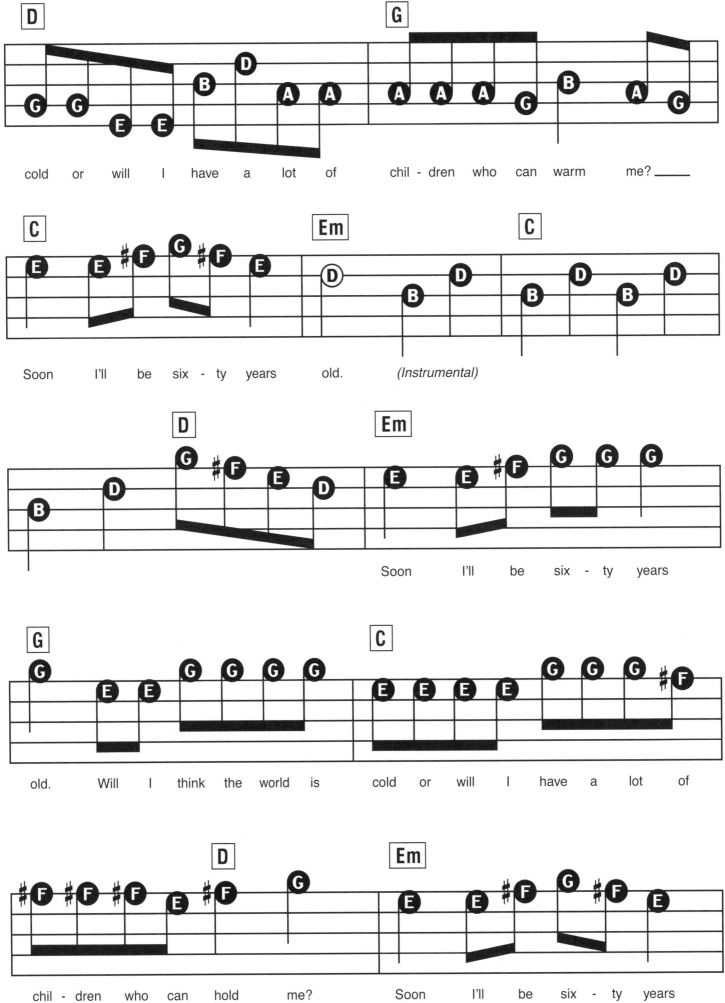

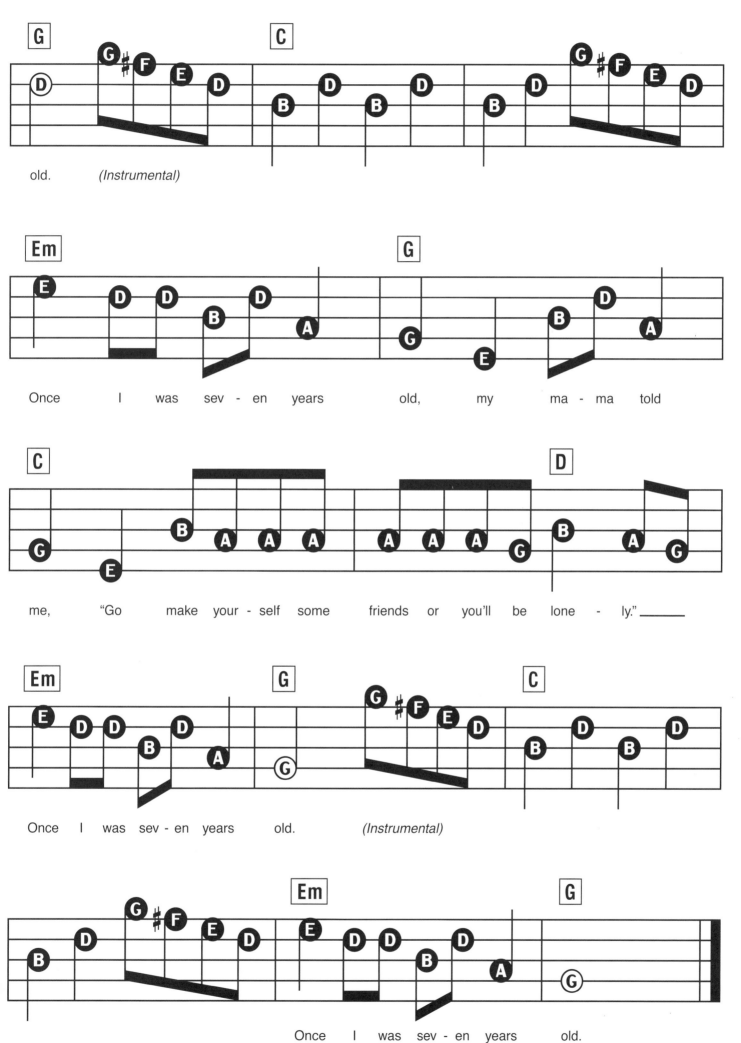

old.   *(Instrumental)*

Once I was sev - en years   old,   my   ma - ma told

me,   "Go   make your - self some   friends or you'll be   lone - ly." _____

Once I was sev - en years   old.   *(Instrumental)*

Once I was sev - en years   old.

Shake It Off

Registration 9
Rhythm: Pop or Dance

Words and Music by Taylor Swift,
Max Martin and Shellback

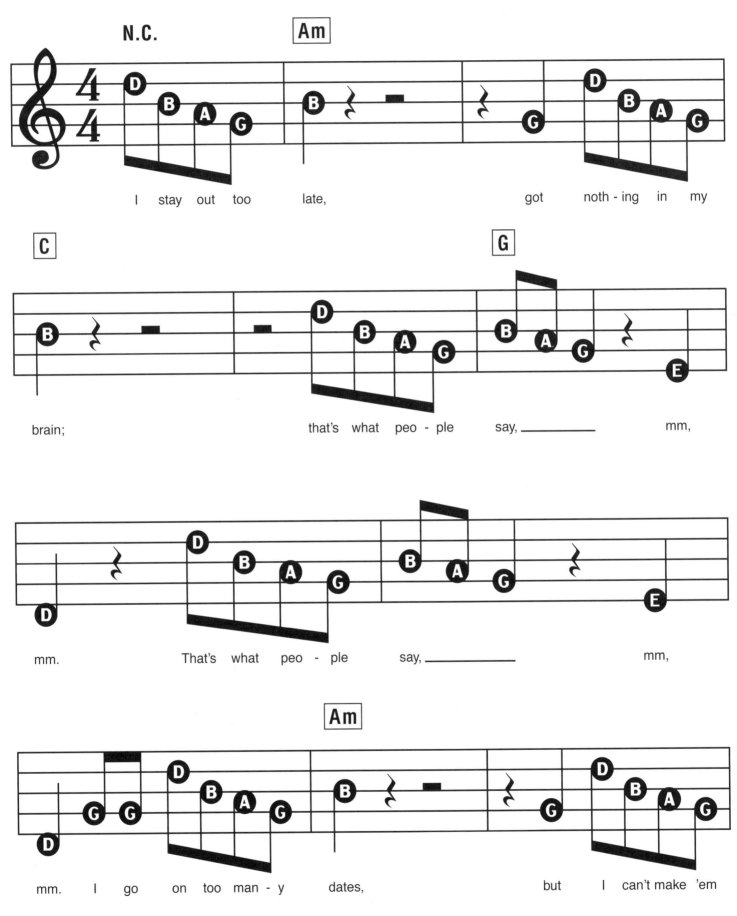

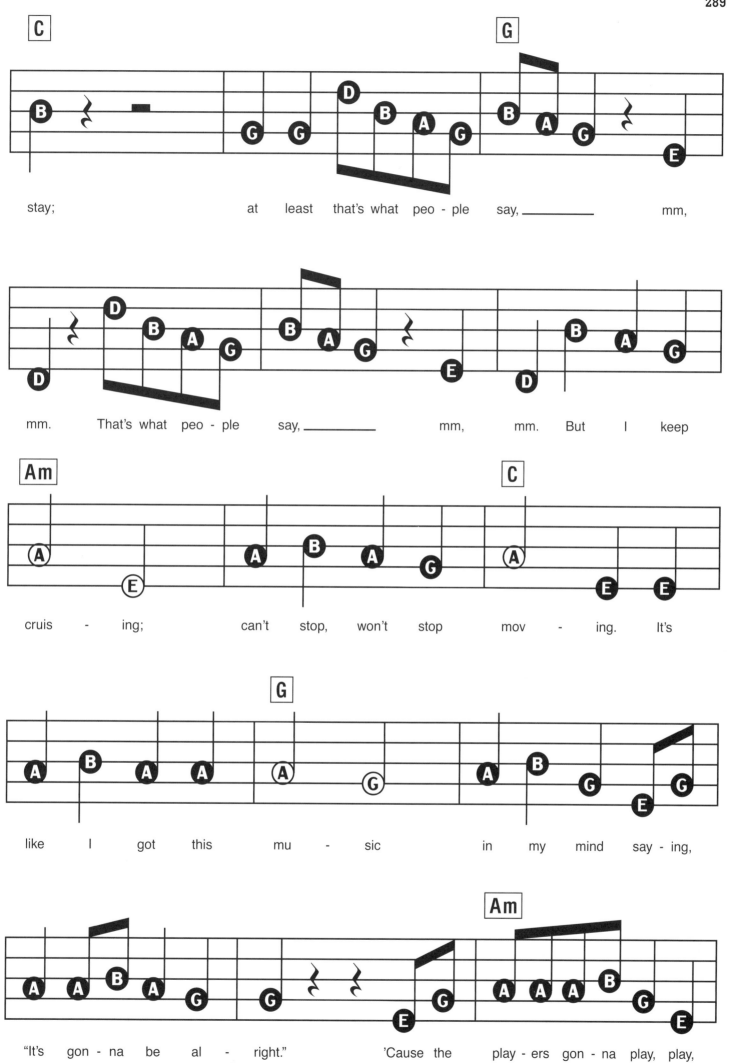

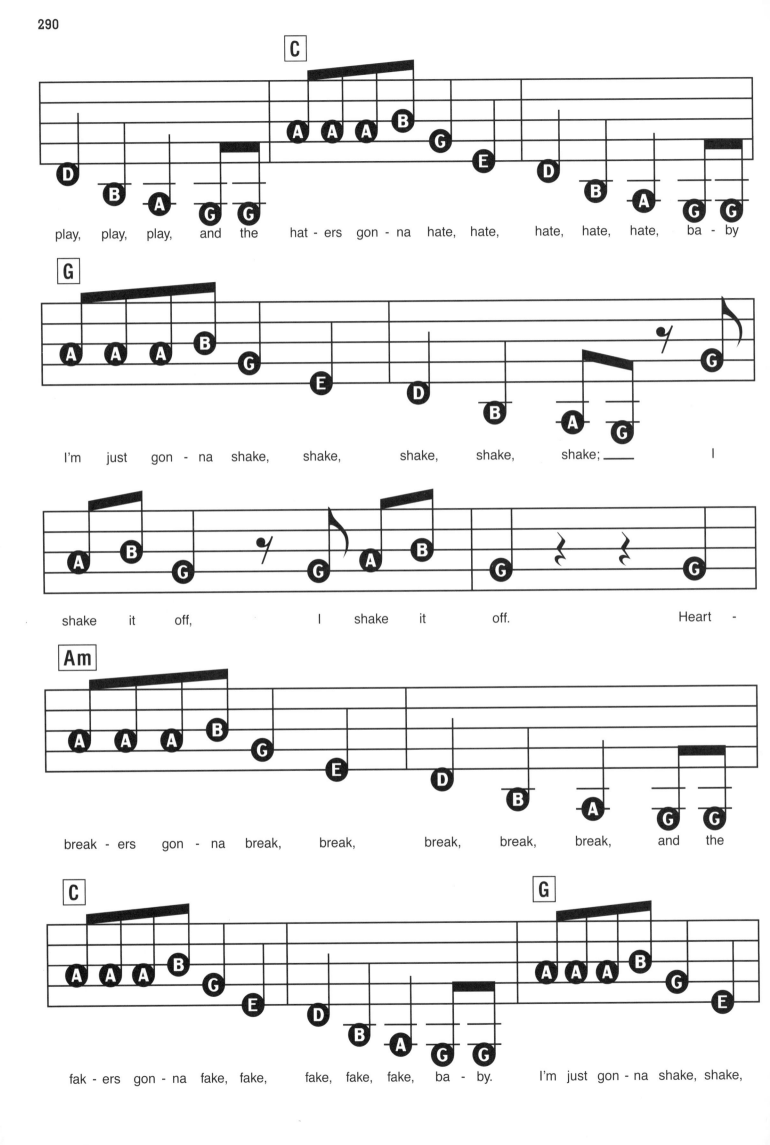

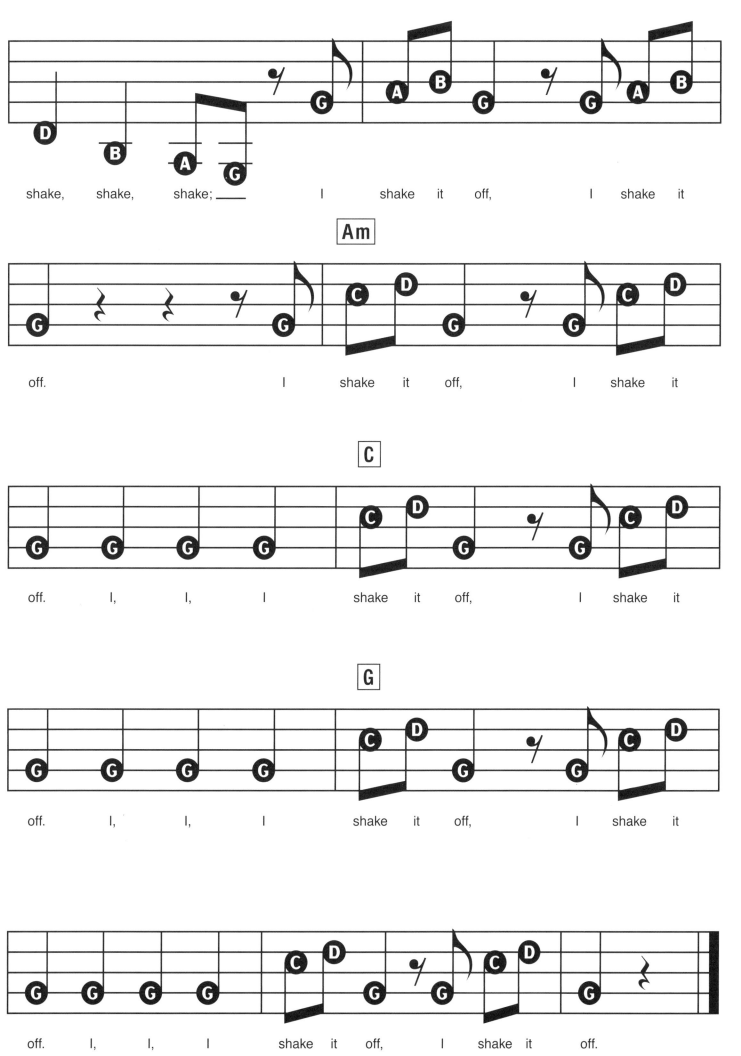

Shallow
from A STAR IS BORN

Registration 4
Rhythm: Folk

Words and Music by Stefani Germanotta,
Mark Ronson, Andrew Wyatt and Anthony Rossomando

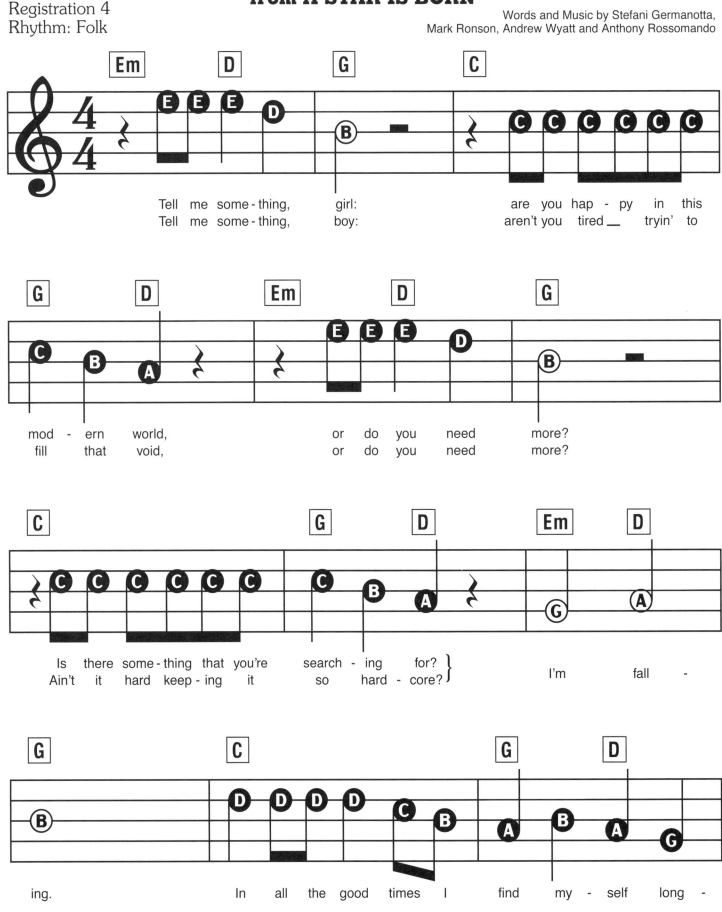

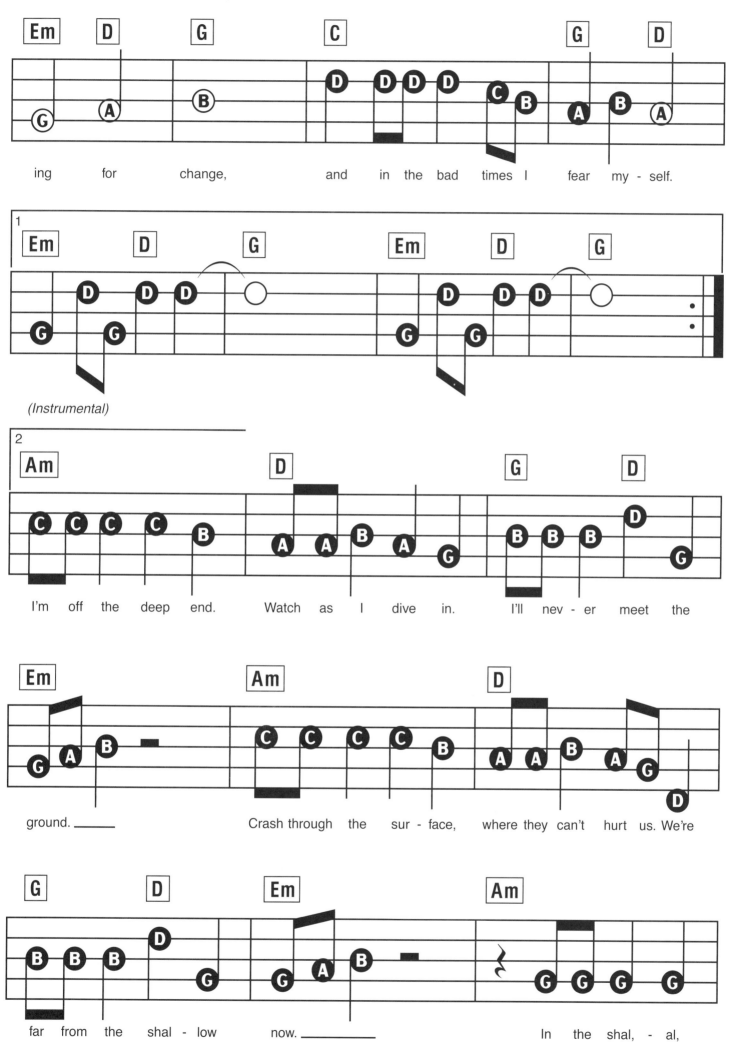

293

294

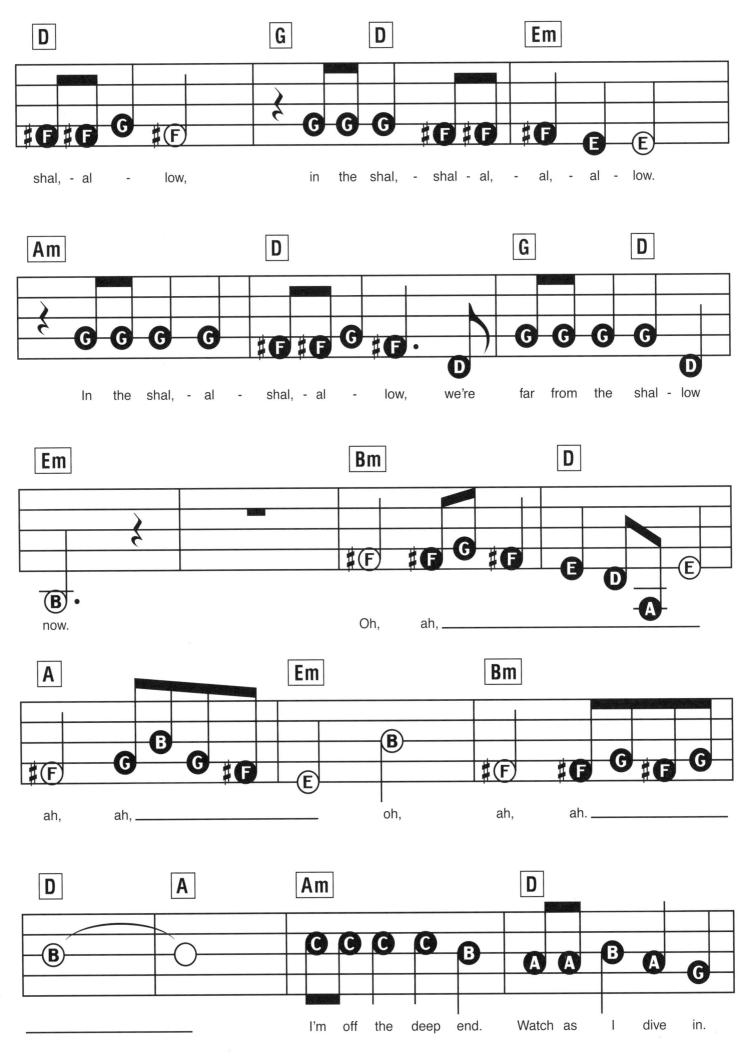

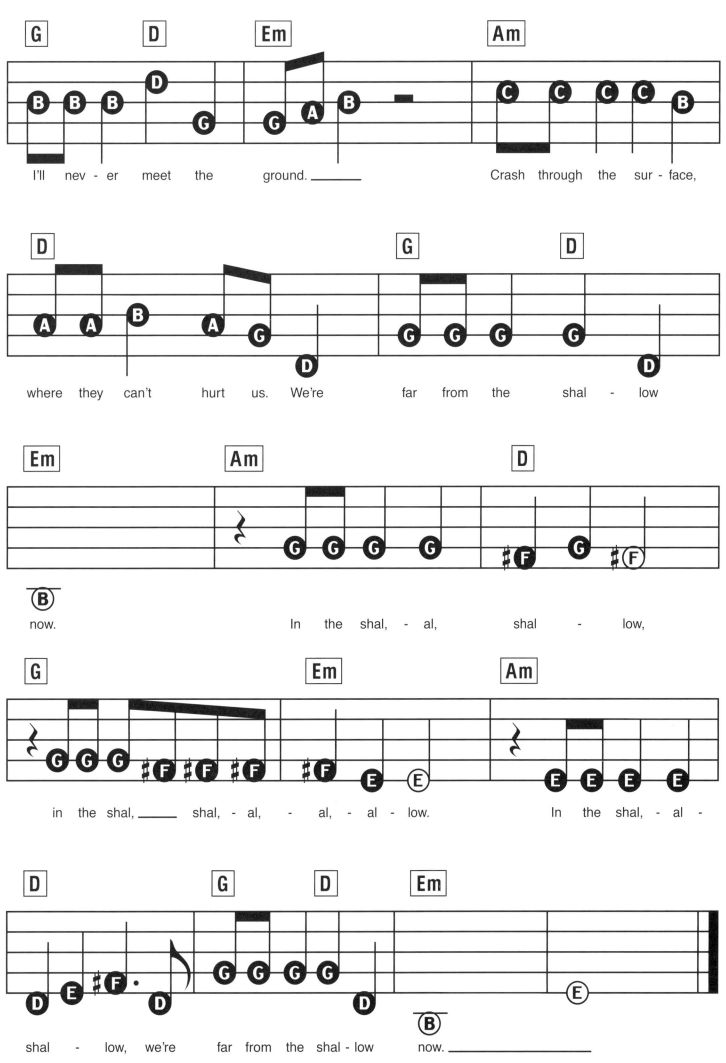

A Sky Full of Stars

Registration 8
Rhythm: Dance or Rock

Words and Music by Guy Berryman,
Jon Buckland, Will Champion,
Chris Martin and Tim Bergling

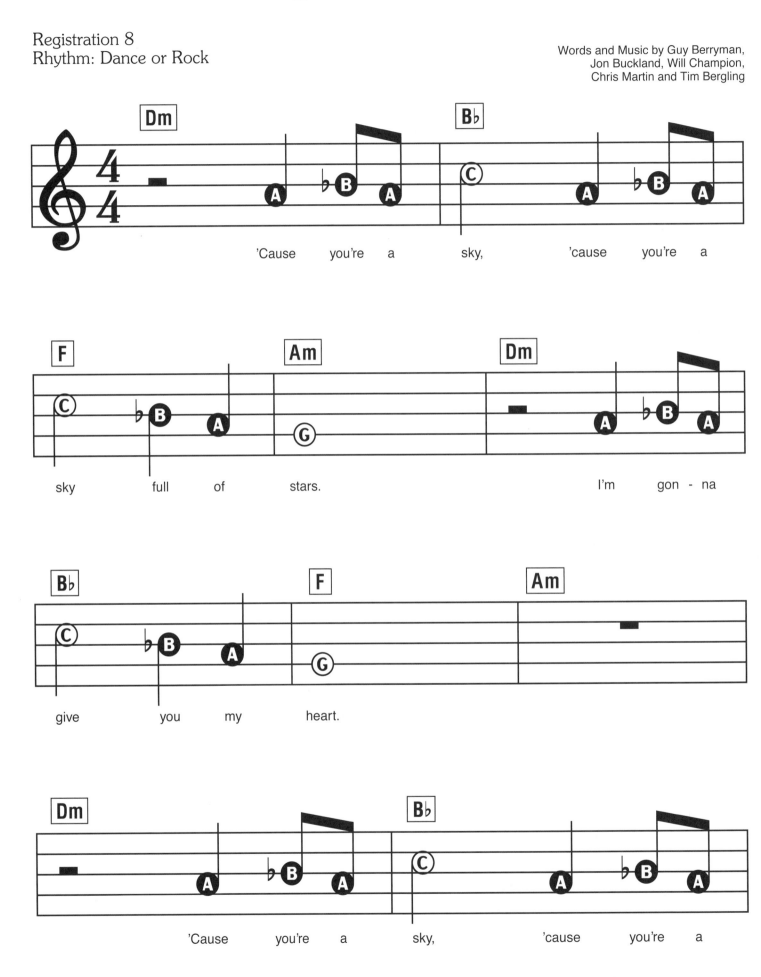

297

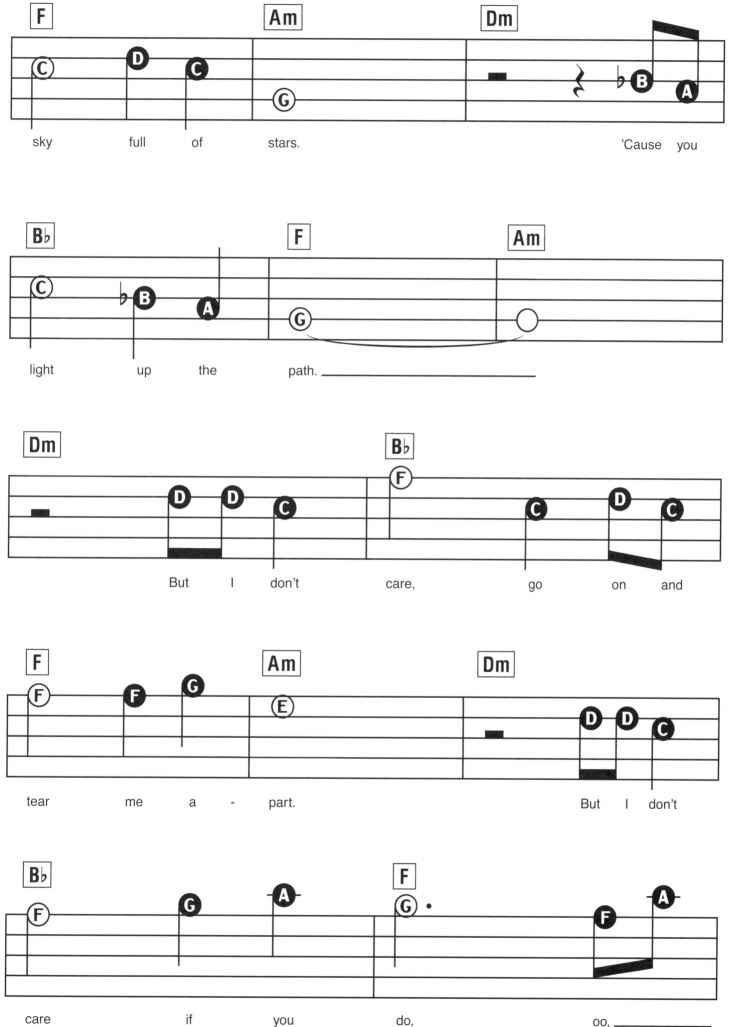

298

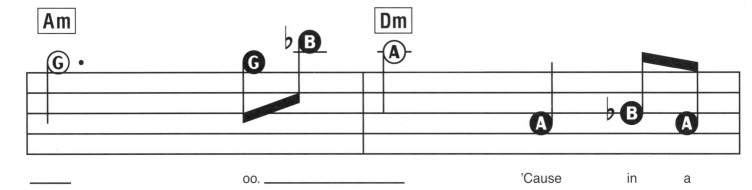

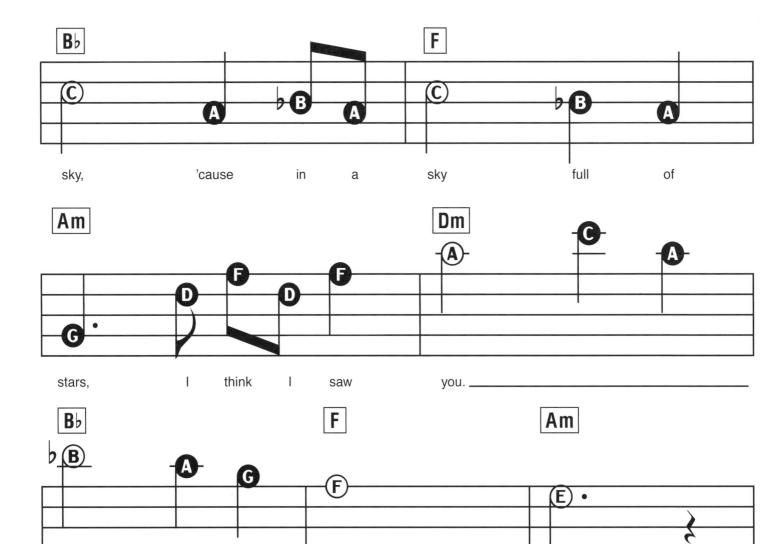

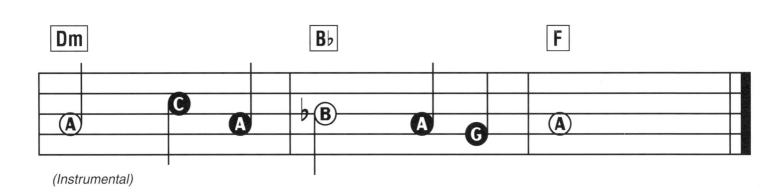

oo. _____ 'Cause in a sky, 'cause in a sky full of stars, I think I saw you. _____

(Instrumental)

There's Nothing Holdin' Me Back

Registration 4
Rhythm: Pop or Rock

Words and Music by Shawn Mendes,
Geoffrey Warburton, Teddy Geiger
and Scott Harris

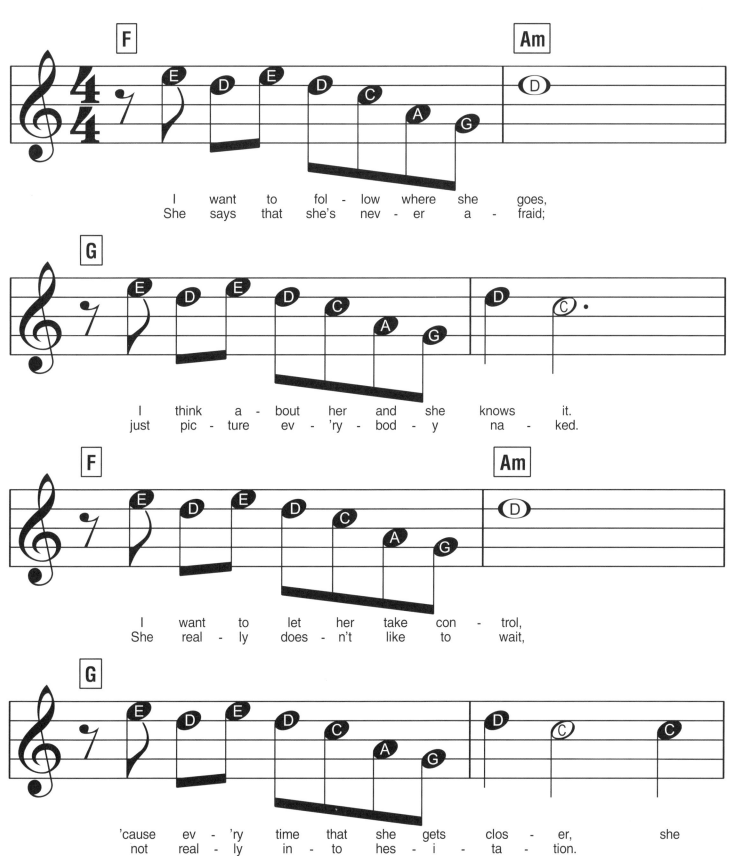

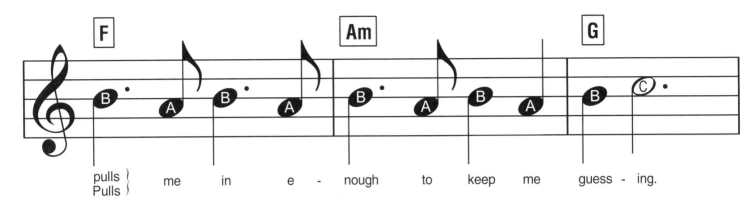

pulls } me in e - nough to keep me guess - ing.
Pulls }

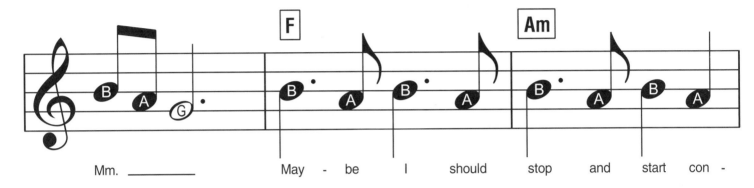

Mm. _____ May - be I should stop and start con -

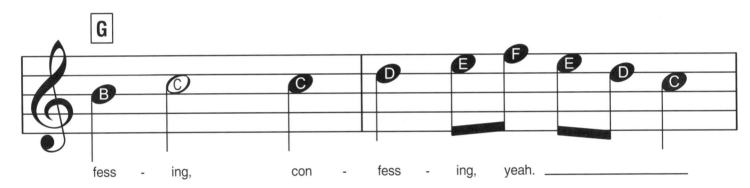

fess - ing, con - fess - ing, yeah. _____

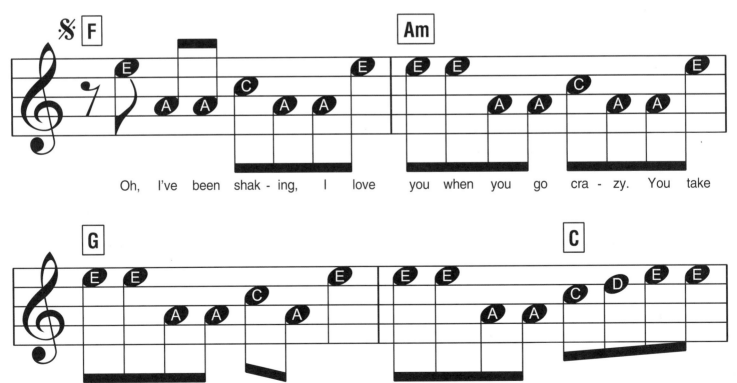

Oh, I've been shak - ing, I love you when you go cra - zy. You take

all my in - hi - bi - tions. Ba - by, there's noth - ing hold - in' me back.

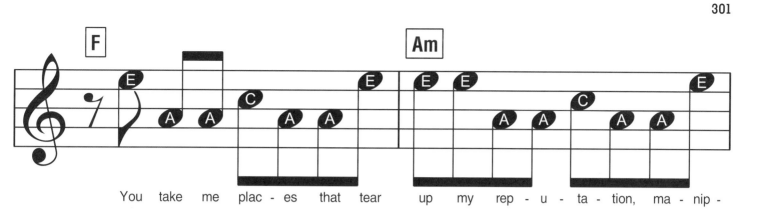

You take me plac - es that tear up my rep - u - ta - tion, ma - nip -

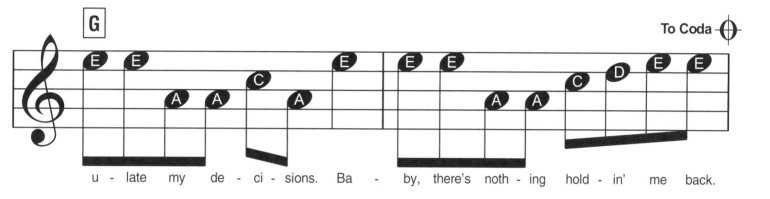

u - late my de - ci - sions. Ba - by, there's noth - ing hold - in' me back.

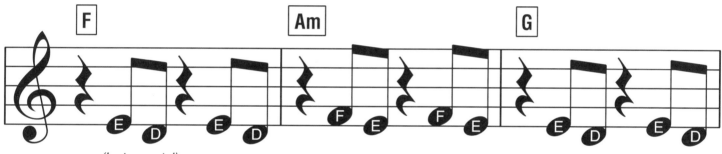

(Instrumental)

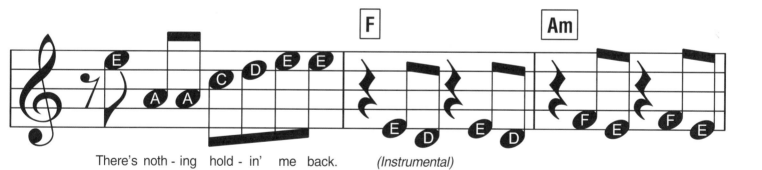

There's noth - ing hold - in' me back. (Instrumental)

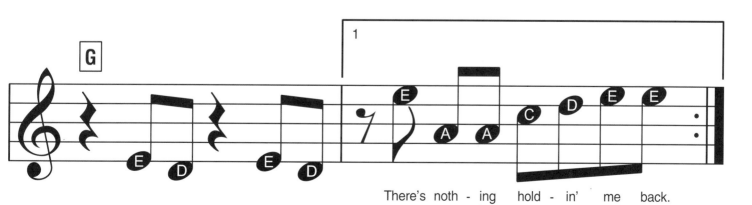

There's noth - ing hold - in' me back.

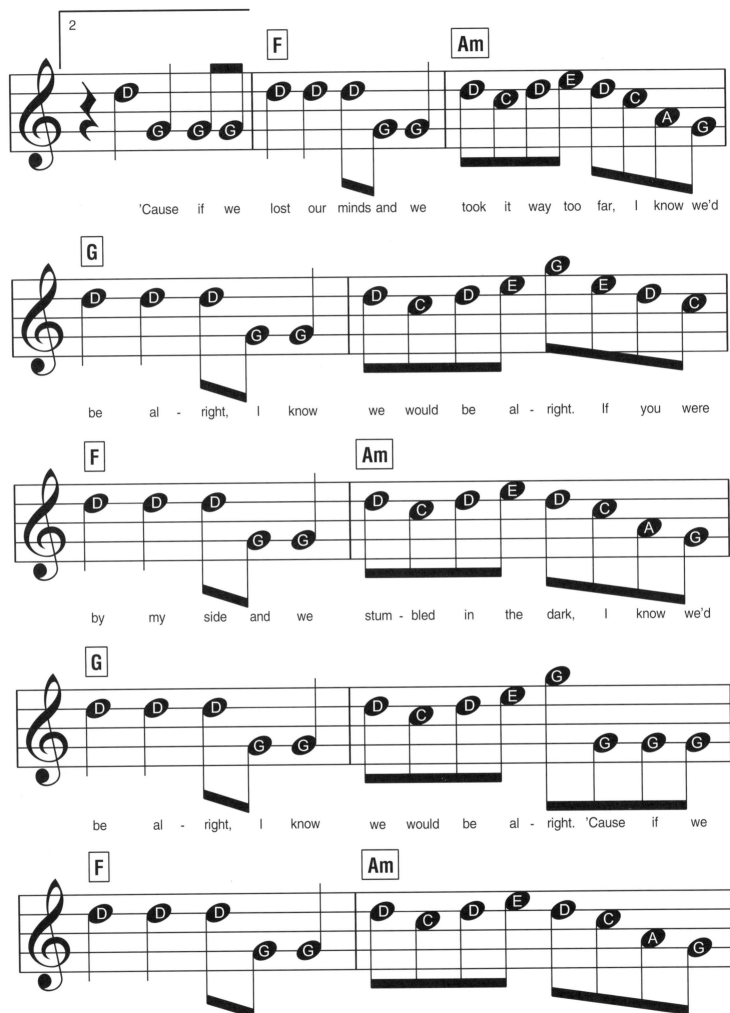

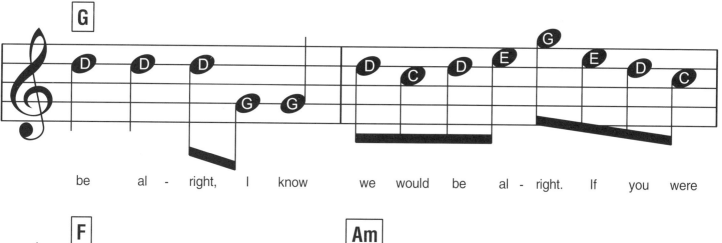

be al - right, I know we would be al - right. If you were

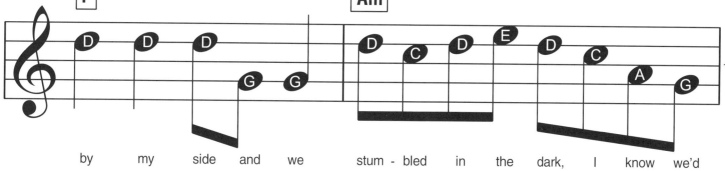

by my side and we stum - bled in the dark, I know we'd

D.S. al Coda
(Return to ℅, play to ⊕ and skip to Coda)

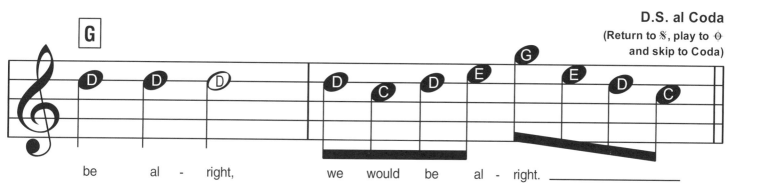

be al - right, we would be al - right. _____

CODA

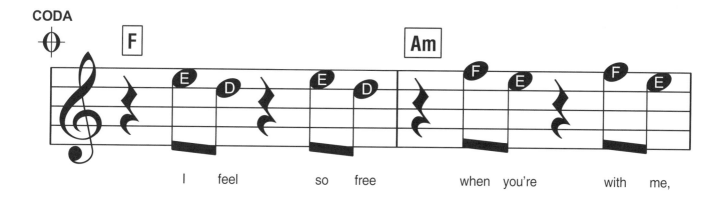

I feel so free when you're with me,

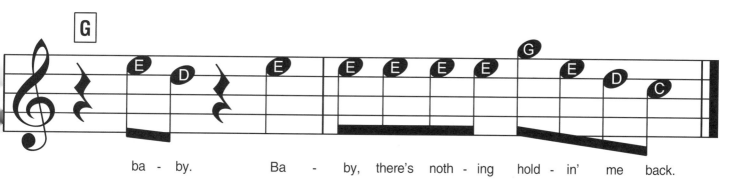

ba - by. Ba - by, there's noth - ing hold - in' me back.

Someone You Loved

Registration 8
Rhythm: Ballad

Words and Music by Lewis Capaldi,
Benjamin Kohn, Peter Kelleher,
Thomas Barnes and Samuel Roman

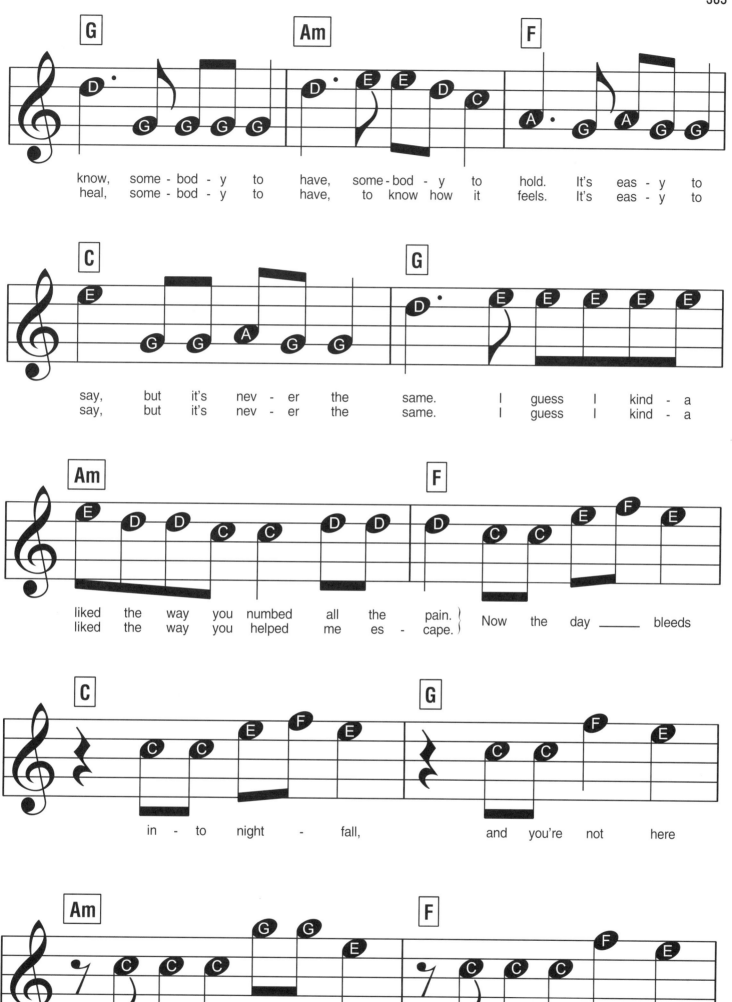

know, some-bod-y to have, some-bod-y to hold. It's eas-y to
heal, some-bod-y to have, to know how it feels. It's eas-y to

say, but it's nev-er the same. I guess I kind-a
say, but it's nev-er the same. I guess I kind-a

liked the way you numbed all the pain. } Now the day _____ bleeds
liked the way you helped me es-cape.

in-to night-fall, and you're not here

to get me through it all. I let my guard down,

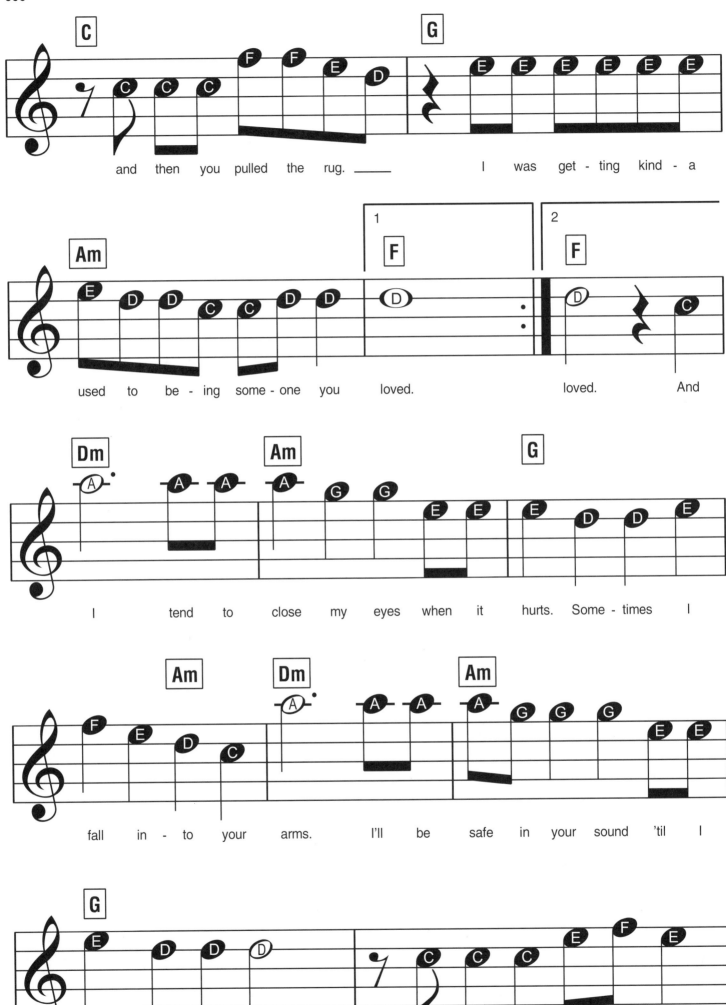

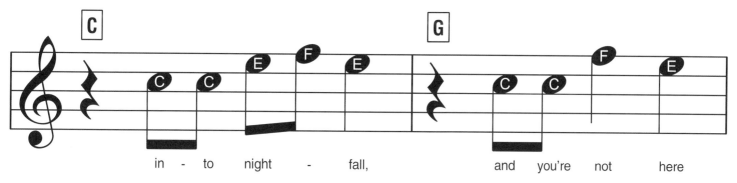

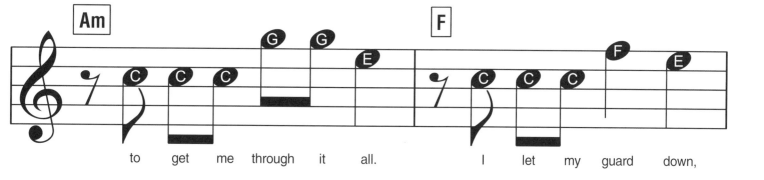

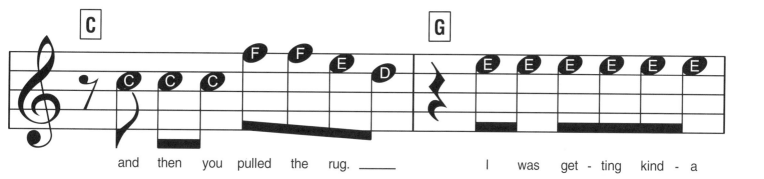

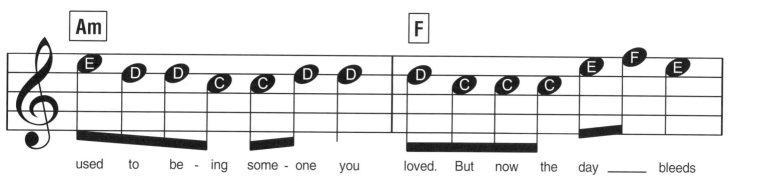

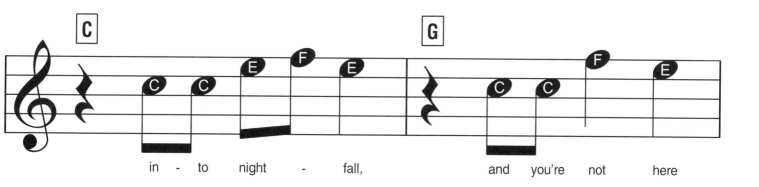

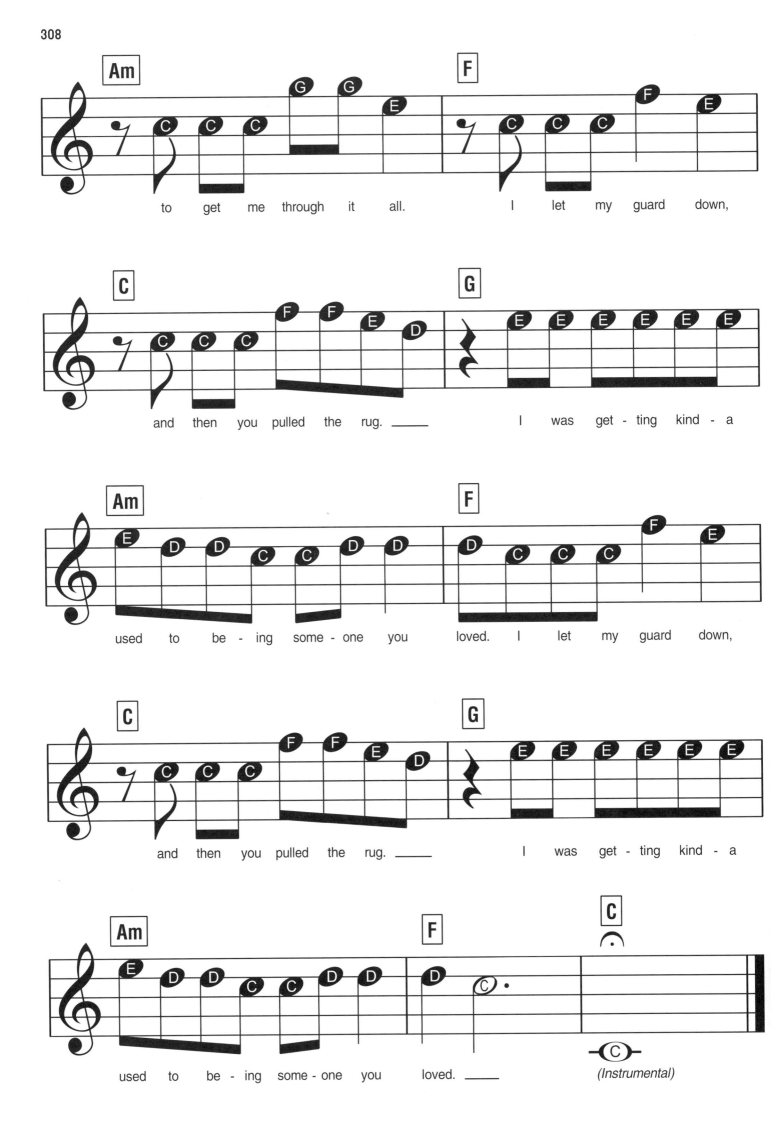

Someone Like You

Registration 2
Rhythm: 4/4 Ballad

Words and Music by Adele Adkins
and Dan Wilson

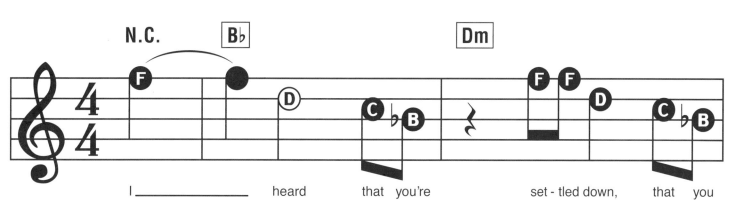

I _____ heard that you're set - tled down, that you

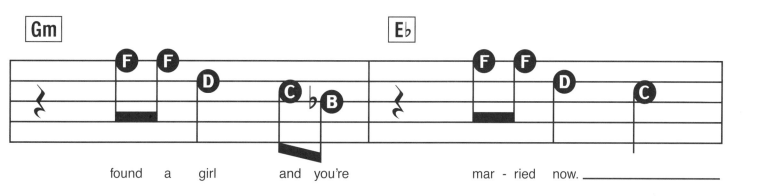

found a girl and you're mar - ried now. _____

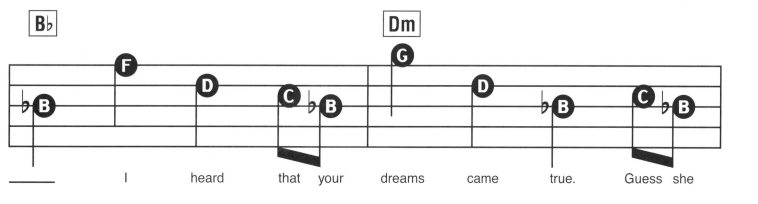

_____ I heard that your dreams came true. Guess she

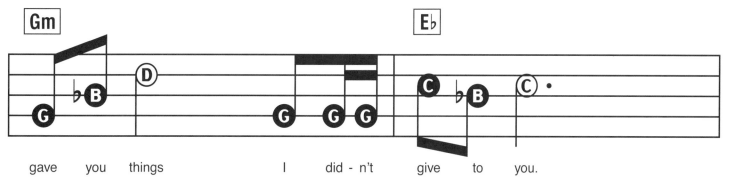

gave you things I did - n't give to you.

310

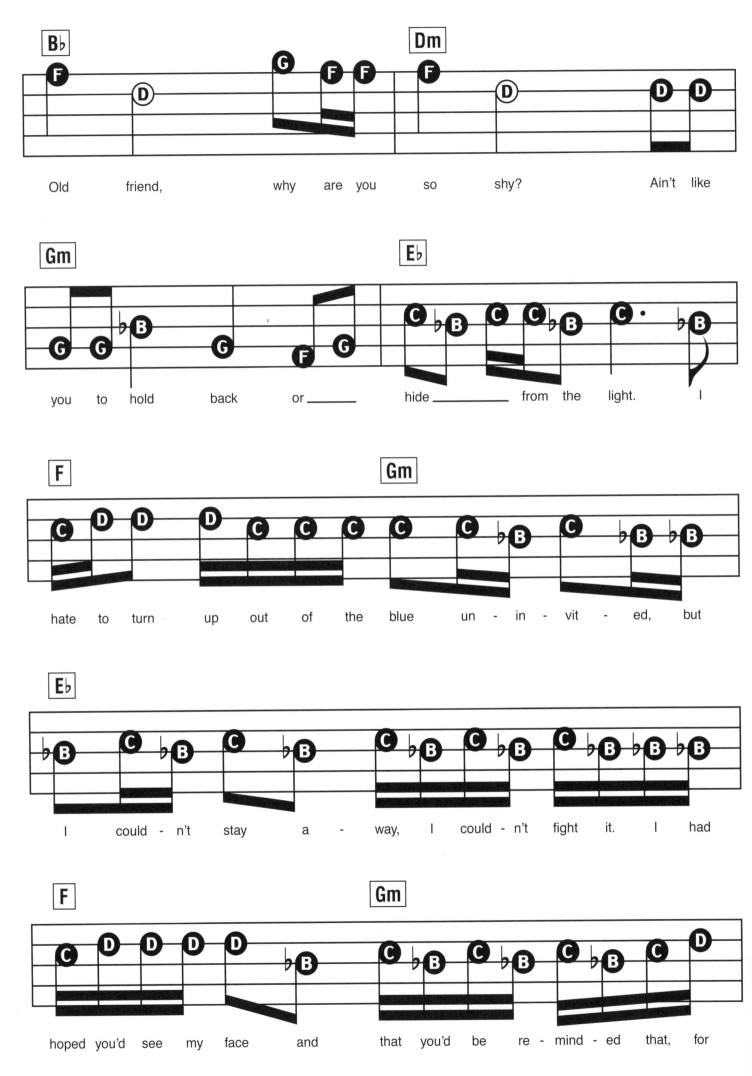

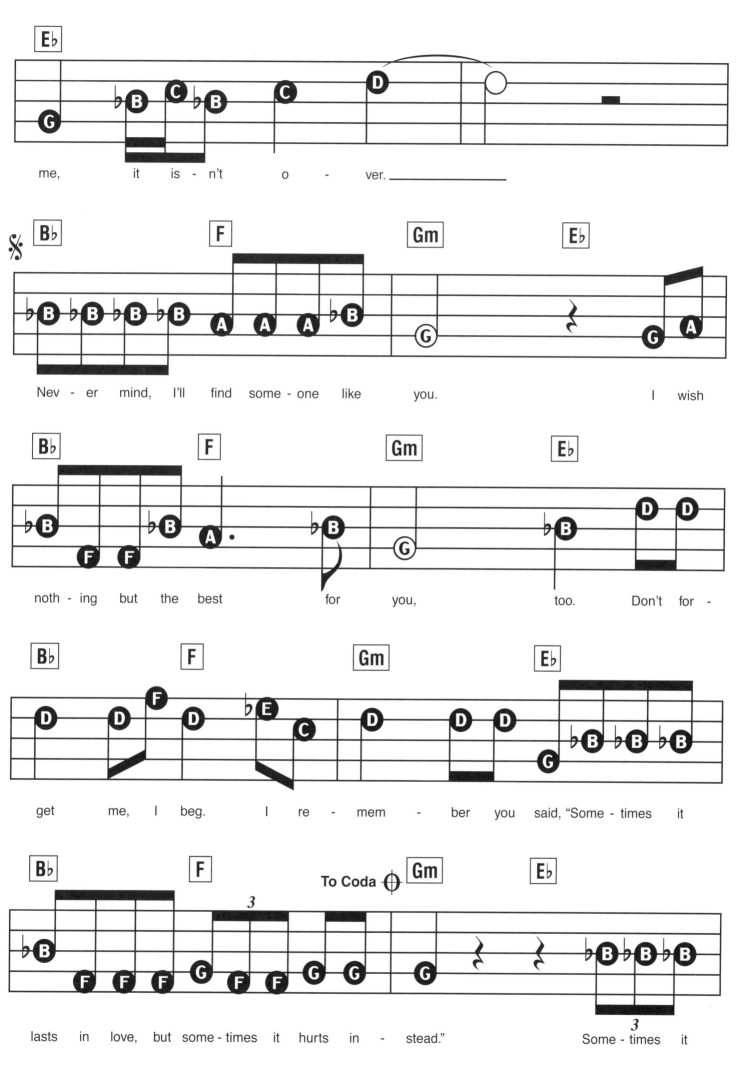

312

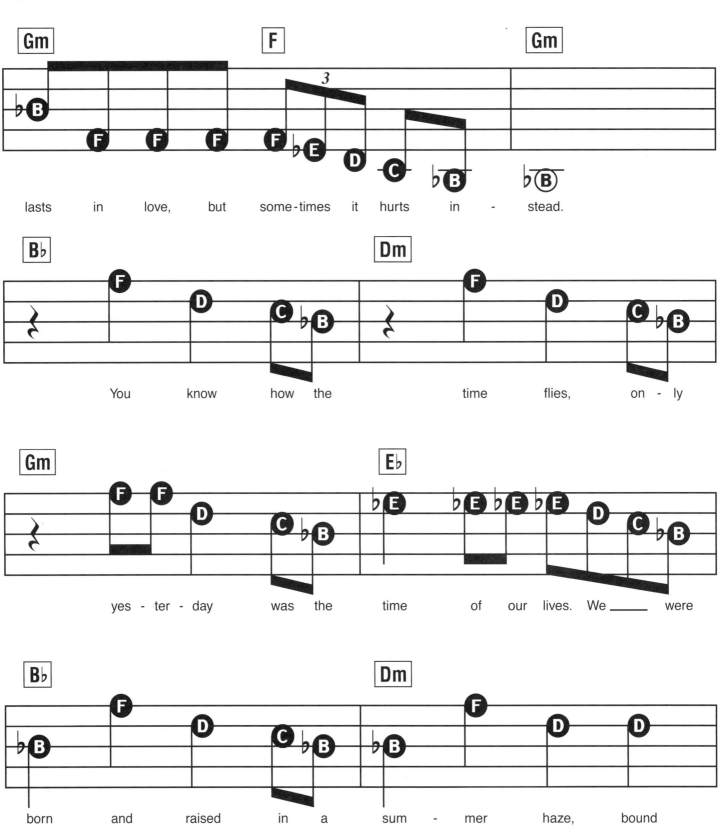

lasts in love, but some-times it hurts in - stead.

You know how the time flies, on - ly

yes - ter - day was the time of our lives. We _____ were

born and raised in a sum - mer haze, bound

by the sur - prise of our glo - ry days. I

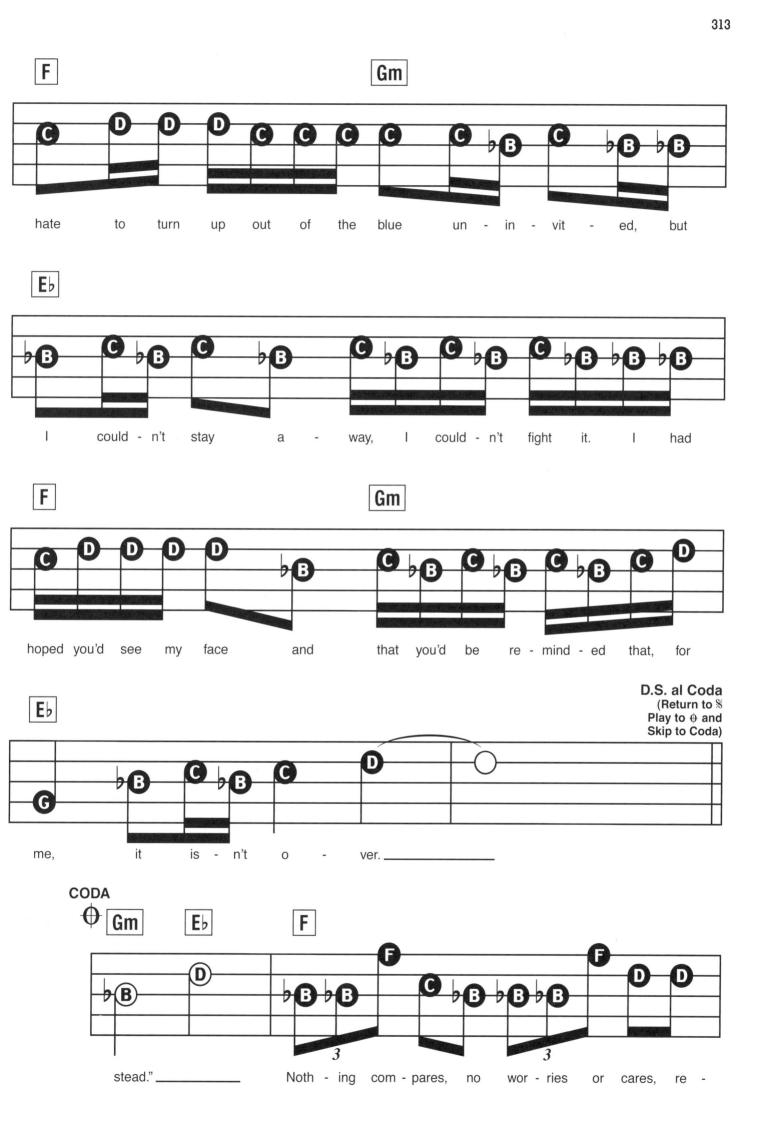

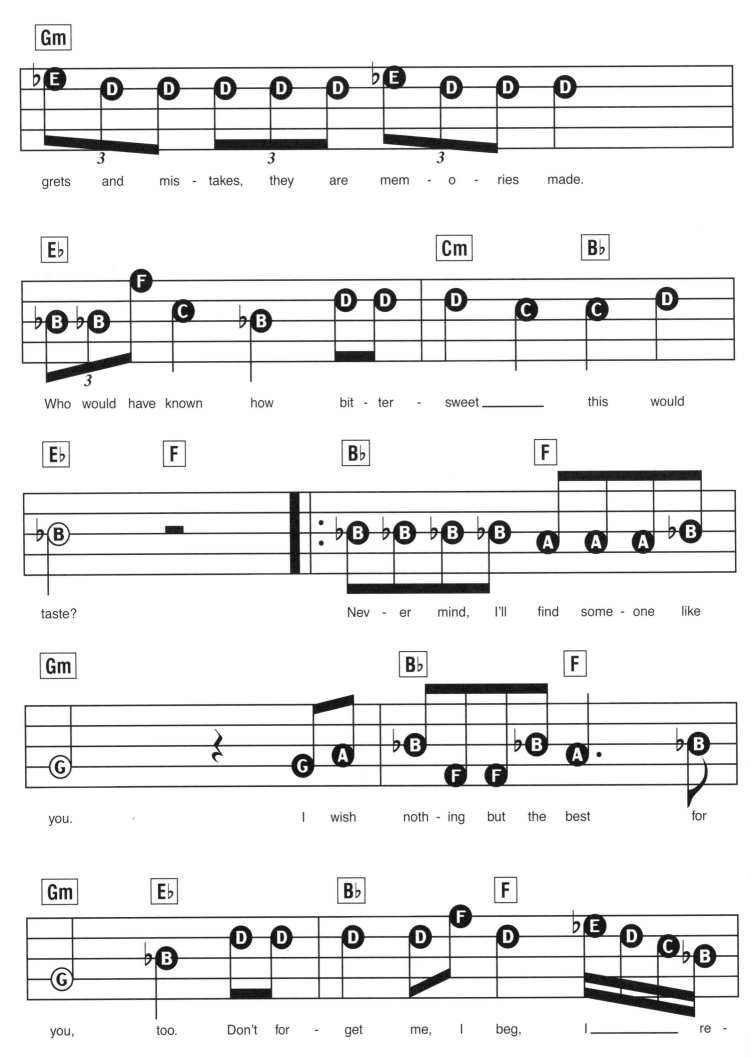

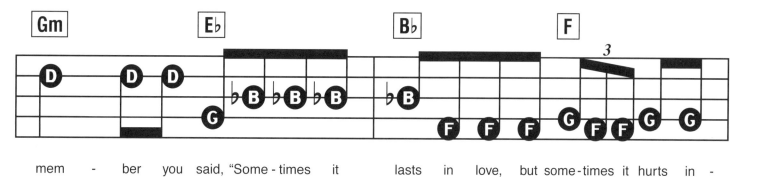

mem - ber you said, "Some - times it lasts in love, but some - times it hurts in -

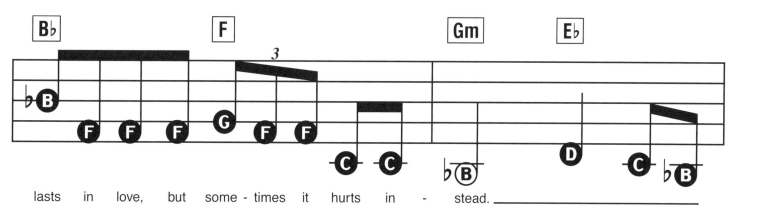

stead." _____

stead." _____ Some - times it

lasts in love, but some - times it hurts in - stead. _____

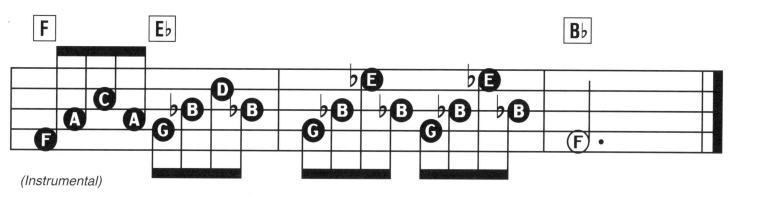

(Instrumental)

Speechless
from ALADDIN

Registration 2
Rhythm: Broadway

Music by Alan Menken
Lyrics by Benj Pasek and Justin Paul

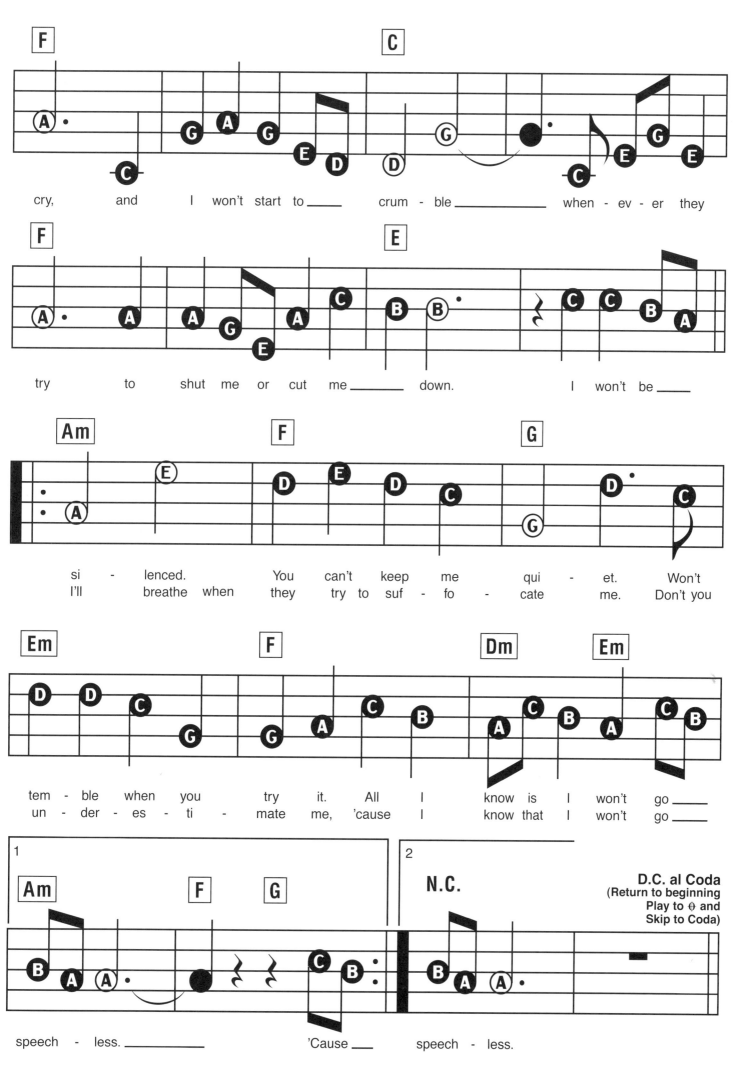

318

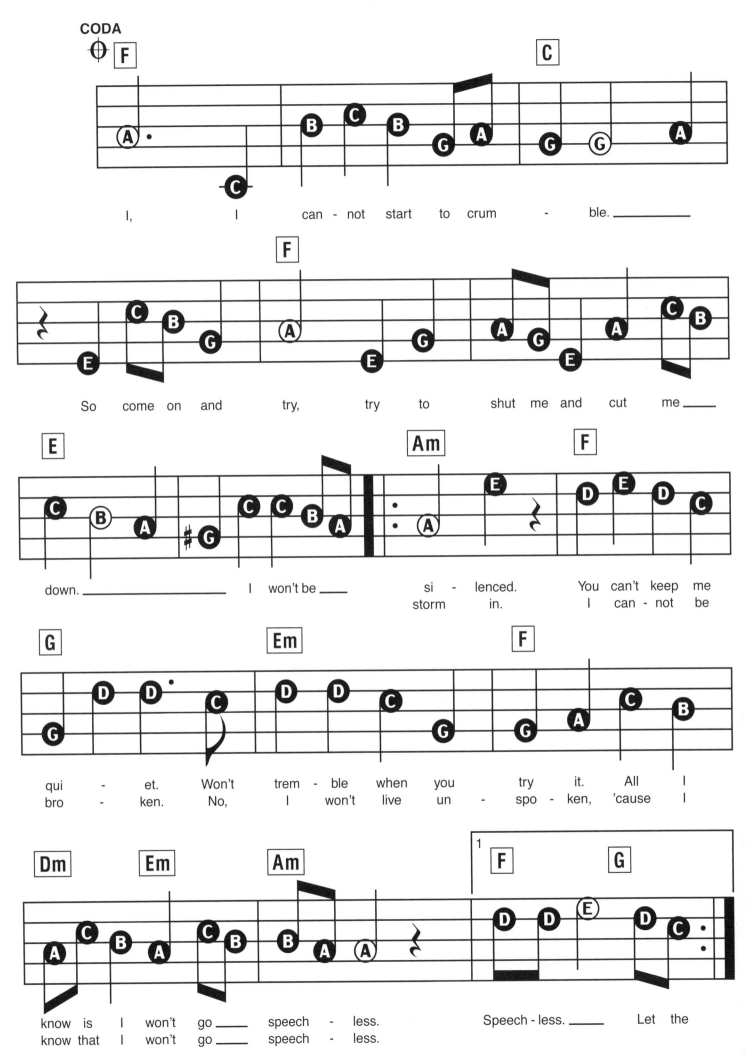

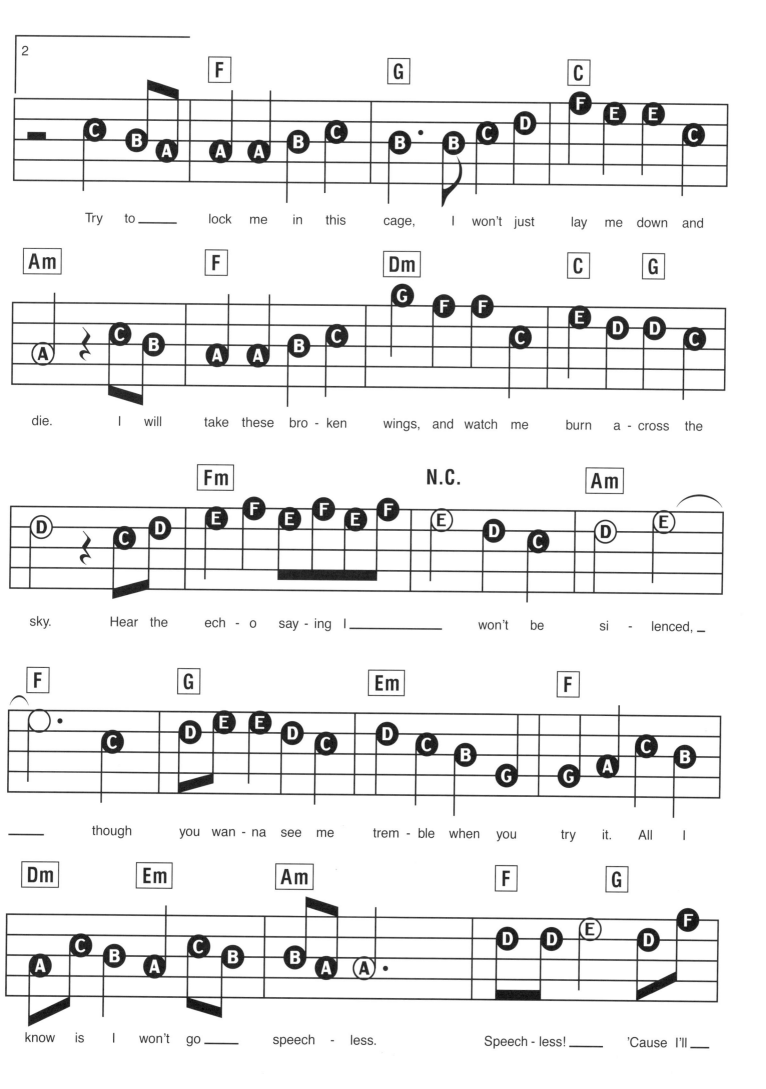

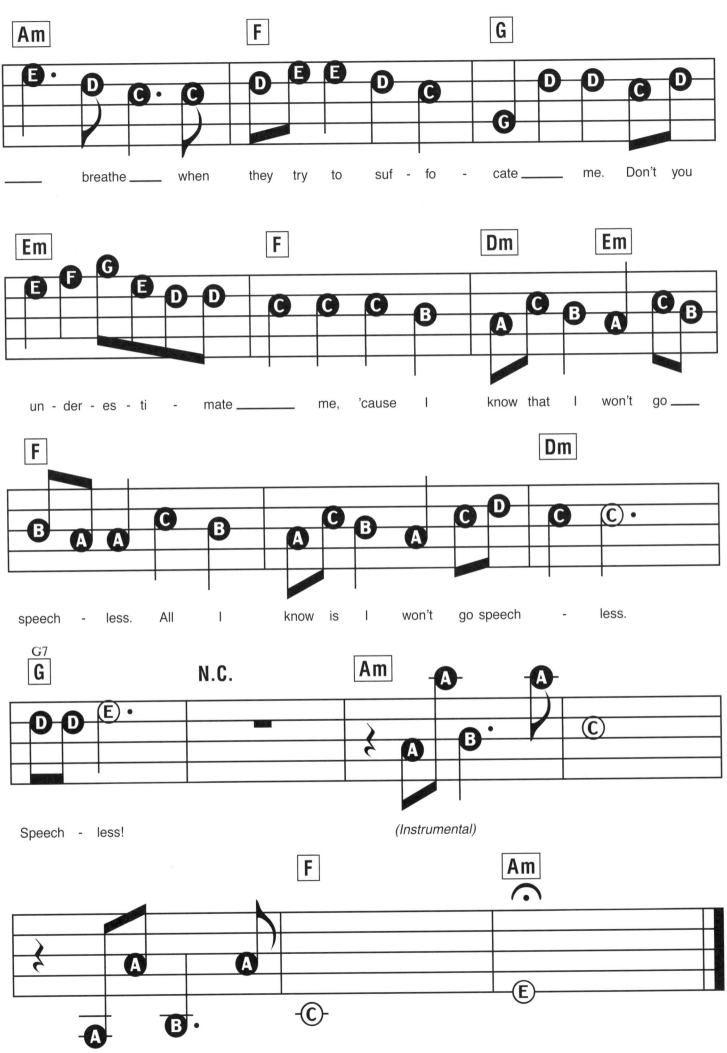

Stay

Registration 8
Rhythm: Ballad

Words and Music by Mikky Ekko
and Justin Parker

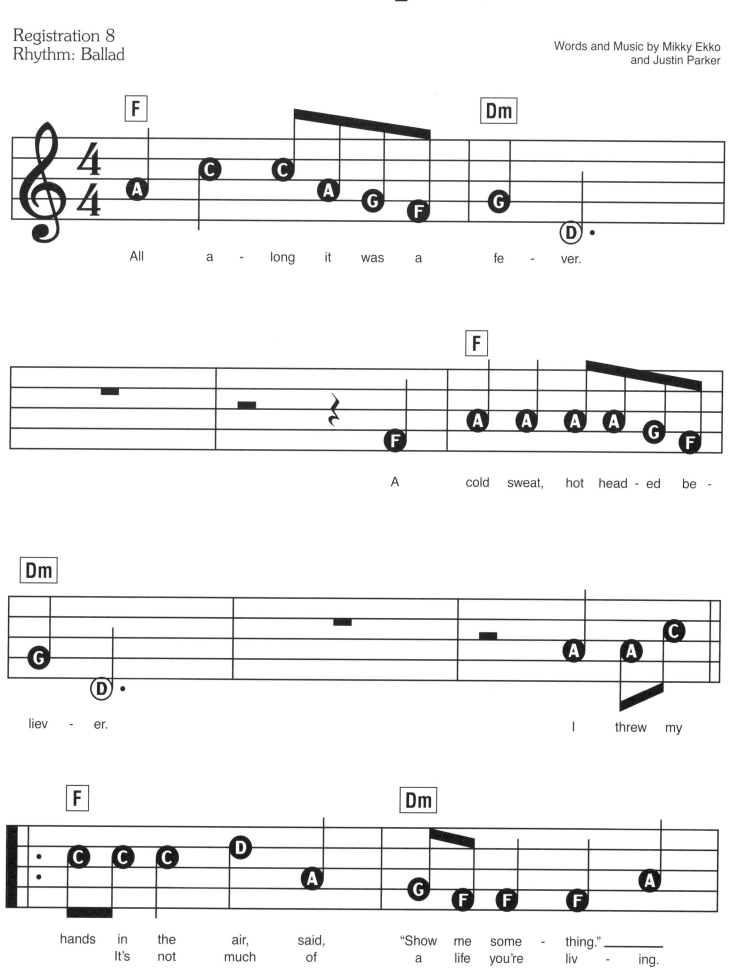

322

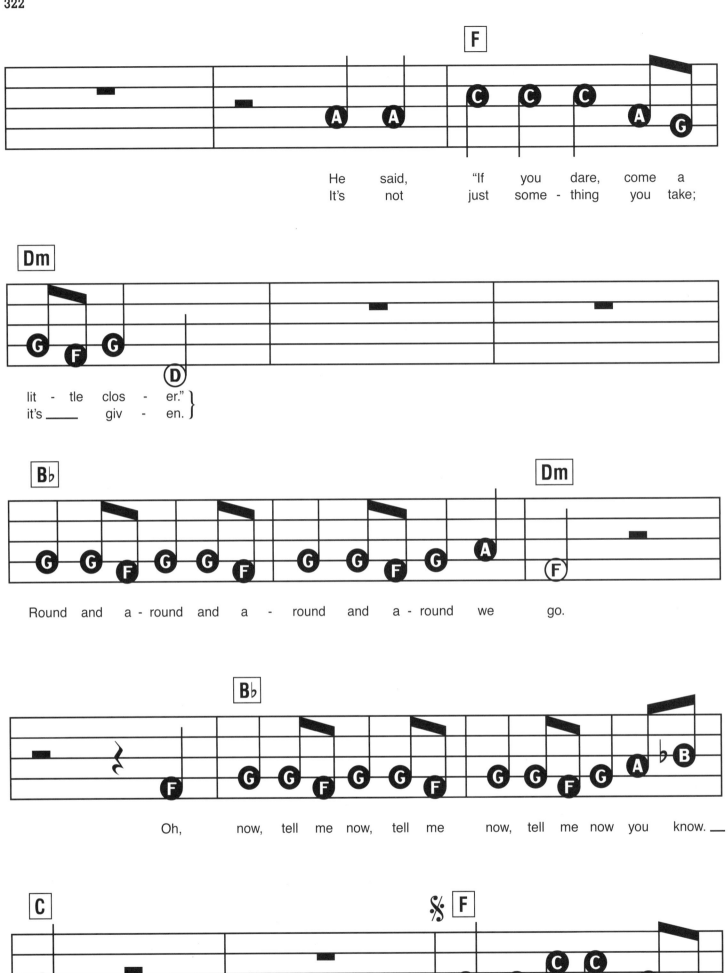

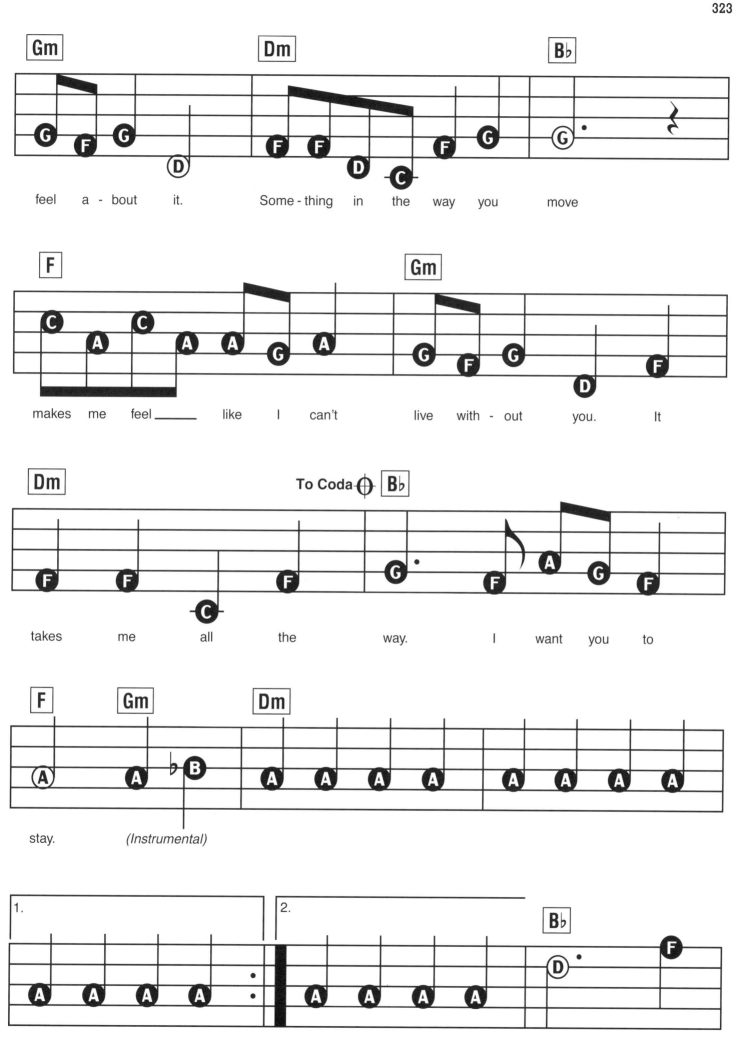

324

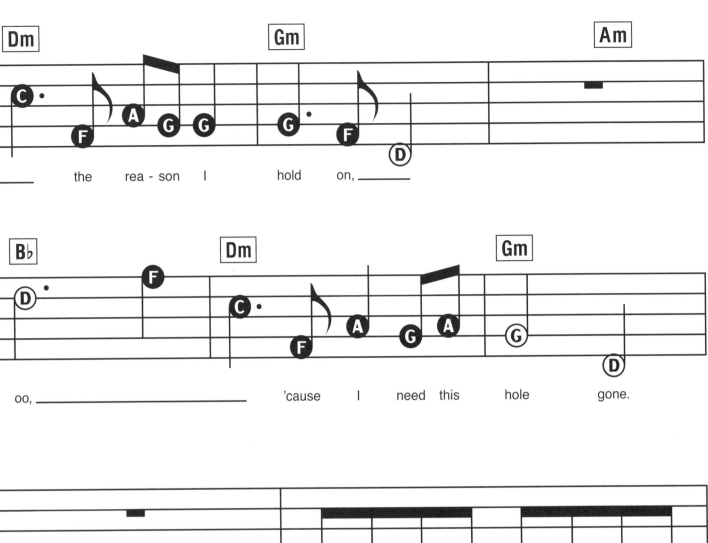

the rea - son I hold on, _____

oo, _____ 'cause I need this hole gone.

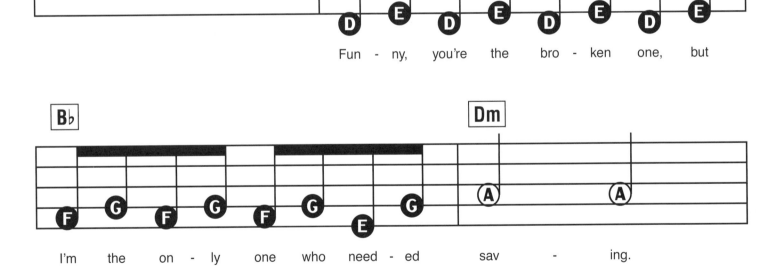

Fun - ny, you're the bro - ken one, but

I'm the on - ly one who need - ed sav - ing.

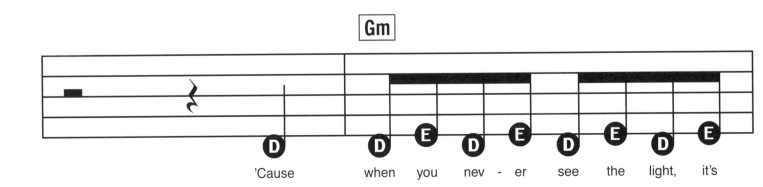

'Cause when you nev - er see the light, it's

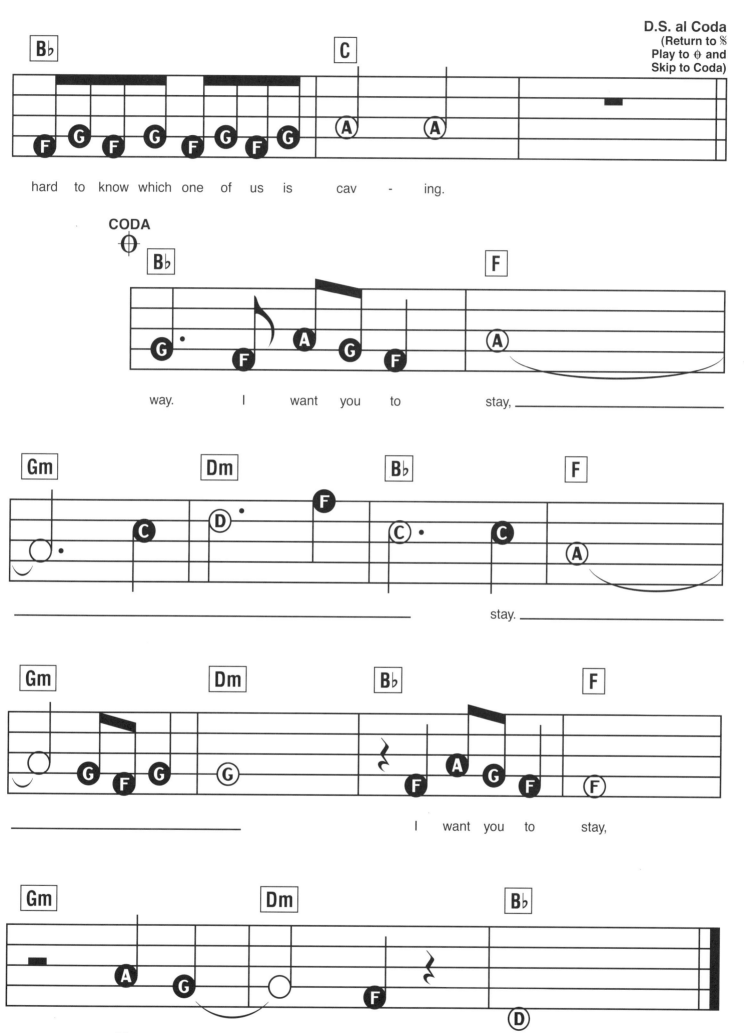

D.S. al Coda
(Return to %
Play to ⊕ and
Skip to Coda)

hard to know which one of us is cav - ing.

CODA

way.　I　want　you　to　stay, _____

stay. _____

I　want　you　to　stay,

oo. _____

Sucker

Registration 9
Rhythm: Pop or Rock

Words and Music by Nick Jonas,
Joseph Jonas, Miles Ale, Mustafa Ahmed,
Ryan Tedder, Louis Bell, Adam Feeney,
Kevin Jonas and Homer Steinweiss

327

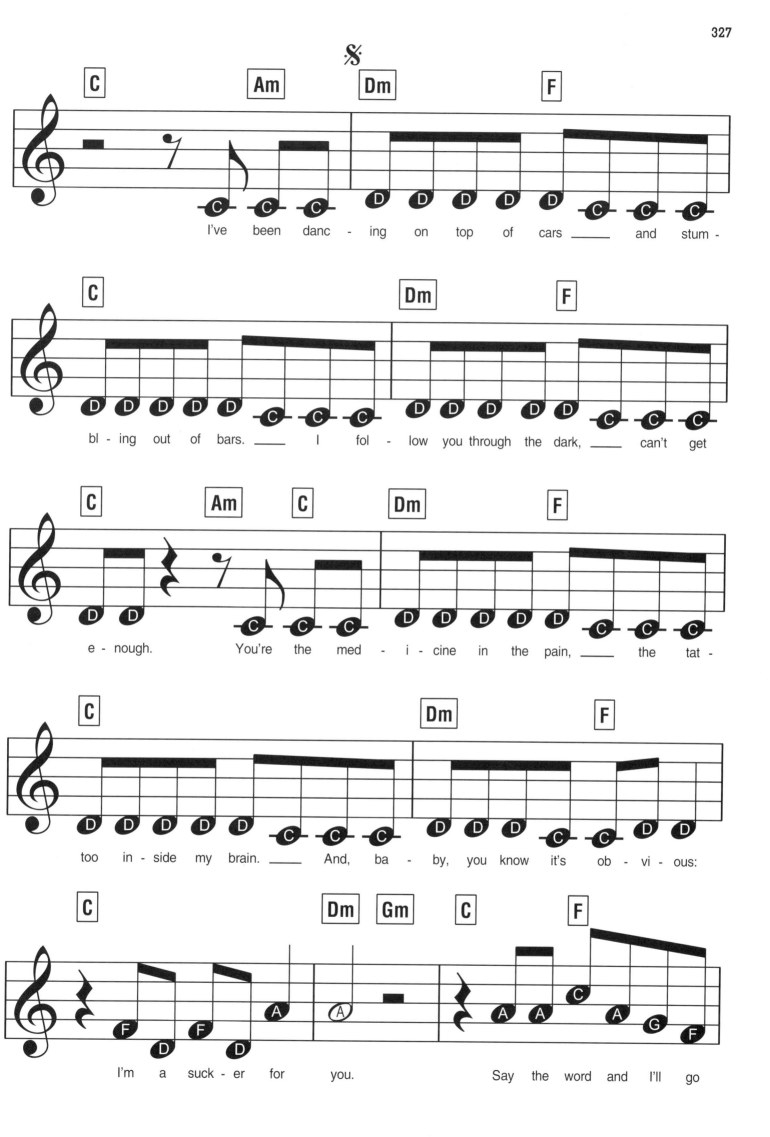

Stay with Me

Registration 2
Rhythm: Ballad

Words and Music by Sam Smith,
James Napier, William Edward Phillips,
Tom Petty and Jeff Lynne

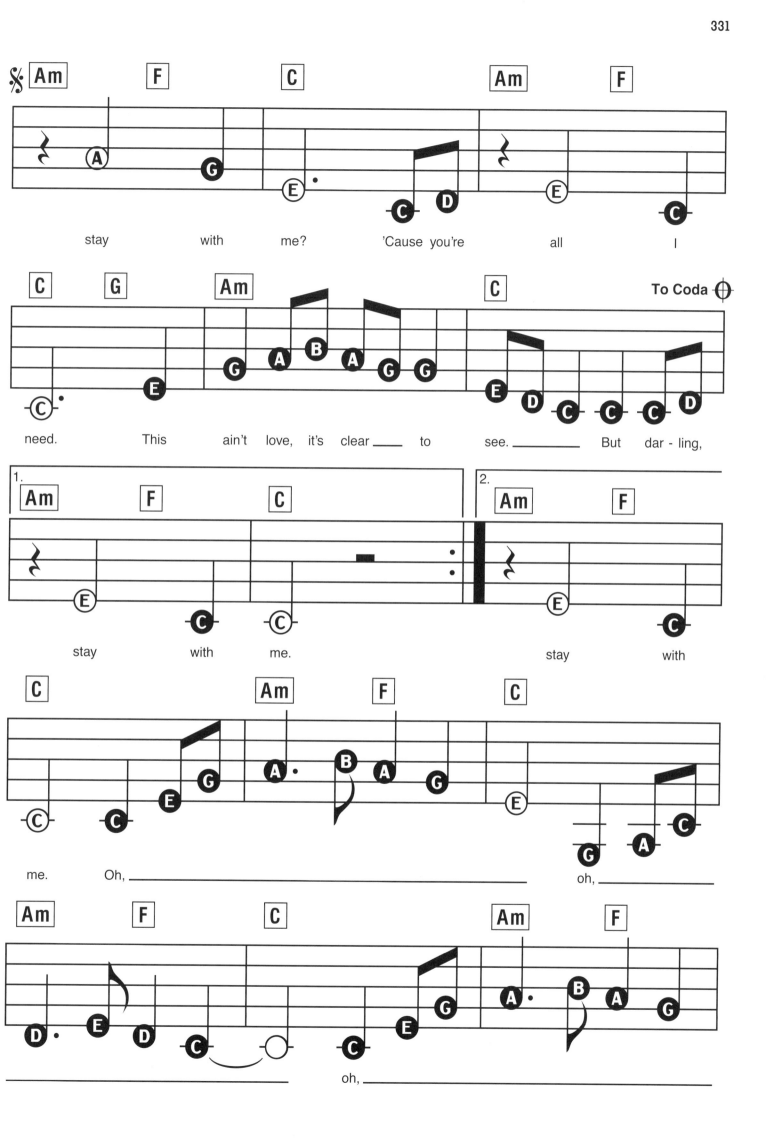

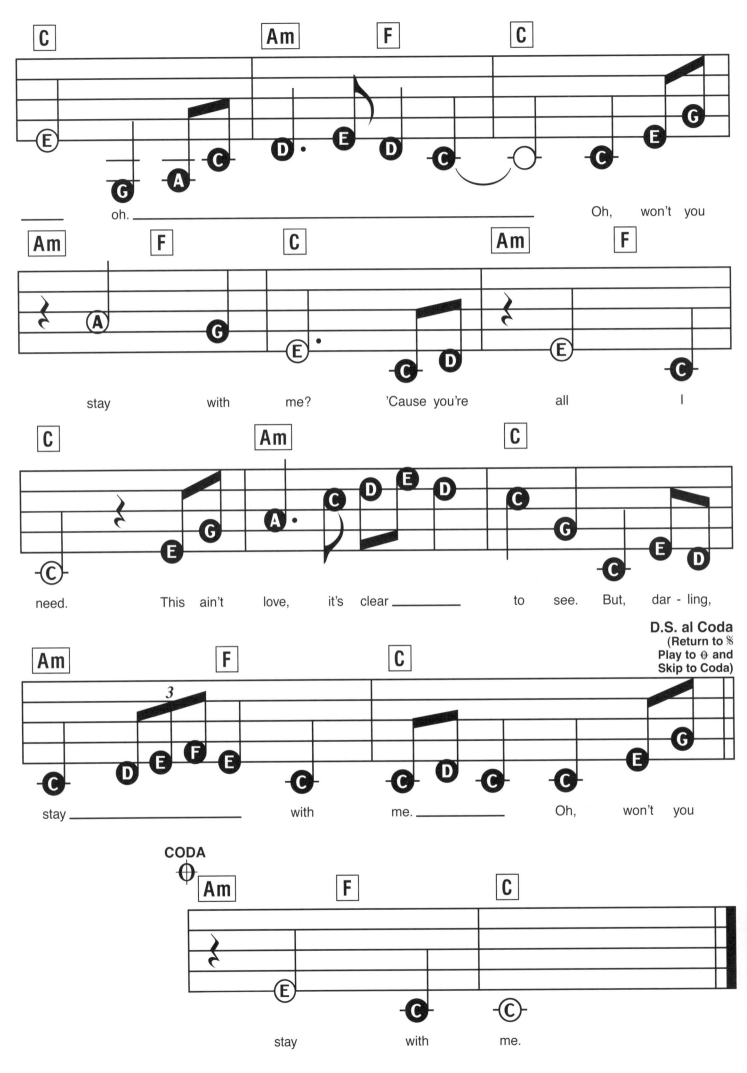

A Thousand Years
from the Summit Entertainment film
THE TWILIGHT SAGA: BREAKING DAWN – PART 1

Registration 8
Rhythm: Waltz

Words and Music by David Hodges
and Christina Perri

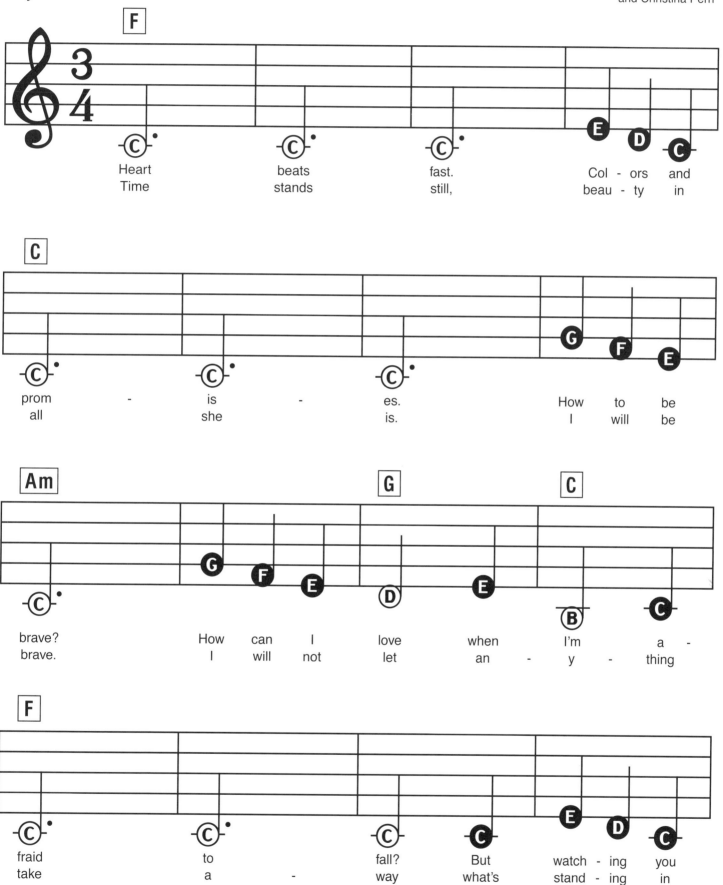

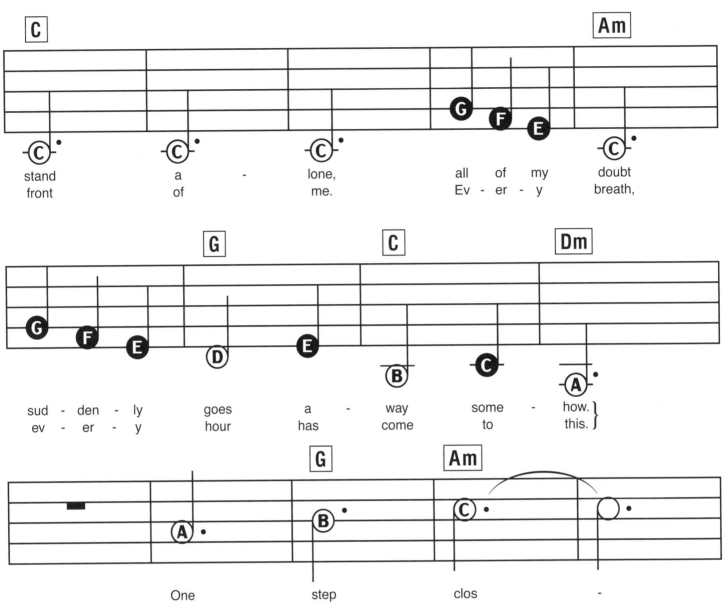

stand a - lone, all of my doubt
front of me. Ev - er - y breath,

sud - den - ly goes a - way some - how.}
ev - er - y hour has come to this.}

One step clos -

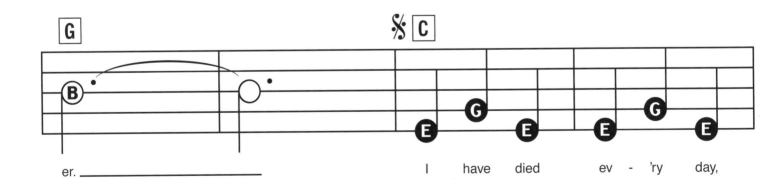

er. _____ I have died ev - 'ry day,

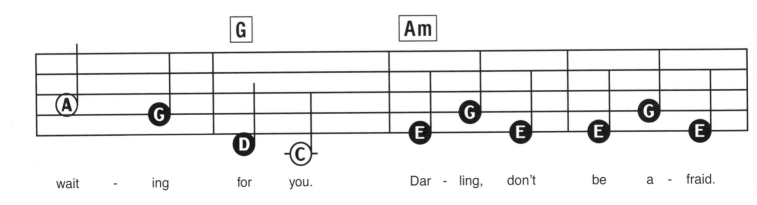

wait - ing for you. Dar - ling, don't be a - fraid.

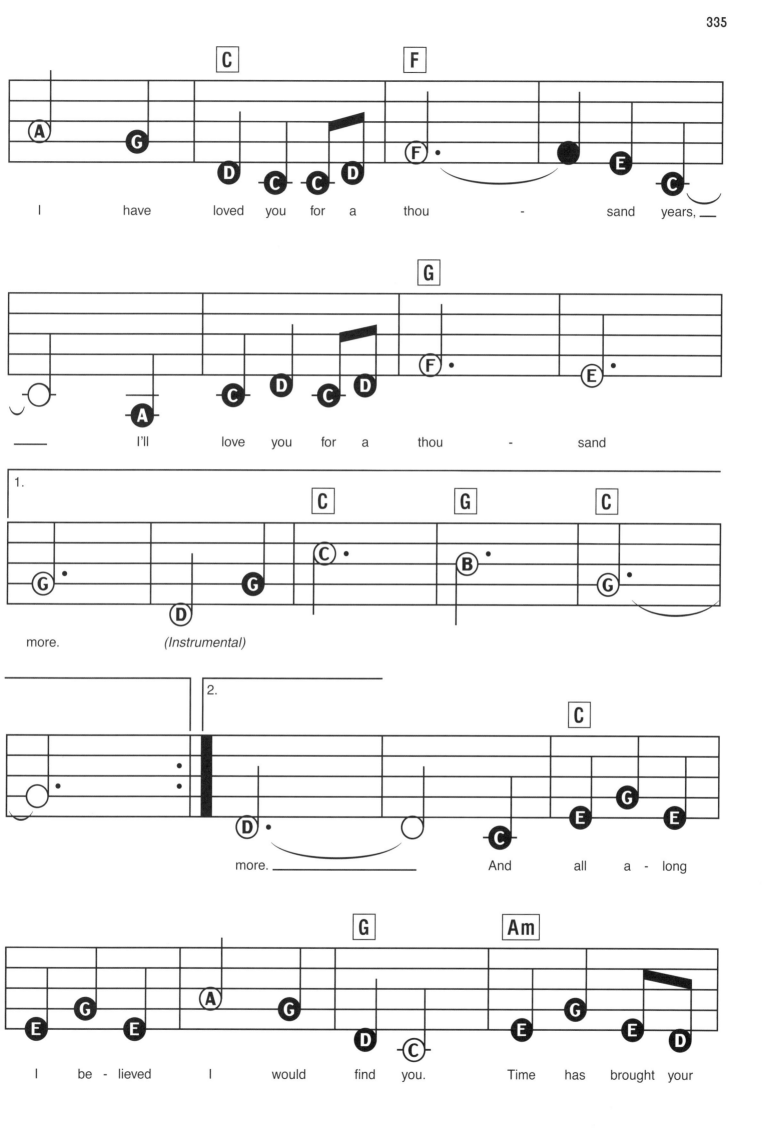

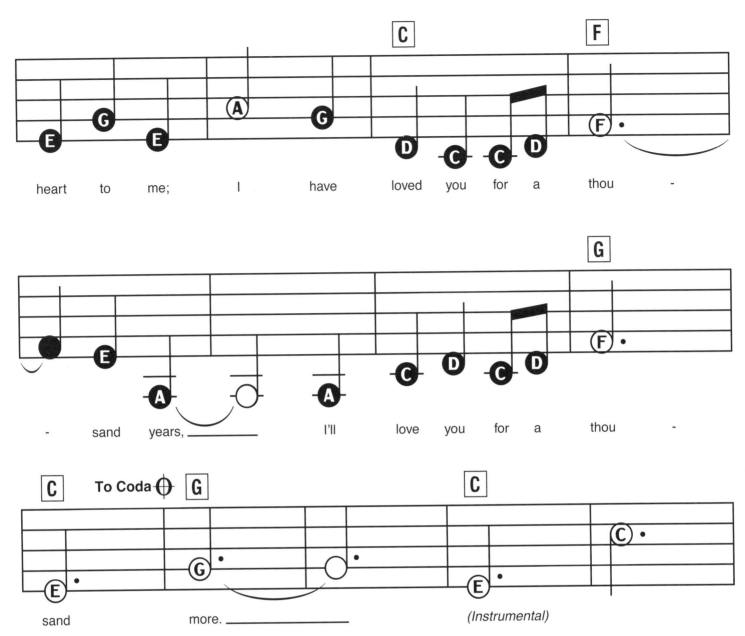

heart to me; I have loved you for a thou -

- sand years, _____ I'll love you for a thou -

sand more. _____ (Instrumental)

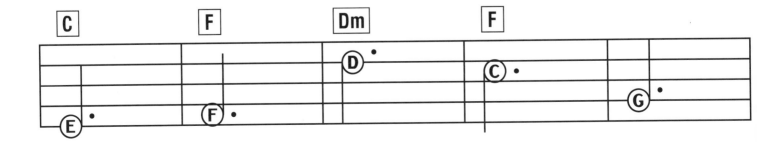

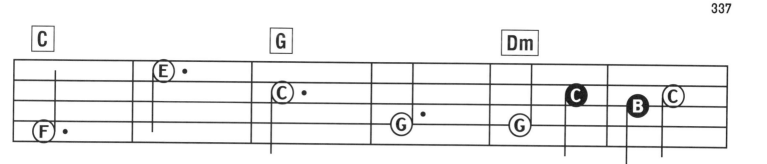

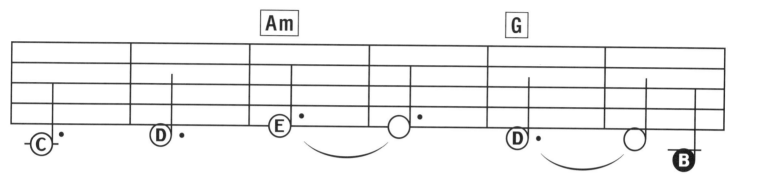

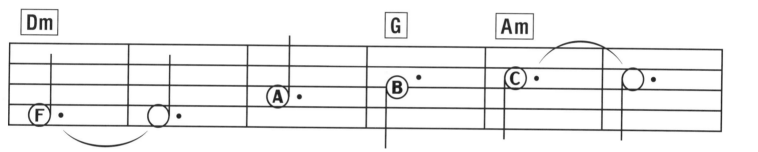

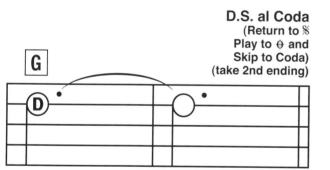

D.S. al Coda
(Return to %
Play to ⊕ and
Skip to Coda)
(take 2nd ending)

CODA

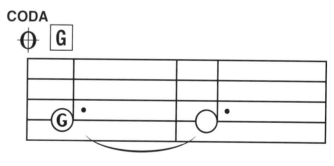

more. _____

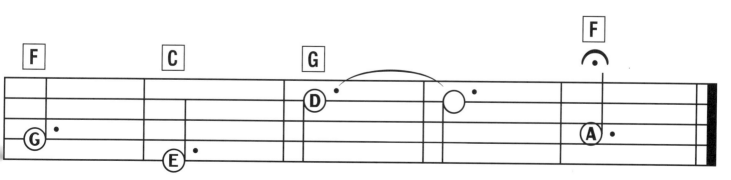

(Instrumental)

Sunflower
from SPIDER-MAN: INTO THE SPIDER-VERSE

Registration 9
Rhythm: Pop

Words and Music by Austin Richard Post,
Carl Austin Rosen, Khalif Brown,
Carter Lang, Louis Bell and Billy Walsh

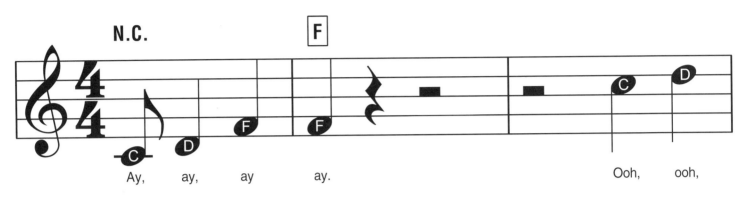

Ay, ay, ay ay. Ooh, ooh,

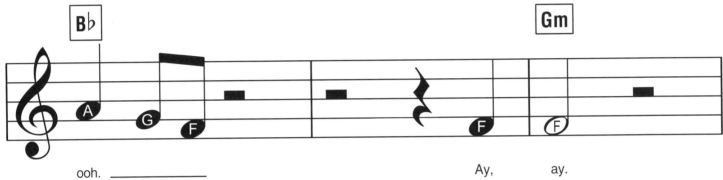

ooh. _____ Ay, ay.

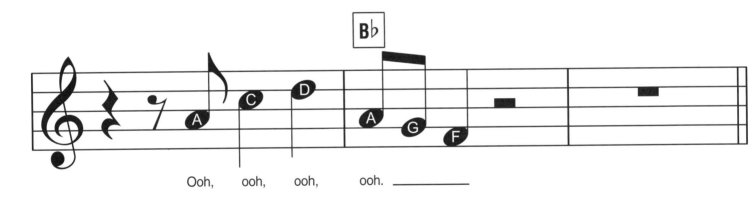

Ooh, ooh, ooh, ooh. _____

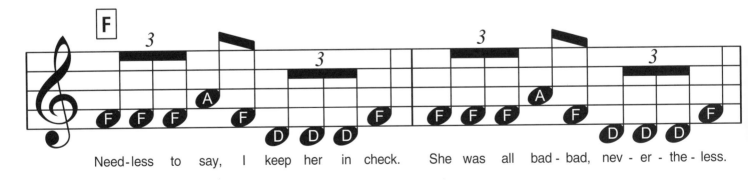

Need-less to say, I keep her in check. She was all bad-bad, nev-er-the-less.

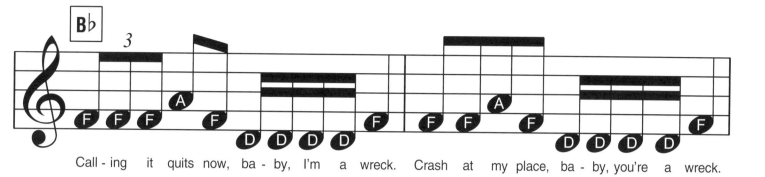

Call-ing it quits now, ba-by, I'm a wreck. Crash at my place, ba-by, you're a wreck.

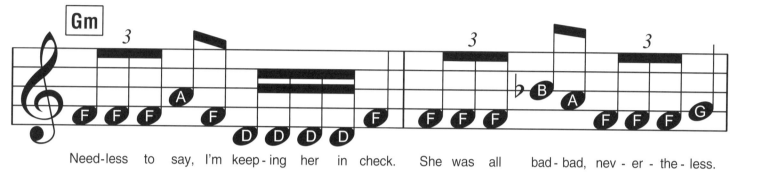

Need-less to say, I'm keep-ing her in check. She was all bad-bad, nev-er-the-less.

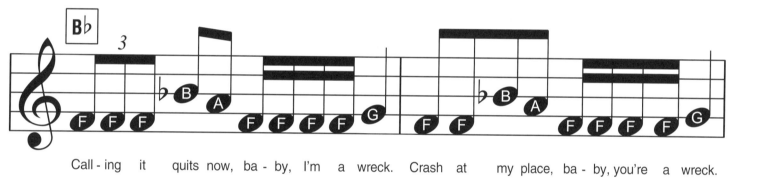

Call-ing it quits now, ba-by, I'm a wreck. Crash at my place, ba-by, you're a wreck.

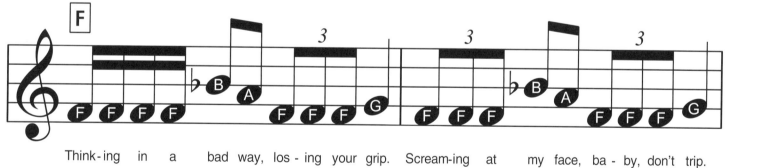

Think-ing in a bad way, los-ing your grip. Scream-ing at my face, ba-by, don't trip.

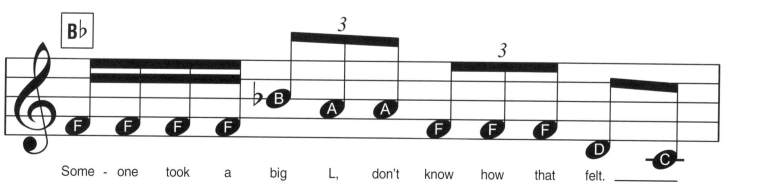

Some-one took a big L, don't know how that felt. _____

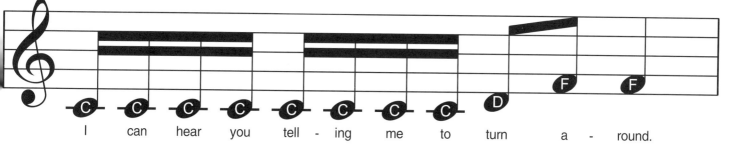

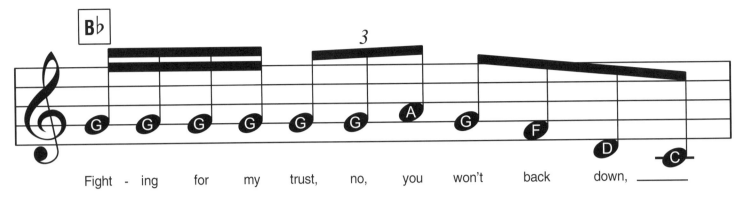

Fight - ing for my trust, no, you won't back down, ____

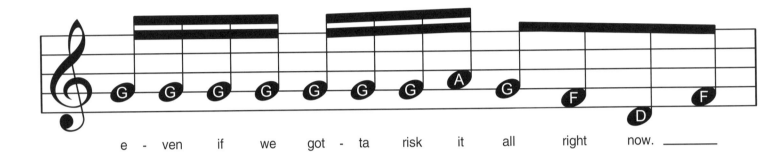

e - ven if we got - ta risk it all right now. ____

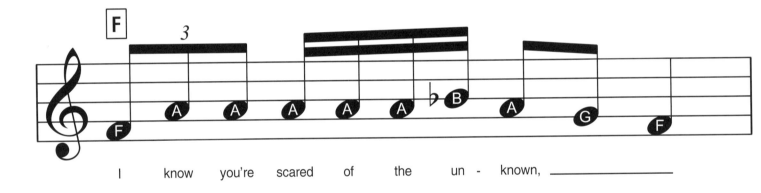

I know you're scared of the un - known, _____

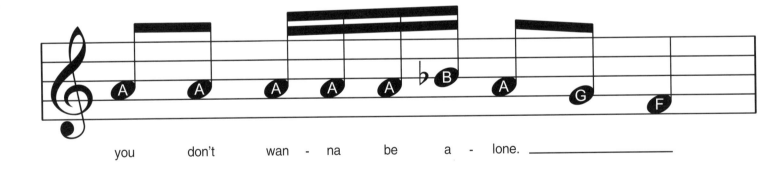

you don't wan - na be a - lone. _____

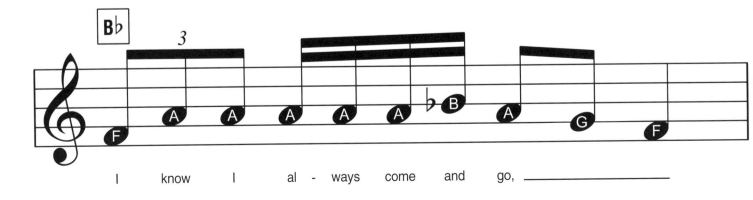

I know I al - ways come and go, _____

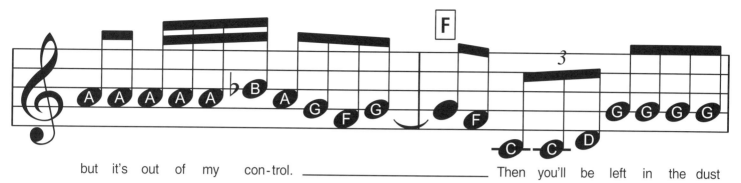

but it's out of my con-trol. _____ Then you'll be left in the dust

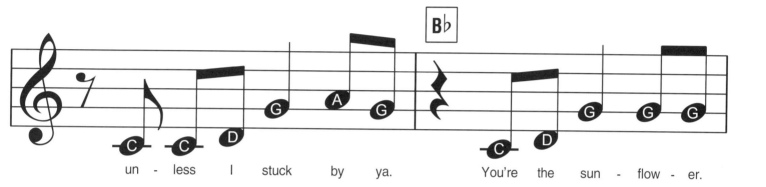

un - less I stuck by ya. You're the sun - flow - er.

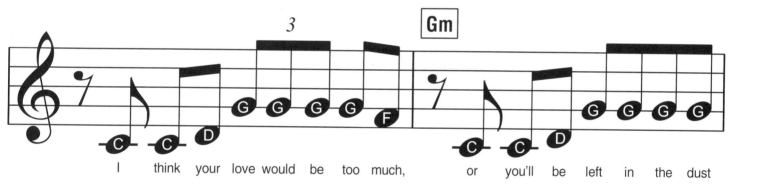

I think your love would be too much, or you'll be left in the dust

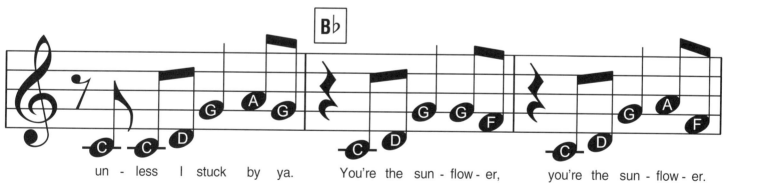

un - less I stuck by ya. You're the sun - flow - er, you're the sun - flow - er.

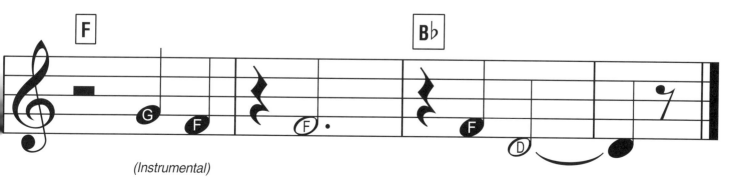

(Instrumental)

Thinking Out Loud

Registration 4
Rhythm: 8-Beat or Rock

Words and Music by Ed Sheeran
and Amy Wadge

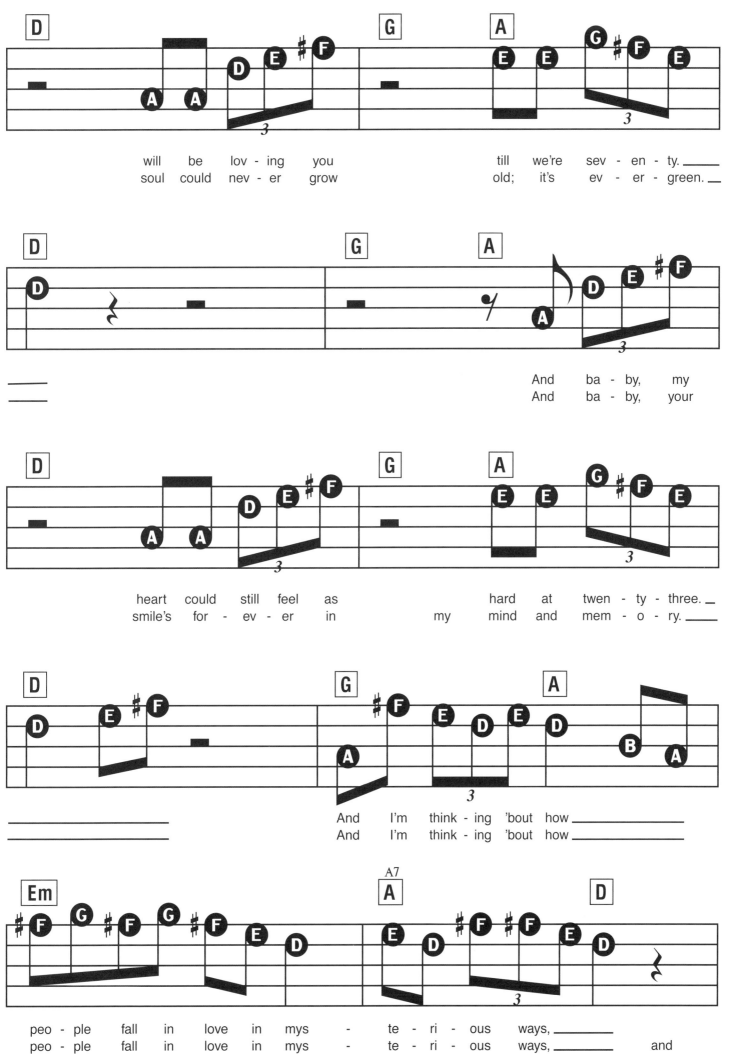

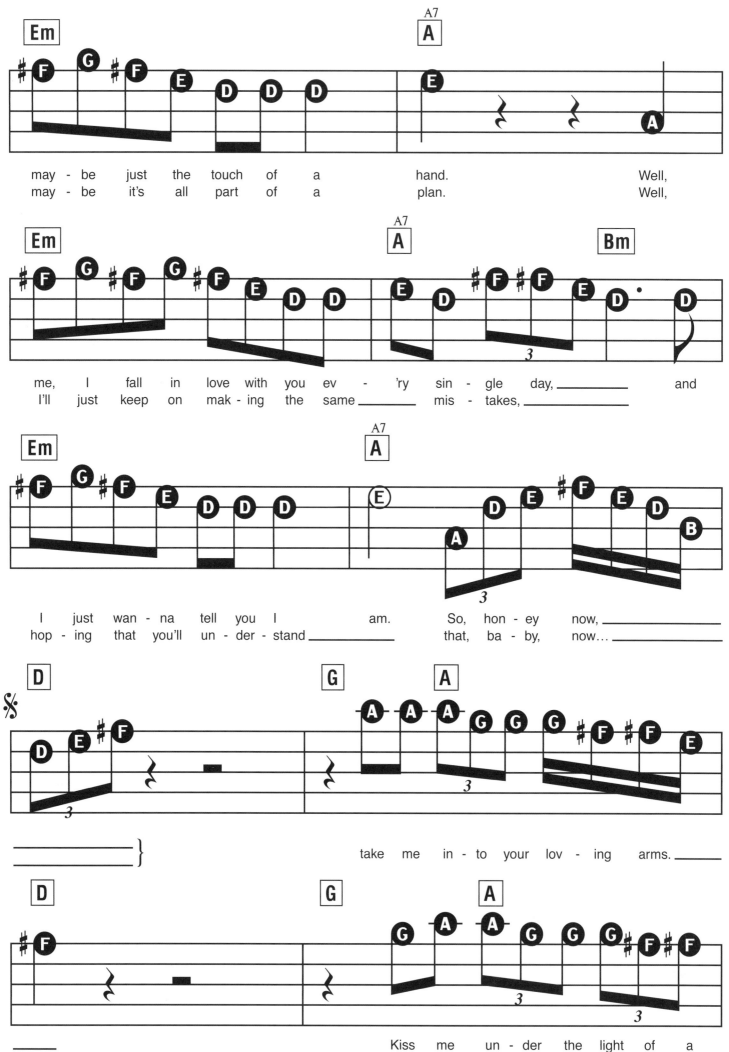

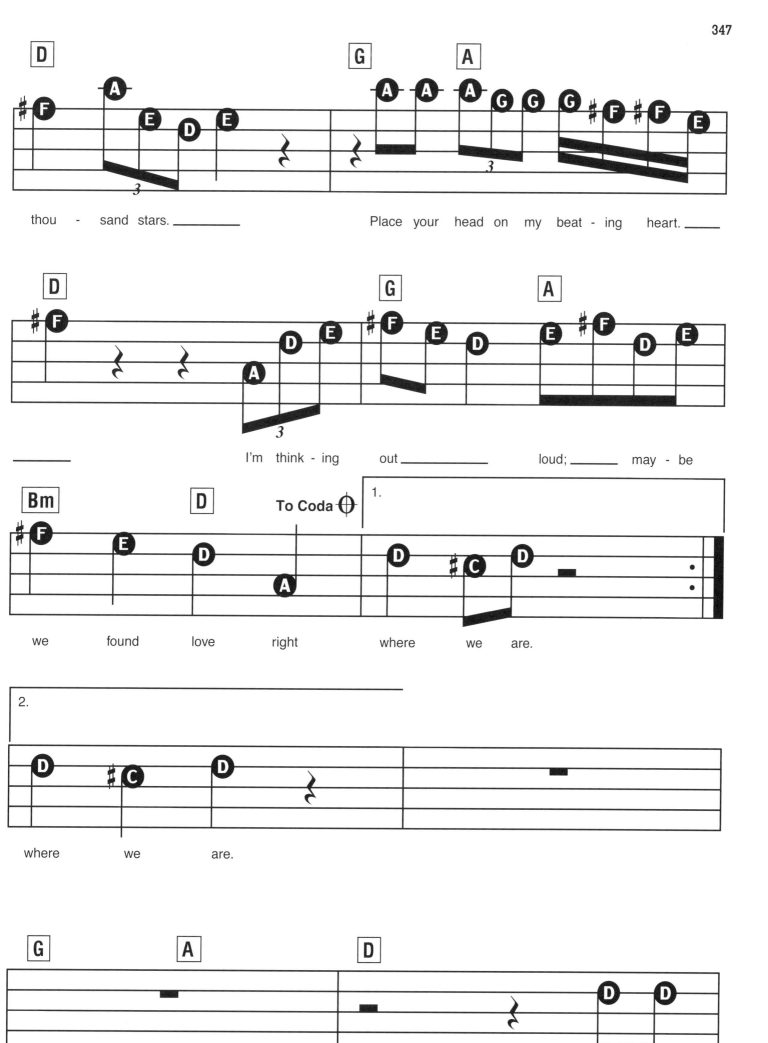

thou - sand stars. _____

Place your head on my beat - ing heart. _____

_____

I'm think - ing out _____ loud; _____ may - be

To Coda ⊕

1.

we found love right where we are.

2.

where we are.

(La, la,

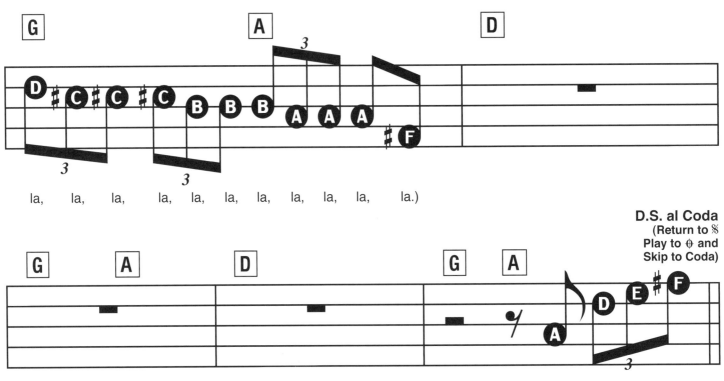

la, la, la, la, la, la, la, la, la, la, la.)

D.S. al Coda
(Return to %
Play to ⊕ and
Skip to Coda)

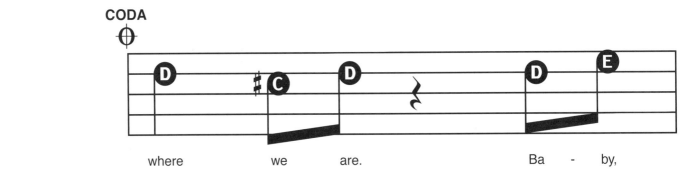

So, ba - by, now, ___

CODA

where we are. Ba - by,

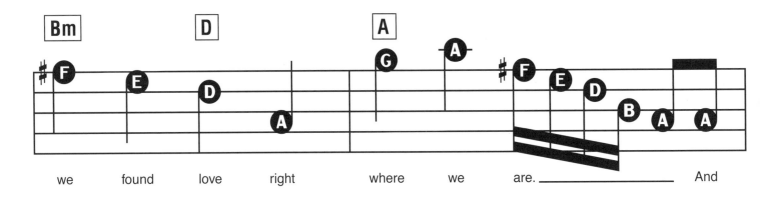

we found love right where we are. ___ And

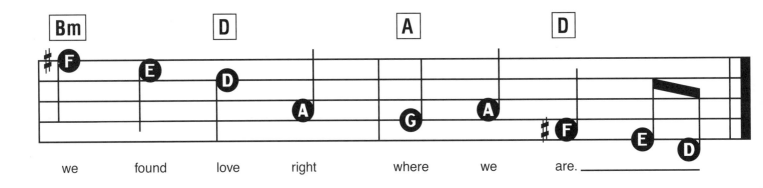

we found love right where we are. ___

Too Good at Goodbyes

Registration 8
Rhythm: Ballad or Pop

Words and Music by Sam Smith,
Tor Hermansen, Mikkel Eriksen
and James Napier

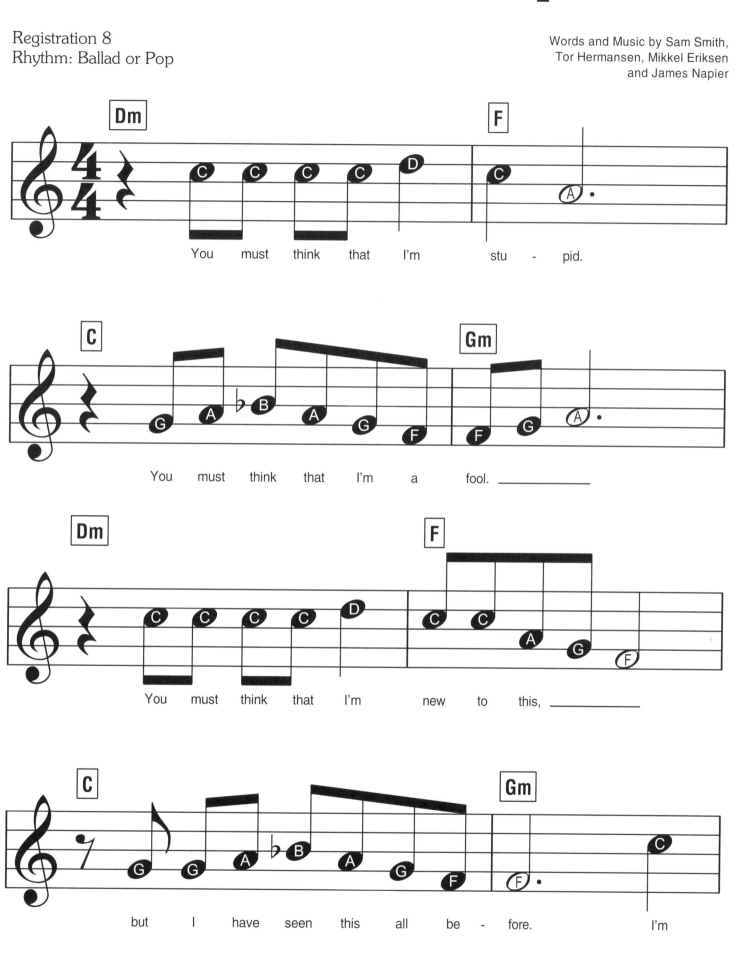

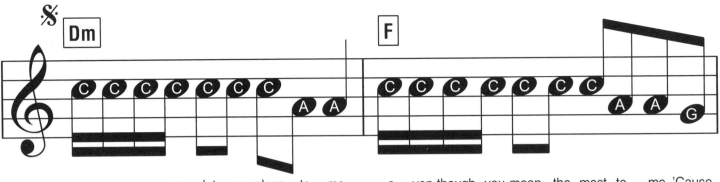

never gon-na let you close to me, e - ven though you mean the most to me. 'Cause

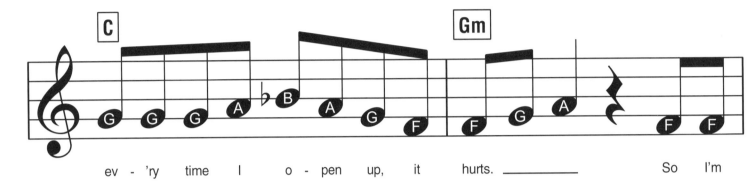

ev - 'ry time I o - pen up, it hurts. _____ So I'm

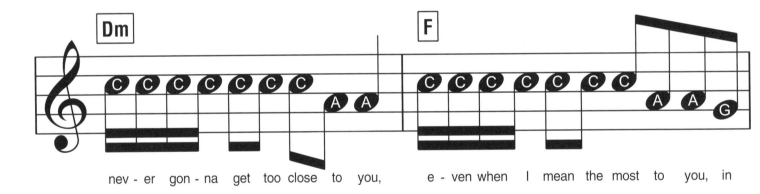

nev - er gon - na get too close to you, e - ven when I mean the most to you, in

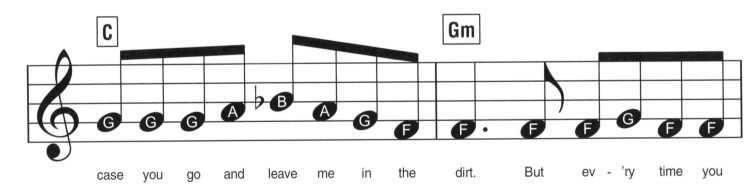

case you go and leave me in the dirt. But ev - 'ry time you

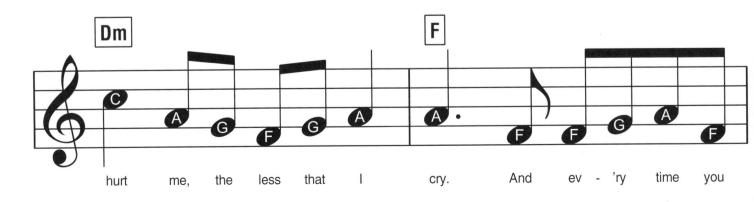

hurt me, the less that I cry. And ev - 'ry time you

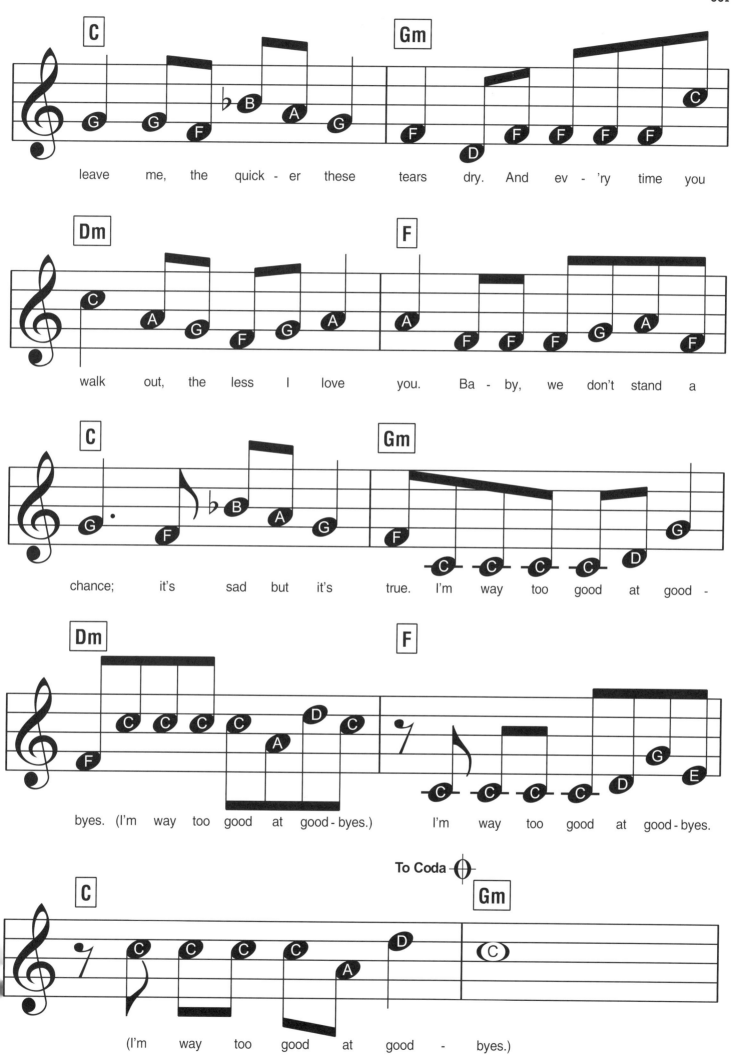

352

354

Uptown Funk

Registration 2
Rhythm: Funk or Rock

Words and Music by Mark Ronson, Bruno Mars,
Philip Lawrence, Jeff Bhasker, Devon Gallaspy,
Nicholaus Williams, Lonnie Simmons, Ronnie Wilson,
Charles Wilson, Rudolph Taylor and Robert Wilson

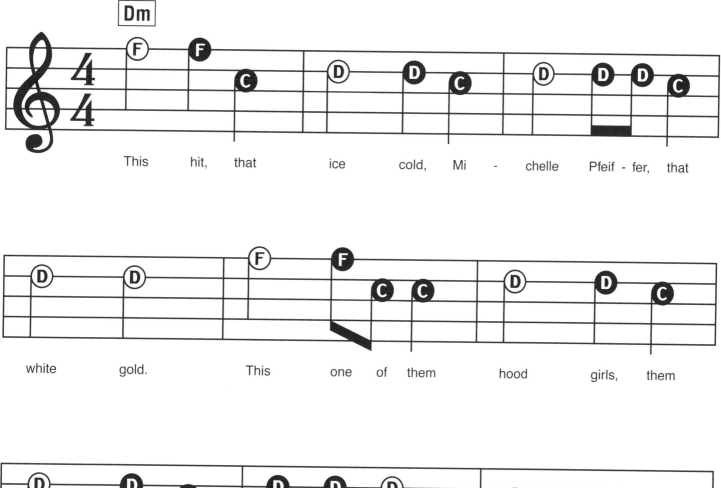

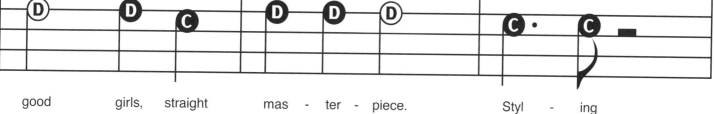

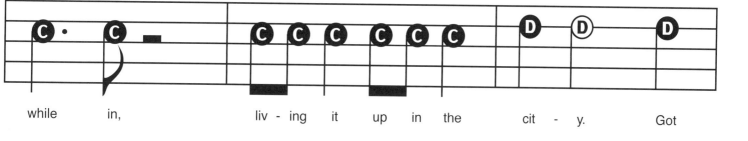

356

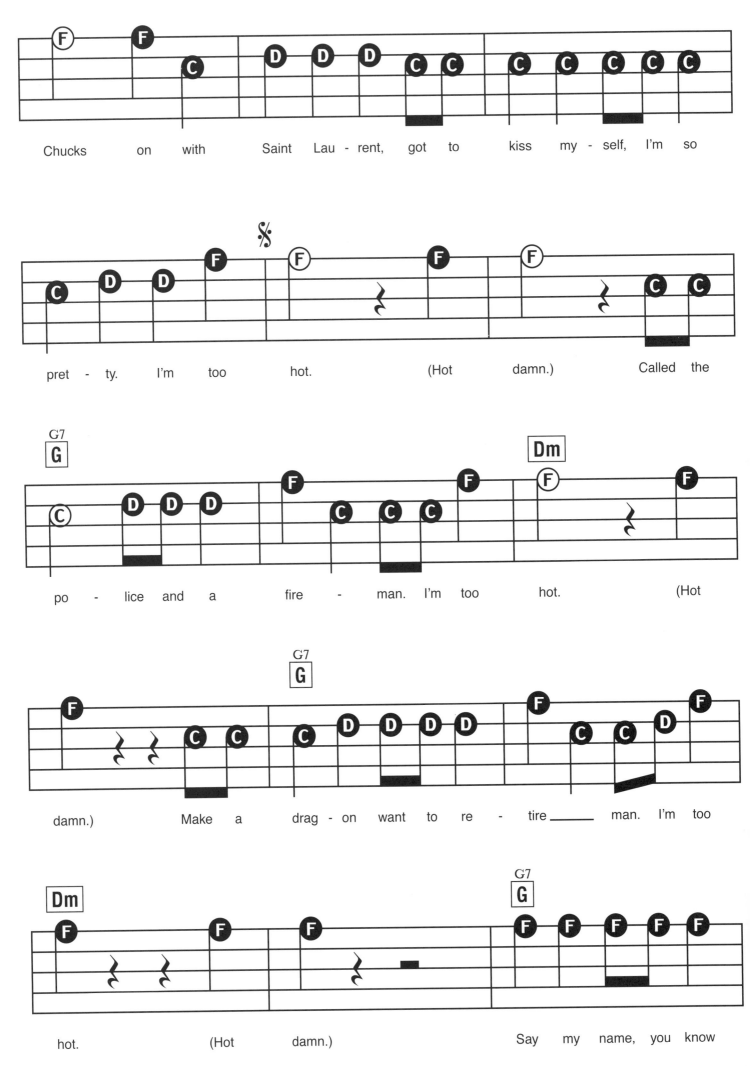

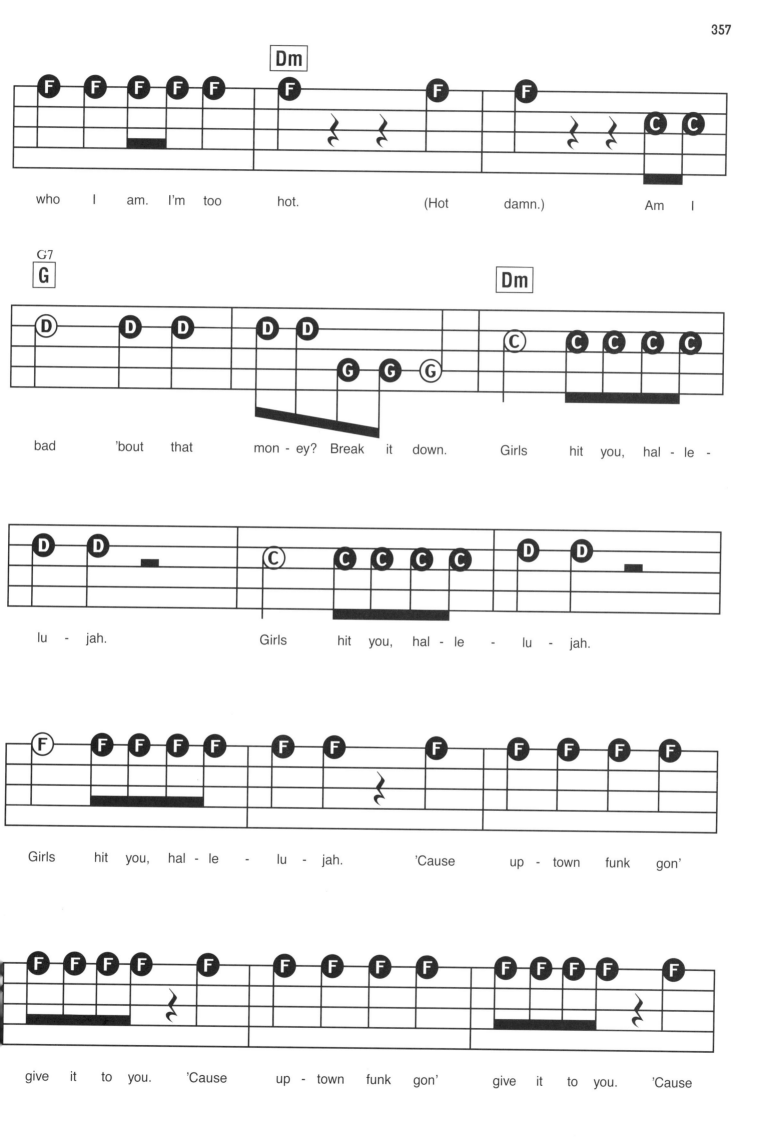

358

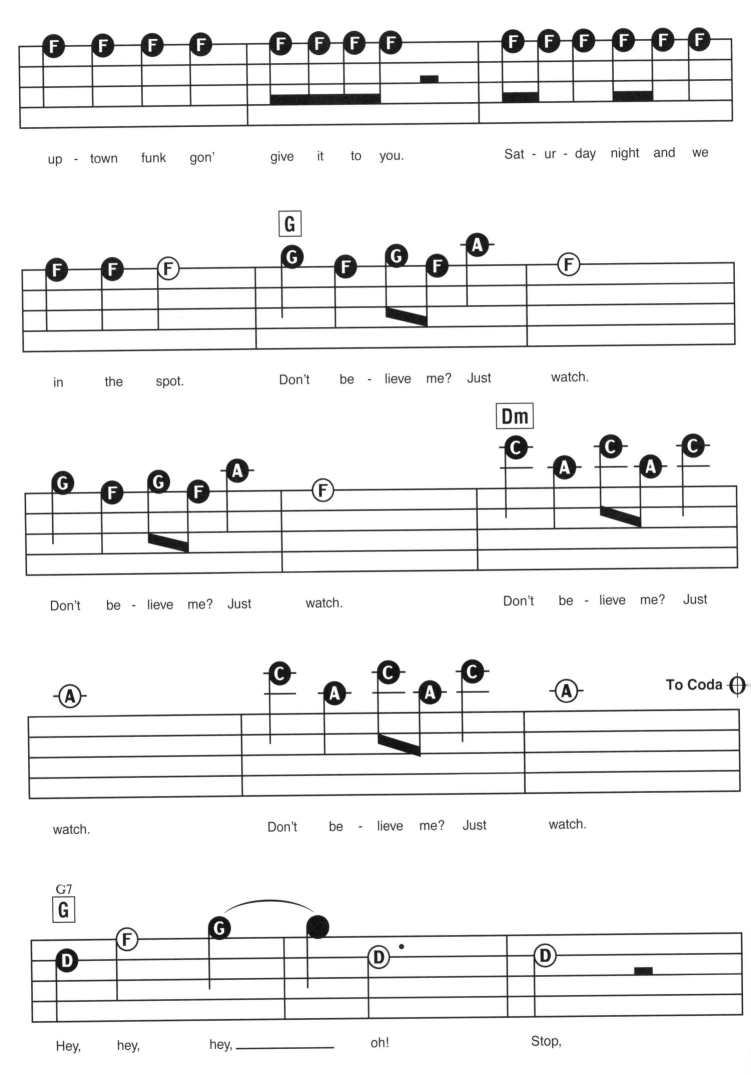

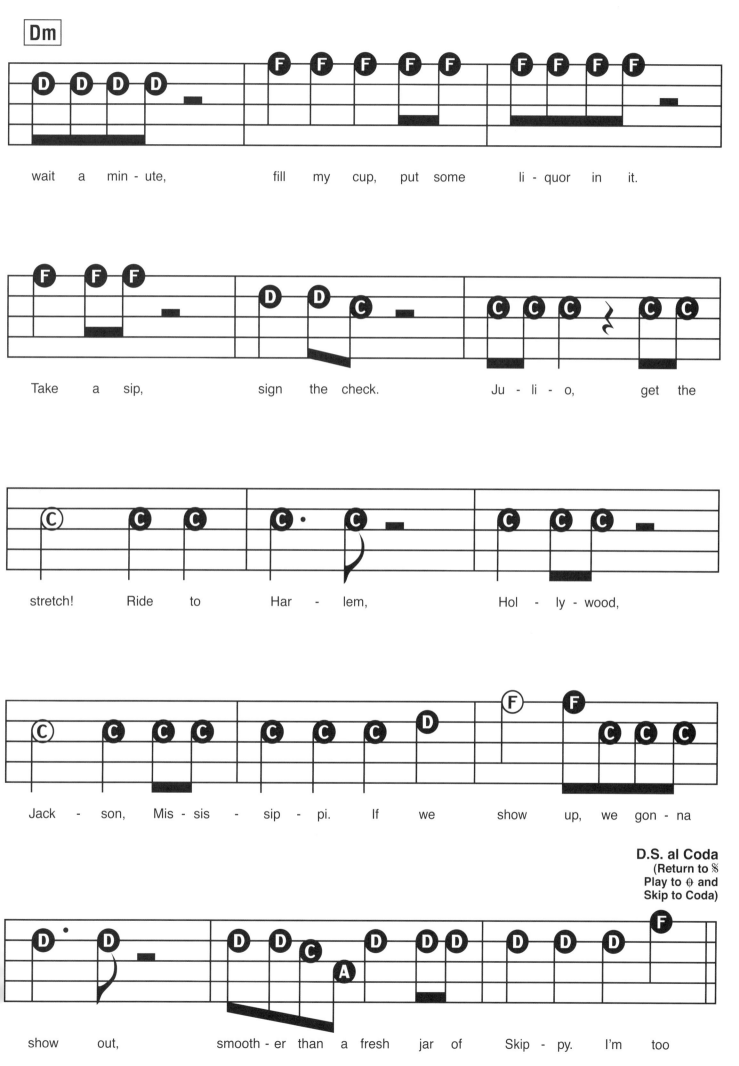

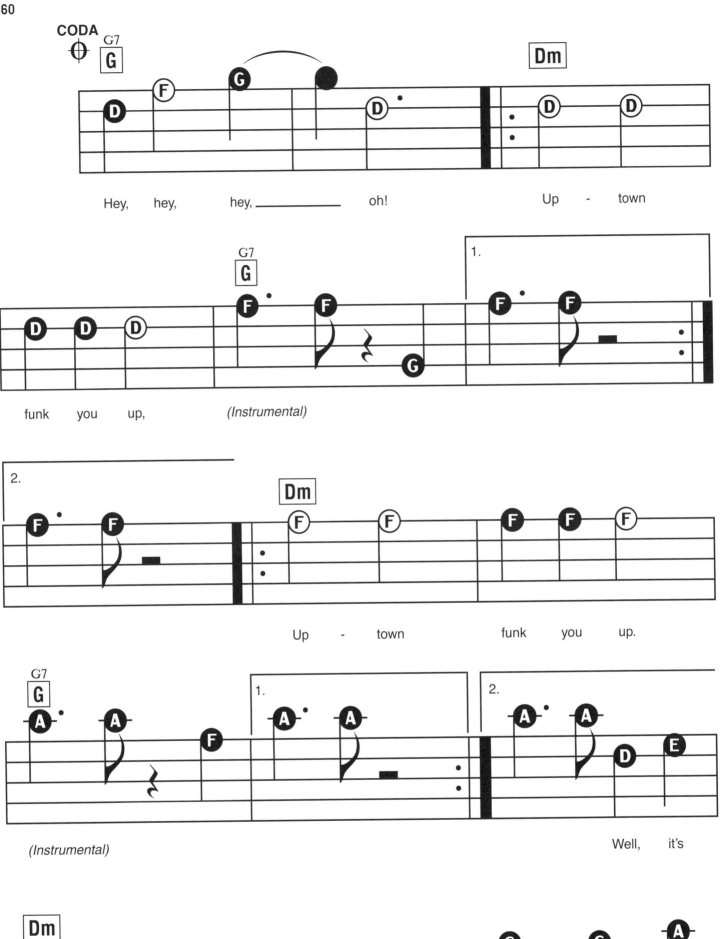

Hey, hey, hey, _____ oh!   Up - town

funk you up,   (Instrumental)

Up - town   funk you up.

(Instrumental)   Well, it's

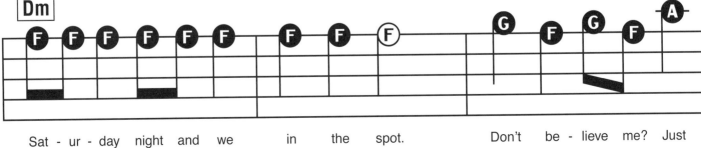

Sat - ur - day night and we   in the spot.   Don't be - lieve me? Just

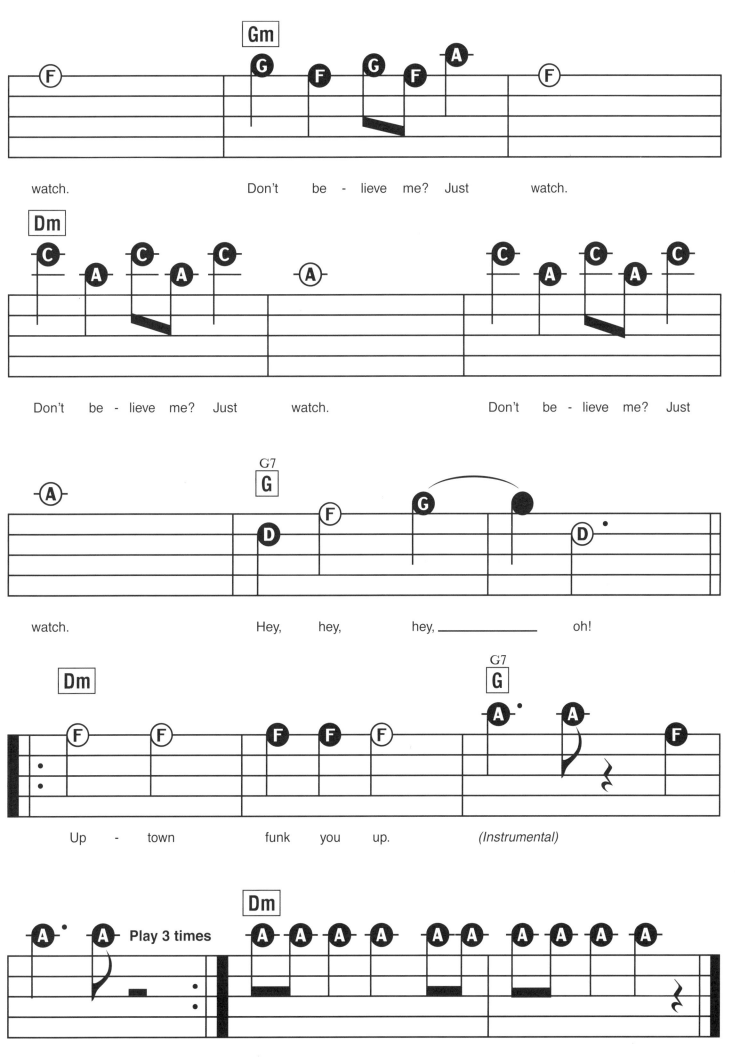

watch.　　Don't　be - lieve me? Just　　watch.

Don't　be - lieve me? Just　　watch.　　　　Don't　be - lieve me? Just

watch.　　　　Hey,　　hey,　　hey, _____ oh!

Up - town　　funk　you　up.　　(Instrumental)

Play 3 times

What Makes You Beautiful

Registration 4
Rhythm: Rock or Pop

Words and Music by Savan Kotecha,
Rami Yacoub and Carl Falk

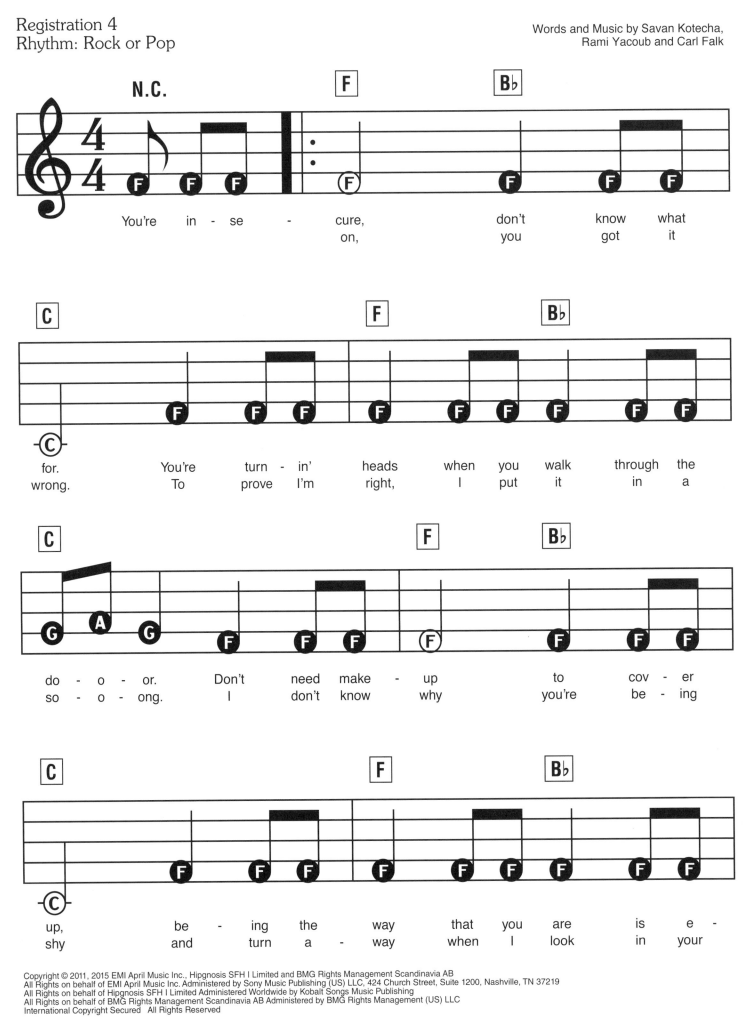

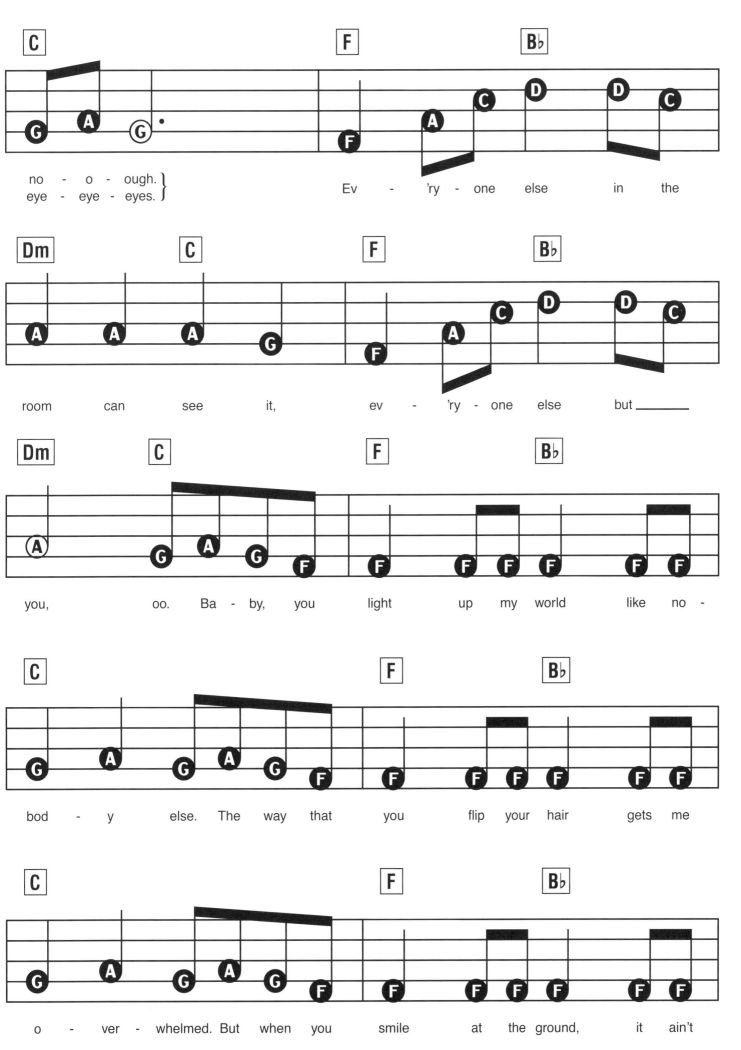

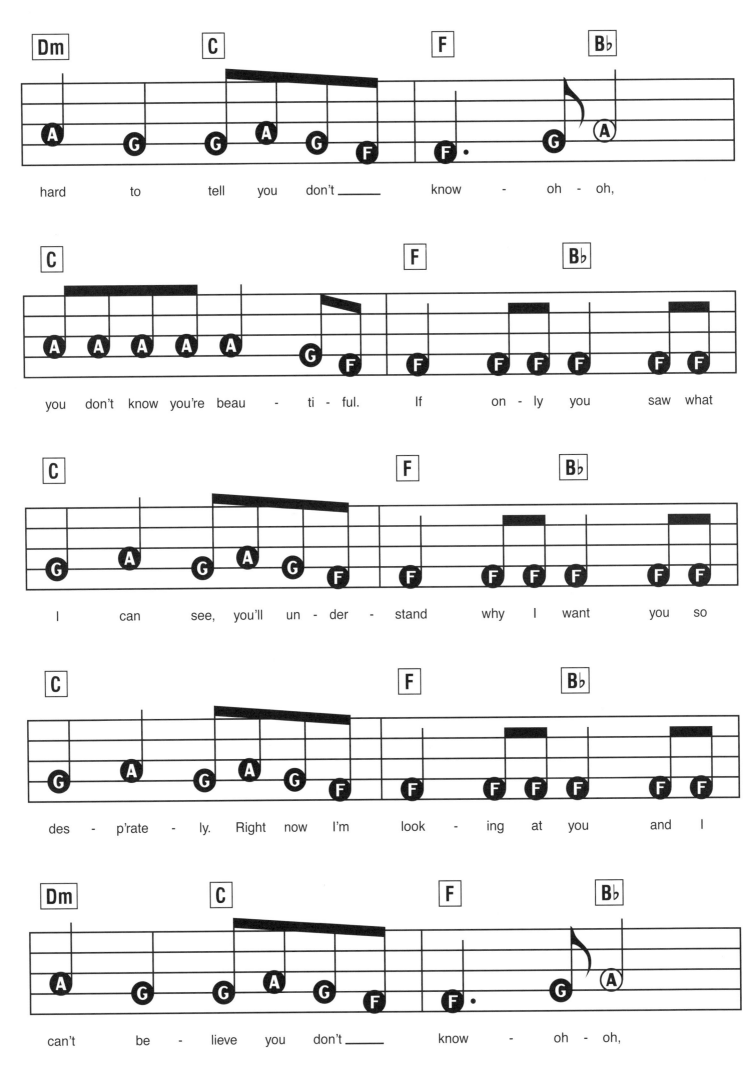

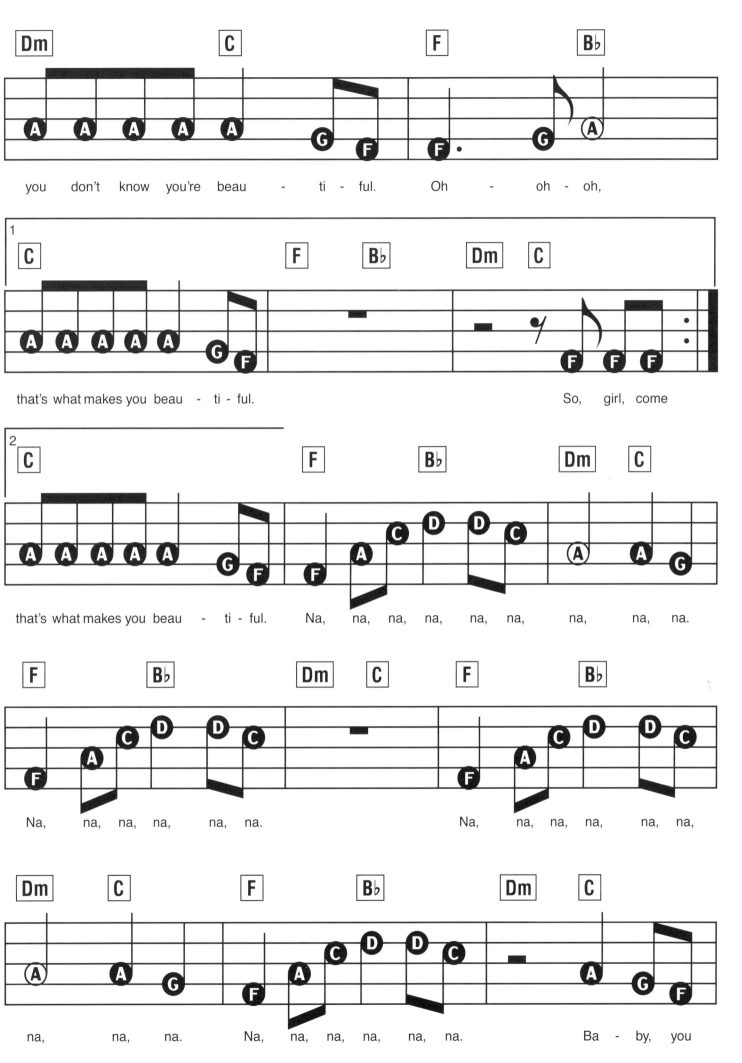

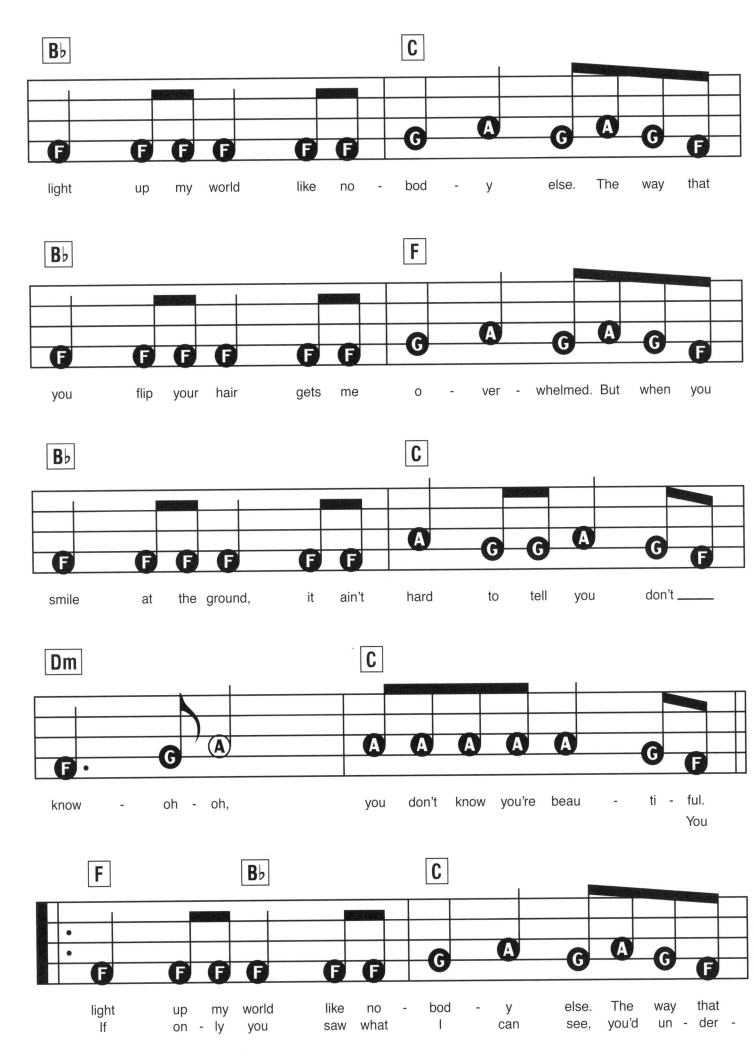

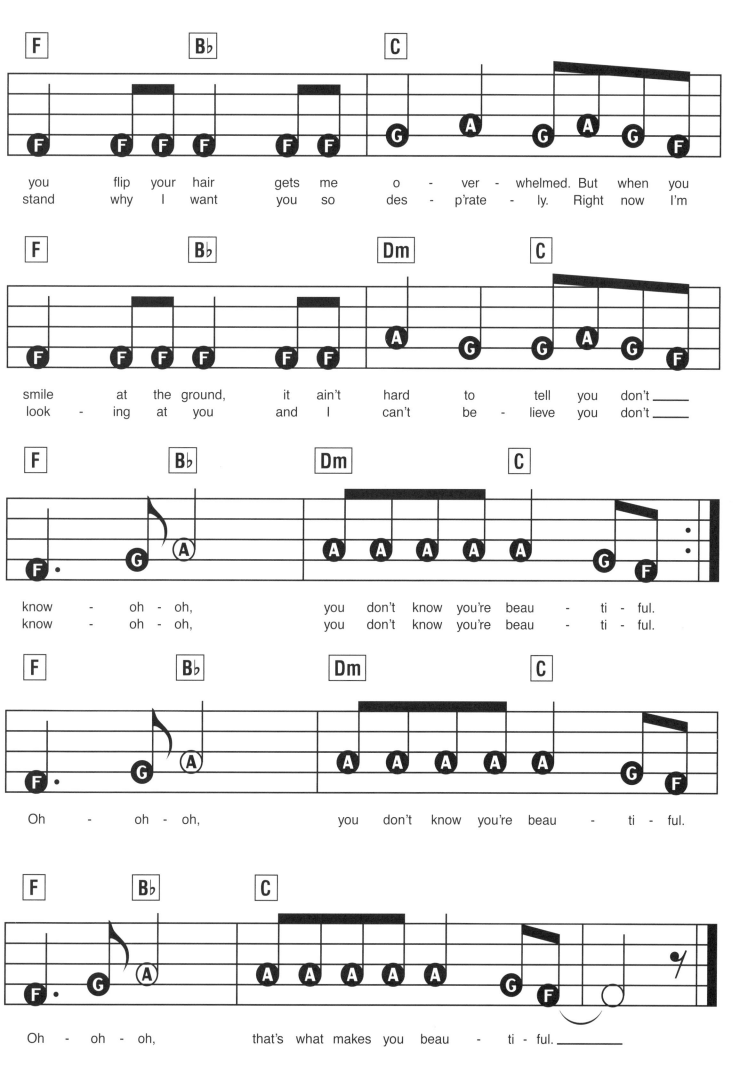

What About Us

Registration 8
Rhythm: Ballad or Pop

Words and Music by Alecia Moore,
Steve Mac and Johnny McDaid

Am ... **F**

C C B B A | A A G G F

La da da da da, la da da da da.

C

C E F G E | C C

Da da da da da. We are

Am **F** **C**

A | G C C C D E | G E E F E

search - lights, we can see in the dark. *(Instrumental)*
prob - lems that we want to be solved.

Am **F**

C F E | A | G C C C D E

We are rock - ets, point - ed up at the
We are chil - dren that need to be

369

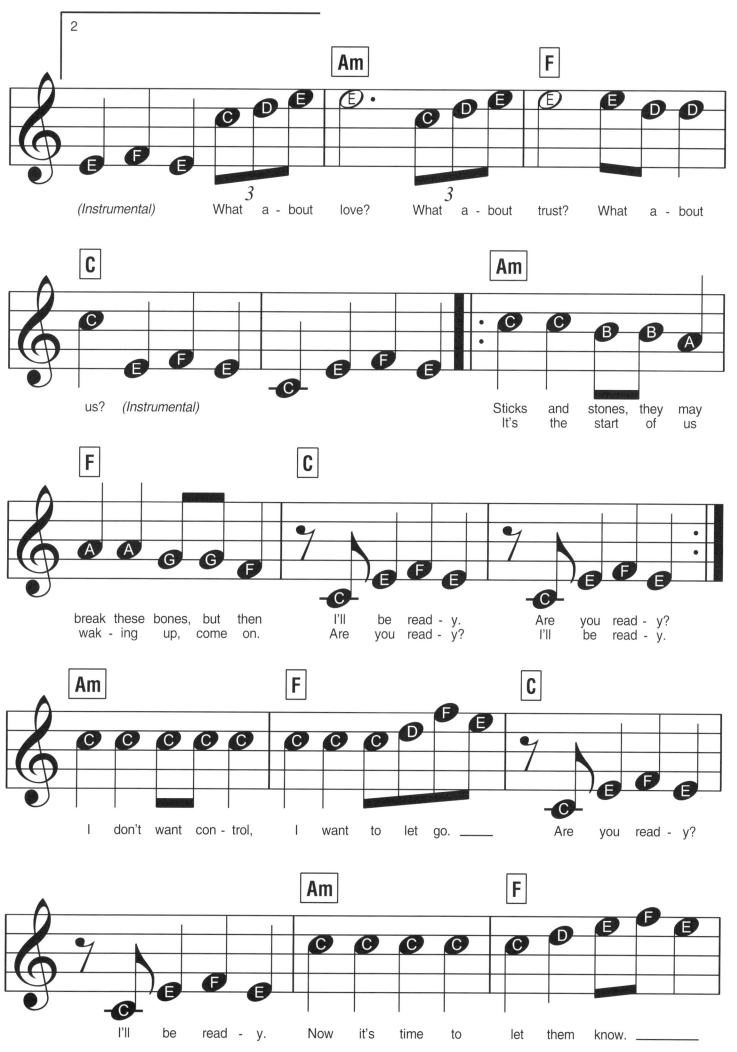

372

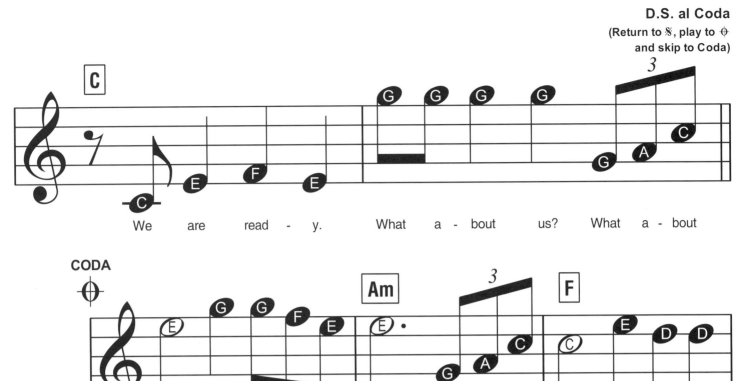

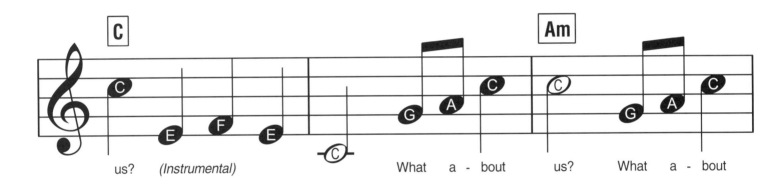

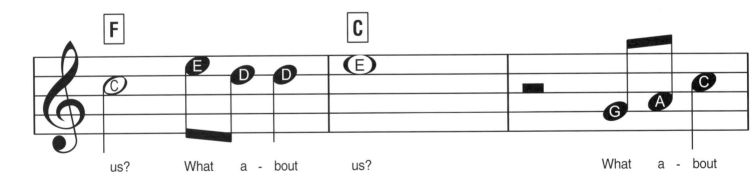

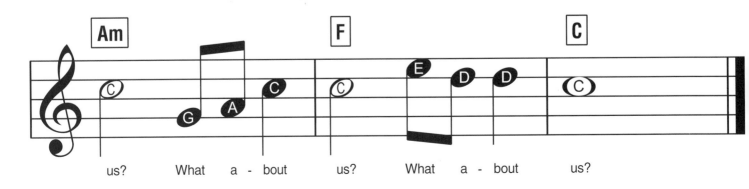

Wake Me Up!

Registration 4
Rhythm: Folk

Words and Music by Aloe Blacc,
Tim Bergling and Michael Einziger

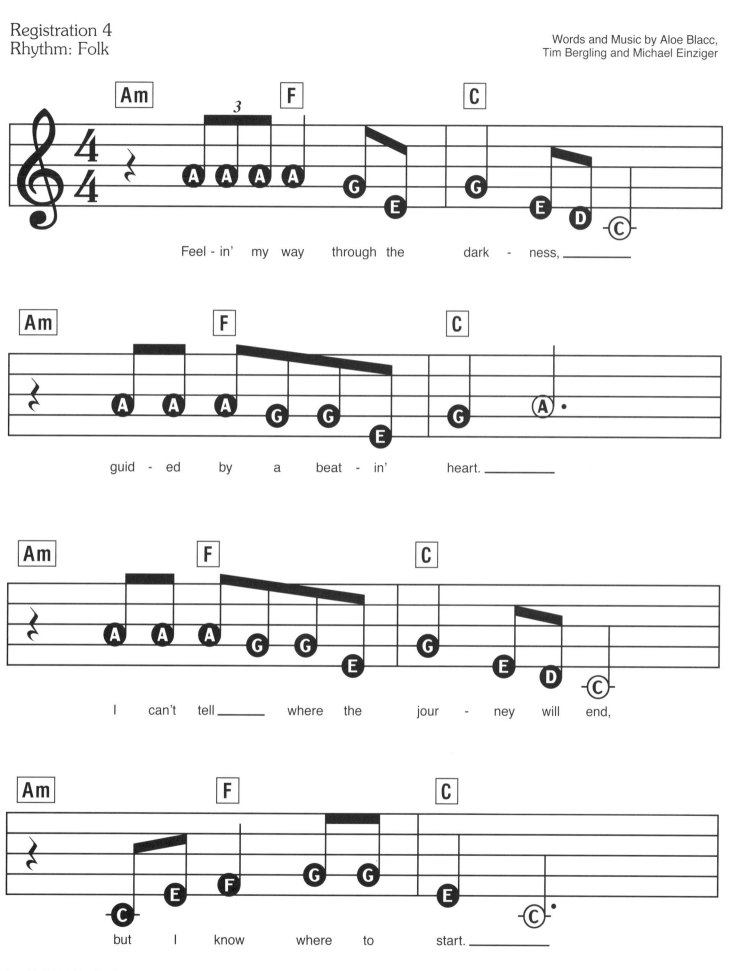

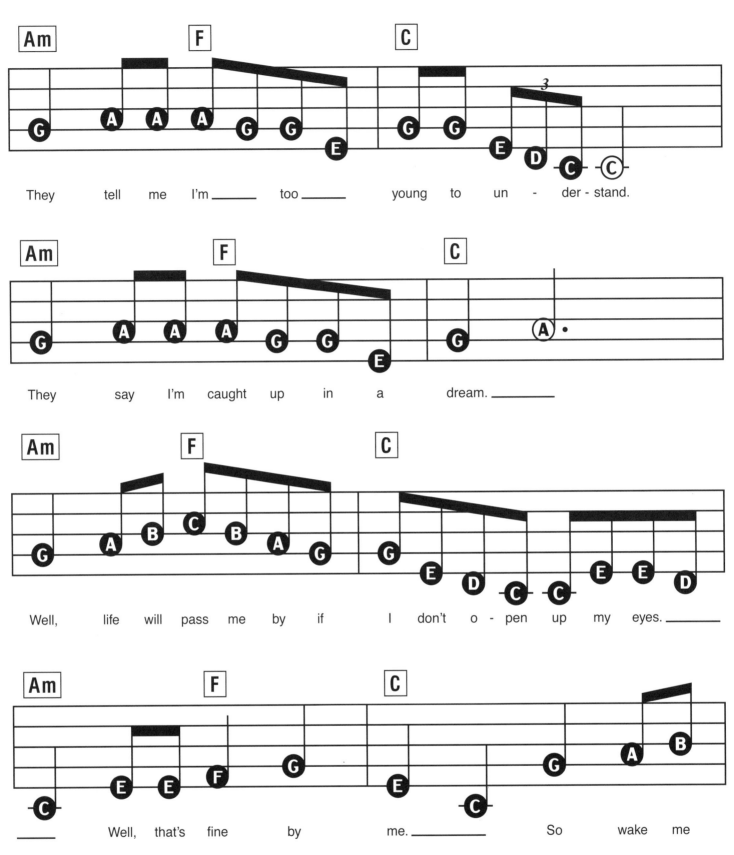

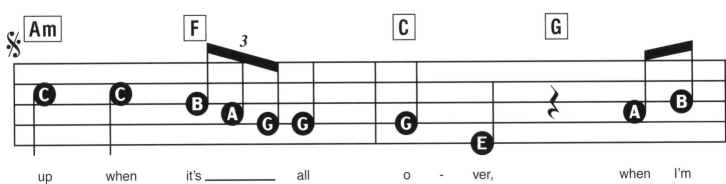

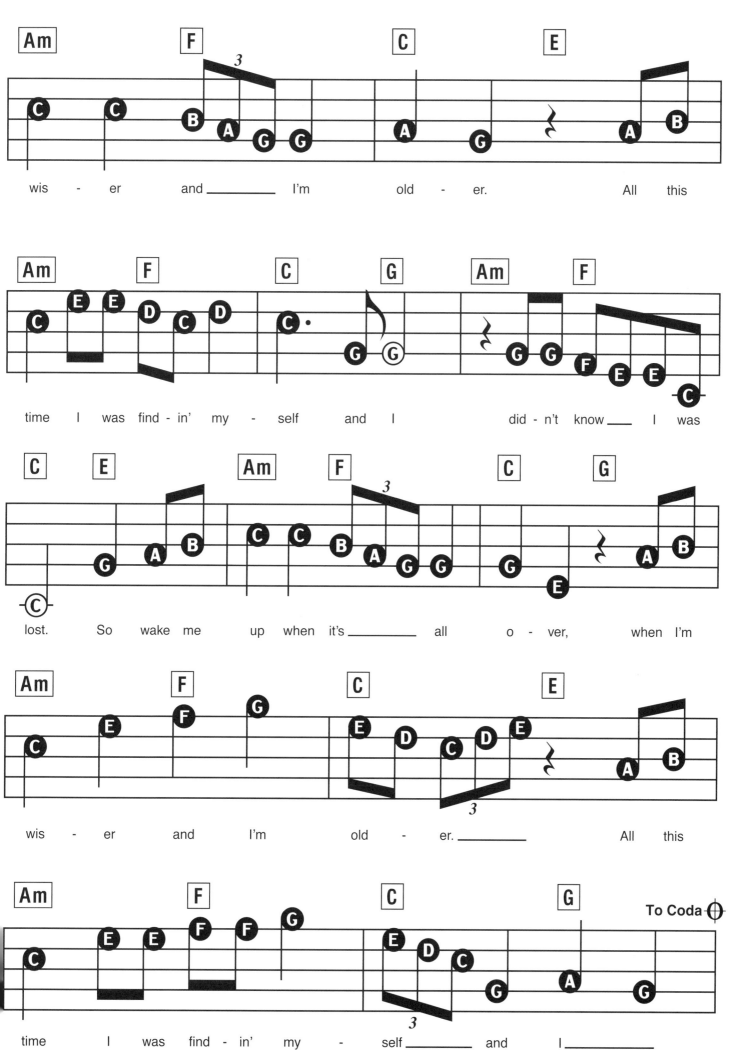

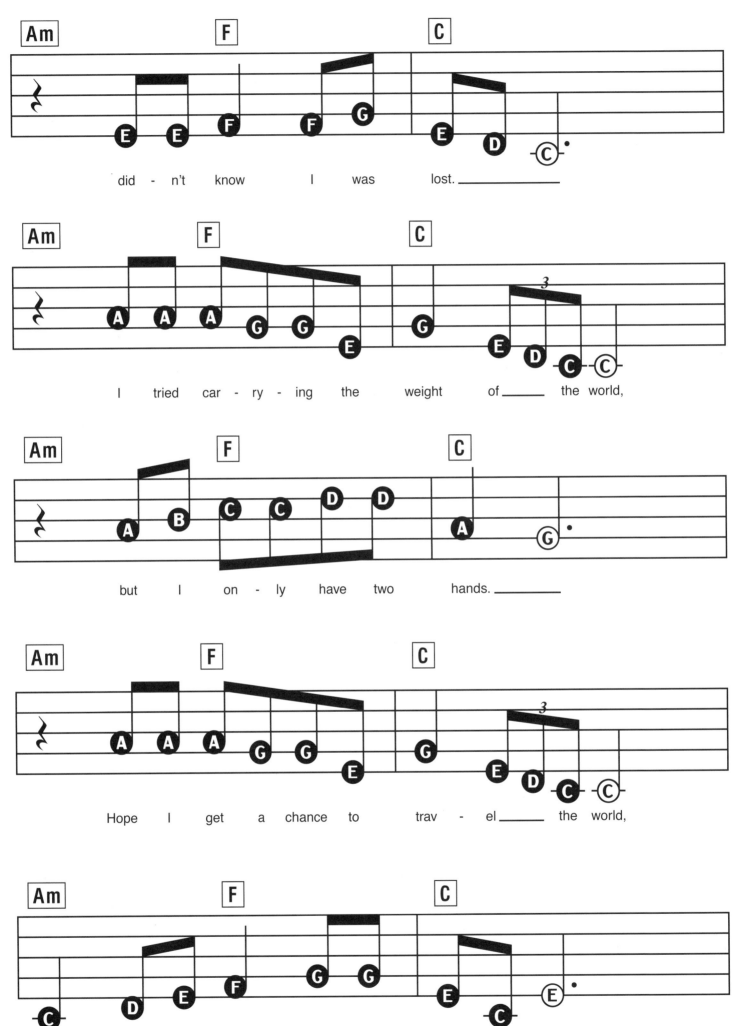

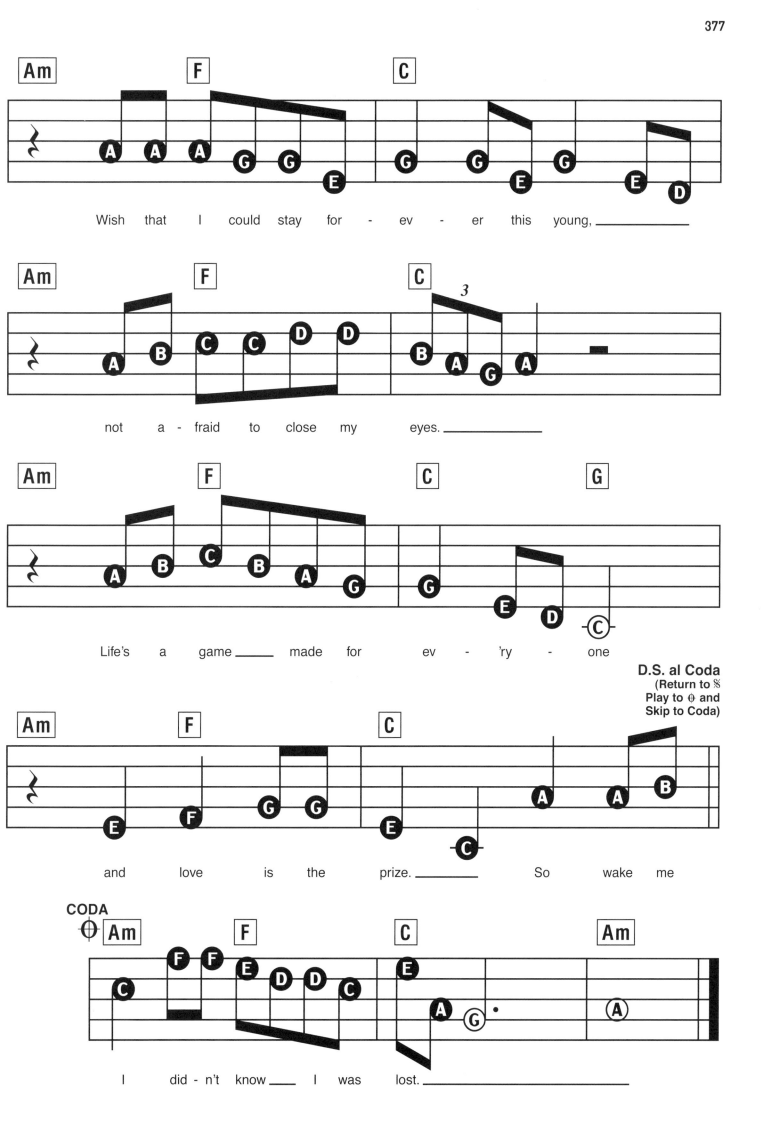

Without Me

Registration 9
Rhythm: Ballad or Pop

Words and Music by Ashley Frangipane,
Brittany Amaradio, Carl Rosen,
Justin Timberlake, Scott Storch, Louis Bell,
Amy Allen and Timothy Mosley

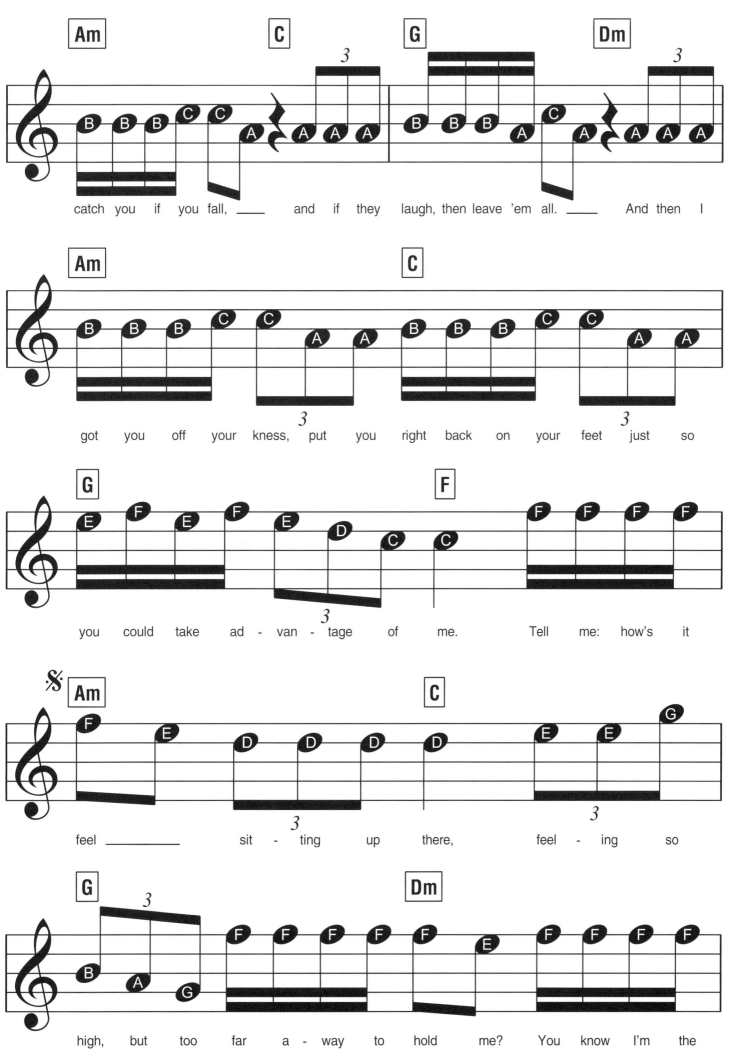

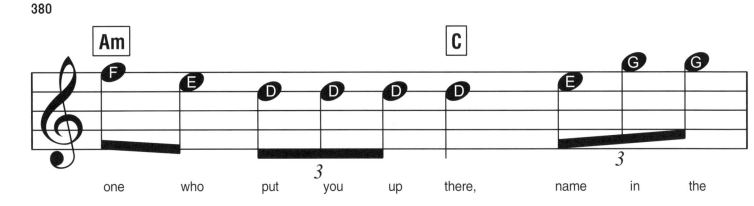

one who put you up there, name in the

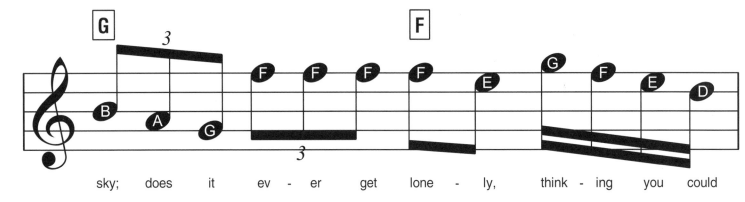

sky; does it ev - er get lone - ly, think - ing you could

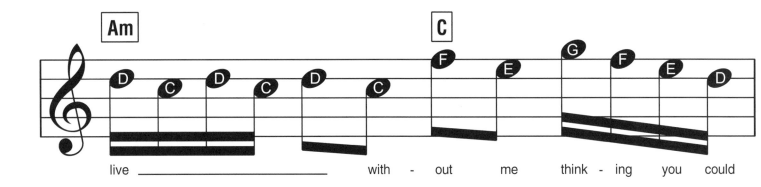

live _____ with - out me think - ing you could

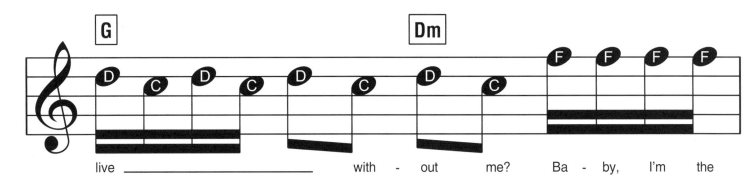

live _____ with - out me? Ba - by, I'm the

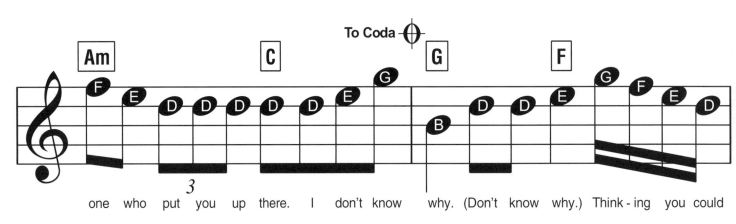

one who put you up there. I don't know why. (Don't know why.) Think - ing you could

Registration Guide

- Match the Registration number on the song to the corresponding numbered category below. Select and activate an instrumental sound available on your instrument.

- Choose an automatic rhythm appropriate to the mood and style of the song. (Consult your Owner's Guide for proper operation of automatic rhythm features.)

- Adjust the tempo and volume controls to comfortable settings.

Registration

1	Mellow	Flutes, Clarinet, Oboe, Flugel Horn, Trombone, French Horn, Organ Flutes
2	Ensemble	Brass Section, Sax Section, Wind Ensemble, Full Organ, Theater Organ
3	Strings	Violin, Viola, Cello, Fiddle, String Ensemble, Pizzicato, Organ Strings
4	Guitars	Acoustic/Electric Guitars, Banjo, Mandolin, Dulcimer, Ukulele, Hawaiian Guitar
5	Mallets	Vibraphone, Marimba, Xylophone, Steel Drums, Bells, Celesta, Chimes
6	Liturgical	Pipe Organ, Hand Bells, Vocal Ensemble, Choir, Organ Flutes
7	Bright	Saxophones, Trumpet, Mute Trumpet, Synth Leads, Jazz/Gospel Organs
8	Piano	Piano, Electric Piano, Honky Tonk Piano, Harpsichord, Clavi
9	Novelty	Melodic Percussion, Wah Trumpet, Synth, Whistle, Kazoo, Perc. Organ
10	Bellows	Accordion, French Accordion, Mussette, Harmonica, Pump Organ, Bagpipes

E-Z PLAY® TODAY SERIES

OVER 300 VOLUMES AVAILABLE!

The E-Z Play® Today songbook series is the shortest distance between beginning music and playing fun! Features of this series include:

- full-size books – large 9" x 12" format features easy-to-read, easy-to-play music

- accurate arrangements – simple enough for the beginner, but with authentic-sounding chords and melody lines

- minimum number of page turns

- thousands of songs – an incredible array of favorites, from classical and country to Christmas and contemporary hits

- lyrics – most arrangements include complete song lyrics

- most up-to-date registrations - books in the series contain a general registration guide, as well as individual song rhythm suggestions for today's electronic keyboards and organs

To see full descriptions of all the books in the series, visit:

HAL•LEONARD®
www.halleonard.com